CW00675907

A Tiny Universe's Companion

A Tiny Universe's Companion

Popular Techniques in Traditional Astrology

Joy Usher

Copyright © 2018 by Joy Usher.

ISBN: Softcover   978-1-5434-0702-0
                 eBook   978-1-5434-0701-3

All rights reserved. No part of this book may be reproduced or transmitted in any form or by any means, electronic or mechanical, including photocopying, recording, or by any information storage and retrieval system, without permission in writing from the copyright owner.

Any people depicted in stock imagery provided by Thinkstock are models, and such images are being used for illustrative purposes only.
Certain stock imagery © Thinkstock.

Print information available on the last page.

Rev. date: 07/06/2018

To order additional copies of this book, contact:
Xlibris
1-800-455-039
www.Xlibris.com.au
Orders@Xlibris.com.au
766423

Contents

To Ian With Love

"The stars men follow have different meanings.
For some people – travellers – the stars are guides.
For others they are merely little lights in the sky.
For others still – the scientists – they are problems to be solved.
But for all these people, the stars are silent.

For you, the stars will be as they are for no one else.
You alone will have stars that can laugh!"

The Little Prince

CHAPTER ONE

The Dignity of Planetary Sect

"Dusk is just an illusion, because the sun is either above the horizon or below it. And that means that day and night are linked in a way that few things are; there cannot be one without the other, yet they cannot exist at the same time.

How would it feel, I remember wondering, to be always together, yet forever apart?"

Nicholas Sparks, *The Notebook*

The dignity known as Planetary Sect was an important cornerstone of traditional astrology, yet sect barely rates a mention when it comes to discussing the nature of the planets in today's modern textbooks.

Robert Hand is a well-known translator of traditional texts who states that the word 'sect' is derived from the Latin *seco* meaning 'to cut' or 'divide'.[1] In astrological terms sect is used to describe the zodiac circle being cut into two halves by a line drawn from the Ascendant to the Descendant. This line from east to west separates the hours of daylight from the hours of darkness when the sun's light is removed from one side of the Earth.

The Greek word for sect provides a slightly different view as *hairesis* means 'acquisition' or 'choice' by definition and *hairesis* describes not just the division itself, but also the critical parts which remain once the division has been achieved.[2]

The two words from different languages combine cutting *(seco)* with acquisition or choice *(hairesis)* thereby suggesting a division which is not

1

only a necessity and a natural partition brought on by the process of Time, but also a requirement for each of the planets to make a choice according to their own nature.

Planetary sect falls under the category of the Accidental Dignities which describe conditions that are exterior to the planet' essence or its natural disposition.

The Accidental Dignities are separate from the five levels of Essential Dignities – Domicile, Exaltation, Triplicity, Term, or Face. These Dignities are concerned with a planet's sign (domicile and exaltation), element (triplicity) or degree (term and face) as these factors determine the level at which a planet has the strength to fulfil its potential 'to be itself' through the twelve zodiac signs.

Accidental dignity is a secondary level of dignity which takes other conditions into consideration, including a planet's environmental preferences, when judging a planet's strengths or weaknesses.

Certain astronomical factors govern some classifications of accidental dignity.

Factors such as the speed and direction in which a planet is travelling, its correct position oriental or occidental to the Sun, its proximity to the Sun so far as a conjunction is concerned, and a planet's aspects to the benefic planets, or to the Moon's North Node.

But celestial astronomy is not the only consideration for accidental dignity and the planet's placement in the chart is vitally important for its expression and its effectiveness.

The Emerald Tablet of Hermes is alleged to be a sacred text containing the secrets of alchemy, that is, the process by which base metal is magically transformed into precious gold. The Tablet commences with the phrase *'The above from the below, and the below from the above – the work of the miracle of the One"* [3] and scholars have studied the Tablet over the span of centuries in an attempt to understand its true meaning.

The connection between the macrocosm *(the above)* and the microcosm *(the below)* is the basis for the tenets of astrology and a combination of the Essential Dignities with the Accidental Dignities grants the greatest insight into the workings of a planet. The Emerald Tablet reinforces astrology's belief that a planet's condition is affected both by its placement in the divine realm (the 'essential' dignities), and also by its situation in the physical environment into which it is thrust when the astrological chart is created (the 'accidental' dignities).

The popular practice of these traditional techniques was built on the foundation that, no matter the purpose or time-span for which the chart was created, the greater connection a planet experiences with its mundane surroundings, the more comfortable it becomes in being able to express itself in a positive manner, and the greater number of possibilities it presents for the chart's potential to come to fruition.

Each of the seven original planets has its own proclivities. It will have an inclination or predisposition towards a particular expression or outcome, and depending on its circumstances, the ability for a planet to fulfil its destiny is largely influenced by its preferences or choices which are inbuilt in its nature (the 'Above' factor).

The chart itself (the 'Below' factor) is the most basic component of a planet's environment once birth has taken place.

The combination of planet and chart is the combination of 'As Above, so Below' and the alchemical process for any astrological practice is driven far more by the metaphysical than it is by the desire to gain financial reward.

There is a fine line between potential and actuality, especially when the planets are involved in the process, and the surroundings in which a planet must fulfil its potential will, with the aid of Essential Dignity, determine the planet's ability to be present, focused and engaged throughout the native's lifetime.

All astrology charts are created by the amalgamation of two units of time – the longer twelve month term when the Sun appears to move through the ecliptic, and the 24-hour period of one day, when the Ascendant degree moves through the zodiac circle.

A combination of the two units of time produces the *Horoskopos,* or Hour of the chart, and this term is used to describe both the Ascendant and the chart itself.

Accidental dignity takes into account the house position of the planet. If the planet is located in one of the angular houses – first, fourth, seventh, or tenth house – it is deemed to be accidentally dignified because it successfully participates in the native's life.

The eleventh and the fifth house can also elevate a planet into dignity as these are both considered to be beneficial houses. The axis of the third and ninth houses is somewhat neutral in benefit as it is often only advantageous for the luminaries (Moon in the third or Sun in the ninth) considering that these are the houses of their joy – another category of Accidental Dignity. The axis is cadent, but as both the third and ninth house receive light from the ascendant, this cancels the normal difficulty of a cadent house.

Planets in the other two cadent houses (derived from the Latin word '*cadaver*' meaning corpse or 'to fall'), that is, the sixth and the twelfth house, are considered to be in 'accidental debility' as the planet's effectiveness is reduced by their weakened position in the chart. Again, there are two exceptions, as Mars is in its joy in the sixth house, and Saturn is in its joy in the twelfth house.

Together, essential and accidental dignity can enhance a planet's abilities and promote its best behaviour.

Under certain circumstances dignity can tone down a malefic's tendency to do harm, and in best case scenarios can utilize a malefic planet's energy so that it becomes an accidental benefic for the native.

Unfortunately, the opposite is also true, and if a planet suffers too greatly from afflictions, or debilities, these will impact on a planet's nature and actions, which means it can becomes a planet of greater malevolence and be the significator of trouble or harm for the native.

Amongst all these rules stands the simplest of classifications, and perhaps the most influential of all accidental dignities. The dignity known as planetary sect divides the planets into two distinct categories dependent on the most basic division of day and night.

In ancient times when Greek philosophers wanted to define an object they would ask

'*What is this thing? What do I see?*'

When they wanted to find context, that is, to find what gives meaning to that object in order to understand how to classify something or group similar things together, they would ask

'*Who made this thing come into being? How does it work? What is its essence?*

What is its purpose?'

These questions form the basis of astrology as '*What do I see?*' begat the worship of the sun as the 'Light-bringer' and the source of life, and during the night, the observation of the heavens and the movement of the planets through the stars.

'*How does it work?*' connected all things under heaven and earth, interweaving mythology with everyday occurrences, and thereby creating the doctrine of astrological lore.

However, at the root of these fundamental questions lies the most basic one of all.

'How do I see?' The answer would be: *'By the Sun's light'*

Which leads to the question, *'Is it day, or is it night?'*

The demarcation between maximum light during the day, and minimum natural light during the night, gives rise to the principle objective of planetary sect.

Sect divides the planets into two distinct camps; those planets which naturally assimilate with daylight functions, and those planets which understand the principles that drive the hours of the night.

Sect complies with both its Latin and Greek names by acknowledging the separation *(seco)* created by Earth's movement around the sun over a twenty four hour period, and by granting the planets the choice *(hairesis)* to decide their preference for day or night.

The observation of planetary sect created two entirely different possibilities.

Solar horoscopes where the Sun is considered to be the most powerful luminary, and lunar horoscopes, a term used by some traditional writers, where the Moon directs life and is examined in greater detail simply because it becomes the leading luminary in a nocturnal (night) chart.

It is not hard to understand how planetary sect became a fundamental principle in traditional astrological practice.

Even without today's knowledge of the sun's effect on our own planet, the ancients worshipped the sun as the source of life, light and energy. Apart from its divine qualities, the sun was also a time keeper, marking the months or the year and the hours of the day. The sun's light made visibility (and the definition of things) easier, and created subtlety and variances in light when objects cast shadows for shifting degrees of 'more light' as opposed to 'less light' according to the hour of the day, eventually disappearing beneath the horizon to leave the world in its reflected light through the moon's changing phases.

Naturally, the astrological Sun prefers the daylight hours, along with Jupiter and Saturn who both choose the warmth, clarity and precision provided by the sun's natural light. Once the sun disappears at sunset, clear definition is lost as boundaries blur and details begin to disappear when light merges with the shadows of night.

"Deep into that darkness peering,
Long I stood there,
Wondering, fearing, doubting,
Dreaming dreams no mortal ever dared to dream before."

Edgar Allan Poe (1809 – 1849)

Without an artificial replacement for light, the night can only provide limited degrees of darkness depending on the moon's phases, and whilst moonlight is flattering for lovers, its lack of clarity means that the philosopher's questions become difficult to answer when sight is restricted and the ability to determine context is drastically compromised.

The hours appear to slow down and the time devoid of the sun's light is spent 'peering into the darkness', emotionally and mentally processing the events of the busy hours of daylight, and dreaming fitfully through the hours of sleep. The Moon, Venus and Mars are the planets which choose darkness and their respective natures are best suited to the hours between dusk and dawn.

Time Division and the Horoscope

"Time is a game played beautifully by children."

Heraclitus (535-475 BCE)

The astrology chart is designed in such a way that it reflects the passage of time through the twenty four hour period when the sun determines the hours of light and dark.

The concept of time and the sun's movement is easy to demonstrate in the Whole Sign chart because each house is equally spaced apart and corresponds to a two hour interval of time, but it is still applicable to quadrant-style houses with unequal houses.

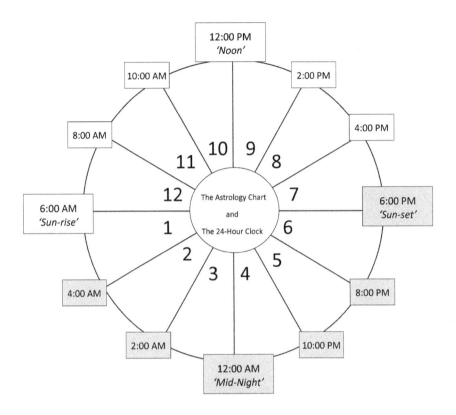

Fig. 1 The 24-hour Clock and the Horoscope

The horizon represents the division between day and night, light and darkness, and the 24-hour clock equates with the astrology chart by placing 6:00 am at the Ascendant and 6:00 pm at the Descendant. High noon occurs at the beginning of the tenth sign, the zenith or highest point of the chart, whilst midnight sits at the position of the nadir at the lowest point of the chart and marks the beginning point of the change in the date from one day to the next.

So far as the astrological chart is concerned, if the birth occurs at midnight, the Sun is on the cusp of the fourth sign at this time. The Sun appears to move in the same direction as the 24-hour clock, so that when the clock displays Local Time (with no Daylight Saving) then the Sun's position in the chart will reflect a similar time of day.

Diurnal motion (shown by the arrow in *Figs. 2-4*) is synonymous with the Sun's apparent movement through both the hours of a day and the horoscope itself, and whilst the times are simply an approximation at each of these stations, it provides the astrologer with the ability to draw up a rough template of the chart.

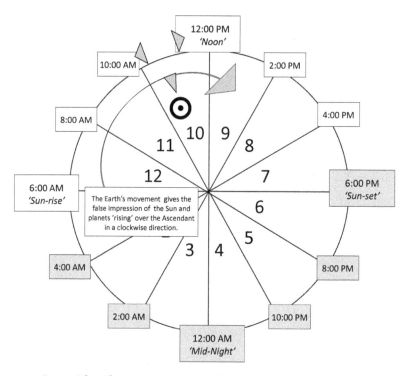

Fig. 2 The Chart:11:00 am Local Time – No Daylight Saving

For example, *Fig 2* shows the Sun's position high in the chart in the tenth house at the same time as indicating that the birth occurred somewhere between 10:00am and 12:00 noon by local time standards.

Daylight saving is a man-made construct which allows the populace to enjoy an 'extra hour' of sunshine during the evenings on summer nights. The movement forward by one hour in some areas of the world during the warmer months is not a true reflection of the sun's position in relation to the clock, and drawing up a quick sketch of a chart when daylight saving is in force requires taking the one hour off and placing the Sun in its correct position in the chart for one hour earlier.

For instance, daylight saving came into operation for most of Australia in 1971, so if the chart for Sydney which is featured in Chart Comparisons *(Fig. 12)* were to be redrawn in the present system, the

Sun in the chart would be in the 2:00 pm position in the ninth house, for a local (summer) time of 3:00 pm on 10th March after 1971.

The following charts *(Fig. 3 and 4)* provide further examples of the correlation between the time on the clock's face and the Sun's position in the chart.

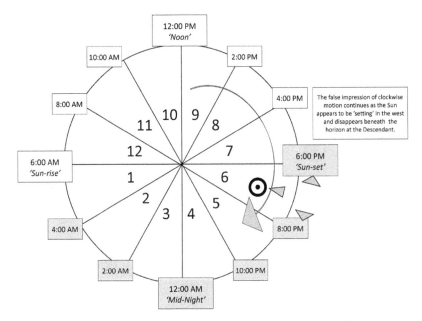

Fig. 3 The Chart: 7:00 pm Local Time – No Daylight Saving

Fig. 4 The Chart: 5:00 am Local Time – No Daylight Saving

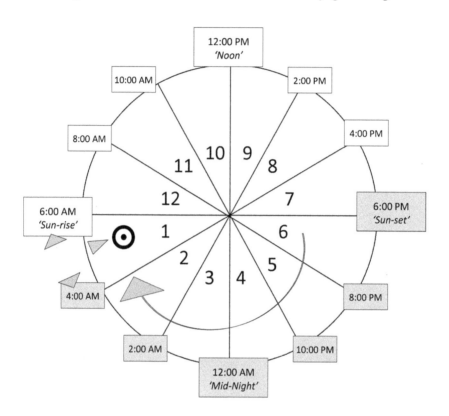

Once the Sun's sign is acknowledged (according to time of year), the signs on the house cusps can also be included to give a rough guide as to what the chart might look like once calculations have constructed an accurate chart.

The same method can be used with a quadrant-style system, although a later degree Sun will suggest a change from one sign on the Ascendant to the following sign simply because the Sun often changes houses when it is in a later degree and a different sign to the house cusp in the quadrant chart.

In the three examples the Sun is located in Pisces in a Whole Sign chart. In *Fig. 5* the Pisces Sun lies in the sixth house when the birth occurs during the first three months of March between the hours of 6:00pm and 8:00pm, and produces an Ascendant in Libra when the signs follow their natural progression from Pisces on the sixth house cusp around to Libra on the first house.

The following chart (*Fig. 6*) has a tenth house Sun in Pisces as the time of the chart is 11:00 am and the signs will follow Pisces on the midheaven in an anti-clockwise direction according to the zodiac. This will place Gemini at the Ascendant of this chart. The last chart has a local time of birth between 4:00 am and 6:00 am in March which produces a Pisces Sun located in the first house and Pisces will be the rising sign in a Whole Sign chart (*Fig. 7*).

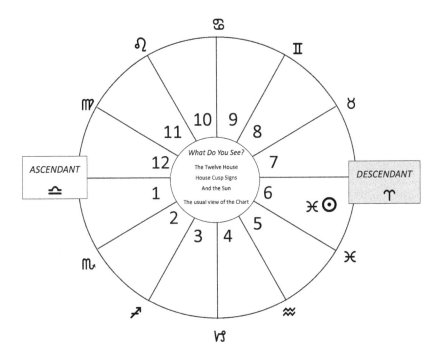

Fig. 5 Pisces Sun: Libra Rising – 7:00 pm Local Time – No Daylight Saving

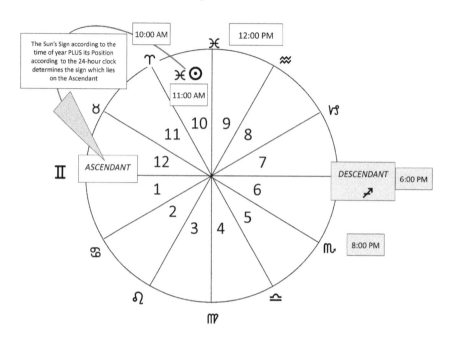

Fig. 6 Pisces Sun: Gemini Rising – 11:00 am Local Time – No Daylight Saving

Note that the signs and the order of the houses appear to run in a counter-clockwise direction, seemingly in the opposite direction to the planets' movement according to the clockwise (and time-wise) activity of diurnal motion. This impression of movement in two different directions is falsely created by the fact that the horizon line in a chart (Ascendant/Descendant) gives the appearance of being stationary, rather than being something which is constantly in motion.

The Sun and the planets appear to move through the chart in the opposite direction from the zodiac belt simply *because the horizon is constantly changing* and the image we receive is one of planets rising over the Ascendant and setting over the Descendant.

'*What do you see?*'

The trick of movement, that is, the comparison between two objects moving at different speeds, is an old problem, as the negative connotations of retrogradation are born from this same principle.

Watching a planet move backwards against the constellations was frightening for our astrological forefathers as it was an omen for them of a terrible event which was about to occur on Earth. A retrograde planet was an abomination to God who had planned everything so beautifully that a rogue planet reversing through the universe was bound to be a warning of impending disaster.

Astronomers, philosophers and scientists of the day concocted elaborate diagrams of complicated cylindrical spheres to try and explain retrograde movement as none could comprehend that it might be due to the fact that the Earth itself was moving, and it was the discrepancy between our planet moving at a faster speed than the one observed out in the universe.

When a planet appears to be is moving in a retrograde motion in the chart it moves back into earlier degrees of the zodiac, and by doing so, it really does comply with the idea of diurnal or clockwise motion – but this is a bad thing and not a sign of natural movement!

A number of astrological software programs allow the user to fast forward a chart and it is suggested that a few examples of speeding up the chart over a twenty four hour period will give a far more accurate account of how movement occurs over the horizon when the Ascendant is passing across the degrees of the zodiac at a rate of approximately one degree in four minutes of time.

The Moon will demonstrate the planets' movement in an identical direction to the Ascendant as the faster luminary will cross approximately fifteen degrees of the zodiac in one day, but the slower movement of the other planets will create the misconception that they are moving against the direction of the zodiac signs.

The image which makes this easier to understand is of the planets being in a relationship to a mobile Ascendant degree which is constantly altering the aspects between the two points which move at a different speed to one another. A planet 'rises' because the Ascendant's degree has come to be in conjunction with the planet's degree. Once the Ascendant has moved past the conjunction, the planet is in an earlier degree and has the impression of being 'pushed' above the horizon. With each passing degree of the Ascendant, the planet appears to rise higher in the chart.

The planets retain the same relationship to one another (with the Moon as the exception) across the day, but their relationship to the horizon continues to shift with the speed of the Earth's movement. Similarly, a planet appears to 'set' simply because it has reached the aspect of opposition to the Ascendant's degree and has crossed the

Descendant, the point in the chart which is an identical degree but in the sign which directly opposes the Ascendant.

The same trick of movement occurs when two cars sit side by side at an intersection waiting for the traffic lights to change. If one car starts to edge forward, the driver in the other car instinctively touches their brakes as they have the impression that they must be moving backwards if the driver in the parallel car has pulled slightly forwards in front of them.

In this scenario, the car moving forwards with speed is the Ascendant's degree, and the stationary or slower moving car is the planet. As the lights change and the first car speeds forward the gap widens between the two vehicles, but because they are both in motion we do not consider one to be reversing or moving in a counter-direction to the other.

However, if we were to somehow make the faster car at the front appear to be in non-motion by freezing its surroundings, then we would get the same impression of two objects of different speeds travelling in two different directions.

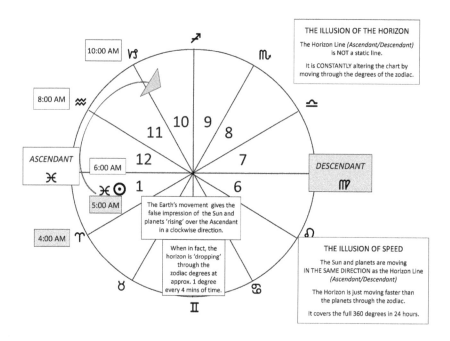

Fig. 7 Pisces Sun: Pisces Rising – 5:00 am Local Time – No Daylight Saving

Time and Movement Across the Globe

Given that the chart is extremely sensitive to the movement of time it would seem a natural progression to expect the horoscope to alter dramatically from one side of the Earth to another. However, this impression is incorrect and misunderstandings often occur over the expectations of what a chart should look like when a significant alteration occurs in the place of birth.

The 24-hour clock is dependent on *local time* which is based on the sun's physical presence in any particular location. For this reason, if the birth occurs at a time which is identical according to the clock, the chart will alter very little when the location changes. The zodiacal position of the planets will change to some degree (the Moon being the most notable) as these calculations are based on Greenwich Mean Time which will be different for each birth, but ultimately the Sun's physical position in the chart will be very similar across the range of birth locations and the type of chart, regardless of whether it is a quadrant-style or a whole sign chart.

For instance, if the birth takes place at 3:00 pm in New York in the United States the chart will be very similar to another person's chart who is born in London in the United Kingdom at 3:00 pm local time, even though there is a great discrepancy between the longitude degrees of both locations. Similarly, the vast difference between both co-ordinates of longitude and latitude in Sydney in Australia and Nairobi in Kenya is not reflected in the charts from these two cities when the birth occurs *at the same local time*, purely because the local time will reflect the sun moving from east to west across the globe.

There will be some minor adjustments as the differing seasons of summer or winter between northern and southern hemispheres will affect the sun's rising and setting times, but basically, the charts of all four nativities will vary very little from one another, as each chart will place the Sun in the eighth house at the 3:00 pm position in the Placidus chart *(Fig. 8-12)*.

DATA: 10TH MARCH 1964 3:00 PM (local time) *Charts Provided Below*	LONDON U.K.	NEW YORK U.S.A.	NAIROBI KENYA	SYDNEY AUSTRALIA
HEMISPHERE	NORTHERN	NORTHERN	SOUTHERN	SOUTHERN
SEASON	WINTER	WINTER	SUMMER	SUMMER
CO-ORDINATES	LAT: 51°N30' LONG: 00°W10'	LAT: 40°N43' LONG: 74°W00'	LAT: 01°S17' LONG: 36°E49'	LAT: 33°S52' LONG: 151°E13'
TIME DIFFERENCE	0:00 (GMT)	5:00 hrs behind GMT	3:00 hrs ahead of GMT	10:00 hrs ahead of GMT
ASCENDANT DEGREE	20♌06	16♌17	22♋41	16♋39
MID-HEAVEN DEGREE	5♉26	6♉51	26♈57	6♉26
SUN'S DEGREE HOUSE	20♓04 8th House	20♓16 8th House	19♓56 8th House	19♓39 8th House
MOON'S DEGREE HOUSE	7♒03 6th House	9♒43 6th House	5♒28 7th House	1♒47 7th House

Fig. 8
Comparison between Charts set for the identical LOCAL TIME of 3:00 pm
(no daylight saving)

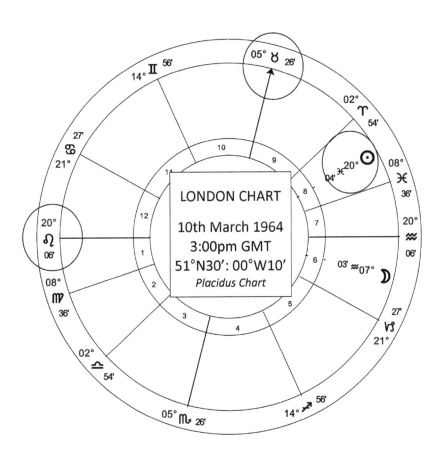

Fig. 9
London Chart

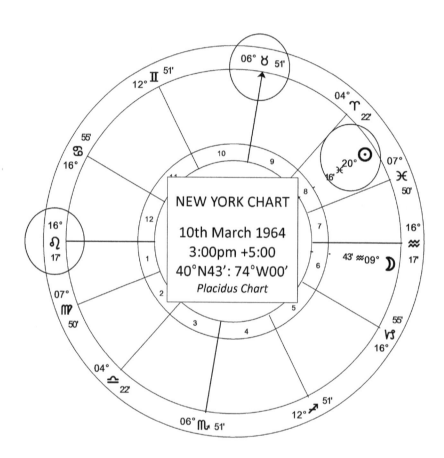

Fig. 10
New York Chart

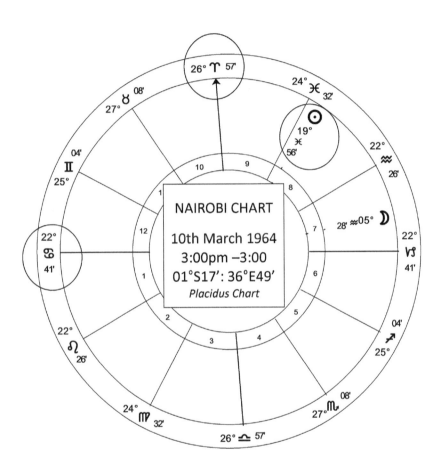

Fig. 11
Nairobi Chart

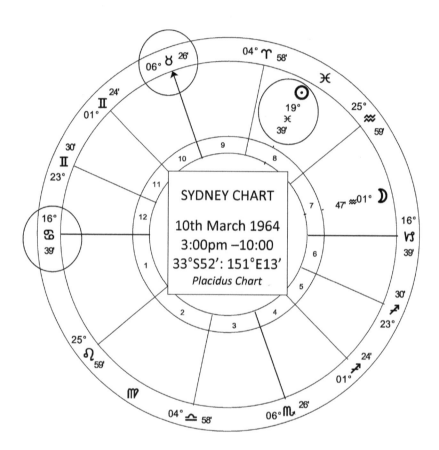

Fig. 12
Sydney Chart (No Daylight Saving)

Sect and the Ascendant
Quadrant-Style Chart vs Whole Sign Chart

In most house systems, such as Placidus, Koch, Campanus, Regiomontanus, or Porphyry, the horizon line is defined by the Ascendant and Descendant axis which cuts the three hundred and sixty degree circle into two perfect halves and creates the division between day and night. These systems are known as quadrant-style house systems and the degrees of the Ascendant and the Midheaven act as house cusps for the angular houses in the chart, with the area between them being divided either by time or by spatial considerations.

The Whole Sign house system is a different and much older way to divide the chart as this system allocates an entire sign per house beginning with zero degrees of the Ascendant's sign and continuing in the order of the eleven remaining signs, with each house at thirty degree intervals.

In the Whole Sign chart the Ascendant is not a horizontal line but rather, it is displayed as a significant point in the first sign of the chart. The number of the Ascendant's degree is marked in a similar fashion to the way in which a planet's position is marked in the chart, so that any aspect from a planet to the Ascendant's degree becomes critical in the analysis of the chart. The ruler of the Ascendant's sign is given the same honour as it is in the quadrant-style chart, being recognised as the Lord of the Chart.

The other crucial point in the chart is the Midheaven which is also identified by its degree and can be found ranging anywhere across the top of the chart, as it no longer lies on the cusp of the tenth house in a Whole Sign chart.

Of the previous four charts based in different countries, three births (London, New York and Nairobi) would have Midheavens placed in their tenth signs and houses, but Sydney's chart would find the Taurus MC in the chart's eleventh house if it was converted from a Placidus chart to a Whole Sign chart as Taurus is eleven signs away from the Cancer Ascendant.

It can be argued that in a Whole Sign chart the Ascendant is more realistically represented as a constantly changing degree which moves in the order of the signs, and whilst it is essential to the manifestation of the chart, it is also shown as a point which changes with incredible speed, especially when compared to the planets' movement over the same period of one day.

In both types of house system, the Ascendant's degree still changes as time moves forward. However, in the quadrant-based chart, the Ascendant never looks to the eye as though it is the point which is doing the action of movement.

It should be noted that in the quadrant house system the Ascendant and Descendant axis clearly defines the difference between the approximation of twelve hours of daylight and twelve hours of the night. In these charts, if the Sun is located in one of the houses in the upper hemisphere from the seventh to the twelfth house, the chart is diurnal. If the Sun is below the Ascendant and Descendant axis in the houses from the first to the sixth house, the chart is nocturnal.

When whole sign charts show the Ascendant as a stationary point and not as a line across the horizon, it requires a certain level of care to avoid misjudging a chart's sect identity if the Sun is anywhere near the Ascendant or Descendant degree.

The two charts below are identical charts calculated for the time of 5:20 pm when the chart is classified as diurnal because the Sun is placed above the horizon in the seventh house for both figures. The Ascendant remains at the same degree of 9 Pisces, but the first chart *(Fig. 13)* is set in the quadrant-style Placidus system, whilst the second is a Whole Sign chart *(Fig. 13 a)* which begins the chart at zero Pisces and shows the Ascendant as a degree in the first house.

The Sun on this day at this particular time is calculated to 18 Virgo. The reason that its position looks slightly different in the two charts – the Sun in *Fig. 13 a)* looks to be higher in the chart and deeper in the seventh house – is due to the fact that the boundaries of the house are different from one system to the other. In the Placidus chart the Sun's position is determined by the Ascendant degree, whilst in the Whole Sign chart the Sun's degree is proportional to where it would lie within the entire thirty degrees of Virgo.

The Sun has not yet crossed the horizon (more accurately, the Descendant has not yet advanced to the Sun's degree), and this is easy to gauge in the Placidus chart. The Whole Sign chart requires careful assessment as crossing the horizon is not so obvious when the descendant is a degree, rather than a horizontal line across the chart's diameter. Mercury belongs to the nocturnal sect in this chart as it is behind the Sun and will set after the Sun, as will Venus and the Moon later in the same night.

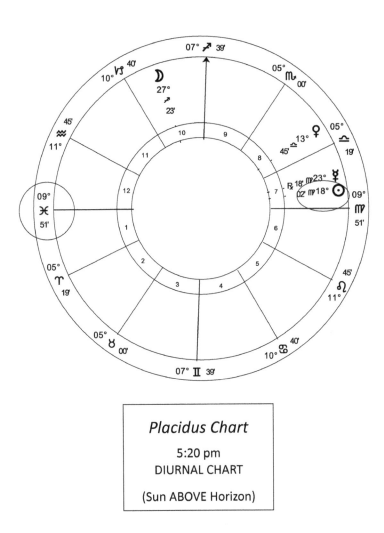

Placidus Chart

5:20 pm
DIURNAL CHART

(Sun ABOVE Horizon)

Fig.13
PLACIDUS Chart for 5:20 pm (Diurnal)

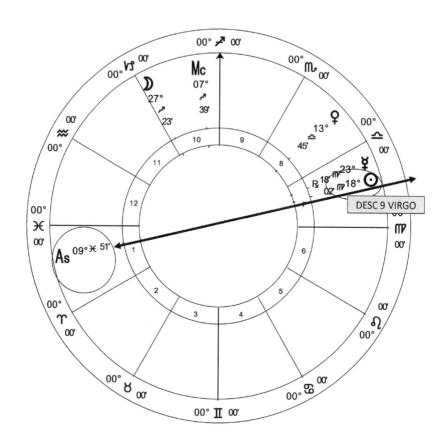

Whole Sign Chart

5:20 pm
DIURNAL CHART

(Sun ABOVE Horizon)

Fig. 13 a)
The same chart in WHOLE SIGN
for 5:20 pm (Diurnal)

"What Do You See?" The following pair of charts are set just over an hour later than the previous chart as the Sun has now set and the chart has changed from being a diurnal chart at 5:20 pm to a nocturnal chart at the time of 6:40 pm on the same day. During the lapsed one hour interval the Ascendant's degree has moved from 9 Pisces *(Fig. 13)*, past the degree which will oppose the Sun's degree at 18 Virgo, and is now at the end of the sign of Pisces at 26 degrees. The Midheaven degree has moved deeper into the sign of Sagittarius so that it now conjuncts the Moon in the late degrees of Sagittarius in the 6:40 pm chart. Once more the two charts are identical in data but not in construction and the change in sect division is much easier to see in the Placidus chart *(Fig. 14)*. The descendant is part of the horizon line and the difference in degrees means that a descendant degree later than the Sun's degree places the Sun beneath the horizon in the Placidus chart's sixth house.

In contrast, the Whole Sign chart *(Fig. 14 a)* retains the Sun's position in the seventh house because the planets will remain within the house of their own sign in this system so as long as the Ascendant remains in Pisces, the Sun will stay in the seventh sign of Virgo.

The Sun's position is not incorrect for this style of chart because the Sun's placement in the house is dependent on where its degree falls in the sign of Virgo, and this has not altered in an hour.

Mercury, at 23 degrees of Virgo, has also set beneath the horizon in this nocturnal chart. In the Placidus chart it is travelling with the Sun in the sixth house because its degrees in Pisces are below the descendant's degree, whilst in the Whole Sign chart Mercury is still featured in the seventh sign with the Sun in Virgo. Venus is yet to set, but will do so once the descendant's degree has progressed beyond 13 degrees Libra, which will happen in ninety minutes at 8:10 pm local time.

In terms of easy recognition between diurnal and nocturnal sect division, the Placidus chart is the preferred style over the Whole Sign chart as in the first chart the Sun *looks* as though it has set and the decision to call a nocturnal chart is made more plausible by the Sun's position in the sixth house.

However, both charts are nocturnal because they are identical, and it should be noted that the Sun at 18 Virgo, is in a lesser degree of the sign than the advanced Descendant at 26 Virgo. For this reason, if there is any question as to whether the Sun has crossed the horizon, it is recommended to hand-draw an axis into the Whole Sign chart to clearly show the distinction between diurnal or nocturnal sect dignity.

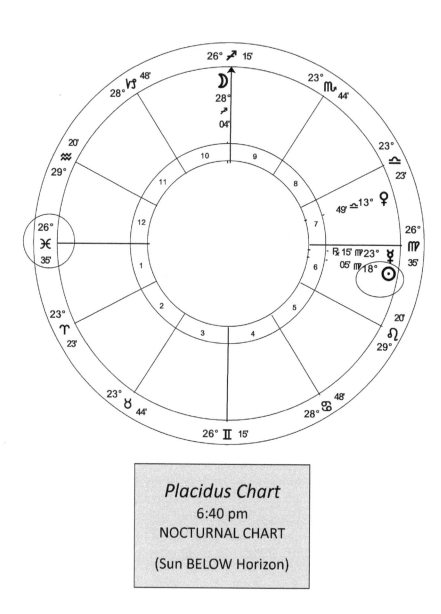

Fig. 14 PLACIDUS Chart for 6:40 pm (Nocturnal)

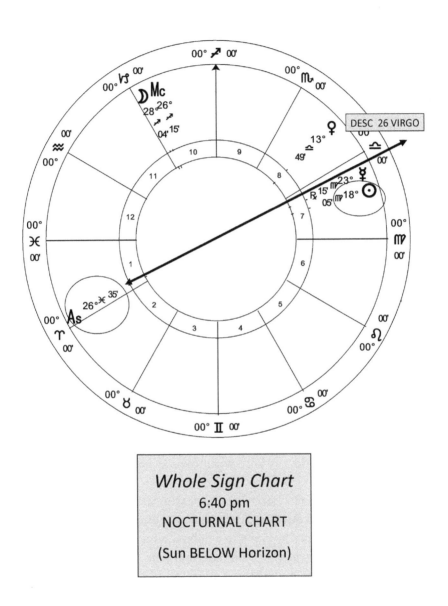

Fig. 14 a) WHOLE SIGN Chart for 6:40 pm (Nocturnal)

The First Division for Sect

When a horoscope's twelve houses also become two hour demarcations of time set by the sun's movement, it clearly demonstrates the importance of the Sun as the sole significator for the division between day and night, and leaves little doubt that where planetary sect is concerned, the Sun is entitled to gain some sort of advantage from this fact.

The first sect division is simple to demonstrate when it is understood that the Sun is the cosmic time-keeper, not only for the four seasons of the year, but also as the defining factor in the construction of the chart, and the determinant in the division between light and dark.

In a quadrant-style chart, the Sun's position above the Ascendant and Descendant axis indicates that the chart belongs to the day-time and is called diurnal.

However, when the Sun is placed below the same axis it is night-time and the chart is classified as nocturnal.

In a Whole Sign the degree of the Ascendant must be taken into account when differentiating between a diurnal and nocturnal chart.

Regardless of which system is in practice, the diurnal chart displays the Sun above the Ascendant and Descendant's sign and degree *(Fig. 15)* whilst a nocturnal chart presents the Sun below the Ascendant and Descendant's sign and degree *(Fig. 16)*.

In the three charts featured earlier in the chapter with a Pisces Sun, *Fig. 6* is a diurnal chart (Sun above the horizon), whilst *Figs. 5 and 7* are nocturnal charts (Sun is below the horizon).

The first rule of Sect is an environmental issue of the most basic kind.

If the environment suits or appeases a planet's nature, its characteristics and its qualities, then that planet is comfortable, and it receives a level of dignity by being in a habitat which is either compatible with, or soothing towards, its own temperament.

When someone or something is in its proper domain then a sense of familiarity creates feelings of confidence, ease, rapport or affinity, and generally encourages acts of self-assuredness performed with a level of good grace.

Under the rules of sect when a planet is situated in congenial surroundings its behaviour has a certain predictability to it because the planet is supported, and knows what to expect from its natural habitat.

The correct sect also places the planet in harmony with its primary luminary, and its position in the chart is strengthened by the protective qualities of either the Sun or the Moon.

Accidental dignity is bestowed on a planet when this happens, and planetary sect boosts whatever the planet receives through the higher level of Essential dignity, as this secondary form of dignity can only be conferred through the 'accident' of birth.

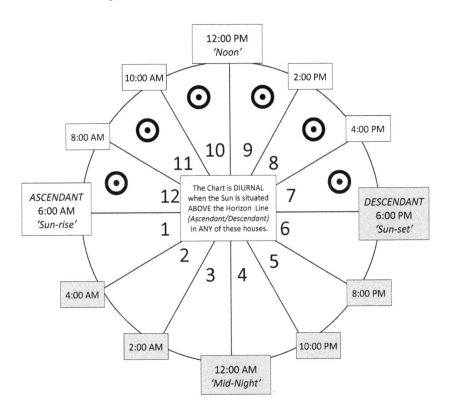

Fig. 15 The Diurnal Chart:
Sun ABOVE the Horizon — The Sun is the Major Luminary of the Chart

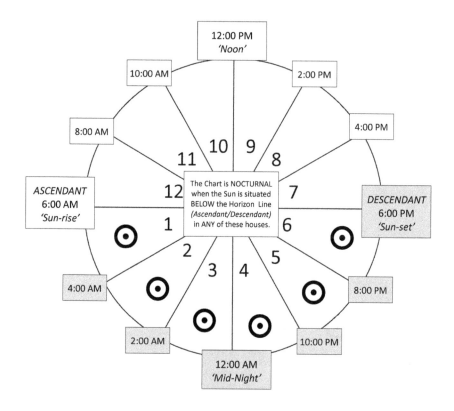

Fig. 16 The Nocturnal Chart:
Sun BELOW the Horizon – The Moon is the Major Luminary of the Chart

The Diurnal Chart: Directed by The Sun

"They who dream by day are cognizant of many things which escape those who dream only at night."

Edgar Allan Poe (1809-1849)

Obviously the Sun prefers the day where it can display its glory and freely broadcast its light.

Jupiter and Saturn are best suited to an environment where warmth is increased and they can bask in the light provided by the Sun during the daylight hours.

The Sun's clarity and visibility provides both planets with the confidence and comfort to drive forward in order to achieve the native's goals, and to stockpile accomplishments, as the native moves through life.

The Sun signifies ambition and a desire for success or public acknowledgement so it expects its two lieutenants to perform their tasks well.

Jupiter provides the vision, the knowledge and simply the good fortune of being in the right place at the right time, whilst Saturn is required to provide the native with the practical side of things, such as timing, discipline, meticulous planning and naturally, the desire to work tirelessly and with repetition until perfection is achieved.

Two of the diurnal planets are Time-keepers. The Sun counts the minutes of an hour, the hours of the day, the days of the week, the weeks of the month and the months of the year.

Saturn is the other significator of Time, its measurements are much larger but not significantly present until years become decades and a life is lived from the cradle to the grave. Many of Saturn's images are of a skeletal figure, usually Death, who carries the scythe, both an agricultural tool and the instrument which symbolically cuts the ties between the body and the spirit.

With two time-keepers active within the diurnal sect, the individual born during the day carries a visionary timeline within their psyche that says 'this should be happening . . . in a week . . . in six months . . . in five years'. Major events in life are measured along this imaginary timeline; events such as my first job, my wedding date, the birth of my first child, my promotion at work, my overseas trip, etc, in whichever random order best suits the individual with a diurnal chart.

Even though Jupiter is not a time-keeper *per se*, it is an accommodating planet and will do all that it can to keep pace with its luminary and its fellow lieutenant. If a timeline is set by the Sun or Saturn, Jupiter will assist in achieving the end-date, but not without adding more to the list, or stressing the other two planets by expanding in several directions at once in an effort to make the most of every opportunity it encounters along the journey.

The Sun has a certain linear quality which is reflected in the way that it continues to present the same circular golden orb, and follows an (almost) identical pathway across the sky as the gentle movement each day is barely noticeable either towards or returning from its maximum angle of 23.5 degrees around the two solstices of Cancer and Capricorn.

Symbolically, the Sun is constantly on the lookout for its own personal version of The Holy Grail in whatever form this represents for the native, and its influence on the daytime chart as the major luminary signifies the need to constantly set goals and put plans in motion in order for the native to capture their envisioned prize. With each prize gained a new challenge is created to ensure that the individual with a diurnal chart will move forwards to the next pursuit once the Grail has been seized and catalogued, embraced or discarded.

In the words of Winston Churchill, *"If you're going through hell, keep going"*, and the Sun may heed this advice when times get tough for its two subordinates as constant movement and organising a way around disaster galvanises Jupiter and Saturn into action when they strike difficulty. Of the two planets, Jupiter is more likely to push through any difficulties as manoeuvring past barriers and hindrances is part of its nature, but Saturn can baulk at the Sun's advice as sometimes resistance can take the place of perseverance if Saturn is in a difficult position in the chart.

A chart motivated and directed by a combination of Sun, Jupiter and Saturn, will usually do what is necessary to push through on a set course of action towards a perceived goal. Sometimes just maintaining forward momentum is exhausting, especially if it means bluffing or intimidating the opposition, or completely ignoring the obstacles placed in front of them.

Some days reaching the other side (whatever that is to the diurnal individual) is enough to claim triumphant victory, in much the same way as the physical sun must, once it has risen, be compelled to keep moving forwards in order to cross the meridian at noon, and set in the west at the close of day.

The Nocturnal Chart: Directed by The Moon

"Things are as they are.
Looking out into the universe at night, we make no
comparisons between right and wrong stars, nor between well
and badly arranged constellations."

Allan Watts, English philosopher (1915-1973)

Regardless of the sign placement of their Sun, night births view the world subjectively and with a nocturnal intuition that even they cannot fully explain to those born during the day.

To say that roughly half the world's population are governed by the Moon, rather than the Sun, would need to be backed up by statistics on the number of daytime births as opposed to night-time births, especially considering the fact that caesarean section births are generally scheduled during the day when the surgeon is free to perform the operation.

However, the numbers or percentages of night births over day births makes a point that so many charts are ruled by the Moon rather than the Sun, and is a factor which is largely overlooked or unappreciated by modern enthusiasts of astrology.

In terms of planetary sect, a lunar horoscope describes a chart which is nocturnal, that is, the Sun is situated below the horizon, and the Moon retains dominance as the chart's major luminary regardless of its position in the chart.

Technically the term *'lunar horoscope'* would describe a specific type of chart which places the Moon's degree as a temporary Ascendant in a whole sign chart, and the Moon would then direct the new chart from its position on the Ascendant. All the other houses would describe something of the Moon's situation and good aspects would sit in strong houses, and planets with no aspect to the Moon would sit in houses which were weak, passive or dark houses.

Firmicus' *Thema Mundi,* one of the well-known Birth-Charts of the Universe, features the Moon with a partile (same degree) conjunction to the chart's ascendant at fifteen degrees of Cancer, so strictly speaking, *Thema Mundi* is a lunar horoscope which is directed by the Moon on the ascendant.

To avoid confusion, the term 'lunar horoscope' should probably be avoided, and instead the chart should simply be referred to as a nocturnal chart.

The Moon is more subtle in the direction of its subordinates than the Sun, and rather than command or dictate its wishes to Venus, Mars and vespertine Mercury, the Moon encourages each nocturnal planet, in their unique manner to explore their desires, and to express their full range of emotions according to their own temperament.

> *"There should be a place where only the things you want to happen, happen."*

> Maurice Sendak, *Where the Wild Things Are*

Two of the diurnal planets are time-keepers. The Sun measures the day and year, and Saturn measures the big events in the period between birth and death. The three nocturnal planets are not particularly good at being aware of time. Driven by emotions, appetites and desires, the Moon, Venus and Mars work on an inner clock of what feels right, and what does not feel right. No amount of prodding, coercion or logical argument from a diurnal source will entice the nocturnal individual to meet a deadline which is not to their liking as this is a person who is driven by emotions and intuition. Long-term goals have little meaning as the journey is more important than the destination for the person born during the night-time hours.

This is not to say that nocturnal births cannot meet deadlines as Saturn and the Sun are still significant players in their chart. But for this person whose main luminary is the Moon, there needs to be a *valid emotional reason* behind beating the restrictions and taking on the stress of time constraints and schedules, and this reason as little to do with feeling good simply because the deadline was met at the appropriate time.

Nocturnal charts are motivated by their Moon, and the Moon is often more satisfied and happier if the purpose behind a deadline means that a service has been performed which has benefitted another human being or created something to which they feel bound. Emotional attachment is the catch-cry of the Moon and if the individual can form a bond with someone or something to which they become close or protective towards, it will ultimately benefit the completion of the task.

Hounding them, praising them, or promising some individual reward, has little effect on the native born during the night. But make it personal for them by connecting through compassion or affection, paint them a verbal picture of another's pleasure, or the promise of relieving another's pain, and the work will be done, and done well.

Diurnal births can be perplexed or experience frustration when they observe loved ones with nocturnal births supposedly making life choices based on random and haphazard decisions.

However, what the diurnal does not comprehend is that for the nocturnally born, emotions nourish the roots of their motivation and it is the possibility of running the gamut of emotions (and not avoiding them), and thereby experiencing a colourful range of random expressions from deep despair to pure delight which captivates and enthrals them.

Nocturnal births are fascinated by all human behaviour which flows from the threefold combination of desire, emotion and knowledge, and it is not part of the lunar landscape which forms their life to make comparisons between what is good or bad, what is healthy and unhealthy, and what is well constructed or poorly designed.

The Source of Wisdom: *Logos* and *Gnosis*

"Human behaviour flows from three sources: desire, emotion, and knowledge"[4]

Quote incorrectly attributed to Plato

Wisdom comes in many forms for the Greeks, but there are two words for knowledge in the Greek language which, individually, describes the personal experiences which help to shape the native's personality.

At the same time, they serve well to illustrate the differences between how, in general terms, a daytime birth seeks knowledge from an external environment whilst a night birth is more inclined to seek knowledge through dialogue with themselves, or through the exploration of their internal landscape.

Logos is not better informed or wiser than *gnosis*, or vice versa – they are simply different forms of knowledge and each has merit in their own right.

The word *'logos'* is a masculine Greek noun derived from the verb *'lego'* meaning "speaking to a conclusion" and has several meanings such as order, pattern, ratio, reason, mediation, and harmony.

Logos became a technical term in philosophy with Heraclitus using the term to describe the link between order and the attainment of knowledge.

Logos is reasoning expressed by words, and describes pure intellectual logic crystallized into argument in order to communicate an opinion supported by fact.

Organised religions adopted *Logos* for their own purpose as many religions used the sun and its light as a basis for their myths and as an image for their divinities.

Philo of Alexandria (c. 25 BCE – 50 CE) was a Hellenistic Jewish philosopher whose work attempted to fuse Plato's teachings with Judaism. To Philo, *Logos* was not an immaterial concept but instead was the name given to the first-born son of God, sent as a mediator to mankind.

Logos was considered to be a bridge to the divine, being both God's envoy to the world, and an advocate who speaks on behalf of humanity.

In Christianity, Jesus Christ was identified as the incarnate *Logos* in the Gospel of John and some gospels link Christ to solar mythology claiming Him as "the light of the world" and the "Sun of Righteousness".

Diurnal charts may be more comfortable with this interpretation of knowledge because *logos* has an external quality of looking to verify information and to search for knowledge, and then to add practical experience to quantify something as 'wisdom'.

It may be argued that the masculine diurnal planets, Sun, Jupiter and Saturn, are attracted to, and work well, under the rules of *Logos* as a principle for knowledge gained through study, discipline, order and reasoning to achieve balance and success in their world.

A completely different approach to knowledge is described by the word *'gnosis'*, a feminine Greek noun derived from the verb *'ginosko'* meaning "to experientially know". This type of knowledge may be more appealing to the nocturnal chart as the route is not direct and an end-result is not part of the process to gaining 'wisdom'.

Gnosis was a word adopted by the Gnostic sects who believed that *Gnosis* was the path to enlightenment through contemplation, inner experience, spiritual epiphanies and the quest for self-knowledge.

Gnosis was the knowledge which freed the individual from their cultural religious indoctrination and then reconciled them to their own personal deity.

Valentinus (100-160 CE) was an early Christian Gnostic theologian who coined the term *'Gnosis Kardias'* meaning 'knowledge of the heart' or 'insights', which could glean the spiritual nature of the cosmos through inner reflection and intuition.

Gnosis is often used to describe personal knowledge, compared with intellectual or theoretical knowledge.

It relates to the study of knowledge retention, or memory, which is unique to the individual, rather than what is commonly known by the masses.

In *gnosis,* the mind chooses what it considers vital to retain as information through memories, which are often linked with emotions or significant past events.

The direct relationship between theory and practice means *gnosis* is born from first-hand personal experience rather than intellectual discourse, and this type of knowledge gains empathy from the nocturnal planets who constantly react with emotional impulses.

The Moon, Venus and Mars are all planets with 'appetite'. They hunger or thirst for connection, they experience strong yearnings and like to form meaningful attachments. It is these nocturnal planets and their *Gnosis* that bond us together and create both our human behaviour and the spiritual freedom to choose our own beliefs.

The Planets and Sect

> *"Saturn, Jupiter and the sun are diurnal and exercise their power during the day.*
>
> *Mars, Venus and the moon are nocturnal and Mercury is either one or the other . . .*
>
> *Every planet assists those resembling it, the diurnal asking assistance from the diurnal and the nocturnal from the nocturnal.*
>
> *The sun is lord of the day and the moon of the night, because their influence is exerted during these periods."*

Al-Biruni, *The Book Of Instruction in the Art of Astrology,*
Notation #386

Sect Preference DIURNAL Planets	Sect Preference NOCTURNAL Planets
☉ Diurnal Luminary	☽ Nocturnal Luminary
Jupiter (benefic)	Venus (benefic)
Saturn (malefic)	Mars (malefic)
DIURNAL MERCURY	NOCTURNAL MERCURY
Rising and Setting BEFORE the Sun	Rising and Setting AFTER the Sun

Fig. 17 Diurnal and Nocturnal Planets

The Accidental Dignity of planetary sect works in two ways. It links benefic planets with like-minded qualities of heat and moisture and the correct gender of their sect.

At the same time, it takes the extreme qualities of the malefic planets and tempers those planets which are nominated as *"noxious and destructive"*[5] through an association with the luminary which best settles their destructive qualities and mitigates their malevolence.

Ptolemy's *Tetrabiblos* allocates gender to the two divisions of time, the night is feminine because the female sex partakes chiefly of moisture, and moisture increases during the night, and the daytime is masculine, because the day has heat and an aptitude for action.

Likewise, the planets themselves were defined according to gender and the three superior planets, that is, those which are higher in the heavens above the Sun, namely Saturn, Jupiter and Mars were all considered to be masculine in gender.

The Sun, which produces heat and moderate dryness, was also considered to be male.

Jupiter's quality is warmth, due to the fact that its sphere is caught between the extreme cold of Saturn and the burning heat of Mars, and the ancients considered the two extremes would tend to neutralise each other to create temperate warmth for Jupiter. Jupiter has some moisture as well, but not as much as the feminine planets, the Moon and Venus.

A combination of male gender and the qualities of heat and dryness justifies the Sun and Jupiter belonging to the diurnal sect.

Saturn is also a male planet, but it does not share the same warm qualities as the Sun and Jupiter. Saturn needs to counterbalance its extreme coldness by absorbing the Sun's heat in the daytime, and for this reason, it belongs to the daytime sect.

So far as gender is concerned, Saturn and Mars are both masculine and rightly should both belong to the masculine diurnal sect. However, Mars' extreme dryness needs the night's moisture to moderate it, and help it to produce a more favourable temperament, and for this reason, it belongs with the Moon in the nocturnal sect division.

Mars is the exception to the rule that gender defines sect, as Mars is both masculine *and* nocturnal.

Ptolemy explains that the malefics (Saturn and Mars) are not allocated to the division of time which parallels their nature, but that instead, they belong to the sect which is contrary to their natures.

The Moon and Venus are feminine because their qualities are principally moist, and in this way, the feminine night and the feminine planets are linked together through a mutual theme of gender classification.

Mercury is common to both genders, and its sect preference will depend on its position relative to the sun.

Mercury has a presence in the morning if it rises before the sun and has an earlier degree in the zodiac, therefore it is deemed to be diurnal *(Fig. 18)*, but if Mercury is behind the sun in a later zodiacal degree, it has a presence in the evening sky after the sun has set, and it belongs to the nocturnal sect *(Fig. 19)*.

Mercury's position is described as matutine when ahead of the sun because it will rise in the morning before the sun and be visible in the east before the sun's light will cause Mercury to be unnoticeable to the human eye.

Mercury rising after the sun is called vespertine because it will be seen for a short time on the western horizon, after the sun has set. A diurnal Mercury has a short period of visibility in the morning, whilst a nocturnal Mercury has small window for visibility once the Sun has sunk beneath the western horizon.

Time of day does not affect Mercury's sect classification – its sect is dependent on its position in regard to the Sun.

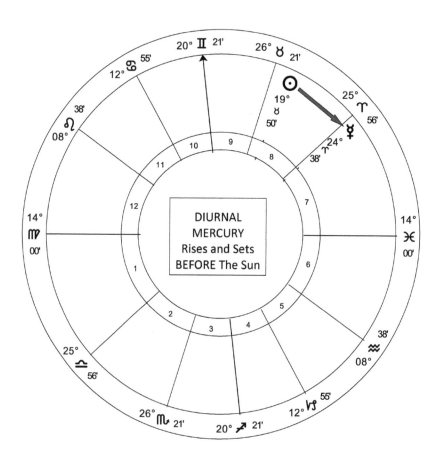

Fig. 18 Mercury in its Diurnal Position

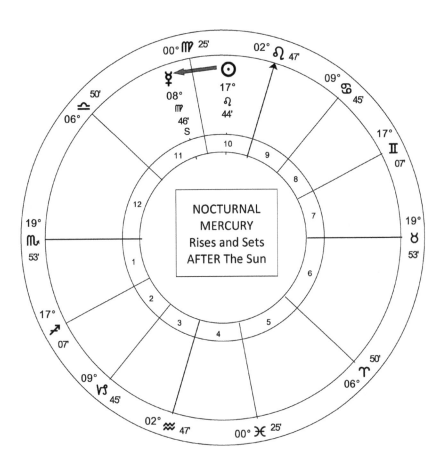

Fig. 19 Mercury in its Nocturnal Position

Practical Application of the First Division of Sect

The following two charts are constructed using the Whole Sign method but they are almost one hour apart. The first chart is calculated for 6:00 am and is a nocturnal chart as the Sun is still below the horizon *(Fig. 20)* whilst the second chart is set at 6:50 am *(Fig. 20a)* and is a diurnal chart because the Sun is featured above the horizon.

In both charts the Sun in the middle degrees of Virgo appears to sit in the centre of the first house. However, the Ascendant's degree at 7 Virgo in *Fig. 20* is the decisive figure in sect division as the 6:00 am chart shows the Ascendant has not yet reached the Sun's 17 degrees of Virgo, and therefore the chart is judged as nocturnal by the first division of sect.

The second chart shows the Ascendant's degree has passed the Sun's degree in the 6:50 am chart, and is now placed at 26 Virgo, giving the impression that the Sun has risen, and that the chart has moved during the intervening fifty minutes from a nocturnal to a diurnal chart.

The two charts set less than an hour apart demonstrate how quickly planetary sect can change from one state to another in the passage of a relatively short time around the periods of sunrise or sunset.

The 6:00 am horoscope is a nocturnal chart *(Fig. 20)* and the Moon would take preference as the main luminary whilst its lieutenants, Venus and Mars, would be in accidental dignity in the chart.

Venus and the Moon are present in both charts and would be considered to be 'in sect' in the first chart which is a nocturnal chart, but not in the second chart which has changed in classification to a diurnal chart.

In contrast, at 6:00 am the diurnal planets, Sun, Jupiter and Saturn would be out of sect according to the first division of sect. The term 'out-of-sect' malefic refers to Saturn in the nocturnal chart as the coldness and the dark environment of the night does not bring out the best in Saturn's nature.

The second chart is set almost one hour later at 6:50 am and shows that the Ascendant has moved deeper into the degrees of Virgo. Its position at 26 Virgo is later than the Sun's degree at 18 Virgo and the Ascendant is now below the Sun's position in the chart *(Fig 20 a)*.

The chart is classified as diurnal and now it is the Sun which has become the major luminary in the second chart.

As the Sun's position in the chart moves from one hemisphere to another, a different set of planets settle more comfortably into their surroundings. When the chart is diurnal, the Sun, Saturn and Jupiter will function with a level of ease and familiarity in this setting. If Mercury had been in a position where it rose before the Sun, it too would be in accidental dignity in a diurnal chart.

This means that in a diurnal chart, the opposite sect (now the nocturnal planets) are left feeling in a less secure position of having to operate in a chart where the territory is foreign to them, and they have to learn to adapt to the conflict between their nature, and their changed environs.

The masculine Jupiter and Saturn have gained accidental dignity in this chart, and had Mercury been ahead of the Sun instead of following it, then Mercury too would be diurnal in nature.

The nocturnal planets (shown here in the chart as the Moon, Venus and Mars) are at a disadvantage in the 6:50 am chart as they would now be out of sect in the diurnal chart. Mars in particular displays less desirable qualities as it has now become the 'out of sect' malefic in the second chart and its behaviour becomes more erratic with its change in sect status. The heat and increased light of daytime exacerbates Mars' tendency to over react to difficult situations and much of its energy is wasted on defending itself against perceived attacks.

"*. . . there cannot be one without the other, yet they cannot exist at the same time*"

The separation of day from night had an incredible impact on Hellenistic astrology, and the battle between the Sun and Moon for superiority over twelve hour divisions of light and dark had significant repercussions for the remaining five planets.

Jupiter and Venus are both benefic planets whose principle role in the chart is to enrich the quality of the native's life.

The level of achievement in this goal is dependent on both the essential and accidental dignity that occurs simultaneously with the moment of birth.

Thankfully, Jupiter and Venus can never truly convert into a force for maleficence, but they are deeply affected by what is going on around them regarding sign, sect, aspect, movement or placement in the chart.

In any given chart, only one benefic can perform its task properly, and this is reliant on whether the chart is diurnal and Jupiter is in sect, or the chart is nocturnal where Venus will be in sect.

Likewise, there are two malefic planets, and one must rise and dominate at the expense of the other.

Saturn and Mars already have a precarious relationship. Mars asks for friendship from Saturn to borrow Capricorn for its sign of exaltation, but Mars also owns Aries, the sign of Saturn's fall, so one could say that the two planets are extremely nervous of one another's motives.

At the first and most basic level of sect, if the birth occurs during the day-time, Saturn would be in sect and has the upper-hand as Mars is the 'out of sect' malefic in the diurnal chart.

The second and third conditions of sect may improve its lot, but these improvements are minor compared with the initial, and most important, division of sect into day or night.

A diurnal chart shows Saturn off to its best advantage.

Loads of opportunity for control and authority for Saturn rankles a displaced Mars who constantly tries to usurp Saturn and ambush its plans for advancement.

If the tables are turned, and the birth occurs during the night-time hours, Mars is in sect and Saturn becomes the 'out of sect' malefic in a nocturnal chart.

Now Mars has the energy, motivation and drive to push forward to claim its advantage, and it is Saturn who creates blockages and disappointments, or undermines Mars' confidence, by questioning the validity of each new decision.

Mercury, as always, has the ability to swing in either direction, so it can befriend either group of planets and commit to either sect depending on its position in relation to the Sun in the chart.

When it comes to planetary sect, the seven planets are destined *"to be always together, yet forever apart"*, and the impact on the chart (and the native) will be huge, as each planet moves towards fulfilling its sect destiny.

Fig 20

WHOLE SIGN CHART: Birth time 6:00 am:
NOCTURNAL SECT, Sun BELOW the horizon

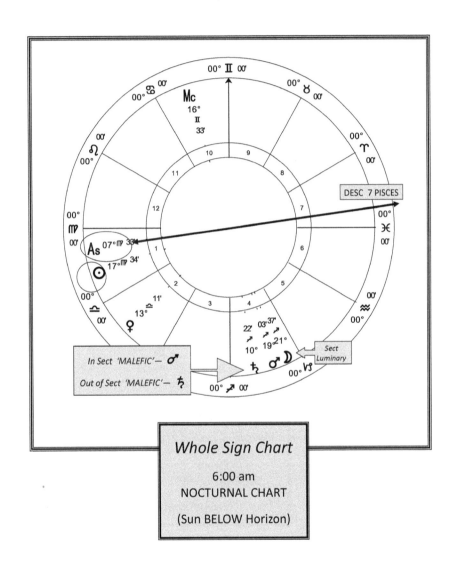

Fig. 20 a)

WHOLE SIGN CHART: Birth time 6:50 am:
DIURNAL SECT, Sun ABOVE the horizon

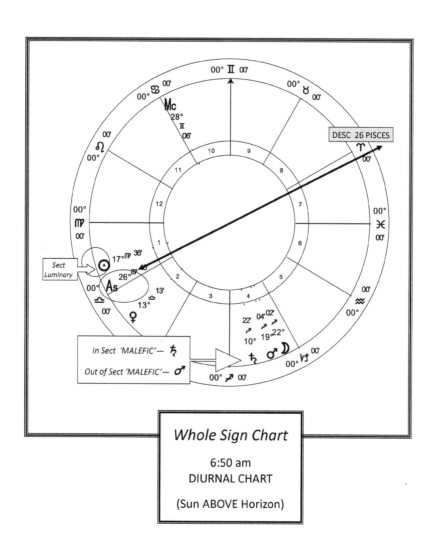

Whole Sign Chart

6:50 am
DIURNAL CHART

(Sun ABOVE Horizon)

The Second Division for Sect
Hemispheres With or Without The Sun

The second sect division can cause confusion amongst those new to the practice of sect, due mainly to the terminology used to describe this particular division in the horoscope.

Once more the Sun plays a major role in determining the second sect division, but this division has little to do with whether the Sun is shining above the horizon or the Moon is providing the night's light when the Sun is beneath the horizon.

In this scenario the circle is still divided into two hemispheres by the line of the horizon, and the Sun's placement in the hemisphere decides the dignity of the second rule of planetary sect.

The hemisphere in which the Sun is located is deemed to belong to the Sun and is called the *Solar Hemisphere or the diurnally placed hemisphere* simply because the Sun is travelling through this area of the chart. In a diurnal chart the Solar Hemisphere is above the horizon and in the nocturnal chart the Solar Hemisphere is beneath the horizon.

Under the rules of the second division, the Sun is the determining factor for the difference between the two hemispheres, and for this reason, **the Sun can never be out of sect according to the second division**, even when in a nocturnal chart the Sun has set below the horizon.

In the Gospel of Matthew, the solar representative of Christianity is Jesus of Nazareth who states, *"Whoever is not with me is against me, and whoever does not gather with me, scatters."*

This polarisation is a perfect example of the second division of planetary sect.

Those planets which *"gather with me"*, that is, with the Sun, are in the part of the chart designated as the *diurnally placed hemisphere*.

Those planets which are *"not with me"*, that is, not travelling with the Sun, are in the hemisphere opposite to the Sun which is called the *nocturnally placed hemisphere or Lunar Hemisphere*. These terms often create confusion as the Lunar Hemisphere does not refer to a night-time chart or even to the hemisphere where the Moon resides, but is used to describe the area of a chart where a planet does not *'gather with the Sun'* and instead *'scatters'* to the other side of the chart.

Diurnal Planets Jupiter and Saturn prefer to gather with the Sun whilst the nocturnal planets, Moon, Venus and Mars prefer to scatter to the opposite hemisphere.

My preference is to use the term 'nocturnally placed hemisphere' in the following diagrams to describe the area in the chart which excludes the Sun, as this can be either the first to sixth houses, or the seventh to twelfth houses, *depending where the Sun is not situated* in the chart.

The simplest way to use the right terminology for the second sect division is to remember that the Ascendant to Descendant axis is the critical diameter of the circle and cuts the circle into two divisions.

Wherever the Sun is placed (either above or below the horizon) instantly becomes the diurnally placed hemisphere, and the opposite half of the circle becomes the nocturnally placed hemisphere.

The Moon's placement is irrelevant to whether the chart is diurnal or nocturnal (Rule Number One of sect), nor does the Moon determine the hemispheres (Rule Number Two of sect) under either of the conditions of planetary sect.

The five planets, plus the Moon, are dependent on the Sun's position in the chart to determine the separation between day or night, whether it be by condition number one, i.e. the physical rising or setting or the Sun, or by condition number two, the Sun's placement in the chart.

All that is needed to find this condition of sect, is to locate which planets travel *on the same side as the Sun* in the same hemisphere, i.e. to determine if they are diurnally placed planets, or to find which planets are travelling *on the opposite side* to the Sun in the other hemisphere, i.e. to decide if they are nocturnally placed planets.

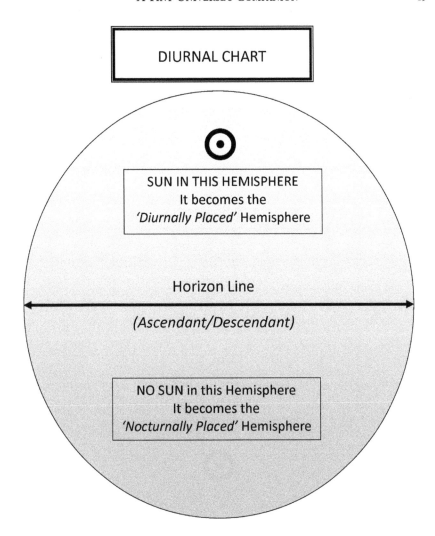

Fig. 21 Diurnal Chart PLUS The Two Hemispheres
(Diurnally Placed and Nocturnally Placed)

JOY USHER

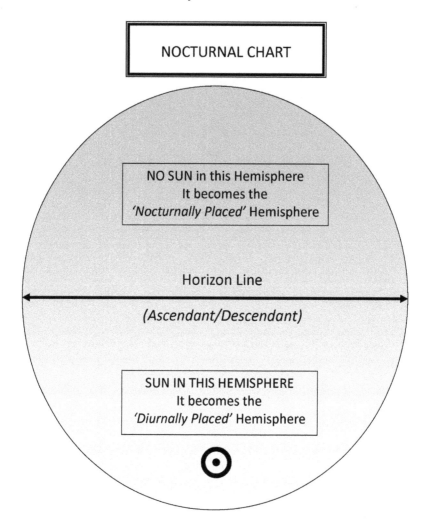

*Fig. 21 a) Nocturnal Chart PLUS The Two Hemispheres
(Diurnally Placed and Nocturnally Placed)*

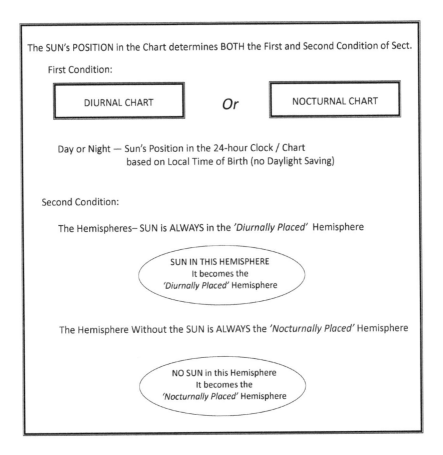

The SUN's POSITION in the Chart determines BOTH the First and Second Condition of Sect.

First Condition:

DIURNAL CHART   *Or*   NOCTURNAL CHART

Day or Night — Sun's Position in the 24-hour Clock / Chart
based on Local Time of Birth (no Daylight Saving)

Second Condition:

The Hemispheres– SUN is ALWAYS in the *'Diurnally Placed'* Hemisphere

SUN IN THIS HEMISPHERE
It becomes the
'Diurnally Placed' Hemisphere

The Hemisphere Without the SUN is ALWAYS the *'Nocturnally Placed'* Hemisphere

NO SUN in this Hemisphere
It becomes the
'Nocturnally Placed' Hemisphere

Fig. 21 b) The First and Second Conditions of Sect Dignity

The following charts are from the examples used earlier – a nocturnal chart calculated for 6:00 am *(Fig. 20)*, and a diurnal chart calculated for 6:50 am *(Fig. 20 a)*. In these diagrams the original seven planets are included in the two charts. The newer planets, Uranus, Neptune and Pluto, have been excluded as they play no part in the accidental dignity of sect.

The first figure *(Fig. 22)* shows all seven planet placed below the horizon in a nocturnal chart.

This means that the Moon is the prime luminary of the chart and that Venus, Mars and the nocturnal Mercury (behind the Sun) have gained accidental dignity because the chart itself matches their sect preference.

By the second classification of sect, the hemisphere below the ascendant becomes the diurnally placed hemisphere, simply because this is where the Sun is situated in the example chart.

In the nocturnal chart, all remaining planets, including the Moon, are situated in the diurnally placed hemisphere and are travelling with the Sun.

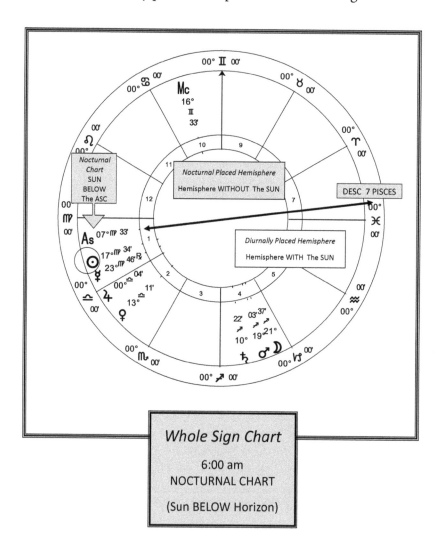

Fig. 22 NOCTURNAL Chart:
The First and Second Conditions of Sect Dignity

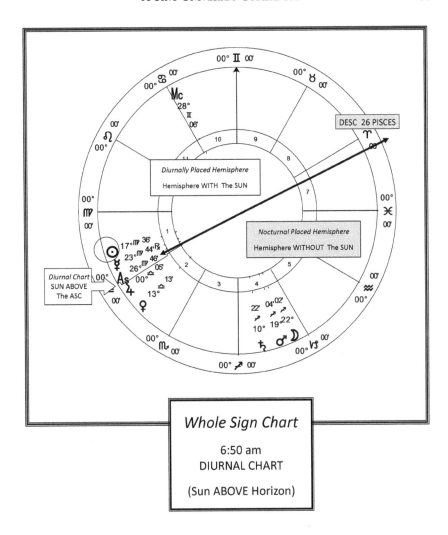

Fig. 22 a) DIURNAL Chart: The First and Second Conditions of Sect Dignity

Once sect dignity has been granted by the primary rule of sect division (primary in both number and in power), that is, the division of day or night, accidental dignity cannot be removed, discarded or diminished if a planet's nature is complimentary to the chart, but its position in the chart does not comply with the second condition of sect.

Non-compliance with the second level of sect *does not remove sect dignity* if it has already been achieved by the critical rule of day or night.

Likewise, a planet which may not have benefitted by the chart, i.e. a diurnal planet in a nocturnal chart or a nocturnal planet in a diurnal chart, has a second opportunity to gain sect dignity through its position in the chart.

Robert Hand, in his book *Night & Day: Planetary Sect in Astrology*, states

"A planet whose sect is not in accord with the chart (Rule One) *is more effective than it would otherwise be if it is correctly placed by hemisphere* (Rule Two) *in the chart."* [6]

The section in Hand's book entitled *General Natures of the Planets According to Sect* discusses principles which can be used as a guideline in delineating the first two rules of sect.

Each of the planets is described as being beneficially enhanced when in agreement with its own sect and Hand suggests that either of the two rules of chart or placement will aid in the planet's expression.

For instance, he says *"Saturn in a diurnal chart or diurnally placed with all other things being equal produces the best qualities of Saturn, discipline, order, and respect."* [7]

The text suggests that either condition will bring out the best in Saturn, and if the first condition is missing, i.e. the chart is nocturnal, then if Saturn is travelling with the Sun in the same hemisphere, it will receive similar blessings from good sect positioning.

In effect, this means that the second rule of sect is put in place as a rule of *inclusion,* rather than as a rule of *exclusion.*

If this is true, then in the 6:00am chart, even though the Moon, Venus, Mars and nocturnal Mercury are situated in the diurnally placed hemisphere (with the Sun) they still *do not lose their sect dignity* because the chart itself is nocturnal.

Jupiter and Saturn in the 6:00am chart *(Fig. 22)* will benefit from the second condition of sect, as whilst the chart is nocturnal, both planets are travelling in the same hemisphere as the Sun, and as diurnal planets, they gain sect dignity by being in the Sun's diurnally placed hemisphere.

In contrast to the first chart, the 6:50 am chart *(Fig. 22 a)* is diurnal because the Sun has moved to the other side of the chart's ascendant.

Of all the planets Mercury loses its sect dignity because its position in regard to the Sun has not altered and it is still a nocturnal planet, but it is now in a diurnal chart and also diurnally placed as it too, has crossed the ascendant with the Sun.

The two diurnal planets, Jupiter and Saturn may be in the opposite hemisphere to the Sun now, but as the chart itself is diurnal, the first rule of sect has blessed these two planets with accidental dignity.

The remaining nocturnal planets, the Moon, Venus and Mars, are out of sect in a diurnal chart, but are helped by the fact that they are in the opposite hemisphere to the Sun now. They gain accidental dignity purely from the fact that they are located in the nocturnally placed hemisphere, away from the Sun.

Spear-Bearers to The Sun and Moon

A number of traditional texts use the term 'rejoicing' to describe a planet in its correct sect division, but there is no traditional term which communicates how a planet reacts when it is in a foreign sect and the planet's nature is out of step with its environment.

Paulus of Alexandria (4th Cent CE) uses the Greek word *'doruphoros'* meaning *'spear bearer'* to describe the type of relationship a planet has with its sect leader.

The Sun has the stars of Kronos and Zeus as spear-bearers and the Moon's spear-bearers are the stars of Ares and Aphrodite.[8]

The term 'spear bearer' suggests elevation in rank - both as an obligation and a privilege – and hints at a planet's pledge to protect its luminary, whether it is Saturn or Jupiter who guards the Sun, or Venus and Mars which honour and serve the Moon as reigning queen of the nocturnal sect.

A planet's ability to perform its duties whether it be loyalty, service, dedication or sacrifice is governed by both the planet's essential and accidental dignities, and the planet will be required to bring its own unique qualities into play.

A benefic tends to serves through reward, assistance or good alliances, whilst the serving malefic, Saturn to the Sun and Mars to the Moon, tends to shrewdly strengthen or fortify its luminary's defences.

Paulus' deliberate use of the term spear-bearer takes planetary sect to another level.

Sect may benefit both the planet and the major luminary of the division when correct sect bestows accidental dignity on the planet, and also benefits the luminary if the planet is able to serve and protect either the Sun or the Moon.

For some translators the Greek *'doruphoros'* became Anglicised as *'doryphory'*, and retained the same meaning as spear-bearers, as is the case in Ashmand's translation of Claudius Ptolemy.

Ptolemy uses *doryphory* as a technique to describe the condition of a native's parents, and lists the conditions under which each sect's spear-bearers, or body guards, can guard their luminary (and the parent) most effectively.

In order for the Sun to benefit from a useful diurnal *doryphory* it requires its same sect attendants, Jupiter, Saturn and Mercury, to rise before him and protect him from frontal attack.

They can either be placed in the same sign as the Sun, but in degrees which precede the Sun, or they can be in the sign immediately before the Sun.

The Moon's best outlook for *doryphory* requires her sect attendants, Venus, Mars and nocturnal Mercury to protect her back and ideally, to rise after her in the degrees of her sign, or in the sign immediately after the Moon's sign.

The concept of planets as spear-bearers to their respective luminary holds interesting nuances for the second division of sect.

If a planet must guard its Lord or Lady, then it makes sense that it can do so much more effectively if it is placed in the correct hemisphere according to its sect.

For instance, Jupiter and Saturn are best to protect the Sun if they are in the same vicinity, so would prefer to be in the diurnally placed hemisphere, travelling alongside the Sun.

If they are nocturnally placed they are of little use as they are removed from the Sun's presence.

There is a phrase known as *'casting the rays'* which refers to a planet having the ability to make its presence known via an aspect, preferably a sextile or trine by Jupiter, and a square or opposition by Saturn, so it is possible for a spear-bearer to protect the Sun from a distance via an aspect, but presumably both planets perform their duties much better if they are visibly present in the same hemisphere as the Sun.

For the nocturnal spear-bearers, their job of shielding the Moon from the rear is not so straight-forward for a number of reasons.

The spear bearers of the Moon would prefer to be in a nocturnally placed hemisphere away from the Sun, but the Moon itself can be close to the Sun when it is completing its twenty nine day lunar cycle or beginning a fresh one at New Moon.

If this is the case, the Moon is more than likely to be located in a diurnally placed hemisphere, and even if the chart itself is nocturnal, she would prefer to be in the opposite location to the Sun.

The further away the Moon moves in her cycle, the more distance she can put between herself and the Sun, and the more comfortable she becomes with Full Moon occurring at the maximum distance of one hundred and eighty degrees between the two luminaries.

Full Moon is the best opportunity for the Moon to be in a nocturnally placed hemisphere, but after the climax of her cycle, the Moon commences her waning phases as she closes the gap between herself and the Sun once more.

Ideally, the Moon would prefer to be in the nocturnally placed hemisphere, far enough away from the Sun to be on the opposite side of the chart, but her nocturnal emissaries may not be fortunate enough to join her there and to serve efficiently as her body guards.

It is possible for Mars to join the Moon in the nocturnal hemisphere because Mars is not tied to the Sun in the geocentrically designed chart and can form the maximum degree aspect of opposition to the Sun thereby putting distance between itself and its contra-sect luminary.

The three planets furthest from Earth in the Chaldean Order are Mars, Jupiter and Saturn who were named as 'superior' because they were on the right-hand side of the Sun and closer to the Ogdoad *(Prime Mover)* in the eighth heaven. Additionally, at least from the chart's perspective, all three superior planets have the ability to move outside of the Sun's direct influence, unlike Venus and Mercury, who are not so fortunate to be free of the Sun.

Along with the Moon, Venus and Mercury were named 'inferior' because of their placement below the Sun and on its left-hand side, and astronomically, Venus and Mercury are situated closer to the Sun than the Earth, and therefore experience limited movement away from the Sun.

Mercury is always less than 30 degrees from the Sun in zodiacal longitude, travelling either in front of the Sun as a diurnal planet or behind the Sun as a nocturnal planet, whilst Venus has a little more freedom, being able of to move a maximum of 48 degrees either side of the Sun.

In terms of sect this means that both planets are more than likely to be found travelling with the Sun in the diurnally placed hemisphere, especially if the birth time is close to midnight creating a nocturnal chart, so at least Venus and nocturnal Mercury have sect dignity, or placed contrary to sect by both rules, when high in the sky in a diurnal chart.

The ability for the nocturnal planets to serve as spear-bearers to the Moon is therefore somewhat limited as they are often trapped in the wrong hemisphere.

A birth near sunset or sunrise can free Venus *(Fig. 22 a)* or a nocturnal Mercury from the Sun's hemisphere, but as the Moon is also caught in a cycle with the Sun, there can be limited opportunities for Venus, Mars or nocturnal Mercury to truly be of much use to the Moon as her nocturnal spear-bearers.

The casting of rays is perhaps the only chance of their being of some use, but if they are uncomfortable in the Sun's presence, or the Moon itself is in the diurnal hemisphere, then the Moon's guards are compromised by one or the other being caught out of sect.

A Dignity Known as '*Halb*'

> "The terms 'hayyiz' and 'halb' are related in meaning, and they share one condition viz. that when a diurnal planet is above the ground by day, and beneath it at night, and when a nocturnal planet is above ground at night and beneath it by day, it is said to be in its halb, and a planet is described as in or not in its halb."

> al-Biruni, *Art of Astrology, Notation #496*

Iranian polymath and astrologer al-Biruni (973-1048 CE) used the term '*halb*' to describe a planet which had the good fortune to be in proper sect according to the second division of sect.

Basically, the diurnal planets, Jupiter and Saturn, prefer to travel with the Sun, so that if either planet is placed above the horizon in a daytime chart, or below the horizon in a night chart, they would be described as being in their *halb (Fig. 23)*.

Likewise, the nocturnal planets, the Moon, Venus or Mars, prefer to travel in the opposite hemisphere to the Sun, so that if any of them are above the horizon at night, or below the horizon during the day, they would be described as being in their *halb* (Fig.23 a).

Mercury can also be in *halb* under the same conditions as the other planets. If it is diurnal (rising before the Sun) it must be above the ground by day and beneath it by night, and if it is nocturnal (rising after the Sun) it must be above the ground by night and below it by day to be classified as being in the sect dignity of *halb*.

The only way the two sect divisions can be achieved at the same time is if diurnal planets, Jupiter and Saturn *(Fig. 23)*, or nocturnal planets, Moon, Venus and Mars *(Fig. 23 a)*, are located in the higher hemisphere above the horizon.

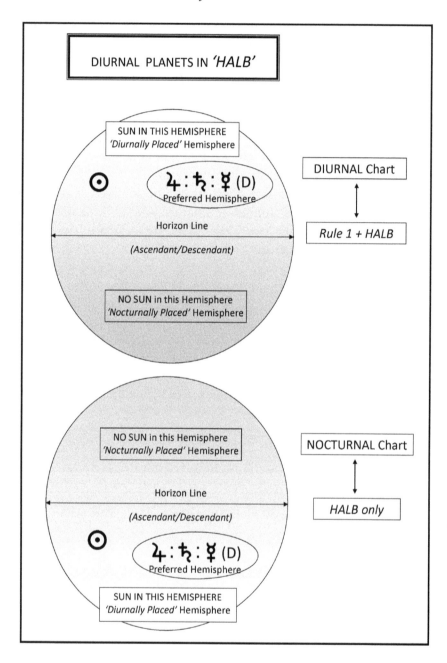

Fig 23 The Condition of HALB for the Diurnal Planets

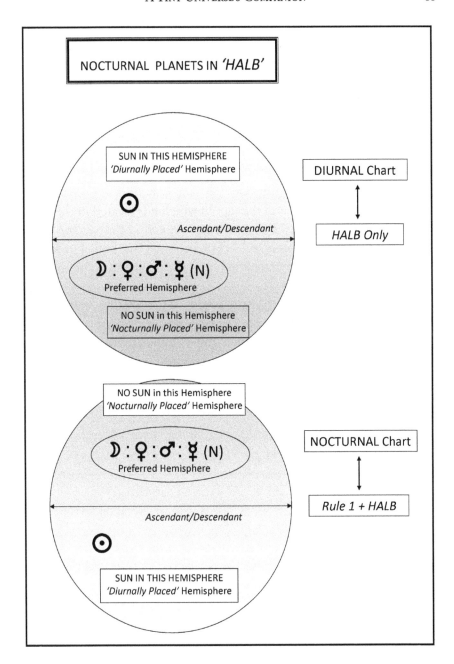

Fig 23 a) The Condition of HALB for the Nocturnal Planets

The Third Division for Sect: The Sign's Gender

"There is a general agreement that all the male signs are diurnal and the female nocturnal.
The diurnal planets are powerful in the day signs and the nocturnal in the night ones."

al-Biruni, Notation #349

The third and final division for sect concerns the correlation between a planet's gender and the sign in which it is located in the chart.

Al-Biruni states that *"The planets are powerful in those signs which resemble them in nature and sex"* [9]. For instance the Sun, Jupiter and Saturn are masculine in gender and prefer their signs to come from the same gender as themselves.

The masculine signs are those whose active quality matches the Sun's heat, that is, the signs from the fire and air element.

The feminine planets, the Moon and Venus, are feminine and they prefer the cold quality signs from the earth and water element.

Mars is the exception to the rule of matching gender with sect, as it is masculine in gender, but nocturnal in sect.

"It should be known that Mars in this matter of hayyiz is different from the other planets, because it is both male and nocturnal."

al-Biruni, Notation #496

For this reason, Mars prefers the masculine signs of fire and air, rather than joining its fellow nocturnal planets, Venus and the Moon which prefer the feminine elements of water and earth.

The earlier authors matched Mars according to its nocturnal sect, citing that it preferred the feminine signs, but al-Biruni clearly states that all three superior planets, Saturn, Jupiter and Mars, are male, adding *"Some people say that Mars is female, but this opinion is not received."* [10]

Modern historian and translator, Robert Hand follows al-Biruni's advice on Mars' situation stating:

"Mars was considered to be in Hayz only when it was in a nocturnal chart, above the horizon (nocturnally placed), in a masculine (diurnal) sign. The logic of sect suggests that this is a later change from an older doctrine in which Mars should have been in a nocturnal (feminine) sign".[11]

Mercury remains its fluid self by adapting to either gender according to its position with the Sun.

If Mercury is oriental, rising before the Sun, it is diurnal, and therefore prefers the masculine diurnal elements of fire and air.

However, should Mercury be occidental, rising after the Sun, it is classified as belonging to the nocturnal sect, and prefers the feminine signs of water and earth.

PLANET	POSITION RELATIVE TO SUN	GENDER	SECT	ELEMENT
☉	—	Masculine	Diurnal	Fire Air
♃	Not Applicable	Masculine	Diurnal	Fire Air
♄	Not Applicable	Masculine	Diurnal	Fire Air
☿	Oriental Occidental	Masculine Feminine	Diurnal Nocturnal	Fire : Air Water : Earth
♂	Not Applicable	Masculine	Nocturnal	Fire Air
♀	Not Applicable	Feminine	Nocturnal	Water Earth
☽	Not Applicable	Feminine	Nocturnal	Water Earth

Fig. 24 Table for the Third Condition of Planetary Sect

The Highest Dignity of Sect:
The Condition Known as *Hayz*

Robert Hand states in his book on sect: *"If a planet's sect is in accordance with the chart, its placement in the chart, and the sect of its sign, it is a quite powerful dignity which is called Hayz."* [12]

It would seem that if all three conditions of sect are fulfilled, that is, the planet is in the correct sect condition according to whether the chart is diurnal or nocturnal, it is placed in the correct hemisphere according to its sect preference (*halb*), and it is in the correct sign according to the planet's gender, then it is considered to be in perfect sect condition, with full dignity intact and is in *Hayz (hayyiz)*.

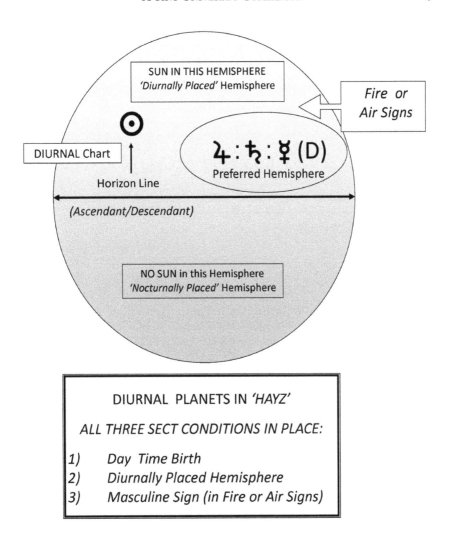

Fig. 25 The Condition of HAYZ for the Diurnal Planets
(Sect Condition One + Two + Three)

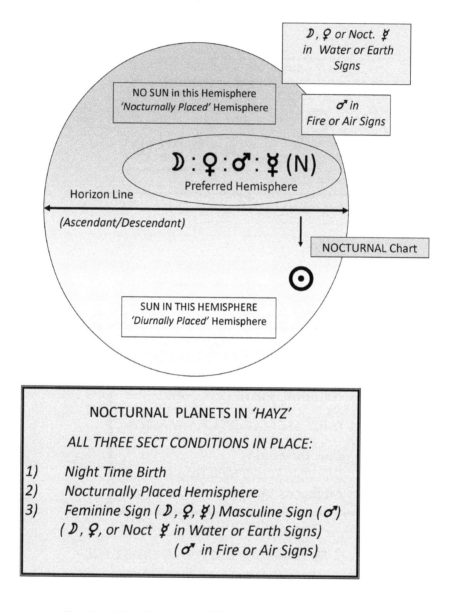

*Fig 25 a) The Condition of HAYZ for the Nocturnal Planets
(Sect Condition One + Two + Three)*

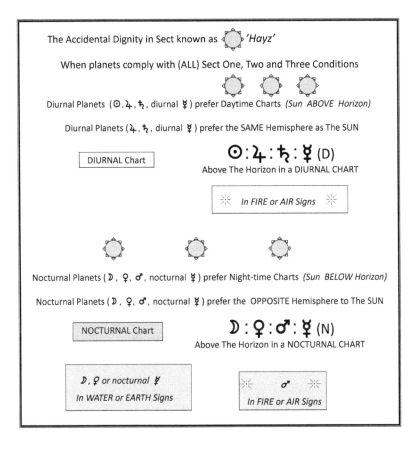

Fig 25 b) The Condition of HAYZ for BOTH Diurnal and Nocturnal Planets (Sect One + Two + Three)

Footnote on *Hayz*
al-Biruni and Valens' Definition on Sect

*"The terms 'hayyiz' and 'halb' are related in meaning, **and they share one condition** viz. that when a diurnal planet is above the ground by day, and beneath it at night, and when a nocturnal planet is above ground at night and beneath it by day, it is said to be in its halb, and a planet is described as in or not in its halb."*

al-Biruni, *Art of Astrology, Notation #496*

The quote cited above is taken from al-Biruni's text concerning sect with reference to the condition known as *halb,* the second condition of planetary sect.

However, it is not the full quote which is complete when al-Biruni continues to define the difference between the condition of *halb* and the more elevated condition of *hayz.*

Concerning *hayz* al-Biruni says:

"When in addition to this (halb) *a planet is male, and in a male sign, or female and in a female sign, the condition is called hayyiz* (hayz), *and a planet is said to be in or not in its hayyiz. Moreover it is obvious that hayyiz is more comprehensive than halb, because every hayyiz is a halb but not every halb a hayyiz."*

These quotes would indicate that so far as al-Biruni is concerned the basic difference between *halb* and *hayz* lies in the matching of the planet's gender with its sign – masculine planets with masculine signs and feminine planets with feminine signs.

As stated previously, Mars is the exception being a masculine planet which belongs to the feminine nocturnal sect, but al-Biruni addresses this discrepancy with the conclusion of Notation #496 saying:

> *"It should be known that Mars in this matter of hayyiz is different from the other planets, because it is both male and nocturnal; if it is above the earth by night and below it by day and in a male sign, it is then in its hayyiz (hayz)."*

> al-Biruni, Notation #496

The relevance of al-Biruni's text is that it does not agree with our perception of what comprises a planet being in the state of *hayz.*

Robert Hand states that all three conditions must be met in order for a planet to be in *hayz* and the astrological community which practices traditional techniques seems to agree with his belief.

However, al-Biruni's text infers that a diurnal planet does no need to be in a diurnal chart to be in *hayz (beneath the ground by night),* nor does a nocturnal planet need a nocturnal chart to receive the blessings of *hayz.* al-Biruni's statement on Mars makes this particularly clear *". . . below it by day and in a male sign, it is then in its hayyiz (hayz)."*

Vettius Valens predates al-Biruni by several centuries, his considerable works of *Anthology* written in Greek in the first century CE and coming from the Hellenistic roots of astrology. The Arabic term *Hayz* is not part of his language but planetary sect is an integral part of his teachings.

In the conclusion to Book II of *Anthology* Valens states:

"It is also necessary to consider the sect of the stars, for the Sun, Zeus, and Kronos rejoice when they are above the earth during the day, below the earth at night. But the Moon, Ares, and Aphrodite rejoice when they are above the earth at night, and below the earth during the day . . ."[13]

The condition that Valens has just described would confer with al-Biruni's later description of planets in *halb*.

Valens continues his text by defining good sect condition for both diurnal and nocturnal sect divisions.

"Whence, for those who are born by day, if someone should be found to have Zeus, the Sun, and Kronos well-figured above the earth, it will be better than having them below the earth.

Similarly also for the nocturnal planets, if someone should have them above the earth (at night), it will be expedient."

Valens has now included the primary rule of sect and is closer to the compliance of all three rules to be classified as *hayz* according to Robert Hand, especially if *"well-figured"* includes the planets' gender or sect preference being correctly aligned with their appropriate sign gender (masculine with masculine signs, fire and air, and feminine planets with feminine signs, earth and water).

Regarding Mercury's sect preference Valens adds an unexpected twist which has no relationship to its position in regard to the Sun (matutine or vespertine). Valens says:

"Hermes goes with the sects of the ruler in whose bounds it lies."

Editor of Valens' Project Hindsight translation Robert Hand adds that this is the first time that this condition for the determination of the sect of Hermes has been seen.[14]

The Egyptian Terms or Bounds *(Fig. 75)* are the fourth level of Essential Dignity which divides the each of the twelve signs into five categories of differing degrees ruled by the five planets (the luminaries are excluded from the Terms).

In many cases the last third of the Terms are ruled by the malefics, either Saturn or Mars, and if Valens' text applies this rule to Mercury it could belong to either the diurnal sect malefic (Saturn) or the nocturnal sect malefic (Mars).

The two benefic planets are also Term Rulers and Mercury can just as easily be classified as a diurnal planet if Jupiter is its ruler, or a nocturnal planet if Mercury is in the terms of Venus.

However, where this system falls down is if Mercury should be in the degrees of a sign where Mercury is the term ruler – no sect dignity can be determined when this is the case so perhaps it is far simpler to observe the later classifications for Mercury's sect identity.

The rediscovery of planetary sect is relatively new to modern astrologers and the gaps in our ancient texts are enormous considering the time-spans involved and the changes in language and methodology over the centuries of astrology's history.

We may never retrieve the bulk of the writings on certain techniques which have been largely ignored or discarded over the years, but it is critical for the future of astrology to be aware of the differences and to keep discussions open to all interpretations both old and new.

Planetary Sect and *Munakara* (Contention)

"Munakara (or contention) is nearly the reverse of hayyiz and occurs when a diurnal planet is in the domicile of a nocturnal one, and the latter is in the domicile of a diurnal one; or when a nocturnal planet is in the domicile of a diurnal one, and the latter is in the domicile of a nocturnal planet." [15]

al-Biruni, *The Art of Astrology*, Notation #497

The accompanying Footnote to al-Biruni's text is provided by the translator, R. Ramsey Wright, with two examples of planets in the state of *munakara*:

"Eg. Saturn in Aries and Mars in Pisces or Mars in Pisces and Jupiter in Taurus"

In order to examine this curious rule the following diagram *(Fig. 26)* is included to illustrate the first example given on *munakara*: *"Saturn in Aries and Mars in Pisces"*

If Saturn is found in Aries, and its dispositor Mars, is in Pisces, it means that Mars itself is disposited by Jupiter, then Saturn (the original planet) is in a state of *'munakara'* or contention.

In other words, *the dispositor* for the first planet *(Diurnal planet – Saturn)* is the second planet *(Nocturnal planet – Mars, the ruler of Aries)* which in turn is disposited by the third planet *(Diurnal planet – Jupiter, ruler of Pisces)*.

If this is the case, then it is the FIRST planet which suffers the fate of *munakara* or contention.

The first example of al-Biruni's *munakara* (CONTENTION)

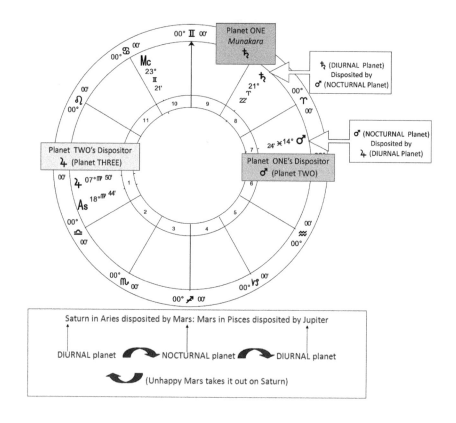

Fig 26 The First Example: Saturn in Munakara

The three planets involved have crossed the sect boundary from Diurnal (Saturn in Aries) to being disposited by a Nocturnal planet (Mars in Pisces), which is in turn is disposited by another counter-sect Diurnal planet (Jupiter, ruler of Pisces).

The effect of *munakara* on Saturn is that presumably, the planet Saturn feels as though it is constantly surrounded by issues of contention or dispute.

Al-Biruni states:

"Munakara (or contention) is nearly the reverse of hayyiz . . ."

If *hayz (hayyiz)* is the most comfortable and at ease state a planet can find itself in, whereby each of the three conditions of sect are in its favour, then we can assume that the opposite occurs for a planet to find themselves in the unfortunate situation of *munakara*.

This would mean that the planet (in this case, Saturn) is extremely uncomfortable in its environment or constantly feels under attack, and therefore becomes super sensitive to interference from an external force. Whatever part of life Saturn signifies in the chart, through its placement, aspects or house rulerships, is an area where the chart's owner feels they are possibly misunderstood or misrepresented, or that their authority will be constantly challenged by others.

It should be noted that whilst *munakara* is determined by whether a planet's nature is classified as either diurnal or nocturnal, the actual state of a planet's sect condition is outside of *munakara*, although presumably, the better a planet's sect condition, the better it is able to handle the difficult situation of contention.

'Mars in Pisces and Jupiter in Taurus'

If Mars *(a nocturnal planet)* is found in Pisces, then its dispositor is Jupiter *(a diurnal planet)*.

If Jupiter is then found to be in Taurus, it means that Jupiter itself is disposited by Venus *(a nocturnal planet)*.

The first planet, **and only the first planet**, in this case Mars, is considered to be in a state of *munakara* or contention.

The second example of al-Biruni's *munakara* (CONTENTION)

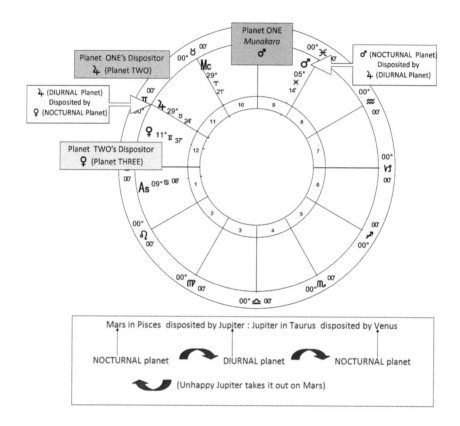

Fig 27 The Second Example: Mars in Munakara

Once more, the three planets involved have crossed the sect boundary from Nocturnal (Mars) to Diurnal (Jupiter, ruler of Pisces) back to Nocturnal (Venus, the ruler of Taurus), and the dispositor of Jupiter.

With the second example of al-Biruni's rule, Mars is in *munakara* in the chart.

This time it is Mars which constantly feels it is surrounded by issues of contention and experiences extreme discomfort in its environment or is constantly on guard against an attack.

Depending on its sect condition (nocturnal or diurnal chart; diurnally or nocturnally placed) the Mars in Pisces would prefer a masculine sign at least to help it overcome its ultra-sensitivity, and whatever part of life Mars signifies in the chart, is an area where the native fears unexpected challenges, or is unsure if they will be a target for dissent or hostility.

It is worth noting that each planet owns two signs apiece, and the state of *munakara* can occur if a planet is located in *either sign* of its opposing sect lord. Mars can just as easily be in *munakara* in Sagittarius as in Pisces, and likewise, Saturn would suffer the same fate had it been in Mars' female sign of Scorpio, rather than its masculine sign of Aries.

A planet can be in *munakara* and still be in the correct chart for its sect, in the right hemisphere for its sect, and in the right gender sign for its sect. In other words, it is technically possible for a planet to be both in *hayz* (perfect sect condition) and in *munakara* (stressed by being in contention).

One situation does not cancel out the other as this is a rule which is dependent on the dispositor, the owner of the sign in which a planet finds itself.

What Does Contention Mean for a Planet?

al-Biruni's text tells us that the closest English translation for *munakara* is 'contention', a word meaning dispute, conflict, strife or disharmony.

There is nothing 'content' or satisfying about a planet being in contention.

The three step process to finding out if a planet is in contention can be likened to a traveller going into hostile territory, or being under the control of someone who wishes them harm, simply because they themselves are quarrelling with their own dispositor/lord.

The link is twofold, but the first and third planets are unrelated, even though they share the same sect.

Munakara goes through the process of dispositor-ship which involves diurnal planet being in the sign of a nocturnal planet which is then in the sign of a diurnal planet (diurnal to nocturnal to diurnal).

Or the original nocturnal planet can be in a sign belonging to a diurnal planet which is in a sign belonging to a nocturnal planet (nocturnal to diurnal to nocturnal).

Circumstances, or the link to the host planet in the centre of the scenario, makes the traveller the likely candidate who gets the short order of the stick, as it becomes the planet on which the central figure can relieve their own frustrations.

It is as if the traveller is in the wrong place at the wrong time, and therefore must suffer the consequences.

The horizon separates two territories – diurnal and nocturnal – and each of the planets chooses one territory over another.

In Example One, Saturn is the 'fall guy' for a disconsolate Mars which finds itself in trouble when its own sign (Pisces) is ruled by Jupiter from an opposing sect.

Even though we find the information by moving from Saturn to Mars to Jupiter, the ultimate penalty is metered out to the one at the beginning who sets the chain in motion.

Munakara or contention only occurs when **both** planets' dispositors belong to the opposite sect.

The chain is broken and *munakara* is avoided if two dispositors share the same sect, i.e. if Saturn was disposited by Sun or Jupiter, rather than Mars, or if Mars was disposited by the Moon or Venus, rather than Jupiter.

The principle of *munakara* demonstrates the rivalry which splits the planets and puts them into opposing camps.

By dispositors swapping camps back and forward, the planet in question is caught in a conflict which removes the comfort it may have found through position in the chart, but this comfort is destroyed or undermined by the ruler of its sign, if it belongs to a foreign territory.

Once more, the importance of dispositor-ship becomes apparent in these older techniques, and the change from one division to the other must occur twice for the repercussions to bounce back on the initial planet.

This condition shows the hierarchy of command.

In a workplace, it is the underling who suffers if their boss is getting a hard time from the boss above them, and each planet looks back and punishes the one below them, purely for their lack of comfort, as in the planet's case, if the condition of the three sects was not duplicated or repeated.

If this were a family situation, the youngest sibling in a family of three children is adversely affected by the behaviour of its immediate predecessor, because they, (the middle child) are getting picked on by the eldest child. The middle child's bad temper goes down the line to the youngest, who finds themselves in a state of *munakara* or contention.

They are feeling downcast or powerless because they are in a hostile environment and have no further outlet by which they can vent their own frustrations because they are the littlest one in the household.

Munakara does not detract from the planets' sect condition, but it does add awareness to the state of a planet's comfort, and therefore if a planet is in contention with its dispositor it will affect its performance in the chart, or will show the chart owner's attitude to trouble around its beleaguered planet.

What does a planet have to contend with?

The whole idea of having to 'contend with' something suggests a level of edginess or a feeling of dread. It can also convey a sense of weariness or exasperation at having to repeat a process or endure a situation with the expectation that it cannot easily reach a resolution.

If the same can be said for a planet in this state, then there is an expectation that whatever the planet signifies (both in its essence and specific to its situation in the chart) will be areas in life where there is a state of agitation, resignation, touchiness or defensive action if the planet considers itself, or its houses, to be under threat.

Controversy can surround a planet in *munakara* and depending on the planet's condition there can be a loss of reputation, a battle, dispute or rivalry in which the native can feel they have unjustly become involved.

Each planet will struggle in their own way with contention as a Moon can battle with health issues whilst the Sun can experience contests and altercations around the person's integrity, their reputation, or even caught up in battles which may have been begun by the father and must be carried on by the child or family member with a Sun in contention.

The following Table *(Fig. 28)* contains suggestions on how a planet might experience *munakara* but as there seems to be very little available on this situation, these are merely guidelines for what may occur, or what the native might experience if they find a planet in their chart is in a situation of *munakara*.

The charts which are examined in detail in Chapter Three are the two Williams sisters, Venus and Serena, and it is interesting to note that both charts have a planet in *munakara*.

Venus Williams has a Leo Moon which is *munakara* and Serena Williams has Mars (also in Leo) in a state of *munakara,* and I believe that both women have experienced circumstances of contention surrounding these planets, one apiece, in their natal charts and in their lives.

Even the synastry between the two planets (Venus' Moon and Serena's Mars are twelve degrees apart) is no co-incidence as the sisters have spent a lifetime playing on opposite sides of a tennis court, in a constant state of contention, across the divide created by a braided net.

How does *munakara* affect a planet's behaviour?

PLANET	*'Munakara'* — The State of Contention
SATURN	The feeling of being under attack from authority figures; having one's authority, expertise or integrity challenged by others; a fearful, disparaging or negative attitude towards father, authority or responsibility; a fascination for secret dealings, or a belief in conspiracy theories concerning governments or powerful organisations.
JUPITER	Physical, social or financial risk taking; excessive behaviour or indulgences which have potentially harmful or addictive consequences; tendency to exaggeration or resentment when challenged by others; obstacles or constant set-backs in achieving success, recognition or ambitions; difficulty with children or money; a feeling of being unprotected or unlucky.
MARS	Suspicion about others' motives; defensive behaviour when threats occur, whether these are real or perceived to be real; experiences of bullying, confrontational or frightening behaviour; attacks on one's masculinity (males), encounters with aggressive or violent males (females); a highly competitive individual who sees personal challenges as full-scale battles.
SUN	Perceived or genuine attacks on the individual's opinions, integrity or reputation; constant need to defend father's actions or feeling the compulsion to justify one's own actions; weakened energy levels or enthusiasm; difficulty in setting goals and maintaining focus or achieving final successful outcome; fear of criticism, public ridicule or humiliation.
VENUS	Fear of unpopularity or public rejection; a sensitivity to hostile environments; perceived or genuine attacks or personal criticism from others; unwarranted attention with sexual connotations; possible scandals; concerns about attractiveness.
MERCURY	Contending with rumours or gossip; cyber-bullying; misunderstandings or arguments; poor communication, reading or writing skills; shyness or speech impediments; suspect money activities or business failings through reading the market incorrectly; challenges in fine motor skills or movement; unresolved issues or conflict with siblings.
MOON	History of the mother (or the native) under attack; a difficult relationship with mother; challenges in maintaining physical strength or mobility; poor health through illness, emotional stress or accidents; a highly sensitive or self-protective individual; fears of separation, alienation or betrayal by loved ones; a need for family to provide an emotional 'buffer' against the outside world; a strong need for privacy or personal space; shyness or withdrawal in public arenas.

Fig 28 The Planets in a State of Contention (Munakara)

CHAPTER TWO

The Planets and Sect Dignity

Vettius Valens (120 – c.175 CE) was a scholar and teacher of astrology whose comprehensive work *Anthologies* [16], contains techniques and chart examples of Hellenistic astrology as it was practised in his day.

THE SUN: Main Luminary of the Diurnal Sect

"In the nativity the all-seeing Sun, nature's fire and intellectual light, the organ of mental perception, indicates kingship, rule, intellect, intelligence, beauty, motion, loftiness of fortune, the ordinance of gods, judgement, public reputation, action, authority over the masses, the father, the master, friendship, noble personages, honours consisting of pictures, statues, and garlands, high priesthoods, rulership over one's country and over other places.

Of the parts of the body, the sun rules the head; of the sense organs, it rules the right eye;

of the trunk, it rules the heart; of the spiritual (i.e. the perceptive) faculties, the nerves.

Of materials, it rules gold; of fruits, it rules wheat and barley.

<u>*It is of the day sect,*</u> *yellowish, bitter in taste."*

Vettius Valens, *Anthologies, Book One*

Condition One – Day or Night
The Sun in Comfort

In a diurnal chart the individual's psyche is geared towards reaching the objectives of the Sun.

The agenda set by the Sun is as clear-cut as the light it provides each day, and as unchanging as the golden orb it presents to the Earth, regardless of the time of year and the opposing seasons.

Fame, fortune, acknowledgement, reputation and advancement are the Sun's desires, so when Jupiter brings good fortune and Saturn provides the planning and time management, the Sun is better able to achieve its objectives.

In a nocturnal chart the Sun is less comfortable when required to step back and take on a secondary role when the Moon becomes the major luminary in the chart.

If the Sun is determined to push its agenda, it must do so with the Moon's blessing, as no amount of success or accolades will keep the native occupied if they feel unhappy or discontent within the bounds of life's daily management.

The Moon is programmed to serve and if its service counts for nothing then fame and fortune will not hold the native to the Sun's agenda.

As the major luminary in a nocturnal chart, the Moon will constantly challenge the Sun and question its motives, as the Sun cannot stay its course if the Moon is dissatisfied or the direction 'does not feel right' to the individual.

Reason and intellect will not prevail over intuition and emotion, and the native will eventually be forced by the Moon's subtle influence to make necessary changes to their life, regardless of how lacking in 'sense' these changes may appear to the rational mind.

That is not to say that a nocturnal birth cannot achieve and maintain success. However, it must be on their terms, and if the individual is prepared to accept and accommodate the Moon's changing patterns, then they will not stress when confronted with the waxing or waning periods of their accomplishments.

A Sun in a feminine sign in a nocturnal chart can be a distinct advantage as it may be more prepared to work under the Moon's supervision and to trust 'in the process' which is guided more by the nocturnal luminary than by its own drive and purpose.

Condition Two – Which Hemisphere?
The Sun's Power

The Sun will *always* be in sect according to the second condition, as it is the Sun which sets the terms in this division between hemispheres.

The Sun's placement above or below the horizon provides the nomenclature for this sect condition, given that the name chosen to describe each area is based on the Sun's presence in the *"diurnally placed hemisphere"* as opposed to the lack of its presence in the *"nocturnally placed hemisphere"*.

One of the common confusions for both sect conditions is the misconception that the Moon should play a role in determining which is a *"nocturnal chart"* or which area is the *"the nocturnally based hemisphere"*.

The Moon has little relevance in the conditions of sect as it is *always* the Sun that determines both sect categories, and unfortunately for nocturnal births, the weight and power of sect lies with the Sun, especially when it comes to the second rule of sect.

In astronomical terms the Moon has no light source and must rely on the Sun's projected light for its own illumination.

The conditions of sect seem to parallel the Moon's situation, and there can be a sense of frustration for nocturnal births when sect appears to favour the Sun in respect to its conditions.

The diagram *(Fig. 29)* illustrates the three possibilities for the Sun to be in *Hayz* – a preference for a daytime chart when it is placed above the horizon (the star), plus the second condition where it claims either hemisphere as its own (the second star), regardless of whether it in above or below the horizon in the chart, and lastly, a preference for the masculine, diurnal signs from either the fire or air element.

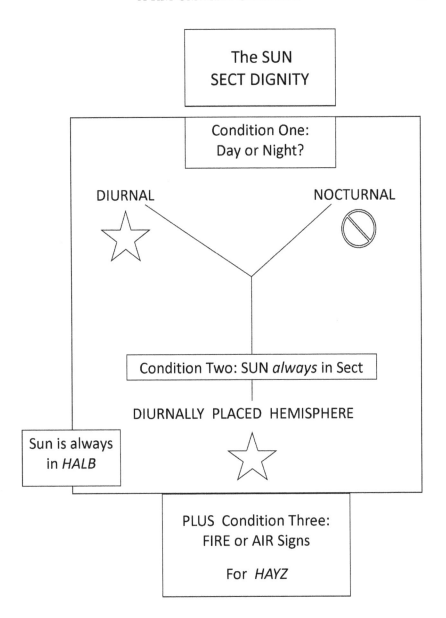

Fig. 29 The Sun in Sect Dignity

The Sun in a State of *Munakara*

Munakara or contention is not dependent on position in the chart, and is totally reliant on the natural selection of a planet's preference for either diurnal or nocturnal categories.

For this reason, the Sun receives no preferential treatment and has as much chance of being in a state of *munakara* as any of the other planets.

The first step towards determining if the Sun is *munakara,* is to look at the Sun's sign, because as a diurnal planet, if it is placed in a sign which belongs to a nocturnal planet, this is the first step towards *munakara.*

This consideration of movement from diurnal to nocturnal via a sign's dispositor has no regard as to the sign's gender, as each of the five planets rules one feminine and one masculine sign.

However, should the Sun be in a sign belonging to a nocturnal planet, the Moon (Cancer), or Venus (Libra/Taurus), or Mars (Aries/Scorpio), as well as possibly to a nocturnal Mercury rising after the Sun (Gemini/Virgo), the Sun's dispositor's sect classification will also need to be examined.

If the Sun's dispositor is itself disposited by a planet from an opposing sect, in this case a different diurnal planet apart from the Sun, then the Sun is judged as being caught in *munakara* or contention, and this state causes significant concern and stress for the luminary.

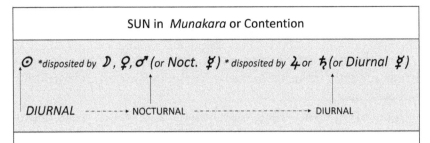

Fig. 30 The Sun in Contention (munakara)

JUPITER: The Benefic of the Diurnal Sect

"Jupiter indicates childbearing, engendering, desire, loves, political ties, acquaintance, friendships with great men, prosperity, salaries, great gifts, an abundance of crops, justice, offices, office-holding ranks, authority over temples, arbitrations, trusts, inheritance, brotherhood, fellowship, beneficence, the secure possession of goods, relief from troubles, release from bonds, freedom, deposits in trust, money, stewardships.

Of the external body parts it rules the thighs and the feet.

Of the internal parts it rules the sperm, the uterus, the liver, the parts of the right side.

Of materials, it rules tin.

It is of the day sect. In colour it is grey verging on white and is sweet in taste."

Condition One – Day or Night
Jupiter in Comfort

In a diurnal chart, Jupiter serves the Sun well by bringing good fortune and great influence to the native through wealth and friendships with great men.

Jupiter is known as the greater benefic, and as such it can nourish the Sun's ambitions by nurturing possibilities and furnishing all the right connections at the most appropriate time.

In a diurnal chart, Jupiter's objectives are clear – promote the native, connect with powerful people, educate and influence those beneath the native in status or wealth, and bring forward children so that the dynasty can live on and prosper in the future.

The Chinese philosopher Confucius once said *"Wherever you go, go with all your heart"* and this would seem to be a 'happy' Jupiter's motto when it serves the human heart's representative, the Sun.

Jupiter is also capable of bringing benefit to a nocturnal chart. However, it can lack the clarity of direction it receives when serving the Sun, and Jupiter by night is often unsure of how best to offer its gifts to the Moon, the dominant luminary in a night-time chart.

Jupiter is still capable of providing abundance, but it does so as an outsider to the nocturnal clan and the comfort and confidence it would usually display is dampened or misunderstood by the three emotion-driven planets of the nocturnal sect.

For this reason, Jupiter in its nervousness, either falls short of expectations, or exaggerates its qualities, and can unintentionally make matters worse for the native.

Jupiter needs the Sun's guidance in determining what associations and friendships are appropriate or advantageous, so that when it brings alliances to a nocturnal chart, these new friendships are not always in the native's best interests and can hinder the native or cause them distress, and even bring about their downfall.

A diurnal Jupiter has the ability to discern who is genuinely capable of expanding the native's horizons, but a nocturnal Jupiter can be impressed by others' bravado and may not be able to discern between who is genuine and who is boasting or *'tooting their own trumpet'*.

A nocturnal Jupiter can also become ensnared by the appetites of the nocturnal planets and can spend more time immersing itself in pleasure, or dreaming up unrealistic scenarios, than in actually being productive, especially if Jupiter is removed from Saturn's discipline or the Sun's watchful eye.

Under certain sect conditions, Jupiter is capable of producing one of life's gamblers whose indulgences become gargantuan, and whose hedonistic lifestyle or narcissistic behaviour, can be extremely destructive for the sensitive individual born during the night-time hours.

As a diurnal planet Jupiter seeks exposure and the room to expand.

It loves grand gestures and the opportunity to show off its intelligence and knowledge, but if this energy is forced upon a shy or introverted native born during the night, they can feel exposed or threatened by Jupiter's propensity for over-sharing personal details.

Shy, introverted people are born during the day too, but the Sun is better equipped to direct Jupiter's enthusiasm towards making plans for the future. The Moon, the nocturnal luminary, is often uncomfortable with Jupiter's need for grand or dramatic displays of wealth or influence.

Condition Two – Which Hemisphere?
Jupiter's Protection of The Sun

Jupiter, diurnally-placed, is both protected by, and protective of, the Sun.

If Jupiter is positioned in the same hemisphere as the Sun, regardless of whether the chart itself is diurnal or nocturnal, then it becomes an effective spear-bearer for the Sun, and the two planets work together to achieve success for the individual.

The best scenario is for Jupiter to be situated above the horizon in a diurnal chart.

In this case Jupiter possesses both the comfort of environment (Sect Division One) and the ability to serve and protect the Sun (Sect Division Two).

It has accidental dignity based on two events – the time of birth, and its position in the zodiac relative to the chart's Ascendant's sign and degree – and the only thing needed to elevate Jupiter to the highest sect dignity of '*hayz*' is placement in a masculine sign of either fire or air element.

If Jupiter is situated in the opposite hemisphere from the Sun, it loses some of its efficiency in being able to aid the Sun in achieving its goals, or making the important connections the Sun needs, in order to advance socially or politically in the world, and financial security can be jeopardised by a nocturnally-placed Jupiter.

Two marks against Jupiter that can impact its ability to deliver, are firstly, being in a nocturnal chart and secondly being nocturnally placed, which makes life even harder for Jupiter.

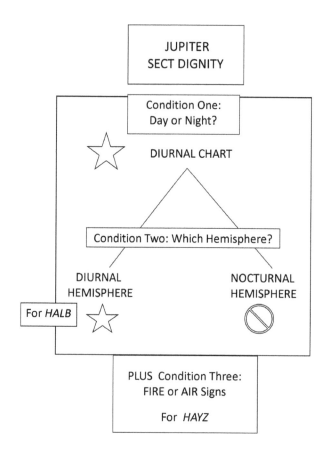

Fig. 31 Jupiter in Sect Dignity

The further Jupiter becomes removed from the Sun, the more its discomfort and a loss of confidence increases as this planet badly needs instruction from the Sun.

An uncomfortable, misdirected Jupiter is still not a malefic, but it does lose consistency and can miss opportunities or blur the boundaries, as it becomes more intertwined with the nocturnal planets.

As the diagram *(Fig.31)* shows Jupiter prefers a diurnal chart and/ or a placement in the same hemisphere as the Sun (*Halb*), and its preference is to be associated with a masculine diurnal sign from either the fire or air elements.

If all three sect conditions are achieved by Jupiter it would be in the maximum quality of sect condition, known as *Hayz*.

The most uncomfortable situation for Jupiter is in a nocturnal chart and in the opposite hemisphere from the Sun, as well as being placed in one of the feminine nocturnal signs of earth or water element.

When none of the three sect conditions are met, Jupiter is completely out of sect. Robert Hand calls this situation *'ex conditione'* (literally 'without the condition of sect').[17]

Jupiter in *Munakara*

If Jupiter is *munakara*, that is, if its dispositor is a nocturnal planet (Moon, Venus, Mars or nocturnal Mercury), and if the nocturnal planet is then disposited by a diurnal planet (Sun, Saturn or diurnal Mercury), this may spoil an otherwise dignified Jupiter.

Jupiter may be exalted in the Moon's sign of Cancer, but if it wants to avoid *munakara*, it had better hope that the Moon in the chart is not disposited by a diurnal planet. If this is the case, Jupiter may have exaltation, but it will have a bundle of trouble to accompany its elevated status.

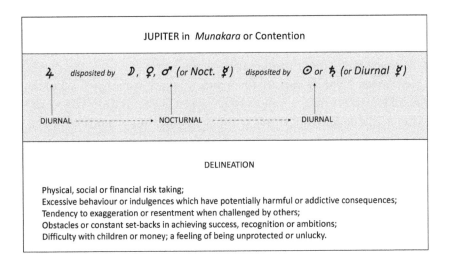

Fig. 32 Jupiter in Contention (munakara)

SATURN: Malefic of the Diurnal Sect

"Saturn causes humblings, sluggishness, unemployment, obstacles in business, interminable lawsuits, subversion of business, secrets, imprisonment, chains, griefs, accusations, tears, bereavement, capture, exposures of children.

It puts into one's hands great ranks and distinguished positions, supervisions, and management of others' property. Of materials, it rules lead, wood, and stone.

Of the limbs of the body, it rules the legs, the knees, the tendons, the lymph, the phlegm, the bladder, the kidneys, and the internal, hidden organs.

Saturn makes bachelors and widows, bereavements, and childlessness.

It causes violent deaths by water, strangulation, imprisonment and dysentery.

It is the star of Nemesis; it is of the day sect. It is like castor in colour and astringent in taste".

Condition One – Day or Night
Saturn in Comfort

Valens paints Saturn as a dark and difficult planet, however, its qualities improve when Saturn becomes a companion to the Sun who brings light to its shadows, and breathes warmth into its cold and distant nature.

Saturn may look like an impediment to the Sun's desires, but it rewards its benefactor's warmth and light with careful planning, hard work and commitment to the task at hand.

Fame and youth makes for a heady combination which only a select few can withstand, and when Saturn is the lord of Time one of its responsibilities in a diurnal chart is to make sure that the timing is right when it comes to achieving the native's dreams without destroying the fabric of their lives.

German writer and statesman Johann Wolfgang von Goethe was born on 28th August 1749 at 12:30pm[18] when Saturn had crossed his Ascendant to join the Sun in the diurnally placed hemisphere where the Sun was culminating at its highest point and conjunct diurnal Mercury.

Goethe was the author of *Faust*, the story of a man who sells his soul to the Devil in order to gain infinite knowledge. *Faust* is a work in two parts which would take Goethe almost sixty years to complete, with

Part One published at his second Saturn Return in 1808 and Part Two completed twenty four years later in 1832, the year of Goethe's death.

A number of Goethe's quotes are reminiscent of a diurnal Saturn on the Ascendant:

"There is strong shadow where there is much light" and *"Everything is hard before it is easy."*

A diurnal chart is the perfect incubator for Saturn's dreams which take time to materialise and Goethe understood Saturn full well when he invented his Faust, an aged scientist disenchanted by a life wasted on trying to unravel the secrets of the universe.

For Faust, fame and rekindled youth are merely by-products of his pact with the Devil, as supreme cosmic knowledge is what he really seeks, and he thinks he has out-witted the Devil who will never be able to collect his soul because Faust has added a side-clause to the contract.

Faust adds the condition that the Devil can only claim his soul if he receives a moment so full of bliss that he does not want it to end – a moment that Faust believes is truly impossible to experience on this earth.

It is easy to see how Saturn morphs into Satan in Goethe's story as he believes nothing that Satan/Saturn gives him will be precious enough to either want to hold onto for eternity, or to cause him to forfeit his soul.

If Faust's tale sounds pretty grim coming from an author with a diurnal Saturn, imagine how it could have progressed if Goethe had been born during the night!

The nocturnal planets relish the inner landscape of emotions and feelings, and love the in-between world of inklings, hunches and sixth senses.

This nocturnal landscape of shadows is no place for Saturn who craves control in its environment and needs the light of day to divide issues simply into black or white.

Saturn does not trust the night. Saturn has trouble recognising and rationalising its fears in a nocturnal chart, it can find the apparent lack of direction and boundaries confusing, and a nocturnal's habit of being gently and subtly directed by the Moon is frustrating for Saturn who needs clear commands from its luminary in order to be its most effective in the chart.

It is true that Saturn's cold and dry qualities become accentuated in a nocturnal chart.

However, it is pure conjecture that Saturn's by-products of depression, anxiety, lethargy or terrors are any worse at night. Or are the reactions of a Saturn in panic – a planet that does not understand its environment or feels powerless to act in foreign territory.

Condition Two – Which Hemisphere?
Saturn's Protection of The Sun

A diurnally placed Saturn is well suited as both a spear-bearer of the Sun and as a tool for guidance and protection.

Saturn has the benefit of the Sun's light and warmth if it is placed on the right side of the blanket with the Sun – it is legal, it has privilege and future promise of entitlement – so there is little wonder that Saturn behaves well and gives its all to benefit the Sun.

It has immunity granted by the Sun so words such as integrity, liberty and responsibility, exclusive rights, prerogative, nobility, sincerity, honesty, decency come easily to the diurnally placed Saturn.

Saturn in a nocturnal hemisphere can jump at shadows, and how troubled or troublesome it becomes for the native, will depend to a great degree on whether the chart itself is diurnal or nocturnal.

If the birth occurs during the day, Saturn still has the benefit of being accidentally dignified, even if it is removed from the Sun by hemisphere, because its sect preference agrees with the light of day.

Saturn is comfortable, but it cannot perform its duty properly when it is so far away from its luminary.

However, if the birth occurs during the night, and Saturn is still removed from the Sun's presence in the opposite hemisphere, Saturn can fret, worry and panic that it is unable to perform its role as guard and spear-bearer to the Sun, especially in an atmosphere which is alien to its own preference.

In this case Saturn is in its worst state when it is removed from light by both sect conditions if the chart is nocturnal, and if, in addition, Saturn is located within the nocturnally placed hemisphere.

Caution becomes terror, and the need to control escalates or blossoms into two distinct categories. A Cronos-like Saturn can be one outcome where the control of all aspects of life feels essential to the individual's safety, and one who sees anyone else's initiative as a threat to their authority. Should something move away from the 'norm', Saturn can mimic the myth by devouring the unknown or unusual and pretending that nothing untoward has happened.

The other Saturn takes an *"if you can't beat them, join them"* attitude, and gives up all pretence at controlling the appetites of the nocturnal planets.

This Saturn takes no responsibility for the native's actions and can spend years denying responsibility for the chaos it creates through its lack of discipline.

These models are two extreme archetypes for the double nocturnal Saturn and in truth only appear in highly stressful situations, but if Saturn continues to carry a chip on its shoulder, it can retreat into its shell where sensitivity turns into despair, and defiance becomes bitterness and self-pity.

With little promise of light from the chart, the double nocturnal Saturn is constantly on the lookout for Light in other forms.

If the individual is vigilant and fights to release Saturn from its dark bonds, the nocturnal planets can direct it towards an external light and provide Saturn with the passion to protect something or someone who represents the Sun's luminance.

Saturn's preferred status according to sect: a diurnal chart with the Sun above the horizon in daylight hours (star), a preference for the diurnal hemisphere (second star), that is, located in the same space as the Sun, and in a masculine diurnal sign, either from the fire or air element *(Fig. 33)*.

Saturn dislikes the cold and darkness which are the properties of the night, and does not like to be removed from the Sun's presence, and is out of sect by sign if it is found in either an earth or a water element sign.

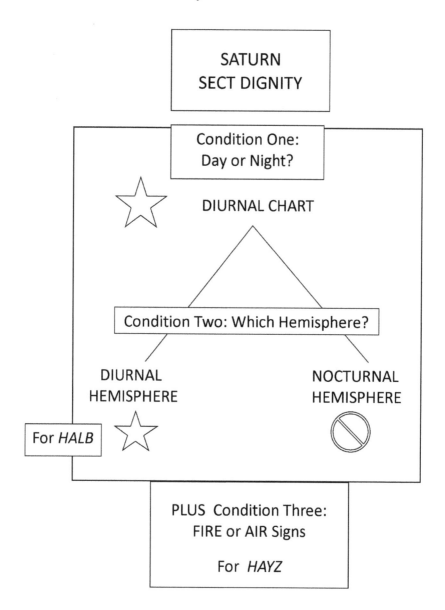

Fig. *33 Saturn in Sect Dignity*

Saturn in *Munakara*

If Saturn is located in a sign belonging to a nocturnal planet –
Moon, Venus, Mars or nocturnal Mercury – and this planet in turn is
disposited by a diurnal planet, then Saturn is judged as being in a state
of contention *(munakara)*.

Contention *(munakara)* can become even more complicated when
Saturn is disposited by the nocturnal planets.

Part of Saturn's discomfort if its dispositor has a change in sect (in
the same manner as Saturn) may have something to do with Saturn's
dependence on the goodwill of its dispositor, especially when some of
the rules have been laid out by the higher level of essential dignity.

The Table of Friendship and Enmity by al-Biruni is discussed in
A Tiny Universe and it is interesting to note that the three nocturnal
planets have a previously established relationship with Saturn – some
of friendship, and some of enmity.

The Moon's sign, Cancer, is one of Saturn's detriment signs, so there
is no love lost between Saturn and the Moon.

Venus' sign of Libra is the sign Saturn seeks for exaltation so there
is a level of cooperation between these two planets.

However, Saturn's relationship with Mars is somewhat ambiguous.
Saturn is in fall in Mars' sign of Aries, so there is some animosity when
Mars is the dispositor of Saturn's sign, but Mars seeks favours from
Saturn when it looks to borrow Capricorn from Saturn for its exaltation.

Contention *(munakara)* is defined as a state of hostility, conflict,
discord, or friction between one party and other, so when Saturn is in
a state of *munakara*, it is a Saturn in direct conflict with its dispositor,
who is experiencing their own problems with their own dispositor.

This condition which al-Biruni says is *"nearly the reverse of hayyiz
(hayz)"*[19] creates a prickly Saturn which is constantly on the lookout for
attack, insult or provocation from its dispositor.

How well it deals with its hyper-sensitivity, will depend largely on
whether the chart itself is diurnal or nocturnal, and whether Saturn is
travelling with the Sun in the same hemisphere, or it is feeling defenceless
and trapped alone in the cold and dark, in the nocturnal hemisphere.

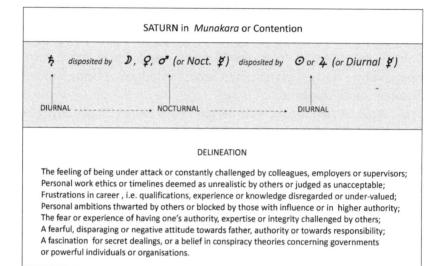

Fig. 34 Saturn in Contention (munakara)

MOON: Main Luminary of the Nocturnal Sect

"The moon, lit by the reflection of the sun's light and possessing a borrowed light, in a nativity indicates man's life, body, the mother, conception, beauty, appearance, sight, living together, nurture, the older brother, housekeeping, the queen, the mistress of the house, and wanderings.

The moon rules the parts of the body as follows: the left eye, the stomach, the breasts, the breath, the spleen, the dura mater, the marrow.

Of materials it rules silver and glass.

<u>*It is of the night sect*</u>*, green in colour and salty in taste".*

Condition One – Day Or Night
The Moon in Comfort

In contrast to the sun, the moon does not consistently hold the same shape, and the fact that it appears to grow in size during its waxing phases and decreases again during its waning phases, sends a message to the psyche that this luminary is more fickle in character than the sun.

In truth the moon is always fully lit, but as it orbits the Earth visibility of its surface varies, and although it receives constant light from the sun, sometimes only as much as 7% of sunlight that hits the moon is actually reflected.

Even when the moon is at its brightest at full moon, it is still only reflecting about 30% of the sun's light.

Nor does the moon's full illumination elevate it to the same honour when it takes on a similar appearance to the sun; full moons supposedly increase criminal activity, sleepwalking, suicide, and violence.

Perhaps the Moon's astronomy created impressions of instability, perhaps being feminine and an agent of the night she engendered suspicion within solar mythology and solar religions and gave rise to whispers of supernatural dealings held under her silvery light. Whatever the reason, the Moon somehow slipped from its own power and influence and became a second-class luminary caught in the shadows of the Sun.

The inequality between the Moon and the Sun continues in the deliberations of planetary sect.

The 24-hour clock may be shared evenly with the Sun but because the Moon is the fastest moving planet it seems to suffer the fate of constantly moving in and out of sect for two reasons.

The Moon is capable of moving up to fourteen degrees in a day and although this movement is minor compared to the Ascendant's movement, it can be enough to alter the Moon's sect condition at certain times of the day.

The Moon's lunar cycle moves through each of its eight phases in almost thirty days, and where it is situated in relation to the Sun can greatly affect how it sits regarding sect quality.

> *"The whole essence of the earthly body is governed by the power of the Moon.*
>
> *Since she is located in the lower regions of the heavens, because of her nearness she has been allotted power over the Earth and the bodies animated by the breath of the Divine Mind.*
>
> *She maintains her course with infinite variety and runs with speed through all the signs, joining herself to all the planets. From different elements she builds up the human body, once conceived, and dissolves it again into its elements."* [20]

Firmicus Maternus, *Matheseos*

In terms of Aristotelian philosophy, the Moon is the last port of call for the soul as it descends from the heavens, and the first planet to meet the soul when it separates from the body at the point of death.

She represents flux and change, her cycle symbolises the corruption of all things on the physical plane, she rules the natural world, and yet she holds little power in solar-based astrology.

With the rediscovery of planetary sect as an integral part of astrology, the Moon is back with a vengeance.

She becomes a sovereign in her own right in the delineation of the lunar horoscope, and with the reintroduction of older predictive systems, such as the first century Persian system known as *Firdaria*, the Moon claims her right as an independent luminary who organises her court and directs the life of the nocturnally born native.

Not only is the Moon comfortable in the nocturnal chart, *she owns it*, and anyone who thinks a female cannot rule, had best look to history to be proven wrong on that opinion.

The Moon in a diurnal chart must prove herself to be a more passive regent, one who works in unison with the Sun to accommodate the wishes of the solar king.

Power in the diurnal chart belongs to the Sun but the Moon still has a say in the proceedings of the chart and as the significator for *"man's life, body, the mother, conception and nurture"*.

The Moon's role in a daytime chart is never minor. She may be the diurnal chart's secondary luminary, but the Moon still has power and influence over the physical body and emotional needs of the native.

The Moon does not possess the ability to openly challenge the Sun in the daytime, but without her support and encouragement, life becomes harder for the individual and no level of outward success will satisfy an unhappy Moon.

The Sun is the driving force in a diurnal chart, but there needs to be a partnership between the two luminaries as the condition of the Moon is highly relevant to the overall strength of the person physically, emotionally and psychologically.

How an individual manages the fluctuating troubles of life – stress, illness, loss, unhappiness, isolation, loneliness, confrontation – are often determined by the resilience of the combined efforts of the Sun and the Moon.

Condition Two – Which Hemisphere?
Self-Protection for The Moon

The Moon can be at odds with its sect preference in the second division by hemisphere as there is no guarantee that it will be in the opposite hemisphere from the Sun.

If the Moon does find itself travelling with the Sun in a diurnal hemisphere, it would prefer the nature of the chart to be nocturnal and to belong to her, as a nocturnal birth will cement her position as the major luminary of the chart.

The Moon holds the power and control but unfortunately during the beginning and end of its lunar cycle it is often poorly placed in the diurnal hemisphere, and even though it must cope with the inconvenience of being trapped in the same hemisphere as the Sun, the Moon has some resilience when it owns the chart.

In a nocturnal chart the Moon achieves accidental dignity, and once blessed with this dignity, it cannot be removed by the second division of sect.

It may be uncomfortable in a diurnally placed hemisphere, but the Moon *has not lost sect dignity* if the chart itself is nocturnal.

A nocturnal chart empowers the Moon's spear-bearers who are at their strongest and most attentive in the night, and any problems the Moon may encounter through poor position in the chart, can often be mitigated by the resilience of her sect lieutenants.

However, if the Moon is diurnally placed in the same hemisphere as the Sun, and the chart is also diurnal, that is, both the Sun and the Moon are located above the horizon, the Moon suffers a double blow through the discrimination of sect.

No dignity for the Moon here, and the only thing she can hope for is that she is placed in a feminine sign in either the earth or water element in order to fulfil the final condition of sect dignity.

Robert Hand says of a Moon so badly dethroned by sect that it is placed at a severe disadvantage, that any aspects from the other planets to the Moon will become a source of difficulty, and that *"the examples from the ancients also suggest that such a Moon is less able to withstand impediments from various sources."* [21]

It would appear that an elevated Moon in the day is weakened in some fashion, and that the native is likely to struggle with, or experience difficulty from, the areas of life covered by the Moon's significations

– body, health, the mother, conception, appearance, nurturing and co-habitation.

The Moon prefers a night-time birth (star), and a hemisphere removed from the Sun's influence (second star) in the feminine signs of either earth or water as these conditions guarantee a state of *hayz* for the accidentally dignified Moon *(Fig. 35)*.

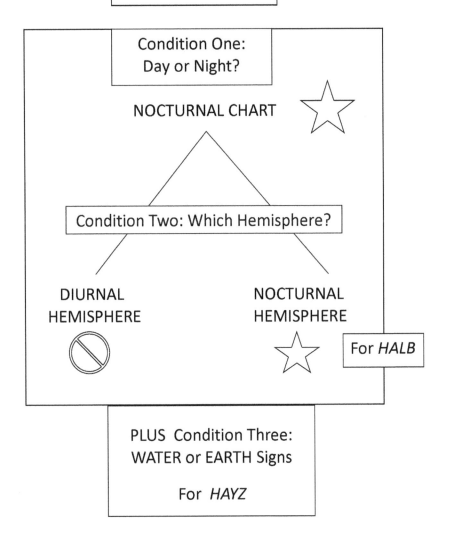

Fig.35 The Moon in Hayz

The Moon's Phasing and Sect

There is one more condition involving the Moon which is worthy of note.

Firmicus Maternus dedicates much of his Book Four in *Matheseos* to the Moon, explaining at the beginning of his chapters,

"We must know how the Moon undertakes the care of the human body and what has been allotted to the power of the Moon. For we feel in our bodies the increases of the waxing Moon and the losses of her waning.

The innermost parts of the human grow when the Moon grows, and when she begins to lose light they languish, fatigued in body; when she grows again, their power of growth comes flooding back."[22]

Firmicus continues by describing what can be expected when the Moon advances to aspect each of the planets, and pays particular attention to whether the Moon is in a waxing or a waning phase.

In terms of astronomy, the moon is waxing when it is gaining in light between a new moon and a full moon, and as soon as the opposition takes place between the sun and the moon at full moon, it begins to lose light and is considered to be in its waning phases until the next new moon.

In astrological lore, an applying aspect from a waxing Moon to a diurnal planet is much more favourable because the concept of strength in light connects the phase to a planet which prefers the daylight. A waning Moon (losing light) in an applying aspect to a diurnal planet is not as effective as the first example.

Likewise, a waning Moon seems to prefer the nocturnal planets (the connection is lack of light) and an applying aspect from a Moon losing light to a nocturnal planet creates a more favourable outcome than if the Moon were to be gaining in light in its waxing phase.

For instance, Maternus tells us that a waxing Moon applying to Jupiter – a growing Moon aspecting a diurnal – indicates a native who is fortunate, famous and rich, but the same aspect from a waning Moon shows a native will be adopted, exposed, or returned to the parents.

Or, a waning Moon moving towards Venus – a reducing Moon aspecting a nocturnal – indicates high position, greatest honours, and trappings of great power.

A waxing Moon coming into aspect to Venus can still bring nobility to the parents, but it also indicates that the native will have a shaky beginning in life as they will be separated from parents and suffer as wretched orphans.[23]

The Moon in *Munakara*

The first step towards the Moon being in a possible state of *munakara* is if it is placed in the signs of the diurnal planets, i.e., the Sun (Leo), Jupiter (Sagittarius: Pisces), Saturn (Capricorn: Aquarius) or a diurnal Mercury (Gemini: Virgo).

The second step involves the Moon's diurnal dispositor being itself placed in a sign which belongs to one of the nocturnal planets, other than the Moon.

If this is the case, and the Moon is in *munakara* (contention), this will create added stress for the Moon and will affect some of her significations in some manner.

The Moon is a highly sensitive planet which does not react well when it is involved in any state of conflict, so that when it is in contention or in disharmony with its own dispositor, then many of the troubles of life mentioned earlier, become a little harder to handle or bounce back from after either physical or psychological setbacks.

If the Moon is in Saturn's sign of Capricorn, and the naturally diurnal Saturn is disposited by one of the other nocturnal planets, then the Moon is in a double bind of difficulty, it is both in detriment in Capricorn, and also in a state of *munakara*.

The long-term ability for a debilitated Moon to keep fighting battles without affecting the native's health or physical and emotional wellbeing are highly unlikely, and there will be periods in the native's life when they will most likely need to withdraw and recoup their strength in order to enter back into the fray of life.

In this scenario a better placed sect condition would be preferable, that is, if the Capricorn Moon were to be in a nocturnal chart and/or placed on the nocturnal hemisphere, away from the Sun.

This would provide some respite for a battle-weary Moon and provide an increase in resilience and hopefully, a more positive outlook on life.

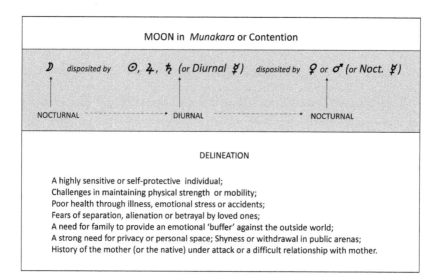

Fig. 36 The Moon in Contention (munakara)

VENUS: Benefic of the Nocturnal Sect

"Venus is desire and love. It indicates the mother and nurture. It makes cheerfulness, friendship, companionship, the acquisition of property, the purchase of ornaments, agreements on favourable terms, marriages, a taste for music, sweet singing, beauty and painting. Venus gives benefits from royal women or from one's own, and brings very high rank when it operates in such affairs.

Of the parts of the body, it rules the neck, the face, the lips, the sense of smell, the front parts from the feet to the head, the parts of intercourse; of the inner parts it rules the lungs.

It is a recipient of support from others and of pleasure.

Of materials it rules precious stones and fancy jewellery.

<u>*It is of the night sect,*</u> *white in colour, very greasy in taste."*

Vettius Valens, *Anthologies,* Book I

Condition One – Day Or Night
Venus in Comfort

Vettius Valens mentions in his descriptions on the planets that both diurnal Jupiter and nocturnal Venus signify friendship, fellowship, acquaintances, and companionship.

The two planets work in opposing sects for the good of the native as two bountiful forces of nature which are similar in that they promote bona fide (L: *"good faith"*) connections, but which have different agendas and separate outcomes for their associations.

Jupiter is a diurnal planet which fosters associations for the native's benefit or advancement. Connections of a political, financial, business or social gain are part of Jupiter's priorities, and whilst the networking and beneficial associations may be made during fun and relaxed social gatherings, Jupiter has an eye towards making the most of opportunities which cement friendships for use in the future.

In these days of social media, Jupiter would represent websites, blogs and podcasts which provide information for promotion, education or professional or political advancement.

The enormous coverage provided by the internet allows Jupiter incredible scope and visibility to see and be seen, and to nurture an incredibly diverse network of influential and powerful individuals.

If the diurnal benefic is really switched on it can take full advantage by gaining knowledge through news broadcasts and professional advertising, as well as taking advantage of random information gathered on a more informal level.

Valens says of Venus, *"It is a recipient of support from others and of pleasure"* and perhaps this is where the two planets diversify into their own planetary sect preferences.

Venus is more immediate in placing demands on its associations, therefore, its pleasures are short-term in nature and Venus will soon tire of maintaining a friendship that does not possess some pleasurable component.

Venus is a nocturnal planet and follows its heart rather than its head when it comes to forming attachments.

It does not understand Jupiter's need for the end-game where only a few pieces remain and there is victory in sight, as Venus would prefer to keep all pieces and players intact, just to keep things entertaining.

In terms of social media, the nocturnally minded Venus would represent blogs of a personal nature, interactive or communication sites such as Twitter, purely entertainment sites like Reddit or artistic and musical videos on You Tube.

The dating sites are designed to draw Venus' attention and mobile applications like Tinder are a goldmine for their creators simply because Venus has such a hold on our desire for love and companionship.

Jupiter may prefer its television to consist of documentaries and discussion panels on varying political views, but Venus devours reality TV, knowing full well that this type of production is designed to amuse and distract the viewer from their own woes.

Venus is also the voyeur, and as much as its audience enjoys its guilty pleasures in the privacy of their own homes, it means that this genre of television is not disappearing from our screens in the near future.

Venus in a nocturnal chart has ample opportunity to explore the diversity of its passions.

For most individuals the night is a time for relaxation, a less frenetic time to get comfortable and to enjoy the slower pace of the evening.

There is time and space to explore and indulge in pleasures as the dark hours are perfect for Venus' playfulness and sensuality.

Venus in a nocturnal chart is more languid, but its languidness is not born from illness or fatigue, but rather as a result of the individual being unembarrassed to take things more easily and to relax whilst diurnal births rush from one job to the next.

Diurnal individuals can find this Venus extremely frustrating in what they see as lack of purpose, but at the same time, they secretly envy the lack of guilt Venus displays in wanting to slow down, enjoy the moment, or simply do nothing.

This is Venus the lover, who rises in the night sky after the Sun has set, who sees no reason to apologise for its self-indulgences, or to excuse itself for behaviour that shocks its prudish diurnal counterpart.

In nocturnal charts Venus has a cat-like quality in terms of movement and physical expression.

Nocturnal Venus likes to think it has mystery and allure, and its feminine qualities, even in a man's chart, are highly developed when it is most comfortable in an environment ruled by the Moon, the only other feminine planet in an otherwise male squad.

There is a sense of genuine camaraderie between Venus and the Moon. A 'sister-hood' of like-minded planets who have no shame in their enthusiasm for exploring the senses, and who happily wander into the nooks and crannies of the mind and the heart, when generally there is no time for such indulgences in the light of day.

Night-time is for confidences, shared whisperings in muted light where romance, capers and mischief are all intriguing prospects, and when Venus is secure in its night-time location, it has plenty of time to explore these delightfully sinful possibilities.

Venus in a diurnal chart is more practically orientated towards the business end of pleasure and a diurnal Venus is inclined towards a work ethic which is constantly heading for some tangible outcome.

Women with Venus out of sect often work in industries and environments where they are expected to constantly prove themselves equal to their male counterparts. It is all very fine to be passionate about something, says Venus in the daytime, but passion requires an end result in order for this Venus to feel justified in possessing these feelings in the first place.

In the harsh light of day, Venus can be made to feel guilty about indulging in the things it loves and the native reprimands themselves for 'wasting' the day (or its sleeping-hours the night before) on leisure, play or social dalliances.

Time-off is frowned upon by the diurnal planets, especially Saturn, who has the upper hand in these charts, so Venus can feel hounded by the industrious collective of diurnals if the individual is not automatically mixing pleasure with business.

The treat Venus enjoyed last night becomes a vehicle for recrimination and self-loathing in the unflattering light of day and this Venus has learnt over time to mask, control or direct its passions so that it can defend the choices it makes to spend time, money or energy on what serious diurnal planets may consider to be a frivolous indulgence.

Venus in a diurnal chart has a more warlike or focused quality, its physical adornment is either played down or used for a specific purpose to impress others, rather than to pamper, or emotionally please, the individual.

Sentimentality is not encouraged by the diurnal planets and they may struggle to understand the anonymous quote:

"What most people need to learn in life is how to love people and use things, instead of using people and loving things."

This Venus tends to lean towards the Jupiterian type of associations, often sacrificing its own friendship preferences when time is limited, and pursuing advantageous relationships with future benefits.

Condition Two – Which Hemisphere?
Venus' Protection of The Moon

Venus in a nocturnal hemisphere is a less likely possibility than finding Venus in the same hemisphere as the Sun.

Venus' orbit is closely connected to the diurnal luminary as Venus' maximum elongation at sunset or sunrise is between 45 and 47 degrees.

This means that there are limited opportunities for Venus to free herself from the diurnal hemisphere, and in fact, this is only possible during the hours of dawn or dusk.

The Greek word *heosphoros* is a name given to the Morning Star, or Venus, literally means 'light-bringer' which was then translated into Latin as *lux* (light) + *ferre* (to bring) – in combination creating the name *'Lucifer'* for Venus when she resides in the sky as the Morning Star.

If Venus rises before the Sun she claims the early hours as her own – she is *Lucifer* – as the Sun has not yet risen to obliterate her light. Morning Venus before sunrise is the herald for the Sun as she is also separated from the Sun by the horizon.

For this reason, Morning Star Venus gains accidental dignity in sect (times two) because technically, the chart is nocturnal, plus Venus is in a different hemisphere from the Sun. Once the Sun has risen, Venus loses both her sect rights, as the chart is now diurnal, and Venus, the Morning Star, is in the same hemisphere (the diurnally placed hemisphere) as the risen Sun at daybreak.

There is only a small window of opportunity for Venus to gain accidental dignity via the first and second rule of planetary sect. That is, to be both in a nocturnal chart and to also reside in the nocturnally placed horizon away from the Sun.

Before Venus and the Sun have risen, Venus gains accidental dignity through the chart being nocturnal, but she is still travelling with the Sun in the diurnally placed hemisphere.

Even at the end of the day, Venus placed ahead of the Sun will set before the diurnal luminary, and has no opportunity to shine in her own light until the next morning when she once more rises ahead of the Sun.

Once the Sun has set, the chart becomes a nocturnal chart once more, but as Venus is ahead of the Sun and has already disappeared beneath the western horizon, she is also in the diurnally placed hemisphere along with the Sun.

The only other chance Venus has to be truly strengthened according to sect is at the other end of her cycle to the Sun.

As the Evening Star Venus sits behind the Sun in zodiacal degrees so that she must wait for dusk when the Sun sets, in order for her to be truly independent once more.

If the Sun is below the horizon in the early evening, and Venus is shining brightly in the night sky, she is doubly dignified, because the chart is nocturnal, and she is in the nocturnally placed hemisphere.

For a short period of time Venus is free of the Sun until she too sets and joins the Sun in the diurnally placed hemisphere.

No other planet truly validates the importance of sect, not just as a theory, but as a living example of what it means for a planet with such a short leash to be free of a master to whom it should never belong.

When next you have the opportunity to observe Venus as either the Morning Star at dawn, or to see her as the Evening Star in the dusk light, think of her as the perfect example of what it means for a planet to have the dignity of sect in its favour, as it is a favour which is both fleeting and constantly changing with the rise and fall of the Earth's horizon.

Venus in a nocturnal hemisphere is more capable of guarding the Moon and acting as its spear-bearer, even though the Moon itself may be in the opposite hemisphere.

Venus' ability to charm its way out of a tense situation or to smooth ruffled feathers is intact in a nocturnally placed hemisphere, so if the Moon becomes fussed or emotionally overwhelmed, this Venus can buy time and even salvage the best from a difficult situation.

Ideally, Venus and the Moon would prefer to be together in the hemisphere opposite to the Sun, but if this is not possible, then under the rules of *doryphory,* a nocturnally placed Venus may have the capability of casting her rays toward the Moon via a sextile or trine aspect, and thereby offering protection to her sovereign.

If the Sun is elevated in the chart and resides near the zenith, then Venus has two problems – she is in a diurnal chart, and more than likely because of her 47 degree maximum separation, she is also in the diurnally placed hemisphere.

Not only will Venus struggle with being able to express herself fully in such a masculine-orientated atmosphere, she will also be poorly placed to be of much assistance to a Moon which may be floundering as much as herself if the Moon joins Venus and the Sun in the diurnal hemisphere.

So far as the native is concerned, this Venus is likely to experience issues and worries with the females in their life.

Relationships may seem to be a luxury rather than a necessity as there is little time to develop intimacy, let alone maintain and nourish a relationship with another human being.

Unfortunately, traditional astrologers often saw a diurnal Venus in a diurnal chart as a mark against a woman's character and there seemed to be little to none in her choice of respectable profession.

However, if a man had Venus in the tenth house Firmicus predicted great fame, good fortune and prizes and wreaths, and if Mercury was situated with Venus the (male) native became clever, inventors of theories and they could easily attain their wishes.

Under certain circumstances, Venus can gain maximum sect dignity and be in *hayz*.

One, if the chart is nocturnal (star) and the Sun is below the horizon.

Two, if the Sun is in a separate hemisphere to Venus, meaning Venus is located in a nocturnally placed hemisphere (second star).

And three, if Venus is moving through a feminine sign, either in a water or an earth element.

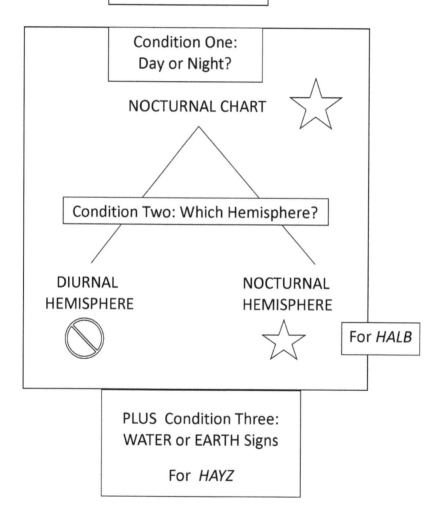

Fig. 37 Venus in Sect Dignity

Ironically, given her name, Venus Williams' Venus and Moon are both completely out of sect according to the three conditions (Venus and Serena Williams' charts are featured in Chapter Three).

For Venus Williams, gaining a steady loving relationship has so far been outside of her reach as her lifestyle and the pressures of maintaining her career as a professional tennis player have taken their toll on her intimate relationships.

Venus herself says that she would like to think about getting married one day, but that she wants to play tennis forever and *"you can't be doing that and have kids."*

For the majority of people the game of tennis is a Venusian pursuit enjoyed in leisure time and played for fun and relaxation.

However, for Venus Williams tennis is a constant battle to win bouts, and improve ranking placement, whilst at the same time battling Sjögren's syndrome, an autoimmune disorder that often causes severe joint pain, dry eyes and constant fatigue, among other symptoms.

The illness has dogged her for years, but it was only in 2011 that doctors finally arrived at the correct diagnosis and identified her condition as Sjögren's syndrome.

In an interview in 2012, Venus said that it was hard for her to accept the restrictions placed on her body by her illness.

"I spent my whole life playing sports and training and pushing myself to the limits," Venus said. *"When you get told that you have a disease, it's like: 'Really? Nah, it's all right. I don't believe that. It must be something else, I'm just making an excuse, let me push harder.'"*

This statement epitomises someone with a Venus out of sect as the pleasures it should naturally be enjoying are fought for and hard-won. Venus Williams may love the game of tennis but it is constantly taking its toll on her body and it will be interesting to see if her beauty products and sponsorships steer her natal Venus in another direction in a future when competitive tennis is no longer an option for Venus to shine in the Sun's light.

Venus in *Munakara*

The first step in Venus being in a possible state of *munakara* would occur if it is placed in the signs belonging to one of the diurnal planets, i.e., the Sun (Leo), Jupiter (Sagittarius: Pisces), Saturn (Capricorn: Aquarius) or a diurnal Mercury (Gemini: Virgo).

The second step involves Venus' diurnal dispositor being itself placed in a sign which belongs to one of the nocturnal planets, other than Venus itself.

If this is the case, and Venus is in *munakara* (contention), this will place tension on the nocturnal benefic which does not aid it in being able to be a positive force in the native's life.

Venus disposited by the Sun adds further problems for a Venus which has trouble getting out from under the Sun's rays, so if the Sun were itself to be disposited by a planet outside of its own sect, means the situation has a domino effect where one planet's discomfort is passed down the line to another planet in its own sign, that is, if Venus were to be in Leo.

This is not a problem if the Sun is situated nearby in the same sign, because it will be in rulership, but should Venus be in Leo, and the Sun in Cancer, then Venus is definitely in a state of *munakara*.

Likewise, if Venus is in Leo and the Sun is in the following sign of Virgo, then it only takes a Mercury to also be behind the Sun, and therefore, nocturnal, for Venus to be placed once more in a difficult position.

Venus disposited by Jupiter can be in exaltation in Pisces, but this exalted state can turn sour if Jupiter is itself disposited by the Moon or Mars or nocturnal Mercury.

Again, the essential dignities will have to be taken into account as should Jupiter be disposited by the Moon it would be in Cancer, which is its sign of exaltation, so whilst both Venus and Jupiter were in exalted signs, the state of *munakara* means that there is a battle going on between them that can have dire repercussions in the chart, and what initially looks like fabulous condition, becomes spoiled by this particular sect rule.

al-Biruni does not specify how significant this rule is when applied to the chart, but it is worth keeping an open mind on its importance, especially if there is evidence in the native's life to support a problem with Venus and Jupiter, or if there are signs of friction or hostility between these two planets which should, by rights, be celebrating one another's fortunate dignity.

It needs to be reiterated that the determination of *munakara* is not dependent on the sect positions of the planets involved. However, their level of sect dignity will advise on which of the planets is likely to be struggling the most – the one actually in *munakara,* or its dispositor.

Venus in Virgo is considered to be in fall, so if Mercury was diurnal in the chart, but disposited by a nocturnal planet (not Venus), then Venus has further problems in surviving the hostilities of a dispositor – Mercury – who is discouraged by the fact that their own ruler is at odds with their sect.

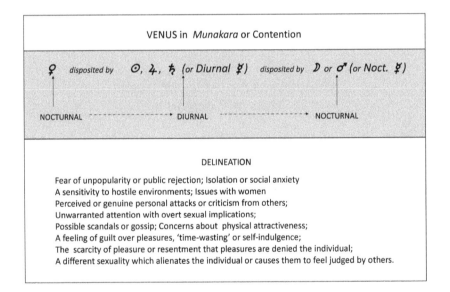

Fig. 38 Venus in Contention (munakara)

MARS: Malefic of the Nocturnal Sect

"Mars indicates force, wars, violence, the loss of property, banishment, exile, alienation from parents, capture, love affairs, marriages, the loss of goods, lies, vain hopes, strong-armed robbery, quarrels among friends, anger, fighting, verbal abuse, hatreds, lawsuits.

Mars brings violent murders, slashings and bloodshed, attacks of fever, burns, masculinity, actions involving fire or iron, craftwork, masonry. In addition Mars causes commands, campaigns, leadership and governorships.

Of the body parts, Mars rules the head, the seat, the genitals; of the internal parts, it rules the blood, the sperm ducts, the bile, the elimination of excrement. It controls the hard and the abrupt.

Of materials, it rules iron, decoration of clothing.
<u>*It is of the night sect,*</u> *red in colour and acid in taste."*

Vettius Valens, *Anthologies*, Book I

Condition One – Day or Night
Mars in Comfort

Mars in a nocturnal chart produces a chivalrous Mars with manners, etiquette, charm, vitality and enthusiasm. Courage rather than aggression is promoted and a quietened or more reserved version of Mars does less mischief in the chart.

This is hard to explain under the umbrella of Valens' description of Mars, but the night soothes the state of aggravation for Mars and takes the edge from its desire to do battle when it feels slighted or ignored.

Perhaps Valens description of Mars causing *"commands, campaigns, leadership and governorships"* is a more positive version of a Mars under the control of the Moon, who directs it with a gentler hand than the Sun.

Even though Mars is the opposite gender to the Moon, it may be surmised that it still respects the lunar dignitary and that Mars works best in a nocturnal horoscope.

Certainly it understands the concept of a planet ruled by its desires, and the link between it and the two feminine planets provides Mars with a similar agenda, but with a different approach to life than Venus and the Moon.

Venus may charm, flirt and flatter to get its own way but Mars is more direct in its approach.

If Mars sees something it wants it has two avenues. Either confront the current owner or contender and take by force (Aries), or wait and bide its time until distraction presents an opportunity to gently entice away something that Mars desires for its own pleasures (Scorpio).

Neither method will be popular with the one who loses their prize and it makes perfect sense to see that Mars in its desire to separate something from its owner/lover/engaged participant, usually ends up creating *"wars, violence, the loss of property, banishment, exile, and alienation"* for both parties involved in the conflict.

Mars in a diurnal chart can be brutally frank and blunt in its execution.

The coaching provided by the Moon and Venus often brings refinement or subtlety to Mars' manners, but without their influence diurnal Mars can lose its thin veneer of social etiquette and become brash or thoughtless when uncomfortable in its environment.

A diurnal Mars can become highly sensitive and take offence at the slightest opportunity, gearing itself up for battle, when a thicker skin, or a little diplomacy, may be more useful in the long run.

Mars needs to pick its battles, but in the warmth of daylight Mars overheats and even minor criticism can enflame Mars causing argument and a defensive or aggressive demeanour on the part of the native.

Unfortunately, this Mars is likely to be less effective in gaining possession over what it desires, and if it does create conflict or offend others, its opponents will take pleasure in blocking and frustrating Mars' aim to win its prize.

The need to curb insolence or impertinent behaviour requires self-control, but when Mars already feels threatened by the strength given to Saturn in the diurnal chart, any form of authority is likely to be met with resentment when Mars finds itself on the wrong side of a powerful diurnal planet.

Any approval Mars seeks from Saturn to sanction its behaviour can evaporate just as quickly as it was granted if Mars misbehaves or breaks the dominant malefic's rules.

The sanctions turn from positive to negative as Saturn punishes Mars for stepping out of line and the native suffers for Mars' audacity when it projects out into life as the individual risks being branded as difficult, rude or deliberately defiant in some way.

Condition Two – Which Hemisphere?

Mars' Protection of The Moon

Mars in a nocturnal hemisphere is saved from the Sun's heat by the protective blanket provided by the Ascendant to Descendant horizon.

Mars in the opposite hemisphere to the Sun is well-behaved and is ready and willing to take up its role as spear-bearer to the Moon.

Its best nature comes to the fore and even Mars' warlike behaviour can be manipulated to work in favour of protecting its queen.

Mars in the nocturnal hemisphere brings out the malefic's nobler characteristics, and even if the chart itself is diurnal, a nocturnally placed Mars can direct its energies towards protection, rather than focusing on ill-advised or inappropriate battles which it is likely to lose in the long run.

The frustration for Mars lies in not being able to reach the Moon if the Moon should happen to be situated in the diurnal hemisphere. Mars may have escaped, but its most important luminary is captured by the Sun.

Hopefully, Mars can use *doryphory* to cast its rays in the direction of the Moon via a square or opposition aspect, and thereby protect the nocturnal luminary, but it is still likely to be fretful and unsettled in a nocturnal hemisphere if the Moon is out of its reach.

Unlike its nocturnal counterparts, Venus and an occidental Mercury (behind the Sun), Mars can travel through the entire zodiac circle without being dependent on the Sun, but it can still find itself in an approaching or separating conjunction to the Sun, and travelling uncomfortably through a diurnal hemisphere.

This Mars is a knight away from its court, moving in a hostile environment in the territory of its enemy.

It is unlikely to be of much assistance to the Moon if it is in this agitated state and usually has to abandon the Moon in order to take care of its own affairs.

This is the condition under which Venus Williams finds her own natal Mars – in a diurnal chart, in a diurnal hemisphere, and in a feminine sign, rather than a more suitable masculine sign which matches its gender rather than its sect.

In Venus Williams' chart Mars is conjunct a powerful Saturn, and although it follows the Moon in correct *doryphory* etiquette, both nocturnal planets are so besieged in this chart, that Mars is unlikely to be of much benefit to a struggling Moon.

Those with the same out of sect Mars as Venus Williams can take heart from the way in which she has been able to utilise an alienated Mars to great effect in her career as a professional tennis player.

Robert Hand describes an out of sect Mars as the planet *"that operates in the worst possible way . . . It would seem that no amount of light can really illuminate Mars. It is a raw, instinctual energy that is never really conscious. All that one can hope for of Mars is that it is restrained by a sense of compassion or feeling."*[24]

There are several reasons why we need to be cautious of taking statements like these into the consulting room, as Venus Williams' chart example demonstrates that all factors together provide the picture, rather than focusing on one planet which is out of sect.

Mars in Venus' chart appears to be directed by the diurnal planets to channel its energy and focus into winning matches against her opponents and accumulating great wealth in the process (Mars rules the 7th and the 2nd house in Venus' chart).

Rob Hand says: *"the perfectly diurnal Mars is one that is ferociously active, but has its feelings completely in check so that it can with perfect discipline and order create mayhem."*

I suppose if you are on the opposite side of the court from Venus Williams, it does feel like mayhem, but Robert's final statement on diurnal Mars needs to be balanced by the entire state of the chart, rather than focusing on just one aspect of Mars.

He finishes by saying: *"It (Mars) is therefore unlucky and unfortunate."*[25]

I would add a footnote to this statement, and that is to be aware of Mars' sect status in charts, but to also view the entire state of the proceedings before predicting calamitous outcomes for an out of sect Mars.

All four of Venus Williams' nocturnal planets are out of sect by the first and second conditions – Venus, the Moon and Mars by the third rule of sign as well – and rather than focusing on just the out of sect malefic, the overall statement of such a significant sect placement for her nocturnal planets is extremely important in understanding what is going on in her chart.

Serena Williams, on the other hand, has her Mars in a much better sect condition.

Serena's chart is nocturnal, and her Mars is in a masculine sign, so her Mars has no problem fighting strategically and aggressively with the aim of winning her tennis matches.

For Mars to be in a state of *Hayz* the chart needs to be nocturnal (star), it needs to be travelling in the opposite hemisphere to the Sun, ideally above the horizon in a nocturnal chart (second star), and preferably in a masculine sign which suits its gender, in a sign from either the fire or air elements.

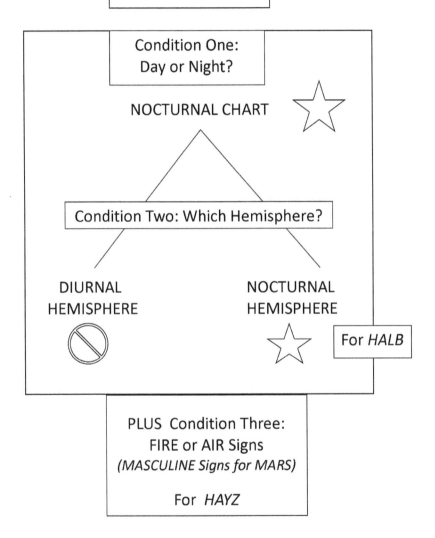

Fig. 39 Mars in Sect Dignity

Mars in *Munakara*

Mars would be one step closer to being in a possible state of *munakara* if its dispositor is one of the diurnal planets; the Sun (Leo), Jupiter (Sagittarius: Pisces), Saturn (Capricorn: Aquarius) or a diurnal Mercury (Gemini: Virgo).

The second step involves Mars' diurnal dispositor being itself placed in a sign which belongs to one of the nocturnal planets - Moon, Venus, or nocturnal Mercury.

If the second dispositor was Mars itself then a state known as *generosity* or *mutual reception* is in force, and *munakara* is not a possibility.

Generosity is a term used to describe two planets in each other's sign with no aspect between them.

Mutual Reception describes two planets in each other's sign who also share a Ptolemaic aspect by degree.

If Mars does happen to be in *munakara* (contention), this will place tension on the nocturnal malefic which does not aid it in being a positive force in the native's life.

The state of *munakara* becomes complicated when Mars finds itself in exaltation in Capricorn, but disposited by the diurnal planet Saturn.

If Saturn in its turn is then in a sign belonging to a different nocturnal planet other than Mars, then Mars is in contention with its exalted ruler.

How difficult life becomes for this Mars will depend on Saturn's situation in the chart, and it is debatable whether it would suit Mars to be in a nocturnal chart which places Saturn out of sect, or to keep Saturn in good humour, but punish Mars by the chart being diurnal in nature.

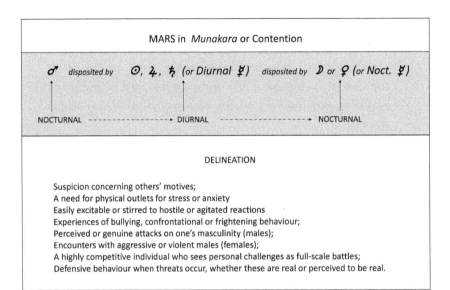

DELINEATION

Suspicion concerning others' motives;
A need for physical outlets for stress or anxiety
Easily excitable or stirred to hostile or agitated reactions
Experiences of bullying, confrontational or frightening behaviour;
Perceived or genuine attacks on one's masculinity (males);
Encounters with aggressive or violent males (females);
A highly competitive individual who sees personal challenges as full-scale battles;
Defensive behaviour when threats occur, whether these are real or perceived to be real.

Fig. 40 Mars in Contention (munakara)

MERCURY: The Planet With Changing Sect

"Mercury indicates education, disputation, reasoning, theft, association, communication, service, gain . . . It is the bestower of forethought and intelligence, the lord of brothers and of younger children, and the creator of all marketing and banking.

This star's effects go in many directions, depending on the changes of the zodiac and the interactions of the stars, and yields quite varied results: knowledge for some, selling for others, service for others, trade or teaching for others, farming or temple service or public employment for still others.

As for the end result – Mercury will make everything capricious in outcome and quite disturbed.

Even more, it causes those having this star in malefic signs or degrees to become even worse.

Of the parts of the body, it rules the hands, the shoulders, the fingers, the joints, the belly, the sense of hearing, arteries, the intestines, the tongue. Of materials, it rules copper and all coins used in buying and selling . . . It is blue in colour and sharp in taste."

Vettius Valens, *Anthologies,* Book I

Condition One – Day or Night
Mercury in Comfort

Valens' omits Mercury's sect preference in his list of Mercury's significations simply because it has the capacity to belong to either diurnal or nocturnal sect, depending on its position in relation to the Sun.

Valens says Mercury's effects go in many directions,*" depending on the changes of the zodiac and the interactions of the stars"*, and Mercury is a chameleon-like planet capable of experiencing all four of the original qualities.

Al-Biruni calls Mercury *"hermaphrodite, being male when associated with the male planets, and female when with the female; when alone it is male in its nature."*[26], meaning that Mercury is capable of turning from hot (male) to cold (female), depending on its circumstances.

Not only can Mercury's gender and its active qualities be altered by its associations, so too can the passive qualities of wet and dry undergo change according to Mercury's circumstances.

Ptolemy says: *"Mercury sometimes produces dryness, and at other times moisture, and each with equal vigour"*[27], explaining that the ambiguity of its qualities, and its ability to move rapidly from one state to the next, is due to the fact that Mercury absorbs moisture and creates dryness being so close to the Sun, yet also produces moisture by bordering on the Moon's sphere.

Mercury's duality follows through into planetary sect when it is common to both divisions of time since in his oriental position – rising before the Sun – he is diurnal, but he turns nocturnal when occidental, or rising after the Sun.

Robert Hand wrote in *Night & Day* (1995) that at the time, the translations showed a distinct lack of delineations for Mercury's sect placements, leaving it open for conjecture as to what impact sect might have on Mercury, but that in his opinion, Mercury was not strongly affected one way or the other by being in or out of sect.[28]

In his latest webinar on sect (July 2015) Hand has not altered his opinion on Mercury's indifference to sect as the accompanying notes state, *"Mercury: Not strongly affected"*[29].

Whilst this may be true, I find it hard to believe that a planet which has the ability to basically alter its fundamental characteristics in attunement with its surroundings, is the same planet that does not react to changes in its physical environment.

Therefore, I suspect it is worth noting Mercury's sect preference according to its position and its compatibility to the chart itself.

For instance, a diurnal Mercury in a diurnal chart is presumably more in synchronization with the Sun's agenda, and therefore will focus its efforts on honing its skills in marketing, banking, trade, and communication with others who are like-minded and whose purpose in life is to achieve success and reputation.

The knowledge sought by the diurnal Mercury will differ from the type of knowledge sought by the nocturnal Mercury and the difference between *Logos* and *Gnosis* becomes more apparent when Mercury serves either the Sun or the Moon, depending on its position in the celestial sphere.

The Greek masculine noun *Logos* seems more suited to a diurnal Mercury considering that its root is translated as "speaking to a conclusion" and has several meanings: order, pattern, ratio, reason and mediation.

On the other hand, the nocturnal Mercury may resonate more comfortably with the Greek feminine noun *Gnosis* whose root verb is translated "to experientially know".

Gnosis often describes intimate and personal knowledge that stands alongside theoretical knowledge. *Gnosis* is highly individual as it incorporates the individual's reactions to memories with corresponding images and emotions evoked by past recollections.

It would seem reasonable to suggest that nocturnal Mercury is more likely to guide the native towards thoughts and pursuits of a more lunar quality; pursuits such as service, trade or teaching, temple service, public employment or dedication to family or community.

In its most simple form, a diurnal Mercury serves the Sun who has a certain level of self-interest, whilst nocturnal Mercury serves the Moon which is other-orientated in its goals.

Perhaps it is not so much the case that Mercury is unaffected by sect, but that simply because of its fluidity, Mercury instinctively adapts to its environment and makes mental adjustments to the behaviour that are taken for granted by the native.

Mercury will need to adjust its thinking according to whether it sits comfortably in sect, or it is in an environment which is alien to its sect preference.

Whatever Mercury's condition, there is always a warning to 'proceed with care' when dealing with Mercury's fickle nature.

Valens states *"As for the end result – Mercury will make everything capricious in outcome and quite disturbed. Even more, it causes those having this star in malefic signs or degrees to become even worse"*, perhaps reminding his readers that Mercury has a reputation for being fickle in its changing fortunes and what start as a good day for Mercury in sect can deteriorate into disaster by evening for a Mercury which has moved to out of sect because of the changing horizon.

Ptolemy wrote around the same time as Valens and says something of the same:

"The Sun and Mercury are neither benefic nor malefic in nature, but are of "common influence" and can produce either good or evil in unison with whatever planets they may be connected with."[30]

In Book II Ptolemy states that Mercury is usually conjoined with one or other of the planets and becomes conformed and assimilated to their natures, but that the effect of the planets on Mercury works in the reverse as well and that there exists a symbiotic relationship between Mercury and the other planets. The text continues with

"yet as, in itself, it (Mercury) presents a certain addition to their power, this planet increases the respective impulses of them all."[31]

In other words, Mercury has the ability to increase the benefic powers of Venus and Jupiter, or to increase the malefic powers of Saturn and Mars if it forms a strong aspect to any of these planets.

If Mercury conjuncts an out of sect malefic then we are likely to see Mercury adding to the problem by *"making everything capricious in outcome"*.

For this reason, it is well worth keeping an eye on Mercury when it comes to sect.

Condition Two – Which Hemisphere?

Mercury's Protection of its Luminary

In terms of visibility, Mercury experiences a similar situation to Venus, except that Mercury's opportunity to shine is much reduced compared with Venus, due to its size, relative lack of brightness, and its proximity to the Sun.

Mercury's maximum elongation from the Sun at sunrise or sunset is between 18 and 28 degrees, so there is very little opportunity for it to be in a separate hemisphere from the Sun.

If Mercury rises before the Sun, it makes sense that it is diurnal, considering that it ushers in the day and holds court for a limited period of time before the Sun's rays obliterate it.

Likewise, if Mercury is situated behind the Sun, it is classified as nocturnal, since when the Sun sets, Mercury has its own tiny piece of the sky in the west, before it too sets below the horizon.

Robert Hand mentions that one possibility for an out of sect Mercury concerns the native's quality of mind or their intelligence, rather than affecting the person's ability to process information.

He says that various descriptions of Mercury suggest two levels of intention.

One which is an elevated level of thought, i.e. high-minded principles and morals (in sect Mercury), and the second level, which indicates a coarser or more vulgar tone in speech, thought and reactions (out of sect Mercury).

Ptolemy writes on Mercury and the Moon being the joint significators of the mind and soul in his *Tetrabiblos* citing that all the spiritual qualities which are rational and intellectual are contemplated by the situation of Mercury, whilst the appetitive soul which is independent of reason, is considered to be the realm of the Moon.[32]

The different conditions of these planets according to essential and accidental dignities make them competent to contribute towards the properties of the mind, and Ptolemy mentions signs, aspects and sect in his judgement of mind and soul.

For instance, if Mercury is oriental to the Sun – a diurnal planet – and happens to be in its joy in the first sign, preferably above the horizon in the diurnal hemisphere, it makes men liberal, frank, self-confident, brave, ingenious, unreserved, and with acute mental faculties.

Diurnal Mercury rising high in the day sky with the Sun or culminating at Midheaven makes men reflective, constant, of good memory, firm, prudent, magnanimous, successful in pursuing their desires, inflexible, powerful in intellect, strict, not easily imposed upon, judicious, active, hostile to crime, and skilful in science.

Ptolemy is very clear in his preference for Mercury to be a diurnal planet in the correct diurnal hemisphere, as his prejudice against a nocturnal Mercury in the diurnal hemisphere definitely colours his view towards the negative in both his descriptions of the mind, and the soul.

For instance, Ptolemy moves directly from elevated diurnal Mercury in *halb*, to describe cadent Mercury in the twelfth house, occidental to the Sun – a nocturnal Mercury – and out of sect according to the first two conditions of sect.

According to Ptolemy a twelfth house nocturnal Mercury situated in a diurnal chart, and also in the diurnal hemisphere with the Sun makes men unsteady, irreverent, imbecile, impatient of labour, easily impressed, humble, doubting, wavering, boastful and cowardly, slothful, lazy, and hard to rouse.

Should the nocturnal Mercury be situated at the base of the chart near the IC, the chart would be nocturnal as the Sun would be close by, but the hemisphere is diurnal as this is where the Sun is situated in the chart. Ptolemy judges this placement of Mercury as rendering the mind to be ingenious and rebellious, but not capable of great recollection, nor very industrious. At the same time, Mercury's position on the IC makes the mind inquisitive in occult matters, such as magic and sacred mysteries, studious of mechanics and mechanical instruments, and addicted to sky-watching, philosophy and prediction techniques, and to the judgement of dreams.

Ptolemy mentions two other conditions which he includes in the same judgement as above, and they both involve diurnal Mercury being out of correct sect placement.

For instance, if Mercury is oriental but it has set before the Sun (*"making a vespertine descension by day"*), then according to sect, both Mercury and the chart are diurnal, but as Mercury has slipped below the horizon, it is now nocturnally placed, which puts it out of sect.

Also, should Mercury be *"rising at night"* it would need to be in an oriental position, rising ahead of the Sun over the horizon.

If so, Mercury would be diurnal, but the chart itself is nocturnal, and Mercury is separated from the Sun by the horizon, and therefore placed in a nocturnal hemisphere.

However, if by a small window of opportunity, Mercury does happen to be in *Hayz* – correct sect times three – and aspecting good planets in rulership, then the mental properties will be rendered exquisite, unimpeded, and successful, especially if these same planets disposit both Mercury and the Moon.

Mercury Rising Before The Sun
Diurnal Mercury

If Mercury rises before the Sun, it prefers a daytime chart (star) and to be travelling with the Sun in the diurnal hemisphere (second star).

Diurnal Mercury's preferred signs are the masculine diurnal signs from either the fire or air element.

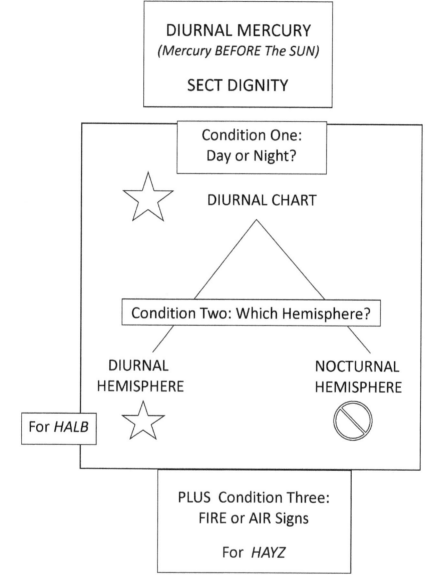

Fig 41 Diurnal Mercury in Sect Dignity

Mercury Rising After The Sun
Nocturnal Mercury

If Mercury rises after the Sun (in occidental position) it prefers the chart to be nocturnal, that is, the Sun being placed below the hemisphere (star).

Although it is difficult for Mercury to achieve, in order for it to be in *Hayz,* it would need to be travelling in the opposite hemisphere to the Sun in the nocturnal hemisphere (second star).

Nocturnal Mercury's ideal evening position is after the Sun has set (nocturnal chart) but before the time when Mercury too slips below the horizon.

Nocturnal Mercury prefers the feminine signs from either the water or earth element.

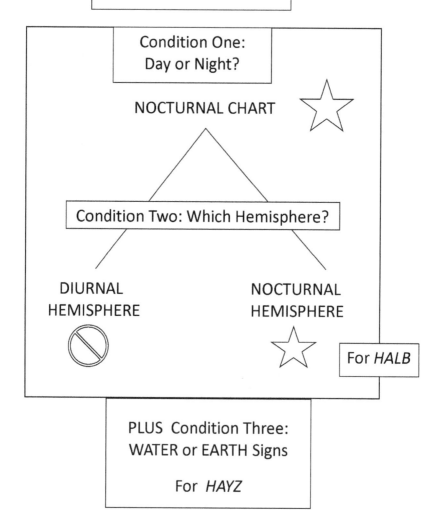

Fig. 42 Nocturnal Mercury in Sect Dignity

Mercury in *Munakara*

If diurnal Mercury is located in a sign belonging to a nocturnal planet – Moon, Venus, Mars – and this planet in turn is disposited by a diurnal planet, then Mercury is judged as being in a state of contention *(munakara)*.

Given the number of variables which affect Mercury, adding the condition of *munakara* can only add to Mercury's confusion, especially if it is essentially diurnal, but has nocturnal influences from a disgruntled dispositor.

The nocturnal Mercury would be in a possible state of *munakara* is if its placed in the signs of the diurnal planets; the Sun (Leo), Jupiter (Sagittarius: Pisces) or Saturn (Capricorn: Aquarius).

The second step involves Mercury's diurnal dispositor being itself placed in a sign which belongs to one of the nocturnal planets, other than the occidental Mercury's sign.

Whilst a diurnal dispositor may bring the nocturnal Mercury back into the reality of the working world and increase its fighting spirit, should Mercury's dispositor be Jupiter, the owner of Mercury's signs of detriment and fall, then it is crucial to be aware of this Mercury's sect conditions.

Presumably, the more uncomfortable Mercury becomes by being out of sect, the more it will create a brash, boasting or defensive disposition whereby the native is either volatile in temperament or extremely careless with their information (Mercury in Sagittarius), or they suffer from a nervous or shy disposition with frayed emotions (Mercury in Pisces), especially if Jupiter also happens to be poorly situated in the chart.

If Jupiter, the owner of Mercury's debilitated signs, is found to be in a sign belonging to a nocturnal planet (Moon, Venus or Mars) then the problem becomes compounded for Mercury when it finds itself in a state of *munakara*.

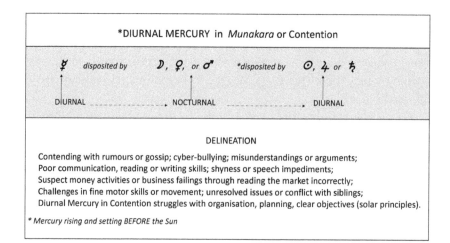

Fig. 43 Diurnal Mercury in Contention (munakara)

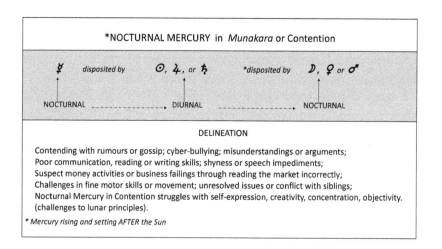

Fig. 44 Nocturnal Mercury in Contention (munakara)

CHAPTER THREE

Two Examples of Planetary Sect
The Williams Sisters

Venus Williams

Venus Ebony Starr Williams (born 17th June, 1980) is an American professional tennis player who is generally regarded as one of the all-time greats of women's tennis and who, along with younger sister Serena Williams, is credited with ushering in a new era of power and athleticism on the women's professional tennis tour.

Venus has been ranked World No. 1 by the Women's Tennis Association on three occasions, for a total of eleven weeks.

She first became the World No. 1 on February 25, 2002, the first African American woman to do so in the Open Era.

Venus is one of four women to have won five or more Wimbledon single titles in the Open Era.

She has won four Olympic gold medals, one in singles and three in women's doubles, and together, Venus and Serena have won more Olympic gold medals than any other tennis player, male or female.

In 2005, Venus Williams met with officials from the French Open and Wimbledon in order to argue that female tennis players should be paid the same amount in prize money as male tennis players.

Venus wrote a sound argument to support her drive for equality in prize money which was published in *The Times* on the eve of Wimbledon in 2006.

In response, British Prime Minister Tony Blair publicly endorsed Williams' arguments.

Under enormous pressure, Wimbledon announced in February 2007 that it would award equal prize money to all competitors in all rounds, and the French Open followed suit a day later.

Venus herself became the first woman to benefit from the equalisation of prize money at Wimbledon, as she won the 2007 tournament and was awarded the same amount as the male winner Roger Federer.

In 2011, Venus Williams was forced to withdraw from the Australian and US Open following the diagnosis of Sjögren's Syndrome, an autoimmune disease that mainly affects the salivary glands and tear ducts and other moisture-producing glands.

Venus has played Serena in 28 professional matches since 1998.

Overall, Serena is 17 – 11 against her sister.

Serena has played Venus 15 times in Grand Slam singles tournaments and 13 times in other tournaments (including 11 finals).

They have met in nine Grand Slam tournament finals, with Serena winning seven times.

Beginning with the 2002 French Open, they played each other in four consecutive Grand Slam singles finals, which was the first time in the open era that the same two players had contested four consecutive major finals.

In the Australian Open in January 2017, Venus advanced to her first Grand Slam final since Wimbledon 2009, and her first Australian Open final since 2003.

In doing so, she set the Open Era record for the longest span (20 years) between grand slam singles final appearances, having first reached a grand slam singles final at the 1997 US Open.

Venus lost the Australian Open final to her younger sister, Serena Williams, who made history by winning her 23rd Grand Slam singles title.

In September 2017 Venus Williams reached the US Open quarter-finals for the second time in three years. If she reaches the final, this will be her third major final for the season, and she could return to the top five for the first time since January 2011.

If she wins the US Open final Venus could finish as high as No. 2 seed.

Venus is the chief executive officer of her interior design firm *V Starr Interiors* and owns her own athletic apparel line *EleVen by Venus Williams*, a collection of active lifestyle clothing which debuted at the 2012 New York fashion week.

Venus has also collaborated with American Express to create the social content series *Ace the Open with Venus Williams* which allows Card Club Members to enter into a multi-sensory tennis activation with Venus as they enter the US Open in 2017.

Venus Williams - Diurnal Chart

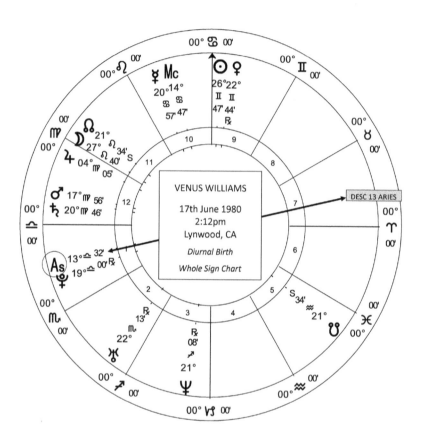

Fig. 45 Diurnal Chart: Venus Williams

Venus Williams: Sect Dignity

VENUS WILLIAMS — Diurnal Chart					
Solar and Diurnal Planets	CONDITION ONE	CONDITION TWO	CONDITION THREE	*MUNAKARA* Contention	TOTAL SECT DIGNITY
☉	✦	✦	✦		Sun in *Hayz* (1 + 2 + 3)
♃	✦	✦	––		Jupiter in *Halb* (1 + 2)
♄	✦	✦	––		Saturn in *Halb* (1 + 2)
☿ (Noct.)	––	––	✦		Sign Only
♂	––	––	––		*Ex Conditione* (no sect dignity)
♀	––	––	––		*Ex Conditione* (no sect dignity)
☽	––	––	––	MOON in *Munakara*	*Ex Conditione* (no sect dignity)
Lunar and Nocturnal Planets					

Fig. 46 Sect Table for Diurnal Chart: Venus Williams

Example One of *Munakara*

Venus Williams

VENUS WILLIAMS — Planets in *Munakara*			
Solar and Diurnal Planets	DISPOSITOR ONE	DISPOSITOR TWO	*MUNAKARA* Contention
♊ ☉ DIURNAL	☿ in ♋ Nocturnal	☽ Nocturnal	No Contention
♍ ♃ DIURNAL	☿ in ♋ Nocturnal	☽ Nocturnal	No Contention
♍ ♄ DIURNAL	☿ in ♋ Nocturnal	☽ Nocturnal	No Contention
♋ ☿ NOCTURNAL	☽ in ♌ Nocturnal	☉ Diurnal	No Contention
♍ ♂ NOCTURNAL	☿ in ♋ Nocturnal	☽ Nocturnal	No Contention
♊ ♀ NOCTURNAL	☿ in ♋ Nocturnal	☽ Nocturnal	No Contention
♌ ☽ NOCTURNAL	☉ in ♊ Diurnal	☿ Nocturnal	MOON in *Munakara*
Lunar and Nocturnal Planets			

Fig. 47 Munakara Table for Diurnal Chart: Venus Williams

Venus Williams

Delineation: Sect and *Munakara*

Venus Williams was born during the day.

Not only does she have a diurnal chart but all seven original planets are placed above the Ascendant in the diurnally placed hemisphere.

This situation automatically gives huge advantage to the diurnal planets whilst at the same time causing distress for the four nocturnal planets.

Mercury in Venus' chart is nocturnal because it travels in the sign behind the Sun, so Mercury joins the Moon, Venus and Mars in being unhappy with the state of their sect dignity in the diurnal chart.

Venus' Gemini Sun is in the best condition according to the accidental dignities of sect and the Joys. It conforms to all three of its sect conditions, and is therefore, in *Hayz,* whilst also finding itself in the house of its joy in the ninth house.

The Sun squares both Saturn and Mars, with Saturn also placed in its joy in the twelfth house.

The elevated Sun in the ninth is the ruler of the beneficial eleventh house, and is also the dispositor for the Moon which is alongside the North Node in the eleventh house.

Saturn rules both the fourth house (father) and the fifth house (leisure and entertainment), and both the Sun and Saturn are indicators for father in the chart.

Undoubtedly both diurnal planets represent Venus' father Richard Williams who trained both of his daughters when they were young and living in Compton, California.

Legend has it that even before the birth of his daughters, Richard saw the amount of prize money awarded to Romania tennis player Virginia Ruzici and became determined to teach himself to play tennis and then to take it upon himself to teach his wife, Oracene, and her three daughters.

Richard alleges he drew up a 78-page plan for rising to the top of the tennis rankings, and when his two youngest daughters Venus and Serena were four and a half and three years old respectively, Richard began their coaching regime.

In one interview Venus jokes that: *"We worked with my dad from conception to now."*

By the time the younger girls picked up a racket both Richard and Oracene had become tennis virtuosos who understood the game perfectly and who could teach and guide the girls to eventually become professional tennis players.

Isha Price, Venus' older stepsister, recalls that training was relentless, *"Life was get up, 6 o'clock in the morning, go to the tennis court, before school. After school, go to tennis. But it was consistency. You just can't be sometimey with it."* [33]

Three nocturnal planets in the chart are described in the table above as *"ex-conditione"* which is a term coined by Robert Hand to describe planets which are totally without sect dignity.

"A planet which is completely out of sect has no traditional name. However, it seems to be an important debility, especially for the malefic. Therefore I have taken the liberty of giving it a name derived from the Latin word for sect, condition. I have simply translated the phrase 'out of sect' into Latin as 'extra conditione'". [34]

It seems ironic that Venus Williams' celestial namesake should be in such terrible condition. Her planet Venus is not only deprived of sect dignity, it is also retrograde, and combust the Sun at four degrees with a conjunction to the major luminary.

Planet Venus may aspect its fellow nocturnal planets with a sextile to the Moon and a square to Mars, but as they all share the same fate, any contact between them is unlikely to be of much benefit to Venus, the owner of this chart.

However, the placement of Venus' Sun and planet Venus in the ninth house gives some insight into how this extraordinary woman works with a planet whose name she shares.

When asked about relationships Venus says: *"I was brought up as a Jehovah's Witness. We are very clear on the role of the female in a marriage situation. Just based on what we believe, a wife is supposed to be submissive (to her husband). And to have a career where you've pretty much done things your way and changed the whole function of a sport, then to come home and have your husband say 'I didn't like this dinner!' You've got to understand that may be a tad bit difficult (for me)."* [35]

Traditionally the Moon in Venus' chart would be classified as void of course (VOC) because it is located in the latest degree in the chart, and therefore, will not make an aspect to another planet before it leaves the sign of Leo.

The Moon's dispositor is strong, being the Sun in accidental dignity, but the Moon itself is struggling to get much relief in the chart so far as feeling emotionally supported or physically comfortable in its surroundings. The Moon rules the MC and the tenth house, but as Leo is blind to Cancer, there are further complications when the VOC Moon cannot see the most elevated point and house in the chart.

The Moon is stretched to its limit and the level of sacrifice it makes to maintain the chart owner's stringent physical training regime is multiplied by the fact that Venus' Moon is also in a state of *munakara*, brought about by the fact that the Moon is disposited by the diurnal Sun, which in turn is disposited by her nocturnal Mercury.

The constant stress that this state creates for a disadvantaged Moon in battle is perfectly displayed in this chart where the Moon is continually facing the emotional and physical rounds of training, competing and recovering, in order to repeat the cycle again in the following months of gruelling tennis tournaments.

Most professional athletes are looking at retirement as they approach their first Saturn Return at twenty eight but when Venus passed this age, she continued to gain strength and resolved to keep playing as long as her body (and her Moon) permitted her to do so.

The year 2011 was a particularly difficult one for both Venus and Serena as the girls were fighting their own battles to regain dropped rankings after illness and injury, yet they allowed cameras into their lives over a period of one year, and the resulting documentary, *Venus and Serena*,[36] provides fascinating insights into both girls' lives and their charts.

The film begins in January 2011 with Serena's operation on a blood clot and Venus' shock withdrawal from the Australian Open with early symptoms of what would be diagnosed later in the year as Sjögren's syndrome, an autoimmune disease that mainly affects salivary glands, tear ducts, and other moisture-producing glands.

Sjögren's syndrome is systemic, which means that it affects the entire body, with symptoms ranging from dry eyes and mouth to fatigue, joint pain, headaches, and swelling and tenderness around the glands. Its progress is unpredictable and there is no cure.

The recommendations for the management of Sjögren's syndrome include a list of challenges for someone who makes their living from an outdoor exercise in the middle of summer. The patient is advised to avoid dry and dusty environments, to keep away from air drafts and to stay indoors during windy weather. If they must go outside, wearing protective glasses is strongly recommended along with constant use of eye lubricants. Reducing stress levels to help maintain overall health to prevent agitating the disease and increasing the effects of fatigue are also urged by medical advisers.

All of these suggestions become laughable for a professional tennis player whose office is the outdoors arena and whose optimum workload occurs during the peak of summer months around the world.

However, they are perfect examples of how a Moon in a completely alien environment is required to find a balance between battling a debilitating disease, whilst at the same time, being driven by powerful diurnal planets to always produce their top game, regardless of the risks to the native's health.

Venus' Moon is in a different sign to the adjoining Jupiter, but there is still less than seven degrees which separate the two planets, and the Moon is approaching Jupiter with the aspect of an out-of-sign conjunction.

In Venus Williams' chart her Moon is waxing as it at the beginning of a new cycle, separating from the Sun in a sextile aspect.

According to Firmicus Maternus' rules on the Moon's phasing and sect, a waxing Moon applying in aspect to a diurnal planet, such as Jupiter, is extremely beneficial for the native

— *"If the waxing Moon is in aspect to Jupiter or is moving towards him, the natives will be fortunate, famous, and rich; masters of many great estates and wide possessions."* [37]

Jupiter has accidental dignity through sect, but is situated in Virgo, the sign of its detriment.

Jupiter is also in the twelfth house in the Whole Sign chart, and it is interesting to note that it rules both the third house of siblings and the sixth house of health's destruction in Venus Williams' chart.

The media hype when the two sisters play each other in Grand Slam finals is unprecedented in women's tennis, and the world's fascination when sister is pitted against sister has been consistently focused upon by many sports magazines, broadcasters, and sports commentators before, during, and after, any major titles game.

The Williams women, Oracene and her five daughters, have always formed an inner circle against the rest of the world, strengthened by their faith as Jehovah's Witnesses, and their collective determination to dominate a sport which has been called "white man's folly".

Oracene quotes Colossians when she describes the sibling's fierce closeness as *"a perfect bond of union"*, so it must be difficult for the family to watch the sisters whilst they are in combat on the tennis court.

In *Venus and Serena* there is a flashback to a 1991 interview with the two girls where an eleven year old Venus is asked, *"What's the toughest match you've ever been in?"*

Initially Venus giggles at the question and plays with her hair, but then she thinks about it and answers *"Probably the one against my sister."*

This answer is immediately followed by the question, *"What was it like?"*

Watching Venus answer this prying question is to see her *ex-conditione* Moon unmasked, and the viewer cannot help but feel for this child who is being asked emotionally charged questions which are way beyond her years, to adequately express her true feelings.

Venus drops her head and quietly whispers *"Horrible. She won 7-6."*

The interviewer thinks Venus has finished, but after a pause of a few seconds Venus adds, *"It was good that she won."*

It is a testament to their close bond that these sisters who are fiercely competitive can make the best of Venus' Jupiter in detriment, that they can lose to one another, and yet still choose to live together when they are both in Florida, to practice together, and to compete for the same prizes and goals in life.

The third house has other meanings besides signifying the siblings, such as describing both the local environment, especially when young, and also, as it sextiles the Ascendant, describes physical gifts which are often natural, unconscious and unrehearsed.

Jupiter in detriment ruling the third house describes Venus' childhood district when the Williams' sisters were growing up in Compton, a tough neighbourhood in Los Angeles County.

"Straight Outta Compton" is one of Richard Williams' catch-cries of which he is extremely proud, but he has a point.

As children the girls would practice on the courts at the local park and when gunshots rang out, they knew to hit the ground instantly.

Years later in 2003, their eldest stepsister's tinted-window car was mistaken for a gangland member's vehicle and Yetunde was shot and killed not far from these same tennis courts in Compton, California.

The rulership of Venus' third house by her diurnal Jupiter also describes her incredible talents as a tennis player, her natural swing, her powerful serve, and her obsession to get things right, no matter how many hours of repetition it takes to get the required results.

In the 2011 documentary Venus argues that the term 'perfectionist' does not apply to her, but rather that she sees herself as 'obsessive'.

She admits that at tournaments when she is allocated practice time on the courts, she is inclined to spend the entire two hour period practising just one single thing over and over again.

This says much about Jupiter in Virgo when it becomes obsessive over one small detail and often to the detriment of the whole larger view.

On the court Venus Williams rarely displays any inkling of strife from her *ex-conditione* Mars.

Serena is more likely to be outspoken or vocally agitated when challenging certain decisions which go against her on the court, but Venus is calm and controlled and the only signs of her displeasure are scowling or chewing the inside of her mouth, or looking dejected in the changeover chair.

Robert Hand describes a severely out of sect Mars as *"belligerent, competitive and selfish in its effects"*[38], so there can be an expectation that Mars is ferocious in its execution in a diurnal chart and when also diurnally placed with the Sun.

But this is not the case for Venus Williams and Mars is almost subdued, or evades any confrontation that may distract it from the contest with her opponent.

Mars rules the seventh house in Venus's chart and it seems all energy is focused in this direction when the seventh house becomes her opponent on the court.

Venus began her tennis career when she was fourteen years old, a girl with African heritage from a poor neighbourhood with none of the privileges that accompany a sport which is usually played at Country Clubs by an elite and wealthy clientele. Venus Williams has come a long way from these beginnings, but an *ex conditione* Mars shows how hard her journey has been over the past twenty plus years.

Mars is conjunct Saturn, which has good sect dignity, and although Mars has struggled to find the right formula for success, and to maintain that success, Saturn has been the discipline and the drive which has channelled Mars' aggression into maintaining focus on the tennis court (7th house) and providing enormous wealth for Venus (2nd house).

Mars rules the second house of money but this is secondary as Venus has said she often does not bother to collect her pay-cheque when she loses a tournament.

Both Mars and Saturn are disposited by Mercury at the top of the chart, and whilst Venus is an extremely private person when she is not playing tennis (Mars and Saturn in the 12th house), Mercury has garnered sponsorships and marketed Venus' image beautifully in the commercial world of advertising.

Again, it requires a huge effort for Mercury to be Venus' public face as nocturnal Mercury is pretty much out of sect dignity, as are her other nocturnal planets.

However, on some deeper level Venus Williams understands that, if handled properly, her nocturnal planets, i.e., Mercury conjunct the MC, the Moon dispositing Mercury, Venus ruling the ascendant and in aspect by trine, and both Mars and Venus disposited by Mercury, have set her up for a comfortable life.

Her nocturnal planets may suffer from weaknesses in sect, but they are an extremely close-knit group and are dependent on one another to rise above their debility and to work together for the good of this individual, even when they have to over-ride physical injury, debilitating illness, negative publicity or hostile opponents.

In *Venus and Serena,* Venus talks candidly about how she felt when Serena was the first of the two sisters to win a major tournament with the 1999 US Open.

There are flashbacks to a jubilant Serena bouncing across the court watched on by the hooded figure of Venus who is caught between being overjoyed for her sister yet at the same time, upset that Serena has claimed this honour before her.

Up until this point Venus had been the darling of the press and the princess of the advertising companies who flocked to sign her up for endorsements when she was just fourteen years old.

When asked about how she felt Venus replies, *"I think at the time not to win the first major was tough for me because I felt like as the older sister I should have been able to step up and do more, be tougher. I didn't know how to win and how to close a match out. I didn't know how to fight, I don't think that it came naturally to me. For Serena – it came more natural to her."*

Perhaps Mars has a choice of two avenues by which it can survive the diurnal chart.

It can either turn up the heat and create a Mars that is *"more active and less feeling"* [39] so there is an expectation for the individual's behaviour to be belligerent, competitive and selfish.

Or the individual can experience Mars in a state of '*hostage mentality*', in that Mars submits to the will of the dominant diurnal planets and forms an empathetic bond with its aggressors, whilst focusing its energy on fulfilling the wishes of the planets in charge.

The second version of Mars does not possess the luxury for self-exploration, but must continue to battle on, having few opportunities to display a more undisciplined version of itself in a diurnal chart.

Venus Williams' chart is a perfect example of how Mercury can slip under the radar in delineation when so much other information is being processed concerning dignities, sect and the possibilities for *munakara*.

In Venus William's chart Mercury sits close to the culminating point, just six degrees from the Midheaven, in the sign of Cancer.

Mercury aspects Saturn and Mars by sextile, Pluto by square, Uranus by trine, and Neptune by quincunx, but in traditional terms the fact that Mercury aspects the three newer planets may go unnoticed, especially if judgement is concentrated on essential or accidental dignities.

So far as sect is concerned, Mercury is nocturnal in Venus' chart as it follows the Sun, and in Venus' diurnal chart, Mercury is diurnally placed in the upper hemisphere with the Sun.

The relevance of Mercury's placement would be easy to overlook, that is, until the chart is closely scrutinised or when accessing the information provided by the three Tables which accompany Venus' chart.

The second column of the *Munakara* Table shows the planet which is the initial dispositor, or the owner of the sign in which of each of the seven planets finds itself.

It is noteworthy that five of Venus' planets are disposited by this nocturnal, feminine-signed Mercury – Sun and Venus in Gemini, and Jupiter, Mars and Saturn in Virgo.

Only the Moon misses out, but she is Mercury's own dispositor, and although the connection is indirect – all roads lead back to this elevated Mercury.

Mercury rules Venus' ninth house where her Sun and Venus reside, and Venus' faith as a Jehovah's Witness provides her with tremendous psychological stability and a haven from the outside world's prying eyes.

True to Mercury's potential, Venus Williams *has* become a household name. Her longevity in professional tennis is amazing and the advertising endorsements which have constantly placed her in the public eye have been financially lucrative, but apart from her commercial fame, Venus has also become an icon for young women who want to break financial, racial or social barriers.

Every aspect of Venus' professional and private life has been under scrutiny since she was a teenager, and it is to her credit that her nocturnal Mercury has been able to maintain Venus' poise and grace, whilst still guarding her privacy over the past twenty years of her career.

Mercury in Cancer has become the linchpin in the chart for this sensitive, intelligent woman.

In Cancer it holds the Williams family together, and astrologically, it is the glue that cements the various elements of a complicated chart.

In Mercury, the nocturnal planets have found both an ally and a protector. Mercury is required to care for Venus and Mars as the dispositor of their signs, and to sympathise with them by being itself nocturnal, and disposited by the lunar luminary.

The remainder of Venus' conversation on Serena pipping her to the post in the 1999 US Open is a pure Mercury moment: *"It was like a defining moment for me, like, how are you going to react to something like that? Am I going to learn from her example or am I going to crumble? I wanted to learn."*

And learn Venus did.

The following year Venus Williams won the 2000 Wimbledon Women's Singles title for the very first time.

Six years later, Venus' Mercury was visible for a different reason when her argument to support equal prize money for women in Open finals was published in *The Times* on the eve of Wimbledon in 2006.

Then British Prime Minister, Tony Blair, publicly endorsed Williams' arguments and equal pay became standard in 2007.

Venus was the first female to directly benefit from the changes, as she went on to become the 2007 Wimbledon Woman's Champion.

Venus' Sun is in the sign of Gemini, disposited by her elevated Mercury on the Midheaven, and the following comment by celebrated American author Gay Talese in the 2011 documentary nicely summarises Venus' complicated relationship with Serena.

Talese says: *"I know they're not twins, but in a way, they are. And their whole life experience has been within the shadow of the other person. There is very little that has happened to one, that the other has not been privy to, maybe even an eye witness to. So if you try and marry into that arrangement it will be very unique – maybe even brothers."*

One sports observer comments that *"They are each other's greatest rivals. If there were no Venus or there were no Serena you could nearly double either of their Grand Slam titles."*

This quote is both the strength and the greatest flaw in the Gemini Sun with the planet Venus as the Ascendant lord – wanting to stand independently in your own glorious circle of light, but also needing the other, the twin, to compete against and inevitably, to share in your limelight.

Serena Williams

Serena Jameka Williams (born 26th September, 1981) is fifteen months younger than her sister Venus Williams.

Serena is also an American professional tennis player who holds the most major titles in singles, doubles, and mixed doubles combined amongst active players.

The Women's Tennis Association (WTA) has ranked her world No. 1 in singles on seven occasions. Serena became the world No. 1 for the first time on 8th July, 2002, and fifteen years later, was ranked world No. 1 for the seventh time after winning the Australian Open on 30th January, 2017.

In total, Serena has been world No. 1 for 311 weeks, which ranks her 3rd in the Open Era among female tennis players. Serena Williams' accomplishments and success in professional tennis have led some commentators, players, and sports writers to regard her as the greatest female tennis player of all time.

Her total of twenty three Grand Slam singles titles marks the record for the most Major wins by a tennis player in the Open Era.

She is the only tennis player to have won ten Grand Slam singles titles in two separate decades. Serena has won fourteen Grand Slam doubles titles with her sister Venus, and the pair are currently unbeaten in Grand Slam doubles finals.

Serena has also won four Olympic gold medals, one in women's singles and three in women's doubles – an all-time record shared with Venus.

The sisters won their first gold medal at the 2000 Sydney Olympics and the last, twelve years later, at the 2012 London Olympics.

At the same Olympics Serena also won the gold medal for women's singles tennis.

Serena has experienced her share of hardship: racist jeers from onlookers during matches, including one incident at Indian Wells in 2001 that caused her to boycott the California tournament for fourteen years. In 2003 Serena underwent knee surgery and in the same year, the sudden loss of her eldest sister Yetunde, caused a deep depression which followed Yetunde's death and the plunge in ranking which followed, taking Serena from No 3 to 139th in the world.

When Serena returned in 2007 for the Grand Slam in Australia, she had fought her way back to being ranked at No. 81, but rather than being supported for her amazing comeback instead she was ridiculed by the press for the extra weight she had gained during her time away from the game.

In 2010 Serena received stitches on both feet after stepping on glass at a restaurant in Munich. Months later, she underwent emergency treatment for a life-threatening blood clot in her lung, which sidelined her for 12 months.

When she returned in 2012 at age 31, Serena returned stronger than ever, rising in the ranks until she became the oldest tennis player to be ranked as No. 1 in the world.

Serena Williams was the highest paid female athlete in 2016, earning $28.9 US million in prize money and endorsements.

Serena retired from tennis for the remainder of the year after announcing in March 2017 that she was expecting a child with her fiancé Alexis Ohanian, the co-founder of Reddit, a social media phenomena. Serena gave birth to a daughter on 31st August, 2017, during the same period as the US Open, a tournament that Serena has won six times and Venus has won twice, was taking place at Flushing Meadows in New York City.

Serena Williams - Nocturnal Chart

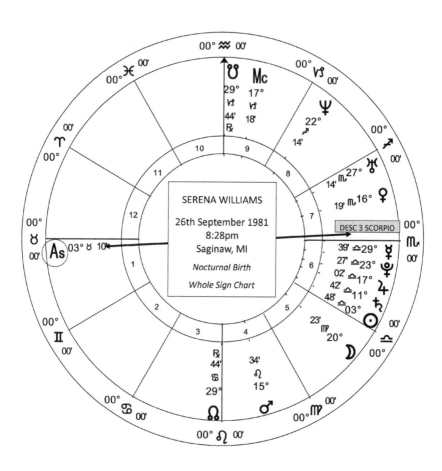

Fig. 48 Nocturnal Chart: Serena Williams

Serena William: Sect Dignity

SERENA WILLIAMS — Nocturnal Chart					

Solar and Diurnal Planets	CONDITION ONE	CONDITION TWO	CONDITION THREE	MUNAKARA *Contention*	TOTAL SECT DIGNITY
☉	––	✦	✦		Sun in *Halb* (2 + 3)
♃	––	✦	✦		Jupiter in *Halb* (2 + 3)
♄	––	✦	✦		Saturn in *Halb* (2 + 3)
☿ (Noct.)	✦	––	––		Chart Only (1)
♂	✦	––	✦	*MARS in Munakara*	(1 + 3)
♀	✦	✦	✦		Venus in *Hayz* (1 + 2 + 3)
☽	✦	––	✦		(1 + 3)

Lunar and Nocturnal Planets

Fig. 49 Sect Table for Nocturnal Chart: Serena Williams

Example Two of *Munakara*

Serena Williams

SERENA WILLIAMS — Planets in *Munakara*			
Solar and Diurnal Planets	DISPOSITOR ONE	DISPOSITOR TWO	*MUNAKARA* Contention
♎☉ DIURNAL	♀ in ♏ *Nocturnal* -------→*Nocturnal*	♂ *Nocturnal*	No Contention
♎♃ DIURNAL	♀ in ♏ *Nocturnal* -------→*Nocturnal*	♂ *Nocturnal*	No Contention
♎♄ DIURNAL	♀ in ♏ *Nocturnal*-------→ *Nocturnal*	♂ *Nocturnal*	No Contention
♎☿ NOCTURNAL	♀ in ♏ *Nocturnal* -------→*Nocturnal*	♂ *Nocturnal*	No Contention
♌♂ NOCTURNAL	☉ in ♎ *Diurnal*	♀ *Nocturnal*	*MARS in Munakara*
♏♀ NOCTURNAL	♂ in ♌ *Nocturnal* -------→ *Diurnal*	☉	No Contention
♍☽ NOCTURNAL	☿ in ♎ *Nocturnal* -------→*Nocturnal*	♀	No Contention
Lunar and Nocturnal Planets			

Fig. 50 Munakara Table for Nocturnal Chart: Serena Williams

Serena Williams

Delineation: Sect and *Munakara*

Serena Williams was born into the opposite sect from her sister, Venus.

Serena's chart is nocturnal, signifying that her main luminary is the Moon, and that her remaining nocturnal planets, Venus, Mars and an occidental Mercury, are all content in their environment and well-pleased with the resultant gift of accidental dignity.

Both girls have an ascendant which is ruled by the planet Venus. Venus Williams has a Libran ascendant with her ruler in Gemini conjunct the Sun in the ninth house whilst Serena's Ascendant is Taurus.

Serena's ascendant has her ruling lord, Venus opposite the first house in Scorpio, and therefore in detriment, in the seventh house of relationships and open enemies.

Strictly speaking Serena's Venus is not in an aspect of opposition to her ascendant as there is a gap of thirteen degrees between the descendant degree (3 Scorpio) and Venus (16 Scorpio).

When asked about relationships in the 2011 documentary film by Maiken Baird, Serena replied, *"I'm married to me. I'm getting very selfish in my ways. It's a shame really, because there are some great guys out there."*

In the same documentary Serena talks playfully about the variety of different personas and their different attitudes that help her Taurean Ascendant to survive the rigours of her very public life.

She explains she projects "Psycho Serena" who is very much a competitive Scorpio Venus who appears during tennis tournaments. Serena says of this character, *"You don't want to meet her.*

She's always on court, she's at practice and she's in the match. She's awesome, she's amazing, and she's a great athlete."

Then there is "Summer Diaz". She is Serena's persona for publicity, and Summer appears in her Venus world of outfits, nails and fashion accessories.

Summer is feminine and flirty, and helps Serena to have the patience to work through her many endorsements and numerous public appearances.

Then there is "Megan" and Serena says she's really mean.

Serena describes Megan as her brash Australian persona and she advises *"You don't want to run into Megan"* as she is apparently outspoken and a bit raunchy.

Lastly, Serena introduces "Taquanda" and this personality is the venomous side to Serena's Venus in Scorpio in the seventh house.

Serena describes Taquanda as rough.

She is not Christian, she's from the Hood.

Serena jokes that it was Taquanda who reacted with a string of verbal abuse aimed at the linesperson who called a foot fault at the 2009 US Open.

Serena smiles sweetly and says that she, Serena, apparently missed the incident, but that she is still paying for Taquanda's outburst with reminders and footage from the media replaying the incident years after it occurred.

Compared to the number of past and present male tennis players who treat the referee to a verbal tirade (from the Italian word *tirata*, meaning "volley"), Serena's slip was minor, and yet Serena's gender or perhaps, her heritage, has meant that she has been called to defend her behaviour many times over.

All of these characters are introduced with fun and a tongue-in-cheek attitude, but for an astrologer looking at Serena's chart with a huge stellium in Libra, there is no doubt that a number of opposing characters are present in this chart, when no less than five planets are disposited by the Venus in Scorpio.

Sun, Saturn, Jupiter, Pluto and Mercury are situated in Libra, in the sign belonging to Venus, so there is plenty of room in Serena's chart for Psycho Serena, Summer Diaz, Megan and Taquanda, as well as her own unique personality, to explore the whimsies of a Libran stellium in this nocturnal chart.

Thankfully, Venus is the most secure of all Serena's planets according to the dignity of sect.

Venus is in *Hayz* with all three conditions – chart, hemisphere and sign – conforming to the correct nocturnal sect.

Serena's comfort and familiarity with her female personas, and indeed her frank appraisal of them, is the measure of a Venus which may not always love its sign of detriment, but is delighted with its sect strength and totally at ease with Serena in her most engaging form, that is, as a strong, confident and powerful African American woman.

As the Sun is beneath the horizon, Serena's Moon becomes the main luminary with sect dignity.

Her Moon gains enormous benefit from its placement in the female sign of Virgo in the fifth house of leisure, sports and entertainment.

Serena's Virgo Moon makes a powerful trine aspect to the Midheaven at 17 degrees Capricorn and the earth element is well represented through the combination of Moon, Midheaven and Ascendant.

The earth element signs are feminine and therefore nocturnal, and could not be better suited to display Serena's dedication to her craft and her ability to only improve with age.

We may possibly see the greatest female tennis player of all time when we watch any of the major Grand Slam tournaments from this century but it has not been an easy road for Serena.

The first house which signifies her physical body is ruled by Venus in detriment, and her three diurnal planets, Sun, Saturn and Jupiter, are placed in the sixth house, a house which is hidden from the Ascendant, and one which can pose an enormous threat to the native's health and wellbeing.

Yet Serena has used her seventh house Venus – the dispositor of her Libra stellium – to confront opponents both on and off the court, especially when the press is often hostile towards her and reporters keep baiting Serena to get a reaction that will provide them with juicy front-page headlines.

The Moon is Serena's main luminary, and whilst many credit Serena's father Richard Williams with the girls' professional success, their mother, Oracene, has had as much impact on both girls, but has played a particularly active role in Serena's career.

Serena wrote in her book that Oracene is one of the best analysts at critiquing her game and it is always her mother who accompanies Serena to the Australian Open, not her father.

When Oracene was interviewed in the documentary *Venus and Serena* she made this comment regarding the girls' coaching during their childhood: *"Venus was on her dad's court, Serena was on mine. He claimed he couldn't handle Serena because she was crazy. I told her different. I made her believe in herself, made her think that she could get to any ball."*

Serena's Moon rules her third house, the house of siblings, childhood community and physical abilities, and so, similar to Venus' statement, but from a different direction, a household of strongly bonded women with a common goal and shared spirituality supports Serena's skill.

Oracene is fiercely proud of her youngest daughter's achievements, and although the Mercury which disposits the Virgo Moon does not aspect it, Mercury is still very much involved in the Libra stellium in Serena's sixth house.

The Sun in Libra is in fall and an exalted Saturn conjuncts her Sun, indicating that her father, Richard, had expectations that were exceedingly high (exalted Saturn) and may have crushed Serena's confidence when she was much younger.

A strong supportive mother in a nocturnal chart can be of enormous benefit in a chart with harsh father statements and for Serena, who was taken under her mother's tuition as a child, her mother's training and her encouragement meant that Serena has been able to override her self-doubt, and with each new success, she claims the exalted Saturn as her own drive for perfection.

Serena's Moon, similar to Venus' Moon, would have traditionally been considered as a difficult 'void of course' Moon (VOC) because it does not aspect any of the other original planets before it leaves the sign of Virgo. The Moon is in the sign alongside Sun, Saturn, Jupiter and Mercury and so it cannot aspect any of these planets and the last aspect the Moon made a few hours prior to Serena's birth was a sextile to Venus in detriment.

The ancients would not have seen the approaching square to Neptune or the Moon's sextile to Uranus, and would have judged this as a difficult Moon for the native.

Both sisters with VOC Moons are an interesting coincidence and perhaps suggests that in order to push their bodies so hard, and so consistently, the Moon, their bodies' significator, must believe that this one match immediately in front of them is "the last chance" and that is why neither sister holds back, regardless of the injuries, the illnesses and the future consequences, when they are on the court.

Perhaps their VOC Moons are one of the few similar signatures in two very different charts that make the Williams sisters the two faces who have changed women's tennis forever.

There are other connections between the two sisters' charts which also suggests that one without the other would not have created the phenomena which is the Williams sisters.

"I know they're not twins, but in a way, they are. And their whole life experience has been within the shadow of the other person. There is very little that has happened to one, that the other has not been privy to, maybe even an eye witness to."

When the two charts are put together the synastry between them is quite unique.

The outer planets will, of course, be very similar, as the births are only fifteen months apart, but there are other similarities which indicate why they are such an integral link in each other's lives and careers.

Venus' Saturn and Mars in Virgo are conjunct Serena's Moon.

Serena's Saturn is conjunct Venus' Ascendant and Serena's Libra stellium lies in Venus' first house.

The nature of Saturn is to relentlessly drive one forwards and the connections between Saturn and Moon, and Saturn and Ascendant indicates that the battles on the court are personal, and a loss by one to the other requires a huge amount of sisterly love to recover from such a blow.

The girls' fourth and tenth axis is reversed, but the degrees are similar. Venus' MC is 14 Cancer which is conjunct Serena's IC at 17 Cancer. Statements about mother and father are interesting when the two share the same parents, but have different memories and attitudes to them. The two girls are very close and share a house in Florida when they are not on the circuit, so it may be difficult for Venus to come to terms with her younger sister's new state of motherhood.

The two feminine planets in Serena's nocturnal chart both represent her elder sibling.

The VOC Moon ruling her third house and the planet Venus represent the sister Venus in Serena's chart, her fiercest opponent and her most treasured loved one.

Serena says in the documentary that it was very difficult being in the shadow of Venus because ever since she remembers Venus was in the newspapers.

There is only fifteen months between the sisters and Venus was fourteen when she moved into the limelight, won a major tournament and became the face of the sports giant, Puma.

All her life Serena has been competing with Venus and only now, in her mid 30's, is Serena beginning to outshine her elder sister.

Serena says: *"I was never supposed to be good. I was never the one that was supposed to be a great player, but I was determined not to become a statistic. So that's the only reason I play tennis. I was a copycat basically."*

Serena's sixth house stellium in Libra consists of the Sun, Saturn, Jupiter, Pluto and Mercury, so there is little doubt that when provoked by others' hostility towards her Serena's forceful Mercury will speak out in order to set the record straight.

Jupiter and Pluto combined with the Libran Mercury strives to gain a level playing field where Serena is concerned, both on the court when she disagrees with poor decisions that affect the game, or in the media room after the match when she is asked to defend her behaviour or answer questions which she feels are irrelevant or accusatory in nature.

Both girls are deeply religious, following their mother's example as Jehovah's Witnesses, but whilst Venus' ninth house of religion contains her Gemini Sun and Venus and is ruled by the planets' overseer, that is her Mercury, Serena has a different lord for her ninth house of religion.

Serena's exalted Saturn rules her ninth house and as Saturn is conjunct Serena's Libran Sun, it is no surprise when she says that her father had always told her as a child that she must put God first, even above her family.

Richard did not convert and has never become a Witness, but all five sisters followed their mother into a religion which has an emphasis on separation from the world, and this has only strengthened the bond between the women.

When Serena lashed out at the linesman at the 2009 US Open she was quietly taken aside and reprimanded by her elders for her abrasive behaviour as they felt that Serena had been a poor ambassador for their religion.

Serena's Sun is in Libra, in fall, conjunct her exalted Saturn, and both planets represent her complicated relationship with an unusual father with incredible talents as a tennis coach.

Venus may have been able to forgive her father's many public outbursts considering that she has a highly visible Sun in its house of joy in the ninth house.

Perhaps her religious teachings that the males in the family are above reproach is enough for her to tolerate her father's extreme behaviour.

After all, he achieved for her all things that he promised in her childhood – fame, fortune and success.

But Serena's chart is a different story.

Her Sun in fall suggests that she is less forgiving of Richard's boxing-promoter language, boasts, exaggerations and misstatements.

Perhaps as the outsider Serena has observed Richard's unreserved glee at Venus' early successes and his behaviour has shown more of the characteristics of the Jupiter and Pluto alongside the exalted Saturn, creating extremes of megalomania and paranoia.

Nor has Richard always been the ideal father, early in the girls' career there were confirmed reports of domestic violence by Richard against Oracene when he broke several of her ribs during an argument.

Serena's Sun rules the fourth house of father so whilst Richard may have been a tennis virtuoso who raised his family in rank and fortune, the father figure Serena might have hoped for, is missing in her chart.

Although there is a difference in Serena's whole sign chart between the MC sign (Capricorn) and the tenth sign (Aquarius), both are ruled by the exalted Saturn in the sixth house, and this may indicate why in post-match remarks Serena firstly thanks Jehovah God, and then both her father (Saturn) and her mother (Saturn-ruled tenth house).

For most successful people accepting awards this is the normal procedure, but for Serena, she is completing the rights of her chart by acknowledging this trinity, which have been the vehicles of her success, in this appropriate manner.

Serena Williams' chart provides an opportunity to examine a second practical application of *munakara,* that is, the switch from one sect to the other and back again.

Serena has her Leo Mars in a state of contention *(munakara)* as Mars is a nocturnal planet but as it is in Leo, it is disposited by the Sun, which is a diurnal planet.

Her Libran Sun is disposited by Venus, a nocturnal planet.

The discomfort felt by the Sun passes back to Mars who must deal with an irate Sun which has its own problems by being in fall and disposited by Venus in detriment.

The Moon's chain of command remains nocturnal, and the planets Venus and Mars are extremely secure as the four planets involved in their chain of command are all nocturnal planets.

It is only when the Sun steps into the middle for Mars that there is a problem.

For this reason, Mars stands alone as the only planet in Serena's chart afflicted by contention, even though four of the seven planets are disposited by Venus, but as Venus herself is disposited by Mars, there is no switch back to diurnal in their case.

Serena's Mars in *munakara,* is a good example of a highly competitive Mars which relishes the battle and it works to her advantage by maintaining her focus on winning, bringing her back from injury, surgery and depression to reinstate her as number 1 in world ranking at a time when most professional tennis players would be retiring from the game.

Serena's Mars is angular in her chart, and although it is in a diurnal hemisphere, it still picks up accidental dignity for the chart being similarly nocturnal, and Mars is placed in the masculine sign of Leo.

Mars has a strong quartile aspect to Venus, which it disposits, and there is a level of control that Mars exerts over the ruler of the Ascendant.

Mars may not aspect the Ascendant directly by degree but Leo squares Taurus, and this may be enough to keep Mars constantly in the picture.

Mars also sextiles both diurnal lieutenants, Jupiter and Saturn, who have good sect condition by travelling with the Sun in a masculine sign.

Mars may not be in direct aspect to the MC, but a good aspect to the MC ruler, that is, an exalted Saturn, can be very useful in pushing a highly motivated Mars towards achieving success in the native's chosen career.

Tennis aficionados comment that Serena's forehand is considered to be among the most powerful shots in women's tennis, as is her double-handed backhand.

Serena's aggressive play is considered to be somewhat "high risk" but it is balanced by her serve, which most believe is the greatest in women's tennis history.

Serena's Mars in *munakara* is perhaps the reason why she is known for producing exceptional comebacks, particularly on the Grand Slam level.

In recent years, Serena has shown an ability to serve aces at critical moments.

One of these instances was the 2013 French Open final, where in the last game of the match, she fired three aces, including one which clocked at 123 mph (198 km/h) on match point.

She repeated the feat similarly against Angelique Kerber in the finals of the 2016 Wimbledon Championships to tie the Open Era record for Grand Slam singles titles.

Williams fired three un-returnable serves in her final service game before winning the match and the title with a casual forehand volley on the next point.

Not bad for a planet in contention.

CHAPTER FOUR

House Rulerships

"One Thing Leads to Another—Everything is Connected"[40]

Artwork by Richard Long, 2009,
on the Jubilee Line of the London Underground

A planet's ownership of a house is an extension of its rulership of a sign.

Wherever a sign is found in the chart, the ruling planet of the sign becomes responsible for the affairs of that house or houses with its sign on the cusp.

The commitment which a planet has to the house it rules, is one of the most basic tenets of Hellenistic astrology.

Within the context of *"Everything is Connected"*, the thoughts and words of the three Greek philosophers, Socrates, Plato and Aristotle, has underpinned astrological theory since 500 BCE.

Their belief, and the beliefs of those who precede them by centuries, in the existence of a living and vibrant Universe being reflected in the lives of people on Earth has led to the astrological practice of connecting the movement of planets with human activity.

In Robert Hand's lecture at the 2005 conference in York in the United Kingdom entitled *On Matter and Form in Astrology*,[41] Robert took Aristotle's four Causes and applied them directly to astrological theory.

The table below *(Fig. 51)* explains the Four Causes in detail. The diagrams on the following pages *(Figs. 54,55)* incorporate Robert Hand's suggestions on linking the Causes to astrology in order to understand how the planets, the signs, and the houses are connected in the chart.

Aristotle's Four Causes

"Plainly, then, these are the causes, and this is how many they are. They are four, and the student of nature should know them all, and it will be his method, when stating an account of what, to get back to them all: the matter, the form, the thing which effects the change, and what the thing is for."[42]

-Aristotle (384-322 BCE)

Aristotle was a Greek philosopher, born in the late fourth century B.C.E., who enrolled in Plato's Academy when he was 17 years old.

In 335 B.C.E. Aristotle founded his own school, the Lyceum in Athens, where he spent most of the rest of his life studying, teaching and writing.

Many of his works were incorporated within Arabic thought and re-introduced to Europe centuries after his death.

The classifications of 'matter and form' were a cornerstone of his philosophy and he believed that the reasons behind things evolving from matter to form or decomposing from form back to matter, could be defined through what he called 'The Four Causes of Being'.

This part of Aristotle's philosophical theory is known as 'Hylomorphism' and is based on the idea that every living organism is capable of possessing an *"essential existence"*[43] which is dependent on the development of a physical presence through the combination of matter (Greek *hyle*) and form (Greek *morph*).

Aristotle named his Four Causes as Material, Efficient, Formal, and Final.

Each of the four Causes asked a question for definition or clarity, and collectively, the answers to these four questions or Causes could describe the nature of something.

What are the questions we must ask in order to understand what something is?

MATERIAL CAUSE asks: *What Am I? Can you describe the material from which I am made?*

The answer may be: clay, stone, wood, plant material etc, but it does not always have to be physical.

Material Cause can be the rough ideas, concepts or imaginings that develop into a Theory.

EFFICIENT CAUSE asks: *What will be the vehicle that takes me from Matter to Form?*

What is my motive? What is the source of my vision?

The answer may be: the potter, the stone-mason, the wood-carver, the apothecary, the scientist or medical researcher, the philosopher.

FORMAL CAUSE asks: *What have I become? What is my form, shape or appearance?*

What do you see? What do you know about me? What is my essence?

The answer may be: a terracotta bowl, a statue, a table, medicine, a Theory, a Scientific Fact.

FINAL CAUSE asks: *What is the purpose, reason or meaning behind my existence? Why do I exist?*

What is my 'for the sake of'? What is the point of my creation?

The answer may be: to drink from, for decoration, for inspiration, for a cure, for safety, for comfort, for clarity, for a basic human need to understand or explain something.

Aristotle believed that together the Four Causes created the stimuli necessary for all matter to undergo constant change, beginning with a material's innate potential to become something else, or to fulfil its actualization into a number of different forms.

These forms were neither permanent nor impenetrable, but could break down over time so that they might once more become matter, and subsequently, commence the cycle of change to re-form again as something quite different.

In Aristotle's mind matter always came first and form followed but once the line of beginnings and endings joins itself to become a cycle of change it leads to the age-old question:

Who came first? The chicken or the egg?

Which one is matter, the chicken or the egg, and which one is form?

The truth is, they are probably both – the material of the hen leads to the formation of an egg, and the material of the egg becomes the form of a chicken, once the egg's shell has been broken by the chick from the inside of the egg.

When this same question was posed to Aristotle he is believed to have answered:

"There could not have been a first egg to give a beginning to birds, or there would have been a first bird which gave a beginning to eggs; for a bird comes from an egg."[44]

Aristotle's final answer was evasive as he maintained that both chicken and egg went infinitely backward, and therefore, both had always existed.

Aristotle's Four Causes of Being

MATERIAL CAUSE "FROM"	EFFICIENT CAUSE "BY"	FORMAL CAUSE "INTO"	FINAL CAUSE "FOR"
POTENTIAL	POTENTIAL	ACTUAL	ACTUAL
- Describes the nature of the raw material 'FROM' which something is made. - The Material Cause takes us directly to the concrete substance of the work. - It provides data on what the possibility might be for a physical end-point of a thing. - Material Cause describes and evaluates something through objective observations – its tactile qualities, its density, malleability, fluidity, etc. - Works in generalisations rather than through personal interpretation. All parties agree on the components of the Material Cause, i.e. wood, stone, clay, or bronze. - Is the original Cause – without Material Cause no other process, action, change, or Cause can take place. - Matter is not restricted to just one type of form. This is where its true potential lies; in its capacity to be limited only by the 'mover' or the force behind the Efficient Cause.	- The vehicle 'BY' which something is changed. - Sometimes called the 'moving cause' because it is the primary source by which matter changes into form. - It is the vision of what could potentially 'be', and the action which is taken for the vision to manifest as reality. - Efficient Cause has a subjective quality. Each person has a different interpretation of what matter should become. - Information is constantly re-evaluated and the vision changes as the object takes shape. - Emotion and imagination drives the Efficient Cause as there must be desire, will-power, and intent for its activation. - For something to take form, there must be a combination of two kinds of potential (Material and Efficient), as well as an objective and subjective purpose behind the change.	- The pattern, form, or arrangement which the raw material has been transformed 'INTO'. - The Formal Cause is the authentic identity of something and is often described as its core "essence". - It embodies all essential attributes and represents what a thing does when it is flourishing. - The object has found its most natural, productive, necessary, or comfortable form in life. - Formal Cause evaluates something by using objectivity to describe details, data, particulars, and measurement. - It is the desired end result or final appearance of something, and falls into the category of having reached its objective purpose or goal. - The movement from 'potential' to 'actual' has occurred and the matter has fulfilled a measure of its potential in the completed form.	- The purpose, end, aim, function or goal 'FOR' which something was created. - It is "telos", the Greek word used to describe something that achieves its final end, its ultimate purpose, the intention made concrete. - The reason behind something's existence. It is 'the point of it all' or the sake for which something was made. - The Final Cause often has practical application, but its merit is highly subjective in nature as each individual will give it different value according to their own opinion and reaction to the form. - The variety of answers to Final Cause's question 'What is it for?' is diverse and far-reaching as Final Cause in itself is highly personal and is affected by the individual's own experiences. - Final Cause evokes a range of emotions and sensations. In the times before science and modern philosophy it provided spiritual or religious meaning to forms.
OBJECTIVE	SUBJECTIVE	OBJECTIVE	SUBJECTIVE

Fig. 51 Table of Aristotle's Four Causes of Being

The Four Causes: Potentiality and Actuality

The Table above *(Fig. 51)* shows that the four Causes can be divided into two sub-categories; Potentiality or Actuality, and Objectivity or Subjectivity.

The first sub-category divides the Causes into what 'could be', that is, what lies dormant in the raw material and what has the likely power or influence to change it (Potentiality), as opposed to what 'manifests' as something tangible in an identifiable form, with a distinct purpose or meaning (Actuality).

If a clay sculpture is used as an example, the beginning stage occurs when a lump of clay has the potential to be moulded into a variety of different forms baked in a kiln, so that the clay holds its form for a substantial period of time.

This matter is the Material Cause from which something can be made, and potentiality describes what lies dormant within the raw material, waiting for the other Causes to transform the potential into actual form and meaning.

The artist who takes the clay and creates a form is described by the Efficient Cause, which also has potentiality because the form is only limited by the personal qualities of the artist and their ability to work within the boundaries of the raw material's potential.

The potter's unique combination of imagination, artistry, desire and commitment together illustrates the invisible potentiality behind the creation of the form and the eventual identity of the sculpture.

The artist's level of skill in working with the raw material, and their competence in completing the task at hand, is the practical side of potentiality as will and intention is fine, but the mastery of skills also defines the potential to create the end result of a comfortable or natural form from the original matter.

Once completed, the sculpture itself has turned into an authentic form, therefore it has become actuality, and this is called Formal Cause in that the viewer can recognise the essence of what the artist was trying to convey to their audience.

The more skilled the artist, the greater is the viewer's ability to relate to the actuality, or completeness, of the form.

A good potter will produce something from the clay which has a natural 'flourishing' form which is pleasant to one or two of the five human senses.

The five senses or faculties – sight, hearing, smell, taste and touch – allow us to experience and interact with our physical environment, and the more senses a form will please or evoke in us, the more likely we are to want to protect that particular form.

The reason behind the sculpture's existence, or the Final Cause, is also actuality in that once the form has been created, both artist and audience finds a meaning behind its existence.

The Final Cause may change its interpretation of something's purpose or meaning, but the form must still exist or maintain its sameness, for the Final Cause to exist.

The two Causes are reliant upon one another's existence, and this is partly a measure of Actuality.

Actuality describes something that persists in holding on to its condition, or works constantly to stay the same (and therefore resists change) so although we cannot see it, both Formal Cause and Final Cause use energy to maintain the end result.

Actuality occurs when the fulfilment of a possibility has occurred, but in Aristotle's mind the form was not a 'dead end' when the process was complete and the form was created.

We can easily see motion, change and activity occurring in Efficient Cause, but these three states of energy also occur in the other Causes.

They are often imperceptible to the human eye but according to Aristotle, Material, Formal and Final Cause are not lacking in activity, change or motion.

The Four Causes: Objectivity and Subjectivity

The second sub-category divides the four Causes into a different set of pairs according to perspective, as two of the Causes will act on objective information, and the other two Causes will use subjective decision-making, as their motivation for change *(Fig. 52)*.

Objectivity describes something which has detachment or the absence of bias as its parameter.

Science uses objective thinking to support theories based on logical analysis, which is the result of measurable experiments with predictable patterns.

The first of Aristotle's Causes, Material Cause, is considered to be objective because the raw material is generally a physical substance which can be measured and analysed for its content.

Formal Cause is also objective in nature because it exists in physical form and is undisputed as the manifestation of matter, regardless of differing opinion or perception.

Formal Cause is usually physical, tangible and has shape, design and structure, so that at the most basic level, both matter and form can be described as objective in principle.

That is, able to be measured, assessed and catalogued, according to similarities or differences in matter or form.

Alternatively, subjectivity is borne from self-knowledge, and takes into account feelings, opinions and personal judgements based on past experiences.

Efficient Cause is the artist who uses the subjectivity of their emotions and their individualised selective process, to create a sculpture which is unique to their skills and their own distinctive interpretation.

In many ways they are the source of inspiration and the creation must please them, before it pleases anyone else.

This is the true nature of subjectivity.

Efficient Cause uses motive (which has a negative connotation) and motivations (a more positive incentive or long-term goal) and is at its most 'efficient' when the primary source has a sound and realistic understanding of its own capabilities, nature and characteristics.

Final Cause is the very personal perception of what gives something a purpose or meaning.

In the case of the clay sculpture, each individual will react to the form differently, and will intuitively search for their own reasons as to why the sculpture exists in this particular form.

Final Cause is subjective in nature, purely because subjectivity means that people will place different values on an object, or will form varying levels of emotional attachments to the sculpture, and unlike objectivity, there is no perfect answer as to why something needs to exist.

Final Cause wants to look beyond the physical form to the metaphysical or spiritual reasons behind existence, and this Cause has often been the driving force behind astrology and the bridge between the Divine and the Mundane.

Robert Hand says of the Final Cause: *"It is the one that modern science and philosophy have most completely thrown out. It asks what is a thing for, or what is a thing trying to, or going to become, or why does it exist . . . Final Cause implies intention and will, and possibly meaning. If the universe is dead and random, there can be no intention and will in the universe."*[45]

Diagram to Illustrate Aristotle's Four Causes [46]

Material and Formal Cause have an objective goal – to produce a maintainable form for a period of time from physical matter.

Material Cause is potential or possibility and form is the actual end result.

Efficient and Final Cause have a subjective goal – to provide motive and motivations to change potential of 'what could be' into the actuality of *telos,* the final end or ultimate purpose of a thing while it holds a particular form.

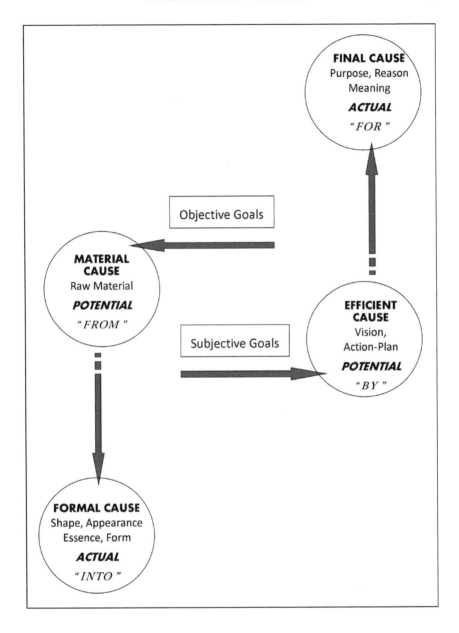

Fig. 52 Aristotle's Four Causes in Diagram

Planets Ruling the Houses

*"Things on earth do not benefit those in heaven, but all
things in heaven benefit things upon earth.*

*Everything that acts or operates is stronger and rules, but
that which is actuated or operated upon is weaker and ruled.*

*That which rules, directs, and governs, is free: but that
which is ruled, is subservient."*

The Divine Pymander to Hermes Trismegistus

What relevance are the Causes to Astrology?

Robert Hand believes Aristotle's Four Causes are relatable to several
important tenets of astrology, including the relationship between a
planet, i.e. *"that which rules, directs and governs"* and its houses, *"that
which is ruled and is subservient."*

Thema Mundi (The Birth-Chart of the Universe) is a mythical chart
which sets the parameters for astrological principles and techniques.

It provides the rules behind the first two levels of Essential Dignity,
whereby a planet's greatest strength lies in its placement in the sign of
its rulership or its exaltation (i.e. Saturn rules Capricorn and Aquarius,
and is exalted in the sign of Libra).

Thema Mundi is constructed in the Whole Sign house system
which begins each house at zero degrees of consecutive signs.

Each of the seven planets is situated at fifteen degrees of a sign of
its rulership: the Moon in Cancer, the Sun in Leo, Mercury in Virgo,
Venus in Libra, Mars in Scorpio, Jupiter in Sagittarius and Saturn in
Capricorn.

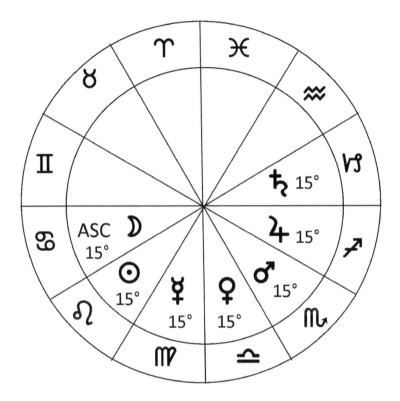

Fig. 53 The Thema Mundi Chart

The remaining five signs are divided between the planets as the two luminaries, the Sun and Moon, rule a singular sign, but the five planets rule two signs apiece.

Saturn takes Aquarius, Jupiter follows by claiming Pisces, Mars rules Aries, Venus becomes the owner of Taurus and finally, Mercury becomes the lord of the last sign, Gemini, in the Thema Mundi chart.

When a planet finds itself in rulership, it is not only dignified, but it is 'in-situ'; that is, the planet is in its original, natural, or appropriate place, in its proper house.

So much so, that the other term given for rulership was a planet's 'domicile' (house, meaning sign).

When a planet is in rulership, its power lies within three related fields of influence: as planet, as house occupant, and as the ruler of both the sign and the house.

Fig. 53a) The Planets' Rulership of the Signs

The term 'dispositor' describes the owner of a sign, and when a planet is in rulership, it is at its maximum level of intensity – it is authentic, pure in essence and *pukka* (in perfect form).

As a planet, it does not need to ask favour from a dispositor when it owns the sign itself.

As the occupant of its own house it can be likened to a king occupying his throne.

And as the ruler of the house, it is present and solidly visible and active within the house, thereby making it highly capable of managing the affairs of its allotted area of life.

Whatever action a planet in rulership begins, it will also be required to finish the matter.

Dignity does not promise an easy life for the native (the chart's owner) as the dignified planet is as true to its own nature as it is ever likely to be, and this is not necessarily good or bad for the individual who has dignified planets in their natal chart.

A modern trend in a chart's interpretation is to use the characteristics of the sign on the house cusp to describe the house itself, or to add specific features to the house's meaning.

This is different to how a Hellenistic astrologer might approach the chart.

In earlier times the sign on a house cusp was exactly that: a signpost or directional indicator that pointed towards a planet which ruled the sign.

Once the planet had been found, the sign was put aside and all focus was diverted to the house's ruling planet.

A judgement on the strength of a house's ruling planet then took place, and the planet's various dignities and debilities were weighed up to determine the house's potential for success or failure in the affairs of life designated to that particular house.

Perhaps the word 'strength' is not totally correct, as in truth, the judgement was more concerned with a planet's 'authenticity' rather than how strong it appeared to be. The closer a planet came to its genuine nature, to the concept of *pukka* (as perfectly formed as a thing can be) or its legitimate claim to being itself, the more likely it could perform the tasks hinted at in the chart.

For instance, Mars rules both of the houses where Aries or Scorpio are found in the chart, and the condition of Mars would dictate whether the native was courageous and understood the difference between brilliance in action or blind stupidity in reaction. Mars could be driven towards success in these areas of their life or it could initiate disaster, depending on its ability to be true to its own nature and impulses. Mars' actions may have begun in its house of occupation but the outcomes of success or failure were experienced in the two houses owned by Mars.

A planet in detriment is a planet in the sign directly opposite to its rulership sign, and this planet's dilemma lies not only in being in a sign which is least likely to express its essence, but it is also placed in the hands of its enemy which now controls and directs the planet through dispositor-ship.

For instance, when Mars is in Taurus or Libra it is in detriment, and its natural opponent Venus owns both the signs.

Al-Biruni's Table (*A Tiny Universe*, Chapter Four) indicates that Mars and Venus are *'mutually hurtful'* towards one another, so this is not good for Mars when Venus, as the owner of Taurus or Libra, becomes the dispositor for Mars when it is in detriment.

Accordingly, while Mars needs Venus' help to operate with some efficiency, it does not mean that it enjoys being dependent on the goodwill of Venus, its natural adversary.

Another problem presents itself when a planet is in detriment, and this relates to its placement in the chart.

It should be remembered that the houses tend to work as an axis of six pairs,

> The cardinal houses of one and seven are the pair of 'myself verses others'.
>
> The other cardinal axis is the fourth and tenth axis which describes the parents, public and private visibility, or past history and future directions.
>
> The succedent houses follow the cardinal or angular houses.
>
> The second and eighth axis is concerned with wealth, mine (2nd) and others' wealth (8th).
>
> The fifth and eleventh axis is one of benefit and good fortune, describing intimate friendships, my children (5th) and their partners or other people's children or social connections (11th).
>
> The cadent houses precede the angular houses and are considered to be the least effective houses when it comes to the business of life.
>
> The third and ninth axis is religious affiliations, siblings and their partners, and safe comings and goings (3rd) or treacherous undertakings into the unknown (9th).
>
> Finally, the difficult axis is the sixth and twelfth axis which covers sorrow, misfortune and removal from life in their own specific way.

In the Whole Sign chart, it is easy to see how the planet in detriment affects this 'six-axes system' when it becomes an occupant of the house opposite to the one that it rules.

The tension between the two opposing houses, and whatever the axis represents, becomes accentuated when the planet can see the issues of its house, but often can do very little to alleviate the tension, or solve the problems, from the other side of the chart.

For instance, if Mars is in Libra in the ninth house it will rule the third house with Aries on the cusp.

Mars will compromise the 3rd/9th axis which is concerned with my siblings and their partners, my learning capacity and my personal safety when journeying.

Mars is in detriment so it will jeopardise the affairs of the third house (Aries on the cusp), at the same time as it destabilises any benefits gained from matters pertaining to the ninth house because it is an occupant of the ninth house, but it is struggling there in the sign of Libra.

A planet's occupancy and its house rulerships are two different matters, but they are definitely interlinked in the chart.

In Whole Sign charts all planets are required to stay within the boundaries of the sign in which they are placed, which means that the ruling planet of the sign, in this instance Mars, is both the manager of the third house _and_ the dispositor of any planets in Aries, in the third house.

Depending on the planets' own peculiar relationship with Mars, it may help or hinder third house relations even further, but ultimately any planets in Aries are at the mercy of their dispositor, which is the debilitated Mars in the ninth house.

The art of using the planets as house rulers brings the chart together cohesively as a vital functioning model with an ecosystem unique unto itself, and this was very much the intention of the traditional astrologer.

Firmicus Maternus says: *"By this* (Thema Mundi) *the ancients wished to prove that the fates of men are arranged in accordance with this birth chart, the conditions of the planets, and the influence they exert on the chart, . . . Thus nothing in the individual charts of men should seem different from the birth chart of the universe."* [47]

The planet's role in ruling a particular house cannot be underestimated, and their level of involvement with their house determines whether a house runs smoothly and with ease, or operates under varying conditions of struggle with disorganisation, stress or neglect.

Whether the planet is in a sign of dignity or debility will give some indication as to how well and how effectively it performs its duty, and the condition of the planet is judged according to the weighted scale of both essential and accidental dignities.

Aristotle's Four Causes in Astrology

In the previous diagram of the Four Causes *(Fig. 52)* the first Objective Goal (on the left) begins with the Material Cause, or the raw material from which potential is drawn in order to become form.

By changing the model to suit astrology's purpose, the Material Cause will correspond to the twelve houses of the horoscope.

Each of the houses has an objective goal and has the potential to affect the native's life.

Most astrologers agree on what constitutes a particular house's area of expertise, so we can say that objectivity exists when it comes to the house in terms of measurability and definition.

The houses are the matter from which form must take place, the 'clay' of the chart which can be moulded into different forms according to the nature of the seven original planets.

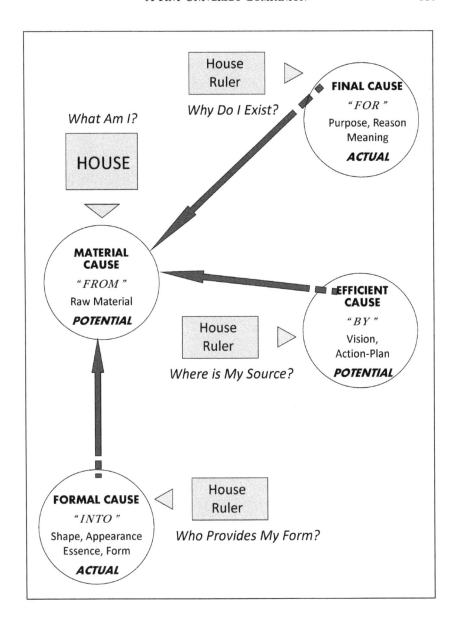

Fig. 54 Astrological Adaption of Aristotle's Four Causes

The questions posed earlier by the four Causes are also relevant to the astrological model which is based on the Four Causes diagram.

MATERIAL CAUSE asks: *What Am I?*

Can you describe the material from which I am made?

The answer becomes – The House – with each of the twelve houses representing a different facet of life (or material)

EFFICIENT CAUSE asks:

What will be the vehicle that takes me from Matter to Form?

What is my motive?

What is the source of my vision?

The answer becomes – The Ruling Planet – each of the seven original planets will have a different motive and a different vision for the house according to who rules the house. It will have the drive, insight and energy to fulfil the tasks needed by the house or area of life

FORMAL CAUSE asks:

What have I become?

What is my form, shape or appearance?

What do you see?

What do you know about me?

What is my essence?

The answer becomes – The Ruling Planet – it will describe the appearance and set the tone for the house and the area of life that it represents. The planet's essence can be seen through the house it rules. For instance, the Sun ruling third house will look different to Saturn or Mars ruling the same house.

FINAL CAUSE asks:

What is the purpose, reason or meaning behind my existence? Why do I exist?

What is my 'for the sake of'?

What is the point of my creation?

The answer becomes – The Ruling Planet – the reasons behind why a house exists will be measured by the planet which rules that house.

For instance, Mercury ruling the seventh house might answer that relationships are designed for communication or intellectual exchange whilst Mars might answer that a partnership is created for protection or to test the individual's strength. The Moon might say that the seventh house is created for affection, a home and a family. The Final Cause will differ depending on which of the planets rules the seventh house, and how well or how efficient the planet is at providing the desired results will depend on its condition in the chart.

An Example of Aristotle's Model:
Gemini on the 2nd House Cusp

If the second house has Gemini on its cusp, the native's finances will consist of the raw material described by Gemini's characteristics as a mutable air sign.

Money and resources come from this house, and any planets in Gemini in the second house will add to the potential of that house to produce wealth.

'*What am I?*' The answer is '*The Second House.*'

'*From what material am I constructed?*'

In this scenario, the material or the matter is '*Gemini.*'

The three remaining Causes, one with an Objective Goal and the other two with Subjective Goals, are defined by the planet which rules the sign on the house's cusp.

In the example, the planet Mercury will be responsible for the Efficient Cause (subjective), the Formal Cause (objective) and the Final Cause (subjective).

Efficient Cause produces the mover, or the thing which effects the change, and this is the initial role of the ruling planet.

In this case, Mercury, the ruler of Gemini, has a vision of how it will achieve wealth for the native.

Depending on its condition in the chart, Mercury may be extremely efficient in bringing the raw material into form, but if Mercury is in poor condition, it may be terrible at creating a form which meets the expectations of the chart's owner.

In the model, the Efficient Cause has a subjective nature, and when Mercury becomes the vehicle by which change is effected, its ability to visualise financial stability can be compromised through unsuitable schemes, poor management or scatter-brained ideas which have little practical application.

When Efficient Cause asks '*Where is my source and by whose hand will I achieve Form?*'

The planet which steps forward in this case answers '*Mercury* ', and it had better have a realistic action plan in mind, if it is going to be an effective, and efficient, ruler of the second house with Gemini on its cusp.

Mercury is also responsible for providing the following Formal Cause, which has taken the potentiality of the first two Causes and created an actual Form from raw material.

When Formal Cause asks: *'Who provides my Form?'*

If Gemini (or Virgo) is found on the cusp of the second house, it is Mercury's identity or essence which defines the second house as it accumulates or squanders the native's wealth.

The structure of the native's finances will be unique to Mercury, when it takes the clay of Gemini (or Virgo) and moulds it into the form of actual wealth for the native.

Formal Cause is objective.

There is no dispute over the bank balance or the incomings and outgoings of money, and Mercury's nature can be well suited towards organising spreadsheets and time-lines, so that information is presented to the individual as plausible facts and data.

When other planets rule the second house, they may not naturally be as proficient in this job as Mercury, but each will blend their unique essence with the house's form according to their own nature and characteristics.

Final Cause deals with the end result of the process.

It asks *'What is the point of second house? What is the purpose behind its existence?'*

'Mercury' is the suitable answer to this question when Gemini or Virgo is on the cusp of the second house, and its powers of reasoning and its understanding of the commercial workings of the world, stands it in good stead to analyse the meaning behind the second house's existence.

When all three Causes are represented by the same planet, in this case, Mercury, it is required to play three roles,

> one as the originator and the driving force behind the achievement of financial security,
>
> two, as the visible 'front of house' man who gives identity and form to the type of wealth sought by the native, and three, tells us why currency exists in this world, on levels ranging from bill-payment to metaphysical meanings on the relevance of money.

The questions of Final Cause vary according to what the native is truly enquiring about, depending on age, circumstances, or their need for money.

Are they asking about the practical implications of Mercury ruling the second house?

Money is needed to live in this world, and Mercury must find some way to earn a living from its repertoire of skills.

But Final Cause is also subjective, so does Mercury remember what it is like to be poor and financially insolvent?

> Does money represent emotional as well as financial security for Mercury?
>
> Does it buy love? Respect? Entertainment? Shoes for the children?

Mercury's position, its sign, its placement and its level of essential or accidental dignity will answer these questions for the enquirer, but it is worth remembering that Mercury *'exists'* in order to fulfil its obligations as the second house's ruling planet. *All things in heaven benefit things upon earth* and no matter how undignified or under attack Mercury may be, it cannot shirk its responsibilities as the lord of the native's finances.

Aristotle says: *". . . the student of nature should know them all (the Causes), and it will be his method to get back to them all: the matter, the form, the thing which effects the change, and what the thing is for."*

The flow from the three houses back to Material Cause *(Fig. 54)* alters the first diagram to illustrate Robert Hand's notion that the house (Material Cause) takes a particular form which is determined by its house ruler (Formal Cause), the planet which effects the change (Efficient), and decides what purpose the house will serve (Final Cause).

In the diagram the relationship between a planet and the house or houses it rules is connected by the three arrows moving from the ruling planet (always the same planet) to the house with the planet's sign on the cusp of the house.

These arrows imply movement, vitality and a flow of energy which is continuous, from the ruling planet to its house of concern.

One thing leads to another, and everything is connected.

This design is deliberate, the house itself, like the clay, has very little energy of its own, given that it will sit as inert matter until something with force and energy comes along, to shift or change its form into something else.

In this manner, the ruling planet can be likened to a puppeteer, and the house it rules to the puppet.

Whilst we often focus on the puppet (house), it is the puppeteer (planet) directing and controlling all the movement and expression for the puppet.

We gain a perspective of the puppet through its handler, and although the puppet may look the same at times, when the handler changes then the puppet's whole nature, demeanour and characteristics change as the new puppeteer has a different essence, and a different vision and purpose for the same puppet.

Once the puppeteer disappears, the life and movement leaves the puppet, and it is merely wood, tangled strings and a pile of colourful material.

The Difference between Location and Rulership

When Planet A is an Occupant (Tenant) and Planet B is the Ruler (Landlord) of a House

The reintroduction of house rulership from Hellenistic principles has changed several critical factors in astrological practice.

Now, so-called 'empty houses' which have no planet in residence are full of meaning when the ruler of the house is examined.

The practice of house rulership by planets reinstates vibrancy in the chart which has been missing in modern practices when delineation focused primarily on the planets' location in the chart.

Thema Mundi becomes a blueprint for every chart and gives it unity, activity and vitality, a constant ebb and flow of energy, rather than pools of still water or stagnation in houses without planets in occupancy.

Planets take on triple roles in this system, as occupants of houses, as rulers of houses, and as dispositors of other planets in their sign and in their house.

Because this triad exists, questions often arise over the differences between the planets' roles and responsibilities in the chart because of this trinity of purpose.

Questions such as,

> 'How does a planet IN the house affect the matters of the house?
>
> How does a planet RULING a house affect the matters of the house?
>
> How does a planet who OWNS the sign of other planets in its house affect the matters of the house?'

Robert Hand uses the matter-form principle to explain the distinction between a planet's role when it is placed in a house (Planet A), as opposed to a planet's role as ruler of the house (Planet B).[48]

The difference between the two activities of the planet is not concerned with importance or the weighting of one planet against another, but rather that their different roles can be defined by the idea of a timeline. In other words:

'Where does this Begin?' Answer – with the Tenant.

'Where will it End?' Answer – with the Landlord.

For instance, the Planet A occupying a house provides a starting point for issues that concern this house.

Planet A not only adds more information as to the material of the house, but it is also responsible for instigating action around the matters of the house.

It may even have an impact on the native in the earlier stages of life, whilst the ruler of the house has the ability to influence the latter stages of life.

For instance, a planet in the seventh house may describe the native's early relationships in their youth, but the ruler of the seventh house will influence their decision on partners during their more mature years.

In a Whole Sign chart, where the house contains the full thirty degrees of a sign, both house and occupying planets will share the same sign, therefore the planet which rules the house *will be the same planet* which is the dispositor for planets contained within its ruled house.

It should be noted that one of the differences between a planet ruling a house, and a planet in the role of dispositor (owner) of the sign, is that in the case of the house ruler, it is ideal if the planet can access the house through aspect, antiscia, contra-antiscia or like-engirdling.

Otherwise, there exists a state of aversion between the signs of the ruler and the sign on the house cusp, and this is not good for the house.

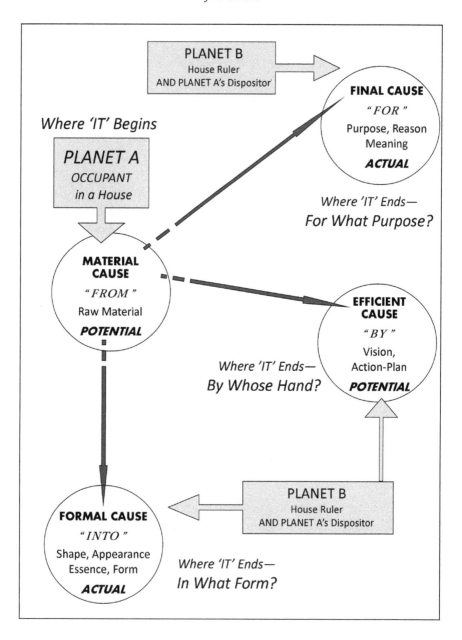

Fig. 55 The Difference between Occupancy,
Dispositorship and Rulership Using Aristotle's Four Causes

However, when there is no aspect or connection between one planet and the dispositor of its occupied sign, *the rules of aversion do not apply.*

So whilst the house itself may be in aversion to its ruler, there is no negative repercussion when planets *located in the house* have no aspect or connection to their dispositor (the owner of the sign).

In defining the difference between a ruling planet and the location of a planet, Robert Hand repeats that Material Cause represents the house and any planets contained within the house, whilst the ruler (and dispositor) is represented by the three remaining Causes.

When the house undergoes any process of change, upset, or needs a particular matter resolved, the planets in the immediate vicinity of the house, that is, planets with occupancy, will begin the process and will represent the 'material' of the early stages.

They may even look like the instigators of the unfolding drama, and as Material Cause has so much potential, these planets can produce a variety of circumstances to commence the necessary change in life.

Where Does it End? By Whose Hand? In What Form? What was its Purpose?

In the earlier astrological model, the house's ruling planet became the representative for the three remaining Causes; Efficient, Formal and Final Cause.

This is still the case when determining the progress and chronological order of unfolding events.

The planet which rules the house and is the dispositor of the planets in occupancy (Planet B), is the one with the final say in matters, and its placement and condition in the chart will show the outcome of any matter begun by planets (Planet A) in its house and sign.

In the diagram of the relationship between a house and its ruler *(Fig. 54)*, three arrows point from the ruling planet (always the same planet) towards the house with its sign on the cusp of the house.

The arrows in *Fig. 55* move in the opposite direction, pointing from the planet in occupancy (Planet A – the Tenant) to the ruler/dispositor of their sign (Planet B – the Landlord).

This direction indicates that whilst the Material Cause is at the hub, it is not the end of the affair, and the result is found elsewhere in the chart, rather than with the original Cause or the planets which began the action.

When the remaining three Causes are examined separately, the same planet is present and active, but has three different functions or tasks in motivating the end result.

When the ruling planet or dispositor (Planet B) represents Efficient Cause, it takes over from the planets in-situ (Planet A) and becomes the guiding hand that will complete the journey to the end in its role as the primary source or the vehicle by which the process of change can occur.

The same ruling planet symbolises Formal Cause wherein the potential suggested by the planets in the house becomes manifest in the form of the ruling planet.

For instance, Venus in Sagittarius may initiate action in the house it occupies, but the end result will take the form of Jupiter in the house where it lies.

Venus may look for acceptance and social interaction, but Jupiter will fulfil the promise given by Venus because it is Jupiter's essence that becomes the stronger influence over a period of time.

The Final Cause also belongs to the planet which owns the sign (Planet B) in which both the house and its tenants which reside within the house.

Whilst there is little dispute over the form which determines the end of the matter, the Final Cause introduces all kinds of subjective interpretations or meanings, behind why the change has ended in a manner which often appears to be so different from its beginnings.

Even experienced practitioners of astrology can get confused over why consistency is lacking when one planet begins the process (Planet A) and another seems to step in and take over the proceedings (Planet B).

This model may help to clarify the question of *'What was that all about? What was the reason behind this change or event ending in this result?'*

Final Cause may help to resolve this question and to guide the chart's reader toward the ruling planet/dispositor, rather than focusing on the dramas created by the planet in the house.

Once again the puppeteer comes to mind as ultimately, they are the one who controls the storyline and it is by their hand, and their imagination, that the variety of puppets play out their roles on the stage.

Connections Between Signs (Planet and House)

There is one more factor which is critical to the smooth running of a house by its ruling planet.

The best connection a planet can have with the house it rules occurs when there is an aspect between the sign on the house cusp and the sign in which its ruling planet is placed in the chart.

The ideal aspects are known as Ptolemaic aspects which are found to exist between the sign on the house cusp and the sign in which the ruler of the house finds itself.

If the ruler of the house occupies the house, technically it creates a same sign situation, and the conjunction is considered to be a position rather than a Ptolemaic aspect.

When a same sign conjunction is not recognised as an aspect then the first Ptolemaic aspect becomes a sextile whereby the two signs are in alternate signs and share the same gender, as in the example of Cancer sextiling Taurus and also in sextile aspect to Virgo *(Fig. 56)*. These three signs belong to the feminine gender as a water sign (in this case Cancer) will always sextile an earth sign and vice versa. Likewise, a masculine fire sign will always sextile masculine air signs either side in alternate signs.

This aspect suggests an ease of connection between the ruling planet and its house as the signs share gender and the aspect is seen as one which is favourable in nature.

The next aspect occurs when the sign on the house squares the sign of its ruler thereby creating a square with the two signs sharing the same modality.

The square aspect denotes some tension between the ruler and its house and can indicate that the ruling planet struggles to meet the needs of its house.

The following Ptolemaic aspect is created when the sign on the house cusp is found in the same element as its ruler, and thereby creates a trine between them.

Trines are easy aspects, so the ruling planet is desirous of meeting its house's needs, but its condition in the chart will indicate whether or not it is successful.

Generally speaking, the ruling planet comprehends what is required for the house and is willing to help, but it may or may not be capable of executing the Efficient, Formal and Final requirements of its house depending on its condition in the chart.

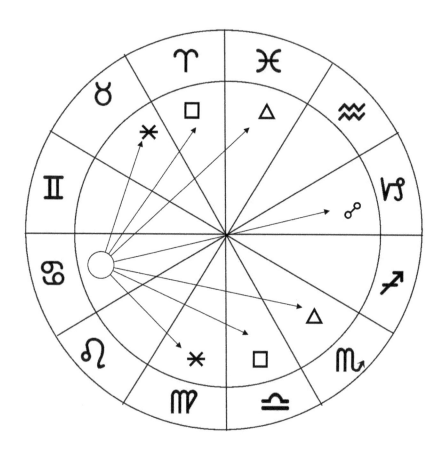

Fig. 56 The Ptolemaic Aspects

The last Ptolemaic aspect is the opposition, but this aspect can create dramas as the ruling planet would have to be in its sign of detriment if the sign on the cusp (its domicile sign) and the planet's temporary sign are opposite one another.

This creates tension between the two signs and their dispositors, as well as emphasising whichever house axis that spans across the chart with the ruler in a house opposite to its own house.

In Thema Mundi Cancer opposes Capricorn, so whilst there is an aspect between the two signs, a Moon in Capricorn can see its house but would battle to complete the tasks of its house, or Saturn in Cancer would aim to build structure or apply discipline to its Capricorn house but would feel like it was sinking into emotional quicksand rather than fortifying its opposing house.

For the sake of simplification in house rulership, only the first level of essential dignity, that is rulership or domicile ruler, has been applied to the rules of house ownership, even though there are five levels of essential dignity in existence.

The second level of essential dignity, exaltation, can be used if the domicile lord has no relationship to its house, but as the exalted lord of a house has some restrictions, it is far better for the domicile lord to aspect its house by sign.

Whilst the Ptolemaic aspects between the signs of house and ruler are the most effective way for the ruling planet to communicate with its house and to effectively manage the affairs of its house, there are other ways by which planets can be in signs which do connect to their houses and these are discussed further into the chapter.

Aversion: When Questions Don't Get Answered

Paulus of Alexandria says that when signs are separated by intervals outside of the accepted channels, they are called averted or unconnected.

The Greek word used in his text is *"apostrophe"* literally meaning 'turning away'[49], and the same word is also translated as "aversion" whereby the signs have no sympathy or lack connection with each other.

This has dire consequences for a ruling planet when it cannot connect with its own house, and there is a sense of blindness and ignorance where the matters of this house are concerned.

The planet is placed in a terrible predicament because it is located in a sign which bears no resemblance or connection to the sign it rules, and therefore to the house with its sign on the cusp.

If this happens the planet effectively loses sight of its house, and even though its intentions are sound and its willingness to fulfil its obligation as house manager still exists, the ruling planet is simply unable to do the right thing by its house.

It should be remembered that there are two consistencies here, and two variables.

The order of the twelve zodiac signs will not alter.

The planets will always rule the same signs.

However, the first variable concerns which sign is rising at the time of birth as this will change the sign on a particular house cusp.

The second variable is that the planets themselves are moving through the zodiac signs, and there will be times when the sign in which they are temporarily located (according to their rate of movement) does not form a Ptolemaic aspect to the sign which they will always rule through their ownership of the sign.

There are three more categories which avoid aversion. These are antiscia, contra-antiscia and like-engirdling, and grids for their conditions are provided later in the text.

One of the earlier diagrams *(Fig. 54)* applied Aristotle's Four Causes to the relationship between the sign on a house's cups and the planet which rules that sign.

Now using the same Four Causes the diagram has been adapted to demonstrate the problems of Aversion and to provide some idea as to why a planet becomes nervous of being caught out in the situation of being unable to manage the affairs of its house *(Fig. 57)*.

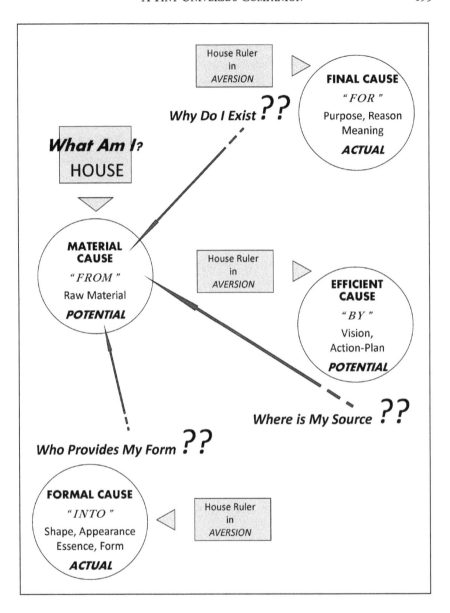

Fig. 57 Ruling Planets in AVERSION

The house was described as the raw material which waits for the process to begin to turn it into Form.

When the house wants input, direction, purpose or even identification, it looks to its ruling planet for an answer.

But if the ruling planet is absent or unable to comprehend the needs of the house, then certain questions go unanswered.

This situation occurs when the sign on the house's cusp (the consistently owned sign) is incompatible with the planet's temporary sign (the variable) and a state of aversion is created.

Ptolemaic Aspects Grid: Signs With and Without Sight

The situation of a planet being in aversion (or blind) to its house requires detailed examination, especially given that it affects both the house, and the ruling planet.

However, before the consequences can be fully discussed it is important to determine how, and under what conditions, a planet may avoid the state of aversion.

For this reason, the following tables have been drawn up to identify if there is a relationship between a planet in a particular sign, and the sign which the planet rules.

The aspect grid *(Fig. 58)* lists the Ptolemaic aspects beginning with Aries on both the horizontal row and the vertical column.

The horizontal row represents the order of the signs as they take their place on the twelve house cusps of a chart.

The blank row above the signs allows for the variable factor of changing house cusps as the chart progresses through a twenty four hour time period.

If the chart is set in the Whole Sign system, each of the signs will occupy one house, but this can differ from quadrant-style systems such as Placidus, when signs can become intercepted in houses.

For instance, Leo may be rising at the time of birth, at which point house number one would be placed in the row above Leo and then the consecutive houses would follow on from this sign;

the second house cusp would be Virgo, the third house cusp would be Libra, in the order of houses to signs with the twelfth house being Cancer on the cusp.

If this were the case, the Sun would ruler the first house, Mercury would rule the second house, Venus would rule the third house, finishing with the Moon ruling the twelfth house as Cancer precedes Leo in the order of the signs.

The vertical row of signs shows the possibility for each planet to enter the sign and to affect the aspect between its sign of placement and the sign that it rules.

The aspect is shown when the row and column intersect.

For instance, Mars rules both Aries and Scorpio.

Aries will be on one house cusp and Scorpio will be on a house cusp which is eight signs and houses away from Aries.

This is consistent.

In the example *(Fig, 58 a)* when Mars is travelling through Sagittarius it will aspect the house with Aries on the cusp by trine (the first arrow), but Mars will be unable to see the house with Scorpio on its cusp as no aspect exists between Sagittarius and Scorpio (the second arrow).

As Mars' sign changes, so too does the aspect change between its placement sign and both Aries and Scorpio.

This is the variable factor.

Similarly, Venus will experience blindness to one of its houses when it is situated in Sagittarius.

With no aspect pending between Sagittarius and Taurus, there is aversion, and Venus will struggle to adequately manage this house (first arrow).

However, the house with Libra on its cusp will fare much better as Libra sees Sagittarius through the aspect of sextile (second arrow), and Venus in Sagittarius can manage the affairs of this house which is six signs and six houses away from Taurus.

The Ptolemaic Aspect Grid *(Fig. 58)* shows that two other planets would struggle to see their rulership signs if they were placed in Sagittarius.

The Moon in Sagittarius would fail to see Cancer and Saturn in Sagittarius would be averse to Capricorn when the aspects between the signs are outside the realm of Ptolemaic aspect.

However, antiscia and contra-antiscia will solve this problem.

Ptolemaic Aspects Grid

Whole Sign Houses Cusp Number (1-12) Varies According to Chart												
Order of Signs *Consistent*	♈	♉	♊	♋	♌	♍	♎	♏	♐	♑	♒	♓
Ruling Planet *Consistent*	♂	♀	☿	☽	☉	☿	♀	♂	♃	♄	♄	♃
Ruling Planet In The Signs ♈	☌	—	✶	□	△	—	☍	—	△	□	✶	—
♉	—	☌	—	✶	□	△	—	☍	—	△	□	✶
♊	✶	—	☌	—	✶	□	△	—	☍	—	△	□
♋	□	✶	—	☌	—	✶	□	△	—	☍	—	△
♌	△	□	✶	—	☌	—	✶	□	△	—	☍	—
♍	—	△	□	✶	—	☌	—	✶	□	△	—	☍
♎	☍	—	△	□	✶	—	☌	—	✶	□	△	—
♏	—	☍	—	△	□	✶	—	☌	—	✶	□	△
♐	△	—	☍	—	△	□	✶	—	☌	—	✶	□
♑	□	△	—	☍	—	△	□	✶	—	☌	—	✶
♒	✶	□	△	—	☍	—	△	□	✶	—	☌	—
♓	—	✶	□	△	—	☍	—	△	□	✶	—	☌

Left column annotations: Ruling Planet In The Signs ***** Varies From Chart to Chart According to Planet's Position *******

Fig. 58 Grid for Ptolemaic Aspects

Ptolemaic Aspects – Example

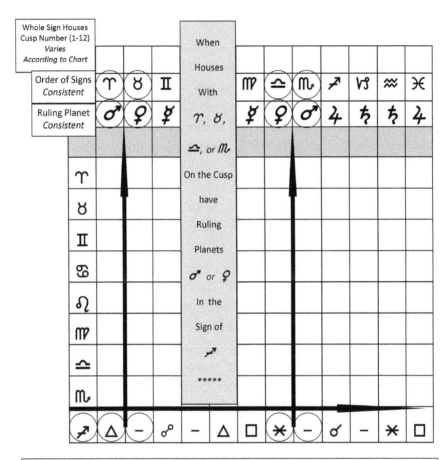

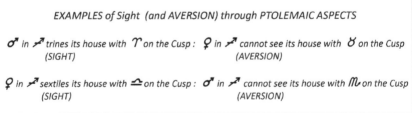

EXAMPLES of Sight (and AVERSION) through PTOLEMAIC ASPECTS

♂ in ♐ trines its house with ♈ on the Cusp : ♀ in ♐ cannot see its house with ♉ on the Cusp
    (SIGHT)   (AVERSION)

♀ in ♐ sextiles its house with ♎ on the Cusp : ♂ in ♐ cannot see its house with ♏ on the Cusp
    (SIGHT)   (AVERSION)

Fig. 58 a) Grid for Ptolemaic Aspects- EXAMPLE

Antiscia: Signs of Equal Light

The theory behind Antiscia is based on the idea of days of equal light either side of the two solstices when the Sun appears to be stationary for three days in the times of the longest day (Cancer in the northern hemisphere and Capricorn in the southern hemisphere) and the shortest day (in Capricorn north of the equator and in Cancer south of the equator. In days leading up to either of the solstice points (zero Cancer and zero Capricorn) the Earth will receive exactly the same amount of light from the Sun, as in the days immediately following the solstice.

For instance, three days before solstice will be equal in length of light to three days after solstice.

Two days before will have the same amount of sunlight as two days after, as will one day before have exactly the same period of light as one day after the solstice occurs.

In this manner the solstice point (0 Cancer or 0 Capricorn) will act as a midpoint for the Sun's degrees as the Sun moves towards its solstice points, makes the connection, and then moves away towards its equinox points at either zero Libra or zero Aries.

Ptolemy states that *"Any two signs, equally distant from either tropical sign* (Cancer/Capricorn), *are equal to each other in power; because the Sun, when present in one, makes day and night, and the divisions of time, respectively **equal in duration** to those which he produces when present in the other."*[50]

Jean Rhys Bram, translator for Firmicus Maternus adds a footnote to Antiscia saying:

*"Earlier names for antiscions are signs of equal power, or signs which see each other. Like aspects, they were **originally measured from sign to sign**, rather than by degree."*[51]

Under the rules of Antiscia, some signs which previously shared no Ptolemaic aspect *(Fig. 58)* have the opportunity to avoid aversion through their antiscia link.

Signs such as
Cancer to Gemini,
Virgo to Aries,
Libra to Pisces and
Sagittarius to Capricorn.

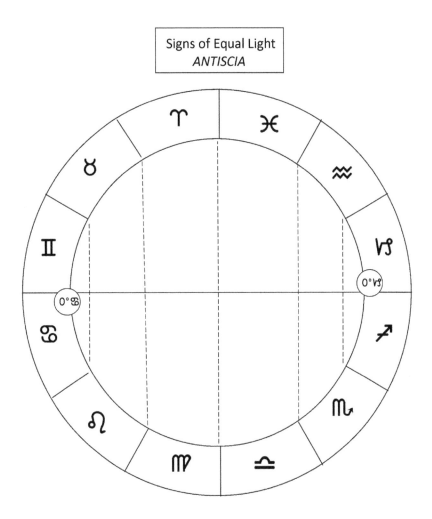

Fig. 59 Signs of Antiscia

The fixed signs gain no further benefit from antiscia as they already connect through the quartile or square aspect.

Signs such as Taurus to Leo and Aquarius to Scorpio are the fixed signs' antiscia connections of equal daylight.

When the antiscia are measured by degrees, the sum of both signs of antiscia must add up to the full number of a sign, i.e. thirty degrees.

That is, 1st degree of one sign (i.e. Taurus) to 29th degree of its antiscia sign (Leo);

or 2nd degree of one sign (Virgo) to 28th degree of its antiscia sign (Aries);

or the 3rd degree of one sign (Capricorn) to 27th degree of its antiscia sign (Sagittarius).

Similarly, the 4th degree of Gemini to 26th degree of its antiscia sign Cancer;

or 5th degree of Scorpio to the 25th degree of its antiscia, Aquarius;

or 6th degree of Libra to the 24th degree of its antiscia sign, Pisces, and so forth through the degrees of a sign.

Contra-Antiscia: Signs of Equal Rising Times

"Two signs equidistant from an equinoctial point (zero Aries or zero Libra) *are said to be equipollent, because the day hours of each are equal to the night hours of the other, and* **their ascensions are equal** *in all places such as Aries and Pisces, Taurus and Aquarius, Gemini and Capricorn, etc."* [52]

The twelve signs can also be divided into pairs according to the time it takes for the sign's degrees to cross the midheaven whilst a sign is completing its rising for the duration of its full thirty degrees.

For instance, at the equator (0 Latitude) the entire signs of Aries and Pisces are quicker than some of the other pairs.

Whilst their thirty degrees are crossing the horizon, a shorter number of degrees (27degs.55) are moving across the midheaven.

The opposite pairing of Libra and Virgo will take the same time to rise at the equator, but this will change as the degrees of latitude increase and there is movement into the northern or southern hemisphere.

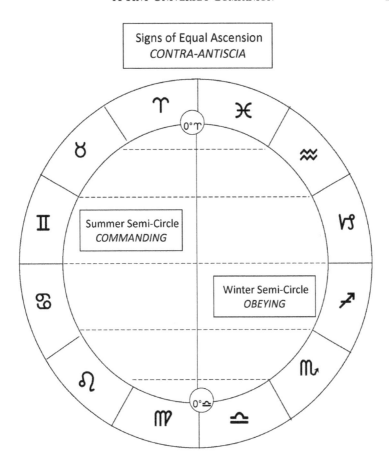

Fig. 60 Signs of Contra-Antiscia

The Table of Ascensional Degrees (*A Tiny Universe*, Chapter Seven) gives the movement of the signs up to 50degs. for northern or southern latitude.

Under the rules of Contra-Antiscia, some signs which previously shared no Ptolemaic aspect have the opportunity to avoid aversion through this specific linking of signs.

"The twelfth-parts which are unsympathetic to one another by aversion have sympathy through like-engirdling and ascending in the same times.

Like-engirdling is when the zoidia happen to be of the same star, while equally-ascending (means that) the ascensions (occur) in equal hours from the unseen to the visible."[53]

It should be noted that the signs of contra-antiscia are signs which oppose antiscia.

For instance, the antiscia for Aries is Virgo, and Aries' contra-antiscia sign is Pisces.

The Latin word *contra* means 'against' or opposite and the two signs which generate from Aries because of the rules of light are signs in opposition, i.e., Virgo and Pisces.

Likewise, Sagittarius sends antiscia to Capricorn and shares contra-antiscia to Cancer – two signs which oppose one another across the zodiacal circle.

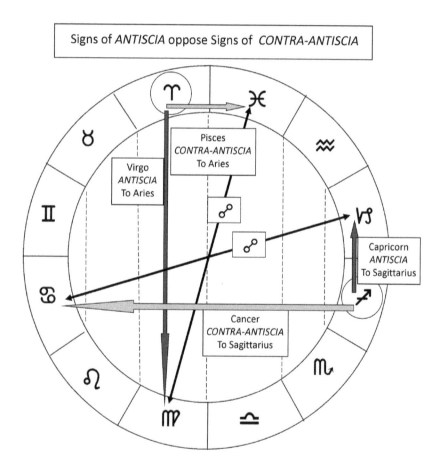

Fig. 61 Signs of Antiscia opposing Contra-Antiscia

The Grid for Antiscia and Contra-Antiscia

Antiscia is a rule which makes it possible for a planet to avoid the problems of aversion, when there is no aspect between a sign that a planet rules, and signs which may not usually share an aspectual relationship with the planet's sign of rulership.

Antiscia means that if two signs share an equal passage of time during the day of sunlight, then they have a kinship which counteracts the aversion, created by the lack of sight through an aspect.

For instance, under the rules of aspecting, two ruled signs of the planets Mercury and Jupiter would struggle to make an aspect to the sign of Aries (marked with a horizontal arrow on the Antiscia Grid).

Under normal circumstances if Mercury is in Aries, it would not connect with Virgo on the cusp as the two signs, Aries and Virgo, are incompatible and therefore do not share a Ptolemaic aspect.

Aries is a masculine fire sign, and Virgo is a feminine earth sign. Aries is cardinal and Virgo is mutable, so the lack of commonality means no light is shared between Aries and Virgo and Mercury's house may have gone unprotected without the rule of antiscia coming in to play.

Under antiscia there is sympathy or equal light between Aries and Virgo, and Mercury in Aries is afforded a pathway through which to manage it own house rather than being powerless to intercede on behalf of its house or would be unable to guide the affairs of its Virgo house.

The contra-antiscia rule is concerned with the pairing of certain signs which take the same amount of time to cross the ascendant in their entirety.

Normally if Jupiter is in Aries it cannot see the adjoining sign of Pisces.

However, contra-antiscia allows for the possibility of a connection between two signs which would otherwise be absent due to a lack of aspect, and this gives Jupiter the ability when it is situated in Aries, to oversee the affairs of the house alongside it, where Pisces is Jupiter's sign on the cusp.

The second example for the Antiscia and Contra-Antiscia Grid (*Fig. 62*) underlines another cardinal sign, Cancer, and highlights issues which may have been present for the same two planets, Mercury and Jupiter.

Mercury in Cancer would normally be 'unsympathetic' (Paulus' term) to the previous sign of Gemini, owned by Mercury, but under the rules of antiscia, Cancer and Gemini share equal light, and therefore are generous towards one another.

This generosity or shared spirit allows Mercury to be situated in Cancer and still be competent to supervise the affairs of its house next door, the one with Gemini on the cusp.

Generosity works both ways, as a Moon in Gemini is able to see Cancer under the same guidelines for antiscia.

Jupiter is exalted in the sign of Cancer, but this may have been of little benefit to its Sagittarian house, were it not for the stipulation of contra-antiscia.

This directive allows Jupiter to enjoy the fruits of exaltation without forfeiting its right to administer to the needs of its house which is five signs away in Sagittarius.

As the signs of antiscia are opposite the signs of contra-antiscia Mercury and Jupiter receive the gift of sight through the signs which oppose both Aries and Cancer. Mercury in Libra can see Virgo whilst Jupiter in Libra can see Pisces by antiscia. Likewise, Mercury in Capricorn can see Gemini whilst Jupiter in Capricorn can see Sagittarius, the sign alongside Capricorn.

Antiscia And Contra-Antiscia Signs

Whole Sign Houses Cusp Number (1-12) Varies According to Chart		♈	♉	♊	♋	♌	♍	♎	♏	♐	♑	♒	♓
Order of Signs Consistent		♈	♉	♊	♋	♌	♍	♎	♏	♐	♑	♒	♓
Ruling Planet Consistent		♂	♀	☿	☽	☉	☿	♀	♂	♃	♄	♄	♃
	♈						Ant						Con Ant
Ruling	♉					Ant						Con Ant	
Planet	♊				Ant						Con Ant		
In	♋			Ant						Con Ant			
The	♌		Ant						Con Ant				
Signs	♍	Ant						Con Ant					
***** Varies From Chart to Chart	♎						Con Ant						Ant
According to Planet's Position	♏					Con Ant						Ant	
	♐				Con Ant						Ant		
	♑			Con Ant						Ant			
*******	♒		Con Ant						Ant				
	♓	Con Ant						Ant					

EXAMPLES of Sight through ANTICIA and CONTRA-ANTISCIA

☿ in ♈ can see its house with ♍ on the Cusp : ♃ in ♈ can see its house with ♓ on the Cusp

☿ in ♋ can see its house with ♊ on the Cusp : ♃ in ♋ can see its house with ♐ on the Cusp

Fig.62 Antiscia and Contra-Antiscia Grid

Like-Engirdling Signs:
Signs with the Same Ruler

"The twelfth-parts which are unsympathetic to one another by aversion have sympathy through like-engirdling and ascending in the same times.

Like-engirdling is when the zoidia happen to be of the same star, while equally-ascending (means that) the ascensions (occur) in equal hours from the unseen to the visible.

And the intervals of the like-engirdling zoidia, by the reckoning of the unconnected (zoidia), are thus: Aries to Scorpio, Scorpio to Aries; Taurus to Libra and Libra to Taurus; Capricorn to Aquarius and Aquarius to Capricorn."[54]

Paulus Alexandrinus

The practice of linking otherwise unconnected signs together through the commonality of their joint ruler is described by Paulus of Alexandria as *'like-engirdling'*[55].

Jupiter and Mercury rule signs which share an aspect outside of rulership.

Sagittarius squares Pisces and Gemini squares Virgo, but the three remaining planets which rule dual signs, have no such aspectual relationship to link their two signs.

For this reason Paulus specifically mentions the signs of Mars, Venus and Saturn.

These three planets have signs which are naturally in aversion to one another.

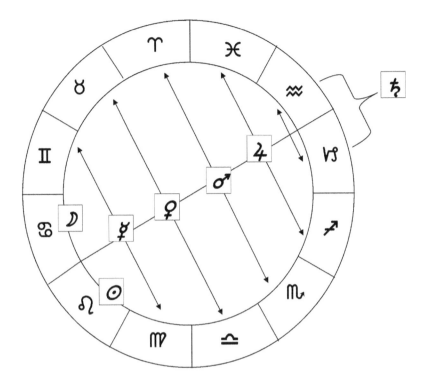

Fig.63 Signs of Like-engirdling

However, under the rules of like-engirdling, the formerly inconjunct signs share a type of sympathy because they are owned by the same ruling planet. Now, Aries links to Scorpio, Taurus links to Libra, and Capricorn links to Aquarius.

Paulus used the term 'like-engirdling' in the late 4th century CE, and there is evidence to suggest that the link between the two signs ruled by the same planet continued to be observed as al-Biruni (11th Century CE) mentions the same practice, although he uses a different term.

al-Biruni in his Note 377 describes Antiscia and Contra-Antiscia, but he also mentions:

"Abu Mashar has called the two signs which have the same presiding planet (ruler) *as 'concordant in itinere', and although this is different from the two kinds of agreement referred to above, it is a relation which has to be considered."* [56]

The term *'concordant in itinere'* roughly means 'travelling along the same road' or taking a corresponding route, i.e., sharing the same ruler.

In the previous grid certain signs receive benefits from antiscia or contra-antiscia.

For instance, Cancer and Sagittarius would otherwise be considered to be *'inconjunct'* (the correct term for two signs without aspect).

However, under the rule of contra-antiscia, they share equal rising times and therefore avoid the problems of aversion.

Likewise, the sign of Libra sees Virgo through contra-antiscia and Pisces through antiscia (equal light).

Often it is the case of signs with different genders and different modalities which profit from these two very old principles of equality between signs.

The exception to this rule is the four fixed signs – Taurus, Leo, Scorpio and Aquarius.

In antiscia and contra-antiscia one fixed sign will always cast to another fixed sign so there is no added advantage from these two states of kinship, as fixed signs already see each other through the ninety degree aspect of a square.

However, the rule of Like-engirdling is a boon for the fixed signs, as three of the four signs are able to gain an extra blessing, and connect to a dissimilar sign because they share the same planetary ruler.

Taurus gains one extra connection to the other Venus-ruled sign, Libra.

Opposite Taurus lies another fixed sign, Scorpio, which 'sees' Aries through both signs being ruled by Mars, and lastly, the fixed sign of Aquarius improves its welfare by connecting to the adjacent sign of Capricorn, because they are both ruled by Saturn.

Leo is the only fixed sign to miss out, simply because its ruler, the Sun, has possession over a singular sign.

For this reason, when the numbers are counted on all the signs, it is the sign of Leo which proves to be a disadvantage to four of the planets – Moon, Mercury, Saturn and Jupiter – who cannot see one of their signs (and houses) when they are situated in Leo.

All four planets dislike their location in Leo as it causes them to be blind to one of their houses.

Saturn is particularly disadvantaged as Leo is also its sign of detriment, so along with being situated in a sign of debility, Saturn is also averse to its house with Capricorn on the cusp.

On the other side, three of the cardinal signs gain the greatest assistance from like-engirdling.

With the exception of Cancer which belongs solely to the Moon, Aries, Libra, and Capricorn will only suffer by being blind to one sign apiece which will be when their lords, Mars, Venus and Saturn, are in signs of aversion to them.

Mars cannot see Aries when it is in Taurus (in detriment), Venus cannot see Libra when it is in Scorpio (in detriment), and Saturn cannot see Capricorn when it is in Leo (in detriment).

Detriment becomes a double-edged sword when it is considered that not only do these three planets suffer by being in a sign opposite to rulership which accentuates the tension of the axis involved, but they are in a terrible predicament when they cannot also see their other house.

The stress caused by this dilemma makes it extremely difficult for Mars, Venus and Saturn to capably deal with both of their houses for different reasons.

It should be noted that their other signs of detriment face this same problem of aversion: Mars in Libra cannot see Scorpio, Venus in Aries cannot see Taurus and Saturn in Cancer cannot see Aquarius.

A planet plays the role of guardian to the houses that it rules, and when any of these three planets find themselves in these particular signs of detriment, then not only do they control unruly and difficult wards, but they themselves are ill-equipped to be competent or protective guardians.

Like-Engirdling Grid: Planets in Rulership

The impact of the link between Aries and Scorpio, or Taurus and Libra is discussed in detail in Chapter Seven on the Mars and Venus Lemniscate.

Likewise, the consequences of Saturn ruling two consecutive signs are featured in Chapter Eight on Saturn's Two Faces.

Perhaps the most important advantage when applying the like-engirdling pattern occurs when any of these three planets are found to be in rulership in the chart.

In the instance of aversion, the impact of like-engirdling is slightly different from aspects or antiscia and contra-antiscia connections, as it will only work in favour of the planet to house relationship when Mars, Venus, or Saturn *are found in one of their signs of rulership*.

For instance, when Mars is found in rulership in Aries it will be able to see Scorpio under the rules of like-engirdling (*Fig. 64*, first horizontal arrow).

This would otherwise not be possible as there is no aspect, or antiscia, between the masculine cardinal fire sign (Aries) and the feminine fixed water sign (Scorpio).

When Mars resides in Scorpio (the fourth horizontal arrow), Mars can see the house with Aries on the cusp, when the rules of the like-engirdling connection are applied to Mars.

The same leniency is shown to both Venus and Saturn which would otherwise rule signs which bear no relation to one another.

Venus in Taurus can see Libra (the second horizontal arrow), and Venus in Libra can see Taurus (the third horizontal arrow), purely because the two mismatched signs share the same ruling planet.

Likewise, Saturn in Capricorn can see Aquarius, and Saturn in Aquarius can see Capricorn (last and shortest horizontal arrow).

The Sun and Moon rule just one sign apiece so the luminaries are not included in the rule on like-engirdling, and Jupiter and Mercury's signs aspect one another, so if either planet is in rulership, it will be able to see both signs and houses.

The inclusion of like-engirdling to signs with sympathy adds another distinct advantage to three planets when they are located in their most powerful signs.

Without this directive which links un-alike signs through the rulers, Venus, Mars and Saturn would have otherwise suffered the fate of being in total control of one house by being in rulership, but would be totally blind to their other house.

For instance, if Mars in Aries could only manage its Aries house it would do this with fabulous insight because it was dignified and situated in its house.

But if like-engirdling did not exist, the same dignified Mars would be terrible at managing its Scorpio house.

In allegory, it could be likened to the parent of two children, one of which it adores and pampers to every whim (Aries' house) and the other child which was completely out of the parent's consciousness and therefore suffered from neglect or poor discipline(Scorpio).

Ultimately, which child is going to feel loved and which will feel angry because it is ignored and therefore not cared for by the parent?

Grid for Like-Engirdling Signs

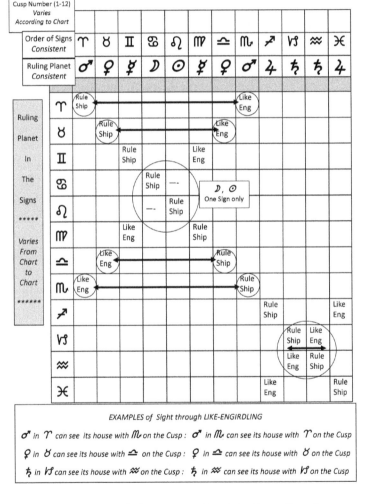

Fig. 64 Signs with the Same Ruler: Like-Engirdling Signs

The Sight Table: Putting it Together

Aspect; Antiscia; Contra-Antiscia; Like-Engirdling and Rulership

When all three of the previous grids are combined the final Table can be daunting until each sign is looked at independently.

The no symbol or prohibition sign (circle with the diagonal line across it) has been used to denote those signs which bear no relation to one another, thereby creating the problems of aversion.

For instance, if the horizontal line of Taurus is examined it can be seen that there are problems with the three signs (and their lords) indicated by the no symbol *(Fig. 66)*.

Two of these no symbols are featured closely together and the first prohibition sign in Taurus indicates that Mars in Taurus will be unable to see the house alongside of it with Aries on the cusp.

Taurus is the fixed earth sign and as it is from the fixed modality, it will not gain any extra benefit from a connection by antiscia or contra-antiscia signs.

When Mars is in detriment in Taurus it cannot see its own masculine cardinal fire sign (Aries) and therefore, is doubly debilitated by sign.

It is difficult for Mars to operate well in the fixed earth sign and often gets bogged down and frustrated in this sign which naturally belongs to Venus.

Added to Mars' frustration is its lack of awareness on how to approach the care of a house it cannot see.

Aversion means blindness and for a weakened and struggling Mars the attempt to care-take the affairs of its Aries' house creates strain and distress for the ruling planet.

There is no issue for Mars with its Scorpio cusp, but whatever the house of Aries represents in the chart, Mars will alternate between being overly anxious or completely oblivious to its requirements.

Aries has an alternate ruler if Mars is unavailable as the Sun is the exalted ruler of Aries according to the second rule of Essential Dignity.

If the Sun's sign in the chart does make an aspect to Aries then Mars may be required to step back and allow the Sun (Aries' exalted lord) to take its place.

Mars does not enjoy relinquishing any of its powers, and a debilitated Mars in Taurus is likely to be less than happy about its state of aversion, and the subsequent loss of its house.

Similarly, the no symbol in the third row of Taurus indicates that when Mercury is situated in Taurus it cannot see its sign of Gemini.

Mercury in Taurus will be able to see Virgo as the two signs are complementary, through both signs belonging to the earth element, but Mercury will be blind to the house with Gemini on its cusp.

The no symbol is also present when the two signs of Taurus and Sagittarius are examined for a link or a shared relationship in the zodiac circle.

A state of aversion exists between these two signs and the house with Sagittarius on the cusp will suffer when its ruler, Jupiter, is found in the sign of Taurus.

Unlike Aries, Gemini and Sagittarius have no exalted ruler to turn to for protection.

Mercury and Jupiter respectively will fret in their own unique way about a house beyond their reach, aversion making them unavailable to provide sustenance or guidance when the house needs the most help from its ruler.

The Sight Table
A Combination of the Three Previous Tables

Whole Sign Houses Cusp Number (1-12) *Varies According to Chart*												
Order of Signs *Consistent*	♈	♉	♊	♋	♌	♍	♎	♏	♐	♑	♒	♓
Ruling Planet *Consistent*	♂	♀	☿	☽	☉	☿	♀	♂	♃	♄	♄	♃
♈	♂	🚫	✳	□	△	Ant	☍	Like Eng	△	□	✳	Con Ant
♉	🚫	♂	🚫	✳	□	△	Like Eng	☍	🚫	△	□	✳
♊	✳	🚫	♂	Ant	✳	□	△	🚫	☍	Con Ant	△	□
♋	□	✳	Ant	♂	🚫	✳	□	△	Con Ant	☍	🚫	△
♌	△	□	✳	🚫	♂	🚫	✳	□	△	🚫	☍	🚫
♍	Ant	△	□	✳	🚫	♂	Con Ant	✳	□	△	🚫	☍
♎	☍	Like Eng	△	□	✳	Con Ant	♂	🚫	✳	□	△	Ant
♏	Like Eng	☍	🚫	△	□	✳	🚫	♂	🚫	✳	□	△
♐	△	🚫	☍	Con Ant	△	□	✳	🚫	♂	Ant	✳	□
♑	□	△	Con Ant	☍	🚫	△	□	✳	Ant	♂	Like Eng	✳
♒	✳	□	△	🚫	☍	🚫	△	□	✳	Like Eng	♂	🚫
♓	Con Ant	✳	□	△	🚫	☍	Ant	△	□	✳	🚫	♂

Left label column: **Ruling Planet In The Signs ***** Varies From Chart to Chart According to Planet's Position *******

Fig.65 The Sight Table: Possibilities for Planets to see their own Signs

The Sight Table – Example

Whole Sign Houses Cusp Number (1-12) *Varies According to Chart*													
Order of Signs *Consistent*		♈	♉	♊	♋	♌	♍	♎	♏	♐	♑	♒	♓
Ruling Planet *Consistent*		♂	♀	☿	☽	☉	☿	♀	♂	♃	♄	♄	♃
Ruling Planet In The Signs *****													
	♉	⊘	☌	⊘	⚹	□	△	Like Eng	☍	⊘	△	□	⚹
	♎	☍	Like Eng	△	□	⚹	*Con Ant*	☌	⊘	⚹	□	△	*Ant*
	♏	Like Eng	☍	⊘	△	□	⚹	⊘	☌	⊘	⚹	□	△
	♐	△	⊘	☍	*Con Ant*	△	□	⚹	⊘	☌	*Ant*	⚹	□

EXAMPLES of AVERSION through THE SIGHT TABLE (Fig. 65)

→ *♂ in ♉ is blind to ♈, ☿ in ♉ is blind to ♊, ♃ in ♉ is blind to ♐ cannot see one of their houses (AVERSION)*

→ *♂ in ♎ is blind to ♏ cannot see one of its houses (AVERSION)*

→ *☿ in ♏ is blind to ♊, ♀ in ♏ is blind to ♎, ♃ in ♏ is blind to ♐ cannot see one of their houses (AVERSION)*

→ *♀ in ♐ is blind to ♉, ♂ in ♐ is blind to ♏ cannot see one of their houses (AVERSION)*

Fig.66 Examples of The Sight Table

Aversion Grid: Signs Without Sight

The Sight Table *(Fig. 65)* shows the signs which struggle to relate to one another.

The Aversion Grid *(Fig. 67)* provides the same information, but instead concentrates on the missing links by removing the contacts the signs do have, and focusing on the lack of sight between signs and their effect on the planet which rules one of these signs.

Once more, the no symbol has been used to denote a lack of sympathy between two signs.

Planets in fixed signs often have more worries with aversion than any of the other two modalities.

The four fixed signs do not gain any further advantage from antiscia and contra-antiscia as the signs which match these rules are already covered by the square aspect.

Four planets struggle with the sign of Leo – the Moon, Mercury, Saturn (in detriment), and Jupiter – and when any one of these find themselves in the fixed fire sign they will be unable to see one of their rulership signs.

Three of these planets also have difficulty with Leo's opposing sign Aquarius as the Moon in either Leo or Aquarius cannot see Cancer, Mercury in Leo or Aquarius cannot see Virgo, and Jupiter in Leo or Aquarius cannot see Pisces.

Only Saturn escapes the same fate because it jointly rules both Capricorn and Aquarius, and whilst it cannot see Capricorn when it is in Leo, under the rules of like-engirdling, when Saturn is in rulership in Aquarius it can, in fact, see its sign of Capricorn.

Aversion Grid: Signs Without Sight

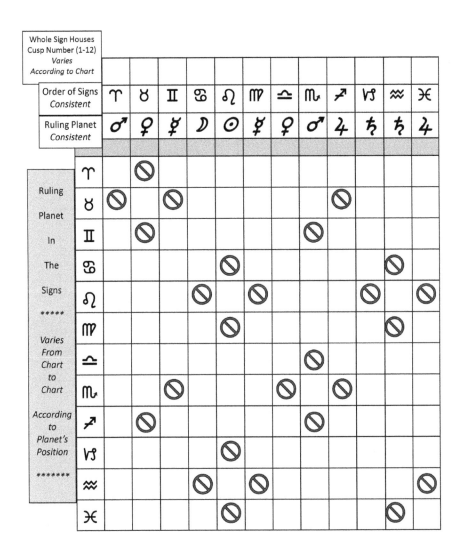

Fig.67 The pattern created by Signs of Aversion

Aversion: Tables of Signs and Planets

SIGN	NO.	PLANETS IN AVERSION	TO THEIR SIGNS (AND HOUSES)
♈	1	VENUS in Aries	VENUS is Blind to TAURUS
♉	3	MARS MERCURY *In* ♉ JUPITER	MARS is Blind to ARIES MERCURY is Blind to GEMINI JUPITER is Blind to SAGITTARIUS
♊	2	VENUS MARS *In* ♊	VENUS is Blind to TAURUS MARS is Blind to SCORPIO
♋	2	SUN SATURN *In* ♋	SUN is Blind to LEO SATURN is Blind to AQUARIUS
♌	4	MOON MERCURY *In* ♌ SATURN JUPITER	MOON is Blind to CANCER MERCURY is Blind to VIRGO SATURN is Blind to CAPRICORN JUPITER is Blind to PISCES
♍	2	SUN SATURN *In* ♍	SUN is Blind to LEO SATURN is Blind to AQUARIUS
♎	1	MARS in Libra	MARS is Blind to SCORPIO
♏	3	MERCURY VENUS *In* ♏ JUPITER	MERCURY is Blind to GEMINI VENUS is Blind to LIBRA JUPITER is Blind to SAGITTARIUS
♐	2	VENUS MARS *In* ♐	VENUS is Blind to TAURUS MARS is Blind to SCORPIO
♑	1	SUN in Capricorn	SUN is Blind to LEO
♒	3	MOON MERCURY *In* ♒ JUPITER	MOON is Blind to CANCER MERCURY is Blind to VIRGO JUPITER is Blind to PISCES
♓	2	SUN SATURN *In* ♓	SUN is Blind to LEO SATURN is Blind to AQUARIUS

Fig. 68 The Twelve Signs and Aversion

		Cannot See *(is in Aversion to)*	
PLANET	**IN THE SIGN OF.......**		**THE SIGN** *(and House)* **THEY RULE**
♄ in FOUR Signs	LEO *(Detriment)*		CAPRICORN
	CANCER or VIRGO or PISCES *(Detriment)*		AQUARIUS
♃ in FOUR Signs	TAURUS or SCORPIO		SAGITTARIUS
	LEO or AQUARIUS *(All Four Fixed Signs)*		PISCES
♂ in FOUR Signs	TAURUS *(Detriment)*		ARIES
	LIBRA or GEMINI or SAGITTARIUS *(Detriment)*		SCORPIO
☉ in FOUR Signs	CANCER or CAPRICORN VIRGO or PISCES *(Four of Six Feminine Signs)*		LEO
♀ in FOUR Signs	ARIES or GEMINI or SAGITTARIUS *(Detriment)*		TAURUS
	SCORPIO *(Detriment)*		LIBRA
☿ in FOUR Signs	TAURUS or SCORPIO		GEMINI
	LEO or AQUARIUS *(All Four Fixed Signs)*		VIRGO
☽ in TWO Signs	LEO or AQUARIUS *(Masculine Signs)*		CANCER

Fig. 69 The Seven Planets in Signs which are Adverse to their own Signs

Patterns in Aversion: The Three Crosses

Cardinal Cross

The Cardinal Cross shows the two pairs of planets which rule the two axes of cardinal signs.

Moon and Saturn rule the Cancer/Capricorn axis. Mars and Venus rule the Aries/ Libra axis.

In charts drawn up in the Whole Sign house system, the cardinal cross can represent the quartile aspect between any of the four houses.

For instance, the four angular houses (the 1st, 4th, 7th, 10th house) can have the cardinal signs on each of their house cusps.

Similarly, the four succedent houses which follow the angular houses (the 2nd, 5th, 8th and 11th house) can be ruled by the four planets listed above.

The four cadent houses (the 3rd, 6th, 9th, 12th house) can have one of each of the cardinal signs on their house cusps.

The Moon and Saturn in Leo will cause both ends of the axis to suffer as both planets are blind to their houses.

They do not need to be in conjunction for aversion to be an issue for their respective houses.

Mars and Venus in each other's fixed signs are both in detriment and have to deal with the difficulty of being unable to reach their cardinal- signed houses.

The problem is accentuated when Mars and Venus are in similar degrees and form an aspect of opposition.

But for the rules of aversion, no aspect need exist for both planets to experience trouble with their cardinal axis.

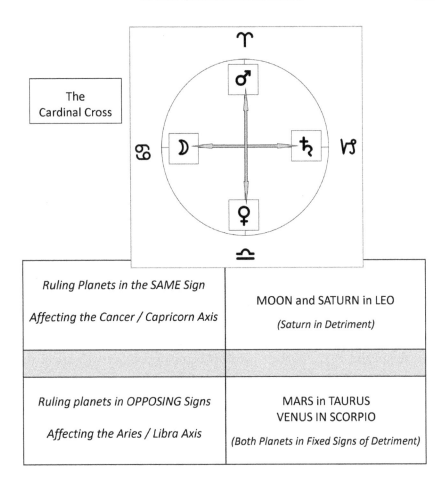

Ruling Planets in the SAME Sign	MOON and SATURN in LEO
Affecting the Cancer / Capricorn Axis	(Saturn in Detriment)
Ruling planets in OPPOSING Signs	MARS in TAURUS
	VENUS IN SCORPIO
Affecting the Aries / Libra Axis	(Both Planets in Fixed Signs of Detriment)

Fig. 70 The Cardinal Cross and Aversion

Fixed Cross

N.B. PLANETS DO NOT NEED TO BE IN ASPECT (SIMILAR DEGREES) TO AFFECT AXIS

The Fixed Cross is ruled by the Sun Saturn combination which rules Leo and Aquarius.

Mars and Venus replicate the conflict shown in the cardinal cross by repeating it through the fixed signs of Scorpio and Taurus.

The following list of zodiacal positions for these two planetary combinations will dictate whether an entire Cross of houses (angular, succedent or cadent) is affected by aversion, or just one of the axes suffers from its ruler's blindness.

Aversion is concerned with sign to sign aspect, not degree to degree, so the pair of planets can be situated in any of the degrees of the sign.

Sun and Saturn in the feminine signs of Cancer, Virgo or Pisces will produce an axis with both sides being neglected by their rulers.

Venus and Mars in the masculine mutable signs of Gemini or Sagittarius will create a similar problem for both planet and house.

Venus and Mars in their cardinal signs of debility will affect the houses with the fixed signs of Taurus and Scorpio on their cusp.

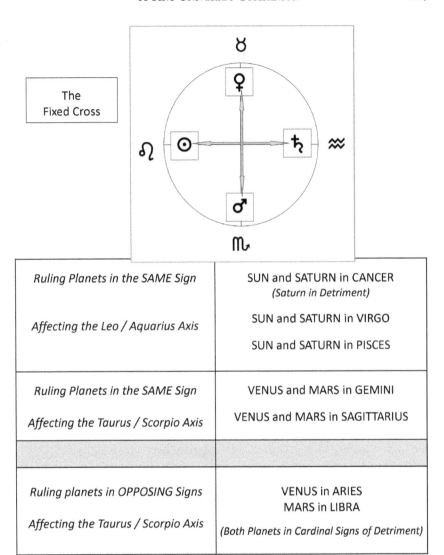

Ruling Planets in the SAME Sign *Affecting the Leo / Aquarius Axis*	SUN and SATURN in CANCER *(Saturn in Detriment)* SUN and SATURN in VIRGO SUN and SATURN in PISCES
Ruling Planets in the SAME Sign *Affecting the Taurus / Scorpio Axis*	VENUS and MARS in GEMINI VENUS and MARS in SAGITTARIUS
Ruling planets in OPPOSING Signs *Affecting the Taurus / Scorpio Axis*	VENUS in ARIES MARS in LIBRA *(Both Planets in Cardinal Signs of Detriment)*

Fig. 71 The Fixed Cross and Aversion

Mutable Cross

N.B. PLANETS DO NOT NEED TO BE IN ASPECT (SIMILAR DEGREES) TO AFFECT AXIS

Together Mercury and Jupiter rule the four mutable signs.

These two planets do not share the same level of animosity which often afflicts the rulers of the cardinal and fixed crosses.

However, the fixed signs are difficult for these two planets as aversion occurs across the axis when Mercury and Jupiter share these four signs.

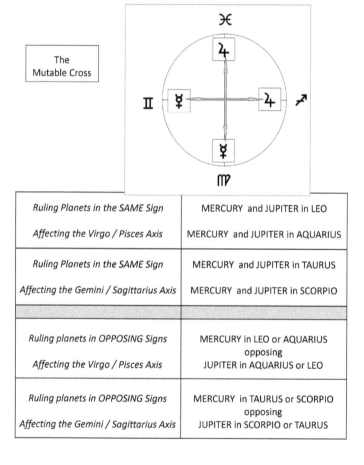

Ruling Planets in the SAME Sign	MERCURY and JUPITER in LEO
Affecting the Virgo / Pisces Axis	MERCURY and JUPITER in AQUARIUS
Ruling Planets in the SAME Sign	MERCURY and JUPITER in TAURUS
Affecting the Gemini / Sagittarius Axis	MERCURY and JUPITER in SCORPIO
Ruling planets in OPPOSING Signs	MERCURY in LEO or AQUARIUS opposing
Affecting the Virgo / Pisces Axis	JUPITER in AQUARIUS or LEO
Ruling planets in OPPOSING Signs	MERCURY in TAURUS or SCORPIO opposing
Affecting the Gemini / Sagittarius Axis	JUPITER in SCORPIO or TAURUS

Fig. 72 The Mutable Cross and Aversion

Sharing Responsibility for a House

It is worth noting that a ruler from a lower level can play the role of house manager if the domicile ruler is absent, so that the exalted ruler can step in for the domicile ruler in aversion and six of the twelve signs can look to rulers by exaltation to relieve the plight of aversion.

For instance, Jupiter can step in for the Moon to rule Cancer, Saturn can watch over the house of Libra if Venus is unavailable, Mars takes the house of Capricorn if Saturn's sign is in aversion to Capricorn.

Venus takes the house of Pisces if Jupiter is blind to this sign, the Sun looks after the house with Aries on the cusp if Mars is 'missing in action' and the Moon takes care of Taurus if its fellow nocturnal planet Venus is unavailable to do its duty by this house.

The following diagram illustrates this idea of a swap in rulers in the primary ruler is in a sign which is averse to its house.

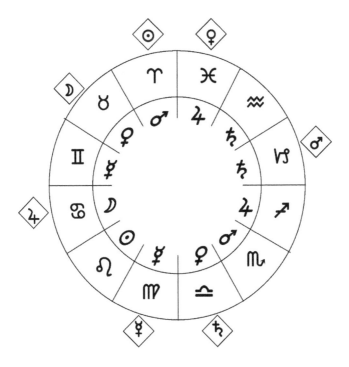

Fig. 73 The domicile and exalted rulers of the signs

In the Whole Sign system the houses have only signs and are not identified by degrees of a sign.

For this reason, there is little point in going further in levels of dignity to find other rulers for a particular sign.

However, the two points which float within the chart are the degree of the Ascendant and the degree of the Midheaven.

These are critical points in the chart and for this reason, it is worthwhile looking further for another ruler if the domicile and the exalted ruler are *in absentia*.

Egyptian Terms or Bounds

The fourth level of dignity is the Egyptian Terms and Bounds *(Fig. 75)* and these divide the degrees of a sign amongst five different rulers.

If the Term ruler's sign aspects the ascendant or MC degree, then these points can be governed by their Term ruler to fulfil their actions, reach their potential or enact their fate in the chart.

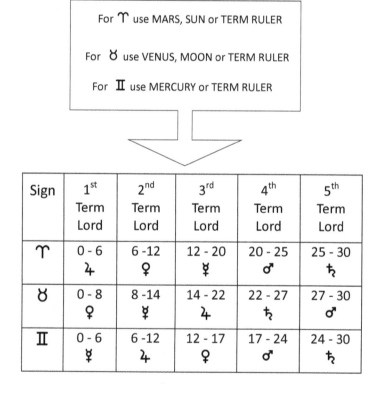

Sign	1st Term Lord	2nd Term Lord	3rd Term Lord	4th Term Lord	5th Term Lord
♈	0 - 6 ♃	6 - 12 ♀	12 - 20 ☿	20 - 25 ♂	25 - 30 ♄
♉	0 - 8 ♀	8 - 14 ☿	14 - 22 ♃	22 - 27 ♄	27 - 30 ♂
♊	0 - 6 ☿	6 - 12 ♃	12 - 17 ♀	17 - 24 ♂	24 - 30 ♄

Fig. 74 An Example of Egyptian Terms as Ruler of the Ascendant or Midheaven

For instance, if the ascendant is in Gemini and Mercury is in a sign which is blind to Gemini, the degree of the ascendant may help to find an alternate guardian by aspecting its term ruler.

Aries and Taurus can fall back on their exalted rulers but as Gemini does not possess an exalted ruler, the Terms may be a saving grace for an otherwise distressed house.

So far as Gemini is concerned, the first term ruler may have already been eliminated because it is the domicile ruler, Mercury, but if the points (ASC or MC) are between the degrees of 6 – 12 Gemini, then it is worth looking to see if Jupiter, the term ruler of these degrees makes an aspect to Gemini.

Similarly, look for Venus if the ASC or MC is between 12 - 17 Gemini or Mars from 17 – 24 Gemini or Saturn for the last six degrees of Gemini.

Sign	1st Term Lord	2nd Term Lord	3rd Term Lord	4th Term Lord	5th Term Lord
♈	0 - 6 ♃	6 -12 ♀	12 - 20 ☿	20 - 25 ♂	25 - 30 ♄
♉	0 - 8 ♀	8 -14 ☿	14 - 22 ♃	22 - 27 ♄	27 - 30 ♂
♊	0 - 6 ☿	6 -12 ♃	12 - 17 ♀	17 - 24 ♂	24 - 30 ♄
♋	0 - 7 ♂	7 -13 ♀	13 - 19 ☿	19 - 26 ♃	26 - 30 ♄
♌	0 - 6 ♃	6 -11 ♀	11 - 18 ♄	18 - 24 ☿	24 - 30 ♂
♍	0 - 7 ☿	7 -17 ♀	17 - 21 ♃	21 - 28 ♂	28 - 30 ♄
♎	0 - 6 ♄	6 -14 ☿	14 - 21 ♃	21 - 28 ♀	28 - 30 ♂
♏	0 - 7 ♂	7 -11 ♀	11 - 19 ☿	19 - 24 ♃	24 - 30 ♄
♐	0 -12 ♃	12-17 ♀	17 - 21 ☿	21 - 26 ♄	26 - 30 ♂
♑	0 - 7 ☿	7 -14 ♃	14 - 22 ♀	22 - 26 ♄	26 - 30 ♂
♒	0 - 7 ☿	7 -13 ♀	13 - 20 ♃	20 - 25 ♂	25 - 30 ♄
♓	0 -12 ♀	12-16 ♃	16 - 19 ☿	19 - 28 ♂	28 - 30 ♄

Fig. 75 The Egyptian Terms or The Bounds : Fourth Level of Essential Dignity

CHAPTER FIVE

Aversion and Its Impact

"Of all the senses, sight must be the most delightful"

Helen Keller (1880-1968)
American author, lecturer and political activist

When sight exists, there is context, comprehension and connection, as often a combination of these three provides security and reassurance, when the mind can identify and categorise something in concrete form.

Identifying a form is necessary for sighted sentient beings (animals and humans alike) in order for them to judge the distance and speed of an approaching object, or to assess the level of danger or impact afforded by a solid object.

In astrology, aversion or lack of sight, is a difficult condition for both a planet and its house.

The word 'domicile' has been used to describe the first preference and highest accreditation level of Essential Dignity and the Latin *'domicilium'* meaning 'house' tells us that when a planet is in its domicile, its first ruling sign, it is as though it is in a place of residence, its natural abode or home-like dwelling.

To put aversion into perspective, imagine a guardianship between an adult and a child.

A guardian is a substitute decision-maker who is responsible for making lifestyle choices in the absence of a parent. They have legally accepted the position of protecting or defending something, or someone, who cannot care adequately for themselves, until they reach a certain age for self-government.

Planets that rule houses are cosmic guardians who manage the mundane affairs of earth through the rulership of their astrological signs and houses.

Trines and sextiles between the signs of a planet's occupation, and its ruling sign, are likened to the guardian with an easier relationship to its ward – there is an understanding or a likeness which means that, in most circumstances, the two parties get along quite well.

This reflects the ease of gender shown by the sextile, or the compatibility of element which exists in a trine aspect.

For instance, if Venus is located in Leo there is a sextile to the house with Libra on the cusp and Venus, as the ruling planet, can easily see to the matters of this house.

Even better if Venus is in an air sign as then there would be a trine between its Libran house and the ruling planet in either Aquarius or Gemini.

If the guardian to child relationship is more challenging, then it might be representative of a more difficult aspect, such as a square or an opposition between the planet's placement sign and its ruled sign.

Venus in Cancer aspects the house with Libra on the cusp from a square position several houses away, and this relationship denotes stress or tension between house and ruler.

A stressed adult with time constraints dealing with a tired child in a hostile environment, such as an airport or a busy department store is the nature of a square aspect.

The needs of a child might be totally unfamiliar to the guardian, so misunderstandings and flare-ups are a trademark of their relationship.

An opposition generally puts the guardian at logger-heads with the child, and the situation is likely to become more explosive with each moment, especially when neither is prepared to give in or abandon the battle.

The guardian may feel that they are completely inadequate as a care-taker and can be daunted by the heaviness of their responsibility for the child.

Even with the best intentions, the guardian feels debilitated in such a situation, and their behaviour may reflect the notion that the guardian suffers a detrimental setback due to their obligation to care for the child's welfare.

This relationship echoes the nature of an opposition in the chart between the ruling planet and its house.

Like any adult who feels out of their depth, the sense of being in detriment is strong, and although the situation may have nothing to do with the child, the ability to be an effective guardian is somewhat diminished.

For example, when Venus is in opposition to its Libran house, it is in Aries, in a sign of its detriment, and both planet and house are feeling uncomfortable, inadequate and unsure as to how events will turn in their favour.

Similar to the young child, a house must be directed by its ruling planet, but the more debilitated a planet feels, the less control it has, and the worse decisions the chart's owner is likely to make when a slight disagreement escalates into full-scale drama.

A child can be fed, put to bed, comforted or put into time-out space, but it is not so simple for a ruling planet to perform these same tasks for its house.

And eventually, the relationship can change for the better when the child will grow into a reasonable human being, or the guardian no longer has to protect their ward.

However, the planet in a chart rules the house for the native's life.

Thankfully, experience and wisdom comes with age, and the tougher relationships between planet and house generally improve with time.

Then there is aversion.

If, for whatever reason, the guardian has agreed to the situation but is incapable of caring for the child's welfare, or is never present in the child's life, or has no knowledge or awareness of its responsibility as guardian, then a state of aversion has occurred.

The guardian (ruling planet) may have all the best intentions, but the child is mostly forgotten as the guardian moves through a life which does not include the care of a child (house).

The guardian (planet) is likely to go through periods of denial, forgetfulness, indifference or ignorance concerning the fate of the child (house), but sometimes there are feelings of guilt, panic and a resolve to improve matters, or to somehow make amends in the future.

The child (house) experiences similar emotions, coupled with a feeling of abandonment, and the desire to understand the reasons behind their situation, and to reconnect with the missing guardian (planet).

Obviously, the human experience is much more sensitive and fraught with emotion than that of a planet and its house, but the general impression exists when a planet is unable to attend to the matters of its house.

How Does Aversion Affect the Delineation of a House?

The preceding metaphor has limitations for two reasons.

A planet is not human, and whilst the analogy may be useful as a symbolic tool to describe aversion, it would be a mistake to confuse human behaviour with planets and houses.

The tendency for *anthropopathism* should be avoided (Gr. *Anthropos* "human" and *pathos* "suffering"), that is, the attribution of human emotions to a deity, or in the case of astrology, to a planet, because it can lead us down the potentially obscure path of planets "causing" things to happen, but not with the same level of clarity and definition as Aristotle's four Causes.

The other reason for caution in relating the metaphor of guardian and child to planet and house is to be aware that aversion is not a matter of choice for the planet.

It occurs because a planet is passing through a particular sign which is at odds with the sign that it rules through the Essential Dignities.

When the native's birth occurs and the horoscope is created, the planet's rulership sign will fall on the cusp of a house, and it is the dilemma of the house, and to some degree of the planet, to cope with the inability of one to see the other.

If the idea of 'domicile' creating a contractual relationship between a planet, its rulership sign, and the cusp of a house is to be considered, then the planet is required to fulfil its contractual obligations and to effectively, or at least to the best of its given ability, to manage whatever the house implies in the chart.

However, in certain signs the planet will be unable to take care of its house, purely because it cannot achieve the contact which is necessary for the undertaking of proper management.

Often the 'lost' house suffers from a lack of direction or discipline because its principle mover, the ruling planet, is blind to its needs.

This tends to result in the native (the chart's owner) vacillating between unintentional neglect, and intense agitation, over the concerns of the house with an absent ruler.

There can be times in an individual's life when a nagging worry can escalate to the borderline of mild paranoia, and when the appropriate house is examined, often an absent ruler can give an indication as to why the native is fixated on a particular part of their lives.

When aversion occurs, the sightless planet has sporadic control over its house whose circumstances are often in a perpetual state of disarray.

The ruling planet is aware of its own shortcomings and is likely to show signs of wear and tear when it comes to the organization of this house's affairs.

The balance between good management and a total lack of awareness unsettles the planet's equilibrium, and this instability is noticeable when the planet oscillates between the extremes of ignoring the house in the hope that its problems will disappear, to overcompensating for the poor performance of its duties by micro-management, thereby increasing tension within the house.

The diagrams on the Four Causes which are featured in the previous chapter demonstrate the reciprocal arrangement between planet and house.

The Four Causes show that the ruling planet has a symbiotic relationship with the house with its sign on the cusp.

Therefore, it makes sense that when there is aversion between the planet's sign of location and its own sign, the planet itself becomes unsettled and struggles to function effectively, or loses the ability to maximise its potential.

Aversion affects the Planet as well as the House

	Responsibilities of the Ruling Planet	Ruling Planets without Sight A Planet's 'Shadows'
♄	Stability; Responsibility; Sound reasoning and judgement; At ease with authority; Expertise and conviction gained through experiment and experience; A good balance of control	♄ in ♋, ♌, ♍ or ♓ Sensitive to blame or guilt; Lack of boundaries or self-control; Overly sensitive or defensive; Possible authority and/or father issue; Procrastination or prevarication on decisions; Poor time management; Laziness; Fearfulness
♃	Benefit; Largesse; Wisdom; Good Humour; Generosity; Confidence; Good Fortune; Authority; Ambition	♃ in ♉, ♏, ♌ or ♒ Sense of opportunities missed; Frustration; Self-indulgent; Disappointments; Issues with authority; Tendency to feel inadequate or exaggerate; Restlessness; Lack of attention to detail; Lack of control or boundaries or awareness of culpability
♂	Competitiveness; Confidence; Action; Masculinity; Courage in adversity; A desire to possess; Independence; Self-motivation	♂ in ♉, ♊, ♎ or ♐ Fits of energy or excessive risk-taking; Frustration; Lack of power or direction; Meekness, passive or aggressive behaviour; Emotional outbursts or destructive acts
☉	Direction; Purpose; Reputation; Vitality; Enthusiasm; Energy; Sense of Self; Authority; Father	☉ in ♋, ♍, ♑ or ♓ Frustration with a lack of recognition or acknowledgement; Authority issues; Lack of confidence; Sensitivity to criticism; Over compensation for errors or perceived weaknesses; Need for approval or feedback from others; Possible father issues; Subjective opinions and emotional decision-making
♀	Ease and comfort with others; Pleasure; Self-confidence; Good social skills; Good Fortune; Beauty; Style or physical grace	♀ in ♈, ♊, ♏ or ♐ Discomfort in areas that should be enjoyable; Limited social skills; Misunderstandings with others; Difficulties or trust issues with women; Lack of control; Hedonistic behaviour or self-denial; Vanity; Lack of self-esteem; Relationship issues
☿	Mind tuned to 'Business at Hand'; Attention to Detail; Good cognitive skills; Memory; Communication skills	☿ in ♉, ♏, ♌ or ♒ Misunderstandings; Envy, resentment or ignorance; poor movement skills; Communication disputes; Frustrations or insecurity in communication on topics concerning Mercury's blind house
☽	At ease with emotions; Comfortable with one's body and the physical world; Physical presence; Nurturing qualities; Sound emotional support	☽ in ♌ or ♒ Discomfort with the body; Lack of physical awareness; emotional misgivings or sensitivity to Moon's house issues; Highly subjective or defensive personality; Mother or nurturing issues; Sense of abandonment or betrayal

Fig. 76 Planets' Shadows: The Effects of Blindness on the Planets

When Angles are Blind to their Rulers

"Come now, prepare an attentive mind for learning the cardinal points (the angles); four in all, they have positions in the firmament permanently fixed and receive in succession the speeding signs.

One looks out from the rising of the heavens as they are born into the world and has the first view of the Earth from the level horizon;

the second faces it from the opposite edge of the sky, the point from which the starry sphere retires and hurtles headlong into Tartarus;

Ascendant *"as they are born into the world, the first view of Earth"*	Descendant *"the second faces it from the opposite edge of the sky"*
Feelings of being ignored or invisible; Fear of exposure or disregard for personal safety	Illness or 'attacks' on the body can show up here due to opposition to Ascendant
Lack of awareness or comfort in physical world; Constant dissatisfaction or discontent with life's circumstances	Relationship inconsistencies or insecurities; Wavering between non-involvement and obsession, neglect to infatuation or fantasy
Disconnected from surroundings; Inability or lack of desire to relate well to the immediate physical environment	Misunderstandings with others resulting in battles or feeling constantly under attack; Feelings of isolation from, or betrayal by others, including loved ones
Actions are misunderstood or misjudged by others; Person can be accused of presenting a 'false identity' where the individual is not conscious of their behaviour or its impact on others	Struggle to discriminate between 'friend' or 'foe' leads to insecurity, confusion, errors in judgement
Insecurities regarding physical body, based on the nature of the planet which is the ruler of the sign on the Ascendant; Mysterious, sudden or unexplained physical ailments	Frustrations, fretting, oscillating behaviour towards others – described by the nature of the planet which is the seventh house ruler

Fig. 77 Table of Aversion for the Lords of the Ascendant or Descendant

a third marks the zenith of high heaven, where wearied Phoebus halts with panting steeds and rests the day and determines the mid-point of shadows;

the fourth occupies the nadir, and has the glory of forming the foundations of the sphere;

in it the stars complete their descent and commence their return.

Mid-Heaven (MC)	Imum Coeli (IC)
"the zenith of high heaven, the mid-point of shadows"	*"the nadir, has the glory of forming the foundations"*
Ignorance, indecision or frustration in life's direction or career goals; Difficulty with authority figures	Family concerns, hidden issues or household secrets; Lack of stability in childhood or family life or place of residence
Public image is misrepresented, distorted or Biased, Possibility of becoming a scapegoat	Mysteries or inconsistencies in family background; Shaky foundations in life
Wavering between despondency towards career, and wanting to devote to a vocation, mission or calling	Inner feelings of 'lacking roots' or insecurity at the base of life; Dispossession or fears of homelessness
Sensitivity, defensiveness or bitterness over perceived 'successes' and 'failures' in life	Property concerns; Family or bloodline squabbles over inheritance, especially land or property orientated bequeathment
If MC lies in the tenth sign, mother or mother's family may be shrouded in mystery, unconnected to father's partner (step-mother issues)	If IC lies in the fourth sign, father or father's family is disconnected from the native, mother's partner (step-father) can define the aversion

Fig. 78 Table of Aversion for the Lords of the MC or IC

These points are charged with exceptional powers, and the influence they exert on fate is the greatest known to our science, because the celestial circle is totally held in position by them as by eternal supports;

did they not receive the circle, sign after sign in succession, flying in its perpetual revolution, and clamp it with fetters at the two sides and lowest and highest extremities of its compass, heaven would fly apart and its fabric disintegrate and perish." [57]

Marcus Manilius (1st c. C.E.)

Aversion and the Ascendant

"He recounts the names and significations of the twelve places of the chart.

For example, that the Hour-Maker ('horoskopos') is both the helm of the life ('oiax biou') and the entrance into physical life ('zoe'), indicative of the soul and behaviour and all such matters." [58]

Antiochus (1ˢᵗ century B.C.E.)

The ascendant is of paramount importance in the design of the astrological chart.

In quadrant-style charts, it sets the horizon and cuts the chart in half to produce the diurnal and nocturnal hemispheres, and in whole sign charts it determines which sign will lead the procession of the signs through the houses.

On a practical level, the ascendant signifies the mortal body; its physical attributes, the robust nature of health, its strength and agility, and its resilience to tangible misfortune from the dark sixth, eighth and twelfth houses.

Under normal circumstances, it falls to the ruling planet of the ascendant's sign to maintain a constant vigilance over the body in order for the native to navigate their way through the mundane affairs of life.

However, when the lord of the ascendant is blind to its house, the individual struggles to come to terms with the care, upkeep, or sometimes the conscious awareness, of their physical body.

For the native with a ruling planet in aversion to the first house, the physical world can feel like a source of constant (and often unsolicited) surprise as external events appear to be out of their control.

The feeling of being constantly blind-sided by circumstances not of their making can mean that the native's own behaviour becomes erratic, overly suspicious or guarded in their responses.

The first house is also likely to be the person's emotional barometer which measures stored emotions and tension levels and when the lord is averse to this house, feelings of calm, peacefulness or well-being are difficult to achieve without an enormous amount of conscious effort on the part of the native.

The effort required for the native to maintain a centred sense of self can be physically and emotionally exhausting, and for this reason, the individual's behaviour and health can reflect their inner conflict.

Aversion in the first house suggests a person's fear of vulnerability, and any feelings of inadequacy can be exposed, especially when sudden changes call for their ruling planet to direct them.

At other times, the individual can seem to others to possess a flagrant disregard for personal safety, almost as though they have little awareness of how rash actions, or inappropriate or unsafe behaviour can have dangerous consequences.

The nature of the behavioural inconsistencies will be dictated by the planet which is the lord of the ascendant.

Although the planet may be unable to communicate with its house, it will still lend its flavour to the type of indiscretions or inconsistent mood swings of which the native is capable, especially when the ascendant is left unguarded or unsupported by its missing lord.

Mercury may be careless in the spoken word, Mars or Jupiter can be excessive risk-takers, while the Sun can be overly critical, highly sensitive or defensive in behaviour.

Saturn can swing between excessive self-protection to having no boundaries at all, whilst the Moon can seem cold and distant when it most needs reassurance and comfort.

Lastly, Venus can display anti-social behaviour or have a tendency to stir up trouble rather than avoiding it, which is its usual method of dealing with the world.

This rash behaviour can be a result of the native feeling ignored, overlooked or invisible to the world, as this is often the remarks made by a person whose ruling lord is in absenteeism.

Feeling disconnected from their surroundings, the individual's interactions with others can be a source of frustration, especially when they are misunderstood or misrepresented by others who accuse them of insincerity or of presenting a 'false' front to the world.

What others can do naturally or unconsciously to protect themselves, the unprotected ascendant finds wearisome and this adds to the exasperation of trying to feel comfortable in their immediate environment.

Sometimes mysterious illness and physical complaints appear unexpectedly, or are difficult to recognise or diagnose, and this situation can be related to an absent first house ruler.

Apart from its practical use as a beginning point to the chart, the ascendant plays a pivotal role in the life's spiritual purpose as well as signifying the physical body.

Antiochus calls the ascendant the 'helm of life' and by extension, the ruling planet is the tiller-man at the helm; the one who is responsible for steering life in the right direction.

The Four Causes in Astrology define the nature of a house and its ruling planet.

The question of *What am I?*

is particularly relevant to the first house, the house of light which represents the native's vitality and direction or purpose in life.

The ruling planet supposedly provides answers for the three remaining questions, but when the lord of the ascendant cannot see its house, then certain questions become difficult to answer with confidence.

Questions originating in the first house, such as:

> *Who am I?*
> *Why do I exist?*
> *What is the purpose of my life?*
> *Where do I belong in this world?*

are painful and vexing when the answers, and even the questions themselves, seem to be beyond our scope of understanding.

This is a large part of the dilemma faced by the individual whose ascendant lord is placed in a sign which is blind to the chart's rising sign.

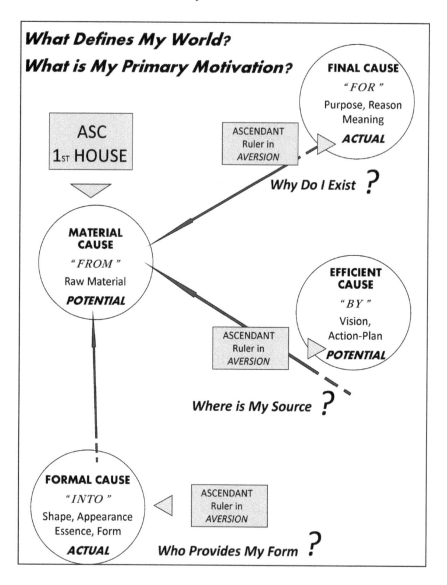

Fig. 79 Aversion and the Ascendant

Aversion and Prime Motivation:

— *The Tiller-man At the Helm of Life*

*"The third cardinal (the Ascendant), which on the same
level as the Earth holds in position the shining dawn, where the
stars first rise, where day returns and divides time into hours, is
for this reason in the Greek world called the Horoscope, and it
declines a foreign name, taking pleasure in its own.*

*Within its domain lies the arbitrament of life and the
formation of character; it will grant success to enterprises, open
up the professions, and decide the early years that await men
from their birth, the education they receive, and the station
to which they are born, according as the planets approve and
mingle their influences."*[59]

Marcus Manilius

Traditional astrologer and translator Robert Zoller used the term
'prime motivation' to describe an individual's principle yearnings in life,
yearnings which could be identified by the sign on the ascendant, and
fulfilled by the planet which ruled that sign.

The inaugural 'primary motivation' occurs when the soul is
motivated to join with its physical form at the moment of birth and
to create not only new life, but also the horoscope for the child's
potentialities in life.

Every new experience or change in life becomes a pale imitation
of this birthing experience and the ascendant is the place where the
native's primary motivations are met, time and time again, throughout
the native's life.

Factors such as the sign, house placement and aspects of the
ascendant's ruling planet are taken into account, as well as any aspects
made by other planets directly to the rising degree.

In this way, the 'birth' of a new phase, direction or purpose in life
will mirror the first breath of life measured at the ascendant's degree.

Each of the elements chooses a different method for meeting its
prime motivation, and the best starting point is to divide the four
elements into two groups of gender-based signs.

The masculine signs of fire and air follow the yang principle (literally, *'sunny side'*), which is characterized as fast, hard, focussed, hot and active.

The ascendants with fire or air signs want to make their mark on the world and are driven by a desire to make an impression on their immediate environment.

Yang is the sword that carves out a niche for itself in the physical realm and declares ownership over its surroundings so that others will follow their lead.

Masculine yang signs will fight for the space to express their primary motivation whenever changing circumstances bring the advent of something new in their lives.

In contrast to the fire and air signs, the feminine elements of water and earth conform to the yin principle (*'shady side'*), characterized by words such as slow, soft, yielding, cold and passive.

The ascendants which fall in either of these feminine elements belong to myths of cauldrons, melting pots, holy grails and magical vessels which protect, hold and maintain life-giving energy, dispersing it whenever it is needed by others to fulfil their tasks.

Yin describes a passive contrariety which flows, replenishes and adjusts to its environment, and so too does an ascendant from the water or earth element learn to survive through adaptation by taking the path of least resistance as the individual is called to constantly adjust to new conditions and modifications to their life.

The ability for any ascendant to adjust or take advantage of change, as well as developing the art of survival, is largely dependent on the levels of dignity which the ruler of the ascendant enjoys in the chart.

When the sign on the ascendant is incompatible with its ruler's temporary sign, there is a state of aversion, and the motivations of the ascendant may be difficult to fulfil.

The two genders and the four elements approach life and change differently, and the individual may struggle with whichever of the Prime Motivation's four principles are relevant to their Ascendant.

For instance, the ascendant in a masculine sign may find it hard to drive themselves to succeed, or feel they cannot recognise the pathway to success or meet challenges as they arise, when it comes to surviving the stress of everyday living.

Aversion for the feminine signs of water and earth can mean that the individual's needs are not being met, either because the individual is not clear in their own minds on what it is that they want or need from life, or because they prioritize others' needs above their own.

Water and earth ascendants are extremely sensitive to external stimuli and can become overly emotional, defensive, or physically exhausted.

Sometimes it seems preferable to withdraw from the world rather than guessing (and missing) what it is that the world expects from them.

For the Greeks the concept of sight was that of light and energy flowing from one object to another, and in the example of the chart, the light flowed out from the ascendant to houses it could see by Ptolemaic aspect.

Houses were given light and life by the ascendant; houses such as the third and eleventh house by a sextile aspect, the tenth and fourth houses by squares, the ninth and fifth by trine, and the seventh house by the aspect of opposition.

This left the four remaining houses which were considered to be dark, foreboding or passive.

In the Whole Sign house system, when the ruler of the ascendant is featured in any one of these houses, then the ruler is unable to reach its house.

This is the case when the ascendant is in aversion to its ruler – the ruling planet is in one of the houses which receive no light from the ascendant.

That is, the second house which carries the burden of money and finances, or the sixth house which denotes the destruction of the native's health, or the eighth house, the house of death or trauma, or the twelfth house which directly precedes the ascendant and brings its own dark visions to the native's ascendant.

Light means energy and when the ascendant does not cast light to certain houses and the ruling planet is featured in any one of those dark houses, then there can be no reciprocal energy sent back from the ruling planet to the ascendant.

Aversion is darkness and a lack of energy and so the ascendant's ruling planet is vexed by having to sit in the dark in a kind of cosmic purgatory, and to contemplate the nature of its sin.

The following phrases describe each element's version of their own Primary Motivation.

The individual with a FIRE Ascendant is motivated by ....

The desire for power and freedom of action

The desire for power and freedom of action is achieved through the differences in fire's modality (cardinal, fixed or mutable), and according to the planet which rules each of the fire signs of Aries, Leo and Sagittarius.

Aries Ascendant ruled by Mars

An Aries ascendant is a cardinal sign and its ruler, Mars, is an initiator who creates opportunities by which it can act freely and independently by seizing the power it desires in order to fulfil its primary motivation.

Whether this is possible, or successful, is governed by Mars through its condition by sign, house position and aspects.

When Mars is in Taurus, it is unable to become the primary motivator for Aries as there is aversion between the two signs of Taurus and Aries.

As Taurus follows Aries in the zodiac Mars will be situated in the second house and its fears or concerns over money will create much of the problems for the ascendant.

Timidity, a miserly attitude or fearfulness over the loss of one's comfort can cause the Aries ascendant to stay too long in a position which compromises the principles of its primary motivation.

If Mars does not connect with the ascendant by Ptolemaic aspects, then the Sun, as the exalted ruler of Aries, can take the position of ascendant ruler in the place of Mars.

Leo Ascendant ruled by The Sun

A Leo Ascendant is dependent on the Sun to achieve it prime motivation, and as has been stated earlier, the Sun has the maximum number of signs by which it will be averse to its sign of Leo.

The Sun in four of the six feminine signs – Cancer, Virgo, Capricorn, or Pisces – will struggle to see the ascendant, and as no planet is exalted in Leo, there is little aid or respite, when the Sun lies in any of these signs.

This can be particularly difficult for the Leo rising individual, as it is very important for the chart owner's self-esteem to appear in control of their world, but it can be both exasperating and exhausting for the native as they struggle to keep up the front of appearing to be invincible, when the planet behind the facade is a Sun with no sight to the ascendant.

The placement of the Sun in the Whole Sign chart will vary according to the Sun's sign, but each of the feminine signs will be in dark houses which are adverse to the Leo ascendant. A Cancer Sun will reside in the twelfth house, a Virgo Sun will have its own issues from the second house, a Capricorn Sun will be blind to the ascendant from its position in the sixth house, and a Pisces Sun will be caught up in the dramas of the eighth house.

Sagittarius Ascendant ruled by Jupiter

The individual with Sagittarius rising at the moment of birth looks to Jupiter to perform well, so that they might achieve their concept of power and freedom of action.

Sagittarius is a mutable sign, and its lord has a love of wide spaces and an open dialogue between itself and the world in general, so the drive for power often comes from energetic exchange or interaction with others. This can be difficult to achieve if Jupiter's sign is averse to Sagittarius, and can result in aimlessness or a sense of missing out rather than finding themselves in the thick of the action.

When Jupiter is located in either Taurus or Scorpio it means the planet bears no relationship to Sagittarius, and the ascendant lord misses out in trying to provide the native's primary motivation.

Similar to Leo, there is no quick back-up plan available from the list of exaltations, and the individual with Sagittarius rising can be frustrated when its lord is held fast in either fixed earth or water signs.

> **The individual with an AIR Ascendant is motivated by....**
>
> **The drive for freedom of movement and communication**

The element of air is a composition of hot and wet qualities, and its desire to quickly connect and move on is very strong in individuals whose rising sign lies in Libra, Aquarius or Gemini.

Libra Ascendant ruled by Venus

The cardinal air sign of Libra will initiate conversation and enjoys any stimulating interaction with others, but as Venus is its lord, it searches for meaningful contact on a person-to-person level.

Libra rising desires to be liked, admired or accepted by the company it keeps, and wants to believe that others are willing and keen to communicate with them on a level of familiarity.

If Venus is in good condition the body's movements are graceful, the voice is pleasing on the ear, and their appearance is attractive and well-constructed, all unconscious ploys to ensure the native is welcomed in a variety of social situations.

There is only one sign which is averse to Libra, and this is Scorpio, the sign of Venus' detriment, so Venus suffers doubly when Libra is rising and Venus is situated in the fixed water sign.

Instead of comfort, freedom and communication, Venus feels hemmed in, agitated and impeded by its sign, and this can be apparent in the individual's defensive or sour demeanour.

A Libran ascendant with Venus in Scorpio is inclined to expect attack rather than acceptance, to perceive social situations as fraught with conflict, or to feel their awkward or self-conscious mannerisms inhibits their personal freedom.

A combination of these factors makes it extremely difficult for the native to relax and communicate with the world around them, or to feel safe enough to venture out into new surroundings.

When Venus in Scorpio is unable to see the ascendant, it is recommended that Saturn be examined to see if it is in a sign which will aspect Libra, or will make a connection through antiscia or contra-antiscia (i.e. Saturn in Virgo or Pisces).

If so, then the exalted lord of Libra, Saturn, may provide a second chance for the individual with Libra rising to meet their primary motivations when Venus is in aversion to Libra in Scorpio.

It should be remembered that even if Saturn does meet the requirements and step up as a secondary ruler, it will manage the first house in a different way from Venus.

Saturn ruling Libra is likely to curb Libra's enthusiasm and to adopt a more austere or distant demeanour than Venus' rulership would have naturally provided for the native.

However, this 'cooling down' effect on the native's behaviour is a small price to pay when another planet is willing to assume the task of guardian if the original owner, Venus, is missing through the predicament of aversion.

Aquarius Ascendant ruled by Saturn

The Aquarian ascendant achieves prime motivation through the condition by house, sign and aspects of its ruler Saturn, and so long as Saturn feels in control of its environment by asking the right questions, finding the most useful information, and moving in areas where it feels safe and protected, there is no problem for this ascendant sign.

However, should Saturn find itself in Cancer (in detriment), Virgo or Pisces, it will be blind to its air sign and the native will be inclined to try to overcompensate for Saturn's loss.

Behaviour such as fretfulness, micro-managing or refusing to take responsibility for their actions can create difficult situations for the chart owner, especially when faced by change which the individual did not initiate, or feels has been forced upon them.

Aquarius may be an air sign, but it is also a fixed sign ruled by a heavy-weight, and if it feels it is being kept in the dark or bullied into change, especially if Saturn is absent, then no amount of reasoning, debate, or cajoling will move this ascendant.

No other planet takes Aquarius for exaltation and without a safety net this Saturn-owned sign can become pedantic or too concerned with literal accuracy, especially if Saturn is in the sign of Virgo.

Left unchecked, the Aquarian ascendant with an aversion to Saturn can create a mind that becomes a mare's nest of intrigues and unsupported conspiracies. The native's conversations can be consumed by the topics of dark dealings by the government, the authorities, or large corporations whose Machiavellian strategies are designed to restrict the world's individuals of their right to freedom.

Gemini Ascendant ruled by Mercury

Gemini is the mutable air sign ruled by Mercury, and although it is more amenable to change than Aquarius, it will still struggle to achieve its primary motivation if Mercury finds itself in the feminine fixed signs of either Taurus or Scorpio.

The mutability of Gemini becomes threatened by a lord which gets entrenched in inflexible thought patterns, and these can lead to attitudes where the native becomes stuck or stubborn, and whose opinions, at least from their perspective, are always right.

The expectation that every Gemini rising individual will be open to new ideas and is willing to change their expectations or modify their behaviour under consideration of other's needs can be an illusion if Mercury is located in the signs of Taurus or Scorpio. The personality is more likely to demonstrate patterns of rigid thinking whereby the individual struggles to consider alternatives to the current situation, cannot cope with optional or differing viewpoints, and is hesitant to try new problem-solving strategies.

This may be attributed to the fixed signs, but it is less likely to occur when Mercury is located in either Leo or Aquarius, as these two masculine fixed signs will form aspects to the Gemini ascendant. Mercury in Leo will sextile Gemini, and Mercury in Aquarius will trine the Gemini rising chart.

The combination of Mercury in two emotionally-charged signs with a blindness to Gemini, has the potential to create thought patterns which are a breeding ground for insecurity, fear and an unhealthy focus on what can go wrong especially when Mercury cannot see its rising sign.

The individual with a WATER Ascendant is motivated by ....

The need for emotional security

The primary motivation for the three water signs of Cancer, Scorpio and Pisces, all of which have a yin perspective on life, turns from the masculine concept of 'drives and desires' to 'needs'.

Everyone has basic human needs – shelter, warmth, nourishment, safety – but emotional needs extend to a connection with others and a need to love and be loved.

Our society is more inclined to admire the yang ascendant individuals who are seen as self-sufficient or self-motivated towards gaining success or achieving their goals. The desire for independence comes naturally for fire and air ascendants, and we can confuse independence with strength of character. Likewise, society is inclined to laud the ability to communicate and to use word-play or a logical argument to sway others' opinions, and to equate cleverness with intelligence, good breeding or an expensive education.

This leaves water and earth ascendants with a distinct disadvantage as communication does not come easily for these individuals who need to feel secure that their ideas will not be rejected, and any sign of a need for connection or emotional support is often judged as being 'needy' or 'clingy'.

Accusations of neediness can cause a person to feel shame or embarrassment for asking for help or support and can short-circuit any attempt to seek appreciation, compassion or affection.

Cancer Ascendant ruled by The Moon

A Cancer ascendant achieves prime motivation through the condition by house, sign and aspects of its ruler the Moon.

The cardinal water sign will go out of its way to nurture those in its immediate environment, with the unspoken or implied agreement that the nurturing process will be reciprocated by the other party.

If the Moon is in good condition in the chart, the person is well thought of by others as loving, kind, compassionate, sensitive and generous in nature. Common sense and practical wisdom are hallmarks of a Moon which is able to see its Cancer ascendant.

However, if the Moon is in poor condition the messages become less clear and the individual may feel constantly let down by the lack of care or concern directed towards them.

Caring becomes a burden, and the Cancer ascendant can be accused of bearing the attitude or demeanour of a martyr.

The Moon also rules the body. The combination of a planet which signifies both physical health and which also rules the house in the chart signifying the body is a double warning to the native to take appropriate care of themselves. The Moon will require gentle and careful management if the person is to avoid exhaustion or burn out from overdoing physical exertion.

If the Moon is situated in the masculine fixed signs of Leo or Aquarius, it is unable to see Cancer on the ascendant, and the experiences of health issues or emotional distress are increased in either of these signs.

The Moon struggles in masculine signs, and the fixed nature of Leo and Aquarius makes it difficult for the individual to break destructive patterns of behaviour when Cancer is rising.

A Leo Moon will be extra sensitive to accusations of neediness and is more likely to swing the other way by hiding its need for emotional security under a cloak of arrogance or bravado. Asking for help or emotional support is hard enough for any Cancer ascendant, but when the Moon is in a sign of aversion, it becomes important for the Leo Moon to be consciously aware of what its needs are, and to not be too proud to ask for them to be fulfilled.

Likewise, the Aquarian Moon is very adept at feigning indifference when it comes to this Cancer ascendant's need for emotional security. Harnessing a Moon which is disposed by Saturn with a state of aversion means that appearances can be deceiving – a cold or dismissive Cancer exterior may be host to a lifetime of accumulated slights, hurts and rejections as the individual believes that biting humour or gruffness can protect them from emotional harm.

If Jupiter is in a sign which can see Cancer, it is capable of stepping in for the Moon, as Jupiter is the exalted lord of Cancer and can act on behalf of the Moon to meet the individual's prime motivation.

If Jupiter replaces the Moon as the secondary lord of the ascendant, the person can send out mixed messages to the world; one moment embracing everyone and volunteering for a multitude of jobs (Jupiter ruling Cancer), and the next being withdrawn or resentful of all the extra work burdening the native (Aquarian or Leo Moon) under their own instigation.

Scorpio Ascendant ruled by Mars

The fixed water sign of Scorpio can become a bubbling cauldron of emotion when driven by its ruling planet.

Mars is the planet of warriors, and may not understand the subtleties of asking others, in a kind or tender manner, to provide the native with the kinds of emotional security Scorpio ascendant needs to survive *"the slings and arrows of outrageous fortune"* (Shakespeare's *Hamlet*).

Rather than making full-frontal demands, the feminine version of Mars instead chooses to entice, mystify and captivate others by being elusive, mysterious and provocative, and if the individual with Scorpio rising asks for information, it gives little back in return.

The stronger Mars' condition, the better equipped Scorpio rising is at collecting admirers, and there is fierce competition to be the one who will provide emotional security for Scorpio's ascendant.

However, should Mars be in detriment in Libra, or Gemini or Sagittarius, the sultry behaviour of the unobtainable Scorpio can backfire, and the chart's owner can find themselves out in the cold so far as emotional support is concerned.

Mars in Libra can create factions rather than friendships, and can find itself getting in and out of messy romances that batter their emotional frailty, rather than strengthen it.

Mars in Sagittarius can overplay its hand and be accused of being a 'drama queen', thereby alienating those whom it seeks for protection or alliance, whilst Mars in Gemini may not understand that its criticisms are harsh or judgmental, its humour is cruel rather than amusing, and any gossip is spreads will come back to bite it.

Mars' version of emotional security demands loyalty, but when the ruler of the ascendant is absent, it is difficult for Mars to know whom it trusts to provide its primary motivation.

Mars in any of the three signs of its aversion to Scorpio will create the opposite effect of what the person is trying to achieve in terms of prime motivation, and it takes time and experience to learn how to achieve a difficult prime motivation when the lord is unable to assist the ascendant.

Pisces Ascendant ruled by Jupiter

Pisces is more adept at achieving emotional security, purely because it is both mutable, and ruled by Jupiter, a planet which is capable of adaptation, change, experimentation and self-preservation.

Pisces rising has the ability to constantly change and adapt its behaviour and mannerisms to mirror its surrounding environment, and as imitation is the best form of flattery, most people are more than happy to provide this water ascendant with the love and appreciation it desires.

Jupiter is also well-versed in being able to discern between needs and neediness, and when it is in good condition, Jupiter is capable of forming strong bonds that connect the native to others and maintaining emotional and physical vibrancy for the individual's well-being.

Water's primary motivation involves the native being cognizant of the fact that they have to be able to understand their needs before they can honour them, and Jupiter (above the Moon and Mars) is the best candidate to be skilled or knowledgeable in this art of self-awareness.

The fact that Venus is its exalted ruler adds to Pisces sociability, and if the mood is filled with fun, good humour and light-heartedness, then Pisces has moved a long way towards earning its prime motivation.

Jupiter in the masculine fixed signs of Leo or Aquarius is unable to see Pisces, and should Venus also be in these signs, then prime motivation becomes difficult when the domicile and exalted lords of the ascendant are caught in signs that bear no relationship to Pisces.

If Jupiter is located in either of these signs the native can find themselves feeling as though they are searching blindly through darkness for why they feel dissatisfied or disillusioned with life.

Jupiter in Leo will pursue honours and try to fulfil the native's ambitions, but if the primary motivation cannot be met, then the individual may feel the accolades have little meaning or bring scant comfort when emotional satisfaction is really the prize they seek.

Likewise, an ambitious Jupiter in Aquarius can reach dizzying heights, but if the only feelings their success invites from others are envy, resentment or jealousy, then the emotional buzz that success provides is not enough to sustain the individual's primary motivation, and rather than providing emotional security, Jupiter in Aquarius can make peace of mind a hard concept to achieve.

> **The individual with an EARTH Ascendant is motivated by....**
>
> **The need for physical security**

The earth element is a combination of cold and dry qualities, and each of its signs struggle in their own way to achieve prime motivation when it comes to repeated 'birthing' experiences.

Earth's interpretation of fulfilling one's needs is a little more practical than the water ascendant as earth signs seek tangible proof that the environment around them is safely secured when they enter its arena.

For this reason, the individual with an earth ascendant will often attach themselves to routine practices, habits, established patterns or repetition in order to feel safe within their own territory.

Checking timetables, travel routes and news reports for possible hazards or obstruction is part of the process, and it is not unknown for the earth ascendant to have small rituals or to carry talismans or good luck charms to help them navigate their way safely through the physical world.

To others observing this behaviour, it may be dismissed as superstition or sentimentality, but to the rising signs of Capricorn, Taurus or Virgo, these items bring comfort and security to their owners, in much the same way as a favoured teddy bear represents a tangible resource, or provides emotional sustenance, for a tired or distressed child.

This comparison is not to say that the earth ascendant is child-like in their emotional or physical needs. Rather, it is the earth ascendant's mostly unconscious desire to surround themselves with objects, people or situations which comfort them through familiarity or predictability and which allows them to have a natural rapport with their physical habitat.

Harmonious surroundings are incredibly important to all three earth ascendants, and for such a visible and tactile element, aversion between the rising sign and the ruling planet's sign can be frightening for someone who seeks reassurance from the normal or the mundane in every situation.

Capricorn Ascendant ruled by Saturn

Even though the cardinal signs supposedly enjoy initiating change, the sign of Capricorn is inclined to hold back or postpone new experiences, favouring tried and true practices over new methods.

When Saturn rules the Capricorn earth sign, it employs caution and moves at a painfully slow pace towards change, as a belief in the security of one's environment is paramount for the native if they are about to start a process which involves transition in their lives.

It makes sense for Saturn, as the lord of the ascendant, to check and re-check all factors before advancing into new and unknown frontiers, especially when Saturn is fearful that rushing headlong into the future has a distinct possibility of danger or failure.

Often the individual will undergo a rite of passage whereby a ceremony or an event will give them the confidence to move forwards into a new role, whether it is a marriage contract, a promotion, becoming a parent for the first time, a shift in home or occupation, or whatever represents a new phase in their lives.

Luckily, there is only one sign whereby Saturn cannot see Capricorn, and this occurs when Saturn is in Leo, a sign of its detriment.

Saturn can feel doubly cheated by Fate when it is not only in debility in Leo, but is also denied access to its earth sign. A Capricorn ascendant with Saturn in Leo can be a timing disaster, as Saturn, the natural lord of Time, is unable to gauge when the most appropriate time is for the native to take action.

Move too soon, and the preparation is incomplete, the action is hasty, and the chance of success is minimised through poorly executed plans.

If the native procrastinates on making a decision, or dithers until the opportunity is lost, or their confidence is so eroded that their decision-making processes are compromised, then failure looms on the horizon.

Wait too long, and Capricorn prevaricates or lies to cover its misgivings or its mistakes. This situation is disastrous for a ruling planet in detriment, i.e., Saturn, which supposedly signifies truth, justice and integrity.

In the King James Version of the Bible Daniel is asked to provide definitions for the writing which appears on the wall at Belshazzar's feast.

The word *'TEKEL'* appears and David explains that the word means: *""You have been weighed on the scales and found wanting." (Daniel Ch 5: verse 27)*

A large part of being *"weighed on the scales"* comes from issues to do with the eighth house as this is where Saturn will reside if it is in Leo and rules a Capricorn ascendant. Others' financial resources or the management of large company investments or public monies will have to be handled carefully by a debilitated Saturn as any misappropriation will become visible through the joint rulership of the first and second houses.

The problems can lie in the fact that aversion can give the false impression that undercover dealings will stay hidden but when Capricorn is on the ascendant the native is unlikely to see their own fall from grace before it happens.

Bluffing through a situation when the ascendant lord is Saturn and is in aversion to its sign is simply not going to work, and the world will soon measure the individual and find them wanting.

Mars is exalted in Capricorn, so should Saturn be in Leo, Mars may be able to move this earth sign forward into a better state of being. Mars' ability to take action to control of a situation which is blocking the individual's feelings of safety in their environment may be the key to moving the Capricorn ascendant out of a frozen state and into a more comfortable position.

Taurus Ascendant ruled by Venus

When Taurus is the sign on the ascendant, the ruling planet Venus will look for friendships, alliances or a pleasant or attractive surrounding, to alleviate the individual's fears of an environment which is hostile or lacks safety for them.

When both ruling planets are people-orientated, that is Venus and the Moon, the exalted lord, then Taurus needs human contact to achieve its prime motivation.

Often the presentation of a pleasing or attractive appearance will hold Taurus in good stead, especially if their adornment includes gifts from loved ones to comfort them when clothing or jewellery are reminders that they are loved, cherished and protected when they move out into their physical surroundings.

When Venus is in detriment in Aries it cannot see Taurus and this means the lord is not only disadvantaged by sign, it is also unable to manage the ascendant, or meet the need for physical security.

Likewise, if Venus is in Gemini or Sagittarius it cannot see Taurus, and although this Venus is sociable, enterprising or adventurous, it risks going too far out on a limb to be able to help its beleaguered ascendant. A Taurean ascendant cannot keep pace with the idiosyncrasies of a Venus in Gemini or Sagittarius as diversity and the absence of uniformity can be challenging for the traditional earth sign that wants nothing more than to blend safely into its surroundings.

These Venus lords of a Taurus ascendant draw way too much attention to the native and this will add to the native's distress if Venus leads them into an uncomfortable situation, only to abandon them because there is no sight between the two signs.

If Venus cannot commit to its duties through blindness, the Moon will be required to stand in for it, and hopefully the nocturnal luminary will be prepared to vouch for Taurus' physical security.

Virgo Ascendant ruled by Mercury

Virgo is a mutable earth sign and as its lord, Mercury will be required to provide the first house with all manner of information by which primary motivation is secured and the native can gain the attainment of a world which is free from danger or trouble.

Mercury is a constant adaptor to the changing variables of life. When road-works block normal driving routes, timetables go out the window, and the working routines of everyday life disintegrate, the lord of the ascendant copes with these fluctuations and springs into action to provide alternate options and new plans.

In the modern era of mobile phones and social media, Virgo is the most likely of the earth signs to be able to adjust to a constantly changing and evolving environment, provided its lord, Mercury, has the ability to communicate and to research, thereby staying one step ahead of disaster.

Mercury in Leo or Aquarius may not be so hazard-free as either sign cannot see Virgo, and as they are from the fixed modality, Mercury can become overly focused or fixated on details which are of little use in avoiding the state of aversion.

Mercury is now performing its tasks wearing a blindfold, and although it is an extremely resourceful planet, it cannot avoid the pitfalls of aversion.

The banditry side of Mercury must be able to appreciate the irony of being robbed of the ability to feel comfortable, and that options are denied to them and that action cannot be taken when needed. If Mercury is unable to manage its sign, and prime motivation for the Virgo rising chart is difficult, it cannot plan ahead and circumvent any worries about a safe and stress-free environment for the native.

Virgo rising with a Mercury in Leo can have trouble with knowing how to present themselves to the world. They may feel as though they are misunderstood as Virgo on the ascendant presents one image and Mercury in Leo in the twelfth house has a completely different concept of who that person really is under the facade.

Mercury in Aquarius has a certain level of alienation from their surroundings and can present as ailments or nervous conditions for the native, considering that Mercury in Aquarius would be in the sixth house from the sign of Virgo on the ascendant.

Aversion and the Descendant

> *"The last point* (the Descendant), *which puts the stars to rest after traversing heaven and, occupying the occident* (west), *looks down upon the submerged half of the sky, is concerned with the consummation of affairs and the conclusion of toil, marriages and banquets and the closing years of life, leisure and social intercourse and worship of the gods."* [60]

Marcus Manilius

The house at the other end of the horizon to the ascendant has a variety of concerns if its ruler lacks sight to the sign on the descendant. The seventh house represents marriages and intimate or supportive relationships, and when the ruler of its sign is absent, there can be dramatic repercussions for the chart's owner who desires a stable, long-term, and relatively drama-free relationship.

The seventh house is also the house of contracts, ranging from spoken, implied, or informal agreements to legally binding indentures.

If the house's sign is in aversion to its ruler's sign, then there are issues with misinterpretation, illusion and mismanagement, especially when it comes to contracts which benefit love, friendship, business or professional concerns.

Even though contact is broken between ruler and house, the ruling planet will still be expected to direct the native's personal and professional relationships. However, the type of setbacks which the seventh house will incur, will be described by the nature and the condition of its ruling planet and each planet, if in aversion to the house, will bring forth different commitment issues when it comes to dealings with other people.

It should be remembered that the descendant is in exact opposition to the ascendant, so the houses which are dark for the ascendant will be the same houses where the beleaguered ruler of the seventh has the potential to be located in the chart. Houses such as the second house, sixth house, eighth house and twelfth house will be the residences for rulers of the descendant who are blind to the seventh house.

When the descendant becomes the focus, the seventh house and any planets contained within it, are associated with Material Cause and ask the question: *From what material am I made?*

The material of the seventh house is made up of relationships, alliances, friendships, civil and personal contracts, as well as people who oppose me, or who display anything from mild irritation to open hostility towards me.

When its ruler aspects the seventh house, the nature of the planet describes Efficient Cause, the source of both allegiances and conflicts, whilst the same planet catalogues Formal Cause by providing details on the appearance, form and essence of the juxtaposition which places enemies and loved ones side by side in the same house.

Lastly, Final Cause is the fountainhead, the reason and purpose behind why I continue to explore a wide variety of relationships with other people, and the ruling planet must provide the answers for any questions posed by the three Causes.

When there is aversion between the planet's sign of rulership and its placement sign the door to relationship confusion and inconsistencies is permanently propped open. The inability to define the needs of a particular relationship causes emotional wavering between avoidance and commitment, or abstinence and infatuation, purely because the individual does not understand what is required of them, or how to explore their own feelings toward loyalty, fidelity or responsibility to an adult who is someone other than themselves.

An obsession to enter into relationships (no matter what the cost) can be borne from an absentee ruler, and an unhealthy focus on the partner, or 'hot and cold' behaviour towards the other party, can result from a ruling planet being blind to what is needed in order to nurture or maintain a vital and productive long-term relationship. Individuals can speak of 'the scales falling from their eyes' or of 'truly seeing someone for the first time' and this type of language can be a hint to what has been happening when the seventh house lord is in aversion to its house.

Seventh house is the umbrella under which one-to-one consultation sits in regards to relationships of a professional nature.

Relationships based on the advice of trained consultants or experts in their field, such as doctors, psychiatrists, dentists, lawyers, or agents acting on the native's behalf, can be tricky when the lord of the descendent cannot see its sign.

Finding the right person to represent you, or who will display the most beneficial knowledge, or who will provide the wisest counsel can be fraught with peril if the native does not trust their advisor, or if the advisor has a hidden agenda, or gives poor advice, as indicated by the ruler which is blind to its house.

Likewise, if the native themselves is the consultant and is engaged in an advisory capacity in exchange for remuneration, they may not feel empowered to make definite decisions. In this capacity they may have a clientele of people who depend exclusively on their instruction, but they can be someone who is 'working without a net' when the governing ruler has no power to direct its house.

If something goes terribly wrong because of their advice, then a civil or criminal court of law can be an alternate (and unpleasant) experience for a missing ruler with no sight to its house.

There are many types of contracts which exist outside the borders of civil or legally binding agreements.

For instance, spoken contracts bind people together through pledges, promises or devotion to one another, but in order to successfully commit to the task, both parties need to be aware of the liabilities and obligations as well as the benefits.

This kind of clarity is often absent when aversion exists between the house and its lord, and there is confusion when the lord of the seventh house cannot tell the difference between a partner who criticises from a place of love and concern, and the frustrated anger of someone who has already vacated the relationship.

At the other end of the scale, where there is discreet or subliminal combat between the native and another person, the absentee ruler of the seventh house struggles to discern between the friend who competes against them, or who uses a subtle form of "negging" (low-grade insults designed to shake a person's self-confidence), or the one who flatters them by imitating the native's actions.

The ruling planet is confused over whether this person is merely a jealous friend whose behaviour is irritating, or whether this is a person who is actually a foe and wishes them harm, or genuinely wants to discredit them.

The ascendant signifies the vitality and well-being of the physical body and an aspect of opposition from the descendant can indicate an attack on the body. Mystery illnesses, injuries and the body's poor performance or slow recovery from illness can occur as a result of a stressed seventh house with its lord in a sign of aversion. Misdiagnosis, or improper or aggressive treatment by a medical practitioner who is 'flying blind' because the symptoms are misleading can exacerbate a health problem and again, this can sometimes be traced back to a missing seventh house lord.

Aversion and the Highest Point (or Medium Coeli)

> *"Each cardinal angle enjoys a different influence; they vary according to their position, and they differ in rank. First place goes to the cardinal which holds sway at the summit of the sky (MC) and divides heaven in two with imperceptible meridian; enthroned on high this post is occupied by Glory so that she may claim all that is pre-eminent, arrogate all distinction, and reign by awarding honours of every kind.*
>
> *Hence comes applause, splendour, and every form of popular favour; hence the power to dispense justice in the courts, to bring the world under the rule of law, to make alliances with foreign nations on one's own terms, and to win fame relative to one's station."*[61]

Marcus Manilius

When the lord of the Midheaven aspects the zenith, or culmination point, the road to *"applause, splendour, and every form of popular favour"* can have a level of ease or difficulty according to the type of aspect. Regardless of the mysterious equation between constant effort and plain good luck, the individual can at least see themselves gaining recognition for their worldly efforts at some time in the future.

Public esteem, ambition, and reputation merge together as the amalgamation of the ruling planet's promised potential and its actualization are realized at the zenith and the highest of the angular houses. In a number of traditional references the mother and her family are signified by the tenth house (rather than the Mid-heaven), simply because it is the house which is opposite to the fourth, the house of the father.

In quadrant-style systems, the Midheaven becomes the beginning of the tenth house and this means that there is a fusion between the significations of the culmination point, and the house at the top of the chart. Therefore, the planet ruling the apex is responsible for the affairs of both the Midheaven and the tenth house.

If the lord is situated in a sign which is adverse to the sign on the Midheaven, then there are likely to be doubts, confusion or frustration over the individual's direction in life.

The individual may swing from one extreme of the 'career pendulum' to the other, vacillating between bouts of apathy or nonchalance regarding their career or future ambitions, to swaying in the opposite direction towards being obsessively focused on their direction in life.

When this occurs the result is likely to be resentment towards dead-end jobs, anger at slights inflicted by superiors and authority figures, and frustration at missed promotions or thwarted opportunities in their given field of work.

With a missing lord of the tenth the native can be robbed of the inner vision of seeing themselves in a position of power or success so that they are bereft of the opportunity to dream or envision what this may feel like to be *"enthroned on high (where) this post is occupied by Glory"* if only for a moment.

At the other end of the scale lies the person with Walter Mitty tendencies. *The Secret Life of Walter Mitty* is a short story written in 1939 by American author James Thurber about an ordinary and often ineffectual man who indulges in fantastic daydreams where he is the hero of the piece.

One famous quote from the book by the main character says:

"To see the world, things dangerous to come to, to see behind walls, draw closer, to find each other, and to feel. That is the purpose of life."

The individual with a ruling planet adverse to the tenth house (or the Midheaven) may be one who has exchanged the boredom or frustration of a dead-end career for the rich inner world of the imagination. Reality may have little to do with their aspirations and the inability to move their lives forward may create a personality which abandons their real-life ambitions for a fantasy world where they become a virtual hero.

Even in his daydreams Walter is robbed of a successful conclusion to his escapades as there are no scenarios which end in triumph and he is snatched from one experience to the next until the story ends with Mitty bravely facing his death before a firing squad. Interestingly, the author James Thurber lost sight in one eye in a childhood accident and when the resultant strain on his good eye became too great Thurber was diagnosed as clinically blind for most of his adult life. It is believed that Thurber suffered from Charles Bonnet syndrome, a neurological condition which causes complex visual hallucinations in people who have suffered some level of visual loss.

The Mid-heaven also signifies one's profile in the public arena and the danger of falsehoods, misrepresentation, malicious gossip, or inappropriate social media posts, is ever present when it comes to damaging or destroying a person's fragile reputation in a world where data and 'false news' is distributed with alarming speed.

In Shakespeare's *Othello* Cassio is a Florentine gentleman's soldier, a man of high morals who is elevated to the rank of lieutenant by Othello. Cassio's colleague is jealous of his success and sets in motion a plot which ruins Cassio's standing and ends in his public disgrace and expulsion from Othello's privileged inner circle.

Cassio has been an instrument of his own destruction through his blindness to his enemy's schemes and he bemoans the price he must pay for his folly.

CASSIO:

"Reputation, reputation, reputation!
O, I have lost my reputation!
I have lost the immortal part of myself, and what remains
is bestial."

Shakespeare's *Othello, Act 2, Scene 3, 281-284*

When the lord of the house of one's reputation is blind and either cannot see the problem, or does not know how to activate damage-control when something negative or offensive appears in public, the individual can be unaware of where the trouble stems from, or how their reaction to it can escalate a minor matter into a major controversy where everyone weighs into a debate over the issue.

The ability to defend oneself from the projections of others is always difficult, but the individual may need to take care that they are not over-sensitive or too defensive if they feel they are being judged or criticised for their opinions or actions, especially when they have no back up or support from the planet which rules the sign on the Midheaven.

The instability that aversion creates for this extremely exposed spot in the chart means that the individual, as a way to survive ridicule or accusation, will be inclined to engage in emotionally defensive manoeuvres designed to play down unsubstantiated claims, or to ward off unwanted feelings of guilt or shame.

They may deny their responsibility in the outcome, they may justify their actions, or they may deflect blame from themselves by briefly accepting responsibility, but then negating it by accusing someone of something far worse than their own behaviour.

All of these defence mechanisms come with a level of risk as the individual jeopardizes their standing if they are caught off-guard when all the facts may be impossible to verify. The nature of a planet which is hindered by its lack of vision means that it cannot fully protect its house and its guardianship is compromised by the fact that it is constantly having to play a game of 'catch-up' where others seem to be better equipped at tearing the native down as soon as they build their protective walls.

Recovering from a disadvantage or a defeat requires constant vigilance against repeated attack, snide remarks or even apathy, where interest has moved on to the next scandal, but the mark against one's name still remains, and sometimes a ruling planet in aversion lacks the energy, the focus or the desire to rebuild again from the beginning.

Midheaven (MC) or Tenth Sign?

When the chart is set in the Whole Sign house system the zenith or apex point can be in another elevated house, and the tenth house and Midheaven may not be sharing the same ruling planet.

If this is the case, both planets will need to be examined, as one may show an improvement over the other, or if the Midheaven's lord is missing through aversion, the lord of the tenth house may be able to stand in as a proxy for the affairs of the career or reputation.

The active or present planet ruling the tenth sign may be capable of diffusing some of the tension created by the absentee Mid-heaven lord, and can give direction when the MC seems lost or abandoned by its ruler.

One of the most noticeable differences between the Midheaven and the tenth sign, is that the tenth house defines the mother and her family heritage, whilst the Midheaven does not represent the female side of the family, if it is not in the tenth house.

The lord of the tenth house in a sign of aversion to its own sign, can be inclined to view mother or father's partner (step-mother) as difficult, treacherous or untrustworthy.

These feelings may be unjustified, but a missing lord is often nervous of a nurturing figure whom they believe has been unavailable or unwilling to care for their emotional or physical needs during their childhood or even as a supporting, loving parent in their adult years.

Aversion and the Lowest Point
(or Imum Coeli)

"The next point, though situate in the lowest point, bears the world poised on its eternal base; in outward aspect its influence is less, but is greater in utility. It controls the foundations of things and governs wealth; it examines to what extent desires are accomplished by the mining of metal and what gain can issue from a hidden source." [62]

Marcus Manilius

The lowest point of the chart is often overlooked when the four angles are examined in regard to the native's direction in life.

The ascendant gains dominance at the beginning of life and continues to occupy focus through its desire or need for primary motivation to be met as life continues to change.

Romance, loyalty, allegiances and conflict complement and oppose the ascendant at every turn, whilst the Midheaven, ten houses or signs further on from the ascendant, brings the culmination of aspirations, and the compulsion to carve a place in the world as an adult.

The traditional meaning for the IC was the place where hidden treasures are found, so when Manilius talks of mining metal, he is being literal, and the idea of claiming back something precious from the earth is associated with the fourth house.

However, the metaphor of digging from the past and finding untold riches, especially from father's ancestry, is part of the glory of the Nadir.

> *"I moved around for work, but I think I also like to move.*
> *Whilst there's a certain rootlessness and solitude to nomadism,*
> *I suppose that I am, as my father asserts, fundamentally a*
> *Bedouin. I am driven to exploration . . ."*

Diana Abu-Jaber, *Origin: A Novel*

The sense of belonging from the IC is much stronger than just the link to father, and the desire to understand where we come from, after generations have passed, not only provides a foundation for the chart, but also a foundation for who we are, and where we are going in life.

When the lord of the IC is missing through the unfortunate reckoning of aversion, then the individual suffers a feeling of disconnection or severance from their genealogy, and although it may not be a dynasty of power, wealth or great influence, there is still a feeling of undirected grief at such a loss.

Father may literally be missing, elusive or difficult to understand or relate to, and this parent may have wounds of their own which are difficult or too painful for healing.

This emotion of rootlessness will have a direct effect on the Midheaven at the top of the chart, as the past and the future are connected, and if the ruling planet of the IC is unable to assist or define the fourth house in the chart, then the unconscious yearnings for belonging in either family, or the world in general, can be hard for the native to express in words.

At worst, it can lead to self-sabotage as the individual may feel that any success, stability or happiness is not truly deserved or earned by them when their grounding, preparation or foundations are missing from their lives.

Imum Coelum (IC) or Fourth Sign?

When the chart is set in the Whole Sign house system, the Nadir can be in a sign other than the fourth sign from the ascendant.

If this is the case, the movement of the Imum Coeli from the fourth sign is either to the preceding third sign, or to the sign following, to that of the fifth sign from the ascendant. If this is the case, then there can be significant changes in how the individual perceives the roots at the lowest point of the chart.

The family can broaden out to include a sense of belonging in the community if the IC falls into the third house, or the history of sibling relationship become especially important to a sense of belonging.

If the IC's lord is situated in a sign which is blind to the IC then the relationships may be painful or any residual tension can be difficult to resolve, even when all parties have reached adulthood.

Even keeping an open dialogue with loved ones can be stressful, if the ruling planet is not able to assist or direct from its position in the chart.

Flare-ups and unresolved jealousies can occur when family inheritances are discussed and reconciliation, which requires tact and forgiveness, can seem almost impossible when there is no direction from a ruling planet.

Blindness to these houses from the ruler shows a sensitivity felt by the individual in how they were treated or viewed by the parent, and the resultant feigned indifference to the parent in question often hides a much deeper feeling of rejection.

The ruling planet of the MC or IC will give some indication as to how the individual felt slighted or ignored by the relevant parent or the parent's partner, and in the case of a Whole Sign chart where the angles differ from the fourth/tenth house cusp, the individual may try to compensate through another planet in the chart.

The difference in rulership between the lord of the IC and the lord of the fourth house can bring resolution to family woes if at least one of these planets aspects its sign. It would be unusual, but not impossible, for both ruling planets to be in aversion to their signs on the IC and the fourth house cusp, but if this does happen, it becomes a major statement of the chart.

When the lowest point of the chart has a ruler in aversion to its sign the effect can have long-term repercussions as Manilius tells us that although *"in outward aspect its influence is less, but is greater in utility. It controls the foundations of things".* When we are unable to understand the foundation of the chart or to negotiate from a starting point the reverberation through the MC and IC axis becomes compromised because if we do not know where we came from we cannot know where we are going in the future.

In the words of writer and philosopher George Santayana *"Those who cannot remember the past are condemned to repeat it"* and a blind ruler of the Imum Coeli may not have the power to stop the mistakes of the past becoming the tragedies of the future.

Aversion and the Other Houses

The remaining eight houses are the succedent and cadent houses and lack of sight by their ruling planet will likely create issues around the following dot points.

The fifth house –

- Difficulty in seeing a benefit from the house of good fortune.
- Can lead to a negative or pessimistic attitude towards life.
- Affects pleasures, entertainments, friendships, and children.
- Difficulty in feeling joys of life can be accessed or fully appreciated.

The eleventh house –

- Misunderstandings with others especially in group or social situations.
- Lack of consistency or success in one's aims or aspirations.
- Isolation from friends, social activities, joint projects, or committees.
- Difficulty in feeling comfortable in group involvement or social situations.
- Blind to social benefits, benefits from mentorship, difficulty in visualising hopes and dreams.

The second house –

- Inability to see resources, money is 'invisible' in some way.
- Money is of no concern or there is no need to provide for oneself, or of great concern.
- Inaccessible or difficult to use, or gain benefit from one's resources.
- Poor balance between money in and money out, according to nature of ruling planet.
- Can be blind-sided by tradesmen or people employed for projects, plumber, builder etc.

The eighth house –

- Difficulty in accessing joint resources – those of the partner, or from joint partnerships.
- Gaining resources from social benefits or financial institutions.
- Poor management in passing funds from 2nd to 8th house or vice versa – i.e. bill paying, gaining loans, tax difficulties.

The third house –

- Blindness concerning short journeys, siblings, learned knowledge, or personal skills.
- Difficulty in learning areas, early education, poor written or collection of information.
- Can be challenged motor skills or poor co-ordination depending on the ruling planet.

The ninth house –

- Misunderstandings, lack of consistency or success, fear or isolation from ninth house representatives, i.e. educators, religious figures, legal or professional people, foreigners.
- Insecurities with higher learning facilities, religious or spiritual concerns.

The sixth house –

- Inconsistencies in management of daily routine, diet or maintenance of health.
- Constantly interrupted patterns and changes in plans or stable work arrangements.
- Unawareness of over-work, stress or exhaustion in achieving work deadlines.

The twelfth house –

- Inability to see oncoming danger, sorrows, bad fortune, imprisonment, illness, depression.
- Unreasonable fear of things or situations that lead to being 'turned away' from life.
- Inconsistency, limited resources or little resilience in dealing with extreme difficulty.
- Feelings of paranoia or persecution towards the unknown or different elements in society.

Aversion: Example Chart – Antoine de Saint-Exupéry

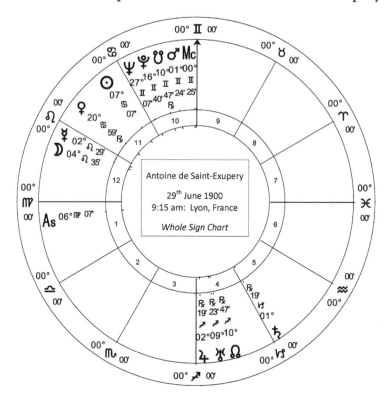

Fig. 81 Chart of Antoine de Saint-Exupéry

Antoine Marie Jean-Baptiste Roger de Saint-Exupéry (1900-1944) was a French aristocrat, writer, poet and pioneering aviator. He is best remembered for his novella *The Little Prince,* which Saint-Exupéry conceived and wrote from December 1940 to April 1943 when he was living in New York, in exile from his home country.

"The Little Prince is a jeu d'espirit (a light-hearted display) *but it has its roots in despair."*[63]

The Little Prince has been translated into over 300 languages. It has become the world's most translated book, with the exception of religious works, including the Bible, which is the current record-holder.[64]

"Born into a large and well-connected Catholic aristocratic family, Antoine spent his childhood within a matriarchal household, in the setting of a large chateau near Lyon, an immense garden and a nearby airfield.

He was to spend much of his life as a young man in the air, intensively so between 1926 and 1932, when he flew for what was later to become the Aéropostale – first carrying the mail from Toulouse to Morocco, then taking charge of a remote and ill-equipped airstrip at Cape Juby (a West African desert outpost bordering the Atlantic).[65]

Aversion Table For Antoine de Saint-Exupéry

House	Sign on Cusp	House's Ruling Planet	Ruling Planet's Sign	Relationship Between The Two Signs (Sight or Aversion)
1	♍	☿	♌	**AVERSION**
2	♎	♀	♋	Aspect (□)
3	♏	♂	♊	**AVERSION**
4	♐	♃	♐	Rulership
5	♑	♄	♑	Rulership
6	♒	♄	♑	Like-Engirdling
7	♓	♃	♐	Aspect (□)
8	♈	♂	♊	Aspect (✶)
9	♉	♀	♋	Aspect (✶)
10	♊	☿	♌	Aspect (✶)
11	♋	☽	♌	**AVERSION**
12	♌	☉	♋	**AVERSION**

Fig. 82 Aversion table for Antoine de Saint-Exupéry

Chart with Houses in Aversion to their Rulers

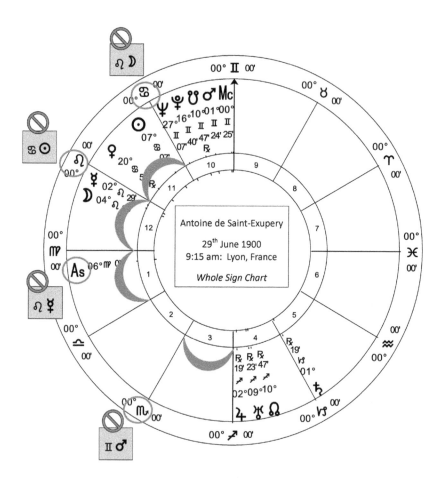

*Fig. 83 Saint-Exupéry's Chart with Four Houses
(11, 12, 1 and 3) and their Lords in a State of Blindness (Aversion)*

Rulers in Aversion to their Houses:
One By One

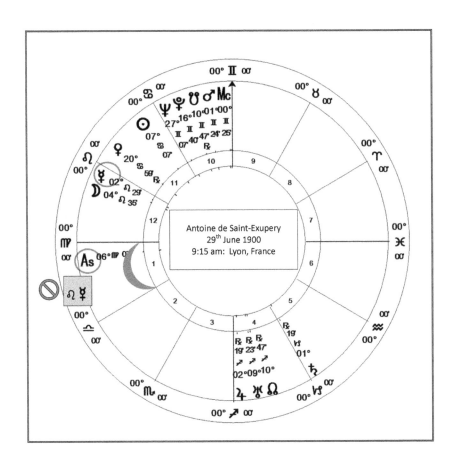

Fig. 84 First House Aversion

Mercury in Leo (In 12th House) Cannot See the Ascendant

The Penguin Classic of *The Little Prince* (1995) introduces the book and the author in the following manner:

"In the case of The Little Prince the circumstances (of its writing) *were urgent and inauspicious, and this charming story was conceived 'in extremis', at the crisis point of an entire life.*

Readers familiar with Saint-Exupéry's life and death have felt that The Little Prince, ostensibly for children, is perhaps a piece of autobiography – an attempt to sublimate the difficulties of his marriage, or to fend off the present for a remembered world of childhood, or even an act of mysterious farewell."

There are two protagonists in *The Little Prince*. The prince who leaves his principality, a tiny asteroid, and wanders the universe until one day he arrives on Earth, and the airman who has crashed into the desert and who is the narrator of the story. Both characters, and even the title itself *(The Little Prince)* relate to Antoine's Mercury in Leo, which is hidden in the twelfth house unable to assist the ascendant. Mercury's reaction to this state is likely to disconnect the author from reality by creating a fantasy world where the dialogue keeps the reader guessing Antoine's true nature.

Tonio (to his friends) has been described as *'loquacious and someone who loved conversation'* and yet he was also an extremely private and reserved man with a strong need for social barriers when others tried to understand the man behind the friendly facade.

Extremes in his behaviour are well-recorded and any Jungian psychologist could fill years trying to determine if Saint-Exupéry was an introverted extrovert or an extroverted introvert. In truth, he was probably both as Leo Mercury yearns for praise and attention, but Mercury's inability to manage the first house of one's behaviour, habits and personality makes this person self-conscious and inhibited in many ways.

His isolation began early in life when his beloved father suffered a fatal stroke on the train station prior to Tonio's fourth birthday, and the family returned to his mother's family home and lived on the goodwill of his father's name and heritage (Mercury is disposited by the Sun and is conjunct the Moon and trining Jupiter and Uranus in the fourth house).

Tonio hid his depression from the world but he could not hide his failing health, his alcoholism, and his physical pain (as a result of his multitude of crashes) with banter and clever dialogue. In his wife's memoirs, published in the late 1990's Consuelo describes him as cruel, negligent, greedy, self-centred and wasteful. These flaws in his character are totally at odds with the characters in *The Little Prince,* especially the prince himself who although constantly perplexed by the adult world, is intrinsically kind, thoughtful and generous in his thoughts and actions. Mercury in Leo describes what Tonio would love to be (the little prince) but he cannot reconcile this image with his own behaviour when Mercury cannot see the first house. His mind is denied the peace he seeks from the stark desert environment, or from the empty skies, or the murder mysteries he reads when he is in the air, and instead splits his world into two very different parts.

In *The Little Prince* there are constant references to things which are concealed or are not what they appear to be. The elephant inside the boa constrictor, the sheep inside the box, the seeds in the earth, the fox in his hole, the secret well in the Sahara, the treasure buried in the old house – all references to the hidden, the unspoken, the complicit.

In parallel to an ascendant with no connection to its ruler, Saint-Exupéry struggled to find a place in the world where he could belong. The primary motivation for earth is a need for physical security, yet Tonio constantly left the earth for the freedom of the skies. He was an impoverished aristocrat who had rejected his family's bigotry and snobbery, a socialist who did not belong with the masses – he hated his mother writing letters addressed to 'The Count' – and an aviator who was rejected by his peers because he broke the golden rule of telling the world about this secret brigade of airmen who lived like pirates of the sky.

All of these experiences create havoc for Mercury who cannot control the vagaries of his mind or the inconsistencies of his personality. Tonio literally crashes into the earth on more than one occasion, breaking his physical body with each new incident, perhaps because he simply cannot see it rushing up to meet him.

Mars in Gemini (In 10ᵗʰ House) Cannot See the Third House

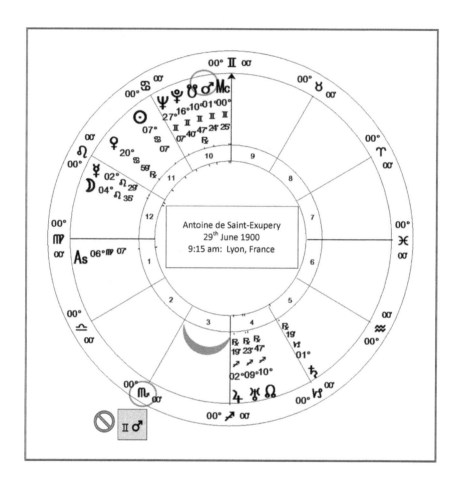

Fig. 85 Third House Aversion

In the introduction, translator, T. Cuffe says: "*Saint-Exupéry claimed in adult life to have been delivered early and irreparably into unhappiness, sent to school in the rigid conservative and royalist establishments of his class and time, where he fared badly.*"[66]

Mars in aversion to one of its houses is likely to show agitation or frustration as it is a planet whose nature is to be constantly on guard, to be both protective and cautious, when it comes to one of its houses.

When Mars can see its houses it is aware of any approaching threat or danger and it prepares its strategy carefully so that both the native, and the affairs of the house, are well looked after.

Blindness means vulnerability or lack of control for Mars, so when Antoine's third house is left unprotected there are certain situations which he cannot control. When Mars has lost sight of its house there can be unresolved anger and feelings of resentment or heartache accompanied by a nagging fear that one's mettle will be tested and one will be found wanting when courage or bravery are badly needed.

One of the most sensitive areas for Saint-Exupéry was his feelings of being robbed of his childhood. The themes of exile and isolation are strong in *The Little Prince*, as Tonio believed he had been exiled from his family, his siblings and his beloved home when he most needed them when he was despatched off to boarding school to gain a decent upper-class education.

Saint-Exupéry once wrote to his mother *"I am not sure that I have lived since childhood"*. The book's introduction continues with this theme saying that all of his works contain highly charge accounts of childhood and that in Antoine's mind escape through flying took him back to a time when he had imagined himself to be happy as a child – *"and flying itself was an art of memory, triggered by hostile and threatening circumstances."*

His removal from his siblings and the security of his mother's love during his formative years left a wound and Tonio needed the little prince, an alien being from a tiny asteroid, to expunge the anger he carried within him for the lost years of his childhood. The fact that Mars in Gemini conjuncts his Midheaven shows the power of his final work, but Saint-Exupéry died before seeing the true effect his little prince would have on the world.

It is easy to see the dashing and reckless aviator turned writer in Antoine's Gemini Mars conjunct his Mid-heaven, but when it is related back to his childhood experiences, the ex-communicated Mars feels bitterness and resentment in being given little choice in the decision to banish him from his home at an early age, and to cast him into a rigid and frightening early education system.

Third house describes our physical skills and the acts we can perform with dexterity and ease. Mars ruling the third house should have equipped this man with lightening reflexes and excellent hand to eye co-ordination. And yet, by all accounts, Antoine was a below-par aviator when it came to actually flying a plane. His crashes were a combination of poor decisions, inattentiveness and a slack compliance to flying protocol, yet he had a sharp, mathematical mind as during the 1930s he patented fourteen inventions for the aircraft industry, including navigation and landing aids.[67]

"On one flight with a failing engine, his mechanic recalled, "Saint-Exupéry simply started doodling cartoons which he handed back to me with a big grin." Lost in thoughts about writing or philosophy, he had a reputation for being absent-minded at the controls."

He suffered permanent disabilities from serious flying accidents, and yet he continued to take terrible risks and to ignore 'third house' instructions on how he could avoid future danger. Mars in Gemini can see its house with Aries on the cusp, the eighth house, and Saint-Exupéry's choice of career meant that he was constantly flirting with death, whereby *"the accident rate in the fragile open-cockpit airplanes was appalling, and downed pilots risked capture and torture by desert tribes if not death by flame or thirst. Yet in flying, Saint-Exupéry found freedom and fulfilment."* [68]

In the last year of his life, when he was exiled from France and he was flying reconnaissance missions for the US Government, *"he clumsily damaged an $80,000 airplane in the middle of the war. Only in the spring of 1944 did he manage to talk his way back into active service, in a plane into which he could not fit, that he could not comfortably fly, communicating with the control tower in a language he could not speak. Over the next months he knew every kind of disaster. He experienced engine trouble and landing difficulties, he fainted in flight, he was pursued by enemy aircraft, he battled a fire on board. Any one of his 1944 missions could have been his last."* [69]

Antoine had to be helped into his pilot's suit because he could not move one side of his body, and part of the plane's control panel was beyond his sight, because after he had been strapped into his seat, he could not turn his head sufficiently to see the dials.

Saint-Exupéry disappeared on 31ˢᵗ July 1944 and his death added to the intrigue of *The Little Prince* until wreckage was found in 1998, but it was 200 kilometres from where Saint-Exupéry was supposed to be taking aerial photos for the military. The family and the French Government debunked the discovery and it took six years for French authorities to confirm in April 2004, that it was indeed his plane. Saint-Exupéry has always been lauded as a national war hero, but a combination of several factors has suggested that Antoine took his own life on his last flight.

His missions were coming to an end, and he must have realized that with this, would be the end of his days as a pilot. The location and the evidence of a vertical crash, the lack of bullet holes or combat damage to the plane, added to his recorded depression, feelings of isolation and ill-health seem to make it less likely that his death was a result of a war skirmish in the skies.

Saint-Exupéry was an avid reader and he would read until take-off, never checking the plane's equipment or gauges but leaving the pilot's duties to the navigator or the engineers. Once the plane had taken off, Antoine continued to read in the sky and throughout the entire journey, and some of his crashes, and there were many, were because he was off-course or low on petrol. When he arrived at his destination, there were stories of him circling the airfield until he had finished reading his book, rather than landing with his reading incomplete.

The third house is our world of familiarity. In the recent past, it described our forays to the local shops, our bill-paying outlets and banking locations. Where we went to the local library or the local pub, but many of these physical locations around the neighbourhood have been replaced by internet shopping and on-line banking. Social media has become the new third house, but in Saint-Exupéry's times, these would have been local areas grown up in, and a familiarity which is repeated in adulthood as people settled into their neighbourhoods and became known around the district.

Saint-Exupéry shunned this familiarity, was excluded from, or did not feel the need to keep in contact with familiar surroundings once he became an airman in his early 20's. Familiarity became foreign dusty lands and constant rovings between Africa, Morocco, Argentina, Patagonia, London (in the early years of the war until he was branded a traitor to France by General Charles De Gaulle), and Northern America, where he wrote *The Little Prince*. His escape from the banal and an ordinary life lay in flying and thereby removing himself from familiarity as often, and as dangerously, as he possibly could.

The third house in a chart signifies 'brotherhood' and Saint-Exupéry certainly loved his fellow airmen and felt bonded to these risk-takers, yet he did not see the damage he would do to this bond by publishing tales about their lives, and breaking the code of silence which was important to these pioneers of aviation. His Mars in Gemini certainly gained notoriety, but he could never heal the wounds and rejoin the brotherhood, and this was yet another mark of rejection and isolation.

Saint-Exupéry had three sisters and a blond-haired brother, two years younger than him named Francois. The two boys were sent to a boarding school in Switzerland during the First World War. When Francois contracted rheumatic fever at age fifteen, Antoine was the sole family member at Francois' deathbed. Saint-Exupery later wrote that Francois *"remained motionless for an instant. He did not cry out. He fell as gently as young tree falls"*.

When the little blond-haired prince dies at the end of the book, Saint-Exupéry recounts the same words to describe the prince's passing as he used for Francois' death. His mother had been a widow since Tonio was four years old, and now, with the death of Francois, he was expected to be the 'man of the house' amongst a household of women.

It is not unknown for a house whose ruler is absent to suffer some major trauma in life, and for the seventeen year old Antoine, the connection to his remaining siblings had been broken with the death of his only brother and closest confidant, a brother who had shared his same misery at being banished from home to attend boarding school in their early years. His anger and despair at bearing the full responsibility of his brother's death is shown by the Mars at the top of his chart and he further alienated his sisters by marrying a foreigner, rather than a fellow French aristocrat, a sin for which they never forgave him for his impetuousness in bringing someone into their family whom they believed was well beneath their station and their bloodline.

Jupiter in rulership in the fourth house has a tight aspect of opposition to the Gemini Mars on the Mid-heaven. Jupiter shows the aristocracy of the family, but it is retrograde, so there is the lack of viable funds as well. Saint-Exupéry died before *The Little Prince* was published in France, and as he had no children, the royalties from the book were shared between Consuelo, his wife, and his three sisters.

Jupiter rules the seventh house as well as the fourth house and Consuelo was required to live in France to be entitled to claim her share of his legacy. The sisters would have nothing to do with her, and even in 2000, on the anniversary celebrations of his birth in France, his sister's family refused to acknowledge Consuelo's existence, and her importance in his life. When asked for the reasons for her exclusion, his great-great niece answered: *"She wasn't a Saint-Exupéry."*[70]

One final story on Mars's inability to see the third house. During World War II Saint-Exupéry flew a number of missions taking reconnaissance photos for the Allies. His colleagues and fellow pilots were alarmed at his poor physical condition and the risks he was increasingly taking and actively planned to keep him grounded.

Together with his commanding officer (Mars on MC) who was also a close friend, the airmen formed a plot to "accidentally" show him the plans for the impending invasion of France, and then to argue that he could not fly in case the Germans shot him down and he became a prisoner of war and revealed the plans under torture. This seemed like a brilliant idea to keep him safe and out of harm's way on the ground (Mars ruling 3rd and 8th house).

Except that on the day of his final flight the commanding officer was ill and absent from duty when Antoine took off in his battered plane. Reportedly, the commanding officer "bawled out" his staff when he learned the grounding scheme hadn't been implemented, but by then, it was too late. Instead, Mars activated the eighth house – Mars in the tenth in aversion to the third house – sometimes all the intentions in the world cannot avoid the problems of a house blind to its ruler.

Moon in Leo (In 12th House) Cannot See the Eleventh House

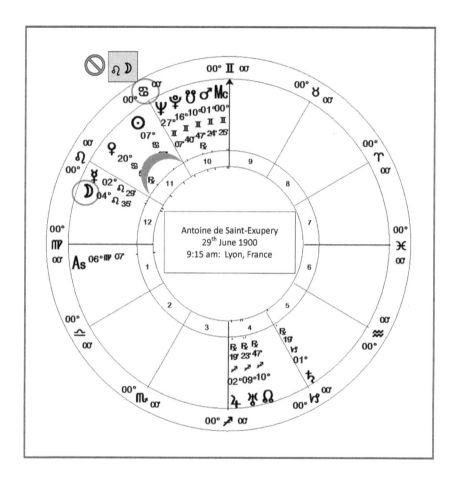

Fig. 86 Eleventh House Aversion

Firmicus Maternus writes: *"The Moon in the twelfth house by day with nothing on the ascendant indicates loss of inheritance, miserable occupations, and journeys."* [71]

A Moon in twelfth house can be a challenge for any individual, but when it cannot see its own house of Cancer, and is also conjunct the lord of the Ascendant (Mercury), which is also blind to its house, then the physical and emotional life of this individual is bound to be marked by injury, illness or emotional pain.

By all accounts, Saint-Exupéry shared a close and loving relationship with his mother (Mercury also rules the tenth sign, the house of mother).

Records of their letters and constant correspondence over the years of his flying show a tender and affectionate bond between mother and son, and Antoine is said to have described his mother as a beautiful, intelligent, and caring woman.[72] Whilst the rest of his family rejected or refused to acknowledge his wife, Consuelo, after his death, his mother maintained contact with Consuelo when she moved to France (Mercury ruler of mother -10th house - trines Jupiter ruler of wife – 7th house) until her own death in 1972, at the age of ninety- two. Consuelo died seven years later in 1979.

Unfortunately, this bond did not extend to his attitude to women in general, and perhaps this natural link between mother and women as an adult (Venus in Cancer is disposited by the Moon), is one of the indications that in social situations, the ruler of the eleventh, the Moon, was blind to its house. Saint-Exupéry was constantly on the prowl for lovers or female companionship and there are several references to Antoine's treatment of women. One commentator writes *"he preached solidarity among men while treating women with contempt."*[73]

The hypocrisy of a man who bragged of making love to several women on the same afternoon, but who complains about his wife's party-going and writes in a letter to Consuelo, *"Why can't you be here to wipe my brow and make my tea?"*[74] is reminiscent of a Moon in Leo which is incapable of comparing one's own behaviour with someone else's and failing to see the similarities.

The first biography published after Saint-Exupéry's death was written by his lover of many years, Nelly de Vogue, under the pseudonym Pierre Chevrier in 1949, five years after his death. In the book Nelly describes him as childish, egotistical, a flier with unimpressive aviation skills, and a compulsive womaniser. She claims that he once forced Benzadrine down her throat so that she could read his new pages with unflagging attention.

However, the distance between past truths and the present realities is interesting as Nelly, aged 92 at the time of the article in 2000, ran the Paris Institute dedicated to his memory, and described Saint-Exupéry as 'Christ-like' when interviewed at his centenary celebrations in 2000.

The conflict between Saint-Exupéry's ego and his desire to show-off his knowledge of a secret society (Moon in Leo in the twelfth) is directly at odds with his Moon's need to be loved and accepted by his friends and his fellow aviators. He brags that he can belong anywhere saying that when he mingled with the working class *"there was no noticeable rank and no social classes"*, yet they were all aware of his family's background.

In one of his books he wrote *"The pilots were joined together by a crusade: the mail had to get through. A postcard to a lover in Rabat was more important than either plane or pilot. The only reward worth having was the recognition of other flyers."*

And yet, Saint-Exupéry risked all this, and lost, by exposing this world to the public, and enjoying the fruits of his own personal success, at the expense of his friends' privacy. So far as they were concerned, he became a social pariah with the exposé of their lifestyle in newspapers and his later books.

Saint-Exupéry's eleventh house is unaspected to the ruling Moon and this creates a state of aversion. However, in his chart, many of the comments on his life overlap between statements which could be attributed to either the Moon in Leo in the twelfth house unaspecting Cancer on the eleventh, or to the Sun in Cancer in the eleventh, with no sight to the twelfth house with Leo on the cusp.

The term 'generosity' is used to describe the situation that two planets are disposited by one another, yet do not share an aspect between them.

Twelfth century Jewish astrologer, Abraham ibn Ezra is believed to be echoing the Latin version of Abu Ma'shar's *Abbreviation* when he writes:

"Generosity *is when two planets are in each other's domicile, or exaltation, or some other rulership; even though they do not join nor aspect one another, there is (still) reception between them."*[75]

Statements such as *"Saint-Exupéry's friends saw a good deal of The Little Prince. The author waved the book around proudly, boyishly, as if handing over a kind of personal manifesto. He demanded reader's reports from those who asked to borrow a precious copy."*[76]

Or, the total inability to take into consideration any inconvenience his behaviour might incur with a self-obsessed Moon in Leo which loves the limelight, yet also wants to hide away in the twelfth house. *"A dinner he was due to attend in Algiers was held up for an hour while the guests watched his plane circle as he finished the last pages of a detective novel."*

So much of the myth has been confused with the man who often struggled to find happiness, peace of mind and even a moral code of decency and compassion.

His literary executor, Frédéric d'Agay, described Antoine in 2000 in the following manner: *"You will never understand Saint-Exupéry unless you see him as a modern knight-errant of the highest moral principles."*[77]

And yet his many weaknesses and human foibles also show a man who is insecure, terrified, and in need of companionship, so much so, that he must find it in an imaginary blond child-prince from an asteroid in the furthermost corner of the universe.

Sun in Cancer (11th House) Cannot See Twelfth House

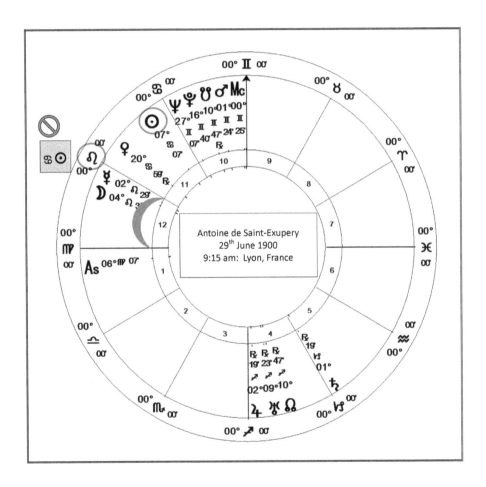

Fig. 87 Twelfth House Aversion

The loss of his father before his fourth birthday is perhaps the first time that Saint-Exupéry's Sun in Cancer is aware that life is filled with terrors, sorrows and losses, and that without sight, there can be no preparation for grief and fatherlessness.

His father may have been well-connected with long-established roots in the French aristocracy but when he suffered a fatal stroke in 1904, he left his family in an unstable financial situation.

After the Viscount died, his wife and five children moved to a castle in Lyon belonging to his mother's aunt, the Countess de Tricaud.

Antoine's Sun rules his twelfth house, and this lack of connection may have added to a number of his weaknesses. In France, he is close to a national saint; he is the only 20th century writer to feature on a French banknote, an airport in Lyon is named after him, as are dozens of avenues, schools and public buildings.

The asteroid 2578 Saint-Exupéry was named in his honour after it was discovered in 1975.

The fictional asteroid which is the home of the little prince, asteroid B612, has been adopted as the name for a non-profit foundation formed for planetary defence against asteroid or near-Earth (NEO) objects colliding with our planet. This connection between what is real and what is myth is a continuous reminder of Saint-Exupéry's Sun and its rulership over the twelfth house.

His disappearance into the ocean in 1944, and the subsequent recovery of his plane and a bracelet bearing his and Consuelo's name sixty years later, only adds to the twelfth house mystery, increases sales of his books, and the legend of his name.

The centenary of Saint-Exupéry's birth was an opportunity to show France's love and appreciation for their own beloved *Little Prince*. One of the organisers, Alain Braun, was quoted as saying that France was always in search of a day of glory and that Saint-Exupéry's own personality reflected France's need for a national hero. *"He was like that. He was a star, a narcissist. He saw himself as a hero and a genius and decided to become a hero and a genius. And then he died for France."*[78]

The articles, books, honours and accolades that continue to follow the myth of Antoine de Saint-Exupéry over seventy years after his death, cannot describe how it felt for his Cancer Sun to crave love and attention, yet at the same time to find that attention repugnant and to fill him with fear at the thought of his exposure to the world. The fear that he would no longer be able to fly, or that he would lose his identity once he lost his flying licence. The fear that he would lose his popularity, his charisma, his sexual attraction, his very sanity, any or all of these fears may have manifested from a variety of sources – his Leo Mercury and Moon unable to see their houses of social interaction with the world, his Gemini Mars caught up in his childhood misery, or his Cancer Sun ruling the dark twelfth house.

The Little Prince contains a number of adult characters whose existence is both ridiculous, and modelled on Tonio's own fears. Before arriving on Earth, the little prince visits six other asteroids, each one occupied by a single absurd figure whose purpose is pointless, and whose actions are blindly disconnected from reality.

A Cancer Sun which cannot see its house – the darkest of the twelve houses – is represented in *The Little Prince* by the author who has created these characters to mimic his own personal demons.

In succession, the little prince meets a king with no subjects, and then a conceited man who (rightly) believes himself to be the most admirable person on his otherwise uninhabited planet.

In reflection of the author's own dependency on alcohol, the prince next travels to an asteroid to find a drunkard who drinks to forget the shame of being a drunkard, after which he lands on an asteroid where a businessman is endlessly counting stars over which he believes to have ownership.

Next, a lamplighter whose futile existence is bound by routine and honour, where he has undertaken to light, extinguish and relight every lamp as his asteroid changes immediately from dark to light to dark again. The play between light and dark is reminiscent of Saint-Exupéry's own Sun (light) which is blind to its house (dark). The last asteroid is the home of an elderly geographer who is so wrapped up in theory that he never actually explores the world that he claims to be mapping, again reflecting the notion of blindness or inability to relate to the real world.

Even the little prince is bound by pointless routine as, when he lives on his own tiny asteroid, he sweeps out three tiny volcanoes and collects the seeds from the baobab trees which threaten to over-run the asteroid's surface. His one meaningful task is to tend to the beautiful rose which lives on his asteroid and which he dearly loves, even though she complains consistently about his care.

The quandary for Saint-Exupéry's Sun, and even his Moon, which are both luminaries averse to their respective houses, is the fact that he both craves attention, and is terrified of it at the same time. Both luminaries' connection to the twelfth house (Sun ruling it and Moon located in it) shows this dilemma, but it is somewhat resolved by the author in *The Little Prince*. The first time the stranded airman meets the little prince, he is woken by a funny little voice saying: *"If you please – draw me a sheep!"*

The airman proceeds to draw a sheep but each time it is dismissed by the little prince. One sheep is deemed to be very sickly, one is a ram with horns, and the third one is too old, and is rejected because the prince wants one that will live a long time.

Finally in exasperation, the airman draws a rectangular box with air-holes and tells the prince that the sheep is tiny and is located inside the box. This drawing delights the little prince as he looks into one of the holes and declares *"He's not as small as all that – Look! He's gone to sleep!"*

For Tonio trying to please everyone – family, fellow aviators, publishers, friends, critics, loved ones – was exhausting and often a futile task (like sweeping out volcanoes). But when one can hide inside an imaginary box, a box that is safe and dark and hidden from the world, then perhaps that is how a man with luminaries fraught with worry learns how to live as a large child in an adult's world.

Not only manages to survive life for forty four years but leaves behind an incredible legacy which touches the hearts of millions who also struggle through life as children trapped in the body of a grown up.

CHAPTER SIX

The Culminations of Mercury and Jupiter

Mercury and Jupiter share a unique relationship in the Thema Mundi chart.

Together they rule the four mutable signs and although they are enemies according to al-Biruni's *Table of Friendship and Enmity (A Tiny Universe,* Chapter Four), there are worse enemies in the chart than Mercury and Jupiter.

Saturn's opposition to both the Sun and the Moon through the rulerships of Capricorn vs. Cancer and Aquarius vs. Leo are much bigger in terms of archetypal combat than Mercury and Jupiter's problems. Saturn pitched against the luminaries is the battle between light and darkness or life and death. The Sun and Moon breathe spirit and energy into a living organism but Saturn as the lord of Time waits patiently in the wings for the physical structure's weaknesses to appear and for its mechanisms to slow and falter until eventually all bodily functions close down at the moment of death.

The quintessential battle between the sexes is apparent in the relationship between the female archetype Venus and its male counterpart Mars as Thema Mundi demonstrates through the tension of Venus and Mars (Love and Strife) beginning with Aries opposing Libra and immediately followed by Taurus opposing Scorpio.

The modality of the cardinal cross accentuates the first battle, and is featured in the four angles of the Thema Mundi chart.

Cancer (Moon) opposes Capricorn (Saturn) across the ascendant and descendant axis, whilst Libra (Venus) on the Imum Coeli opposes Aries (Mars) on the Midheaven in Thema Mundi's vertical axis.

The fixed modality cross follows the cardinal signs' cross, and features three of the four planets from the cardinal cross.

However, in the fixed sign model, the Sun has been substituted for the Moon, and the battlegrounds may be fresh but the campaign remains the same.

Leo (Sun) opposes Aquarius (Saturn) and Scorpio (Mars) opposes Taurus (Venus) again giving Birth and Death, as well as Love and Strife the statement of being always together, yet forever apart.

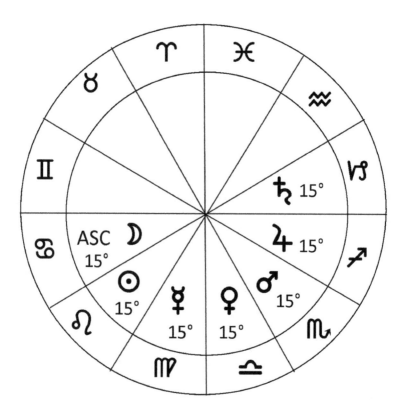

Fig. 88 Thema Mundi

Compared to the warfare which has raged between these powerful adversaries over the centuries and which still continues, Mercury and Jupiter's oppositions are gentle skirmishes that take place between breakfast and tea-time on the side-lines of the planetary battlefield.

And even then, there is a feeling that the weapons are quills and parchment rather than swords and maces.

Perhaps it is true that 'the pen is mightier than the sword', but I doubt that the other planets would agree with this statement.

There may be jibes hurled back and forth and plenty of name-calling, but Mercury likes to get on with the business of life.

It is the merchant or the amusing raconteur who loves to spin stories from everyday life, even the thief or trickster, whereas Jupiter's lofty sights are set higher as the star gazer, the philosopher, the lawyer, the adventurer or the zealot.

The two planets would prefer to politely ignore one another rather than openly engage in battle as unless commerce involves the sale of deadly weapons, Mercury and Jupiter agree that in theory at least, war is bad for business.

The Top of the Chart: The Importance of Culmination

In principle, the ascendant or the first house, is the location for the starting point of life.

Fourth century astrologer Julius Firmicus Maternus says of the first house:

"In this house is to be found the life and vital spirit of men; from this house the basic character of the entire nativity is determined."[79]

When life begins at the first sign of the ascendant the waning square ten signs away stipulates where the native might find the control and strength to manage their adult life.

Theoretically, ten signs away from the ascendant is the highest pinnacle, the culmination of life, and even if the Midheaven is found in another sign, this tenth place in the chart is a critical destination in terms of the native having the authority and power to control their own lives.

To quote Firmicus: *"The tenth house is located in the tenth sign from the ascendant. This place is the first in importance and has the greatest influence of all of the angles. In this house we find life and vital spirit, all our actions, country, home, all our dealings with others, professional careers, and whatever our choice of career brings us. The influence of this house is aspected to the ascendant very powerfully, for it can be seen to be in square aspect to the ascendant."*[80]

The repetition of the phrase *"we find life and vital spirit"* in both his description of the first house, and of the tenth house, is assumed to be deliberate on Firmicus' part.

The blessings of life and vital spirit are given at the ascendant, but the other, at the tenth sign, requires input by the native plus a level of toil and dedication.

This tenth house is the consummation of all the native's efforts which accumulate at the apex of the chart. Failures as well as successes and accomplishments of life are noted here, along with the satisfaction and fulfilment of the vital spirit for a life well lived, which only occurs at the zenith of the chart.

On initial view of Maternus' version of Thema Mundi, the Birth-chart of the Universe, the first question for modern astrologers tends to be,

Why isn't Aries the sign on the Thema Mundi's ascendant?

In other astrological practices, Aries the Ram is considered to lead the signs of the zodiac.

Mars' cardinal sign marks the Vernal Equinox in the northern hemisphere at zero degrees of Aries in late March and is seen as the place of commencement for the astrological calendar.

Medical astrology starts at the head with Aries and follows the body down to the feet at Pisces. For many years astrologers have mistakenly associated Aries with the first house in a chart and *A Tiny Universe* addresses the flaws in this system by comparing it with traditional values of the houses in Chapter Seven on the Houses.

In his discussion on Thema Mundi, Firmicus says that in all charts, the place at the top of the chart is the principle place and the basis of the whole chart.

"We must now discuss why they begin the twelve signs with Aries. In the book of principles that question could not be discussed until the birth chart of the universe had been explained.

In the chart of the universe, which we have said was invented by very learned men, the MC (Medium Caelum) is found to be in Aries. This is because frequently, or rather always, in all charts, the MC holds the principal place, and from this we deduce the basis of the whole chart, especially since most of the planets and the luminaries, the Sun and Moon, send their influence toward this sign." [81]

With these words, Firmicus has given a completely different perspective as to how Thema Mundi might be viewed.

The Moon on the ascendant, and the six planets which follow the Moon, usually draw major focus as these are the alleged positions of the planets in the hypothetical chart of the universe's beginnings.

The planets' positions in seven of the zodiac signs set the model for rulership or domicile, the first level of the Essential Dignities.

Generally speaking, Aries receives very little attention in Thema Mundi, purely because none of the planets are featured in this sign at the top of the chart.

The hypothesis which supports the sign of Cancer rising in Thema Mundi (along with its ruling planet the Moon) tends to emphasise Cancer as a symbol of fertility and nurturance as well as being suggestive of the vulnerability of the birth process. The Moon's position on the ascendant in a place of power reinforces the Moon as the luminary which rules physical matter and the body.

The moment of birth is the commencement of any chart whether it represents a living being or a moment in time, and the Greek word *horoskopos, horo* 'time' + *skopos* 'observer', is synonymous with astrology and the chart.

However, Firmicus is making the point that the chart actually *begins with Aries* in prominence at the zenith of the chart where events culminate and wherein the true repository of power and glory lies.

With Maternus' words we gain insight into the idea that most of the planets *"send their influence toward this sign"* is one of the most significant statements being made by this chart.

Certainly the Moon and Saturn square Aries, Sun and Jupiter trine Aries, Venus opposes it, and from Scorpio Mars exerts its power as the lord of both signs.

The planet which misses its connection with Aries is Mercury in Virgo, but this omission has been covered by the rules of antiscia, as Aries and Virgo are signs of equal light, and therefore can connect through this pathway.

Thirteenth century astrologer Guido Bonatti and the astrologer-scholar Johannes Schoener (1477-1547) both mention the planets as co-significators of the houses in the Chaldean Order and Mars is named as the co-significator of the tenth house when Saturn at the ascendant begins the procession of the planets in their roles as co-significators of the houses.[82]

A Tiny Universe looks at this practice in more detail as each of the seven planets shares a bond with at least one, and sometimes two of the houses in a chart. Even without a planet present in Aries in Thema Mundi, its ruler Mars, is symbolic of the crusade to reach the summit, and then to continue battling to maintain power for as long as it can possibly hold its place and the meekest of professions still requires Mars' courage, cunning or assertiveness to stay on top.

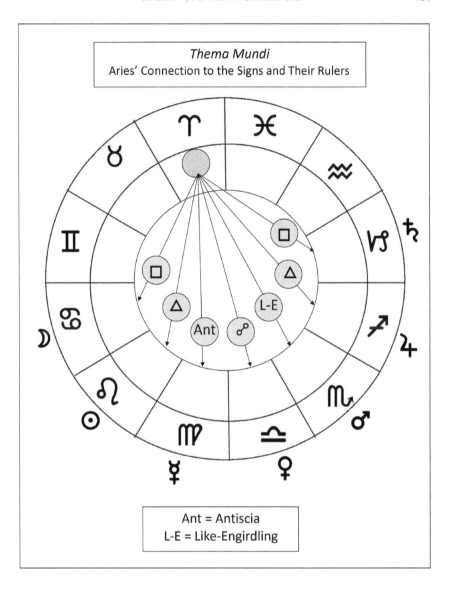

Fig. 89 Thema Mundi's Connections to Aries

The Relevance of a Square Aspect

Within the Thema Mundi chart, there are four quartile or square aspects which connect certain planets.

The Moon in Cancer squares Venus in Libra and the only two female planets in astrology form a relationship through the square aspect.

The Sun in Leo squares Mars in Scorpio as the two masculine planets reach a gentleman's agreement through the quartile aspect.

Mercury in Virgo squares Jupiter in Sagittarius.

Venus in Libra squares Saturn in Capricorn and although their genders are mismatched the two planets share a relationship born from the Essential Dignities.

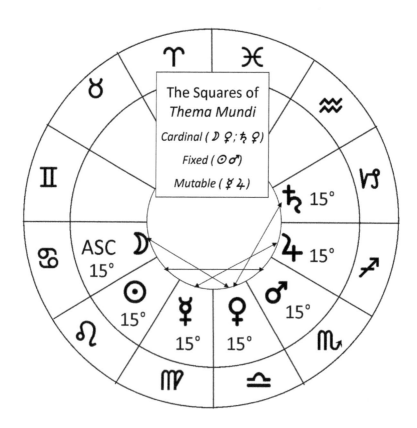

Fig. 90 Thema Mundi Aspects by Square (90 degree angles)

al-Biruni's *Table of Friendship and Enmity* (*A Tiny Universe*, Chapter Four)[83] describes the process known as '*offering or asking for friendship*' whereby planets cooperate with one another under the need to share signs through the second level of Essential Dignity, known as Exaltation, as one planet must borrow another's sign for their exaltation.

The Moon asks for friendship from Venus to borrow Taurus for its exaltation and the square aspect supports this agreement.

The Sun asks for friendship from Mars to borrow Aries for its exaltation and Thema Mundi's square between these two planets is a part of their gentleman's agreement.

Saturn asks for friendship from Venus to borrow Libra for its exaltation and the square once more fortifies their relationship.

This business agreement of sharing signs suggests that at least one participant of the square is required to act with grace and good manners towards the planet which owns its sign and that the connection by square aspect cements this bond.

And then there is Mercury and Jupiter.

Mercury '*neither offers nor asks friendship*' simply because it keeps its own sign, Virgo, for rulership and exaltation.

Jupiter lends its sign of Pisces to Venus for exaltation, but so far as Mercury is concerned, the two planets are '*mutually hurtful*' towards one another and perhaps their relationship is more hostile than first impressions indicate about these two rulers of the mutable signs.

Mercury and Jupiter also share the unique position of being the only two planets whose signs of rulership echo the square aspect which exists in Thema Mundi.

The usual observation of Mercury's signs is that Gemini is the first of its signs and Virgo follows on four signs away in a quartile square. Similarly, Sagittarius comes before Pisces in the zodiac wheel and the ninety degree space which separates them is taken up by planets ruling the intermediate signs.

Each of the four mutable signs are ruled by either Mercury or Jupiter and this creates its own pattern in the chart. For instance, if we start at Gemini we find a Mercury ruled sign. Four signs away is Virgo, once more ruled by Mercury. Four signs from Virgo is Sagittarius, this time ruled by Jupiter. Four signs from Sagittarius is Pisces, once more ruled by Jupiter. Four signs from Pisces is Gemini, ruled by Mercury. The square aspect is reinforced over and over and one is reminded of the dexter and sinister squares mentioned in *A Tiny Universe*.

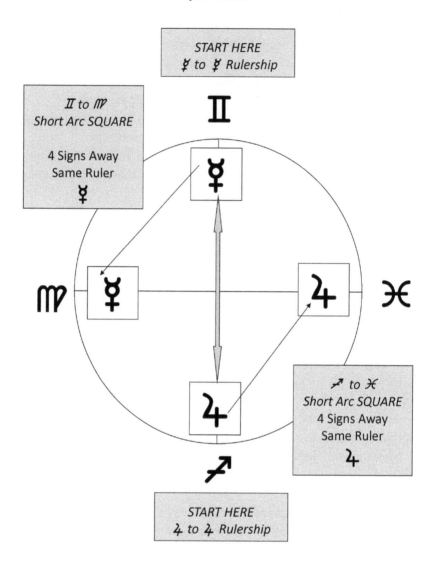

Fig. 91 The Squares of the Mutable Signs

A dexter square occurs on the right-hand side of a sign or planet as viewed from the centre of the circle, and a sinister square occurs on the left-hand side of a sign or planet. In *Fig. 91* Gemini will rise before Virgo and will be in the dexter position to Virgo. Both signs are ruled by Mercury but a planet in Gemini would 'over-power' a planet located in Virgo. Hence the idea of dexter/right-hand being a superior position to sinister/left-hand in the ninety degree aspect of a square.

Likewise, Sagittarius will rise before Pisces in the order of the signs. A planet in Sagittarius (dexter square) would over-power a planet in Pisces (sinister square).

Direction demonstrates superiority or strength and supports the idea that for the dual signs of Mercury and Jupiter at least, culmination ten signs away is a place which according to Firmicus, *'is first in importance and has the greatest influence of all the angles'*.

This quick example on the difference between the two directions of a square creates two important observations.

One is that a dexter square shows who rises first over the ascendant so far as the zodiac signs are concerned, and that secondly, there are two directions a square can take and this brings us to the relevance of short arc and long arc aspects especially where the quartile or square aspects are concerned.

The Short and Long Arc Squares of Mercury and Jupiter

Squares can show strength in two different directions. In the order of the signs, whichever rises first will take the dexter position and whichever rises second will assume the weaker sinister position. In the case of Mercury's two signs the long arc to the right of Virgo places Gemini ten signs away in the order of the zodiac, whilst the short arc to the left of Gemini finds Virgo situated four signs away.

Most aspects in the chart measure distances where the degrees fall under the diameter of the circle at 180 degrees and are known as short arc because of the smaller number of degrees. However, a long arc aspect can be just as useful as the Moon's synodic cycle with the Sun demonstrates.

The Moon's synodic cycle with the Sun shows a different use for the square aspect as a waxing square between the signs of the Moon and Sun occurs when the Moon has moved ninety degrees away from the Sun and the Earth experiences a first quarter moon. The number of degrees accumulate in the Moon's lunar cycle as the moon moves further from the sun and rather than turning the number back at 180 degrees when full moon occurs the degrees continue to mount as the moon moves into its waning phases. By the time the third quarter phase is reached the measurement between the Sun and the fast-moving moon is 270 degrees and the Moon need only move a further ninety degrees to complete its cycle with the Sun.

The lunar cycle is a series of aspects between the faster moving Moon and the Sun, but the same concept can be applied to the distance between the signs.

For instance, the short arc square between Mercury's signs of Gemini and Virgo is a measurement of ninety degrees. If one planet is found in Gemini and another is ninety degrees away in Virgo then the aspect is classified as a waxing square.

If the circle was continued and the measurement made from the sign of Virgo all the way around to Gemini the distance covered would be two hundred and seventy degrees (360 minus 90) and the long arc square would be a waning square ten signs away in Gemini.

Traditional astrologers paid attention to the difference between a waxing square and a waning square as they were well aware of the movement of planets and the variant speeds of the planets. In the works attributed to Dorotheus of Sidon in the early centuries there is much discussion on the delineation of a faster planet moving away from a slower-moving planet to form a short arc square compared to a planet moving away from the slower-moving planet to form a long arc square.

An identical situation is created for Jupiter's two signs *(Fig. 92)*. A measurement from Sagittarius to Pisces finds a waxing square at ninety degrees and a measurement from Pisces to Sagittarius finds a waning square at two hundred and seventy degrees.

It should be noted that in both cases a measurement from each planet's masculine diurnal sign, that is, Gemini or Sagittarius, to the feminine nocturnal signs of Virgo or Pisces always results in a difference of four signs and a short arc angle of ninety degrees.

However, a movement from the feminine nocturnal signs (Virgo or Pisces) to the masculine diurnal signs (Gemini and Sagittarius) covers the distance of ten signs and is a long arc angle of two hundred and seventy degrees.

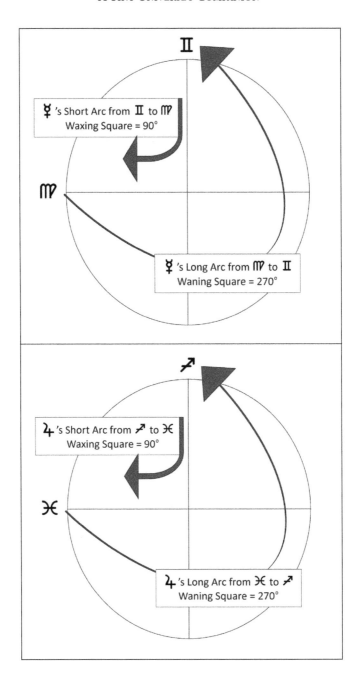

Fig. 92 Mutable short and Long Arc Squares of Mercury and Jupiter

Ptolemy's Aphorism #37

This advantage of shared signs by both short arc (waxing square) and long arc (waning square) exists solely for Mercury and Jupiter and was noted by first century CE writer Claudius Ptolemy in Appendix III of his Tetrabiblos, known as *'The Centiloquy, or One Hundred Aphorisms of Claudius Ptolemy.*[84]

There is some dispute as to whether these astrological principles were actually penned by Ptolemy, or have been added in later periods under his esteemed name to grant them credibility.

However, regardless of the true author, the Aphorisms have worth if only for the length of their tenure.

Ptolemy's *Aphorism 37* states,

"If Virgo or Pisces be on the ascendant, the native will create his own dignity."[85]

Aphorism 37 places Virgo on the ascendant which means that Gemini will fall ten signs away at the Midheaven.

The culmination of life occurs at the place of honours in the house ten signs from the first house and as Mercury rules both the ascendant and the MC, *"the native will create his own dignity"*.

When this is the case Mercury will be responsible for both the beginning of life and the native's actions.

Ptolemy's inclusion of Jupiter in Aphorism 37 means that the same rule which applies for Mercury, can just as easily be adapted for the native's benefit when Jupiter rules both signs. *"If Virgo or Pisces be on the ascendant, the native will create his own dignity"*

Jupiter experiences the same dynamic as Mercury, bringing success through the native's own actions with Pisces on the ascendant and Sagittarius on the tenth house cusp *(Fig. 93)*.

Jupiter's signs can also be measured by the short arc of a waxing square from Sagittarius to Pisces, or by the long arc of a waning square, measuring from Pisces, crossing the boundary at Aries, and continuing until arrival at Sagittarius.

In each case, if either Virgo or Pisces is rising, the ruling planet is responsible for the tenth sign as well, so the native creates his own dignity or destiny (from his actions at the ascendant) which is dependent on the condition of the signs' ruling planet (Mercury or Jupiter) to bring either success or ruin at the apex sign.

Note that in each instance in Ptolemy's Aphorism #37 it is the planet's feminine signs which begin the action, and its masculine signs which dominate the outcome.

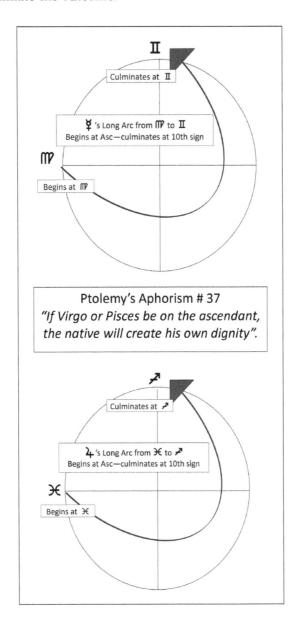

Fig. 93 Ptolemy's Aphorism #37: Virgo and Pisces Rising

The Culmination of Mutable Signs on Angular Houses

The possibility of Ptolemy's Aphorism being taken one step further is tantalising, and is the springboard for the ideas put forward in this chapter on Mercury or Jupiter's culmination points.

The concept of a crest or summit occurring ten signs away is potentially available for either Mercury or Jupiter, and may extend beyond Virgo on the ascendant culminating at Gemini at the zenith of the chart, or a Pisces rising chart experiencing its rewards with Sagittarius on the midheaven.

Any of the twelve houses which form a quartile square by Whole Sign can potentially express the same idea of a culmination point ten signs away, especially when it is the same planet (Mercury or Jupiter) which is ultimately responsible for the two houses concerned.

For Mercury, the house with Gemini on the cusp becomes the culmination point of whatever began at Virgo's house, and for Jupiter, the house which has Sagittarius on its cusp will be the crowning glory for Jupiter's aspirations which began at the house with Pisces on the cusp.

If Virgo moves to the IC, Gemini will fall ten signs away at the first house *(Fig. 94)*, and the ascendant becomes the finishing point for the fourth house if we apply the principle of 'tenth sign culmination'.

Hence, YOU, are depicted by the ascendant, as you are the end result of your father's seed.

Any hereditary benefits, be they entitlements, inherited positions, titles or property, will pass to you in the first house, presumably as you carry your father's name.

The ascendant is also the house of the body, so physical resemblance to the father can be perfected here at the first house.

The development of any biological flaw, and any natural weakness descended from a genetic inheritance can be the 'reward' bestowed by Mercury which began at the fourth and culminated with the first house.

So whilst ideally your health and vitality (1st H) are the very best possible result which originates from the family's genetic pool (4th), the culmination of father's history can be fraught with difficulties, especially if the planet which rules both points, is in poor zodiacal state.

Jupiter can create the same benefits or difficulties when Pisces is on the fourth house and Sagittarius is the sign on the ascendant *(Fig. 97)*.

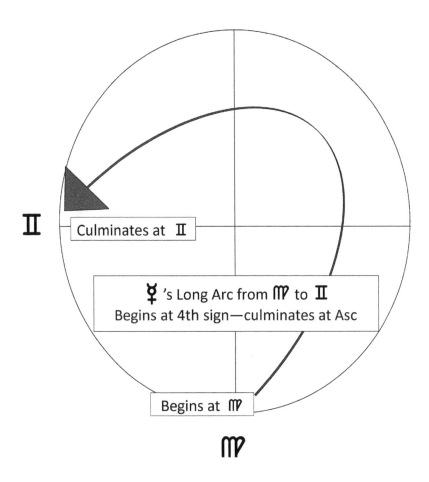

Fig. 94 Virgo on the fourth house culminating 10 signs away at the ascendant

When the feminine signs of Virgo or Pisces are placed on the seventh house cusp their culminating male signs of Gemini and Sagittarius will fall at the fourth house.

This scenario would indicate that for the mutable Cross of Matter with either of these placements the prime target for a committed relationship is to form a home base with the person of their choice.

This may seem obvious for everyone in a relationship to wish for the same outcome, but in a cardinal or a fixed Cross of Matter there will always be two planets involved (one ruling the seventh and one ruling the fourth), and getting them to work together, or even to aspect one another, can be a real trial for the native.

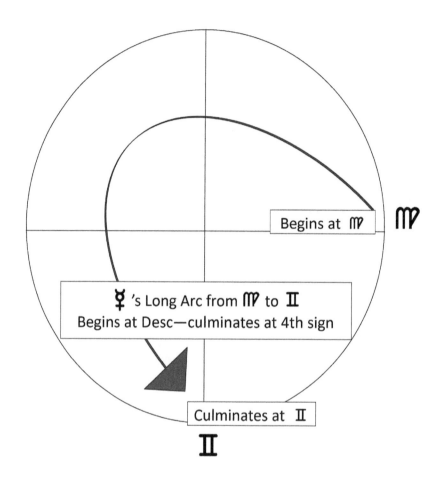

*Fig. 95 Virgo on the seventh house culminating
10 signs away at the fourth house*

The same scenario of separate rulership for the two angles will also take place if the masculine signs of either Mercury or Jupiter are found on the seventh house cusp.

Gemini on the seventh will mean Mercury rules the house of relationships, whilst Jupiter rules the fourth house with Pisces on the cusp, and the chart will replicate the example below with Virgo on the MC *(Fig. 96)*.

However, if either of the feminine mutable signs are found on the seventh house cusp, the same planet, Mercury or Jupiter, will be required to fulfil both roles and to bring to fruition the best possible outcome for the house of relationships via the fourth house.

Even if the house at the base of the chart does not represent a physical abode for the relationship, the cycle moves on by attempting to create another 'father' or parent from this house to ensure the procreation of the next generation.

When feminine signs of Mercury or Jupiter are relocated to the tenth sign, their masculine counterparts will reside a further ten signs away on the seventh house cusp.

The house which culminates in honours and success is also capable of providing a relationship for the native.

Whenever award presentations bring forth a parade of the top guns from any industry, those judged by society as possessing successful tenth houses, are often accompanied by stunningly attractive partners with whom they share their success (and the limelight).

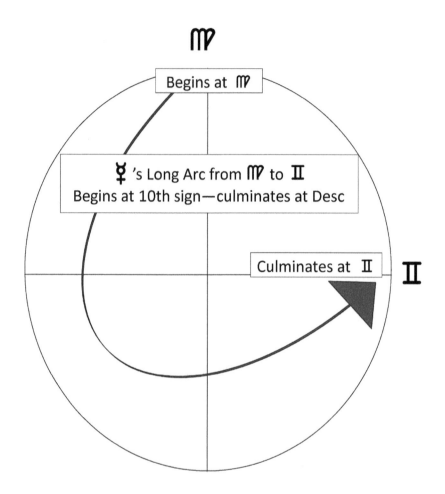

Fig. 96 Virgo on the tenth house culminates 10 signs away at the seventh house

It would seem that one of the high points for the leaders of society is the opportunity to choose a partner who reflects their own wealth, status or notoriety.

Whilst this opinion may appear cynical, it should be noted that social media and entertainment magazines thrive on 'culmination points' of the rich and famous, and will dedicate pages of print and internet space to open speculation on who will become the next love interest of a high profile individual.

Pisces on the tenth house tends to elevate Jupiter-like men and women who rise through the ranks of their own professional field, whilst

Virgo on the tenth house is generally commercial success, popularity or bank-ability, as good self-marketing is Mercury's trademark.

Before proceeding further with this concept, it is important to remember that whilst the two planets share a commonality in having signs which are in waning squares from one another, the similarity ends here, as Mercury and Jupiter are two very different planets.

The matter from which they spring is essentially different, and the possible forms that their summits and peaks (and troughs) will take, will be in keeping with the characteristics and nature of the planet involved in the process of culmination at either Gemini for Mercury, or Sagittarius for Jupiter.

The following list of the two planets' significations from Vettius Valens is featured in Chapter Two on planetary sect.

They have been replicated here as a reminder that Mercury will want to produce different outcomes from Jupiter, and vice versa.

Mercury's list comes with a timely warning on the capricious nature of this planet, as the house where Gemini resides may encounter unusual, unexpected or undesired outcomes which begun in the house where Virgo lies on the cusp.

Mercury is classified as an inferior planet beneath the Sun in the Chaldean Order and therefore greatly influenced by the other planets. Jupiter on the other hand is superior residing higher in the heavens than the Sun and therefore is less likely to be influenced by the other planets. When Mercury aspects either benefic or malefic planets it will adopt some of their characteristics and this can affect its outcomes. Both planets will need to consider the essential and accidental dignities which will affect both the process at the beginning, as well as the apex house at the end of their ten-sign journey.

"Mercury indicates education, disputation, reasoning, theft, association, communication, service, gain . . . It is the bestower of forethought and intelligence, the lord of brothers and of younger children, and the creator of all marketing and banking.

This star's effects go in many directions, depending on the changes of the zodiac and the interactions of the stars, and yields quite varied results: knowledge for some, selling for others, service for others, trade or teaching for others, farming or temple service or public employment for still others.

> *As for the end result — Mercury will make everything*
> *capricious in outcome and quite disturbed. Even more, it causes*
> *those having this star in malefic signs or degrees* (rulership
> according to Egyptian Terms) *to become even worse."*

Vettius Valens, Anthologies, Book I

Despite the fact that ten signs separate the waning square, this journey is not concerned with meandering through the other signs to pick up thoughts and helpful hints along the way.

It moves directly and efficiently from one point to the other, sometimes with breathtaking speed as the impact of actions taken in Virgo's house can have immediate repercussions for Gemini's house.

The journey can take only minutes as Mercury is capable of adroitly assessing a situation when it does not appreciate the outcome, sending messages to its beginning point to try again to see if a change in pattern in Virgo's house will alter the result at Gemini's doorstop.

Virgo is an earth sign, as such it is a nocturnal sign, feminine in gender and its combined qualities are cold and dry.

Virgo is a cautious and careful sign that appreciates patterns and does not like to be rushed, even by its ruling planet.

Even though Mercury is its lord Virgo can be a frustrating sign, especially if Mercury in the chart is itself located in the heated elements of fire or air. However, Mercury can appreciate that it is not a bad thing to start a journey by being well-prepared and the accumulation of facts and options can be extremely useful, especially when the culmination is not pleasant and the process must begin again in the hope of finding a better outcome.

> *"Jupiter indicates childbearing, engendering, desire,*
> *loves, political ties, acquaintance, friendships with great men,*
> *prosperity, salaries, great gifts, an abundance of crops, justice,*
> *offices, office-holding ranks, authority over temples, arbitrations,*
> *trusts, inheritance, brotherhood, fellowship, beneficence, the*
> *secure possession of goods, relief from troubles, release from*
> *bonds, freedom, deposits in trust, money, stewardships."*

Vettius Valens, Anthologies, Book I

Jupiter's natural motion is not as fast as Mercury so it may be prepared to work a little longer on the outcome in order to gain a greater level of success, but again, the rewards or consequences of Jupiter's actions can still manifest quite suddenly.

If actions concerning Jupiter and its houses are foolhardy, unrealistic or extreme, or the native's decisions lack wisdom, care or forethought, then there will be consequences in the house where Sagittarius lies on the cusp.

Another difference between the two planets is the fact that Mercury's actions begin with an earth sign, whilst Jupiter has its starting point in Pisces, a water sign.

Both earth and water are female signs and their active quality is coldness, but Pisces varies from Virgo in the fact that it has a wet passive quality whilst Virgo has a dry passive quality.

The house where Pisces lies will not lack for imagination or creative skills, but emotions can bog down the affairs of this house and Jupiter may be impatient with running the emotional gamut when it wants to see a result to the journey.

Jupiter is a planet that values compassion and prides itself on its philanthropic or humanitarian projects, however it may not appreciate sentimentality or self-pity which stays its hand or gets in the way of its ambitions.

Jupiter's list of significations is far loftier than Mercury's, and it may take extra time to foster *'friendships with great men'* or to find the appropriate time management to achieve vaulted positions in *'justice, offices, office-holding ranks, authority over temples, arbitrations, and trusts'* as Valens suggests in his significations of Jupiter.

Mercury looks for the little victories in life, but Jupiter sets its sights much higher and is familiar with the phrase 'the higher the climb, the harder the fall'.

Jupiter's culminating sign is Sagittarius, and although the house with Pisces on the cusp will want Jupiter to retreat in order to lick its wounds and restore its dignity, a mutable fire sign will be more than happy to send the message back to Pisces' house to *'try again, but this time, try better'*.

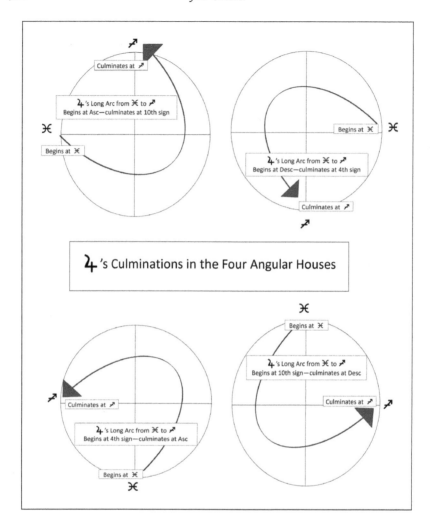

Fig. 97 Jupiter's Four Possible Culminations for Angular Houses

a) *Starts in 1ˢᵗ house with Pisces – culminates in 10ᵗʰ house with Sagittarius (top left)*
b) *Starts in 4ᵗʰ house with Pisces – culminates in 1ˢᵗ house with Sagittarius (bottom left)*
c) *Starts in 7ᵗʰ house with Pisces – culminates in 4ᵗʰ house with Sagittarius (top right)*
d) *Starts in 10ᵗʰ house with Pisces – culminates in 7ᵗʰ house with Sagittarius (bottom right)*

The Combination of Mercury and Jupiter Rulerships

Culmination Axes: The Angular Houses

Practitioners of natal astrology can take a little time to grasp the implications of such a possibility, as culminations points for either Mercury or Jupiter can take some time to manifest in a person's life, but horary astrologers are likely to be using this idea already, although perhaps not consciously aware of doing so.

Horary astrology is the chart of the moment, as a question asked of the astrologer creates a temporary chart by which to supply an answer, and the notion of finding an outcome to a particular situation in another part of the chart is not new to the horary astrologer.

If the house where Virgo or Pisces lies is the focus house then either Mercury or Jupiter will step in as the significators of a question.

Surely looking at where Gemini or Sagittarius is located in the chart might be worth the effort to help find an outcome for the temporary situation or as an answer to a posed question. The concept of culmination is similar to the idea of turning the chart, sometimes known as deriving the chart, wherein houses are counted from a particular point of commencement which is not always the ascendant.

The original chart, called the radical chart, can be turned to represent a multitude of different individuals and life situations, and the culminations for Mercury at Gemini or Jupiter at Sagittarius ten signs away from the Virgo house or the Pisces house respectively, may be useful to the horary astrologer.

The ability for Mercury's signs to have the capacity to reach a culmination point when moving from feminine sign to masculine sign is an interesting concept.

When it is realised that Jupiter has exactly the same capability since its signs too are placed in a quartile square in the chart, adds even further interest when together, the two rulerships complete the mutable Cross of Matter.

If Virgo is on the ascendant and culminates with Gemini at the tenth sign, then on the same axis across the chart from Virgo is Pisces on the descendant which will culminate at Sagittarius on the fourth sign.

This means that on a cross of mutable signs, wherever the feminine signs (earth and water) are situated *there are two points of beginning*, with the masculine signs (air and fire) as the points *for two culminations* for rulers Mercury and Jupiter, that is, *two planets with different natures and agendas.*

Suddenly a relatively simple idea becomes more complicated, as although the timing is not the same for both planets (remember Mercury and Jupiter will move at their own speed), and their objectives and methods are vastly different, any mutable cross will duplicate the notion that both Mercury and Jupiter are trying to do something positive with their rulership houses, and what begins at their feminine signs of mutable earth or water will culminate at their respective masculine signs of mutable air or fire.

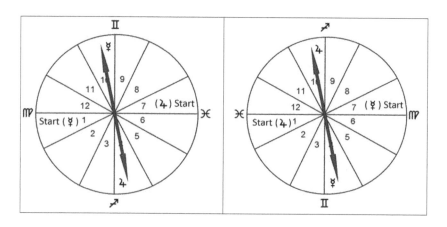

Fig. 98 Combinations of Jupiter and Mercury
ruled Angles – Ptolemy's Aphorism #37

a) *Mercury starts with 1ˢᵗ – culminates in 10ᵗʰ; Jupiter starts in 7ᵗʰ – culminates in 4ᵗʰ H (left wheel)*
b) *Jupiter starts with 1ˢᵗ – culminates in 10ᵗʰ; Mercury starts in 7ᵗʰ – culminates in 4ᵗʰ H (right)*

The four diagrams shown here *(Figs. 98 and 99)* combine the axes of Mercury and Jupiter signs to create four possibilities when the mutable signs reside on a chart's angular houses.

Each diagram shows the starting point at the female signs' axis of Virgo and Pisces which culminates at the male signs' axis of Gemini and Sagittarius.

The ruling planet is featured in parentheses in the house which is the springboard for Mercury or Jupiter which has the female element on the house cusp.

The double-headed arrow shows the culmination points for both planets, and in the following chart examples the same arrow is included to indicate which house axis is accentuate by the combination of Mercury and Jupiter's air and fire signs.

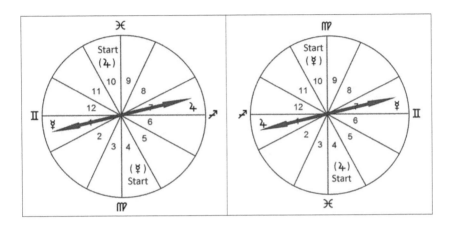

Fig. 99 Combinations of Jupiter and Mercury ruled Angles

a) *Mercury starts with 4ᵗʰ – culminates in 1ˢᵗ; Jupiter starts in 10ᵗʰ – culminates in 7ᵗʰ (left)*
b) *Jupiter starts with 4ᵗʰ – culminates in 1ˢᵗ; Mercury starts in 10ᵗʰ – culminates in 7ᵗʰ (right)*

Example Chart One : Marlon Brando

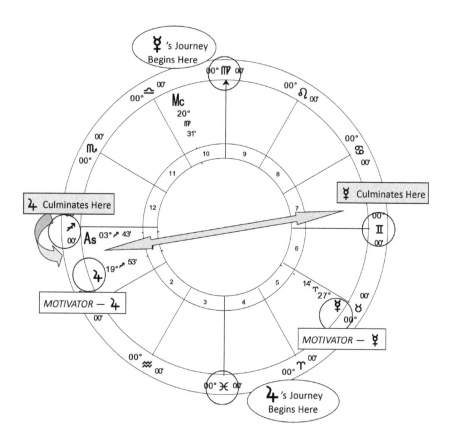

Fig. 100 Culminations of the Angular Houses: Marlon Brando[86]

Marlon Brando (1924-2004) was an American actor, film director and activist. He was a charismatic actor known for his raw passion and emotional truth whom some say changed forever the way we look at acting. Jupiter in rulership is in the house of its culmination in the first house and Mercury is located in the 5th house with its culminating house as the seventh house. Jupiter in Sagittarius trines Mercury in Aries.

Both parents are represented by the fourth and tenth axis where the female signs of Jupiter and Mercury are present. Both Marlon's parents were alcoholics and both were promiscuous. Their relationship was volatile and they separated several times during their marriage but always reconciled and this may be shown by the trine aspect between Jupiter and Mercury. Marlon Jr. was named after his father but he hated him as his father was a bully who delighted in taunting his son.

Brando would say in an interview late in his life,

"I was his namesake, but nothing I did ever pleased or even interested him. He enjoyed telling me I couldn't do anything right. He had a habit of telling me I would never amount to anything."

From these painful beginnings (Pisces on 4th house) of wanting to prove his father wrong Marlon drew his emotional depths and the passion for which he became known as an actor. Many critics believed he had perfected the Stanislavski technique of acting known as The Method but Marlon denied this saying that he drew on his own inner rage towards his father to create the reality seen on the screen.

Jupiter in rulership in the first house demonstrates how a planet in dignity can rise and claim success but it can also go too far. Brando was famous for his petulant behaviour on set, his refusal to memorise lines, his failure to adhere to time schedules and his erratic insubordinate behaviour. He was particularly truculent during the filming of *"Mutiny on the Bounty"* but he fell in love with Polynesia during filming and eventually bought the 12-island atoll of Teti-aroa where his fourth house finally found peace.

In his later years Jupiter in the first allowed him to claim ridiculous amounts of money for small cameo roles that would bankroll his lifestyle and the rebuilding of his home and environmental resort on the atoll. He also built an environmental laboratory to protect seabirds and turtles which was used for many years as a teaching base for students. Tragically much of it was destroyed during a hurricane in 1983.

Brandon's notoriety as a difficult and demanding actor, his troubled family life and his obesity attracted more attention than his late acting career and many critics believed he sold out when he withdrew from acting but Marlon was not as impervious to criticism as he was reported to be.

"They can hit you every day and you have no way of fighting back. I was very convincing in my pose of indifference, but I was very sensitive and it hurt a lot."

Mercury's culmination occurs in the seventh house and part of Brando's notoriety comes from his famous array of relationships.

Brando never denied the rumours that he was bisexual and part of his erotic appeal came from his dismissal of the prudish attitudes of Hollywood during the early years of his career. He was both a social and a sexual rebel throughout his life as he had multiple relationships, many marriages and girlfriends and reportedly fathered up to seventeen children to a variety of women.

Mercury's Virgo on the tenth sign creates a number of screen roles to initiate the adoration and availability of partners both on and off the screen. Mercury in Aries in the fifth house allows Brando to fully explore his creativity and although he was criticised for being unprofessional in not learning his lines he defended his choice saying that instead he preferred to bring realism and spontaneity to the role.

"If you don't know what the words are but you have a general idea of what they are, then you look at the cue card and it gives the feeling to the viewer, hopefully, that the person is really searching for what he is going to say – that he doesn't know what to say."

A man who changed screen acting with his magnetic and empathetic performances must surely have been drawn to the profession at a young age. Yet Marlon Brando fell into acting because he had no skills or training to provide other career options. In fact he followed his older sister into acting (Mercury is the significator for siblings) by an impulse but Mercury's culminating house soon gave him a reason to gather all the information he needed for a successful career. Acting did provide the opportunity for a variety of beautiful partners, but it gave him something else as well. Fellow actor and friend George Englund once said that Brando fell into acting in New York because *"he was accepted there. He wasn't criticized. It was the first time in his life that he heard good things about himself."*

The profile Brando gained from his career as a famous and newsworthy figure was channelled into other activities of a seventh house nature which were close to Brando's heart. It gave him a voice to express his affinity with civil rights leaders such as Martin Luther King, Jr., and American Indian activist Sacheen Littlefeather who appeared in his place at the 1973 Academy Awards to refuse the statue in protest of the depiction of American Indians in the film industry.

Brando joined fellow actor Paul Newman on the Freedom Rides in the early '60s, riding interstate buses in the South with mixed racial groups to challenge local laws or customs that enforced segregation in seating.

Brando also had a special relationship with the equally reclusive singer Michael Jackson, perhaps because both men had come from traumatic childhoods and both needed sanctuary from their fame and a space away the prying eyes of the world. Despite their age gap, Brando and Jackson were close and the actor's son who was Jackson's bodyguard says that Michael was instrumental in helping his father through the last few years of his life.

Perhaps the final comment on Marlon Brando's combination of Jupiter and Mercury's culminating axis across the first and seventh houses should be left to one of his biographers Peter Manso who commented on Brando's inner struggle and his eventual withdrawal from the world,

"On the one hand, being a celebrity allowed Marlon to take his revenge on the world that had so deeply hurt him, so deeply scarred him. On the other hand he hated it because he knew it was false and ephemeral."

Culminating Points in Other Axes: The Succedent and Cadent Houses

The aspect with a right angle is called quartile (quarter of a circle) or square, and part of the reason is that it connects signs which have little in common with one another besides the fact that they share modality.

By a square aspect, cardinal will link to cardinal, fixed sign to another fixed sign, and mutable to mutable.

A square aspect will link a female sign to a male sign meaning that one sign will have a cold quality (female) whilst the other sign has a hot quality (male).

This may sound like a small difference, but being incompatible in the active quality is extremely stressful for any two planets which find themselves in this position.

The planet in the cold feminine sign will want to slow events down, ignore the escalating tension, or withdraw from conflict, whilst the planet in a hot masculine sign will want to push ahead to resolve the pressure created by the quartile aspect.

The difference in attitudes, protection modes and desired speed of activity towards resolution will only aggravate the aspect, and usually it will blow out a situation until it affects the affairs of both houses containing the planets in square aspect.

This results in the individual becoming stressed, or so uncomfortable in both areas of life, that they are forced to resolve the issue.

The best way to describe a square in the chart is a feeling of embarrassment, heightened emotionality or guilt. That which began as a minor irritation has resulted in the native over-reacting and feeling slightly ashamed about their behaviour.

Squares abound with recriminations, apologies and promises to never repeat the same mistakes, that is, until the next time the same square is activated by the same planets in a scenario which looks very different, but basically harbours the same problems.

No other Ptolemaic aspect does this, and only the modern aspect known as a quincunx has the problem of mismatched signs, and even then, quincunxes are known for being an aspect of blindness for both the planets involved, thereby rendering the aspect's resolution practically impossible for the native.

In a Whole Sign chart square aspects will connect houses from the same classification, i.e. a planet in an angular house will square a planet in another angular house, ninety degrees away. Likewise, a planet in a succedent house will form a right angle aspect to a planet in the last or the next succedent house and the same situation will occur for planets in cadent houses.

An opposition will also link the houses from the same strata level together, but an opposition does not have the same tension as a square, simply because the two signs share a similar active quality. Both signs will be either feminine or masculine in gender and so they will have similar problem-solving techniques, unlike the square aspect which crosses gender classifications and emphasises the tension between masculine and feminine signs.

An opposition will also emphasise a particular houses axis (1st to 7th, or 3rd to 9th), which a quartile aspect does not experience because the angle between the two signs is too small.

When it is the signs themselves which form a square aspect to one another and are connected by the rule of like-engirdling, that is, they share the same ruling planet, then two houses from the same classification (angular, succedent, cadent) will be linked together.

Mutability (and the same ruler) is the only common denominator for Virgo and Gemini, and the same thing happens when Pisces is in quartile aspect to Sagittarius.

The houses where the two signs lie on the cusp can have vastly different agendas and meanings, and it often requires resourceful planets like Mercury or Jupiter to provide options where both houses' needs are adequately catered for.

Problem-solving through intelligence, prudence or common sense is vital for these two planets if the native is going to gain a level of success in the house where the planet's wishes are fulfilled.

Culmination Axes of the Succedent Houses

The twelve houses of the horoscope are grouped according to three categories: angular (1,4,7,10), succedent (2,5,8,11) and cadent (3, 6, 9, 12).

Traditional authors, such as thirteenth century astrologer Guido Bonatti, agree that planets in the angular houses are judged as strong, planets located in the succedent houses are mediocre in strength and are compromised in their ability to function well, and planets placed in the cadent houses are considered to be ineffectual or weakened by their position in the chart.[87]

The chapter on Houses (*A Tiny Universe*) discusses the concept that each house's strength, meaning and the significations of the house are dependent on receiving light from the Ascendant through the aspects of the signs.

All angles are considered to be strong houses since each angle aspects the ascendant, and four other houses besides the angles are deemed to be beneficial because they receive light from the ascendant.

However, if there is no aspect from the Ascendant, then there is no light sent to the house, and the four remaining houses, namely the second, eighth, sixth and twelfth house are considered to be dark houses simply because there is no Ptolemaic aspect (sextile, square, trine or opposition) between themselves and the ascendant.

The four succedent houses have two houses which receive light from the ascendant (fifth and eleventh house) and two houses which remain in the dark as no light reaches them from the ascendant.

Firmicus Maternus calls both the second and the eighth 'feeble' houses and their Greek names translate into English as the Gates of Hell.

The eighth house is *Epicataphora,* meaning Casting down into the Underworld and the second house is *Anafora,* meaning Rising up from the Underworld.[88]

In the advent of Mercury and Jupiter's two signs being featured on the succedent cross of houses, that is, the second, fifth, eighth and eleventh houses, there will be a combination of one light and one dark house when the square aspect between the planets' signs are taken into account.

In the first set of circumstances *(Fig. 101),* the feminine mutable signs begin in the feeble or passive houses (according to Maternus) and are the axis of the second and eighth houses.

Money concerns, resources, access to financial backing for large projects, inheritances, mortgages and insurance, or merely balancing the budget to pay the weekly bills can be the concerns of the two ruling planets of Virgo and Pisces.

The fifth house is the house of Good Fortune and its house on the opposite side of the axis is known as the house of the Good Daemon.

Both of these houses receive light from the ascendant – the fifth house by trine and the eleventh house by a sextile aspect.

When the culminations occur in these houses then relief may be gained or burdens lifted when Mercury and Jupiter rule the masculine signs of mutability on this beneficial house axis.

In the second set of circumstances when the axes are flipped *(Fig. 104)* and the culminations occur in the dark houses the journey may start well for Mercury and Jupiter but may become bogged down at the end by financial restraints or legal wrangling.

The feminine mutable signs located on the positive and productive axis of the fifth and eleventh houses have the potential for either planet to extend its boundaries and move forth into the world with confidence and a sound business plan. Virgo will work hard for Mercury in the fifth house by constructing plans and objectives based on the enthusiasm of this creative house. Or it may network from the eleventh house to promote ideas and look for financial backing amongst its peer group.

Pisces is Jupiter's feminine sign so passion and intuition in the fifth house may guide it towards its goal of financial independence in the second house.

Mentors and individuals with authority or public standing may be influenced by Jupiter's emotive and persuasive skills when Pisces is located on the eleventh house so that the goal or culmination point in the eighth house is access to large amounts of money from an external source to enable Jupiter's dream to come to fruition.

However, constant good fortune may not be guaranteed when the houses of culmination are dark in nature and the affairs of these money houses begins to cause concern for the native if the budget is stretched too thin or financial backers start to clamour for returns to their investments.

The condition of the two ruling planets will have a huge influence on the shades of light and darkness in these houses and part of understanding the process of culmination involves an awareness of Mercury and Jupiter's levels of dignity or debility in the chart.

Succedent Houses moving from Dark to Light

2nd House Culminates in the 11th House
8th House Culminates in the 5th House

With Virgo or Pisces on the second house cusp, and Gemini or Sagittarius on the eleventh house cusp, the two planets journey from a commencement place with no light from the ascendant to find the house of the Good Daemon.

Jupiter is naturally bountiful and therefore more suited to provide wealth for the native, but even Mercury's good condition can provide a good wage (2nd) and the end result can be influential friends or money to subsidise a lively social life (11th).

On the other side of the chart, Pisces or Virgo indicate a starting point from the eighth house, and this can entice money from outside sources provided Mercury or Jupiter's condition aids in bringing successful investment from this house.

The two planets rule opposing houses of wealth, therefore, the planet ruling the eighth house needs to know that its opposing partner (ruling the second house) can afford to make repayments or pay debts when they become due.

If one planet overextends the other's resources (by borrowing too much or by wasting money), then the culmination may be a reduction of pleasures in the two houses of light (5th and 11th house) because the luxuries of these houses are no longer affordable by the native's tightening or unrealistic budget.

Virgo or Pisces on the eighth house means that external financial support or a living made from professions of an eighth house nature can entitle the native to fully develop fifth house leisure activities and creative pursuits, but if the ruler which links these two houses is in a difficult position there is a likelihood that maturation results in hardship or despair.

For instance, if divorce proceedings are tying up joint resources or child support from the partner (8th house) is not forthcoming, the outcome is not pleasant as the native's children will likely suffer as a consequence.

The culmination for the dark second house, which deals with money, is the more beneficial eleventh house so if Virgo or Pisces is situated on the second house cusp money spent or earned can bring benefits through the eleventh house of the Good Daemon.

However, if Virgo or Pisces are located on the second house cusp and money is constantly leaving via the second house this can shatter hopes for a brighter future and lead to a mindset of poverty and a feeling that hopes and dreams may never be achieved (poor outcomes for the 11th house).

Mercury may provide ideas or gain sound financial advice from mentors or friends and accumulate wealth in the second, so the square swings back and forth to benefit the native.

If Mercury is not well situated in the chart the benefits of the eleventh house may be lost and these will subsequently affect the finances.

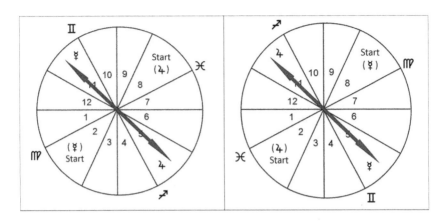

Fig. 101 SUCCEDENT Jupiter and Mercury Ruled
Squares Culminating in Houses of Light

Leo or Aquarius Ascendant

a) *Mercury starts with 2nd – culminates in 11th; Jupiter starts in 8th – culminates in 5th H (left)*
b) *Jupiter starts with 2nd – culminates in 11th; Mercury starts in 8th – culminates in 5th H (right)*

Example Chart Two : Paul Gauguin (1848-1903)

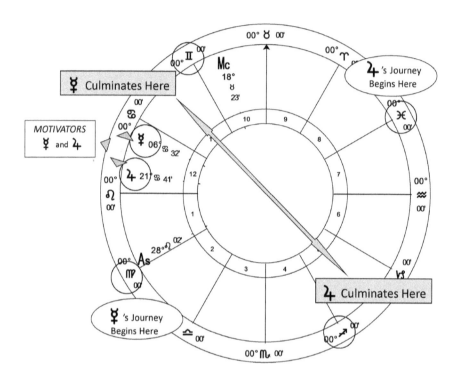

Fig. 102 Succedent Houses from Dark to Light: Paul Gauguin[89]

Paul Gauguin was a French Post-Impressionist artist who lived his life in abject poverty. Gauguin had Mercury and Jupiter in Cancer in the twelfth house. Mercury rules his second house in Virgo and eleventh house in Gemini and Jupiter rules his eighth house in Pisces and his fifth house in Sagittarius.

On two occasions critical to his artistic career, Gauguin had the opportunity for patronage which would have provided him and his family with an easy life of wealth and fame. However, financial assistance was revoked when he quarrelled with his wealthy patron, and he wrote of his bitter disappointment, when lesser skilled artists became rich from sales on the American markets.

When his need was the greatest he lost a lucrative commission to paint for the French Colonialists because he spoke out against their treatment of the native Polynesians, and the authorities revoked the lease on his Crown land when he was unable to pay the rent because he no longer had government employment.

In both instances his financial support was cut short by hidden enemies and lost causes from the ruling planets in the twelfth house. Jupiter may be in exaltation but sometimes high ideals and vocal opinions can spoil the outcome for the beneficial houses which should provide good luck and a rise to fame.

Nor does dignified Jupiter fare any better in the twelfth house as Gauguin's creative efforts were savaged by the art critics who became his hidden enemies with the influence to prevent him from selling his paintings in Paris or borrowing money against his art to feed or clothe his family.

His Danish wife was supported by her own family who were willing to help him financially, but only if he promised to abandon his painting and return to work as a successful stockbroker.

His pride and the belief in his own artistic talent (Jupiter's culminating in the 5th) prevented him from taking their financial handouts (8th house) and eventually the family split when his wife and children returned to Denmark.

Gauguin wrote copious amounts of letters to his influential friends in France whilst he was living in French Polynesia begging them to buy his work so that he could afford to continue to paint, but the letters were largely ignored and when he sent consignments back to France he rarely received payments for his work. Mercury's culmination in the eleventh house was erratic and unpredictable and the journals published after Paul's death (still available today) are a sad witness to the effect his friends' abandonment had on his mental state during the final years of his life.

When Gauguin received the crushing news of the death of the beloved daughter named after his mother Aline from pneumonia (ruler of 5th, Jupiter is eight signs away in 12th house) Gauguin painted what he believed was his greatest work, and dedicated it to Aline.

The painting is entitled *Where Do we Come From? What Are We? Where Are We Going?*

Painted in 1897, the year of Aline's death, it is a rich and beautiful depiction of various elements of Tahitian life.

He said of this painting *"I believe that this canvas not only surpasses all my preceding ones, but that I shall never do anything better – or even like it."*

In the same period Gauguin's land was repossessed as he had borrowed heavily to build an extravagant wooden house with beautiful views of the mountains and the sea.

Debt, illness and grief ended in Gauguin taking what he believed to be a lethal dose of arsenic when he completed this work but rather than ending his life the effects of the poison only accentuated his misery and he laments in his journal that he fails at even this task.

When Gauguin finished '*Where Do We Come From?*', he sent it back by ship to a friend and art dealer in Paris, but the painting remained unsold until 1901, two years before his death, and Gauguin received very little money from the sale of perhaps his most exquisite work.

The painting was intended to be read from right to left as the first question *Where Do We Come From?* is posed by three women and an infant at the beginning of life.

What Are We? is symbolized by the young adults in the centre of the painting and

Where Are We Going? is the question posed by the old woman approaching death in the left-hand corner.

The painting was sold to the Museum of Fine Arts in Boston in 1936 for $80,000US and still resides there for public viewing.

When Gauguin died a trunkful of his paintings were tipped into the sea as they were considered worthless, and his painted canvases were found tattered and filthy as floor coverings in nearby huts when he had sold them for a handful of coins.

His canvasses were considered more valuable as substitute shoe leather than they were as masterpieces and his stunning Polynesian landscapes ended up on the soles of his friends' feet.

For Gauguin the eleventh house culminated in rejection and ridicule for his paintings, and his emotional outbursts earned him enemies instead of friends, never providing for his second house, and almost destroying a brilliant artist's lifelong work.

The culmination of Jupiter's efforts in the fifth house were of little use to Gauguin whilst he was alive, and his artwork only began to make money and to provide an inheritance for his family after his miserable death.

As the example for Gauguin indicates, culmination in good houses, does not necessarily assure success and happiness, and reaching the summit can produce both swings of the pendulum.

Sometimes the climax is quite magical, but is born from pain and loss as in the case of Gauguin's famous painting, and other times not all things are guaranteed to end well when they reach their conclusion.

For example, Gauguin was both excited and flattered when asked by his friend Vincent Van Gogh to join him in the south of France so that they could both paint the beautiful country landscape.

Gauguin was penniless at the time, and Van Gogh had paid for his train ticket, but Gauguin's arrogant manner (and exalted Jupiter) got the better of him, and when the two friends fell into heavy drinking sessions Gauguin was so cruel and dismissive of Van Gogh's work that after a particularly violent evening Van Gogh attacked him with a knife.

Gauguin fled, and Van Gogh, tortured by deep remorse, self-mutilated by removing part of his own ear.

Example Chart Three : Richard Branson (1950-)

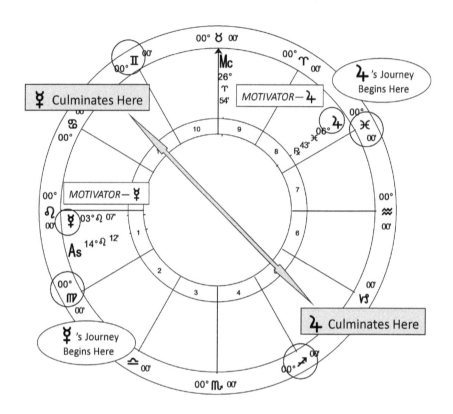

Fig. 103 Houses from Dark to Light: Richard Branson[90]

English entrepreneur Richard Branson, creator of Virgin Airlines, has Mercury in Leo in his first house with Virgo on the second and Gemini on the eleventh house.

Although Branson is a multi-millionaire, it is not the second house that he desires, but the culmination of his eleventh house that reaches towards far-reaching goals and the manifestation of his dreams.

He is quoted as saying *"Above all, you want to make something you are proud of. That's always been my philosophy of business. I can honestly say that I have never gone into any business purely to make money. If that is the sole motive, then I believe you are better off doing nothing."*[91]

Branson's Jupiter is in Pisces in its rulership house in the eighth but also ruling the fifth house.

His rise to fame and riches is of happier circumstance than Gauguin, as Branson used his own money as a teenager to start his 'Student' magazine, randomly phoning advertisers to ask for finance from a public telephone.

By age twenty he had a thriving business and forty employees.

His financial management of the Sex Pistols (8th) cemented his position in the music industry (5th), and when he used that money to garner large amounts of finance from a dignified Jupiter in its eighth house, he ploughed it into the pursuit of entertainment and leisure by creating an airline for ordinary people to afford, a culmination of Sagittarius on his fifth house cusp.

Branson is quoted in many self-made success books and lectures with quotes such as:

"A business has to be involving, it has to be fun, and it has to exercise your creative instincts."[92]

In March 2000, Branson was knighted at Buckingham Palace for "services to entrepreneurship".

For his work in retail, music, travel and transport, his taste for adventure, and for his humanitarian work, he became a prominent figure easily identified around the world.

Succedent Houses moving from Light to Dark

5th House Culminates in the 2nd House
11th House Culminates in the 8th House

If the signs are swapped for this same set of four succedent houses and the feminine signs of Virgo and Pisces are placed at the fifth or eleventh house axis the culmination of these two houses becomes the money axis of second and eighth house.

Fifth house affairs will culminate in the second house, and eleventh house beginnings will culminate in the eighth house when a combination of Virgo opposing Pisces is on these cusps.

Fifth house children can constantly erode the finances, but as it is generally a labour of love to spend money on one's children, the outcome is not particularly bleak.

Extra curriculum activities can cost large amounts of money but a parent is willing to spend this to develop a child's talents and interests.

Occasionally, the child's talents are enough to put money back into the coffers or even provide an income for the native if the child is especially lucky or skilled.

The dark houses do not necessarily bode bad things as this example shows.

They may be dark, but they can produce wealth, and a life of relative ease, if the original starting point of fifth or eleventh house had produced some benefit either from Good Fortune or with help from the Good Daemon.

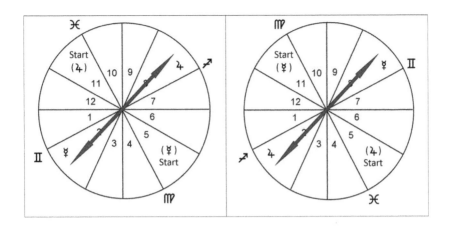

*Fig. 104 SUCCEDENT Jupiter and Mercury Ruled
Squares Culminating in Dark Houses*

Taurus or Scorpio Ascendant

a) *Mercury starts with 5th – culminates in 2nd; Jupiter starts in 11th – culminates in 8th H (left)*
b) *Jupiter starts with 5th – culminates in 2nd; Mercury starts in 11th – culminates in 8th H (right)*

Example Chart Four : Rodney King

Mercury's Houses: Starts in 5th – culminates in 2nd house
Jupiter's Houses: Starts in 11th – culminates in 8th house

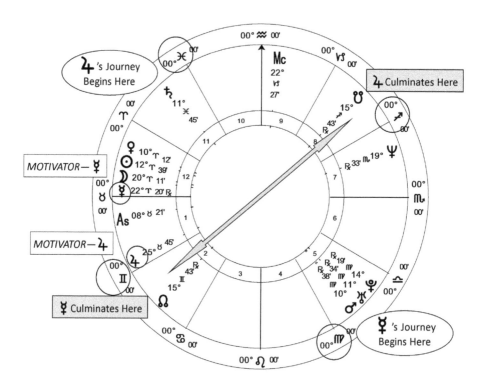

Fig. 105 Whole Sign Chart with Mercury and Jupiter Houses – Rodney King [93]

Simple examples are useful for demonstrating Mercury and Jupiter rulerships however the full story is rarely as clear-cut as the examples provided earlier in the chapter.

A more in-depth exploration of the path from beginning to culmination ten signs away is needed to truly appreciate the impact these planets (and their culminations) can have on an individual's life.

Rodney King (1965-2012) was an African-American construction worker who was savagely beaten by police officers in early 1991 following a high-speed car chase in Los Angeles, California.

The event was filmed by a local citizen who witnessed the incident from his balcony and presented the videotape to a local television station who broadcast the beating worldwide.

Three surgeons operated on King in surgery lasting five hours that morning and the beating fractured him both physically and mentally as King suffered debilitating brain damage and ongoing emotional trauma for the rest of his life.

Four police officers were charged with use of excessive force but were acquitted on 29th April 1992. When news broke of their acquittal, rioting followed which was to last for six days. A record which still stands as the most devastating single urban riot in U.S. history.

During the 1992 L.A. riots fifty three people were killed, over 2,000 were injured, 7,000 fires were lit causing damage to 3,000 businesses and costing the city nearly $1 billion in financial losses.

Over twenty years later many of the districts affected by the riots have still not recovered and are an urban wasteland.

In Rodney King's chart *(Fig.105)* the succedent houses are ruled jointly by Mercury and Jupiter. Mercury rules the fifth house and is the dispositor of three planets located in the fifth house in Virgo, planets Mars, Uranus and Pluto – all capable of producing violence which escalates at an alarming rate.

Rodney King was born during the period in the mid to late 1960's when Uranus was conjunct Pluto in Virgo.

Early 1965 was particularly harsh so far as synodic cycles are concerned as Saturn was also travelling through a critical point in its own synodic cycles with both Pluto and Uranus, and when King was born in April 1965 Saturn was in partile (same degree) opposition to Uranus. Mercury and Jupiter became embroiled in these cycles as these two planets are the dispositors for the planets in Virgo and Pisces.

The unfortunate addition of Mars in Virgo at the time of King's birth accelerates the potential for violence and the stellium in Aries (disposited by Mars) became even more volatile in King's twelfth house.

Mercury, the ruler of the second and fifth houses, is situated in the Aries stellium in the twelfth house.

The fact that Mercury and Mars are each other's dispositor, that is Mars is in Virgo whilst Mercury is in Aries, is known as 'generosity' between the two planets – not mutual reception as there is no aspect which binds Aries to Virgo.

But this is not necessarily a 'generosity' that you want in your life.

The beating that King received resulted in damage to his brain (Mercury conjunct Moon in Aries) and the bouncing act between the excesses of Mars with Uranus and Pluto and the damaged Mercury led to excessive binge drinking, convictions of spousal abuse and repeated car crashes, one which broke his pelvis and gave him a permanent limp.

On 3rd March 1991 King and two friends spent the night watching a basketball game and drinking at a private residence before jumping into King's car around midnight to go for a drive to get more beers. Simple fifth house entertainments such as King was enjoying that night became the catalyst for the Virgo stellium as a simple act from this house began the circumstances which would change King's life forever.

King later admitted to trying to lose the police because he suspected he was above the alcohol limit and a charge of driving under the influence would violate his parole from a previous robbery conviction. With the fear of incarceration Mars in the fifth house ruling the house of imprisonment (12th) was put into play by his actions in using speed to try and outrun the pursuing police car.

When he was finally stopped Saturn in Pisces in the eleventh house opposing the stellium in Virgo in the fifth house erupted into violence which went way beyond the bounds of restraining and arresting King for drinking charges.

The four officers are represented by Saturn (archetypically the authorities) but also agents of the government through the eleventh house, in the same way as in traditional accounts the eleventh house belongs to the 'king's court' or those immediately under his control.

Saturn in Pisces in hard aspect to Mars, Uranus and Pluto in Virgo depict how both Mercury and Jupiter become involved through house rulership and by being the dispositors of this aspect.

Jupiter in the first house is very visible and is opposite Neptune bringing forth the triangle of victim, saviour and persecutor with the strange coincidence of King being caught on camera and both parties acting out all three of these archetypes.

Whilst the two feminine signs of Mercury and Jupiter show the beginning through their houses and the planets contained with them, the rulers of the signs and houses tell us what happens next.

Jupiter in the first indicates King's own erratic behaviour by speeding and resisting arrest, but Jupiter also shows how the incident became so public, so very quickly when images of the incident were beamed around the world and seen by millions of television viewers.

Mercury in the Aries stellium in the twelfth shows the rage and feelings of injustice unleashed by the police officers' acquittal and the ensuing destruction which followed, creating more victims and pitting one underprivileged minority group against another.

The maximum amount of damage did not occur in the rich end of town, but rather the looting and burnings and most of the deaths took place in the poorer Korean and Hispanic shopping areas.

On day three of the riots King appeared in public as a spokesperson for the same system which had seen him beaten by the authorities, and whose representatives in the courts had subsequently acquitted his assailants.

The footage shows a man surrounded by city officials, a man whose spirit is broken and who is both embarrassed and humiliated at being dragged out into the public and forced to play the role of compliant mouthpiece for the authorities who so viciously abused him and then cheated him by denying a conviction.

In the footage King keeps his eyes to the ground the entire time and whispers in a shaky and tearful voice *"People, I just want to say, you know, can we all get along? Can we stop making it horrible for the older people and the kids?"*

For this piece of propaganda King was branded by the African American community as a coward and a traitor to the cause of social equality and freedom from persecution, and King was ostracized for most of his life.

Jupiter's actions start in the eleventh house of public and social groups, and culminates in the eighth house.

For King, life would never be the same and his public display of 'loyalty' to the authorities (Saturn in Pisces in the 11th) ended his life in ways which were much more damaging to his spirit than any beating his body could have taken on that night.

For the city of L.A. there were significant consequences which followed the riots such as a no-holds-barred analysis of the general political and economical atmosphere that contributed to the riots, and an overhaul of the LAPD which included additional funding (8th H) for an increased quota of police officers with backgrounds from minority groups.

As for King, the acquittal and riots led to a civil case two years later and he was awarded $3.8 million dollars by the city of Los Angeles. The culmination of the act which began with violence in the fifth and eleventh houses did indeed became a second house benefit, that is, financial compensation for brutality at the hands of the police.

King's money gained from public funds (2nd/8th axis) bounced back to the fifth house when he invested most of it in a hip-hop record label Straight Alta-Pazz Records the profits of which he had intended to go to the kids from poor L.A. neighbourhoods, but poor management and no musical skills finally settled back in the second house when he lost his money in the venture.

In an interview in 2012 King told NPR Books that he had wanted to start the label to employ otherwise unemployable black and Hispanic youths.

Everyone involved had good intentions, but ultimately Mercury's entrepreneurial skills were tested and found wanting and as King's friends had no experience in the musical industry the whole enterprise became a critical blunder that would ensure the label's failure.[94]

The undue force used by Saturn in the eleventh house ruled by Jupiter also culminated with Jupiter's eighth house.

King's own mortality was threatened on that fateful night and Jupiter's ability to protect his body through its house placement was destroyed. The large sum of money awarded when King sued the city for compensation for injuries inflicted by its officers is a culmination of Jupiter's eighth house.

King had been close to death and although he survived, his Jupiter had been tested and had failed and the incident left him a victim of post-traumatic stress for the rest of his life.

King's nodal axis lies across the culmination axis of 2nd/8th and the volatile 5th/11th house opposition of Saturn to the Mars Uranus Pluto stellium is squaring the nodes.

Even though the event is deeply personal for King himself he becomes an agent and a public figure (first house Jupiter) for events which triggered mob violence driven by a minority group's accelerating fear of police violence coupled with the despair of poverty and unemployment (twelfth house Mercury).

Rodney King died on 17th June 2012 from accidental drowning after suffering a cardiac arrest and falling into the swimming pool at his home.

At the time King had been promoting his book *"The Riot Within: My Journey from Rebellion to Redemption"* published on the 20th anniversary of his arrest and the 1992 L.A. riots.

Alcohol and a mixture of drugs found in his system were believed to have been a contributing factor to his death.

Jupiter in the first and the ruler of his eighth house shows a sad outcome for a man who was caught in something bigger than he could control and which ultimately destroyed him.

In an interview with the Los Angeles Times just weeks before his death, King said:

"I sometimes feel like I'm caught in a vice. Some people feel like I'm some kind of hero. Others hate me. They say I deserved it. Other people, I can hear them mocking me for when I called for an end to the destruction, like I'm a fool for believing in peace."

Cadent Houses moving from Light to Dark

3rd House Culminates in the 12th House
9th House Culminates in the 6th House

In reality Mercury or Jupiter's high point on the most difficult axis in the chart can create situations where withdrawal from life is a choice rather than a penalty, or even a gift to mankind, as is the case for Alexander Fleming, the scientist who discovered penicillin.

Practical application of these cadent culminations can take some careful thought but it is not impossible to imagine how they may work.

God asks for duty, humility and sacrifice from the ninth house, and the climax at the sixth, which could be considered 'the house of the monk' results in someone who takes a lifelong vow of diligence, studious contemplation and steadfast obedience in order to serve their God.

Nor does the state of service need to be triggered by devotion to a divine entity. Study in the ninth house can bring a career where commitment and belief can turn into self-imposed drudgery or ridiculously long working hours which can have a long-term effect on the native's health.

Foreign travel in the ninth can expose the individual to viruses and illnesses that may have a chronic effect on the native's health. Unexpected accidents whilst travelling overseas can have similar repercussions.

Likewise, the twelfth house is an unsettling place for the third house to culminate but the familiarity of the third house should never be taken for granted when the possibility is that actions taken in the third house can end in one's undoing by either Jupiter or Mercury's rulerships.

Third house in our times represents social media outlets and once comments are made and opinions are voiced they remain on the records and vilification or cyber-bullying are criminal offences with possible prison terms when their impact on total strangers has caused death or devastation for the recipient.

However, the work of the third house can illuminate the twelfth house so that communication organised through the same avenues of social media can help to highlight the plight of those who cannot defend themselves or who would otherwise remain hidden in the shadows of society.

The 2015 image of drowned Syrian toddler Alyan Kurdi on a Turkish beach went viral on the Internet, and changed the attitude of Europe in its treatment of Syrian refugees, opening channels of asylum for thousands of desperate souls who believed the world had forgotten them.

In late 2017 the Australian postal vote to decide on same sex marriage uncovered both positive and negative culminations in the twelfth house, as one side displayed the multi-coloured rainbow for a 'Yes' vote, whilst the other side ran television campaigns aimed at parents to generate homophobic fears of a terrible future for their children in order to force a 'No' vote from the Australian public.

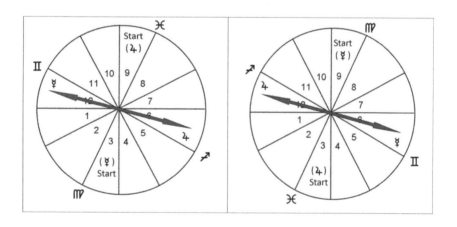

Fig. 106 CADENT Jupiter and Mercury Ruled
Squares Culminating in Dark Houses

Cancer or Capricorn Ascendant

a) *Mercury starts with 3rd – culminates in 12th; Jupiter starts in 9th – culminates in 6th H (left)*

b) *Jupiter starts with 3rd – culminates in 12th; Mercury starts in 9th – culminates in 6th H(right)*

Example Chart Five : Alexander Fleming

Mercury's Houses: Starts in 3ʳᵈ – culminates in 12ᵗʰ house

Jupiter's Houses: Starts in 9ᵗʰ – culminates in 6ᵗʰ house

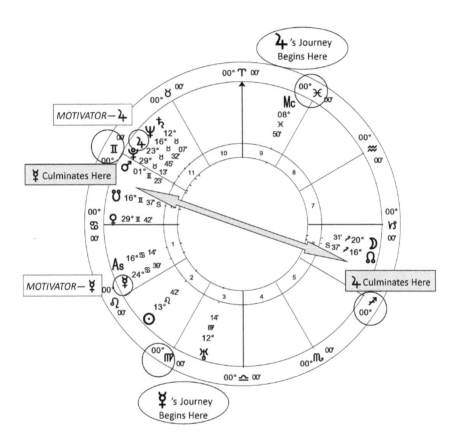

*Fig. 107 Whole Sign Chart with Mercury and
Jupiter Houses: Alexander Fleming*[95]

Alexander Fleming (1881-1955) was a Scottish bacteriologist and
Nobel Prize winner, best known for his discovery of penicillin in 1928.

His discovery was purely accidental as the mould which would become a lifesaver began in an unwashed culture dish and developed completely without supervision whilst Fleming was on leave for a month.

When he returned, he noticed that mould that had developed on the dishes, and had created a bacteria-free circle around itself.

Fleming experimented further with his 'mould juice' and eventually named the active substance penicillin.[96]

Fleming's chart has Mercury conjunct his Cancer ascendant which sextiles Jupiter in Taurus.

Both planets are in their houses of joy, Mercury rejoices in the first, and Jupiter rejoices in the eleventh house.

Both planets in sextile separately form a quincunx aspect to the Moon in the sixth house, creating a modern major aspect pattern known as the Yod.

The Yod is called 'the finger of God': people with Yods *"are in the deepest sense pioneers of the future"*[97] and Fleming used his Yod through its three active planets to discover the world's most efficient life-saving drug.

The Moon is the lord of the ascendant, but Mercury's rulership of the third house uses Fleming's unique skills as a disorganised bacteriologist to fulfil its culmination via Gemini on the twelfth house cusp. Fleming's brilliance lies in his ability to recognise the growth for what it is, and with a scientist's precision to repeat the experiment and to record his findings until they could be published and the drug could be manufactured as an anti-biotic.

Penicillin released millions from the imprisonment of disease conquering *"some of mankind's most ancient scourges, including syphilis, gangrene and tuberculosis"*[98] proving that sometimes a twelfth house culmination in darkness can have a tremendously beneficial effect on human evolution.

Fleming's Jupiter lies in the eleventh house ruling the ninth and sixth houses.

Jupiter expressed itself in the eleventh house by representing his various honours, including the Nobel Prize, and his academic influence in the field of medicine.

Jupiter's ninth house rulership can be seen as the beginning and the sixth house as the end result, which seems like a backward move from an eminent house to a cadent house that lies in the dark.

Fleming was trained at St Mary's Hospital Medical School at the University of London and his dream was to become a surgeon, especially after winning the gold medal in 1908 for top medical student.[99]

However, the ninth house culminates in the sixth, and a series of circumstances meant Fleming became a researcher who chose the dogged repetition of the laboratory where public recognition is often denied instead of the honours of a prestigious career as chief surgeon in an operating theatre.

Although brilliant in his field, Fleming's research was less glamorous than the world of a top surgeon, as patience, repetition and persistence are signatures of the sixth house rather than the highly visible houses at the Midheaven.

Example Chart Six : John Belushi

Jupiter's Houses: Starts in 3rd – culminates in 12th house
Mercury's Houses: Starts in 9th – culminates in 6th house

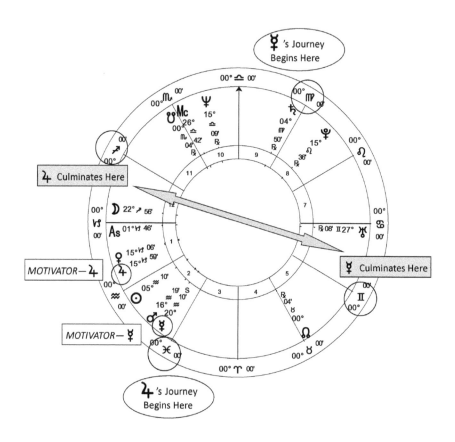

Fig. 108 Whole Sign Chart with Mercury and Jupiter Houses: John Belushi[100]

John Belushi (1949-1982) was an American comedian, actor, and musician who was known for his manic behaviour, intense energy, irreverent humour and raucous attitude towards life.

He was one of the original cast members of the popular television show Saturday Night Live, and gained fame from his role in the 1978 American cult movie *Animal House* and with his musical performances in the Blues Brothers.

Belushi's Jupiter is in the first house in its fall sign, Capricorn, with Venus, and squares Neptune in the tenth house, suggesting his passion for excessive partying when it came to pleasure and his need for escape despite his obvious success.

Jupiter rules the third house (hence, the Blues Brothers, but he also has a famous younger brother, Jim Belushi) and culminates with Sagittarius in the twelfth house.

Sadly, Belushi's natural comedic talent and his fame was not enough to save him from the miseries of the twelfth house as he was a long-term user of narcotics and died at age thirty three from a drug overdose.

Mercury, the other ruler of his cadent houses, does little to relieve his inner demons as whilst it definitely brought wealth from its placement in the second house, it is conjunct Mars and opposing Pluto. With these aspects there is little space for quiet or calm within his mind and his substance abuse may have given him temporary peace, but ultimately climaxed in the destruction of his health.

Mercury is in Aquarius, Saturn's sign, and like many comedians, Belushi had a dry cutting humour when observing life and when this bordered on bleakness or despair he would sink into bouts of depression.

Saturn is disposited by Mercury but there is no mutual reception as no aspect exists between the two signs and one does not ease the other.

The traditionalists used the term 'generosity' to describe two planets which were in each other's sign but made no aspect.

Sometimes this generosity works well for the two planets and the chart's owner, but at other times it compounds a problem and allows little escape from anxiety or a troubled soul.

Mercury and Saturn may share generosity and create moments of comedic madness with perfect timing and excellent execution, but if Saturn in Virgo descends into depression, there is very little that Mercury in Aquarius can do to lift spirits or drive away dark or oppressive thought-patterns.

The debilitated Jupiter in fall in the first house finds little relief as ruler of the twelfth house, especially when it is Sagittarius, its male sign of culmination which sits on the cusp of the twelfth.

Belushi may have shared his feelings with his brother but he also may have hidden his anxiety from the world or cloaked it in humour and wild partying.

Saturn is situated in Mercury's ninth house, and although Belushi produced work that is still held up as being iconic in its content, culmination in Mercury's dark sixth house suggests that Belushi himself may have doubted his own skill or felt unappreciated by his peers, or perhaps feared that he would one day disappear into anonymity, Mars driving his Mercury deeper into depression and drug abuse.

Cadent Houses moving from Dark to Light

12th House Culminates in the 9th House
6th House Culminates in the 3rd House

In theory there should be some redemption in having a cadent house with no light from the ascendant (6th /12th axis) gaining some sense of hope by rising above hardship to be delivered into houses with good aspects and positive relationships with the ascendant.

The process of movement from a dark house portrayed as either the Bad Daemon (12th) or Bad Fortune (6th) climaxing in houses of God (9th) or Goddess (3rd) appears to suggest spiritual deliverance, but not all experiences will manifest in a metaphysical result.

In the following chart examples the journey began with fear and darkness, but in each case the chart's owner rose above their personal despair to achieve their individual mark of victory over the twelfth house.

Part of the process for both Coretta Scott King and Jean-Dominique Bauby involved meeting their own version of the sixth house in order to gain benefits from the third house, and one of the most significant threads which tie these two charts together is the fact that their destiny was not of their own choice, but born from exterior circumstances begun in the dark houses.

Negative stereotypes can sometimes be created by the twelfth to ninth culmination, whereby fear and shadows from the twelfth house can result in the broadcasting of information through the ninth which is misleading, prejudiced or destructive, such as hate-filled rants against race or religion, or bullying by social media where identity can be masked and there are no legal ramifications for the untraceable perpetrator.

The condition of Mercury ruling these two houses will supply information on how troubling are these manifestations, whereas Jupiter, as a natural benefic, can provide some protection against darkness when it rules the twelfth house, and once conquered and turned towards more positive goals, the elevated and well-aspected ninth house of study, religion and travel is an optimistic place for Jupiter's twelfth house beginnings to reach their endgame.

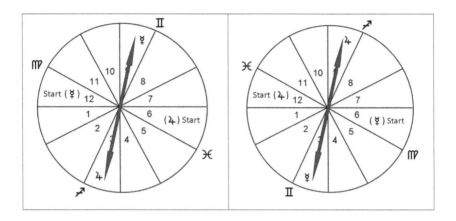

Fig. 109 CADENT Jupiter and Mercury Ruled
Squares Culmination in Houses of Light

Libra or Aries Ascendant

a) *Mercury starts with 12th – culminates in 9th; Jupiter starts in 6th – culminates in 3rd (left)*

b) *Jupiter starts with 12th – culminates in 9th; Mercury starts in 6th – culminates in 3rd (right)*

Example Chart Seven : Coretta Scott King

Mercury's Houses: Starts in 12th – culminates in 9th house
Jupiter's Houses: Starts in 6th – culminates in 3rd house

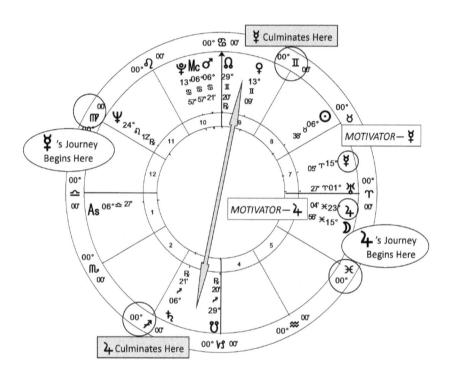

*Fig. 110 Whole Sign Chart with Mercury and
Jupiter Houses: Coretta Scott King*[101]

Coretta Scott King (1927-2006) was an American author, activist, and civil rights leader and the wife of Martin Luther King Jr. from 1953 until his death in 1968.

Coretta's Mercury is situated in the house of her partnerships, and whilst her husband discouraged her participation in the American Civil Rights Movement during his lifetime, Coretta became its leader after his assassination, heading a planned demonstration of sanitation workers just four days after his death and reading directly from his notes prepared prior to the march.

Her seventh house Aries Mercury squares Pluto in the tenth house, rules her cadent twelfth with Virgo on the cusp and culminates with Gemini on the ninth house cusp.

Coretta devoted her life to social justice and demonstrated Mercury's dual rulership when travelling throughout the world speaking out on behalf or racial and economic justice, women's and children's rights, gay and lesbian dignity, religious freedom, the needs of the poor and homeless, nuclear disarmament and environmental justice.[102]

Mercury's ninth house rulership brought special moments in history as Coretta stood with Nelson Mandela in Johannesburg when he became South Africa's first democratically-elected president.

Her husband may have begun the fight for Coretta's seventh house Mercury, but when she became the first woman to deliver the class day address at Harvard, and was the first woman to preach at a statutory service in Saint Paul's Cathedral in London, UK, Coretta's Mercury claimed the ninth house as its own, and her Mercury was triumphant in culmination here in the house of faith and religion.

Coretta Scott King has a Pisces Moon and Jupiter conjunct in the sixth house and both planets trine Pluto in the tenth house.

With a Jupiter in dignity, Coretta's belief in justice and equality for all meant her passion for the cause and her ability to inspire others often drove her body to the point of exhaustion.

Jupiter's masculine sign is ten signs from Pisces at the third house, and indicates one of Coretta's greatest achievements concerning education as Saturn is placed in Jupiter's house.

Coretta believed in the dream of 'a beloved community' where her husband's philosophies could be taught, and for this reason Coretta founded and developed programs for the Atlanta-based Martin Luther King Jr. Center for Nonviolent Social Change in loving memory of Martin Luther King Jr.'s dream of social justice.

Housed within the King Center is the largest collection of documents from the Civil Rights Movement and amongst them are the original notes from her husband's most famous speeches.

Coretta dedicated much of her energy and her later years to the King Center and to the pursuit of decent education programs for poor children.

Both houses of Mercury and Jupiter's culmination hold important planets.

Saturn in Sagittarius fights to make the dream a reality, which goes beyond her lifetime and Venus, the ruler of her ascendant is in Gemini in the ninth house.

Venus gives her the voice, the persona, and her love for God by which she takes these dreams to fruition and carries on the work of her late husband until her own death at the age of seventy nine.

Example Chart Eight : Jean-Dominique Bauby

Mercury's Houses: Starts in 6th – culminates in 3rd house
Jupiter's Houses: Starts in 12th – culminates in 9th house

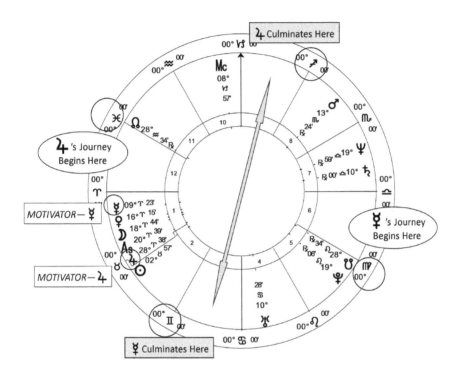

*Fig. 111 Whole Sign Chart with Mercury and
Jupiter Houses: Jean-Dominique Bauby*[103]

Jean-Dominique Bauby (1952-1997) was a well-known French actor, author and editor of the French fashion magazine, Elle.

Jean-Do to his friends, he was a charismatic charmer, a talented journalist who loved fast cars, good food, and reading what he thought of as the hilarious English tabloids.[104]

Bauby has four planets, including Mercury and Jupiter in Aries in the first house, which together rule the four cadent houses.

Bauby experienced the full impact of Mercury and Jupiter beginning his final journey from the debilitated 6th/12th axis when, on 8th December

1995, a massive stroke left him crippled with locked-in syndrome, a rare neurological condition in which his mind was clear and alert but the body was completely frozen. When Jean-Do woke from a coma twenty days after the stroke the only muscle he could move was the one in his left eyelid.

Imprisonment of the worst kind was Jean-Do's fate as a T-square from Mercury opposing Saturn with an apex Uranus in the fourth house conjunct IC metamorphosed a man full of vitality into a helpless invalid in an instant.

Bauby's Mercury culminates horrifically with the third house, a house which sextiles the ascendant and describes the body's ability to perform tasks that are so automatic that they are executed without conscious thought. Jean-Do's reflexes no longer worked, his motor skills were destroyed and he was completely bereft of physical movement.

Most people would give up completely after such a devastating event, but Bauby's Aries stellium kicked into overdrive and he was determined to learn how to communicate in whatever fashion was still available to him. Mercury at the beginning and Jupiter as the last planet of the Aries stellium created a culmination between them that shows the strength and resourcefulness of the human spirit when it is subjected to trauma and crisis.

In spite of his paralysis Bauby learnt to communicate using a method known as the Silent Alphabet where an accomplice slowly reads the alphabet out loud and the listener blinks on the letter which will form part of a word. The process requires enormous patience on the part of both parties as the letters must be re-read each time in order to find the right one which instigates the action of a single eyelid.

Note that exalted Saturn in Libra opposes his Aries Mercury and the skill and dedication required by the reader is enormous as not only do they recite the alphabet, but at the same time they are required to watch the listener so as not to miss the flutter of an eyelid.

In this manner Bauby wrote an entire book over the period of several months by blinking his eyelid to depict the letters of words, one by one. It took him 200,000 blinks to complete the book, *"The Diving Bell and the Butterfly: A Memoir of Life in Death"*.

In the book he explains that the Diving Bell represents the corporeal trap his once active body had now become, and the Butterfly is the imagination of his mind which he uses to flee the terrors of his frozen body: *"There is so much to do. You can wander off in space or in time, set out for Tierra del Fuego or for King Midas' court."*

Jean-Dominique has Jupiter in Aries in the first ruling the twelfth house with Pisces on the cusp, and culminates with Sagittarius at the ninth house of publication.

The fear, the isolation and the entrapment of total paralysis can only be imagined by the able-bodied but Bauby fought for the entire fifteen month period when he suffered under his condition.

The New York Times reviewed his book in June 1997 stating: *"The author cultivates strong feelings, especially anger, to keep his spirit from atrophying along with his limbs."*[105]

They could just as easily have been describing the connection between Jupiter and the Moon which straddle Bauby's Aries ascendant. Jean-Do's French publication date was 7th March 1997: the same date as transiting Jupiter at 9 Aquarius was in a sextile aspect to his natal Mercury at 9 Aries.

He would have no idea that his book would become an international best seller as he died suddenly from pneumonia two days after publication on 9th March 1997 when transiting Jupiter released him from his torment.

Mercury and Jupiter Culminations

Your Chart

If you are interested in finding where commencement starts for these two planets in your own chart, locate the feminine signs, Virgo for Mercury and Pisces for Jupiter, and begin here to track the path to their culmination points at the masculine signs of Gemini and Sagittarius respectively.

Mercury's commencement begins with the feminine earth sign and culminates at the masculine air sign, suggesting that Mercury moves through the process by beginning at a sign which is cautious by nature and inclined towards introspection.

Feminine signs are inclined to be self-protective and in echo of Macrobius' declaration, the soul learns *'expression and interpretation of feelings'* from entering Mercury's sphere.

Wherever the earth sign of Virgo sits in the horoscope, it is creating a commencement point, born of analysis and the exploration of feelings through its reactions to the physical world.

Virgo will take all the time it needs before Mercury can move to completion at the more outgoing station of Gemini.

Air signs are more extroverted in their expression than earth signs, more inclined towards movement and a desire for activity or positive outcome.

Mercury has various levels by which it is equipped to take the experiences learned from Virgo and perfect them through increasing its rank, power or quality at the culminating point of Gemini, and its condition in the chart will give clues as to how this can be achieved.

Jupiter's culmination also begins with a feminine sign and ends at the masculine.

Jupiter is required to harness the dispersive qualities of mutable water and come to grips with its inner landscape, in order to achieve a prosperous termination ten signs away at the mutable fire sign of Sagittarius.

Whilst Mercury is somewhat ambiguous in conferring favours, Jupiter is known as the greater benefic and presumably promises rewards for at least going through the process of moving ten signs from Pisces to Sagittarius.

Macrobius says that the soul as it descends learns *reasoning and theorizing* at Saturn's level but it is when the soul meets Jupiter that it is educated in the power of putting Saturn's gift into practice.

This idea of culmination is unique to these two planets as Mercury and Jupiter alone possess signs in square aspect, and constant movement from one side of the square to the other, either through the long arc to the tenth sign, or the more direct route via the short arc to the fourth sign, fulfils the promise of two planets attempting to achieve authenticity.

Mercury and Jupiter may be problematic for each other being placed in a square aspect and ruling opposing signs according to Thema Mundi, but they do share a passion for mind games.

Each planet in their own way tries to stay one step ahead so that every decision made in the present can gain the greatest advantage for the future.

The only way they can achieve this is through mobility, adaptability and perpetual change as each new set of circumstances arises.

A multitude of options are a way of life for these two planets fascinated by the end-game, and the placement of their masculine signs in the chart can pinpoint exactly how they arrived from Point A to Point B in the native's life.

CHAPTER SEVEN

The Venus and Mars Lemniscate

"See first, think later, then test.
But always see first.
Otherwise, you will only see what you were expecting.
Most scientists forget that."

Douglas Adams (1952–2001)
Author of *The Hitchhiker's Guide to the Galaxy*

Fourth century astrologer Paulus of Alexandria uses the curious term *'like-engirdling'* to describe the relationship between two signs which are bound by the common thread of the same planetary ruler.

Signs which under normal circumstances would bear no relationship to one another are suddenly connected, not through the usual avenues of gender, quality or modality, but rather through the authority of *Thema Mundi*.

Paulus says in his *Introductory Matters*:

"Like-engirdling is whenever the zoidia (signs) happen to be of the same star . . .

The intervals of the like-engirdling zoidia, **in accordance with the count of the unconnected zoidia,** *are as follows: Aries to Scorpio, Scorpio to Aries; Taurus to Libra and Libra to Taurus; Capricorn to Aquarius and Aquarius to Capricorn."*[106]

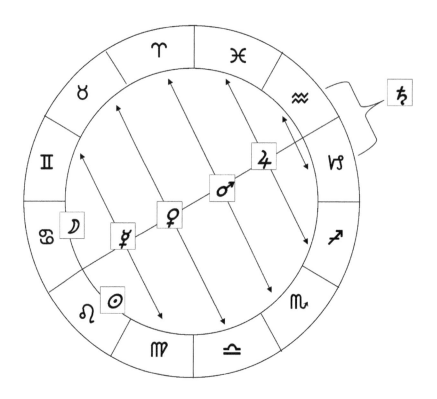

Fig. 112 Signs of Like-Engirdling: Same Planet ruling Two Signs

The term *'like-engirdling'* is extremely descriptive for planets that bind signs together for a common cause.

In earlier times a girdle was not simply an item of clothing or a belt to gather together loose clothing.

In many mythologies the girdle was both a symbol of fertility and a source of protection for women.

The Babylonian goddess Ishtar wore a fertility girdle which, when it was removed, rendered the universe barren.

In Greek mythology Hippolyte the Queen of the Amazons wore a magnificent girdle given to her by the god Ares. Hercules was sent to steal the girdle and in the ensuing battle Hippolyte and her warriors were slaughtered by Hercules who took the girdle with him to the battle of Troy.

The girdle was also sacred to men as it was a symbol of power, strength and victory.

Warriors and soldiers wore their combat girdle on the battlefield to help them overcome their enemies in times of war.

The expression *"to gird one's loins"* is a term which has two meanings.

On a practical level, it meant to collect the material of the long tunic worn during Hebrew times and tie it out of the way using a girdle so that movement became easier for the wearer to fight on the battlefield or toil in the fields in times of peace.

But it was also a term that was used as a warning to get ready for danger or to prepare yourself, physically, mentally and even spiritually, for hard times or dangerous situations when you might need to stand and fight your enemy.

In later times, the Christian Church adopted the girdle as part of their representative's attire as together the girdle and cassock symbolised the holy man's readiness to abandon an ordinary life in order to serve God.

Monks in Catholic Orders would knot the end of their girdle three times to remind themselves of their sacred vows of poverty, chastity and obedience.

In the Old Testament, the Book of Isaiah mentions that girdles of sackcloth were worn as a token of sorrow or physical reminders that the wearer was in a state of mourning.

The girdle was also a symbol of Christ's spiritual strength and virtue.

From Isaiah Ch. 11 v. 5: *"Righteousness and faithfulness are the girdle of the Messiah."*

The circular girdle is not so far removed from the circle of eternity, the Cosmic Egg, or the Gnostic image of the world serpent forming a circle with its tail in its mouth.

The Hindu catechism embodies the idea of the circle as a spiritual symbol saying that the One is "an unbroken circle with no circumference, for it is nowhere and everywhere".

Venus and Mars

The Figure-Eight: Infinity Symbol: The Lemniscate

"Opposition unites.
From what draws apart results the most beautiful harmony.
All things take place by strife."

Heraclitus (504 BCE)

Paulus' text on like-engirdling gives the impression that there exists a flow of energy between two signs ruled by the same planet.

The quartile aspects which exist between the rulership signs of Mercury and Jupiter gives rise to culmination points for these two planets, but for other planets the relationship between planet and signs becomes more complicated.

Mars rules Aries, a masculine cardinal fire sign and also rules Scorpio, a feminine fixed water sign. These two signs have no commonality as they share neither gender, nor modality, nor element, and would hardly know the other one existed if it were not for the connection through their ruler.

Venus also rules signs alien to one another, with Taurus, a feminine fixed earth sign, and Libra, a masculine cardinal air sign.

The flow of energy which exists between Aries and Scorpio for Mars' rulership signs, is immediately followed (or preceded), by a flow of energy in the adjoining signs of Taurus and Libra, which both belong to the planet Venus.

The two examples of like-engirdling should be separate and dissociated from one another, in the same fashion as Saturn minds its own business in the like-engirdling of its two signs (Capricorn and Aquarius) and has no interaction or common link with either Venus or Mars.

And this would be true for Venus and Mars, except for one thing.

The two signs belonging to Mars, and the two signs of Venus, sit in opposition to one another, and therefore, together, the two planets rule axes that lie side by side in the chart.

The connections between the adjoining signs and the oppositions create the crossover from one sign to another and from one ruling planet to another in an angular version of the infinity symbol or figure eight *(Fig. 113).*

When the connecting lines become curves the infinity loop is much easier to see *(Fig. 114)* and the image is one which is reminiscent of the sacred girdle from mythology.

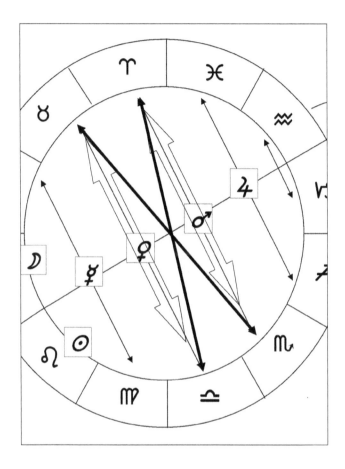

Fig. 113 The Unique Relationship between the Signs of Venus and Mars

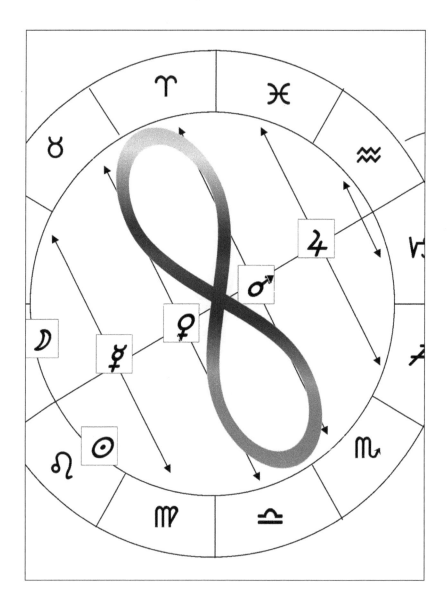

Fig. 114 The Figure-Eight: Infinity Symbol: The Lemniscate

The infinity symbol or the figure-eight lying on its side originates from the Indian religion and similar to the sacred girdle is yet another symbol of a circle depicting infinity or completeness because it is composed of a clockwise circle and an anti-clockwise circle: that is, a male, solar, right-hand half united with a female, lunar, left-hand half.

Like the figure eight that it resembles, the infinity sign originally signified sexual union and the sense of perfection: two becoming one.[107]

Another less well-known term for the infinity symbol is a lemniscate, derived from a word which comes from the Latin *"lemniscatus"* and meaning *"decorated with ribbons"* as it originated from the Greek island of Lemnos where ribbons were worn as decorations.

The lemniscate is a figure-eight consisting of two loops that meet at a central point, and this is exactly what happens for Venus and Mars – they have their own agenda but they meeting and crossing over in a symbolic union of male and female, and this affects how the four houses ruled by the two planets become inexorably linked with one another.

Aphrodite would approve of the idea of ribbons entwined for decoration to represent her planet as it suggests adornment, gaiety, the desire to attract attention, and ultimately the public celebration of union.

But ribbons are also the decorations of war and just as suitable for Mars as it was the French general Napoleon Bonaparte who once remarked: *"A soldier will fight long and hard for a bit of coloured ribbon."*

For these reason, the lemniscate, or entwined ribbon, is a perfect description for the energy which flows non-stop between Venus and Mars.

Venus and Mars – The Oldest Soap Opera in the Universe

One way to describe the complications which arise from the sign rulerships of Venus and Mars is to introduce a scenario which best fits their energies, both independently and as the pair of planets which represent the female and male archetype.

When pondering on the circumstances of Venus and Mars, think *Coronation Street* (1960 – present), *General Hospital* (1963 – present), *Neighbours* (1985 – present), or any *telenovela* (television novel), the Latin American version of soap operas, where in Spain they are also known as *culebrones* ("long snakes") in reference to their convoluted plots.

The term 'soap opera' became the collective title for serial dramas which took snippets of ordinary life and enlarged them into scenarios full of extraordinarily situations and melodramatic events. Tangled interpersonal relationships were the basis of these continuing sagas as they were originally written for daytime radio in the 1920s to entertain women at home.

The early serials were packed with advertisements, and leading soap manufacturing companies of that time, such as Proctor & Gamble, Colgate-Palmolive and Lever Brothers, were the first to realise that they had a captive audience for their home products, and rushed to sponsor these popular on-going programs on the radio. Hence, the name 'soap opera'.

If the lemniscate represented by Mars and Venus were to feature as a popular soap opera there would be four main characters in the cast.

Aries, whom we are going to call Bert

Taurus, who is Alice

Libra, who is Jennifer

Scorpio, who is Tom

In Thema Mundi the sign of Aries is opposite to the sign of Libra.

In the corresponding soap opera, Bert (Aries) is married to Jennifer (Libra).

The sign of Taurus is opposite to the sign of Scorpio.

So Alice (Taurus) is married to Tom (Scorpio)

Bert and Jennifer (Aries opposing Libra) live in the house next door to Alice and Tom (Taurus opposing Scorpio).

In Thema Mundi, Taurus and Libra are both ruled by Venus and linked through Like-Engirdling.

The two women Alice (Taurus) and Jennifer (Libra) are best friends.

Similarly, Aries and Scorpio are linked because both signs are ruled by the planet Mars and can relate to one another via the rules of Like-Engirdling.

The two men, Bert (Aries) and Tom (Scorpio) are therefore best friends.

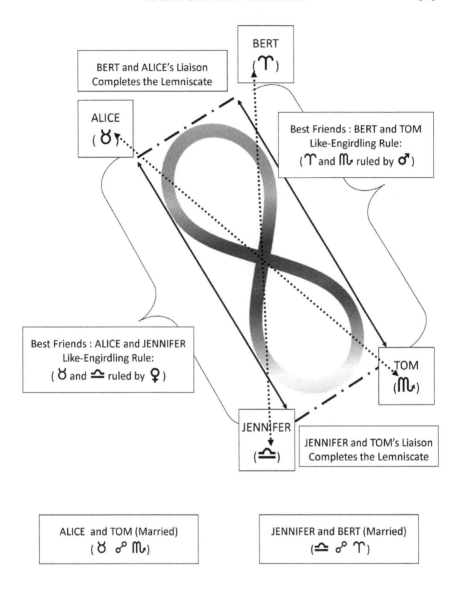

Fig. 115 Thema Mundi: The Rulerships of Venus and Mars (Soap Opera style)

To Recap:

Neighbours Bert (Aries) and Alice (Taurus) reside in houses which are situated side by side in their street.

Bert is married to Jennifer (Aries opposes Libra) and Alice is married to Tom (Taurus opposes Scorpio), so they live in houses which are next door to one another.

I will leave it to the reader's imagination to assign personality traits to these two couples, but suffice to say, the two marriages create the aspect of opposition from Aries to Libra (Bert and Jennifer) and from Taurus to Scorpio (Alice and Tom).

The two women, Alice and Jennifer, are different in personality but are best friends, as are Bert and Tom (again, two very dissimilar men), and the women enjoy spending time together whilst the men enjoy outdoor sports.

The two 'friendships' are the like-engirdled signs, which are different in all four qualities, but are ruled by the same planet, i.e., the friendship between the two women, Alice and Jennifer (Taurus and Libra are ruled by Venus) or the friendship that exists between the two men, Bert and Tom (Aries and Scorpio are ruled by Mars).

Constant contact between the women and the men (like-engirdling) means that the two couples (opposing signs) spend a great deal of time together.

As we are talking about a soap opera here it soon becomes obvious that this closeness between friends and partners incites passion and a desire for change, and one night the four characters, Bert married to Jennifer, and Alice married to Tom, decide to engage in partner-swapping.

Through their liaisons Bert (Aries) is now in love with Alice (Taurus) and this means that Aries is now connected to Taurus.

Meanwhile, Jennifer (Libra) and Tom (Scorpio) have also decided to become a couple which means there is now a female to male connection between Libra and Scorpio.

This may be confusing for the rest of the street, but the couples (in original marriages or in new partnerships) always holiday together, and the girls (and boys) are still best friends.

In true soap opera style, Alice and Jennifer are probably lovers as well as friends, as are Bert and Tom.

The relationships between the four main characters in this planetary soap opera are particularly complicated.

That is, Aries (Bert), Taurus (Alice), Libra (Jennifer) and Scorpio (Tom), are interconnected simply because of the relationship which exists between opposing planets, Mars and Venus, who jointly rule these four zodiac signs.

And also due to the fact that there are relationships between like-engirdling signs which are ruled by the same planet.

The swapping of gender partnerships works two ways in *Thema Mundi*.

Aries, the masculine sign of Mars (the significator of the male gender) now links to Taurus, the feminine sign of Venus (the significator of the female gender).

On the opposite side of *Thema Mundi*, the masculine sign, Libra, which belongs to Venus (the significator of the female gender), now links to Scorpio, the feminine sign of Mars (the significator of the male gender).

There are twelve possibilities but only six lemniscates which can manifest in the chart, but in each case the initiating gender does not change and the following gender does not change on the consecutive house cusp.

Aries/Libra must always lead and will be placed on the first of the consecutive houses, whilst Taurus/Scorpio will always follow on the second consecutive house cusp.

However, on one side of the chart Mars always leads with its masculine sign Aries, and on the opposite side Venus always leads with its masculine sign Libra.

The way in which the signs follow one another in the zodiac circle means that *the masculine signs will always lead the lemniscate* and determine the order of the first of the consecutive houses, and *the feminine signs will always follow* or be found on the second consecutive house on the other side of the circle.

But the first ruler of one side will swap places with the second ruler of the lemniscate, depending on which of the signs, Aries or Libra, comes first.

This is the crux of the Mars and Venus Lemniscate.

In other words, a flow of energy between two very dissimilar planets, ruling two very dissimilar signs apiece, but with connections that constantly drive them together (or into each other's arms, and in whatever order, in the case of Bert and Alice and Jennifer and Tom).

Gender classification becomes very important when describing these two planets.

Mars is a masculine planet, Venus is a feminine planet, and together they create the roots, or elements, of astrology through their separate rulerships of Aries – fire, Taurus – earth, Libra – air, and Scorpio – water.

The worldwide symbol for male (♂) is Mars, and the recognised symbol for female (♀) is the same astrological sigil for Venus.

The two planets belonging to the nocturnal sect share a flow of energy which possesses a raw, creative, and sexual quality that inclines Mars and Venus towards instinctual action and reaction.

These two planets are the archetypes for Love and Strife, the two divine powers described by Empedocles as the reason behind why the elements, and physical matter, keep changing in the world.

Love (Venus) is the force by which things are attracted, and Strife (Mars) is the force by which things repel one another.

According to Empedocles, in the time before these two powers were connected the world was inert and lifeless because there was no change.

When the two divine agents were encased within their own separate worlds, Love would allow nothing to separate, and Strife would allow nothing to come together.

It is only when these two forces are joined, that Life is created.

Similar to the couple who move totally in-sync with one another on the dance floor, Venus and Mars (or Love and Strife) move to an intimate rhythm, made even more insistent when the two planets share an aspect in the chart.

Without an aspect to connect them, the dance movements are not so smooth or automatic, but the dance still exists without an aspect because their rulership signs face one another across the chart, and therefore, Venus/Love and Mars/Strife are forced to acknowledge one another's existence.

Mars and Venus will act according to their own nature in order to produce results for their ruled houses which means that the two planets will react differently to the frustrations experienced by their own houses which experience an inconjunct aspect.

The rule of like-engirdling may assist the planets in overseeing the affairs of their houses, particularly when the planet is in the dignity of rulership, but the houses themselves, and what they represent in the native's life, can be at odds with one another because the two signs still have incompatible qualities.

For Mars, the frustration will build into anger, and this fiery planet is likely to confront from its placement sign, in a way which will reflect the aspect it has to both of its rulership signs.

For instance, if the sign where Mars is located has an aspect to Aries but not Scorpio, (this can happen when Mars is in Gemini, Libra or Sagittarius), Mars will feel confident to manage the affairs of its Aries house (Gemini sextiles Aries, Libra opposes Aries, and Sagittarius trines Aries).

Mars may not be particularly happy in detriment in Libra managing its own house by opposition but at least there is contact and visibility, even if the aspect is hostile in nature.

However, Gemini and Sagittarius do not aspect Scorpio, and Mars is likely to panic or to push too hard for a solution in the house with Scorpio on the cusp which, rather than resolving the issue, is likely to cause Scorpion-like disruptions further down the track in the related area of life.

Venus, on the other hand, would rather find a less confrontational solution, either by trying to appease both houses, or by choosing to ignore one where there is discomfort through aversion, it will favour the affairs of the other house.

This approach by Venus to any dilemma in its houses may find temporary solutions which band-aid the problem, but unless Venus is willing to get ruthless, which is Mars-like behaviour, it is unlikely to produce a practical long-term solution and the issue will keep cropping up in varying forms from Venus' houses with either Taurus or Libra on the cusp.

Venus and Mars belong to the nocturnal sect, meaning that their natures both display highly emotive behaviour, and they are planets which are desire-driven in their objectives.

Neither planet is particularly good at sacrificing themselves or showing restraint where their desires are concerned.

Venus may be a little coy in its approach, but it is just as determined as Mars to get its own way, and dealing with these wayward, and often irrational planetary energies, can be like trying to reason with two petulant children.

Neither planet is prepared to compromise or capitulate, and the fact that their signs face off against one another across the diameter of the chart, not once but twice, means that often the individual bounces from one side to the other, constantly projecting onto the other party and believing them to be totally unreasonable.

Thema Mundi and The Lemniscate: Houses with Light

> *"Every action of your life touches on some chord that will vibrate in eternity."*

Edwin Hubbel Chaplin (1814-1880)

Thema Mundi demonstrates the unique relationship which exists between Mars and Venus as both have signs placed one hundred and fifty degrees apart.

Mars rules both the tenth and the fifth house as Aries is the sign on the Midheaven and Mars itself is located in the fifth sign of Scorpio.

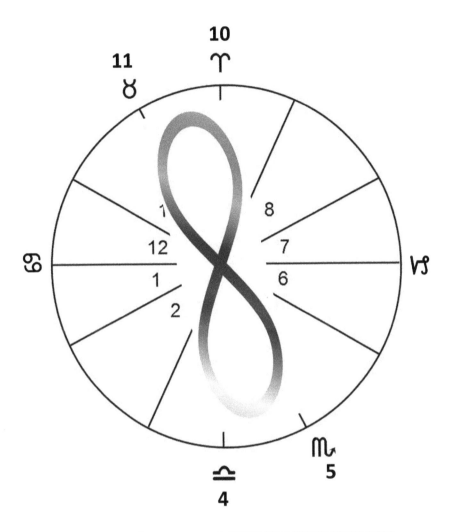

The Lemniscate in THEMA MUNDI
VENUS and MARS Rulerships

Fig. 116 Venus and Mars' rulership houses in Thema Mundi across the 10th/ 4th and the 11th/5th axis

Normally these two houses struggle to connect in the Whole Sign system as there is no aspect from the fifth house of leisure to the tenth house of career.

This means that the two houses are mutually exclusive and this causes glitches in the smooth running of the houses.

The native is required to remove themselves from a focus on one in order to concentrate on the other, so whilst having children or taking time off for leisure (Scorpio or Taurus on the 5ᵗʰ H) lends balance to the life in the long-term, it is unlikely to directly benefit the career (Aries or Libra on the 10ᵗʰ H).

The opposite is also true. If focus is only directed towards the career ambitions or promotion or defending one's position then the fifth house interests can suffer. "Cats in the Cradle" is a 1974 folk song written by Harry Chapin to remind parents of the 'karma' which can happen when a career takes precedence over time spent with their children and is a perfect example of the dilemma between these inconjunct houses ruled by the same planet.

The planets themselves must provide a bridge for these two houses to assimilate. Otherwise one area of life can thwart the other until the native decides to forfeit one house in order to focus on the other, sometimes for life and sometimes for a predetermined period of time.

In Mars' case in *Thema Mundi,* if this were a client's chart, it may be that having children is put on hold for the career, or the career can be temporarily sacrificed in favour of becoming a parent.

It was deemed by society in the last century and beyond to be a perfect solution when it was decided that a woman's career *was her children.* Or, if the family was wealthy, a full-time nanny was engaged to care for the children while the wife entertained, did charity work or supported the public standing of the father.

But this is no longer the case and juggling between the two, career and children, can be exhausting for both parents who seek to find a workable solution to the affairs of two inconjunct houses.

In the *Thema Mundi* Mars must keep an eye on both the fifth and tenth houses at the same time as Venus is also trying to find a balance between the fourth and eleventh houses through its two signs, Libra and Taurus.

It should be noted that the same neighbouring axes are activated when the chart is reversed and Capricorn is on the Ascendant rather than Cancer. When this is the case, Mars and Venus will still rule the combination houses of 4th/10th and 5th/11th but now Aries will be on the fourth house cusp opposing Libra on the tenth and Taurus will be the sign on the fifth house opposing Scorpio on the eleventh house cusp. Now Venus will rule the fifth and tenth houses and Mars will rule the fourth and eleventh houses. This swapping of the two rulers but not the house axes concerned is the same scenario for the diagrams with flowing lemniscates *(Figs.116 - 121)* and the reason why there are twelve possibilities but only six lemniscates in the examples.

The sign, house position, and aspects of both Mars and Venus will describe the natural flow or the strain incurred by the lemniscate created by adjoining axes and can cause the chart's owner to feel like a mouse caught on a running wheel.

The native performs mental gymnastics as they race from one neighbouring (and opposing) house to the other, to rekindle tattered relationships and put out fires that Mars has deliberately lit and Venus is politely trying to ignore.

For example, a natal chart with the same layout as *Thema Mundi* has dynamic Mars in charge of the tenth and fifth, whilst Venus is attempting to pacify both the eleventh and fourth houses.

The horizontal figure eight demonstrated by the lemniscate in this scenario has Venus and Mars jointly sharing the 4th/10th house axis and the 5th/11th house axis.

The loop pattern then develops issues which overlap and become inter-connected, with the native finding themselves moving back and forwards between dilemmas which are not exclusive to one singular axis.

Life situations become extremely wearing on body and soul when separate issues become bound together and the native often feels overwhelmed by constantly trying to find a solution which will satisfy both axes.

Independently the planets can cope adequately with their rulerships.

For instance, trying to balance a social life (11th) with wanting to stay home (4th) for a quiet night is not too difficult for Venus and sometimes one preference will over-ride the other, depending on which feels more comfortable, or desirable, when the time comes to choose between a night in on the couch or a night out with friends.

Trying to balance the demands of a busy career (10th) whilst fretting over the children (5th) is a conundrum which challenges working parents the world over, but when Mars rules both, the native can easily become frazzled and snap at the children when they press for more time, or lose their temper in an inappropriate moment at work when distracted by parental concerns.

Individual rulership can be tricky as the balance between one house and another ruled by the same planet requires effort and planning.

However, complications arise when the lemniscate or figure-eight comes into play and the concerns of two separate axes begin to overlap.

Mars' stress suddenly accelerates with the dilemma of a sick child, especially when the tenth house not only represents the career, but also the house of a child's illness when counting six houses forward from the child's house (turning the chart with the fifth as the first house + six houses = 10th house).

Both houses belong to Mars and a child's sudden illness can disrupt any busy working schedule. But if that illness becomes serious or chronic Mars battles to keep both houses satisfied, whilst at the same time being challenged to come up with a solution.

The house itself may aid in the solution as the native's mother (10th) might step in to help with the child's care, but being Mars-ruled there is likely to be tension between either the grandmother and the child, or the native themselves and their mother.

The infinity loop becomes activated when the opposing side of each axis introduces Venus through its rulership of the fourth and eleventh houses.

The mother may need to move into the native's home to care for the child properly and this starts to infringe on the native's privacy (4th H), or the father may feel neglected and resent the time his wife spends away from him when the fourth house comes into play through Venus.

The native may grow accustomed to the freedom afforded by at-home childcare and decides to spend more time socialising with friends or attending group activities (11th) which upsets both the parents who feel they are being taken advantage of (4th/ 10th axis) and the child who begins to fret for its parent (5th / 11th axis).

Tension builds within the home, there are arguments, the mother moves out or the father objects, and career, social life and family all suffer – the native is back where they started with the same problem, feeling emotionally drained and guilt-ridden, only now with limited options.

Work is unhappy that their employee is constantly taking time off or the individual's work standards have dropped, and the relationships with the mother, father or child, or realistically all three, are now strained.

The loop continues, and is only broken when the child's health improves or the native sacrifices the career, reconnects with the parents, or finds a completely new solution that ultimately brings different stresses, i.e. a friend suggests a live-in nanny (Venus ruling the 11th and 4th house), but the child or mother, or both, doesn't like the new nanny and arguments abound (Mars ruling 5th and 10th house).

There are a number of interactions involved in the lemniscate which involve complicated relationships, and often the perceived root of the problem becomes projected on to the other party.

In this scenario, the native perceives mother to be overly sensitive, work to be excessively demanding, friends to rely on them too much, and the child to be relentlessly seeking love and attention.

Cancer ascendant gets defensive, Mars gets angry, Venus smoulders resentment, and with no reasonable solution in sight, the loop continues in the same fashion, or creates problems of a different kind if none of the parties are willing to take responsibility for their actions.

The *Thema Mundi* lemniscate has Cancer rising squaring the leading masculine sign of Aries on the tenth opposing Libra, also a masculine sign, on the fourth house.

The feminine signs of Taurus on the eleventh house follow Aries and Scorpio on the fifth house cusp follows Libra.

Although the angle of the lemniscate drawn in the centre of the circle will not change as the same house axes are involved in the figure eight, the reversal of signs is not going to produce an identical reaction from the lemniscate.

Now Capricorn rising places Aries on the fourth house opposing Libra on the tenth, and Taurus on the fifth house opposing Scorpio on the eleventh house means that Mars now rules the fourth and eleventh houses, and Venus' house rulerships have altered to the fifth and tenth houses.

A Saturn ruled ascendant will want control over the native's circumstances and Mars will have a completely different way of managing the fourth and eleventh than Venus, and the same applies to Venus when she takes over from Mars to rule the fifth and tenth houses.

The following five diagrams illustrate the possibilities for connections between two consecutive house axes in the chart.

In the hope of avoiding repetition the signs at each of the house cusps have an either/or possibility.

The masculine sign leading the lemniscate is either Aries or Libra and the feminine sign following and completing the figure eight is either Taurus or Scorpio.

Attention needs to be drawn to the fact that only six of a possible twelve diagrams are included here.

The reader needs to be aware that the ruling planets of these signs can utilise the same lemniscate as a double axis *from either side of the chart,* but it is important to note whether Mars is ruling the first sign on one side of the lemniscate (Aries), or Venus is ruling the first sign of the lemniscate (Libra).

Even though the sign gender does not change, the reversal of planetary rulership will have a huge impact on how the lemniscate, and the chart itself, will be read by the astrologer.

Other Examples of the Lemniscate in Practice

Coloured Ribbons of Light: 3ʳᵈ/9ᵗʰ Axis and the 4ᵗʰ/10ᵗʰ Axis

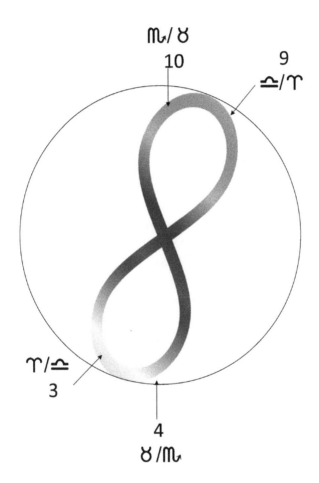

*Fig. 117 **Aquarius or Leo Ascendant***
Lemniscate with Houses of 'Light' – 3ʳᵈ /9ᵗʰ axis
combined with 4ᵗʰ /10ᵗʰ house axis

The positions of the signs in *Thema Mundi* presents just one example of the lemniscate pattern and in total there are six possible combinations which connect two consecutive house axes ruled by Venus and Mars.

The remaining five possibilities present varying degrees of difficulty, simply because some house combinations are more challenging than others.

The exploration of Mercury and Jupiter's culmination patterns in the previous chapter gave examples between houses of the same strength, angular to angular, succedent to succedent, and cadent to cadent, differing only between houses which aspect the ascendant and houses which received no light from the ascendant.

The Mars and Venus lemniscate provide a contrast to the Mercury Jupiter pattern. The lemniscate joins houses in sequence which connect not by square but by inconjunct meaning that the loop will constantly cross boundaries from angular to succedent houses, angular to cadent houses, or cadent to succedent houses.

Nor is the flow of energy always smooth and momentum gained or lost as the figure-eight shifts from one axis to another can be quite off-putting, even for two axes that are not debilitated by cadency or darkness, as in the case of the four houses in the *Thema Mundi* chart.

The only other lemniscate which has all four houses aspecting the ascendant apart from *Thema Mundi* is the one which flows from the $3^{rd}/9^{th}$ and $4^{th}/10^{th}$ axes, and whilst the third to ninth axis involves cadent houses, they still receive easy aspects of sextile and trine to the Aquarius or Leo ascendant.

For this reason two of the six lemniscates are considered to be more fortunate in their house axes than the remaining four lemniscates, as the native may be able to 'see the light' and find their own solutions to the possible issues created by Mars and Venus.

In both cases the lemniscates with light connect consecutive houses which are family-orientated.

The third house of siblings and the siblings' partners (9th H) is joined to the father/mother axis by the lemniscate, so the theme of family relationships is a strong focus for Venus and Mars in both lemniscates where all four houses aspect the ascendant.

The second figure-eight shown here *(Fig. 117)* produces a theme where the home (comfort and security) verses travel or local verses exotic (excitement and adventure).

The lemniscate can also highlight dramas in the study and religion axis (3rd/9th) in competition with family attitudes to education or a pull between career/family obligations verses freedom and personal growth.

This will very much depend on which of the inconjunct signs and houses are ruled by Mars or Venus.

Ribbons of Dark and Light:

12th /6th Axis and the 1st/7th Axis

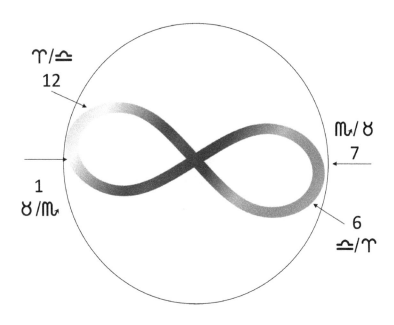

Fig. 118 Lemniscate with 'Best of the Best' house axis connected by Venus and Mars with the 'Worst of the Worst' house axis – 1st /7th axis combined with 12h /6th house axis

Two of the most difficult combinations involve the 6th/12th house axis as the figure-eight pattern has the potential to involve axes on either side of it.

The lemniscate connects the difficult cadent axis with the ascendant and descendant suggesting a shift back and forwards from extremes in shadow and light and this shift can be confronting for the individual with the feminine Taurus or Scorpio signs on the ascendant.

The cardinal masculine signs will be located on the sixth and twelfth axis, and the only difference will be whether Mars rules the twelfth house with Aries on the cusp, or the roles are reversed and Venus rules the twelfth with Libra on the cusp.

The fears, sorrows and mental or physical imprisonments which accompany the twelfth house are likely to show themselves in the very public first house or in the relationship-orientated seventh house.

The difference will be marked as to how the two opposing planets will react to their dealings in the twelfth house.

If Aries is on the cusp the individual may fear violence, cruelty, their own and others' rage, and hidden enemies who are men or who display Martian qualities.

With Mars also ruling the seventh house these fears can be carried through to the individual's personal or business relationships or in dealings with other people.

The lemniscate comes into play when Venus ruling the ascendant through its sign of Taurus – who should look to make friends and form strong bonds – is instead haunted by Mars' fears in the twelfth house.

Feelings of isolation can be a signature of this lemniscate as withdrawal from the cadent houses frustrates the need to connect with other people through the houses ruled by Venus.

As the twelfth house is also the house of my partner's illness, accidents or work commitments (7th house + 6 houses), there can be times when Mars needs to deal with the dilemmas created by its dual rulerships.

Aries on the twelfth and Taurus on the ascendant finds Venus ruling both the first and sixth houses and sometimes the native is dealing with their own physical dilemmas at the same time as their partner is stressed by poor health or tight work schedules.

This lemniscate can be exhausting for both players and the couple can be robbed of the time and energy to fully enjoy their relationship.

If Libra is on the twelfth house cusp, the native fears social alienation, loneliness, aging or ugliness (lack of attractiveness), and its hidden enemies are women, loved ones and those who appear to be friends, but who work against them in private.

Scorpio will follow on the first house cusp, and although it is a water sign and seeks emotional safety, the lemniscate links it to the twelfth house which worries the native that the people whom it loves may secretly wish them harm.

This makes Scorpio rising more secretive and closed, as Mars ruling the sign is likely to search for any advancing harm rather than trying to make friends.

The opposing seventh house is in a dilemma either way – if Taurus is on the ascendant Mars rules the descendant, and if Scorpio is on the ascendant, Venus will rule the descendant, but its worries about the twelfth house are likely to spoil close relationships.

And so the soap opera of Mars and Venus continues.

The example chart at the end of this section for Rodney King *(Fig. 122)* features this lemniscate as Rodney has Taurus rising with Libra on the sixth house cusp and spent a lifetime coping with exposure to issues dealing with health, physical injury and self-sacrifice according to the state of Venus in his chart.

Mars rules his descendant and twelfth house, and Rodney's interactions with others moulded how he dealt with a house which holds the individual's and society's projections of fear, alienation, social injustice, and repression.

Ribbons of Light and Dark:
11th /5th Axis and the 12th/6th Axis

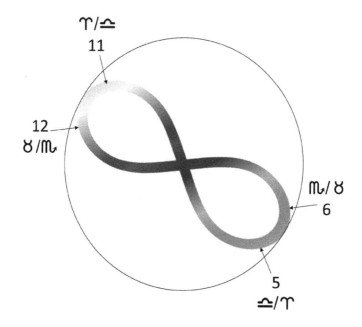

*Fig. 119 **Gemini or Sagittarius Ascendant***
Lemniscate for Light and Dark Axes – 5th/11th axis and 6th/12th axis

The other lemniscate which involves the dark and debilitated house axis of the 6th /12th houses also pulls in the 5th/11th house axis of good fortune and the good Daemon respectively.

In this scenario the masculine axis of Aries and Libra will be on the cusp at either end of the social houses of the fifth and eleventh.

Without an awareness of the lemniscate Venus ruling the eleventh with Libra on the cusp looks pretty good.

Social activities, friends, partying and good times seem to be on Venus' agenda, except that Taurus will be on the sixth house, and all this socialising may just be a nice dream of what I will do when I finally have the time, energy and desire to participate in all this merriment.

Venus may get so bogged down by work schedules or over commitment made by promises to others that there is little time for friendships or group activities.

If Venus is having too good a time too often in the eleventh, then the health can suffer and over-indulgence can cause problems which may seem temporary, but if the excesses persist there can be long-term consequences, especially when Mars is brought into the picture through the flowing lemniscate.

Mars will rule the adjoining houses of the fifth (Aries) and the twelfth (Scorpio) when Libra is on the eleventh, and suddenly friendships don't look so friendly.

Competition between peer group members, or arguments over the behaviour of children starts to spoil good times, and the old saying 'what starts in giggles ends in tears' comes to mind when the axis of good fortune and the good daemon (5th/ 11th axis) is tied to the axis of bad fortune and the evil daemon (6th /12th axis), especially when it is considered that Mars, a malefic planet, must own one end of both axes.

It is hard to say if one would prefer Mars to rule good fortune (Aries on 5th) and thereby spoil it as Mars would also rule the house of the evil daemon (Scorpio on 12th).

Or does one want Mars to rule or ruin the good daemon (Aries on 11th) and also revel in the woes of bad fortune (Scorpio on 6th)?

On the other end of the figure-eight, if Libra is on the fifth it will mean Taurus is on the twelfth house, and this can be a killjoy for Venus.

The other indication for the fifth and eleventh house axis signifies children and this has been mentioned in the discussion on the lemniscate which borrows from the *Thema Mundi* chart.

Any combination of the fifth and eleventh houses (the fifth as my children, and the eleventh as other people's children, or my partner's children, or my child's partner, or my child's enemy) with the sixth and twelfth house can deliver one's own exhaustion, depression or night terrors over the complications of progeny.

It should be remembered that both of the planets involved are creative in their own way and sometimes this particular lemniscate is an ideal expression of the committed artist who finds their inspiration in the fifth and eleventh axis (ruled by either Venus or Mars) and who then withdraws into the sixth and twelfth house axis to dedicate themselves to their art.

Hopefully, this results in beautiful melodies in music, writing or poetry, or stunning and insightful work in the visual arts, but it also can have a touch of the tortured artist who martyrs themselves to their art if passion overrides reason or reality. Both Venus and Mars are nocturnal planets and the chart as a whole will need to have equal balance from the diurnal planets to provide a grounded approach to the individual's creative skills.

Ribbons of Light and Dark:

1st /7th Axis and the 2nd/8th Axis

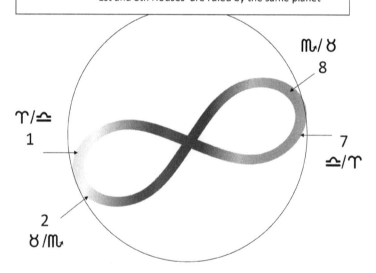

Ptolemy's *Aphorism 37 (second part)* :

"but if Aries or Libra is on the ascendant, he will cause his own death."

Both signs (♈/ ♏ or ♎/ ♉) are ruled by the same planet

1st and 8th Houses are ruled by the same planet

Fig. 120 Lemniscate of Ptolemy's Aphorism 37 – 1ˢᵗ /7ᵗʰ axis combined with 2ⁿᵈ/8ᵗʰ house axis

Ptolemy's Aphorism 37 contains two separate statements: *"If Virgo or Pisces be on the ascendant, the native will create his own dignity: but if Aries or Libra is on the ascendant, he will cause his own death.*

This dire prediction can only occur when the masculine signs of Mars or Venus are placed on the relating axis and are followed by their feminine signs on the succedent second to eighth house axis.

In this diagram either Mars or Venus ruling the ascendant will lead back to the same planet also ruling the eighth house hence the native (1) causes his own death (8).

Hearing this for the first time can cause consternation for those individuals with Libra or Aries on the ascendant but it should be remembered that the eighth house is not a one-use house and has many other meanings. Besides representing one's own death (which comes to all of us regardless of whether we helped it along or not) the eighth house also signifies the wealth of others (2nd from 7th), my partner's wealth, lending institutions, taxation and inheritances.

Libra on the ascendant ruling the first and eighth may mean my indulgences or stress over my love-life bring about my demise, but it is more likely that I borrow money or overextend my credit card to improve my appearance, to buy beautiful things for adornment or I spend too much money in my immediate environment on the ones I admire, wish to impress, or those for whom I genuinely hold affection.

Ptolemy's warning may have been geared more towards Aries rising as Mars ruling the first and eighth houses was more likely to produce sharp objects, swords, knives, even poison, as the individual attracted enemies or their behaviour tended towards dangerous behaviour and therefore the consequences of their Martian antics led them to pay the ultimate price.

Again no need for concern, as Mars ruling these houses may be a little more active or challenge orientated than Venus ruling the first and eighth houses, but the risks are just as likely to involve debt as they are risk to life and limb.

This lemniscate ties together the houses of money with the relating axis, and both Venus and Mars will be concerned with money changing hands as both independent (2nd H) and joint resources (8th H) are affected by their condition and aspects in the chart.

There is the ability to draw large amounts of money and investment towards oneself and one's partners if the cause is right and moves people to put their hand in their pocket.

This is certainly the case for Coretta Scott King *(Fig. 123)* the wife of Martin Luther King Jr. who became the leader of the civil rights movement in the United States after her husband was assassinated.

It took Coretta years of dedicated fundraising to finance and build The Martin Luther King Jr. Center for Nonviolent Social Change in Atlanta, Georgia. The King Centre is a non-profit organisation which still runs on donations and receives over one million visitors a year who come to see the exhibits of MLK Jr.'s photos, artefacts and memorabilia from the years leading up to his death in 1968.

Ribbons of Dark and Light:

2nd/8th Axis and the 3rd /9th Axis

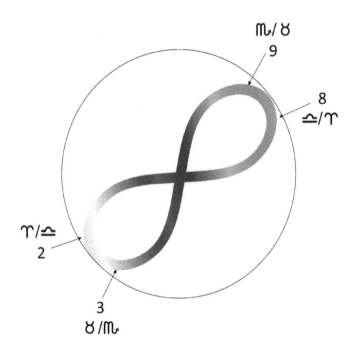

*Fig. 121 **Pisces or Virgo Ascendant***
Lemniscate for Dark and Light Axes – 2nd /8th axis and 3rd /9th axis

The final figure-eight involves the money houses with the cadent third and ninth house axis.

The native or their partner no longer directs the flow of money which was the case in the previous lemniscate *(Fig. 120)*, and the desire-driven nature of Venus and Mars may mean that money is often spent on the 3rd/9th axis.

A more frugal approach would involve money being earned from the skills these two good houses provide for the native rather than money being spent on frivolous pursuits that strain the finances.

Once more family dynamics can come into play in this lemniscate as the house of the siblings (3rd) and their respective partners (9th) can be charged with drama, especially if business dealings, money lending or inheritance is moving back and forth over the second and eighth house axis.

Inheritance is a particularly touchy subject as the last thing Venus or Mars needs to enflame their already emotional tendencies is squabbles over family finances, especially when the territory becomes tricky and the monetary value begins to slide into parental preferences of one child over another. So often the reading of the will becomes about which one of the children was more 'valuable' in the eyes of the parent as the division of assets reopens old wounds and past jealousies amongst the siblings.

Battle lines may have been drawn long before the death of the parent as wrangles over the sale of the family home, power of attorney and other legal documents, and the expenses incurred by aged care facilities or hospitalization are all possibilities which cause strain between siblings in this final lemniscate.

Families often close ranks against the world when this happens as Venus does not like to be thought of as mean-spirited or an unjust or unappreciative child and Mars has a short fuse where family finances are concerned, often wavering between long-winded defensive explanations or indignant outburst which make the native feel they have broken the code of silence and exposed family secrets.

The two planets' signs are not helped by being a combination of cardinal signs (Aries/Libra) and fixed signs (Taurus/Scorpio) so both modalities like to see themselves as powerful forces who will initiate and create change through their masculine signs, but then refuse to capitulate when their feminine signs are tested, preferring instead to use passive aggressive tactics to hold their own.

The choice between swapping to alternate houses or riding the same axis is especially difficult if Mars and Venus happen to be in a hard aspect (conjunction, square or opposition) to one another in the chart.

The archetypal female (Venus) is doubly at war with the archetypal male (Mars) through their signs of opposition. The last thing any lemniscate needs is for the two cosmic adversaries to be placed in signs which create a difficult aspect.

It seems appropriate to add Ptolemy's *Aphorism 12: "Love and hatred prohibit the true accomplishment of judgements; and, inasmuch as they lessen the most important, so likewise they magnify the most trivial things."*[108]

Presumably Ptolemy was reflecting on life rather than making an astrological statement, but its relevance is not lost on two planets signifying the principles of Love and Strife. The native risks their happiness and peace of mind if the conflict between Venus and Mars affects the person's judgement by making a big deal about nothing, and consequently missing the most important things in life.

The Two Kings:
Rodney King and Coretta Scott King

"I existed from all eternity and, behold, I am here; and I shall exist till the end of time, for my being has no end."

Kahlil Gibran (1813-1931)

Rodney King has the fixed signs of Venus and Mars on his first and seventh house axis. Taurus is on the ascendant and its ruling planet Venus is in detriment in the twelfth house. Unfortunately, Venus is in aversion to the first house and Rodney King suffers many of the problems described in Chapter Five on Aversion when the Ascendant lord is blind to its house.

Venus' other house is the sixth house of accident and poor health and when Venus is in detriment it opposes the house with Libra on the cusp.

Rodney's Mars rules the difficult combination of twelfth house and seventh house and is situated in the fifth house in Virgo with Uranus and Pluto with all three planets in a tight opposition to Saturn in Pisces. Mars is also the dispositor for the stellium in the twelfth house. Mars in Virgo can see its Aries house through the rules of Antiscia, and although Rodney tried hard to fight his demons he kept falling back into old habits and destructive relationships which kept feeding the vicious cycle of his lemniscate.

Coretta Scott King also has Venus ruling her Ascendant. However, the cardinal sign of Libra changes the angle of her lemniscate to include the second and eighth houses of wealth.

Venus is in the sign of Gemini in the ninth house and trines the Ascendant degree. As Gemini is the sign directly after Taurus, Coretta's Venus is blind to the eighth house.

The other planet which involves the lemniscate is Mars which in Coretta's chart is located in the sign of its fall in Cancer and in partile (identical) degree to the Midheaven.

Although Mars is debilitated in Cancer it can see both of its houses by being trine to Scorpio and square to Aries and this can be a huge advantage for such a prominent Mars at the zenith.

Mars rules Scorpio on the second house cusp and Aries on the seventh house cusp.

The history of the Two Kings is vastly different and their lifetimes occur in different times – Rodney was only three years old when Martin Luther King Jr. was assassinated – but they each played a pivotal role in the history of the civil rights movement in America.

Both individuals have lemniscates which feature the axis of the first and seventh houses and both have Venus ruling their Ascendant. However, the difference between a cardinal sign ruled by Venus and a fixed sign ruled by the same planet means that the other axis which completes the flowing ribbon will be different in each case. Both charts bring together an axis of light (the Ascendant Descendant axis) intermingled with one of darkness and it could be argued that Rodney King suffered a crueller fate with the planets' situation and the involvement of the sixth and twelfth house axis.

But choice is also involved in any aspect of the chart, including the lemniscate. The problem lies in the fact that a never-ending loop circling through the chart can be hard to leave when the nature of its two ruling planets are passionate, illogical and unpredictably driven by desires that change from one moment to the next. Lemniscates, particularly destructive ones, require a huge amount of discipline and self-knowledge to break their cycle and sometimes the individual does not have the strength or the will-power to alter their course especially when they are used by the greater Fate as a pawn on history's chess-board.

The Chart of Rodney King

Venus Ruled Houses: Taurus on the 1ˢᵗ/ Libra on the 6ᵗʰ

Mars Ruled Houses: Scorpio on the 7ᵗʰ/ Aries on the 12ᵗʰ

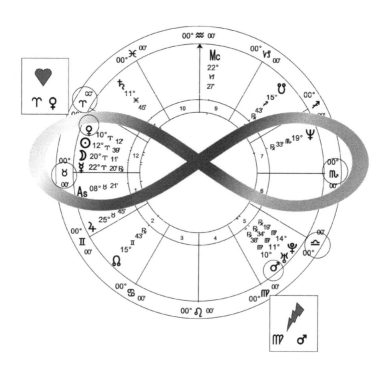

*Fig.122 Whole Sign Chart with Venus and Mars
Lemniscate – RODNEY KING*[109]

The Lemniscate of Rodney King

Rodney's ascendant ruler is Venus in detriment in the 12ᵗʰ house, so the loop created by Venus and Mars is even more accentuated in his chart, when Mars is the dispositor of his Venus, and Venus is situated in one of the houses involved in the lemniscate, because it is in the sign belonging to Mars.

Rodney's physical appearance as a member of an ethnic minority (Venus ruling Ascendant in detriment in Mars-ruled 12th H) and the reaction of the arresting officers to his appearance (Mars-ruled 7th) and his subsequent behaviour is shown by the relating axis owned jointly by Venus and Mars.

Sometimes the action around a lemniscate can quickly accelerate from a harmless night at home with friends drinking and watching sports (Venus ruling the ascendant and Mars, ruling the descendant in 5th H) into one of terror and brutality (Mars conjunct Uranus and Pluto opposing Saturn and ruling 12th house) where life after a major incident is never quite the same.

The beating which King received at the hands of the four officers is an appalling way for the flow of energy released by the lemniscate to manifest, and its impact is so severe that it leaves King with permanent physical and psychological damage. When the flow moves from the sixth house to the twelfth and collects the ascendant and descendant in the process it is not hard to see how the authorities become King's open enemies and their subsequent acquittal becomes the catalyst for the rage and frustration of a small number of the African-American population to explode into violence in the poorer areas of Los Angeles (Venus in Aries in 12th House ruling ascendant, and 6th house of injuries; Mars ruling 7th and 12th house).

Eventually Rodney won settlement in a civil court case (7th) but he was unable to control his destructive behaviour or to pacify his inner demons and his drinking, violent episodes and drug abuse grew worse as time passed.

Venus rules his 6th house cusp but again it is contained within the 12th house ruled by Mars, and the quincunx aspect (150 degrees) between Venus and Mars does nothing to relieve their tension or provide peace for the chart's owner.

The non- aspect of an inconjunct suggests Rodney's inability to escape an infinity loop that is particularly vicious.

Every few years the lemniscate seemed to put King back before the public eye and his history was once more dredged up by the media. In 1993, two years after the L.A. riots, King crashed his car into a brick wall and was convicted of driving under the influence of alcohol. In 1995 he was arrested by police for hitting his wife with a car and knocking her to the ground. In 2003 King was arrested for speeding after he evaded a police chase and eventually crashed into a house, breaking his pelvis and resulting in a permanent limp. In 2007 King was shot in the face, arms and back with pellets from a shotgun whilst he was riding his bike.

There were also times when King did try to break the vicious cycle produced by the lemniscate in his chart. In 2008 he appeared in two reality shows on American television, *Celebrity Rehab with Dr Drew* and *Sober House* to publicly work on his addiction and the lingering trauma of the beating by retracing King's steps on the night and eventually reaching the spot where it happened, ironically the site of the Children's Museum of Los Angeles (Mars in Virgo in the 5th). Sixteen months later in a much publicised charity boxing match King beat an ex-police officer in the boxing ring, and appeared as a panel speaker to a new group of addicts at the Pasadena Recovery Center in the next year's season of *Celeb Rehab*.

In 2010 King announced his engagement to Cynthia Kelly, a woman he had met when she was a juror in the civil suit against the city of Los Angeles and it looked as though Rodney had finally turned his life around for the good.

But the demons were never far away.

On the 3rd March 2011, twenty years to the day since his very public assault, King was stopped by the Los Angeles Police Department for driving erratically, leading to a misdemeanour conviction for reckless driving just months before his death.

In April 2012 Rodney published his memoir entitled *The Riot Within: My Journey from Rebellion to Redemption*, a title which admirably sums up his Venus Mars lemniscate.

Two months later on June 17, 2012 Cynthia locked Rodney out of his house in the early hours of the morning when he became abusive towards her after a heavy drinking session.

At 5:30am Cynthia went outside to check on King and found him at the bottom of his swimming pool. Medics were unable to revive him and he was pronounced dead. King's autopsy revealed that a combination of alcohol, cocaine and marijuana plus a heart condition had contributed to his death by accidental drowning.

The Chart of Coretta Scott King

Venus Ruled Houses: Libra on the 1st/ Taurus on the 8th

Mars Ruled Houses: Scorpio on the 2nd / Aries on the 7th

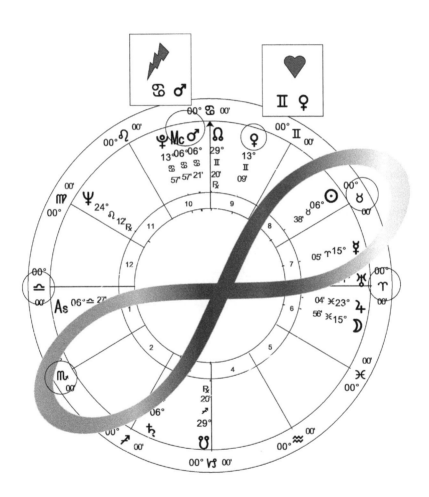

*Fig.123 Whole Sign Chart with Venus and Mars
Lemniscate – CORETTA SCOTT KING*[110]

The Lemniscate of Coretta Scott King

Coretta Scott King was born in the last few days of April and whilst Rodney King was also born in April, his Sun was in Aries whilst Coretta has a Sun in Taurus. For both of these individuals the lemniscate became part of who they were as Mars was the dispositor of Rodney's Sun and Venus was the ruler of Coretta's Sun. In both Whole Sign charts the Sun is featured in one of the houses of their lemniscate.

Coretta also has Venus ruling her ascendant, but Libra is the masculine sign belonging to Venus whilst Rodney has Venus' feminine sign of Taurus on his ascendant.

This change in signs will mean that Coretta's lemniscate will also involve the ascendant and descendant axis, but instead of the cadent axis preceding the ascendant, her lemniscate will involve the money axis of the second and eighth houses.

Venus will rule the first and eighth houses and Mars will rule the second and seventh houses.

Both ruling planets are situated high in the chart with Venus in Gemini in the ninth sign and Mars in Cancer in the tenth house in the same degree as her Midheaven.

Coretta came to the attention of the world in the 1960s through her marriage to American civil rights activist the Reverend Martin Luther King Jr. (elevated Mars ruling 7th h). The Mars in Cancer is in fall and indicates a situation where the person (and their spouse) is greatly disadvantaged within society's social class system and this was certainly the case when MLK Jr. came to fame during the 1955 Montgomery bus boycott.

Coretta won a fellowship to the New England Conservatory of Music in Boston the city where she met Martin Luther King Jr. (Venus in Gemini in 9th house). She was a soprano and was intending a career in music but was warned by Martin's father this would be unsuitable for a Baptist minister's wife.

The couple were married in 1953 and although Coretta abandoned thoughts of a career after marriage, she conceived and performed in a series of favourably reviewed Freedom Concerts which combined prose and poetry narration with musical selection. The Concerts served as significant fundraisers for the Southern Christian Leadership Conference, the direct action organisation of which Dr. King served as first president.

Coretta's lemniscate flows from the first and seventh axis (herself and MLK Jr.) to the axis of money and Coretta's early fundraising efforts were incorporated with her singing and her Venusian talents.

During King's lifetime he discouraged Coretta's involvement with the civil rights movement preferring her to stay home as a traditional mother and raise their four children.

Yet Coretta was hugely instrumental in raising money for the cause and for acknowledging the role that women played in the civil rights movement. During the 385 days of the bus boycott when African-Americans refused to ride the segregated buses, it was grassroots communities of women who financially supported those who lost their jobs during this period.

Coretta publicly criticized the sexism of the Civil Right Movement in Jan 1966, two years before her husband's death in an interview with a woman's magazine saying *"Not enough attention has been focused on the roles played by women in the struggle. By and large, men have formed the leadership in the civil rights struggle but women have been the backbone of the whole civil rights movement."*

King travelled extensively during the years of their marriage and there were always rumours of extramarital affairs of which Coretta became publicly aware when the FBI deliberately sent tapes of his infidelities to Coretta whilst King was travelling knowing full well that Coretta opened all his correspondence whilst he was away. This act confirmed that the FBI knew from surveillance that the combination of the two was incredibly powerful – King spoke to the men but it was Coretta who moved and inspired the women but the tapes did not break the marriage or discredit her husband. After Martin's death Coretta commented *"all that other business just doesn't have a place in the very high level relationship we enjoyed".*

The year after Martin Luther King was assassinated Coretta published a book entitled *My Life with Martin Luther King Jr*. The FBI spent considerable time studying the book as rather than the Movement collapsing after Martin's death, Coretta was proving herself to be just as powerful and charismatic as her late husband. The FBI report concluded that her "selfless, magnanimous, decorous attitude is belied by her actual shrewd, calculating business-like activities."

Coretta's lemniscate could not be better summed up than by this statement. Not only did she have the poise, grace and passion for the politics behind the Movement but she was able to find financial backers who would provide the money needed to bankroll the struggle for racial equality.

Mars rules Coretta's seventh house and her grief certainly fuelled her determination to fulfill her late husband's dreams and keep his memory alive. Four days after his death Coretta marched with the sanitation workers for fair pay and work conditions, reading from the speech taken from the suit that Martin was wearing when he was shot. Mars also rules the second house, and whilst money is generally the theme associated with this house, the second house is also the house of my husband's death (seventh house + 8).

Martin Luther King Jr. was an advocate for non-violence yet he lived a dangerous life. There were countless death threats, imprisonment for civil disobedience, marches that often turned to violence, a firebomb and shots fired directly into the family home and a stab wound at a book signing.

All of these terrifying events were part of Coretta's marriage to MLK Jr. and a mark of Mars in fall on the Midheaven.

There is no record of the same threats being made against Coretta's life when she took his place as the president of the SCLC. Coretta broadened the range of her civil rights, including women's rights, LGBT equality, her opposition to apartheid and her commitment to the peace movement.

In regards to equal rights for women Coretta once said *"I believe all Americans who believe in freedom, tolerance and human rights have a responsibility to oppose bigotry and prejudice based on sexual orientation."*

Coretta raised the funds to build The Martin Luther King Jr. Center for Nonviolent Social Change and served as the Center's president and CEO from its inception. Situated in the Freedom Hall complex encircling Dr King's tomb, the King Centre is today located inside of a 23-acre natural historic park which includes his birth home. The Centre contains thousands of documents including her husband's speeches and notes and finances education for children from poor communities as well as supporting civil rights movements across the globe.

The King family under Coretta's control and even after her death was often publicly criticized for the handling of King's estate and Coretta instigated several civil cases in her term as president of The King Centre. In 1987 Coretta began a lawsuit against the Boston University for the return of 83,000 documents which she believed belonged with the King's archives. In 1992 she sued a Californian auction house for the sale of stolen documents and requested punitive damages (2nd/8th house axis) for the theft. In 1994 Coretta sued and won a court case against *US Today* for using King's famous "I Have a Dream" speech without her permission, and instigated a similar lawsuit in 1996 against CBS for copyright infringement. In 1998 Coretta met the Attorney General four days after the thirtieth anniversary of her husband's assassination to pressure the Justice Department into investigating claims made by Loyd Jowers that he had been paid to hire an assassin to kill MLK Jr. Coretta also filed a lawsuit seeking unspecified damages against Jowers and his co-conspirators.

Coretta remained constantly in the limelight campaigned for years for her husband's birthday to become a national holiday and in January 1986 she oversaw the first legal holiday in honour of her late husband. By the year 2000 fifty States of America commemorate King's birthday. Years after Coretta's death her youngest child Bernice King said "that in many respects her mother paved the way and made it possible for the most hated man in America in 1968 to now being one of the most revered and loved men in the world."

There are many facets of Coretta's chart which display her determination but it is hard to ignore the success of her lemniscate which crosses the double axis and draws together four houses that may otherwise have been overlooked as a dynamic vehicle for her tremendous drive and passion.

In 1959 the couple were sponsored by the American Friends Service to travel to India on a month-long pilgrimage to visit disciples and sites around the country associated with Mahatma Gandhi. It was here that the two forged their plans to base their own battle with inequality and racial hate on Gandhi's principles of nonviolence.

Coretta would carry through with these principles after her husband's death and for the rest of her life, and although their beliefs often put the King marriage under huge strain, it also created a partnership which changed the face of the Civil Rights Movement, not just in America, but around the world.

CHAPTER EIGHT

Saturn's Two Faces

January – The Poet's Calendar

"Janus am I; oldest of potentates,
Forward I look, and backward, and below
I count, as god of avenues and gates,
the years that through my portals come and go."
Henry Wadsworth Longfellow (1807-1882)

Saturn and Janus: Gods of Beginnings and Endings

Janus is a Roman god whose epithet *'Geminus' or 'two-faced'* refers to both his physical appearance and his ability to look in both directions at the same time.

His special gift of divinity allowed him to view the past whilst being able to see into the future and the Romans believed Janus was the god who best represented Time.

The windows to the past and the future were open to Janus but the present was of little interest to him. The concerns of today were of little consequence, as this time demarcation merely served as a midway point between 'what was, and what will be.'

Today was both yesterday's future and tomorrow's past, and this level of unconcern gave Janus an impartiality which raised him above other gods whom the Romans embroiled in their daily dramas of life.

Janus was the god of beginnings and endings. He was worshipped as an agricultural god at the season's plantings and celebrated at harvest festivals when the crops were reapt and prayers were offered up to him at the start and end of each day's business.

Janus was present at all human rites of passage.

He was the immortal honoured guest at every celebration concerning births and marriages, and most importantly, he was the divine representative at funerals when he performed his duty by guiding the soul to its final resting place after death.

He was paramount to every important event in a human's life, and Ovid called him the 'gatekeeper of the heavenly mansion', because he watched over the eastern gate at the beginning of life at birth and the western gate at the end of life.[111]

The Romans believed Janus held the key to Heaven and was honoured by all other gods, so when prayers or religious ceremonies were enacted, custom required that Janus be invoked first before approaching another god so that he alone could act as an intermediary between the mundane and the divine.

In the physical world, Janus ruled the daily alternation of light and darkness at each new day's dawn.

He presided over household doorways and portals keeping families safe within their homes, and for the community in general, his effigy marked the boundaries at city gates and throughout the districts of Rome.

Both Janus and Saturn were patron gods of sailors and both were agricultural gods.

The stories of these two gods are intertwined in Roman mythology.

Janus was the Beginner, the first king of Old Latium who received Saturn when he was expelled by Jupiter from Heaven, and who offered sanctuary to the deposed god when he was shipwrecked on Latium's shores.

The two gods became firm friends, Saturn teaching Janus the art of agriculture, and Janus sharing his kingdom with Saturn in reward for his guest's instruction on the seasons and land management.

January, one of the months belonging to Saturn, is named after Janus and each year the Romans paid homage to the two-faced god on New Year's Day.

The early hours of business were dedicated to Janus as men rose from their beds to start what could be called their Saturnian rounds, their daily activities and business obligations, so much so that Horace called Janus *'Matutine Pater'* or Morning Father.

As well as carrying the name of Father, Janus was also called the Creator, as it was believed he was present at the beginning of Time, which granted him the right to be called the Guardian of the Gates of Heaven.

'Consivius' or Sower, was another epithet given to Janus, not only to honour him as a god of agricultural, but also to gain his favour at conception, as Augustine states: *"In fact Janus himself first, when pregnancy is conceived . . . opens the way to receiving the semen."*[112]

Again this is reminiscent of Saturn's part at the beginning of the nine months of gestation when Omar of Tiberius states in his Disposition of the Months before birth: *"When the seed falls into the vulva in the first month, it happens in the disposition of Saturn, and he disposes of the native by means of cold"*[113]

Saturn-Like Images of Janus

The Romans dedicated much artwork in the form of statues and mosaics to Janus' two faces.

In many instances the two faces were not identical. In fact, artists took great pains to emphasise the difference between the face of the past, and the face of the future. The image below *(Fig. 124)* is one of a series of sketches from Dom Bernard de Montfaucon's original work in the 1700s and demonstrates the concept of two markedly different faces looking in opposite directions.

In de Montfaucon's Janus the face on the right side of the image is set in shadows and its features suggest a much older man who has gained wisdom and experience with age.

The face of advanced age holds a passive and somewhat dreamy gaze which seems to be without judgement or condemnation.

His lips gently press together, not in disapproval, but merely waiting patiently for the face's owner to quietly express his own opinions when others have finished voicing their own views on life.

The older man's face is bearded and his hair is slightly unkempt, naturally following the contours of his face, rather than styled in any particular fashion.

In contrast, the face on the left side is clear and bright, seemingly facing the sun rather than being cloaked in shade.

This face is clean-shaven and younger in appearance, adorned in an elaborate headdress, or a centurion's helmet, which implies authority and elevated social standing.

Behind the headdress the hair is carefully manicured, and the face holds a gaze that appears sharper or more focused than its companion face who is in a state of contemplative reverie.

The younger man's face has his eye tilted upwards, literally looking forward to a bright future, rather than being downcast and somewhat resigned to life's vagaries.

There is almost a caricature quality to the young man's face as all the features are sharply chiselled to the point of being exaggerated, with the chin, single ear, lips and nose being all clearly defined in the print.

The differences in nose shape even suggest a difference in background or ethnicity from the man on the right side of the image.

Presumably this intention is meant to accentuate youth, or perhaps to add an air of handsomeness. In comparison to the brightness of the youth the features on the attached face to the right are worn and blunt almost as though Time has produced a more careworn countenance.

The myth of Janus says that he is a god of the future and a god of the past, but which face represents which time period?

It would be easy to say that the older face is a reminder of years gone by and therefore represents the past, and that the youthful face with a steady eye is symbolic of the future, but it may not be as simple as equating an older face with the past and a youth with the future.

If this is an interpretation of an immortal god, then when viewed by a mortal it may be a gentle reminder that youth does not last forever as it will fade into the past, and it will not be many years before the fresh face on the left becomes the old man in the future.

Either way, Janus is a reminder of Time passing and he is perfect for Saturn, the planet which also marks Time and also bears two countenances through the signs of Capricorn and Aquarius.

> *"The past gives you an identity and the future holds the promise of salvation, of fulfilment in whatever form. Both are illusions."*

> Eckhart Tolle (1948-)

Fig. 124

Janus image, a print of French Benedictine monk
Dom Bernard de Montfaucon (1655-1741).[114]

The Two Faces of Saturn

Saturn holds a unique position within *Thema Mundi* as it is the only
planet which rules two consecutive signs in the chart.

Saturn's two signs are linked through the rule of like-engirdling
which states that there is a shared sympathy between two signs ruled
by the same planet.

This gives Saturn a 'Janus effect' as its two faces, Capricorn and
Aquarius, are attached to the one planet through like-engirdling, but

their countenances face in different directions because they share nothing in common.

Capricorn is a feminine nocturnal sign with cold and dry qualities, and Aquarius is a masculine diurnal sign with hot and wet qualities.

They are as unrelated as Janus' dual visages, but the laws of astrology command that they work together for Saturn their mutual dispositor.

The key to the two faces of Saturn lies within its signs, Capricorn and Aquarius.

Similar to Janus' riddle over which face is the past and which is the future, it would be too simple to associate the older face of Janus with the cold earth sign of Capricorn, and say that Capricorn represents the past, or to think that the aristocratic younger image is analogous of Saturn's air sign, Aquarius, with the hot, wet qualities of youth, who represents the future.

Both roles are reversible and Capricorn may just as easily be seen as the future image of old age whilst Aquarius is the past, reminding us that once upon a time we were all fresh-faced young with sure opinions and idealistic notions of how the world could be changed for the better if only the older generation would listen.

Fig.125 Saturn's Janus-effect in Thema Mundi

Qualities, Signs and Rulers

Signs which are adjacent in the zodiac circle bear little resemblance and share little in common with one another.

They alternate in the active qualities of hot or cold (in the outer circle in *Fig. 126*), are different in element and modality, and, with the exception of Saturn, are ruled by different planets.

The only repetition occurs when the passive qualities of wet or dry (in the inner circle in *Fig. 126*) are doubled between sign changes as this pattern allows for the discrepancies which create the tension of an opposition.

Signs with the same active quality (hot or cold) face across from signs with different passive qualities (wet and dry) and allow for the creation of four elements.

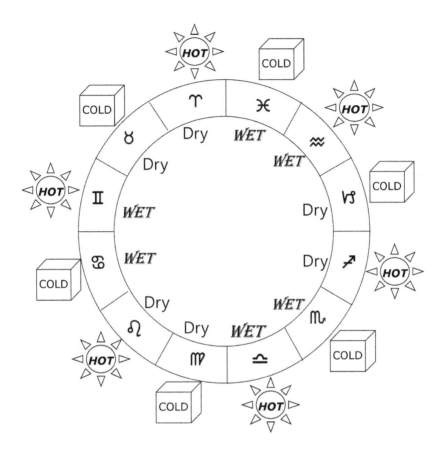

Fig. 126 Thema Mundi's Patterns of Active and Passive Qualities

If the passive qualities of wet and dry were in alternate order like their active brethren, then only two elements can be created and there would be no such thing as an opposition.

For instance, Aries begins the zodiac circle at Vernal Equinox with its hot and dry qualities as it is a fire element.

If both qualities then changed order, Taurus would be cold and wet, and rather than maintaining its element as earth (cold and dry), it would now become water.

The following change in both qualities to hot and dry creates fire, eliminating air completely from the elements, and the following change will create water once more.

This means that only two elements are possible when the inner circle of passive qualities is alternated, rather than being presented as pairs.

If we had started the same hypothetical process at Aries' opposite sign of Libra, then air (hot and wet) and earth (cold and dry) would exist and would be alternate elements around the chart, but the elements of fire and water would be eliminated under this system.

This pattern of constantly switching the active contrariety of hot or cold, and rotating the pairing of the dry and wet passive contrariety, is a clever system which ensures that each of the five planets receives the benefit of experiencing the four qualities through rulership of two signs apiece *(Fig. 127)*.

Mercury rules Gemini, an air sign with hot and wet qualities, and also rules Virgo, an earth sign with cold and dry qualities.

Jupiter rules the opposing signs to Mercury, being Sagittarius, a sign belonging to the fire element (hot and dry) and Pisces, which is a water sign (cold and wet).

Similar to Mercury, Venus rules an air element sign, Libra, and an earth element sign, Taurus, whilst its opponent Mars copies Jupiter and rules both a fire and a water sign (Aries and Scorpio).

This leaves Saturn to rule two consecutive signs with differing qualities: Capricorn, cold and dry, and Aquarius, hot and wet.

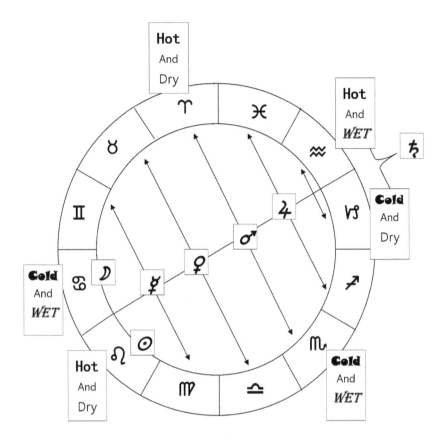

Fig. 127 Saturn's Signs in Thema Mundi's Patterns of the Qualities

The luminaries are exempt from this rule as they are lords of singular signs.

The Sun rules Leo, a fire sign with hot and dry qualities, and the Moon takes the opposite standpoint with her qualities being cold and wet as Cancer is a water sign.

Signs which are adjacent in the zodiac are similar to unfriendly neighbours who choose to ignore one another and interact with strained civility only when one encroaches on the other's territory.

In the situation where Venus and Mars are fated to own adjacent signs (Aries/Taurus; Libra/Scorpio) the relationship between the two planets is tantamount to warring neighbours who are forced to live side by side as neither can voluntarily relocate. Or to find a resolution by creating the figure-eight as suggested in Chapter Seven on the Venus and Mars Lemniscate.

Their one similarity lies in the fact that the signs of Mars and Venus, that is, Aries and Taurus, share a common passive quality as they are both dry, and Libra and Scorpio both have the passive quality of wetness.

This means that the two adjoining signs of Mars and Venus tend to approach issues from a like-minded point of view, and to have the ability to pass through obstacles when they have similar problem-solving techniques.

Sharing the qualities of the passive contrariety can make a huge difference to signs which would otherwise have no common ground.

(Ah! Now we know why Bert was attracted to Alice, and Jennifer found Tom so appealing!

Bert and Alice were both 'dry', whilst Jennifer and Tom were both 'wet'!)

Any aspect between Mars and Venus in the chart will indicate whether they can find a suitable compromise (a trine or sextile aspect), or if they will be in a state of constant aggravation (a conjunction, square or opposition), bearing in mind that Mars will always have the upper hand as it is a superior planet by being placed above the Sun in the Chaldean Order, and can occasionally turn into the neighbour from Hell for Venus.

The situation for Saturn is different as it is parent to both signs and its own circumstances will imply which of its two children it tends to favour in any particular chart.

For instance, if Saturn is located in the sign of Taurus, it will form a trine to its sign Capricorn because both signs are from the earth element, at the same time as it squares Aquarius which shares the fixed modality with Taurus.

Therefore, we need to ask ourselves, does Saturn's management of the Capricorn house flow easily, whilst it has greater strain in controlling the matters described by the Aquarian house?

Each of the five planets faces the same dilemma.

They will often be in signs which form aspects that are more compatible with one rulership sign than the other.

But in the case of Saturn, its two signs are way too close, and any inequalities will be glaringly obvious when one sign runs into the next, suggesting that the problems of one will naturally infringe on the other.

"The worst thing about crossing a line, is when you don't know you already have."

Kuiltje

It seems ironic that Saturn, a planet which signifies boundaries, should have to constantly retain the boundaries of signs under its own jurisdiction, and to secure some imaginary space between Capricorn and Aquarius.

Perhaps it is the Cosmos' constant reminder to Saturn to be ever vigilant of the dangers of crossing boundaries – when the line is crossed it ceases to be a line and becomes a squeaky gate where one can pass back and forth at one's discretion.

Saturn may need to take advantage of what seems to be a random incident to drive a wedge between the two houses and what they signify in the native's chart in order to re-establish the line and to find some breathing space to recuperate before it enters the fray once again.

In modern astrological practice there seems to be a tendency to want to keep the affairs of one house completely separate from those of another house by the reluctance to use the old system of planetary house rulership.

Yet examples given by Ptolemy's Aphorism #37 on Mercury and Jupiter (Chapter Six), and on the signs of Venus and Mars (Chapter Seven) suggest that this was not the case in traditional astrology.

Saturn is the planet which signifies separation, isolation and division, so by definition alone it should be perfectly capable of managing the affairs of two houses that determine two entirely unrelated walks of life.

However, the face of Janus suggests otherwise, and the following delineations on Saturn two-faced house rulerships are based on the premise that Saturn is either incapable or unwilling to separate the affairs of the house of Capricorn from its neighbouring house of Aquarius.

Like-engirdling implies that the affairs of one sign will share sympathy with the other and that Saturn's involvement with one house, and one area of life, will have immediate repercussions on its next door neighbour.

The walls can be very thin in Saturn's houses, and 'leakage' is not unknown to happen when one area of life impacts on the next.

Other planets need aspects, house placement or dispositorship to link houses which lie side by side in a chart but Saturn is a loner in this task, and this makes its situation unique in the delineation of a chart.

Saturn Ruling Adjacent Houses

A reproduction from Maternus' *Matheseos, Book II* features a diagram of singular meanings for each of the twelve houses *(Fig. 128)* and is used in Saturn's three Tables *(Fig. 129, 134 and 139)* to keep descriptions of the houses down to one word significations.[115]

A wider variety of meanings is described in the chapter on Houses in *A Tiny Universe*, but for the purpose of demonstrating Saturn's rulership of contiguous houses, a more simplified label is a good place to start the process of relating one house to the next in zodiacal order.

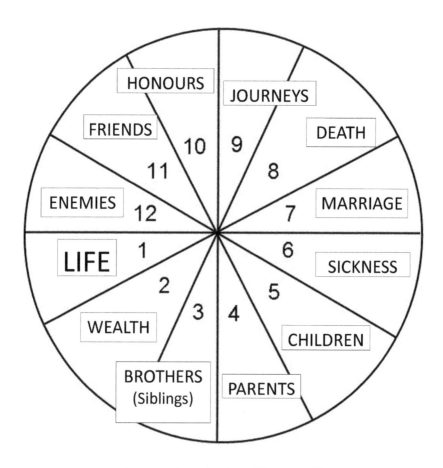

Fig. 128 Reproduction of Diagram V:

The Twelve Houses from Firmicus Maternus' Matheseos Liber Secundus (Book Two)

There are definite advantages and disadvantages as to where the two signs of Saturn occupy the chart when the Whole Sign system is applied to this theory.

In Whole Sign, the two signs will occupy adjacent houses, but in a quadrant based system, the same sign may be located on two houses in a row so that Saturn can take possession of one extra house.

For instance, a low degree of Capricorn may claim the initial cusp, whilst a high degree of Capricorn on the following cusp means that Saturn will rule not one, but two houses through Capricorn, as well as the following house with Aquarius on the cusp.

Likewise, if one of Saturn's signs is intercepted in a house, it may appear as if Saturn rules only one house rather than two because of the interception.

The diagrams and Tables which complete this chapter demonstrate Saturn's involvement in consecutive houses through its rulership of Capricorn and Aquarius.

The first Table *(Fig. 129)* gives four examples where the light from the ascendant shines on both of Saturn's houses and the diagrams which follow shows what this looks like in the chart.

The second Table *(Fig. 134)* has been named as Saturn's Series One and shows four examples of rising signs which create a Saturn house in the dark alongside its partner house in the light and suggests ideas as to what this might imply for Saturn and its two houses.

Series One features the houses on the eastern side of the chart and includes the Ascendant in this series.

The third Table *(Fig. 139)* is Series Two which includes the last four possibilities in Saturn's rulership of dual connecting houses. The diagrams which follow show the four signs which will produce Saturn's alternate light and dark house, or vice versa, from the perspective of the western side of the chart and includes the Descendant in this series of charts.

Saturn's Rulership of the Houses

THE JANUS EFFECT ♄ Ruling Adjacent Houses With Light Looking in Both Directions With Clarity			
♈ on ASC	♑	10th House	HONOURS
	♒	11th House	Combines With FRIENDS
♎ on ASC	♑	4th House	PARENTS
	♒	5th House	Combines With CHILDREN
♉ on ASC	♑	9th House	JOURNEYS
	♒	10th House	Combines With HONOURS
♏ on ASC	♑	3rd House	SIBLINGS
	♒	4th House	Combines With PARENTS

Fig. 129 Table of Saturn's Houses with Light

Saturn's Houses with Light from the Ascendant

The Table above *(Fig. 129)* demonstrates four combinations which tie together consecutive houses ruled by Saturn with light from the ascendant.

Two of these combinations will involve the fourth house and the houses either side of the angular fourth house, and two combinations of Saturn's rulership of neighbouring signs will involve the tenth house, with the house to the left or right benefiting from an aspect to the ascendant as well as the angular tenth house.

Saturn Ruling Angular 4th House and The Beneficial 3rd House

To illustrate the benefits of the four preferred options, place the sign of Capricorn on the third house cusp with Aquarius on the fourth cusp.

Both houses are within sight of a Scorpio ascendant – Capricorn by sextile, Aquarius by square – so according to Maternus' label for each house *(Fig. 128)* Saturn would jointly rule over the house of brothers (or sisters) and the house of parents.

A longer list of significations of the third house would include siblings in general, neighbours, short journeys, written communication and the native's physical skills.

The fourth house would extend to include the physical home, including its monetary value as fourth house represents non-movable assets, property, hidden treasures, and father or grandfather.

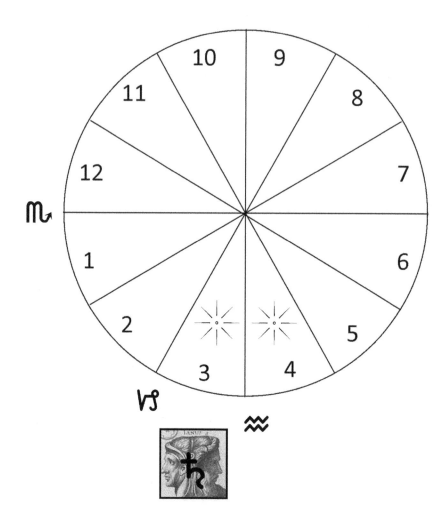

Fig. 130 Scorpio on the Ascendant: Saturn ruling
'Light Houses' Three and Four

If Saturn's condition is good then Saturn's rulership of the third and fourth houses joins these two houses through commitment or responsibility for both types of blood relatives, that is, siblings and parents. However, if Saturn's condition is poor, Saturn can drive a wedge between the members of the family causing separation, isolation or distance due to 'bad blood', fights over inheritance, care of aging parents, or past transgressions or secrets within the family unit.

The native may desire to move away completely from the family and start life in a new community (3rd) but the family, or the family property, may keep drawing them back into the fold (4th).

The nature of the problem will be evident through Saturn's circumstances in the chart, but either way, the native is conscious of what is happening and has some choice in the matter, as both houses form an aspect to the Ascendant.

Saturn ruling Angular 4th House and The 5th House of Good Fortune

In the next example, Saturn ruling the fourth and fifth houses draws them together through their mutual ruler.

Parents or home are linked in a Saturnian fashion to children, leisure or good fortune, so there may be plenty of hard work in the home environment, but the individual is likely to willingly take it on board, as they can either see a future advantage to their commitment, or they consider it is worth the effort because they receive pleasure or acknowledgement for their efforts.

This is a good example of the 'Janus-effect' of Saturn rulership, whereby the face turned to the past (4th house) can pass on the benefits to its mate who looks into the future through the fifth house.

Capricorn on the fourth and Aquarius on the fifth by Whole Sign will give an ascendant of Libra, and sometimes this combination works particularly well because Saturn will also rule the Ascendant through the secondary dignity of exaltation.

This means that Saturn has the ability to tie all three houses together through rulership as well as having the advantage of houses which aspect the Libran ascendant.

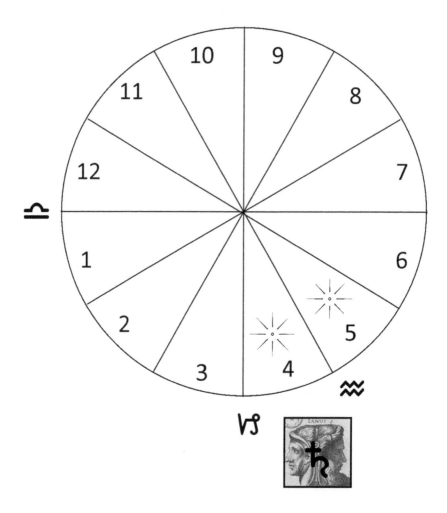

Fig. 131 Libra on the Ascendant: Saturn ruling 'Light Houses' Four and Five

In the previous chapter on Lemniscates Coretta Scott King's chart became an example of the working relationship between Mars and Venus. Coretta's chart *(Fig. 123)* features a Libran ascendant with Capricorn on the fourth and Aquarius on the fifth house. Saturn is located in Sagittarius in the third house and forms a T-square with an opposition to her Venus in Gemini in the ninth house and her Pisces Moon in the sixth house.

Coretta's Saturn aspect gave her the strength and determination to make sure that her husband's dreams would not die and that his legacy would live on through the establishment of The King Centre in his birthplace of Alabama. In 1968, two days after her husband's funeral Coretta started the organization in the basement of the couple's home and began planning a budget of $15 million US dollars to pay for the memorial which would centre on her husband's birthplace. She financed the building of the complex in 1981 which would house thousands of documents on the civil rights movement including her husband's papers and his handwritten notes and speeches.

Saturn in Sagittarius ruling the fourth and fifth houses meant that Coretta's four children (whom she raised alone) were also involved in the running of The King Center and her son Dexter Scott King initially took over as CEO when Coretta's health began to fail but resigned four months later when differences with his mother undermined his presidency. During his tenure Dexter reduced the staff from 70 to 14 employees and closed a child care centre within the facility which his mother had founded.

In 2012 Coretta's youngest child and daughter Bernice King became the current president and CEO of the King Centre. Coretta's children fell out when older sister Yolanda and Dexter had wanted to sell The King Centre but Martin Luther King III and Bernice refused to allow the sale to continue and pass out of the family's control.

Saturn Ruling Angular 10th and The Beneficial 9th House

Further around the chart, if Capricorn is on the cusp of the ninth house and Aquarius follows it at the tenth, Saturn again rules two houses which aspect an ascendant in the sign of Taurus.

In Maternus' model this joint rulership connects journeys with honours, or by extension, any number of cross references between study, travel or spiritual leanings (9th) with career, mother, social obligations or public status (10th).

Any of these combinations between ninth and tenth houses provide Saturn with the opportunity to apply Capricorn's dedication to so many different possibilities, if only the tenth house with Aquarius on the cusp can focus on how best to achieve the potential promised by Saturn.

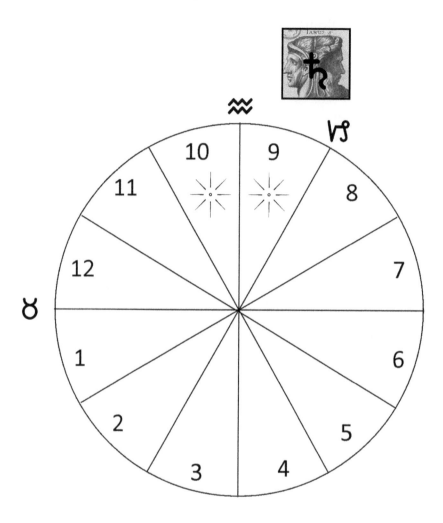

Fig. 132 Taurus on the Ascendant: Saturn ruling 'Light Houses' Nine and Ten

Once again this combination is reminiscent of Janus's two faces, with past and future bound together to create a bright future, if in the past the necessary preparation has been done in order to achieve the required results.

It would be an over-simplification to only apply Janus' past face to Capricorn and the future visage to Aquarius in every scenario as the faces of Janus change direction constantly. The Janus-effect between the two houses should have the ability to flow back and forward in a like manner to his altering countenance. After all, the Roman god's jurisdiction is both beginnings and endings, and sometimes in the thick of things it is difficult to deduce where the initiating process began.

– Is this situation the end of the beginning? Or is it the beginning of the end?

Saturn is a master at forcing these questions to the front of the mind, usually accompanied by remorse and self-doubt or guilt about lost opportunities or poorly timed decisions which resulted in failure.

Capricorn may be more hesitant and fearful when it views the future, and Aquarius may seem more suited to a leap of faith, but Capricorn's caution can be a good thing especially when Aquarius has blundered in the past by alienating others with its strong opinions, or tried to force unworkable visions into reality.

Rodney King's chart *(Fig. 122)* has Taurus rising and Saturn rules both his ninth and tenth houses. Saturn is located in Pisces in the eleventh house and opposes King's terrible conjunction of Mars, Uranus, and Pluto in Virgo in the fifth house. All four planets including Saturn are situated at the Nodal square known as the Bendings and his Moon's Nodes cut across the second and eighth house axis.

In 1996 when the high court reversed the lower court's ruling and it appeared that King would press for punitive damages, Los Angeles mayor Tom Bradley offered Rodney $200,000 and a four-year college education funded by the city of Los Angeles. King rejected the offer and sued the city instead, winning $3.8 million in damages for his ordeal. In hindsight, and given Saturn's rulership of the ninth and tenth houses, perhaps King might have fared better in life if he had taken the Saturn option, rather than pushing for Jupiter which ultimately helped to ruin his health and his life (Jupiter in the first house is the dispositor of King's Saturn and rules his eighth and eleventh houses).

Saturn ruling Angular 10th House and The 11th House of the *Good Daemon*

The final combination when Saturn's two houses will aspect the ascendant occurs when Capricorn is on the tenth and Aquarius on the eleventh house cusp. This scenario results in an ascendant with the cardinal sign of Aries on the first house cusp.

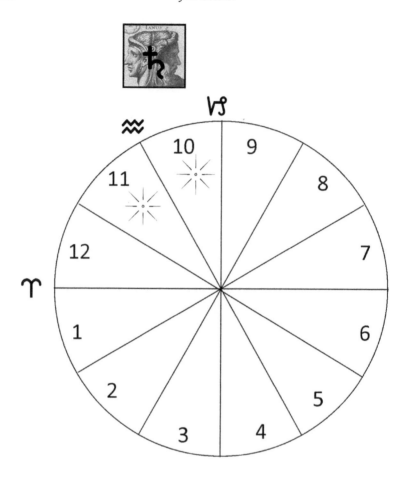

Fig. 133 Aries on the Ascendant: Saturn ruling 'Light Houses' Ten and Eleven

Once again, the pivotal tenth house is involved, but this time Capricorn has moved on to the angular house of culmination, and Aquarius has moved to the eleventh house, on the other side from the previous ninth house.

A combination of honours and friends, colleagues and mentors has a potential for the Janus-effect to work to the native's advantage, as these two houses can go hand in hand if Saturn is playing nicely in the chart.

The more elevated the ruler of status and honours received (in this case Saturn), the higher the rank of influence enjoyed by the individual and a well-placed Saturn can enjoy the fruits of its labours when ruling these two elevated houses.

In traditional astrology these two houses would be the king (10th) and the knights of his court (11th), and this situation augurs well if the native is in the king's favour or the king is a decent monarch.

Saturn in good condition would confirm this, but Saturn in terrible condition would indicate that the king and his court are toxic, or the native is so far removed from them that he is invisible in their eyes.

Saturn may take the role of regent for himself and the individual would be wise to make sure that their 'court' in the eleventh house is also satisfied with the quality of leadership that Saturn provides.

Without the friendship and support of others from the eleventh house, Saturn may not be able to maintain the person's elevated rank.

The square from Capricorn to Aries and sextile to Aquarius from the ascendant may give some promise, but if Saturn, the ruler of the two adjacent houses, is badly placed or is debilitated then the aspect can do little to save the native's frustration or humiliation.

The native can see what is happening, but can do very little to improve their own situation.

The hopes and dreams which are cherished in the eleventh house are fed by Saturn, who can take each new promotion and accolade, and add to the eleventh house's feelings of being satisfied and content that dreams are manifesting at the appropriate time, and Saturn is putting the plans of the eleventh into good use in its elevated house next door.

Series One:

Saturn's Consecutive Rulership with 12th and 2nd House Involvement

		SERIES ONE : 11th to 3rd House Involvement ♄ Ruling Adjacent Houses of Light and Dark	
♓ on ASC	♑	11th House	FRIENDS
	♒	12th House	Combines With ENEMIES
♒ on ASC	♑	12th House	ENEMIES
	♒	1st House	Combines With LIFE
♑ on ASC	♑	1st House	LIFE
	♒	2nd House	Combines With WEALTH
♐ on ASC	♑	2nd House	WEALTH
	♒	3rd House	Combines With SIBLINGS

Fig. 134 Saturn's Series One

The remaining eight conditions shown in Series One and Two will involve one of Saturn's houses aspecting the ascendant, whilst the other house does not receive light from the ascendant.

The wheels show a division between light house and dark house and in each diagram Saturn's dark house is marked by the shaded triangle. The shape of a solid base combined with a peak is intended to parodize Saturn's battle to constantly strive to climb to the top even though the sharp angles cause slippage with every forward movement.

The Series One diagrams show that the shading does not follow the sign itself but is concerned with the house that is in darkness.

As the chart is turned and a new ascendant sign appears, circumstances will change as to whether it is Capricorn or Aquarius' house which is experiencing the difficulty of blindness to the ascendant.

Series One connects eleventh to twelfth house; twelfth to first house; first to second house; and second to third house through the dual rulership of Saturn for these houses and in this way it will illustrate four possibilities. Two will feature the twelfth house, which has two strikes against it, being both cadent and unaspected to the ascendant, and two will feature the second house, which whilst still unaspected to the ascendant is succedent and therefore a slight improvement on the twelfth house.

In two of these cases Saturn will be the Lord of the Ascendant, regardless of whether Capricorn or Aquarius is the rising sign at the creation of the chart, and under the guise of rulership, will automatically bind the Ascendant Lord to a difficult house whether it is the twelfth or the second house.

Saturn Ruling 11th and Cadent 12th House

In Maternus' language Saturn ruling both the eleventh and twelfth houses will create a mix of friends and hidden enemies and the native can struggle to differentiate one from the other when lines need to be drawn between friend and foe.

On a more esoteric level Saturn jointly rules the *Cacos Daemon* (Bad Spirit) with the *Agathos Daemon* (Good Spirit) binding the house of sorrows to the house of hopes and dreams, and suggesting battles of monumental proportions within the chart owner's psyche.

This example will place the mutable water sign Pisces on the ascendant and the fine balance between extreme sensitivity and emotional stability may be upset if Saturn's involvement with groups and friends leads to being blind-sided by the woes of the twelfth house.

The shaded triangle is symbolic of the shadows which can haunt the twelfth house that receives no light from the ascendant.

Saturn is no stranger to the twelfth house, as the traditionalists believed the darkest house in the chart was the place where Saturn found its joy.

And not because Saturn was better behaved here, but that the significations of both the house, and the malefic planet were in alignment, and that Saturn 'rejoiced' here because it could cause great mischief.

The combination of Saturn's rulership over both the eleventh and the twelfth house means that Saturn is likely to be nervous of groups, social gatherings, or friendships and associations especially if it is testing the members of these groups in an effort to flush out the native's hidden enemies.

Unfortunately for Saturn, this behaviour by the Pisces rising individual is only going to make them feel more isolated from others as Saturn's caution is a probably a waste of its valuable time.

The point of hidden enemies is just that – they are impossible to predict as they act as friends in the light, but do their best damage in the darkness of the twelfth house.

The individual with this chart would do better to treat everyone the same and avoid being paranoid by seeing shadows and innuendos when they do not exist, or by being overly-sensitive and taking offence to others' words or actions.

Otherwise, Saturn risks becoming a self-fulfilling prophecy, withdrawing from groups and friends, and isolating itself by being consumed with twelfth house fears and sorrows.

The lack of aspectual relationship between Pisces and Aquarius which creates blindness between the twelfth and first house may be relieved if the two lords of the signs are related in some way in the chart. Saturn and Jupiter are allies from the diurnal sect so perhaps Jupiter may be able to calm Saturn's nerves if needed and there is contact in the chart between the two planets.

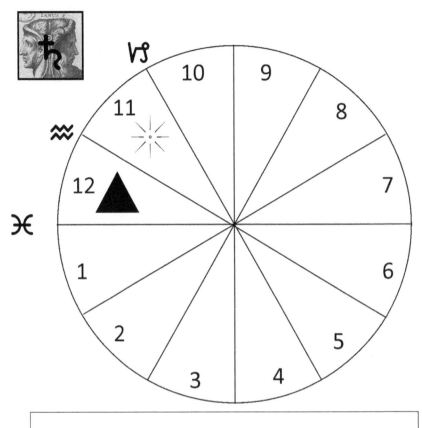

SERIES ONE

♄ Ruling A Light House (11th) Followed by A Dark House (12th)

*Fig. 135 Pisces on the Ascendant: Saturn ruling
the Eleventh and Twelfth Houses*

Saturn Ruling Cadent 12ᵗʰ and Ascendant

The battle to keep the demons at bay can be arduous when Capricorn is on the twelfth house cusp and Aquarius is the sign on the ascendant.

Saturn's mask slips more often in this scenario as the ability to keep the two houses separate through different planets ruling the two houses, is lost to the chart when Saturn must control the movements of both houses.

How well Saturn is able to perform this task will depend on its condition in the chart, and the sign in which it is located, as the aspects between its temporary sign and Capricorn or Aquarius will give clues as to which house Saturn favours as its ruler.

The presumption that Saturn might prefer a better aspect to Aquarius, and therefore be a more competent ruler of the ascendant, may be assuming too much and there are many factors that will need to be taken into account before jumping to this conclusion.

The Roman god Janus's two-faced image comes to mind in this Saturn combination of houses.

The shadowy face that prefers to be hidden from the light, must also accept that it is only one of two characters, and the other side of the countenance will be just as keen to actively seek the light, wanting the world to know that they exist.

As a fixed air sign, Aquarius is fated to communicate with the immediate environment, but this can work to Saturn's advantage if Aquarius constantly re-evaluates its situation through the collection and dissemination of information, so that it feels like it is in control of any situation.

If Saturn feels it has covered all eventualities through the Aquarian ascendant, then it may be able to quiet the nervous rumblings from Capricorn in the twelfth house.

Maternus labels the twelfth as enemies and the first as life but if Saturn rules both, can he stop the individual from becoming their own worst enemy?

There are more positive expressions for Saturn ruling twelfth and first house.

An innate responsibility to personally help those who cannot help themselves is one viable solution for this combination, but the level of exposure or the burden of carrying such a weight can be extremely difficult.

The Janus-effect for this combination can feel like it is a bleak view indeed, whether the person is looking back to the past or gazing forward into the future.

Saturn's circumstances in the chart will indicate the heaviness of the burden, and this combination of twelfth and first house rulership is particularly harsh if Saturn is in debility or in hard aspect with Neptune or Pluto, as both of these newer planets can create their own private Hell for Saturn.

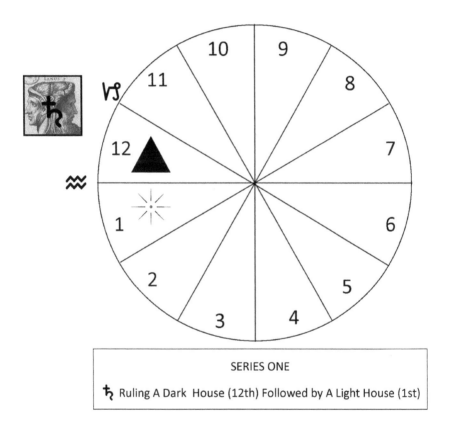

SERIES ONE

♄ Ruling A Dark House (12th) Followed by A Light House (1st)

Fig. 136 Aquarius on the Ascendant: Saturn ruling Twelfth and First Houses

Saturn Ruling Ascendant and Passive 2nd House

Saturn's earth sign of Capricorn is featured on the ascendant and the second house obligates Saturn to tend to the finances as well as the general welfare of the native through the first house.

Saturn ruling both of these houses suggests a seriousness towards all things physical, whether it is trying to fit into the immediate environment, or working through how to provide for themselves on a practical level.

This individual may learn very early in life the value the world puts on wealth, and yet, may not know how to go about finding it for themselves if Saturn as its lord is unable to see the second house.

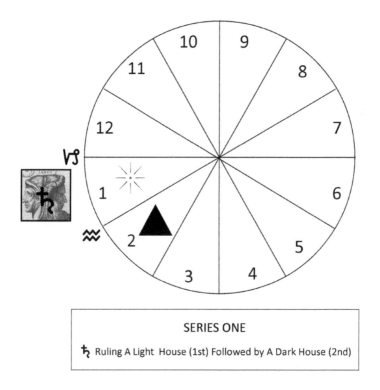

SERIES ONE

♄ Ruling A Light House (1st) Followed by A Dark House (2nd)

Fig. 137 Capricorn on the Ascendant: Saturn ruling First and Second Houses

Janus was responsible for overseeing rites of passage, and Saturn may not be as sharp or as quick at cutting and severing as fellow malefic

Mars, but it does know that separation and removal are a part of any rite of passage.

Saturn's involvement with houses at the beginning of the chart often means the individual learns from a young age the value of having to let go and move on, even though earth sign Capricorn will want to hang on for as long as possible to what is safe or familiar or comfortable.

Depending on Saturn's situation in the chart, the individual born with this strong Saturn statement will thrive in an environment where they are allowed to take charge of their lives, and their preference is to earn money (and respect) from their actions or behaviour at the same time.

Unfortunately, this may be one of those rare examples of money and self-esteem being tied together through Saturn's joint rulership.

If the responsible adult cannot pay their bills, suffers from long-term unemployment, or feels the experiences or qualifications they have struggled to achieve are not financially rewarded, then Saturn can add a touch of bitterness to this combination.

Being born with Saturn ruling the ascendant is tough enough, but the Capricorn rising individual with an earth sign on the ascendant is seeking security from their physical surroundings, and this can be doubly hard, if no money is coming in to pay the bills or put a roof over their family's heads.

Finance, money worries and fiscal planning are conversations the Capricorn rising can find themselves repeating to anyone who will listen. There is hope that as Saturn progresses through its twenty eight year cycle the individual with this combination will begin to relax, and know that all their earlier preparation will look after them financially, as they grow deeper and more confidently into their Capricorn skin.

Saturn Ruling Passive 2nd and 3rd House

A chart with Sagittarius rising will place Capricorn on the second house and Aquarius on the third in a Whole Sign house system.

Once more Jupiter rules the ascendant but this combination may not be as invasive for the individual as Jupiter's other sign of Pisces, where Saturn was the joint ruler of the eleventh and the twelfth houses (*Fig. 135*).

Saturn's involvement with the second rather than the twelfth house somewhat lightens the relationship between Saturn and Jupiter, and if the two diurnal planet can come to a 'gentleman's agreement' through aspecting one another in the chart, then Saturn may not suffer too badly from the darkness which exists between the ascendant and the second house.

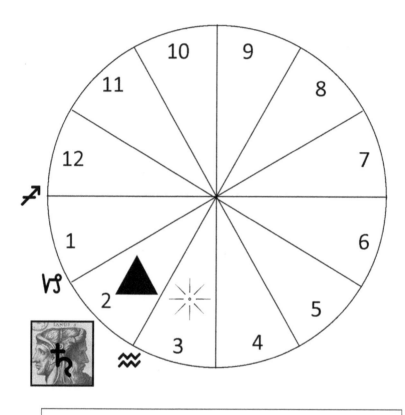

SERIES ONE

♄ Ruling A Dark House (2nd) Followed by A Light House (3rd)

Fig. 138 Sagittarius on the Ascendant: Saturn ruling Second and Third Houses

Saturn ruling the house of wealth and also the house of brothers combines money making schemes with the involvement of siblings in Maternus' short-hand text, but an extension of the third house in particular may provide a broader range of possibilities.

Third house involves local community, communication, written language, early learning, basic skills, neighbours, and short journeys.

Any one, or a combination of several of these significations, has the ability to take full advantage of the Janus-effect to gather financial strength from Capricorn on the second house cusp, and to move toward benefiting from pursuits described by the following house in the future.

Either a benefit or a curse, money can be squandered on unrealistic or expensive third house dreams and schemes, money spent on the neighbour's fence or damage incurred due to their behaviour, wasting money via the internet, or risky business plans which Saturn may not bring to fruition are all possible expressions for this combination of houses.

Saturn can hinder the native by creating a poverty mentality and a state of miserliness through its rulership of the money house, especially if the third house pursuits burn a hole in the pocket.

Or it can help by steadily accumulating resources (otherwise known as good old fashioned 'saving') that will benefit or support the third house concerns.

The difficulty for Saturn ruling a house unaspected to the ascendant is that the chart's owner is unlikely to reconcile their money issues with their own behaviour, unless Saturn itself aspects Jupiter, the ruler of Sagittarius, and the two planets can set up a conversation which will over-rule the lack of sight between the first and second houses.

Series Two:

Saturn's Consecutive Rulership with 6th and 8th House Involvement

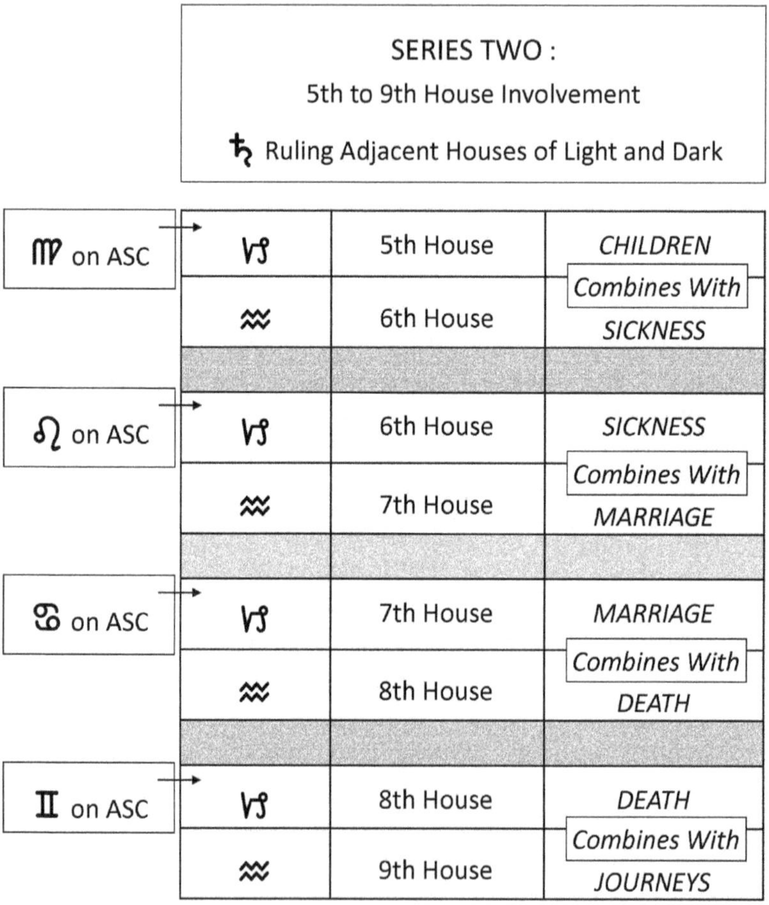

SERIES TWO : 5th to 9th House Involvement ♄ Ruling Adjacent Houses of Light and Dark			
♍ on ASC	♑	5th House	*CHILDREN*
	♒	6th House	*Combines With* *SICKNESS*
♌ on ASC	♑	6th House	*SICKNESS*
	♒	7th House	*Combines With* *MARRIAGE*
♋ on ASC	♑	7th House	*MARRIAGE*
	♒	8th House	*Combines With* *DEATH*
♊ on ASC	♑	8th House	*DEATH*
	♒	9th House	*Combines With* *JOURNEYS*

Fig. 139 Saturn's Series Two

Series Two moves away from the ascendant to address four possible combinations on the other side of the chart.

The passive houses are those with no aspect to the ascendant, and the two houses which fall either side of the descendant, i.e. the sixth and the eighth house both fall into this category.

Saturn Ruling 5ᵗʰ and Cadent 6ᵗʰ House

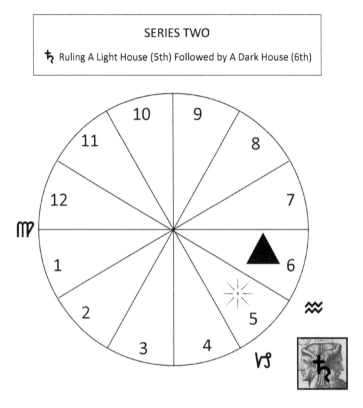

Fig. 140 Virgo on the Ascendant: Saturn ruling Fifth and Sixth Houses

The combination of Saturn ruled signs on the fifth house and the sixth ties together two houses of fortune: *Agathe Tyche*, Good Luck and *Cace Tyche*, Bad Luck.

The link between these two houses is likely to have several repercussions.

Firstly, the difficulty in determining whether or not there are strings attached to something that at Janus' first glance looks good, but may be more trouble than it is worth.

This can make the individual extremely wary of Good Luck, and the fact that if it is a cautionary or even cynical Saturn ruling this house and the next, some opportunities may be lost due to hesitation or nervousness on the part of the native.

Secondly, what should be a rather light-filled house which trines the ascendant can lose its playfulness under the stern gaze of Saturn.

One frustrating scenario between the dual rulership by Saturn of the fifth and sixth houses links the blessings of children with illness or toil.

This can be particularly heartbreaking for the (often single) parent who is trying to raise children, have fun and share light-hearted moments, and at the same time, be desperately trying to adequately provide for their progeny.

Time is tight, work commitments are a constant drain, and overwhelming tiredness or poor health makes it difficult to be a fun parent who is available and energetic enough to join in the games and play with offspring who clamour for attention.

Guilt, the trademark of Saturn, can easily creep in and the parent finds the children's demands suffocating or self-recrimination exhausting as the individual constantly plays catch-up with their duties as a parent and an employee.

In this example, a chart set in Whole Sign will have Virgo on the ascendant and may compound the individual's feelings of self-doubt or the conversation where they feel they have to defend their actions if they are facing outside criticism on their parenting skills.

To balance the scales on this combination of Saturn's houses is to remember that this can be an excellent extension of one's creative talents being transferred to the house of hard work and commitment. A person who is artistic or creative can use the fifth house for inspiration and freedom of expression and then dedicate the sixth house in making sure that something concrete is produced by this combination.

Time slips away in the sixth house if the writer, visual artist, poet or musically talented individual spends hours perfecting their art through the rulership of Saturn. But there needs to be awareness that the body also needs nourishment (Virgo on the ascendant) and time must be put away for the basic needs of sufficient sleep and a good diet.

If this is ignored too often then the sixth house creates a Saturnian problem by the annoyance of reoccurring illness or physical injury through exhaustion and as Saturn rules so much of the body in the skeletal system, the joints, the skin and the lungs, it would be wise for the individual to balance the passion of the fifth house with the obsession of Saturn's sixth house activities.

Saturn Ruling Cadent 6ᵗʰ and the Descendant

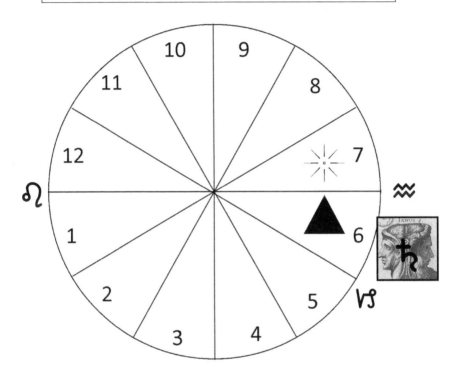

Fig. 141 Leo on the Ascendant: Saturn ruling Sixth and Seventh Houses

When Saturn rules the sixth and the seventh house Maternus would perhaps say that the native's illness impacted on the marriage, or vice versa.

Aquarius on the seventh house cusp opposes the ascendant in Leo implying that marriage or partnerships have a Saturnian influence on the individual.

The partner may be older or authoritarian in nature, and if the person's health is determined by Saturn, often an indicator for poor health, the partner may be required to take on a controlling position in order to care for the person.

However, the two houses both ruled by Saturn may indicate that the marriage or partnership has put such a strain on the native, that poor health has resulted from the association.

The state of Saturn in the chart, and even of the Sun itself as the ruler of Leo will give an indication as to the vitality of the ascendant, or the level of damage a relationship may invite or alleviate for the individual.

Likewise, seventh house can describe a professional relationship between doctor and patient especially when Saturn is involved, so that Capricorn indicates the past and Aquarius produces the future according to how brilliant or incompetent are the level of the professional's skills.

Saturn Ruling the Descendant and Passive 8th House

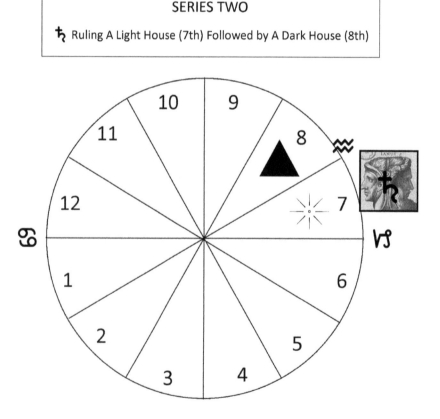

Fig. 142 Cancer on the Ascendant: Saturn ruling Seventh and Eighth Houses

On the other side of the seventh house lies the house of death so that Maternus might be tempted to connect these two topics through his brief list of house meanings.

The potential is always there, but it may be more useful to examine the partner's resources before jumping to frightening or macabre associations between the two houses.

Saturn ruling seventh and eighth houses will place the Moon's sign Cancer on the ascendant and this scenario is identical to the *Thema Mundi* chart.

Saturn's two signs will always oppose both luminaries' signs, Cancer and Leo, and if the house that signifies life is the first house, then it makes sense to oppose life via the seventh house, and to continue the theme in the eighth house, given that Saturn rules beginnings and endings.

As in the case of the previous chart with Leo rising, it is a good idea to be aware of the condition of the opposing luminary in the chart as the Moon's position in the Cancer rising chart will help to evaluate the overall health and well-being of the chart's owner.

Saturn will be the ruler of relationships at the same time as ruling joint finances, and this may concern the workings or the dynamics of both intimate relationships and business partnerships.

Divorce settlements, child support, arguments over how money will be split both during the marriage, or after, should it fail to survive Saturn's strain – these are all areas which Saturn can explore when it rules both of these houses.

Even the native's wills and testaments, and entitlements by the spouse, will be included if the eighth house should be called into play as the house of death.

Care in choosing one's business partners is also covered by Saturn when it rules these two neighbouring houses, and it would be a good idea to put Saturn to good use by keeping track of the money – that is, provided that Saturn's sign is in aspect to Aquarius.

The eighth house can also signify the resources belonging to the partner separate from the native, and Saturn may represent formal contracts involving pre-nuptial agreements, if the partner is concerned about the division of their wealth should the marriage fail in the future.

The seventh house is also the house of civil litigation and there may be times when poor advice from professionals in the seventh house will create legal proceedings where punitive damages are sought by the plaintiff.

If this is the case the native should proceed with caution as if a poorly placed or debilitated Saturn led to the situation in the first place (by rulership of 7th house), the same Saturn may not be able to offer an adequate amount of compensation for its loss or distress and the costs of the court may add to financial woes if Saturn cannot win the case for the native (rulership of 8th house).

Saturn Ruling Passive 8ᵗʰ and 9ᵗʰ House

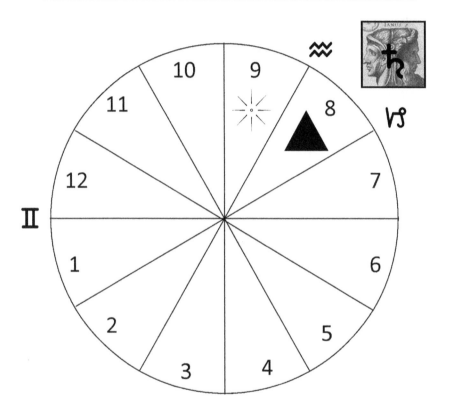

Fig. 143 *Gemini on the Ascendant: Saturn ruling Eighth and Ninth Houses*

Saturn ruling both the eighth and ninth house often requires a staunch or practical attitude towards drama, crisis and even death.

A house of philosophy, spirituality, religion and higher learning often produces individuals who choose to take responsibility for other peoples' messes.

Saturn may feel it has greater control over life if it can direct its energy towards educating the native from the ninth house of education so that the individual has an air of authority or competence when it comes to the chaos created by the eighth house.

Janus in this combination often looks to the ninth house to provide meaning or order through finding a spiritual or metaphysical support system in the ninth house to make sense of a chaotic eighth house.

The pre-Saturn Return individual is usually not particularly interested in what happens after death, but Saturn's cycle at one of its seven year squares may have introduced death even at a young age.

If this happens, the individual with Saturn ruling both houses is forced to find a model to fit their experiences, whether that model is religious, spiritual, scientific or intellectual.

Whatever model Saturn chooses to provide can bring comfort and stability for this awkward and sometimes painful Saturn-ruled combination.

The individual with this combination will have Gemini rising in the Whole Sign house system and Mercury is likely to hunt for answers and will do so alongside Saturn, if the two planets are related by sign or aspect in the chart.

Student loans are another way for Saturn to encompass the affairs of both houses as money borrowed for extended studies or education loans subsidised by the government are ways for Saturn to teach the individual about responsibility and financial accountability.

Money borrowed for overseas travel may bring a solution to being able to explore foreign worlds and cultures but ultimately Saturn and the lending institution will require that the money be reimbursed sometime in the future. A debilitated Saturn may struggle with repayments if the person has overextended themselves or has no real plan or budget to reduce a debt spiralling out of control through interest rates on the loan.

CHAPTER NINE

A Square, A Lemniscate and
A Two-Faced God

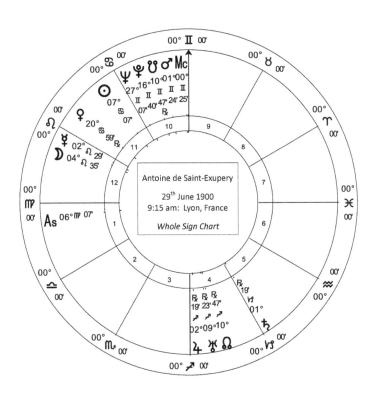

Fig. 144 Natal Chart for Antoine de Saint-Exupéry

Antoine de Saint-Exupéry (1900-1944) was a French aristocrat, writer, poet and pioneering aviator. He became a laureate of several of France's highest literary awards and also won the U.S. National Book Award in 1939. He is best remembered for his novella *The Little Prince*.

The Little Prince has been described as a tender tale of loneliness, friendship, love, and loss, in the form of a young alien prince fallen to Earth from a tiny asteroid.

"It is an allegory of Saint-Exupéry's own life – his search for childhood certainties and interior peace, his mysticism, his belief in human courage and brotherhood, and his deep love for Consuelo, but also an allusion to the tortured nature of their relationship."[116]

Aversion Table for Saint-Exupéry

ANTOINE de SAINT-EXUPÉRY Author of "The Little Prince"				
House	Sign on Cusp	House's Ruling Planet	Ruling Planet's Sign	Relationship Between The Two Signs *(Sight or Aversion)*
1	♍	☿	♌	**AVERSION**
2	♎	♀	♋	Aspect (□)
3	♏	♂	♊	**AVERSION**
4	♐	♃	♐	Rulership
5	♑	♄	♑	Rulership
6	♒	♄	♑	Like-Engirdling
7	♓	♃	♐	Aspect (□)
8	♈	♂	♊	Aspect (✶)
9	♉	♀	♋	Aspect (✶)
10	♊	☿	♌	Aspect (✶)
11	♋	☽	♌	**AVERSION**
12	♌	☉	♋	**AVERSION**

Fig. 145 Aversion Table for Antoine de Saint-Exupéry

Sect Table for Saint-Exupéry

ANTOINE de SAINT-EXUPÉRY — Planetary Sect					
Solar and Diurnal Planets	CONDITION ONE	CONDITION TWO	CONDITION THREE	*MUNAKARA* Contention	TOTAL SECT DIGNITY
☉	✦	✦	— —		Sun in *Halb* (1 + 2)
♃	✦	— —	✦		(1 + 3)
♄	✦	— —	— —		(1 only—Diurnal Chart)
☿ (Noct.)	— —	— —	— —	MERCURY in *Munakara*	*Ex Conditione* (no sect dignity)
♂	— —	— —	✦		(3 only—Masculine Sign)
♀	— —	— —	✦		(3 only—Feminine Sign)
☽	— —	— —	— —		*Ex Conditione* (no sect dignity)
Lunar and Nocturnal Planets					

Fig. 146 Sect Table for Antoine de Saint-Exupéry

Munakara Table for Saint-Exupéry

ANTOINE de SAINT-EXUPÉRY — Planets in *Munakara*			

Solar and Diurnal Planets	DISPOSITOR ONE	DISPOSITOR TWO	MUNAKARA Contention
♋︎☉ DIURNAL	☽ in ♌︎ *Nocturnal*	*'Generosity' Each other's dispositor But No Aspect*	No Contention
♐︎♃ DIURNAL	*In Rulership No Dispositor*	—	No Contention
♑︎♄ DIURNAL	*In Rulership No Dispositor*	—	No Contention
♌︎☿ NOCTURNAL	☉ in ♋︎ *Diurnal*	☽ *Nocturnal*	MERCURY in Munakara
♊︎♂ NOCTURNAL	☿ in ♌︎ *Nocturnal*	☉ *Diurnal*	No Contention
♋︎♀ NOCTURNAL	☽ in ♌︎ *Nocturnal*	☉ *Diurnal*	No Contention
♌︎☽ NOCTURNAL	☉ in ♋︎ *Diurnal*	*'Generosity' Each other's dispositor But No Aspect*	No Contention

Lunar and Nocturnal Planets

Fig. 147 Munakara Table for Antoine de Saint-Exupéry

The Culminations of Mercury and Jupiter

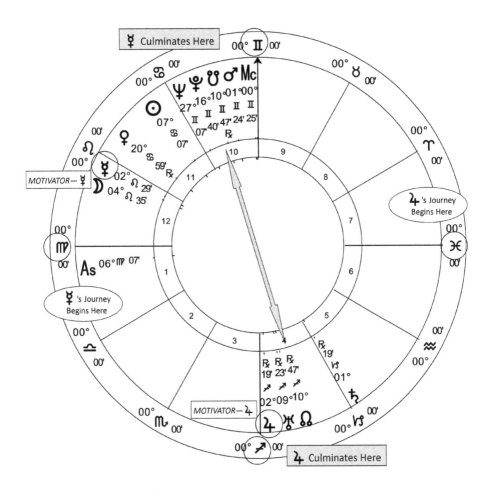

Fig. 148 Culminations for Mercury and Jupiter for Antoine de Saint-Exupéry

Mercury in Leo in the 12th

Ruling 1st House (Beginnings) and
10th House (Culminations)

Ptolemy's *Aphorism 37: "If Virgo be on the ascendant, the
native will create his own dignity."*

This sounds like a wonderful prediction from Ptolemy for Tonio,
as he was known to his friends, but there are a number of problems
in the chart for the mutual ruler of these two angles. Tonio has a
nocturnal Mercury because it is placed behind the Sun in the chart. It
is completely out of sect as it would prefer to be in a nocturnal chart, in
a different hemisphere from the Sun, and in a feminine sign – all three
sect conditions are missing for Mercury. The lack of sect puts Mercury
in an uncomfortable position as everything it wants from this critical
accidental dignity is missing. Tonio may have been a brilliant writer
but he was also childish, cruel and vulgar and an *ex conditione* Mercury
can display huge chasms in knowing when some communication is
appropriate and when it is not, especially for someone whose Mercury
rules the two most visible houses in the chart.

To add to the worries of *ex conditione* Mercury, the ruler of his
Ascendant and his Midheaven is in a state of *munakara* in his chart.

The translation for this Arabic word is 'contention' and it creates the
feeling of a planet, and what it represents, being constantly harassed,
criticised or under attack.

His Mercury is nocturnal and is disposited by the Sun, which is a
diurnal planet. This is not ideal, but the fact that the Sun itself is in
Cancer means that it is disposited by a nocturnal planet, the Moon and
so we have the second crossover from one sect to the other.

Nocturnal (Leo Mercury) – Diurnal (Cancer Sun) – Nocturnal
(Moon). No-one is happy but the buck stops at Mercury which
constantly worries about what it has to contend with throughout life.

In Chapter Two I described Nocturnal Mercury in *munakara* as
struggling with self-expression, creativity, concentration or objectivity.
Antoine certainly mastered creativity, but he did struggle with keeping
his mind on task, and in his writing and in his life objectivity was
certainly not part of his mental tool-kit. Antoine was desperate for
acceptance and understanding and he tried to express himself in a way

that made him feel valued and loved – this could have been the sign of Leo – but his desperation to be accepted was the signature of all the components of an out of sect Mercury in contention and blind to Virgo on the Ascendant.

Mercury's culmination occurs in the tenth sign and Tonio was lauded for his books on early aviation during his lifetime. However, he would not live to see that his greatest triumph was a book about a little boy from an alien world. A book written for children but one that strikes a chord in anyone who has ever felt that they did not fit in this world. Even with the praise, the prizes and the parties thrown in his honour, Tonio's insecurities about his writing never receded or assuaged his fear of being exposed as a 'light-weight intellectual' with no sound basis to his politics or philosophies on life. The sky and the empty desert were the only places of safety in Tonio's mind and in his later life he yearned for the peace of his younger years. Mercury did produce amazing success in the Gemini tenth house but the more attention he gained the more he needed to chase the demons from his mind.

The Firdaria Timeline *(Fig. 151)* mentions that in his late teens and early twenties Tonio's academic record was appalling despite having had the best education in private academies and expensive boarding schools around Europe in his schooling years. Even though he had a good mind for engineering, Tonio's job prospects were not good without formal qualifications, and he returned to flying as this adventurous lifestyle really was the best option for him (Mars in Mercury's sign on MC).

The wisest character in *The Little Prince* is the fox who makes social comments on relationships, commitment, life and love, and over the years much energy has been put into deciphering the meaning behind the fox's oblique statements.

Tonio's debilitated Mercury is apparent when the fox tells the prince *"I shall watch you out of the corner of my eye and you will say nothing; words are the source of misunderstandings" (page 69, 70).*

Misunderstandings abound for his Mercury when it cannot properly rule the Ascendant because it is blind to its own sign. A narrator guides the reader through *The Little Prince* but before we meet the prince the narrator tells us something about himself. He begins with a story about his own childhood and says that he loved to draw and the picture of which he is most proud features a boa constrictor swallowing an elephant whole. When he shows the snake with an extended belly to the adults in his life they think it is a hat and advise him to abandon his drawing and do something else when he grows up. Sadly he gives up on drawing, and on adults. The narrator says *"Grown ups never understand anything by themselves, and it is exhausting for children always and forever to be giving explanations"* and from that moment *"I kept my own company, without anyone whom I could really talk* "[117]. That is, until he meets the little prince in the desert.

To the outside world Tonio was a brilliant writer, but this is not how he felt about himself. For every book he wrote there was three times the amount of writing thrown into the bin. He was a poor student who constantly failed exams. He was exiled during the German occupation of France and isolated himself in the United States during the war because he refused to learn English, saying that he still had not mastered his native French language.

The argument between the aviator and the little prince on page 27 ... *"I did not really know what to say. I felt like a blundering idiot. I did not know how to reach him, where to catch up with him. It is such a secret place, the land of tears"* aptly describing (without knowing it) his Leo Mercury in the cadent twelfth house in aversion to his Virgo ascendant.

By all traditional standards this Mercury is appalling. It does create the legend of Saint-Exupéry as a dashing pilot and a successful author, but he is also a man who drank heavily, who suffered from long bouts of depression, and whose body (1st house) was broken by his constant crashes as he was reported to be a terrible pilot who often misjudged his landings, had poor navigational skills and often ran out of fuel because he was too busy reading when he was airborne to notice much of what was going on in his surroundings.

Mercury had its final say when the wreck of a missing plane was discovered off the coast of Marseilles in 1998 and a bracelet was authenticated to be Saint-Exupery's engraved by his loving wife Consuelo. For over fifty years the missing pilot had been hailed as a national war hero but the angle of the wreck plus the fact that it was found hundreds of miles from where it should have been once more threw his Mercury into a state of contention. Fame of a different kind began to surface as the culmination of a difficult Mercury suggested dishonour and an act of cowardice, and as his family prepared for celebrations for the centennial of his birth in 2000 speculation abounded on whether Saint-Exupéry's final mission had been the suicidal actions of a desperately unhappy man.

Jupiter in Sagittarius in the 4th House

Ruling 7th House (Beginnings) and 4th House (Culminations)

Fortunately for Tonio Jupiter is better placed in the chart, and may have even improved Mercury's chances of fame considering that there is a partile (same degree) fire trine between the two lords of the angles. Jupiter is a diurnal planet so it is in good sect dignity because Tonio was born during the daytime. Jupiter in the chart is essentially dignified in Sagittarius and has good placement in an angular house. Jupiter describes the long aristocratic lineage of Tonio's father and himself, but the retrogradation, the conjunction to Uranus and the opposition to Mars describe Tonio's father suddenly dying at the train station when Tonio was only three years old. Whilst the biographies talk of an idyllic childhood in the family chateau, the family was impoverished, Tonio was shipped off to a boarding school at an early age, and his words as an adult indicated that he felt he had been robbed of his childhood.

Tonio's Jupiter beginnings are in the seventh house, describing his passionate but obsessive love for Consuelo, his Salvadorean wife. The two met in Buenos Aires and Tonio proposed marriage to Consuelo hours after meeting her when he took her flying in his plane. Consuelo was certainly his muse, but Tonio was constantly unfaithful to her, as she was to him.

In *The Little Prince* the boy talks about a beautiful rose that he tends back on his tiny asteroid. He gives her water, picks the bugs from her leaves and builds her a special glass dome to keep the cold wind from hurting her petals during the cold nights. But he says that she is never satisfied (retrograde Jupiter opposing Mars) and the reason he has wandered the universe rather than stay on his asteroid is because he can no longer cope with her increasing demands.

When the little prince is at home tending to his rose, he thinks she is unique, the only one of her kind in the universe. But when he finds gardens of countless roses on Earth (dignified Jupiter in the 4th) he feels he wants to know and love them all and that his rose, in the end, is not so special.

It is only when the fox points out that *"you can only see clearly with your heart"* that the little prince realizes the love he has for his precious rose.

Saint-Exupéry's main character and his identification with the golden-haired prince has Jupiter's touch of royalty, and this is exactly what Saint-Exupéry becomes with the publication of *The Little Prince* in France – but only after his mysterious death at sea. (Jupiter culminating in the 4th)

In a strange twist of fate, Saint-Exupéry regained honour, prestige and financial security for his aristocratic family but they were appalled at his profession which seemed common in their eyes.

Nor did they approve of Consuelo, calling her a "tart" and saying that she was not "Saint-Exupéry" material so far as they were concerned. When in 2000 France celebrated the centenary of Tonio's birth, the family refused to have any of Consuelo's photos on display, and yet, as Tonio's muse and the model for the little prince's beautiful rose, it was she whom the family should have thanked for their improved circumstances.

The culmination of Tonio's Jupiter is in the fourth house, a house which is often seen as the end of life and even hidden treasure. This gift of *The Little Prince* was Tonio's hidden treasure as it was ultimately what he brought back to the family as his legacy. Consuelo died in 1979, thirty five years after her beloved Tonio, but her memoirs were found and published in the same year as the centenary of his birth. She was scathing in her criticism of her husband and many people believed she betrayed him in the end, but she remains his disgruntled rose well after both had left this earth.

The Lemniscate of Mars and Venus

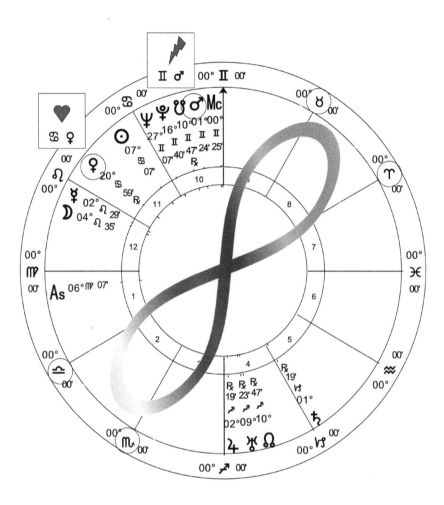

Fig. 149 Mars and Venus Lemniscate for Antoine de Saint-Exupéry

Mars in Leo in 10th House
(Conjunct MC)
Ruling 3rd and 8th House

Venus in Cancer in 11th House Ruling 2nd and 9th House

For Tonio one side of his lemniscate combines his love of adventure and his passion for foreign lands (9th) with his constant near-death experiences (8th house) from crashing numerous times to almost perishing in an African desert in the Paris to Saigon air race in 1935. Mars combines rulership over the third and eighth houses as he became a pioneer of international postal flight delivering the mail (3rd) which flew between Toulouse, France and Dakar in Senegal.

He considered his fellow pilots as brothers who together travelled the skies delivering mail, finding freedom and fulfilment in flying as *"The only reward worth having was the recognition of the other pilots"*. But when he published his books on aviation many turned against him because he had broken the unspoken code of secrecy and made them characters who were sold out in his desire to publish and make money through the telling of his beloved comrades' exploits (Cancer Venus in 11th rules 2nd and 9th houses). A mark against Mars which rules the third but is in aversion to its house and also a retrograde Venus which rules his second house.

As a pioneering pilot who flew the airmail routes of northwest Africa, the South Atlantic and South America, Tonio wrote books and newspaper articles about his adventures and Mars in Gemini at the Midheaven must have been in its element. In truth, however, Mars is not in its element, nor in its proper sect, which probably describes how Saint-Exupéry managed to break so many bones and crash so many aeroplanes in his career.

Part of the reason for Tonio's constant brushes with death in the desert was basically the fact that he lacked the necessary skills to fly these death traps with wings. Mars rules the third house but it is in aversion to its house – there is only blindness between Gemini and Scorpio – and stories abound of Tonio failing to check instruments, fuel or flight plans before takeoff, preferring instead to read his favourite detective stories up until the very last minute the plane left the ground. On his last flights in 1943 during the war Antoine flew reconnaissance missions in planes that should have been grounded in a flying suit that he needed help in donning because his body was so damaged by past accidents. He was literally flying blind as he had limited movement and sight and could not read the dashboard instruments.

His mind was rarely on the job. He once misread his dials and flew a new plane up 10,000 metres rather than 10,000 feet and blacked out. During the war he returned from a reconnaissance mission with pictures of a French Chateau that reminded him of his childhood home rather than pictures of the enemy and the total destruction of a much needed military plane grounded him for months whilst he begged the American Air Force to be given another chance to fly one of their planes.

Tonio knew time was running out for him and that it would be his last chance in the air so perhaps it was not so surprising when he did not return from his last mission.

Venus ruling the second house seems out of place in the lemniscate as finances seem an unlikely fit with the rest of the players in this figure-eight pattern. That is, until we look a little closer. Tonio came from an aristocratic background whose family had inherited a beautiful country house in Lyon, but there was very little cash. He learnt early in life that nourishing friendships with his class of people and relying on family connections (Venus is in Cancer) meant not having to pay his own way and when he joined the air service he had little need for money as travel was cheap and he preferred the rough but simple life style of his fellow pilots. He later wrote: *"I have worked eight years* (Venus cycle) *of my life, day and night, with working men. I have found myself sharing their table. I know very well what I am talking about when I speak of working-class people, and I love them."*

When Tonio met Consuelo she was financially very well off, having recently collected a widow's pension in Buenos Aires. In her published memoirs she maintains that each time Tonio was threatened with divorce proceedings over his infidelities he would initiate a reconciliation by claiming his undying love for her. On at least one occasion by means of trickery, on another proceedings were halted after one of his near-fatal crashes, but in many cases, by Tonio deliberately thwarting her plans to disentangle their finances. On his visits to the United States Tonio was adored by the women of American high society who threw lavish parties in his honour (Venus in 11th ruling 9th H). Rarely was Consuelo invited to these soirees where her husband would be surrounded by beautiful women who resented Consuelo's presence at their parties. But money from book sales was minimal during his lifetime and Tonio needed Consuelo's financial support to once more live the life of a French aristocrat. When they met Consuelo she was a wealthy widow and an author in her own right but she seems to have been eclipsed by Saint-Exupéry. She wrote *"Nothing is more personal to an artist than his creation. Even if you have given him your youth, your money, your love, your courage, nothing belongs to you."*

His estate improved substantially after *The Little Prince* was published but as it occurred posthumously, it was Consuelo who benefited from sales of the book which proved to be Tonio's most financially lucrative project. The lemniscate includes the money axis and Consuelo uprooted her life and moved to France where she was perceived as a foreigner and was largely ignored as the great war hero's wife but where she was entitled to his legacy, provided she stayed in the country and kept his money where the French authorities thought it belonged. Even after death Tonio's lemniscates continues to affect Consuela as his 8th and 9th houses still control his beloved's fate decades after his demise.

When she died Consuelo left her house and half the royalties from Saint-Exupéry's books to her companion-gardener, Martinez Fructuoso. A touch of irony perhaps for the woman who was immortalized as a rose.

The gardener who inherited from Consuelo recalls how she lived her life once Tonio was gone.

"He was her passion, the love of her life. From the moment of Saint-Exupéry's death, she was obsessed by him. But in the official story, she was a bit forgotten. Biographers wouldn't even come and interview her, yet she was the cornerstone of his life."

Similar to the solitary rose on the little prince's asteroid, Tonio's Venus sits completely alone in his eleventh house. It aspects no other planet and its only companion is the Cancer Sun which is in the same house, but not close by. Venus' dispositor sits in the twelfth house, and although Venus can see both of its signs it seems like a lonely planet which is a bit lost in the chart.

Saint-Exupéry's lemniscate winds through the two axes of money and death, adventure and brotherhood but perhaps the most significant impact of Tonio's flowing ribbon of destiny was the love hate relationship between this man/prince and his beautiful but wayward woman/rose.

The Two Faces of Saturn

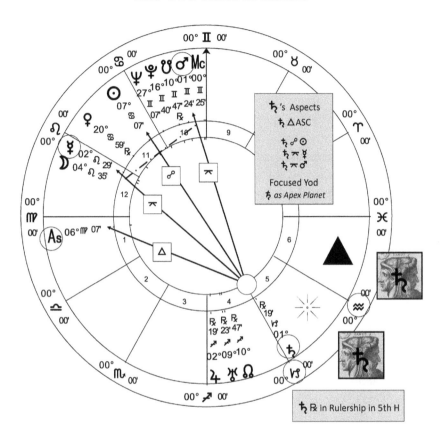

Fig. 150 Saturn's Activity and Houses in Antoine de Saint-Exupéry's Chart

Saturn in Capricorn Ruling 5ᵗʰ and 6ᵗʰ House

Saturn's story is much simpler than planets that culminate and ribbons that wind through charts in circles of infinity. Saturn is a solitary planet that looks in two opposite directions at the same time.

Tonio's Saturn resides in the fifth house of children, leisure and in modern terms, creativity. His books are his Saturn, not just the ones he writes, but his voracious appetite for reading is shown by the dignified Saturn in the fifth house.

Saturn in Capricorn opposes his Cancer Sun, and although Tonio did not father children, the little prince is as much his protégé as any living child could be. The disappearance of the prince at the end of the book is dignified and under-stated - a complete opposite to how Tonio's death was to manifest before the book was published in France in 1945.

Saturn also rules the house alongside the fifth house with Aquarius on the cusp. For all the light that was granted to a dignified Saturn in a house of good fortune, there was pain and misery in equal amount meted out to the sixth house with Aquarius on the cusp. By the age of forty three Tonio was a broken man. His body was crippled from so many broken bones and in constant torment from the damage to his internal organs caused by his reckless way of life. His spirit was also broken, depressed by the thought of no longer flying and dispirited by a ruined relationship with the only woman he had ever truly loved.

Even though Saturn is dignified in the chart and makes a strong aspect to the ascendant's degree, it still brought its own level of despair and misery for this man. Saturn also forms the apex of a modern aspect known as the Yod, sometimes called the Finger of God. In his chart, the Yod is comprised of two planets at the base, Mercury and Mars, and the addition of an opposition to the Cancer Sun elevates this aspect to the position of a Focussed Yod whereby all four elements are featured in this aspectual pattern.

The Focussed Yod is one of those rare times that all three patterns come together in an aspect which speaks of God and fate and destiny. Sometimes a level of arrogance or devil-may-care attitude accompanies such a powerful aspect. The fact that Saturn is in dignity and that his official title was 'The Count' because he came from a long line of French aristocrats added to certain aspects of his personality which were less than pleasant.

The literary legacy of *The Little Prince* will live on purely because it is a book that requires an afternoon of reading, but takes a lifetime to understand. Tonio's Saturn in the fifth gave something to the world that even he did not comprehend and perhaps it is for the best that he did not survive to see its success. The other side of the Focussed Yod involving Saturn, Mars and Mercury, and even the Cancer Sun ruling the twelfth house, is a challenge to the mental stability of the individual. A lifetime of depression was the Yod's bi-product and perhaps the greatest gift of *the Little Prince* is that Tonio poured his emotional anguish into his last book and the world responded by embracing his tiny hero.

The final page of *The Little Prince* signifies Tonio's Saturn ruling one house of light and one house of darkness as it contains two strokes to show the horizon and one lone star in the sky.

The text reads

> *"This, to me, is the loveliest and saddest landscape in the world . . . It was here that the little prince appeared on Earth, and then disappeared.*
>
> *And if you happen to pass this spot, I beg you not to hurry, but wait for a moment directly beneath the star! And if a child comes up to you, and laughs, and has golden hair, and does not answer your questions, you shall easily guess who it is."* [118]

Antoine de Saint-Exupery: Timeline of a Diurnal Firdaria

☉/☉	29 June 1900	0.0
☉/♀	3 Dec 1901	1.4
☉/☿	8 May 1903	2.9
☉/☽	11 Oct 1904	4.3
☉/♄	17 Mar 1906	5.7
☉/♃	21 Aug 1907	7.1
☉/♂	24 Jan 1909	8.6
♀/♀	29 June 1910	10.0
♀/☿	21 Aug 1911	11.1
♀/☽	11 Oct 1912	12.3
♀/♄	3 Dec 1913	13.4
♀/♃	24 Jan 1915	14.6
♀/♂	16 Mar 1916	15.7
♀/☉	8 May 1917	16.9
☿/☿	29 June 1918	18.0
☿/☽	8 May 1920	19.9
☿/♄	17 Mar 1922	21.7
☿/♃	24 Jan 1924	23.6
☿/♂	2 Dec 1925	25.4
☿/☉	12 Oct 1927	27.3
☿/♀	20 Aug 1929	29.1
☽/☽	29 June 1931	31.0
☽/♄	11 Oct 1932	32.3
☽/♃	24 Jan 1934	33.6
☽/♂	8 May 1935	34.9
☽/☉	20 Aug 1936	36.1
☽/♀	2 Dec 1937	37.4
☽/☿	17 Mar 1939	38.7
♄/♄	29 June 1940	40.0
♄/♃	24 Jan 1942	41.6
♄/♂	20 Aug 1943	43.1
♄/☉	16 Mar 1945	44.7

Fig. 151 Diurnal Firdaria for Antoine de Saint-Exupéry

Sun's Firdaria: 1900 – 1910

2nd Oct 1904 – Death of father from a stroke

Venus' Firdaria: 1910 – 1918

1912 – First flight in an aeroplane, vows to become a pilot

1915 – Sent to Jesuit school in Switzerland with Francois

1917 – Death of Francois in Switzerland, Antoine expelled for poor performance in examinations

Mercury's Firdaria: 1918 – 1931

1919 – Joined naval preparatory school but fails exams

1920 – Enrols in university to study architecture but fails exams

1921 – Began two year service in military as a mechanic.

Gained his pilot's licence by secretly taking flying lessons.

Fractures his skull in plane crash, leaves the armed forces.

1926 – His first short story *The Aviator* is published. Returns to flying becoming a pilot for *Aéropostal* taking mail from Toulouse to Dakar.

1927 – Accepts post as airfield chief for Cape Juby in Southern Morocco.

Began work on his first book *Southern Mail.*

1929 – *Southern Mail* published. Moves to Argentina.

1930 – Awarded the Légion d'honneur by French Government for negotiations in the release of captured French pilots in Africa

Moon's Firdaria: 1931 – 1940

1931 – Meets and marries Consuelo Suncin.

Published second book *Night Flight*, wins prestigious Prix Femina

1935 – Crashes in Libyan desert with navigator whilst in Paris to Saigon Air Race. Saved from death by Bedouin caravan.

1938 – Another serious plane crash confines him to hospital

1939 – *Wind, Sand and Stars* published.

Awarded the Grand Prize for Fiction and US National Book Award.

Becomes a military reconnaissance pilot.

Saturn's Firdaria: 1940 – 1951

1940 – Fall of France. He leaves France to live in exile in US.

1942 – *Flight to Arras* and *Letter to a Hostage* published.

Writes *The Little Prince* whilst living in exile in New York.

1943 – *The Little Prince* published in US.

He rejoins his French air squadron in Northern Africa.

1944 – Antoine sets out from Corsica to survey France but never returns from his mission.

Antoine de Saint-Exupéry: A Life Lived in Firdaria

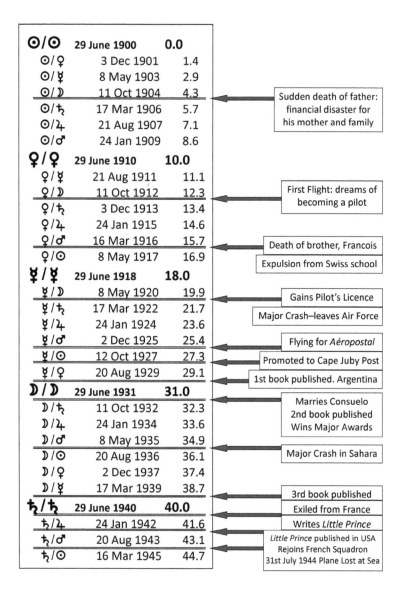

☉/☉	29 June 1900	0.0	
☉/♀	3 Dec 1901	1.4	
☉/☿	8 May 1903	2.9	
☉/☽	11 Oct 1904	4.3	Sudden death of father: financial disaster for his mother and family
☉/♄	17 Mar 1906	5.7	
☉/♃	21 Aug 1907	7.1	
☉/♂	24 Jan 1909	8.6	
♀/♀	29 June 1910	10.0	
♀/☿	21 Aug 1911	11.1	
♀/☽	11 Oct 1912	12.3	First Flight: dreams of becoming a pilot
♀/♄	3 Dec 1913	13.4	
♀/♃	24 Jan 1915	14.6	
♀/♂	16 Mar 1916	15.7	Death of brother, Francois
♀/☉	8 May 1917	16.9	Expulsion from Swiss school
☿/☿	29 June 1918	18.0	
☿/☽	8 May 1920	19.9	Gains Pilot's Licence
☿/♄	17 Mar 1922	21.7	Major Crash—leaves Air Force
☿/♃	24 Jan 1924	23.6	
☿/♂	2 Dec 1925	25.4	Flying for *Aéropostal*
☿/☉	12 Oct 1927	27.3	Promoted to Cape Juby Post
☿/♀	20 Aug 1929	29.1	1st book published. Argentina
☽/☽	29 June 1931	31.0	Marries Consuelo 2nd book published Wins Major Awards
☽/♄	11 Oct 1932	32.3	
☽/♃	24 Jan 1934	33.6	
☽/♂	8 May 1935	34.9	
☽/☉	20 Aug 1936	36.1	Major Crash in Sahara
☽/♀	2 Dec 1937	37.4	
☽/☿	17 Mar 1939	38.7	3rd book published
♄/♄	29 June 1940	40.0	Exiled from France
♄/♃	24 Jan 1942	41.6	Writes *Little Prince*
♄/♂	20 Aug 1943	43.1	*Little Prince* published in USA Rejoins French Squadron
♄/☉	16 Mar 1945	44.7	31st July 1944 Plane Lost at Sea

Fig. 152 Firdaria Timeline for Antoine de Saint-Exupéry

Antoine de Saint-Exupéry: A Life Lived in Firdaria

There is often merit in looking back at life and wondering if we could have joined the dots so that we might see the big picture whilst life was being lived.

Sometimes, looking at a person's Firdaria can be of great benefit towards understanding the complex patterns of a person's life using this fascinating tool which is new to our predictive astrology techniques.

Not 'new' in terms of generations of astrologers who have previously used the technique, but 'new' so far as we are concerned, as we are now rediscovering its value after so much time when it was concealed in texts we could not access or comprehend.

The arrows in Tonio's Diurnal Firdaria point to significant events in his life and there is a reoccurring theme to his Firdaria, as often occurs in other charts I have examined over the past few years.

When working with this technique it should be remembered that Firdaria does not work like planetary transits. Firdarias mark periods of time and the dates given in its Table are times when the Firdaria lords change places or a new period is starting.

For instance, the first period marked in Tonio's Firdaria is the Sun major period with the Moon as the minor sub-lord for the shorter period of time *(identified as Sun/Moon in Fig. 152)*. The Moon's period begins on 11th October 1904 and ends on 17th March 1906 and the Moon will be the governor over this period which runs for seventeen months.

This means that the entire period can identify major events which change the course of the native's life. Even though this Moon period occurs at such a young age and Tonio would barely remember the circumstances, it is described by his two luminaries, his father and mother, and the changes that occurred due to his father's sudden death.

Often when the Firdaria is viewed as a whole, patterns between certain planets start to become obvious when the events of the past are examined. Sometimes traumatic events reoccur when a particular planet is in charge, or benefits arrive and success marks a time when the same planet appears as a time lord.

The two sub-period lords who constantly turn up in Tonio's Firdaria are the nocturnal planets, the Moon and Mars.

The Moon is the Sun's sub-lord when Tonio's father dies when he is not yet four years old.

In his chart, the Sun and Moon are in a state known as 'generosity'. This means that they are each other's dispositor and both planets have a strong link to his twelfth house.

Grief, uncertainty, and the fact that he has no recollection of his father are the legacies of this Firdaria term.

The Moon reappears in the sub-Firdaria periods in happier times in his life – his first flight which he later said was what made him want to be a pilot when he grew up. The next Moon sub-period finds Tonio taking secret flying lessons to gain his pilot's license, and the following one (a Moon/Moon Firdaria) in 1931 sees him falling in love and marrying Consuelo as well as receiving accolades for his second book.

Antoine does not live to see another Moon sub-period.

Mars is also heavily featured in the sub-periods of Tonio's Firdaria.

Mars appears at the death of his brother Francois (Mars rules third house of siblings), is there again when Tonio gains his pilot's license (Mars conjunct MC), and features as a sub-lord in 1925 when he gets his first job as a pilot delivering mail from Toulouse to Dakar.

Mars is back again when Antoine crashes his plane during an air race and wanders for three days in the desert, nearly dying of thirst until rescued by a passing caravan and given a rehydrating drink to save his life. Mars is the last sub-period Saint-Exupéry experiences in his life, as this is the period when his final flight saw him crash into the ocean.

If Firdaria is a new experience to you, these may seem like incredible coincidences, and whilst Saint-Exupéry's Firdaria shows experiences which are unique to his life, there are many times I have seen these time periods work in parallel with an individual's life.

Firdaria is an amazing predictive technique and deserves to be one of the major tools in an astrologer's predictive kit-bag.

The final three chapters are dedicated to the Firdaria system as it is one which will only continue to rise in popularity in the future as more astrologers experiment with it in their own lives, and hopefully carry into the consulting room to review their clients' charts.

CHAPTER TEN

Time Lords: The Firdaria

The Persian technique known as Firdar, Firdaria or Alfridaries[119] makes good use of the Chaldean Order to provide a framework for a system which counts the years of a person's life according to whether they were born during the daytime or during the night.

The Chaldean Order of the Planets lists the seven original planets from the slowest planet to the fastest in the following order: Saturn, Jupiter, Mars, Sun, Venus, Mercury and the Moon.

The Firdar has two possible commencement points as the sect of the chart is critical as to where the Firdar will begin at the individual's birth.

The Diurnal Firdaria

A daytime birth belongs to the Sun, and if the Sun is found in either of the two southern quadrants, that is, the houses found above the horizon governed by the Ascendant and Descendant axis, the chart is said to be diurnal.

Under the first condition of planetary sect, the Sun becomes the major luminary of the chart.

In accordance with this rule, the Firdaria system for a diurnal chart begins at the central point of the Chaldean Order where the Sun is situated *(Fig. 153)*.

The Sun's guardianship begins at birth and lasts for a ten year period which is instrumental in the development of the native's life from infancy to pre-pubescence.

When the child turns ten years of age, the planet next in line in the descending Chaldean Order is Venus, which becomes the time-lord for the next eight years of the native's life.

Venus will be the primary lord of the period between ten and eighteen years of life for the diurnal chart.

Mercury will be the next lord which follows Venus in the Chaldean Order. Its rule will last from the age of eighteen until the thirty first birthday, and holds sway over the longest of the planets' periods as it governs the native's life for a period of thirteen years.

After Mercury's period has passed, the Moon takes over and will direct the native's life from the age of thirty one until their fortieth birthday.

At the age of forty, Saturn takes up the mantle as the Firdaria lord in the diurnal chart's timeline.

Saturn will influence the direction of the native's life from forty to fifty one years of age.

At fifty one years of age Saturn hands over to Jupiter whose role it is to supervise the next twelve years until the native turns sixty three years of age.

Mars is the last planet in the Chaldean Order to fulfil its role as Firdaria lord for the diurnal chart. Mars' time period is seven years and will finish on the individual's seventieth birthday.

The Moon's Nodes will guide the Firdaria from seventy to seventy three (North Node), and from seventy three to seventy five years of age (South Node).

After the Nodes the cycle commences again with the Sun's Firdaria at seventy five years for a ten year period.

Diurnal Firdaria

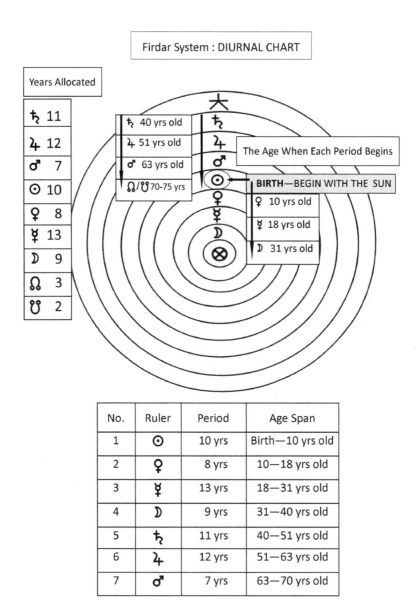

Firdar System : DIURNAL CHART

Years Allocated

♄	11
♃	12
♂	7
☉	10
♀	8
☿	13
☽	9
☊	3
☋	2

♄ 40 yrs old
♃ 51 yrs old
♂ 63 yrs old
☊/☋ 70-75 yrs

The Age When Each Period Begins

BIRTH—BEGIN WITH THE SUN
♀ 10 yrs old
☿ 18 yrs old
☽ 31 yrs old

No.	Ruler	Period	Age Span
1	☉	10 yrs	Birth—10 yrs old
2	♀	8 yrs	10—18 yrs old
3	☿	13 yrs	18—31 yrs old
4	☽	9 yrs	31—40 yrs old
5	♄	11 yrs	40—51 yrs old
6	♃	12 yrs	51—63 yrs old
7	♂	7 yrs	63—70 yrs old

Fig. 153 Diurnal Firdaria

The Nocturnal Firdaria

When the birth takes place after the Sun has set beneath the Descendant, the chart is deemed to be nocturnal until the Sun rises over the eastern horizon at the ascendant, approximately twelve hours later.

In the horoscope, the Sun will be placed beneath the horizon in the houses from the first to the sixth house in quadrant-style houses, but the Sun can also be located in the seventh house in a Whole Sign chart if it is below the degrees of the descendant (Chapter One on Sect).

If this is the case, the chart is called nocturnal, and as such, it comes under the jurisdiction of the second luminary, the Moon.

The Moon is considered to be the major luminary in the nocturnal chart.

For nocturnal births, the Firdar system starts at the Moon, which rules from birth to nine years of age *(Fig. 154)*.

In the Chaldean Order the Moon is the last of the planets the soul will visit, on its journey from the higher heavens, the Ogdoad, to its arrival on Earth.

As the Moon is the lowest placed planet, the order of the Firdaria must move from the Moon to Saturn, the first of the planets at the most elevated position at the beginning of the Order.

Saturn will become the representative for change and growth in the next period of the native's life following their ninth birthday until the twentieth birthday.

Saturn is responsible for directing the native's life through the years of puberty in a nocturnal chart for a period of eleven years.

Jupiter will follow Saturn at twenty and guide the native's life for the next twelve years until the thirty second birthday.

Mars is the fourth lord in the Firdaria system for the nocturnal birth and has the shortest period of all the planets at seven years. This means that Mars is in charge from age of thirty two to thirty nine years of age.

The Sun is the secondary luminary in a night-time chart and steps up to govern the native's life for ten years from thirty nine to forty nine years of age.

Venus is the sixth Firdaria lord and will manage the affairs of the native from the ages of forty nine to fifty seven years, for a period of eight years' duration.

The final lord in the nocturnal Firdaria, Mercury, is the planet which has the longest jurisdiction, with thirteen years taking the native from the age of fifty seven to their seventieth birthday.

The cycle of planets is now complete, and the next five years belongs to the North and South Nodes, with the North Node, a benefic, bringing fortune for three years, and its shadow, the South Node, subsequently taking the fortune away during its own two year reign.

After the Nodes, the planetary periods begin once more with the Moon for a nocturnal birth at the age of seventy five years.

Nocturnal Firdaria

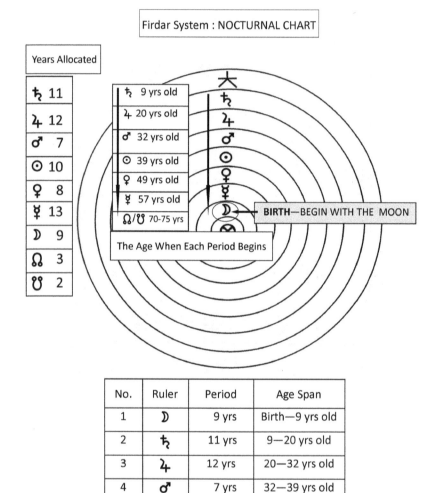

Fig. 154 Nocturnal Firdaria

Diurnal and Nocturnal Firdaria: Side by Side

MAJOR FIRDAR PERIODS	Diurnal Firdaria Planetary Lord No. of Years		Nocturnal Firdaria Planetary Lord No. of Years
1	☉ 10		☽ 9
2	♀ 8		♄ 11
3	☿ 13		♃ 12
4	☽ 9		♂ 7
5	♄ 11		☉ 10
6	♃ 12		♀ 8
7	♂ 7		☿ 13

Fig. 155 Firdar System of Planetary Periods: Comparison between Diurnal and Nocturnal Order

Regardless of whether the birth occurs during the day and the chart is diurnal, or during the night-time when the chart is nocturnal, the time periods allotted to the planets remains the same in the Firdaria system *(Fig. 155).*

Each of the planets will have dominion over a set number or years and the sequence will follow in a representation of the Chaldean Order.

Apart from Mercury which has the largest period of thirteen years, the diurnal planets, Sun, Saturn and Jupiter collectively govern a greater number of years in life.

The Sun rules ten years, Saturn is eleven years, and Jupiter has twelve years in the Firdaria System, giving them a total of thirty three years in a management role.

The nocturnal planets receive a lesser number of years: the Moon (nine years), Venus (eight years) and Mars (seven years) giving the night-time rulers a total of twenty four of the seventy five years before the Nodes take over and the process begins once more.

The following Table *(Fig. 156)* lists the number of years allotted to each of the planets according to whether they are diurnal or nocturnal planets. Mercury is also listed as the planet which receives the maximum number of years.

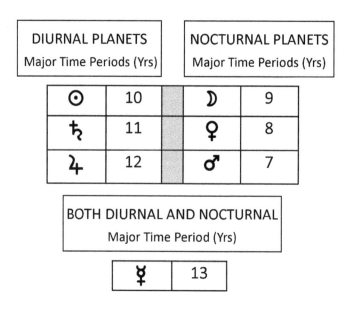

Fig. 156 Time Periods and Ages of the Diurnal and Nocturnal Firdaria

The Table below *(Fig. 157)* lists the diurnal planets on the left-hand side, along with the span of their longer time period, and their commencement and completion ages.

The right-hand side lists the alternate system of Firdar which applies to night-time births with commencement and completion ages for the nocturnal charts where the Sun was below the horizon when the birth took place after sunset during the evening or before sunrise the next morning.

Over the past twenty years there has been discussion over differences in the order of the nocturnal Firdaria.

Initially, the translations of Alcabitius and Guido Bonatti seemed to support an interruption in the planets' order for the night-time birth in that the Nodes were believed to intercept between the Mars Firdaria period and the Sun's Firdaria period.

However, a later translation of Alcabitius in 2004[120], makes it clear that each of the planets must complete their sequencing before the Nodal period at the age of seventy years.

Robert Hand makes this point in his article on the Firdar (revised June 2012), saying that *"Apparently the Latin translator filled in the blanks for the diurnal sequence and then neglected to do so with the nocturnal."*[121]

The passage where Bonatti appears to support the interruption in the nocturnal Firdaria is believed by Hand to be a mistranslation from the Latin text.

	Diurnal Firdaria Ruler of Years	Age Span		Nocturnal Firdaria Ruler of Years	Age Span
1	☉ 10	Birth—10 yrs old		☽ 9	Birth—9 yrs old
2	♀ 8	10—18 yrs old		♄ 11	9—20 yrs old
3	☿ 13	18—31 yrs old		♃ 12	20—32 yrs old
4	☽ 9	31—40 yrs old		♂ 7	32—39 yrs old
5	♄ 11	40—51 yrs old		☉ 10	39—49 yrs old
6	♃ 12	51—63 yrs old		♀ 8	49—57 yrs old
7	♂ 7	63—70 yrs old		☿ 13	57—70 yrs old
	☊ 3	70—73 yrs old		☊ 3	70—73 yrs old
	☋ 2	73—75 yrs old		☋ 2	73—75 yrs old
1	☉ 10	75— 85 yrs old		☽ 9	75—84 yrs old
2	♀ 8	85—93 yrs old		♄ 11	84—95 yrs old

Fig. 157 Firdar System of Planetary Periods: Comparison between Diurnal and Nocturnal Order

Planetary Sect and Life's Timeline

The one thing which becomes crystal clear in Firdaria is the importance of Planetary Sect.

It would appear from this predictive system of allocated time lords that sect is the most crucial factor in traditional astrological practices. Sect changes everything.

The way in which a chart is read.

The way in which the Sun and the Moon have the capacity to be the major luminary in a chart.

The way in which planets are divided into one sect or the other according to their sect preference. The way in which the dispositor will affect a planet if it belongs to the opposite sect.

So much of our modern astrology needs to be reinterpreted if we are going to allow sect to return to its original force in astrological lore.

The inclusion of planetary periods which are dominated by sect has the potential to change the way in which we interpret the past, the present, and the future purely because the life is lived differently *according to whether the chart is diurnal or nocturnal.*

A planet's sect will affect the way in which the Firdaria is interpreted.

For instance, the Sun, Saturn and Jupiter will bring their best game to the Diurnal Firdaria, simply because the chart itself is diurnal.

Similarly, the nocturnal planets, the Moon, Venus and Mars will gladly engage in the proceedings of a Nocturnal Firdaria because they have become accidentally dignified in the night-time chart.

Mercury rising ahead of the Sun is diurnal, and will therefore perform well in the Diurnal Firdaria, but when Mercury rises after the Sun it is nocturnal, and will function best in the Nocturnal Firdaria.

The switch over from one lord to the next – whether it be for the longer period of years or for the shorter period of sub-lords – often involves not only a change in planetary nature, but also a change in the sect preference of a planet.

To all intents and purposes, planets will produce their best work within an environment which is familiar, comfortable and fitting for their own sect dignity.

Firdaria and The Diurnal Timeline

The sequencing of the planets in a diurnal birth has a tendency to follow a certain 'natural' order of development from infancy to maturation which is not so evident in the nocturnal order of Firdaria.

For instance, the Sun which receives considerable attention in the Sun-sign Astrology of newspaper columns, daytime television and many social media sites, is the dominant figure for the first ten years of life.

Perhaps this honour is richly deserved considering that the Sun is vitality, light, warmth and the gained attention of others – all factors which teach a child how to gain favour, praise and attention, both within the family unit and in the community so that they may perform well within the expected norms of society.

The father figure is often represented as the Sun, so the solar individual is likely to observe the dominant male figure in their lives in order to emulate them when they reach maturity.

The father's strengths and weaknesses will be unconsciously absorbed by the child, and at an early age, the diurnal chart will begin to make choices over what it likes or dislikes about their solar model.

The movement from Sun to Venus at ten years of age is complementary with the process of forming friendships and social groups as the diurnal child reaches puberty.

The angst of fitting in or being socially isolated is well within the nature of Venus' explorative nature to determine what is acceptable behaviour in the company of others when peers play such a huge role in the individual's life.

It is worth remembering that whilst Venus' nature seems comparatively amenable as a benefic planet, it is a nocturnal planet in a diurnal chart, and if it has not escaped the Sun's hemisphere (the second rule of sect) Venus can struggle during its eight years as Firdaria lord.

The next period are the years belonging to Mercury from the ages of eighteen to thirty one and if Mercury is a diurnal planet (rising ahead of the Sun in the chart), then these years are mostly exciting and beneficial for the native's future years.

Learning experiences abound for the young adult as education may be extended to include university or college years, or young adulthood with first jobs, employment or travel opportunities and learning to live as an adult away from family influences.

Mercury's period will include the decisive years of Saturn's waning square at twenty one and its return at twenty seven, so there is ample opportunity to learn about oneself and one's environment.

The fourth period of a diurnal chart's Firdaria journey involves the Moon, the luminary which governs the opposite sect.

This nine-year period in the diurnal chart has a certain 'foreign' quality to it as the Sun may not always enjoy the internalised process of working through emotions and questions that concern happiness, satisfaction in life, or indeed, one's purpose in being on the planet.

If the solar journey until just over the age of thirty has been one of skimming the surface and getting through on light-hearted banter, good fortune and a pretty face (both male and female), then the Moon's Firdaria period can come as a rude shock to the 30-something adult.

The Moon is the alternate luminary (the prime luminary of the nocturnal sect) and this period of nine years can be a time when the changes in the native's life are coloured by decisions which involve parenthood, emotional turmoil, family concerns, or periods when the care of the body in terms of physical ailments or sudden illnesses can feature in the native's life.

The Moon's placement and its position as the house ruler of Cancer will indicate the types of challenges posed by this luminary, and whilst the period may bring the joys of becoming a parent, or the care of young children, there can be times when the secondary lord can quite suddenly change the circumstances of life.

The Moon can manifest in any number of emotional or physical entanglements and these will be described by the Moon's condition regarding the essential and accidental dignities or debilities.

The relationship it shares with the other planets will also be incredibly important as the Moon can be highly susceptible to their influence especially if it is completely out-of-sect (*ex-conditione*) in the chart.

The chart's owner can be in for an enlightening nine year period where self-examination is part of this period's journey, and the criticism of others can be brutally honest, especially if past acts or inconsiderate behaviour delivers a few home truths.

In the modernised words of Geoffrey Chaucer (1343 – 1400) in *The Parson's Tale:*

"And oft times which cursing wrongfully returneth again to him that curseth, as a bird that returneth again to his own nest."

Chaucer's line refers to a bird returning to its nest at nightfall, a familiar sight to his medieval audience with a warning of repercussions.

Similarly, the lord of nightfall can be a testing planet for the diurnal chart if past acts are 'returning again to one's own nest', but is a necessary process in assimilating the diurnal and the nocturnal aspects of the personality in order to attain wholeness or balance within the life.

The individual born during the daytime meets Saturn after its stint with the Moon, but as Saturn is in sect in the diurnal chart, the period from forty to fifty one can be one where the individual feels they have a modicum of success and control over their lives.

Jupiter follows Saturn in the Chaldean Order and has dominion over the next twelve years from fifty one to sixty years of age.

Similar to Saturn, Jupiter belongs to the diurnal sect and so is likely to be performing well over these years when the native is hopefully strong, healthy and in command of their lives.

The seventh and final planetary period before the Nodes belongs to Mars for seven years and each sub-period begins at the celebration of a new birthday.

After the previous two Firdaria lords Mars changes sect and the last period belongs to a naturally nocturnal planet.

If Mars has some sect dignity in the chart, the years between sixty three and seventy can be fruitful and active if the native has maintained their health, drive and energy levels.

However, if Mars is in poor condition and debilitated by essential and accidental dignity (including sect), then these years can be trying for the diurnal chart.

Disputes, resentments and bitterness can be hallmarks of a disgruntled Mars which feels that it is losing power or control over life.

If Mars is somehow connected to the Moon, and the Moon is also out-of-sect, then illness or accident can mar this period or test the individual's strength, motivation or temperament.

The houses which Mars rules, and Mars' placement in the chart, can also indicate troubles or issues of malcontent.

Firdaria and The Nocturnal Timeline

The nocturnal chart begins life with the Moon as the natural protector over the first nine years of life.

The individual born during the night learns to be aware of the environment in which they find themselves after birth.

The soul learns to come to terms with the weight and implications of the physical body, and whilst a diurnal infant learns the lessons of knowledge through *logos* or learning with the mind, the nocturnal chart experiments with *gnosis* or learning through the heart.

Regardless of the sect dignity, each of the sect infants learns survival skills, but they are different skills according to whether the Sun or the Moon is the primary luminary of the chart.

The diurnal chart learns cleverness and intelligence through display, connecting information, or learning how to copy the actions of the adults which surround them.

From this source comes praise and rewards in the form of attention or affection, and this helps to kindle the fire within, which will one day provide the warm glow of self-worth.

The nocturnal chart learns through attachment and connection.

It tests the boundaries and the safety of its surroundings, and learns whom and what it can trust in its environment.

The nocturnal child observes the female gender in their lives and judges whether the nurturer is worthy of their affections.

This may sound cold and calculating, but the astronomy of these two luminaries should not be overlooked in the analysis of their differences and how this has an effect on their sect dignity.

The sun is at the centre of the solar system.

We live in a world which is dependent on the sun's energy for our survival.

The sun is the source of its own light and warmth.

The moon is a tiny satellite of Earth which looks deceptively similar in size to the sun when it rises on a full moon once a month purely because it is so much closer to Earth that the dimensions of the two which dominate our world seem comparative to one another.

The moon has no light source of its own and any light it does project is reflected light from the sun. This is always the same amount, but because the Moon and Earth rotate the sun, we see different phases on the moon over a period of one month.

Who can blame the nocturnal child for their sense of insecurity in their early years when the astrological Moon is the primary initiator for life?

And sometimes, it takes a while for the nocturnal child to relax and enjoy this world as the second period of the nocturnal Firdaria progresses under the watchful eye of Saturn.

After the Moon's period of nine years, the Chaldean Order reverts back to the highest planet and a nine year old learns from Saturn for the next eleven years.

Saturn also teaches the child about the physical restrictions of their world, but unlike the Moon which has sect dignity, Saturn is functioning away from its own sect preference in a nocturnal chart. Saturn's lessons may be about exclusion rather than inclusion, and to meet a cold dark Saturn at such a young age seems a little unfair on the child.

The child's only experience of the Saturn cycle prior to the second Firdaria is the waxing square at six or seven years of age, when they separate from one authority, their parents, to attach to another set of authorities, their educational providers.

For the nocturnal birth, Saturn is the guardian from nine to twenty years of age and although the experiences are valuable, the teacher during this period can be a little harsh in its delivery.

The opposition of Saturn's cycle occurs during its Firdaria period around the age of fourteen or fifteen and may intensify any feelings of separation, isolation or rebellion against authority or anyone else who attempts to threaten or challenge the teenager.

Jupiter is a welcome respite after Saturn, but it should be remembered that Jupiter too is a diurnal planet, and may be hampered by its own lack of sect dignity in the chart.

Jupiter rules for twelve years and helps the young adult through the passage of time from twenty to thirty two years of age.

Mars becomes the seven-year lord from thirty two to thirty nine years of age for the nocturnal chart. Mars is in sect in the night-time chart and although there will always be challenges from this planet, the nocturnal individual may experience a sense of happiness and gratitude at finally arriving back at a planet and a period where they feel more at home and in command of their life choices.

At the age of thirty nine the crossover from Mars to the Sun, the other sect luminary, illuminates the individual's life in a way that can make the nocturnal chart extremely uncomfortable in the sudden glare of the Sun's light.

The Sun's Firdaria can feel like too much exposure for the nocturnal chart as although both sects enjoy success and a high profile, the methods and the reasons behind them can come from opposing sources.

The Sun is mostly a benefic planet, except when planets are placed directly alongside it, and there can be times during its Firdaria when the individual wonders whether they have chosen the best pathway for themselves.

Any self-doubt can result in swaps in their professional direction and are still viable options at this time of their lives, so long as the individual understands why they are making the shifts in the first place.

At forty nine years of age the sixth Firdaria begins for the nocturnal chart.

Diurnal charts experience the giddiness of Venus' Firdaria as first loves, crushes, romantic idealism and passionate friendship ties, but this individual is nearly fifty so the Venus experience must come from a more mature reflection on relationships.

Venus is in essence a nocturnal planet, and the opportunity presents itself at this age to be confident enough in oneself to know what gives pleasure in life, and what does not.

During the eight years when Venus is the Firdaria lord, it is likely to promote the socializing, relationships, activities and female company the native truly enjoys, and to gently weed out from their lives, the socializing, relationships, activities and female company that causes pain, distress, discomfort or boredom.

If the previous ten years of the Sun's Firdaria has taught the nocturnal person anything, it is that clarity is one asset the Moon's people often lack, and that action and decisiveness are weapons which are important to the diurnal way of life.

Part of the process of the passage through the Firdaria timeline, for either side of sect dignity, is the lesson of learning to look at life from both sides of light and dark.

Whether it is the diurnal person who has moved through the Moon's period and had to learn to trust their own instincts in the dark of the Moon's Firdaria to reach the age of forty, or the nocturnal person who has taken a little longer to get there at forty nine, but has learnt that exposure to light can bring forth epiphanies which are both extremely painful and freeing to the spirit at the same time.

The nocturnal chart's reward for starting life hard with an out of sect malefic, Saturn, as its second Firdaria lord, is to receive Venus' benefits at a more conscious age than at the breathless self-absorption of youth at ten to eighteen years of age when every relationship feels 'permanent' and essential to their happiness.

One drawback of Venus' period in the early fifties of one's life is if the nocturnal individual has become too reliant on physical appearance to provide them with love, admiration and security. Venus' period then becomes the fear of aging, of losing one's attractiveness or competing with younger, supple bodies who now receive more attention than themselves.

The first period when the Moon ruled the life before puberty can give clues as to how the individual felt about love, security and nurturance, and if these have been unsteady or frightening lessons, then Venus' period can be either a reassessment on one's inner beauty as a middle-aged adult, or it can be a nightmare of insecurities concerning one's fading looks.

The seventh and last Firdaria contains the longest number of years and belongs to Mercury.

From fifty seven to seventy years of age Mercury gives the nocturnal chart the opportunity to write, study, communicate, evaluate and learn from past experiences.

The greatest wisdom or the greatest foolishness, or a mixture of both, are possibilities for a random planet such as Mercury.

Some learning institutions may claim that the person in their sixties is too old to absorb new knowledge and information, and that perhaps Mercury was better served by the diurnal chart which experienced its Firdaria during the native's twenties.

The point is open to debate as it could easily be argued that for the diurnal chart, a Mercury which scouts ahead of the Sun is diurnal and rises before the Sun in the east. Its role is to gather information for the future and cannot differentiate between what will be useful and what will be discarded in the future.

A nocturnal Mercury travels behind the Sun and covers ground that the Sun has already passed by.

This Mercury has its 'alone time' after the Sun has set in the West, and is beautiful if visible on the western horizon at dusk.

Similarly, the Mercury Firdaria in the nocturnal chart looks back at the life in reflection, not because life is over, but because this type of wisdom which the nocturnal began learning at birth is *gnosis;* knowledge from within, knowledge born from intuition, pain, sadness, joy or sometimes pure freedom whereby I understand that I do not understand.

Mercury shifts and changes in nature, qualities and characteristics but it serves each Firdaria perfectly well, purely because it embraces diversity but comprehends human nature's desire for knowledge and self-acceptance.

Vettius Valens and Time-Lords

Long-Term and Short-Term Time Lords

The Firdar system includes a second level of control whereby each planet takes a turn during the longer time period allotted to each planet.

The time period for each of the planets, i.e., Saturn (11 years), Jupiter (12 years), Mars (7 years), Sun (10 years), Venus (8 years), Mercury (13 years), and Moon (9 years), can be broken down once more into smaller increments of time.

Each period is divided by the number seven, and each of these smaller evenly-numbered periods, is divided amongst the seven planets.

The first of each smaller time, known as a sub-period, begins with the original owner of the larger period.

For instance, the Sun will be the initial sub-ruler of its ten years, Venus will be the first sub-ruler of its eight years and Mercury will be the first sub-ruler of its thirteen year period.

The seven planets begin with the initial lord and then follow in correct sequence according to the Chaldean Order.

The division of the larger period known as the 'major period' creates an equality for each 'minor period' but can be tricky to calculate, as the division breaks into years, months and days.

Only Mars is easy to calculate as, being seven years in duration, each sub-period will begin and end at the native's birthday.

Robert Hand writes in his Introduction to Book IV of the *Anthology* of second century astrologer, Vettius Valens, that the Greek astrologers would never have used the terms 'major lord' or 'minor lord' to differentiate between the two planets as in his opinion, this is misleading terminology suggesting the longer serving lord (major) has the greater power or influence over the entire period of its rulership.[122]

He believes that these particular terms have caused confusion over who has the greatest input in the Firdaria system and that most astrologers using the Firdaria system as a predictive technique would consider the so-called 'minor lord' or short-term ruler, to have the greater impact of the two planets over the length of their shorter time period.

Hand recommends avoiding the use of major and minor to describe the time lapse differences between the ruling lords as the traditional Greek astrologers would have been more comfortable considering the two planets in the terms of Aristotle's philosophy on 'matter' and 'form'.

Simply put, 'matter' is the potential for something to 'become', and cannot in itself function alone, as matter requires some sort of physical action to allow the 'matter' to take a 'form'.

Matter always precedes form but can only hint at the possibilities that form might become in the future.

"Perfection is achieved, not when there is nothing more to add, but when there is nothing left to take away."

Antoine de Saint-Exupéry (1900-1944)

Saint-Exupéry's definition of perfection is a good example of how matter and form co-exist in the physical world.

In a world where there is always an excess of matter the variety in forms is almost infinite. However, the form only becomes truly perfect, that is, comes closest to its authentic self, once all excess matter has been sheared away.

To become separated suddenly by sheer force is to take something back to its pristine form and it is this almost violent or ruthless action that gives form the opportunity to reach perfection.

The sculptor takes a block of stone and chips away at it until the form that they perceive to exist within that particular material is released. They use knowledge, skill and intuition to create the perfect form – not so much aesthetically perfect, but perfect so far as what was promised by the material and by the artist's vision.

If this analogy is applied to the Firdar's planetary periods, the lords of the major periods become seven individual base materials, i.e. one is stone, another wood, marble, clay, metal or wax.

The material of each planet is different and unique in both its qualities and its possibilities.

The material that each native or individual is provided with is similar, but not the same.

The difference between the material we all expect, and the material provided lies in the state of the planet, that is, its condition in terms of essential and accidental dignities, so that the material is somewhat flawed or personalised even before the chipping away process begins.

During the major planet's longer term, each sub-lord must find its own form within the material provided by the major planet, and create a form which is unique to its own nature.

Each form will change and mutate according to the state of the sub-period planet, and when the longer period is finished, a new material is presented for seven different forms to take their place.

The process is multi-faceted and extremely personal, so there is little wonder that it takes a lifetime for a person to come to terms with their true nature.

The sculptor in this work is also many things: fate, destiny, faith, love, good luck, bad luck, even the native themselves, as events tumble over one another in their eagerness to make an impact on the process of reduction. Choices are made constantly, sometimes randomly and sometimes with purpose during the creation of the closest thing to the soul's perfection here on Earth.

Robert Hand adds another term to the concept of the two sharing lords of a Firdaria and he suggests that the longer serving lords are the 'donating' lords. The long-term lord donates the larger period of years to be broken down (the matter) which is shared amongst the shorter serving lords who are the 'recipient' lords. The short-term lords then have the opportunity to create change or bring something to fruition (the form), as the major lord cannot provide this service themselves over the longer period. Remember that the long-term ruler sets the agenda by leading as the first short-term ruler of its period.

After the first sub-period the short-term lords each in their turn become the recipients of the governing lord's matter, but can only give a form which is unique to their own particular nature (i.e., Saturn provides a Saturnian form or Venus provides a Venusian form).

In Robert Hand's explanation of Firdaria lords, the material is carved from the donor, and the form created from the material, is provided by the recipient. The terms donating and recipient are reminiscent of a medical procedure where there is a handover of a living organ.

Without the 'donation' of the wood, metal, marble, or really any material including a living organ, the form can never exist, so the symbiotic relationship between the two planets is dependent on the first action of the longer serving planet.

This sounds like a wonderful concept if the two planets are willing to cooperate and the flow from matter to form is without agitation – the donor wants to give and the recipient wants to receive and create its best form from the material. However, imagine if the material donated is incompatible with the form that is desired, and the sub-lord is incapable or unwilling to work within the parameters of a particular material.

The frustration of the sculptor, surgeon or chart owner becomes the over-riding factor as the Firdaria order attempts to bring together the potential of one force which is rejected by the second party. In likelihood the tension between the two parties creates problems and although the resultant form looks anything but perfect, it is both parties who are equally to blame for the poor workmanship.

For instance, the Sun and Saturn are considered to be mutually hurtful to one another because they sit opposite one another in Thema Mundi, and rule signs which naturally are in opposition.

Not only is their position difficult, but they represent different principles, with the Sun promoting life, energy, warmth and light, and Saturn signifying restrictions on life, coldness, and darkness or the absence of light.

It is very difficult then for the Sun to hand over its matter to a Saturnian form which does not support the principles of what the matter is trying to become.

Where the Sun's material needs delicate and subtle treatment, instead Saturn provides a heaviness and a solidity that the Sun does not require from its sub-lord.

The resultant form breaks or tarnishes easily, or in a non-perfect way represents the material from whence it came.

It is irrelevant that the long-term ruler, the Sun, requires its best solar work for the native. When it comes the time for Saturn to be the short-term lord, then the Saturnian form it has taken is a poor representative for the Sun's material, and neither planet (nor the chart owner) is satisfied with the result. The better sect dignity that Saturn possesses the better the form will be but if the chart is nocturnal and Saturn is out of sect then difficulties arise in the native's life during this period.

According to Robert Hand, the major or donating lord, provides several crucial elements for the minor or recipient lord, and together they bring about action and change in the native's life.

Firstly, the donating lord sets the boundary which defines the time in which a particular process or activity must occur. This is the division by seven of the donating lord's long-term period.

Secondly, the donating lord has a range of potentials or possibilities from which the recipient must choose one most suitable to its own need.

In other words, the major or long-term lord has a substantial list of generic significations from which the minor lord may choose a specific one that is appropriate to its own nature.

Imagine you are part of a working bee and the organiser gathers everyone to read out a list of random tasks that need to be accomplished within a certain time-frame.

The organiser does not care who chooses what task, they just want the list to be completed within the appropriate time.

He is 'donating' these tasks to you collectively and asking you to choose one.

You will most likely choose a task that you feel makes best use of your skill set, is most likely to be completely successfully, is more appealing to you, and is a task which you think is specifically designed to suit your own nature.

You are the 'recipient' of the task and the better you choose, the more likely you are to be a successful, efficient and worthwhile member of the working bee.

For instance, in a nocturnal chart when the Sun is the major lord from ages thirty nine to forty nine, its significations are honour, reputation, intellect, the father, public aspirations and so forth.

From this list each minor lord must choose one solar purpose most suited to it; the Moon may choose popularity, Mars may choose ambition and competition, Jupiter may choose cultivating friendships with important people, etc, and then each planet will attempt to bring about action to complete its task. In a diurnal chart the Sun's major period begins at birth so the planets will each need to choose more appropriate tasks for this age. They are likely to choose projections of their energies to imprint on the young child's psyche.

The difficulty lies in the possibility that the suggested tasks are so foreign to your skill set or your own nature, that you feel threatened, undermined or incapable of assistance, and this is when discomfort turns to trouble.

Rather than being useful or productive, you become 'an enemy of the list' and your negative contribution means that the outcomes you are generating are annoying and counter-productive in their nature.

This can mean that the other members of the team feel they must work that bit harder to undo your efforts in order to achieve success for the whole project.

Astrologically, this happens when the intrinsic nature of the two lords is incompatible and their principles are naturally in conflict, i.e. the Sun and Saturn.

The expression will change according to who owns the longer period, and who is the short-term ruler, but on the most basic level, it matters little who is the donating lord and who is the recipient, as nothing will bring about an amicable working relationship between these ancient adversaries.

Another defining factor which determines the level of success for both parties is their respective situations in the natal chart.

The condition of both planets is critical to the success of the mission. In other words, the donation of healthy organs is the best material for a successful transplant to a strong recipient. For this reason, dignity through sign and degree, house placement, movement and aspects to either benefics or malefics will need to be examined thoroughly to determine the outcome of each short-term period.

To sum up, if the list (of organs or tasks, or matter) provided by the donating lord is damaged, unrealistic, impossible to achieve, or has limited potential, then the entire project is in jeopardy and the recipient will be struggling to effectively achieve its own specific task.

Likewise, if the donor is in excellent shape and has high expectations, but the recipient is blighted in some way, then the task it sets for itself may be suitable to its nature, but the planet may be so inefficient that it cannot possibly fulfil what it has initially promised.

There is a modern practice in large corporations or government departments of the temporary movement of skilled employees from one division to another, and this practice can be used to illustrate the working relationship between the two Firdar lords.

The practice is known as 'Secondment', and happens when an experienced official or employee is temporarily transferred to another position where their skills are required, for a defined period of time, and for a specific purpose, to the mutual benefit of all parties.

If the concept of Firdaria is considered in this context, then 'head office' is the major lord who requests and oversees the secondment and the 'expert' is the minor lord, who is being seconded as they have the skill-set to accomplish the required workload, and the native is the 'all parties' who hope to benefit from the secondment.

The results of the combination will differ according to which planet is organising the secondment, and which planet is actually doing the work required.

The material in the following two chapters on the Diurnal Firdar sub-periods (Chapter Eleven) and the Nocturnal Firdar sub-periods (Chapter Twelve) has been adapted from Valens *Anthologies*, Book VI[123] which was originally written for a different predictive system known as Profection.

Valens' delineations were intended to predict incidents in the adult's life and for this reason the first period of either the Sun (diurnal births) or the Moon (nocturnal births) has been reshaped to provide practical observations on childhood periods based on Valens' text.

Also, Valens uses the terms '*handing over, giving over, or distributing*', to describe the relationship between the two planets involved in the process, and these terms would normally not be applied to the Persian Firdaria system.

Robert Hand in his editorship of Valens' translation explains that in the case of both profection and planetary period systems (such as Firdaria), the order of the planets directly affects the description of the period.

Robert Hand states: *"And there appears to be the same relationship between the ruler of a long planetary period and that of the planet that rules the sub-period; as a result the so-called minor period lord may actually be the more important of the two because it is the determinant of the eidos (form) of the event."*[124]

In a later article on Firdar[125] Hand includes a complete set of Firdar delineations by 15th century astrologer Johannes Schoener from his *Three Books on the Judgement of Nativities*, Book III.

When Schoener's text is compared to the earlier works of Valens there are distinct similarities, but this should be no surprise as both delineations are based on a system of first principles of the planets, and this is the foundation for both predictive techniques.

It should be noted that Valens defines each planet's sect in the following description of their significations, for instance: *"Sun . . . Saturn . . . Jupiter . . . is of the day sect"* and *"Moon . . . Mars . . . Venus . . . is of the night sect"*, but he does not take sect into account when he predicts the effects of one planet handing over to another in his delineations.

In his conclusions on the planets he mentions the following text on how sect affects the planets, especially the malefics:

"The benefic stars which are appropriately and favourably situated bring about their proper effects according to their own nature and the nature of their sign, with the aspects and conjunctions of each star being blended.

*If however they are unfavourably situated, they are indicative of reversals. In the same way even the malefic stars, when they are operative in appropriate places **in their own sect**, are bestowers of good and indicative of the greatest positions and success; when they are inoperative, they bring about disasters and accusations."*[126]

Valens' quote makes a distinction between the effects of sect on the malefic, where the correct sect can have a positive effect on the planet, is subtly different from the benefics, who are more affected by sign, rather than planetary sect.

Accordingly, Saturn in the diurnal chart benefits from the Sun's warmth and light and consequently, its expression and significations are improved for daytime births. By extension the Firdar in which Saturn is involved, either during its own major period, or when it takes the role of sub-period lord, are also improved in circumstances which favour the diurnal chart.

The opposite occurs in a night-time chart when Saturn, who is described by Valens as *"a servant of evil and of downfall, and a depriver of years of life."*[127] is colder and darker when it is removed from the Sun's influence.

Likewise, Mars, whom Valens describes as *"the bane of nativities"*, will be considered to be out-of-sect in a diurnal chart under the first rule of Sect (Chapter Two on Planetary Sect) and will be more inflamed and volatile in the chart of someone born during the day.

However, should the birth occur in the night hours Mars is soothed by the Moon's coolness and moisture and is more cautious and calmer in its actions.

LONG PERIOD	SHORT PERIOD
Minimum - 7 yrs (♂) : Maximum - 13 yrs (☿)	Minimum - 1 yr (♂) : Maximum - 1yr 10 months (☿)
'Major' Lord *(in terms of Time but not Importance)*	*'Minor'* Lord *(in terms of Time but not Importance)*
Matter	Form
Donor (giving)	Recipient (taking)
List of 'organs' available: Tasks required or expected: Significations according to its nature and its condition in the chart *Long-term planet's wish-list*	Body choosing organs: Ability to complete tasks: Significations peculiar to the recipient planet's nature and its condition in the chart *Capability or Desire to fulfil tasks according to its relationship with the long-term ruler - both its innate relationship (Thema Mundi Dignities) and its own chart-specific relationship*
Potential for growth and experience: The planet's potential indicated by the chart to be realised during its long-term period: Opportunity for Change	Seven different possibilities *(including its own short period):* Unique versions of how the long-term planet's potential may be achieved: Outcome or manifestation of Change

Fig. 158 Comparison between Major and Minor Time Periods in the Firdar System

Firdaria Time Periods in Life

The following Tables *(Fig. 159–165)* provide the long and short term periods for the Firdaria of both Diurnal and Nocturnal births.

The Tables are listed according to the lords of the seven longer periods (major periods) which differ according to whether the birth occurred during daylight or in the hours of the night.

The diurnal birth commences with the Sun as the first major time lord in the Firdaria system and is followed by Venus (2nd lord), Mercury (3rd lord), Moon (4th lord), Saturn (5th lord), Jupiter (6th lord), and Mars (7th lord).

The nocturnal birth commences with the Moon as the first major time lord in the Firdaria system and is followed by Saturn (2nd lord), Jupiter (3rd lord), Mars (4th lord), Sun (5th lord), Venus (6th lord), and Mercury (7th lord).

Both Firdars will then complete their cycle with the five year period of the Nodes, before commencement again in the same order at seventy five years of age.

The Five Year Nodal Period

Neither Valens or Schoener refer to the periods belonging to the Nodes. For this reason it is best to remember that the North Node is a benefic and the South Node is a malefic. Three years of good fortune followed by two years of possible retrospection may be the nature of the five years between seventy and seventy five. The two rulers of their opposing axis will determine the flavor of these two periods, as will the house axis across which the Nodes lie in the chart. Planets either conjunct the Nodes or at the Bendings at the halfway mark of a square will also play a large part in the proceedings of the Nodal Firdaria.

Firdaria: FIRST Major Time Period For Diurnal and Nocturnal Births				
	DIURNAL CHARTS Time Lords for *Daytime Births*	☉ 10 year MAJOR Period * 1 yr 5 months MINOR Period	NOCTURNAL CHARTS Time Lords for *Night-time Births*	☽ 9 year MAJOR Period * 1 yr 3 months MINOR Period
1	☉/☉	BIRTH – 1.4	☽ / ☽	BIRTH – 1.3
2	☉/♀	1.4 – 2.9	☽/♄	1.3 – 2.6
3	☉/☿	2.9 – 4.3	☽/♃	2.6 – 3.9
4	☉/☽	4.3 – 5.7	☽/♂	3.9 – 5.1
5	☉/♄	5.7 – 7.1	☽/☉	5.1 – 6.4
6	☉/♃	7.1 – 8.6	☽/♀	6.4 – 7.7
7	☉/♂	8.6 – 10.0	☽/☿	7.7 – 9.0

*Figs. 159 to 165 The Seven Major and Minor Time
Periods for Diurnal and Nocturnal Charts*

		Firdaria: SECOND Major Time Period For Diurnal and Nocturnal Births				
	DIURNAL CHARTS Time Lords for *Daytime Births*	♀ 8 year MAJOR Period * 1 yr 1 month MINOR Period		NOCTURNAL CHARTS Time Lords for *Night-time Births*	♄ 11 year MAJOR Period * 1 yr 6 months MINOR Period	
1	♀/♀	10.0 – 11.1		♄/♄	9.0 – 10.6	
2	♀/☿	11.1 – 12.3		♄/♃	10.6 – 12.1	
3	♀/☽	12.3 – 13.4		♄/♂	12.1 – 13.7	
4	♀/♄	13.4 – 14.6		♄/☉	13.7 – 15.3	
5	♀/♃	14.6 – 15.7		♄/♀	15.3 – 16.9	
6	♀/♂	15.7 – 16.9		♄/☿	16.9 – 18.4	
7	♀/☉	16.9 – 18.0		♄/☽	18.4 – 20.0	

Fig. 160

	DIURNAL CHARTS Time Lords for *Daytime Births*	☿ 13 year MAJOR Period * 1 yr 10 months MINOR Period		NOCTURNAL CHARTS Time Lords for *Night-time Births*	♃ 12 year MAJOR Period * 1 yr 8 months MINOR Period
1	☿ / ☿	18.0 – 19.9		♃ / ♃	20.0 – 21.7
2	☿ / ☽	19.9 – 21.7		♃ / ♂	21.7 – 23.4
3	☿ / ♄	21.7 – 23.6		♃ / ☉	23.4 – 25.1
4	☿ / ♃	23.6 – 25.4		♃ / ♀	25.1 – 26.9
5	☿ / ♂	25.4 – 27.3		♃ / ☿	26.9 – 28.6
6	☿ / ☉	27.3 – 29.1		♃ / ☽	28.6 – 30.3
7	☿ / ♀	29.1 – 31.0		♃ / ♄	30.3 – 32.0

Firdaria: THIRD Major Time Period
For Diurnal and Nocturnal Births

Fig. 161

	DIURNAL CHARTS Time Lords for *Daytime Births*	☽ 9 year MAJOR Period * 1 yr 3 months MINOR Period		NOCTURNAL CHARTS Time Lords for *Night-time Births*	♂ 7 year MAJOR Period * 1 year MINOR Period	
1	☽ / ☽	**31.0 – 32.3**		♂ / ♂	**32.0 – 33.0**	
2	☽ / ♄	32.3 – 33.6		♂ / ☉	33.0 – 34.0	
3	☽ / ♃	33.6 – 34.9		♂ / ♀	34.0 – 35.0	
4	☽ / ♂	34.9 – 36.1		♂ / ☿	35.0 – 36.0	
5	☽ / ☉	36.1 – 37.4		♂ / ☽	36.0 – 37.0	
6	☽ / ♀	37.4 – 38.7		♂ / ♄	37.0 – 38.0	
7	☽ / ☿	38.7 – 40.0		♂ / ♃	38.0 – 39.0	

Firdaria: FOURTH Major Time Period
For Diurnal and Nocturnal Births

Fig. 162

	DIURNAL CHARTS Time Lords for *Daytime Births*	♄ 11 year MAJOR Period * 1 yr 6 months MINOR Period		NOCTURNAL CHARTS Time Lords for *Night-time Births*	☉ 10 year MAJOR Period * 1 yr 5 months MINOR Period
		Firdaria: FIFTH Major Time Period For Diurnal and Nocturnal Births			
1	♄ / ♄	**40.0 – 41.6**		☉ / ☉	**39.0 – 40.4**
2	♄ / ♃	41.6 – 43.1		☉ / ♀	40.4 – 41.9
3	♄ / ♂	43.1 – 44.7		☉ / ☿	41.9 – 43.3
4	♄ / ☉	44.7 – 46.3		☉ / ☽	43.3 – 44.7
5	♄ / ♀	46.3 – 47.9		☉ / ♄	44.7 – 46.1
6	♄ / ☿	47.9 – 49.4		☉ / ♃	46.1 – 47.6
7	♄ / ☽	49.4 – 51.0		☉ / ♂	47.6 – 49.0

Fig. 163

	DIURNAL CHARTS Time Lords for *Daytime Births*	♃ 12 year MAJOR Period * 1 yr 8 months MINOR Period		NOCTURNAL CHARTS Time Lords for *Night-time Births*	♀ 8 year MAJOR Period * 1 yr 1 month MINOR Period
1	♃ / ♃	**51.0 – 52.7**		♀ / ♀	**49.0 – 50.1**
2	♃ / ♂	52.7 – 54.4		♀ / ☿	50.1 – 51.3
3	♃ / ☉	54.4 – 56.1		♀ / ☽	51.3 – 52.4
4	♃ / ♀	56.1 – 57.9		♀ / ♄	52.4 – 53.6
5	♃ / ☿	57.9 – 59.6		♀ / ♃	53.6 – 54.7
6	♃ / ☽	59.6 – 61.3		♀ / ♂	54.7 – 55.9
7	♃ / ♄	61.3 – 63.0		♀ / ☉	55.9 – 57.0

Firdaria: SIXTH Major Time Period
For Diurnal and Nocturnal Births

Fig. 164

Firdaria: SEVENTH Major Time Period					
For Diurnal and Nocturnal Births					

	DIURNAL CHARTS Time Lords for *Daytime Births*	♂ 7 year MAJOR Period * 1 year MINOR Period		NOCTURNAL CHARTS Time Lords for *Night-time Births*	☿ 13 year MAJOR Period * 1 yr 10 months MINOR Period
1	♂ / ♂	63.0 – 64.0		☿ / ☿	57.0 – 58.9
2	♂ / ☉	64.0 – 65.0		☿ / ☽	58.9 – 60.7
3	♂ / ♀	65.0 – 66.0		☿ / ♄	60.7 – 62.6
4	♂ / ☿	66.0 – 67.0		☿ / ♃	62.6 – 64.4
5	♂ / ☽	67.0 – 68.0		☿ / ♂	64.4 – 66.3
6	♂ / ♄	68.0 – 69.0		☿ / ☉	66.3 – 68.1
7	♂ / ♃	69.0 – 70.0		☿ / ♀	68.1 – 70.0

Fig. 165

The Moon's Nodes at the End of Both Full Firdaria Periods

Firdaria: THE NODES Time Period				
SAME For Diurnal and Nocturnal Births				
DIURNAL CHARTS Time Lords for *Daytime Births*	☊ 3 year Time Period * ☋ 2 year Time Period		NOCTURNAL CHARTS Time Lords for *Night-time Births*	☊ 3 year Time Period * ☋ 2 year Time Period
1	☊	70.0 – 73.0	☊	70.0 – 73.0
2	☋	73.0 – 75.0	☋	73.0 – 75.0

Fig. 166 The Nodal years of the Firdar System

The Egyptian Terms

The Terms or Bounds are the fourth level of Essential Dignity and are reproduced in the Table below as Valens includes references to the Terms in his delineations on planetary periods or handings-over.

The degrees of a sign are divided into groups of five for the purpose of allotting one of the five planets as ruler over the sign's degrees. The two luminaries, the Sun and Moon, are exempt from the Terms.

The late degrees of most signs are in Terms belonging to the malefic planets, either Saturn or Mars, and Valens warns of these degrees as the Term Ruler of a planet's degrees can affect its situation and the outcomes of an event during a planet's major or minor Firdar period.

Sign	1st Term Lord	2nd Term Lord	3rd Term Lord	4th Term Lord	5th Term Lord
♈	0 - 6 ♃	6 -12 ♀	12 - 20 ☿	20 - 25 ♂	25 - 30 ♄
♉	0 - 8 ♀	8 -14 ☿	14 - 22 ♃	22 - 27 ♄	27 - 30 ♂
♊	0 - 6 ☿	6 -12 ♃	12 - 17 ♀	17 - 24 ♂	24 - 30 ♄
♋	0 - 7 ♂	7 -13 ♀	13 - 19 ☿	19 - 26 ♃	26 - 30 ♄
♌	0 - 6 ♃	6 -11 ♀	11 - 18 ♄	18 - 24 ☿	24 - 30 ♂
♍	0 - 7 ☿	7 -17 ♀	17 - 21 ♃	21 - 28 ♂	28 - 30 ♄
♎	0 - 6 ♄	6 -14 ☿	14 - 21 ♃	21 - 28 ♀	28 - 30 ♂
♏	0 - 7 ♂	7 -11 ♀	11 - 19 ☿	19 - 24 ♃	24 - 30 ♄
♐	0 -12 ♃	12-17 ♀	17 - 21 ☿	21 - 26 ♄	26 - 30 ♂
♑	0 - 7 ☿	7 -14 ♃	14 - 22 ♀	22 - 26 ♄	26 - 30 ♂
♒	0 - 7 ☿	7 -13 ♀	13 - 20 ♃	20 - 25 ♂	25 - 30 ♄
♓	0 -12 ♀	12-16 ♃	16 - 19 ☿	19 - 28 ♂	28 - 30 ♄

Fig. 167 The Egyptian Terms

CHAPTER ELEVEN

The Solar Journey

The Firdaria and the Diurnal Chart

In the story of *The Little Prince* the wandering boy from another planet meets a number of characters on other tiny asteroids before finally arriving on Earth.

Many of these characters are adults whose lives seems futile and somewhat meaningless to the little stranger.

A king with no subjects, a business man who spends his time counting stars which he believes are his property, a geographer who never leaves his desk or consults a map, a lamplighter who constantly lights and extinguishes lamps and a station master who speaks of passengers on trains who rush madly from one place to the other simply because, *"One is never happy where one is"*[128].

Only the children passengers take an interest in the journey, looking out of the train windows at the world whizzing by and squealing with delight at the passing parade.

Even the prince's own life at home on his tiny asteroid would seem to have a certain pointlessness to the casual observer, as his time is spent sweeping the ash from volcanoes, weeding out unwanted baobab seeds which sprout overnight and tending to a single petulant rose who ignores him and takes his care for granted.

When questioned by the airman about his routine, the little prince answers that it's a question of discipline, *"When you finish washing and dressing each morning, you must carefully wash and dress your planet . . . It is very tedious work, but it is very easy."*[129]

Sometimes the journey through life feels a bit this way.

Routines and ritual bind us to our lives, and the choices we make sometimes feel as though they have a foregone conclusion.

But there are also times when life's rhythm is interrupted, events change life, and we do pause to look out of the train window, or to decide to enjoy the journey, or change the destination.

Looking back at these moments and comparing them to the passage in the Firdaria system from the perspective of both long-term and short-term lords, is an enlightening experience for the philosopher or the astrologer.

Being aware of the present Firdaria situation, or an approaching change in either the major period lord, or the shorter (not-so-minor) lord can be of tremendous value in the consulting room as clients often sense change is on the way, but are unsure on how to act on it.

When the little prince takes his leave from the fox whom he has befriended, the fox gives him a secret which helps the wanderer to understand more about his life. The fox tells him

"It is the time you have wasted for your rose that makes your rose so important."[130]

The little prince realises that he has resented the time spent on his asteroid performing tedious tasks such as watering his rose, placing her under the glass dome at night, removing the caterpillars from her leaves, and listening to her when she complained or boasted about her own beauty.

But with the fox's words, he sees that no time was ever wasted on something (or someone) that he has loved.

We all have passions, we all have people and things we love and are responsible for, and sometimes it takes the Firdaria's changing guard to play the role of the fox, and to remind us that time spent with them was never wasted.

Like everyone else on the planet, Antoine's roses were numerous throughout his life.

His passion for flying, his love of adventure, his dedication to his younger brother Francois and the grief at his loss, his philosophies on man's state, his fellow airman, his politics, his books, and perhaps the rose which caused him the greatest consternation and who became immortalized in *The Little Prince* is the love of his life, his wife Consuelo.

Life's journey in the Diurnal Firdaria occurs in the order of the planets' governance over life – Sun, Venus, Mercury, Moon, Saturn, Jupiter, Mars and the Nodes.

Each of these major periods can be divided into sub-periods and the headings in this chapter are the time divisions of both major and minor Firdaria periods. The descriptions which accompany each sub-period have been adapted from the joint delineations of planetary periods by Vettius Valens (1st century CE) and Johannes Schoener (late 15th/ early 16th century CE).

I have tried to relate these texts to modern experiences of the Firdaria and I have used a combination of sources to demonstrate that astrologers from later times and different languages were familiar with the concept of planetary periods. Surprisingly, given the time-span between texts and the difficulties with translation, it is interesting to note that there are very few differences between the two delineations.

The diagram below *(Fig. 168)* shows the periods in years of the long-term Firdaria lords in their correct order.

Diurnal Firdaria

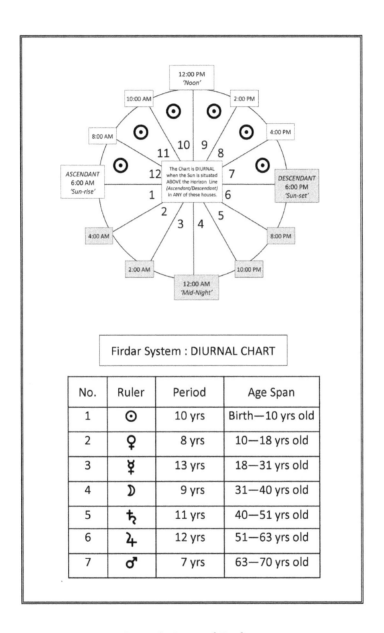

Fig. 168 Diurnal Firdaria

Pure Radiance ... THE SUN

"my mother
is pure radiance.
she is the sun
i can touch
and kiss
and hold
without
getting burnt."

- Sanober Khan

First Diurnal Major Period lasts for 10 Years

The Sun is Lord from Birth – 10ᵗʰ Birthday

The Sun's Matter and Significations:

Brilliance	Action	Self-awareness	Good fortune
Father	Respect	Power	Acknowledgement
Intelligence	Authority	Judgement	Public Reputation

In a Diurnal Firdaria the Sun becomes the major lord for the first ten years of life, and when this portion of time is divided by seven, the resultant term for each sub-lord is approximately seventeen months in duration.

The initial stage after birth belongs to the Sun, who hands over to Venus, the next descending planet in the Chaldean Order, then Mercury, followed by the Moon, Saturn, Jupiter and Mars.

Each planet becomes recipient of the Sun's material for a period of seventeen months, after which the ten years is finished and the Sun's major period has come to an end.

It seems out of place for the Sun to begin the journey of life, when so many of the Sun's significations are inconsistent with the timing of its rulership in a diurnal chart.

In fact, the majority of Valens' delineations for the Sun's handover[131] are far more suitable for a nocturnal birth which experiences the Sun's Firdaria in adulthood, from the ages of thirty nine to forty nine years of age.

Public reputation or friendship with noble personages is not exactly on the agenda for a newborn babe, but it does not mean that assessing the potential of the Sun as a donating principle is without value at the commencement of life.

Firstly, the social position and situation of both parents measures the ease or difficulty of these first few years.

The material provided by the Sun indicates both the external and the internal landscape of the child's existence; namely the social, political, economical and religious affiliations will determine the class structure to which the parents belong, and whether they can maintain or improve their situation.

Many traditional texts discuss these possibilities in length as the situations experienced by the parent will directly affect the safety and well-being of the infant and child. Therefore, each sub-lord period needs to be examined in the light of *both* participating lords' condition and situation in the chart, in order to identify any immediate danger to the infant's survival and also to evaluate how the first major period (or its sub-lord) will affect the native in adulthood.

This thread between the parent and the child's life was efficiently demonstrated in Antoine de Saint-Exupéry's life when his father suddenly died from a heart attack at the time that Antoine was in the Sun's major period with the Moon as its recipient. Nor is it unique to Saint-Exupéry's experience at such a young age. There have been a number of times in the consulting room when I have found that the first long-term period of either the Sun in a diurnal chart (ten years) or the Moon in a nocturnal chart (nine years) has set the stage for a planet ruling the sub-period to keep reverberating in the individual's life whenever it appears in further Firdaria patterns later in life.

Regardless of gender, the daylight individual will want to ensure that when they reach adulthood they can duplicate or improve on father's success in providing for the family.

The catalyst may occur when the Sun becomes a sub-period lord for one of the other planets in adult years and opportunities which present themselves trigger memories from the first major period of life.

Each generation strives to improve on the last, and a diurnal nativity will apply the qualities of its Sun to elevate themselves in reputation or authority, especially if they believe that father has made a poor job of it during their own childhood.

If the wounds of father are more internalised, the native may reject father entirely and try to heal any psychological or emotional wounds inflicted during the Sun's term of office using a later time when the Sun is a sub-lord for one of the remaining six planets.

The delineations listed below for the Sun's major period, can apply as much to the father or the family situation as it does for the infant, as the natal chart will indicate the strength of the Sun, and its relationship with the other planets.

For this reason, the Sun's field of expertise is listed below as Valens' indications of intellect, intelligence, judgement and good actions still have significance, especially if they are the groundwork for the seeds of potential which are lain down within the child's psyche during the first ten years of life.

In many classifications, the Sun is associated directly with the father, rather than the child's mother.

However, the condition of both the luminaries and their relationship in the natal chart needs to be taken into account, as the actions of father will have a direct influence on the mother, and vice versa, and this will ultimately affect how the child perceives both parents, either individually, or as a dual nurturing unit.

The poem by Sanober Khan has been deliberately chosen to challenge the concept of the Sun's qualities being aligned solely with father, as the Sun is shown as accessible to the child through the mother's radiance rather than being the remote figure that father can present when he is associated with the more fearsome and powerful image of the Sun.

The Sun's ten year period may include another addition to the family unit and the jealously that a new sibling instils in the older brother or sister can be overwhelming for a diurnal child who does not wish to share the limelight with an intruder. For parents with young children in this Firdaria it is important to know who is the sub-period lord so that this planet can be examined during the settling in period of a new baby's arrival.

For instance, in Antoine de Saint-Exupéry's example there was a gap of two years between Tonio and his beloved brother Francois

(1902-1917) who would have arrived in Tonio's life during his Sun Venus period (from 1.4 to 2.9 years). In Saint-Exupéry's chart Venus is in Cancer with the Sun in his eleventh house suggesting Tonio bonded immediately with his newborn brother.

There are many times during the first Sun period when mother steps in as the solar image and family units are no longer as traditional as in the past or as gender restrictive as they used to be, so although I have used 'father' more often in following the terms of Valens and Schoener, be advised that it can apply to either parent playing a dominant role in the child's early years.

FIRST Major Firdaria for the Diurnal Chart
☉ — 10 years
10 years divided by 7 = 1 year 5 months 4 days

Major SUN 10 yrs Sub-Period	Combination of Major (1st) and Minor (2nd) Time Lords	Minor Time Period BEGINS—ENDS for 1 yr 5 months *(1.4) *months as %
1	☉/☉	Birth – 1.4
2	☉/♀	1.4 – 2.9
3	☉/☿	2.9 – 4.3
4	☉/☽	4.3 – 5.7
5	☉/♄	5.7 – 7.1
6	☉/♃	7.1 – 8.6
7	☉/♂	8.6 – 10.0

Fig. 169 The Sun's Firdaria in the Diurnal Chart

First Sub-Period
Donor – SUN : Recipient – SUN
(Birth – 1.4 Years)

The common rule for all Firdar sub-periods is that the long-term major lord also becomes the initial minor lord for the first of the seven periods.

In an act synonymous with 'leading by example', the major lord sets the agenda for the planets which are destined to follow in its stead.

In this case, the Sun is both the matter and the form for the first seventeen months of life, and as it is the primary luminary in a day-time chart, it has the dignity of Sect on its side.

The Sun's power as the sole source of light and heat means that if the Sun is in reasonable condition in the natal chart, the child's vitality is assured as there is a strong desire for the spirit's representative, the Sun, to protect the frailty of the body during the initial months of life.

As life expectancy increases with modern medical advancements, and healthier lifestyles maintain the native's vitality throughout the later years, it is worth mentioning that a second tour of the planets begins again with the Sun's Firdaria for a diurnal birth at the age of seventy five years.

Valens directs his delineations on the Sun towards the adult, rather than the child, so that when he says that a well figured Sun can produce brilliant acclamations and actions, alliances with superiors and unexpected benefits, especially if benefics add to the Sun's good condition, these conditions may apply for the father at the child's birth.

They can also be used for the native with the diurnal chart for the Sun's major period a second time around and can be extremely beneficial if they have the interest and vitality to pursue personal ambitions later in life.

Second Sub-Period
Donor – SUN : Recipient – VENUS
(1.4 – 2.9 Years)

The planet Venus is a suitable recipient for Sun's material as she is happy to provide an amenable form by which the Sun can gain the love and attention of those family members who surround the infant.

Venus adds further beauty to the Sun, and generally speaking Valens says that her time indicates a good and pleasing period with gifts and delights in abundance.

In diurnal charts both Venus and the Moon represent the mother, so nurturing is usually assured during Venus' sub-period, assuming the planet itself is in good condition in the natal chart.

It should be remembered however, that Venus is naturally a nocturnal planet and is likely to be out of sect by the first two rules of sect dignity, and this may dampen some of Venus' enthusiasm to produce a baby who is prepared to leave the mother's side and venture further from the nurturing source.

Third Sub-Period
Donor – SUN : Recipient – MERCURY
(2.9 – 4.3 Years)

The potential hinted at by the Sun starts to move through the form of Mercury and the native's temperament echoes the nature of this capricious, changeable planet.

Just as Mercury is easily influenced by the planets around it, so too is the child affected by external stimuli, as developing language and primitive reasoning become the signature for this sub-period.

Mercury rules the hands, fingers, tongue and the sense of hearing, so the form that Mercury has chosen to take from the Sun's material is the desire to explore the world and to learn basic lessons in self-awareness and individuation.

The one drawback to Mercury's nature is not in its willingness to explore the child's world, but in its susceptibility to outside influence, and should it be badly affected by a malefic in the chart, this may translate as difficulty of a Mercurial kind for the child, so that movement or early communication may be frustrated or restricted in some way.

Fourth Sub-Period
Donor – SUN : Recipient – MOON
(4.3 – 5.7 Years)

Robert Hand says of this period that the material of the Sun is bent to the tasks of the Moon, and the resultant action brings a time for developing relationships through a growing awareness of others, as the child develops compassion and has a desire to care for someone other than themselves.

The combination of the luminaries is a good balance between the idealistic matter of the Sun and the practical form of the Moon, and if all is well with the Moon's condition natally, the child should continue to mature in physical, behavioural and emotional character.

Fifth Sub-Period
Donor – SUN : Recipient – SATURN
(5.7 – 7.1 Years)

The opposition which exists between the Sun's sign of Cancer and Saturn's Capricorn in Thema Mundi, is paralleled when the body of Saturn chooses to reject every material organ the Sun is nervously offering to what it sees as an unworthy recipient.

The incompatibility between donor and recipient is reflected in this phase when Valens predicts a grievously difficult period, but some of Saturn's worst qualities may be mitigated by the fact that this is a diurnal chart which suits Saturn's temperament and its need for warmth and light from the Sun.

Given that this phase occurs in the latter part of the child's sixth year (at age 5.7 years) and continues until just after their seventh birthday, at best Saturn's contributes growth through the schooling experience.

The child separates from its nurturing source and learns that there are external authority figures operating outside of the family, and that they are now required to conform to rules laid down by other adults besides their own parents.

The Sun may secretly rejoice in this sudden leap towards a development in the child's potential, but the nature of Saturn, especially on the heels of the Moon, is more likely to flavour the experience with a child's sadness at being away from home or their nurturing parent, being in an alien atmosphere, frustration with learning, or potential bullying by other children.

The Saturn may also represent the father figure so that there may be calamities for father, change and disruption, and sometimes even illness for either child or father, especially if Saturn is poorly situated in the chart.

Sixth Sub-Period
Donor – SUN : Recipient – JUPITER
(7.1 – 8.6 Years)

This recipient lord is far more agreeable than the previous one.

Diurnal Jupiter is keen and eager to improve the child's lot, and chooses tasks which bring an improvement in both the father and the child's lives as Valens tells us that it indicates a brilliant year and fame for the native's father.

Jupiter is far more sympathetic to the Sun's wish-list and willing to provide an agreeable form of action, which is both positive and self-affirming for the growing child.

Jupiter brings friendships and the forging of alliances with someone stronger than the child who is willing to protect and advance the native, even if it is only in the school yard or on the sports field.

These experiences may be mundane at this age, but they have a far-reaching effect on the psyche's self-belief, and act as a cosmic Petri dish for the growth of qualities such as confidence, integrity, wisdom and strength of character.

Seventh Sub-Period
Donor – SUN : Recipient – MARS
(8.6 – 10 Years)

Mars is the final lord of the first seven sub-periods of life under the direction of the Sun, and it seems a shame that the Sun should finish on an allotment ruled by the malefic which is most uncomfortable in a diurnal chart.

Mars becomes more irrational and aggressive under the heat of the Sun's rays, so that when Valens describes its period as unhealthy and precarious, he may be addressing the fact that the success or failing of the completion of Sun's tasks is jeopardised by Mars' hasty and unpredictable nature.

Mars is a poor recipient for the Sun's material strivings toward self-government, and the child may not understand that these desires are premature given their young age.

It would be a fine thing to use Mars' energy to encourage to child to experiment with leadership roles or to direct them towards productive pursuits such as sport or extra curriculum activities, but instead Mars may create jealousies, rivalries, injuries, physical challenges, bleeding, and possible alienation from the father.

The child's behaviour can become wilful, destructive or volatile under Mars' direction, and the more malefic Mars becomes in the natal chart, the more difficult (for everyone, including the child) are the final seventeen months of the Sun's Firdaria.

The one shining light in the Mars sub-period is that the two planets, the Sun and Mars, have a connection through the shared sign of Aries, but as it is the Sun which must ask for favours from Mars to borrow its sign for exaltation, it is more likely that the reversal of roles, i.e. Mars/Sun Firdaria works much better in the mix than Mars, which owes no favours to the solar luminary, being seconded for the Sun's benefit in the final seventeen months of its reign.

Yearning for Love . . . VENUS

"It's a sad thing, that we all want so desperately to be loved,
that we forget to love ourselves."

- William C. Hannan

Second Diurnal Major Period lasts for 8 Years

Venus is Lord From 10 – 18ᵗʰ Birthday

Venus' Matter and Significations:

Social graces	Women	Self-appreciation	Mother
Relationships	Acceptance	Femininity	Pleasures
Beauty	Movement	Adornment	Artistic skills

The second period of rulership for a day-time birth belongs to Venus which covers eight years of the native's life.

Venus teaches the social skills needed for the diurnal individual to develop a 'sunny' disposition and to take advantage of the years between ten and eighteen to experience how different peer groups operate, and how to choose a social model that provides them with the greatest degree of comfort or security.

For the diurnal nativity Venus is the bridge between childhood and adulthood, and she supposedly softens this time with friendship, music, dance, movement, and physical pleasures that bring brief periods of ease and happiness during these awkward and often frightening years of puberty.

Mostly, Venus continues on from the Sun's previous Firdaria, and adds her own special flair in the native's striving for individuation, and the desire to be noticed and appreciated by the world. Venus teaches the teenager how to attract confidantes and partners, practices adornment for self-expression, and encourages refinement of skills that will come in handy later in life.

Whilst Venus will always remain a benefic planet, placing it in a sect which is alien to its own nature can have its difficulties.

Adults often remember these years with affection and a touch of nostalgia, but puberty is a tough time when you are caught in this age range belonging to an out of sect Venus.

Valens' predictions for happiness and *"a good and pleasing time"* during Venus' sub-period are insulting to the teenager who has been ostracised by their peers, is bombarded with unrealistic images everywhere they look, or is being relentlessly bullied at school or on social media.

In William Shakespeare's love tragedy *Romeo and Juliet,* the two lovers are teenagers.

Juliet takes her own life ten days before her fourteenth birthday, and whilst Romeo's age is not specifically mentioned in the play, he is presumed by those who study Shakespeare to be a few years older, making him sixteen at the time when he first meets Juliet and falls in love.

If Shakespeare had been aware of Firdaria, it would mean that Juliet loved and died during her Venus Saturn period, whilst Romeo loved, fought and died during his Venus Mars period.

That is provided they were both born during the day-light hours!

By today's standards Juliet would be legally classified as a minor in most countries, as she is below the age of consent at thirteen years of age, whilst Romeo would also be a minor had the romance taken place in Malta, Turkey, Guatemala, Haiti or the Vatican City, all of which apply the age of eighteen to their own country's age of consent.

Therefore for the purpose of legality, Venus' last three sub-period lords, that is Jupiter, Mars and the Sun, who rule between the ages of fourteen to eighteen years, are the years when most countries accept that sexual experimentation is part of the process of growing up.

In astrological terms, encounters of a sexual nature will provide a more concrete idea of Venus' wish-list of pleasures as the native learns, often through heartache and teenage angst, something of what appeals to them and how they will seek sexual gratification as an adult.

Many of Valens' indications for Venus are well beyond the years allotted to her in the diurnal chart, and like the Sun, Venus is best suited to the nocturnal chart which will experience the Venus Firdaria in adulthood.

However, that does not prevent Venus from setting up a framework through the adolescent crushes and the agony of unrequited love in puberty. Hopefully, a framework from which the native can build more realistic and fulfilling relationships in adulthood.

SECOND Major Firdaria for the Diurnal Chart
♀ —8 years
8 years divided by 7 = 1 year 1 month 22 days

Major VENUS 8 yrs Sub-Period	Combination of Major (1st) and Minor (2nd) Time Lords	Minor Time Period BEGINS—ENDS for 1 yr 2 months *(1.1) *months as %
1	♀ / ♀	10.0 – 11.1
2	♀ / ☿	11.1 – 12.3
3	♀ / ☽	12.3 – 13.4
4	♀ / ♄	13.4 – 14.6
5	♀ / ♃	14.6 – 15.7
6	♀ / ♂	15.7 – 16.9
7	♀ / ☉	16.9 – 18.0

Fig. 170 Venus' Firdaria in the Diurnal Chart

First Sub-Period
Donor – VENUS : Recipient – VENUS
(10 – 11.1 Years)

Venus is both the donor and the recipient for the first fourteen months and if she is well situated in the chart according to sign, dignity (apart from sect), house placement and aspect, she will support friendships, even though the child is only ten years of age.

Pleasures and benefits, gifts and a happy family atmosphere are all taken care of by Venus, so that the change-over from Sun as the major lord to Venus as the major lord will hopefully be a smooth transition.

However, should Saturn or Mars become involved with Venus in the chart, the level of comfort and ease diminishes rapidly, and instead suggests a time in the child's life when conflicting feelings, loneliness or alienation from other children or loved ones occurs, especially if there is a major transition, a new school, relocation, or a change in the family situation during Venus' minor period.

Venus ruling both major and minor periods means that Venus is doubled in both pleasure or pain – present according to both the matter she provides, and the form that she creates from the very same matter. This chapter in Venus' period can be tricky if Venus is in poor condition at a time when any ten year old should be enjoying childhood, not surrounded by quarrels and heartache, or frightened by disruption and familial breakdown.

Second Sub-Period
Donor – VENUS : Recipient – MERCURY
(11.1 – 12.3 Years)

Valens is very encouraging of the following period when Venus graciously donates and Mercury is the willing recipient.

If the previous year of Venus was difficult, then Mercury provides a different form for Venus, one which brings some good news or a change in circumstances which delivers a new focal point for the child.

When the two planets liaise effectively, the result produces a love of movement in the form of dance, drama, physical expression, or sporting acumen, and this physical release can bring the native back to social interaction with others their age, or be an outlet for the child's frustration if the current situation of their life is troubled by external circumstances.

The child may feel they truly understand a skill and are on the way to mastering something which was previously beyond them in their younger years.

Communication and learning during Mercury's period can become a source of joy and feelings of self-worth grow in this planet's short phase.

Valens warns that there can be worries if Mercury is found in either the Terms of Saturn or Mars in final degrees of a number of signs (Table of Terms at the end of Chapter Ten). Or if Mercury is aspected by either of the malefic planets, in which case movement, communication and learning are likely to be aggravated by Mars, or restricted by Saturn, and these effects can be harmful to Venus' general well-being.

Third Sub-Period
Donor – VENUS : Recipient – MOON
(12.3 – 13.4 Years)

This period is very much determined by the Moon's situation in the chart, and by the fact that both of these planets belong to the nocturnal sect, and yet are operating in the Diurnal Firdaria.

As both Venus and the Moon represent the mother, this fourteen month period will incorporate what is happening in the life of the person usually described as the dominant nurturer.

If the Moon is free from stress, the time should be one of ease and comfort with benefits from friends and family, but Valens warns that another may be watching on with envy, and their actions can somewhat mar the happy times.

However, if the Moon is troubled in the natal chart, then the matter provided by Venus is spoiled by feelings of mistreatment or neglect on the part of others, and the child's emotional or physical state suffers during the Moon's period.

Family disputes, or conflict within the child's social groups can leave them feeling alienated, and depending on where the Moon lies in the chart, and how sever its disability is, the child's emotional outbursts will not help its cause, but instead is likely to make the situation worse for them in the long run.

Fourth Sub-Period
Donor – VENUS : Recipient – SATURN
(13.4 – 14.6 Years)

Saturn takes over from the Moon, and the nature of this difficult planet may indicate decisions or changes initiated by the diurnal Saturn, to sever a situation where the Moon has been in torment in the previous period.

Strictly speaking, Venus and Saturn are not natural enemies as they share the same sign according to different levels in essential dignity.

Venus is the domicile ruler of Libra, whilst Saturn is exalted in Libra, and there are a number of traditional texts which see this combination of planets as a strength, rather than as an aspect of negativity.

However, a problem arises in Firdaria when Venus is responsible for providing the material by which her needs are to be met, and hands it over to Saturn who does not necessarily understand Venus' brief.

When Valens describes Venus' works in progress as love, desire, cheerfulness, companionship, and sweet singing, Saturn must look mournfully at the list and scratch his head in confusion and dismay.

How can he possibly meld his own unique form to Venus' matter when her list of qualities is so alien to his own?

This is a case of good organ, poor recipient – it does not matter how much she tries to infuse him with her positivity, it is outside of his capabilities to apply it to the native's advantage.

Instead, Saturn's term mid-way through the child's fourteenth year can be a miserable year, especially if Saturn uproots the child whose family environment is disintegrating. Valens says Saturn indicates a time which is both suspenseful and harmful, bringing on separations, fights, outrages and injustices because of the mother or females. Venus in the diurnal chart can signify mother whilst Saturn is the secondary signifier for a male member of the family, usually father, but sometimes the maternal or paternal grandfather. This period may bring changes or concerns born from disputes or tensions between female and male members of the immediate or extended family unit.

Saturn in the form of authority figures are unavailable as a resource if the child is distrustful or shy in the presence of adults, feels that their life has spun out of control, or is resentful of restrictions or decisions made without their consent or consultation (remember Juliet?).

Fifth Sub-Period
Donor – VENUS : Recipient – JUPITER
(14.6 – 15.7 Years)

The fifth sub-period sees Venus' matter given to the form of Jupiter who applies his qualities to bring relief after Saturn's trying term.

At last a planet presents itself to help Venus' dreams come true, and as Jupiter operates to its best advantage in a diurnal chart, then it is delighted to introduce the teenager to the full impact of love and desire, with no restraint or responsibility for what is to follow during this fourteen month period.

Pleasure and company, and a time suitable for spending money makes Jupiter's term a good one for Venus, and Valens even goes so far as to say it brings forth *"loveliness for those who make the attempt!"* [132]

Sixth Sub-Period
Donor – VENUS : Recipient – MARS
(15.7 – 16.9 Years)

The second to last sub-period for Venus brings a year which takes Jupiter's easy format and drastically transforms it to suit Mars' temperament and form.

Venus and Mars rule signs which are in opposition in Thema Mundi, and this surely gives Venus some nervous moments when she is forced to place her needs in the hands of her adversary.

Mars' intolerant nature becomes more inflamed in a diurnal chart, so it is probable that he will have little patience for the subtle nuances of Venus, and is therefore liable to produce a year full of vexation and suspense.

Romeo once more comes to mind in Mars' period, and should romance occur during an over-heated malefic's reign, it will to be one heightened by smouldering sexual tension, but also peppered with spectacular fights, emotional outbursts, petty jealousies and almost certainly break-up songs that set to music all the angst of a broken romance.

Valens warns that separations will be invoked by prayer (yesteryear's version of social media), but that *"they keep notorious scandals alive because of certain hopes that they harbor."*[133]

Valens wrote his text almost 2,000 years ago, but nothing in human nature and the transition from child to adult has really changed, and teenage romance was just as painful in his day as it is today, in an age when privacy is sacrificed and heartache becomes entertainment for the masses.

This is the period during which Antoine lost Francois who died from rheumatic fever at age fifteen and tragically, it is Mars' aversion to the third house in his chart (siblings) which is activated in this sad time of his life.

Seventh Sub-Period
Donor – VENUS : Recipient – SUN
(16.9 – 18 Years)

The Sun is the final receptacle for Venus' ambrosia as her desire for love and acceptance turns into a form which takes her principles and directs it towards his own solar purposes of high office, wealth and public display.

Venus' last fourteen months becomes preoccupied with future gains and advantages, and the Sun scouts for those who can give the native an introduction to superiors and mentors who will guide and nurture the young adult.

Teenage companionship becomes more competitive as an awareness of others' ambitions ignites both envy and rivalry, when social elevation and powerful alliances can aid the native in future advancement by opening the right doors for the diurnal nativity moving into Mercury's major period.

The Sun's task is to sort through friendships and to judge them according to future value and worth, so it is no coincidence that during this last year groups start to drift apart, and what may have been a tight-knit bunch of troubadours at school, suddenly begins to fracture and break apart.

It seems clinical to weigh and discard friendships which have been so important over the past few years, but this is the nature of the Sun and his period serves a dual purpose.

It ties up any loose ends from Venus' major period, especially if they risk being awkward or embarrassing in the future, and at the same time clears space to allow for the changes which are about to take place when Mercury steps in as the next major lord at the age of eighteen years.

The Sun also represents father, so the forming of alliances may be instigated by the father rather than the young adult, as father may call in favours or pull strings to ease the way for his child's future.

If the Sun is stressed in the chart, this period can terrify the native, as he or she may have greatly enjoyed Venus' pleasures, and unlike their more ambitious friends, may wish the party was ongoing.

The child's unwillingness or incapacity to take responsibility for themselves can create tension with the father who wants them to earn a wage or make plans to enter the adult world, and rather than finishing on a high note, Venus' eight years can terminate swiftly in arguments and banishment from the family home.

The Freedom of the Mind . . . MERCURY

"I know but one freedom and that is the freedom of the mind."

Antoine de Saint-Exupéry

Third Diurnal Major Period lasts for 13 Years

Mercury is Lord from 18 – 31st Birthday

Mercury's Matter and Significations:

Intelligence	Memory	Rational thought	Opinions
Education	Reasoning	Business pursuits	Speech
Numbers	Sport	Supervision	Marketing

In the Firdar system, Mercury holds the highest number of years as it is master for thirteen years.

Valens says *"This star's effects go in many directions"*, so perhaps it is fitting that Mercury should rule for the longest period, especially considering the sheer volume and variety of tasks it sets for this time period in the diurnal nativity's life.

There is so much happening during the third decade from eighteen to thirty one years of age.

The thirteen years, when divided by seven, means that each minor lord will have the longest sub-period (twenty two months) in which to fulfil Mercury's potential through the lens of their own nature.

This term of almost two years provides each planet with the opportunity to settle in to their role as recipients to Mercury's material. There is potential for the sub-lord to either bring events and actions to a successfully conclusion or to cause so much havoc that the native is forced to make Mercury's changes in a wide and varied manner.

Mercury craves activity so when this stage in life involves constant changes in employment, lifestyle choices, relationships, or home, work and social environment, Mercury is happy to include experimentation and risk-taking in its list of accomplishments.

For the most part, Mercury will happily allow the sub-period lords to create opportunities and act according to their own natures, as each planet will play their role in offering a variety of choices to the native throughout their second decade of life.

True to its nature, Mercury is both versatile and capricious.

In its sect definition Mercury has the capacity to be included in either sect division as it is not dependent on its own qualities to define sect – which is the case for the other planets – but rather on its position in relation to the Sun.

If Mercury rises before the Sun it is deemed to be diurnal, but if Mercury rises after the Sun it is judged as a nocturnal planet.

For this reason, the natal Mercury can be either diurnal or nocturnal and it may not make a great deal of difference to Mercury's behaviour in either version of Firdaria, that is, according to whether it is complementary to the sect of the chart or is opposing it.

Mercury is not greatly affected by planetary sect as its behaviour does not appear to be significantly changed according to whether it is in-sect, or is out-of-sect in the chart.

Robert Hand says that lack of sect dignity can bring forth the meaner qualities of Mercury.[134]

An out of sect Mercury is described in the Greek by Paulus as common, vulgar or debased in some way and is demonstrated through crude humour, sarcasm or imbecilic behaviour, but it is hard to tell which one is really acting the fool – the undignified Mercury – or the child-adult in their 20s who still delights in shocking their parents and older authorities.

Of the seven original planets Mercury appears to be the most susceptible to the degree rulers under the essential dignity known as Egyptian Terms. Valens makes a special point of adding Term Rulers when he speaks of Mercury so it is worthwhile checking The Terms in Chapter Ten *(Fig. 167)* to see if Mercury in the chart is in late degrees of a sign. For many signs Saturn and Mars rule the last ten degrees between them.

This is the case if Mercury is situated in the middle to late degrees of Aries, Taurus, Gemini, Virgo, Sagittarius, Capricorn, Aquarius and Pisces. Sometimes the fourth term ruler is an improved planet as in the case of Cancer (Jupiter), Leo (Mercury), Libra (Venus) and Scorpio (Jupiter), but even in these signs, the fifth and final Term Ruler is always Saturn (Cancer and Scorpio) or Mars (Leo or Libra).

Mercury is the third planet to step forward in the diurnal Firdaria model, and its timing in life means that it arrives after two other major periods involving first the Sun, and then Venus.

Presumably, the native has a general idea of firstly, the seeds of *who they want to be* through the Sun Firdaria, and secondly, *who they want to be with,* in the exploration of relationships during the Venus Firdaria.

Mercury's major period adds to the experiences of both its predecessors by deliberately engaging the mind to mould *who the person will ultimately become* after their thirty first birthday when the impressions of their childhood and youth solidify to create the adult they will be for the rest of their lives.

Mercury's one request to all of its recipients is a call to explore all avenues, to search for information, to find answers to its questions, and to report back to Mercury so that the individual's mind can find its own unique concept of freedom in a world of physical restraints and obligations.

THIRD Major Firdaria for the Diurnal Chart

☿ —13 years

13 years divided by 7 = 1 year 10 months 9 days

Major MERCURY 13 yrs Sub-Period	Combination of Major (1st) and Minor (2nd) Time Lords	Minor Time Period BEGINS—ENDS for 1 yr 10 months *(1.9) *months as %
1	☿ / ☿	18.0 – 19.9
2	☿ / ☽	19.9 – 21.7
3	☿ / ♄	21.7 – 23.6
4	☿ / ♃	23.6 – 25.4
5	☿ / ♂	25.4 – 27.3
6	☿ / ☉	27.3 – 29.1
7	☿ / ♀	29.1 – 31.0

Fig. 171 Mercury's Firdaria in the Diurnal Chart

First Sub-Period
Donor – MERCURY : Recipient – MERCURY
(18 – 19.9 Years)

At eighteen years of age, the young adult is beginning to make plans on where their life will lead in the future.

Questions on how they will earn a living as an adult involve making decisions on work prospects, apprenticeship terms, further study or travel, so that when the first period belongs to Mercury, it is this planet's task to set the agenda for the next thirteen years of life.

Valens says that a double Mercury period is effectual and beneficial, and that it makes the native shrewd concerning whatever he puts his hand to, and that Mercury produces good verbal delivery and makes the native more excellent than their opponents.

Presumably Mercury's sub-period is the ideal spring board for Mercury's extensive list of professions by developing skills such as working with numbers and accounts, marketing skills, supervisory or communication skills, . . . the list goes on.

Those individuals who are confident in speech or mathematical calculation are well served in Mercury's sub-period, especially if Mercury should be in a favourable sign or in aspect to Jupiter or Venus.

However, if the malefics aspect Mercury in the natal chart, or if Mercury is in the Terms of either Mars of Saturn *(Fig. 167)*, then this planet can become the prophet of false hope.

The mind becomes fearful or uncertain, and the advantages gained by Mercury can also be lost, so much so that debt instead of gain can occur with amazing speed leaving the individual wondering where it all went wrong. Mercury's nature is fickle and the anticipated outcome may evaporate or never come to fruition if malefics enter into the equation.

Luckily Mercury's changeable nature – and the fact that it has a decade to still run its course as Firdar lord – means that it usually commends the youth for their courage and enthusiasm, and a new plan will quickly replace the one which has so recently failed.

Second Sub-Period
Donor – MERCURY : Recipient – MOON
(19.9 – 21.7 Years)

The following sub-period for Mercury belongs to the Moon and good fortune will very much depend on how the Moon is situated in the chart.

The Moon is not always comfortable in a diurnal nativity, however, if it is well-placed in the chart the Moon becomes a worthy recipient for Mercury's wishes, and Valens predicts profitable alliances and prosperity.

If the Moon is in a good situation, both planets feel content with the relationship during this phase when Mercury strives constantly for expression and for success, and the Moon feels self-satisfied and happy if it is able to be of service to Mercury.

As a result, troublesome matters may rectify themselves, and the native encounters sympathy from others who support their cause.

However, should the Moon *"be uncongenially situated"* (Valens' term), or if it aspects Saturn or Mars, then it becomes a poor recipient for what it perceives to be a difficult, demanding or unstable Mercury.

Poor judgements (often clouded by emotion or based on youthful ignorance or inexperience) can invite the insults or threats of superiors, and the Moon's allotted time becomes one of extreme sensitivity, fear, hesitation, second guessing and inconsistent decision-making as the native, who is barely twenty years old, is likely to fall deeper into a trap of their own making.

The Moon signifies both the native's body and the native's mother, so a stressed Moon can indicate worries from either of these sources.

Anxiety over a family situation can bounce back as illness and a weakening of the body especially if these areas are signified by Mercury in the natal chart.

If Mercury is stretching itself thin through overwork, study, or excessive partying, it will exhaust both the mind and the body and the Moon's duration as Firdar lord can show the negative effect of this strain.

Saturn will follow the Moon's period and if there has been some drama occur during transiting Saturn's square to natal Saturn at the age of twenty one – which occurs during this period – then there can be a flow-on effect during the two years following the Moon's term when Saturn steps up to the plate and becomes Mercury's next sub-period lord.

Third Sub-Period
Donor – MERCURY : Recipient – SATURN
(21.7 – 23.6 Years)

If the previous period of the Moon has been difficult due to a natal Moon under threat, then the period belonging to Saturn may not provide much relief if the young adult is trying to avoid responsibility for their earlier actions, or cannot control emotional outbursts encouraged by an out-of-sect Moon in the previous Firdar.

The potential suggested by Mercury is unlikely to find a sympathetic recipient in Saturn, that is unless Saturn is in an excellent condition by sign as it is definitely improved by its placement in a diurnal chart.

If this is the case, there is promise of an improvement in reputation, status, or studies, although there are likely frustrations brought on by delays, postponements and unexpected expenditure involved in the process of Saturn's twenty two month period.

If the previous Moon's period has been satisfying, then Saturn's chapter may bring the native back to Earth with a thump because Saturn in poor condition by sign indicates a year full of danger and trouble according to Valens.

The nature of Mercury's matter means that this planet signifies communication, accounting, writings, business dealings and commerce.

Saturn is concerned with integrity and honesty – it will find the cracks if there are any to be found and expose them mercilessly – so the native needs to be very clear and honest in their dealings with others.

Saturn's form is often one of accountability or responsibility for one's actions, and if Mercury has played the role of trickster, or has been genuinely naive in the previous two sub-periods, then the native can come under the scrutiny of those in authority as their activity incurs losses, insults, or the dismantling of a structure.

Although Mercury and Saturn are not natural enemies, Valens states that Saturn's sub-period can manifest in a state of mental or physical weakness, or wasting and disease, and perhaps there is merit in this determination as the Firdar can combine the natures of the two planets to produce results which can be worrying for the native.

Mercury, who signifies the workings of the mind, and Saturn, which can cloak the mind in darkness, can result in anxiety, exhaustion or depression, especially if there has been an on-going health issue during the Moon's previous term.

Fourth Sub-Period
Donor – MERCURY : Recipient – JUPITER
(23.6 – 25.4 Years)

When Jupiter is seconded by Mercury to fulfil some of its tasks over the next two years, it is expected to relieve the tension created by Saturn and the Moon, and to provide the native with adequate breathing space to reset Mercury, and to get the native back on task so far as their professional and personal lives are concerned.

Jupiter's term occurs at the midpoint of Mercury's thirteen years, so perhaps it is a happy coincidence that during this time Jupiter will complete its second revolution of the zodiac.

Hopefully a Jupiter Return will mean that this planet will prove to be a more encouraging recipient for Mercury's list of possibilities, and that Jupiter's natural propensity to bring good fortune will put projects back on track or introduce new ventures, thereby restoring confidence as well as improving finances.

Reputation and health can steadily be restored during Jupiter's interval, and if isolation has been a theme of the past few years, the diurnal Jupiter in sect dignity has the ability to rebuild friendships and encourage new alliances which may be to Mercury's advantage in the future.

If the individual's ambitions involve administration, commerce or any profession indicated by Mercury, then Jupiter's term can be productive in supporting these ambitions.

It is worth mentioning one shadow on Jupiter's otherwise shining horizon, and that involves the fact that these two planets are not always *simpatico* in desiring the same outcomes.

Thema Mundi shows Gemini opposing Sagittarius, whilst Virgo opposes Pisces, and this tension between Mercury and Jupiter is reflected in Valens' closing statement on the sub-period, when Jupiter is expected to work hard on behalf of Mercury, its employer in this sequence of Firdaria.

Valens warns that the native will be greatly troubled among crowds, and that there will be unexpected expenditures.

They may experience both scandals and fears during this time, and relations with family can become unsettled or strained.

It seems as though Jupiter transfers his benefits to aid Mercury, but there is some resentment on its part to serve its natural enemy, and an exchange between the two planets is not always friendly or of an easy-going nature.

Fifth Sub-Period
Donor – MERCURY : Recipient – MARS
(25.4 – 27.3 Years)

For the diurnal chart, Mercury's fifth sub-period begins after the native turns twenty five years old and when Mars becomes the sub-period lord it is not surprising that the predictions for a Mercury/Mars period are not good.

Mars is a poor recipient for Mercury as this is a planet which is famous for its volatility and lack of grace, especially when it is out-of-sect and operating in a diurnal chart.

Mars prefers a night-time chart, so when it is away from its true sect it is inclined to create a multitude of opportunities for arguments, upsets, betrayals, losses and disputes amongst family members.

Valens predicts a terrible time, and even darkly hints at villainy. Valens suggests that illegal or immoral dealings are both visited on the native, or performed by them, and he warns that rash or thoughtless behaviour will be heavily penalised.

At this time in life the individual is fast approaching their first Saturn Return which will occur within the next Mercury sub-period belonging to the Sun, so it would be wise not to go out on a ledge in business dealings, or risk building something shaky which may collapse during the next two years following Mars' term.

Mars is a planet known for its quickness in temper and a desire for battle, so Mercury supplying Mars with reasons to over-react or start an argument is not good.

If the native is constantly expecting trouble they will be suspicious of others' motives and actions, and this constant stress can build into an explosion if the individual cannot hold their tongue or they allow their thoughts to lead them into reckless and foolhardy behaviour.

Sixth Sub-Period
Donor – MERCURY : Recipient – SUN
(27.3 – 29.1 Years)

The Sun is the recipient for Mercury in the sixth sub-period and the meeting of two like-minded planets suggests a relationship which has the potential to work well for the native, given that the Sun's form is naturally inclined towards bestowing honours, fame and reputation.

For this reason, the Sun's sub-period indicates a two year period when the native is shrewd in their business dealings when the Sun's significations for intelligence and good judgement affords the gift of being able to differentiate between decisions which harm, and those which bring benefit.

Superiors may start to take notice of the individual, and advancement and a rise in social status bring benefits and a bright light in Mercury's somewhat fickle-fortuned Firdaria.

Study or education may be coming to completion during the Sun's Firdaria bringing rewards as certificates, qualifications and titles are the solar luminary's way of displaying both intelligence and a commitment to knowledge.

Saturn may cast a shadow on this period as, although Saturn's Return between twenty seven and twenty nine years of age is external to the Firdaria, it does occur during the Sun's sub-period.

The Sun is naturally optimistic and is careful to guard the native's reputation.

However, the malefic nature of Saturn can mean the Sun's rewards count for nothing, or have the potential to be diminished or removed by Saturn as quickly as they were granted by the Sun's own efforts.

Seventh Sub-Period
Donor – MERCURY : Recipient – VENUS
(29.1 – 31 Years)

The final placement in the longest major period in the Firdaria system belongs to Venus, and even when she is out-of-sect, she is usually happy to provide an upbeat finish to a thirteen year period which has experienced plenty of ups and downs in the diurnal native's Mercury Firdaria.

Venus takes Mercury's list of possibilities and turns them into occasion for celebration, and a time for giving and receiving gifts and adornments.

Venus provides a beneficial time for advancement under Mercury's banner of speech, education or administration, and even adds her own quality by hinting at a new love interest as, according to Valens, she encourages amorous intercourse for the native who gains additional new alliances, fresh intimacies and novel friendships with both men and women under her rule.

Moving from Light into Darkness . . . THE MOON

"Everyone is a moon, and has a dark side which he never shows to anybody."

Mark Twain (1835-1910)

Fourth Diurnal Major Period lasts for 9 Years

The Moon is Lord From 31 – 40ᵗʰ Birthday

The Moon's Matter and Significations:

Life	Body	Mother	Physical environment
Appearance	Family	Children	Short journeys
Emotional state	Health	Women	Female relatives

The nine year stretch which belongs to the Moon is quite challenging for the individual living life within the guidelines of a Firdaria designed for the diurnal nativity.

For the past three decades they have been changing and growing according to the pattern placed before them by the Sun.

Now they will need to take a new approach for the next decade and experience life from the other side of the Firdaria planetary system.

Part of this new experience has to do with the relationship between the Sun and Moon, as it is unique in terms of traditional astrological lore.

Whilst both are considered to be luminaries rather than planets, the Sun is the main luminary who rules the day, and the Moon is responsible for ruling the night.

The division known as Planetary Sect is discussed in detail in the first three chapters of this book.

However, for the purposes of Firdaria, the differences between the two luminaries goes beyond mere visual distinction between the light of day and its absence during the night-time hours.

The sun brings to this world its light and warmth during the day, promoting the process of life on so many levels, as the sun's energising force is the only reason Earth survives, and its removal would mean death to this planet.

For this reason, humankind has worshipped the sun and constructed mythologies and world religions around its yearly and daily cycle since Time began, and whilst the physical shape of the Sun does not alter, the length of the day's light has been measured, worried and celebrated over for dozens of past centuries.

In contrast to the Sun, the Moon's shape does alter.

She does not warm the Earth, and even first century astrologers such as Valens knew that she does not possess her own light source.

Rather, her light is a reflection of the Sun's light, in effect making her a huge cosmic mirror.

It is thought that the early Gnostics believed there was a threefold association between the concept of light, the soul, and the intellect.

In contrast, they associated darkness with matter and physical incarnation[135], so that it seems appropriate that at the mid-point years of the diurnal chart's seven-period Firdaria that the Sun would hold up its light against the dark matter of the Moon in order to see its own reflection.

During the Moon's nine year period the coming together of the soul and intellect with the physical world of matter will occur at a time in life when the native has passed through three of its seven major periods.

The Sun, Venus and Mercury have played their parts, and in a mirror image of the Sun, the Moon will stand in the centre of the Firdaria cycle, and will be followed by Saturn, Jupiter and Mars in correct Chaldean Order.

The Moon's Firdaria is the central pivotal point for the diurnal nativity. This is an opportunity to experience on a sub-conscious level the instinctual movement away from the light, which is much more than accolades, fame and status, towards the darkness of matter and physical incarnation. It may feel like an abyss with no beginning or end but there is a fascination for the diurnal individual to explore the soul and the intellect safely through the lens of reflected light, in much the same way as we watch a solar eclipse through a mirrored reflection without damaging our sight by looking directly at the Sun.

When the Moon's Firdaria is completed at the glorious age of forty the diurnal individual will pass through three more major planets periods before coming to the period governed by the North and South Nodes. The way in which the individual comes into the Moon's Firdaria is not the same as when they leave it. Clients over the age of forty may reminisce over the brief period when Saturn was returning to meet its natal position, but this is not the time which seems to leave the greatest impression on an individual. The decade between the ages of thirty and forty are exhausting, challenging and emotionally a rollercoaster for the person born during daylight hours.

The Moon travels through eight phases in its journey with the Sun and this luminary reflects the constant shifts and changes which occur during this period of a person's life. Whilst the Moon is the instigator for the diurnal chart, on the other side of sect the Fourth Firdaria lord is Mars who is busy causing havoc in the nocturnal's life. The time-span may be similar in that both diurnal and nocturnal charts are challenged by their middle Firdaria, but there are obvious differences which divide them as well.

In the nocturnal chart Mars is in sect so the central period is governed by a planet which is complementary to the chart. Mars is inclined to be kinder to the nocturnal individual so whilst the seven year period does have touches of high drama and crisis, it is accompanied by a sense of familiarity or purpose and can be used to clean out the emotional cobwebs and make some significant changes in life.

In a diurnal chart the Moon is an alien planet. It pits itself against the Sun and even Valens warns that when the Sun becomes the sub-period lord things don't always work out well. There is an expectation for Saturn's sub-period to denote hard times because the Moon and Saturn's signs oppose one another across the ascendant descendant axis in Thema Mundi, but it may come as a surprise that the Sun creates its own problems for the Moon.

Valens lists amongst the Moon's body parts the *'dura mater'*, the Latin term for 'hard mother', which is the tough fibrous membrane forming the outermost of the three coverings of the brain and the spinal cord. If this membrane is pierced death is not far away.

In the same way as the Moon provides a body which reflects the Sun's glorious light, so too does she provide the physical mass on which the divine spirit can be reflected, and the *'dura mater'* is a perfect example for this symbiotic relationship in that the Sun may be nature's fire and intellectual light, but it is the Moon that possesses the material vessel for this light.

For this reason, the native can struggle with the nine years when the Moon's Firdaria is in effect. Mirrors do not always show us what we want to see, and if the Moon uses brutal honesty to drive its message home, then even a tiny glimpse of the soul's true nature can be a wake-up call for the native to make some significant changes as they journey through the centre of the Diurnal Firdaria.

FOURTH Major Firdaria for the Diurnal Chart
☽ — 9 years
9 years divided by 7 = 1 year 3 months 13 days

Major MOON 9 yrs Sub-Period	Combination of Major (1st) and Minor (2nd) Time Lords	Minor Time Period BEGINS—ENDS for 1 yr 3 months *(1.3) *months as %
1	☽ / ☽	31.0 – 32.3
2	☽ / ♄	32.3 – 33.6
3	☽ / ♃	33.6 – 34.9
4	☽ / ♂	34.9 – 36.1
5	☽ / ☉	36.1 – 37.4
6	☽ / ♀	37.4 – 38.7
7	☽ / ☿	38.7 – 40.0

Fig. 172
The Moon's Firdaria in the Diurnal Chart

First Sub-Period
Donor – MOON : Recipient – MOON
(31 – 32.3 Years)

The initial sub-period for the Moon lacks a certain level of stability, as the Moon possesses the power over matter and tries to imprint her natural capacity for unrest and change onto the native's life.

Valens says of this period that it is unpleasant.

It brings enemies and lawsuits from powerful people, and unsteadiness and fluctuations in livelihood as well as confrontations with relatives and the partner.

Valens is an astrologer not a psychologist, so he is not concerned with the inner landscape of the individual who, perhaps after striving though their twenties for recognition, honours and reputation, is starting to wonder if the cost was worth the prize, or if indeed, they are truly happy with their lives.

This soul-searching is part of the crossroads in both the years of life, and the seven major Firdaria periods, and the Moon's portion can be likened to walking from a life of sunlight, and suddenly turning the corner to meet the pitch black of a dark starless night.

The landscape is both familiar, yet at the same time strangely foreign, and the native experiences the emotional equivalent to the condition of vertigo, whereby the environment starts whirling about and the result is dizziness and disorientation.

There is a frailty to the Moon which reflects both its connection to the human body and astrologically, to the planets which surround it.

For instance, the content and experiences of the entire period of the Moon's Firdaria is hugely affected by the state of the Moon in the natal chart.

This double period is just the beginning of what can be major changes in the native's life as Valens says that if the Moon is in aspect to a malefic it will produce bodily weakness and sudden dangers.

Planets transiting over the natal Moon throughout the Moon's Firdaria will have a drastic effect on any actions, events or outcomes during the nine years, as the Moon is easily affected by external influences, producing both good and bad outcomes.

Physical illness or exhaustion, fear, uncertainty and a sense of yearning for something different, are hallmark emotions for the first period, which is confronting for the native who has temporarily left the Sun's light, and is moving towards the dark side of the Moon.

Second Sub-Period
Donor – MOON : Recipient – SATURN
(32.3 – 33.6 Years)

The Moon lies at the base of the Chaldean Order so when her period is complete, the task goes to the most elevated planet, Saturn, to care for the Moon's needs.

Unfortunately this is not an easy transition as these two planets are diametrically opposed in placement and principle in Thema Mundi.

The Moon's sign of Cancer opposes Saturn's sign of Capricorn, thereby creating a tension between the two planets and hinting that their fundamental incompatibility is not going to bode well for the native.

Saturn may be a diurnal planet that would normally work well within the guidelines of the Diurnal Firdaria but it does not enjoy taking its orders from the lord of the opposite sect.

This is a case where the Moon as the donor is offering a rich variety of matter, but Saturn is a dismal recipient who is more inclined to spoil the riches, and is unlikely to promote the Moon's mercy or its loving kindness during its own sub-period.

Valens predicts this interval will produce a year that is diverse and suspenseful.

He says that it will be a bad time for the native's mother, and, that Saturn produces a period of unfriendliness and alienation from others when enemies gather to destroy the native.

Valens also predicts a possible re-location or separation, and a time of withdrawal, illness and frustrations.

In other words, Saturn is likely to bring a fifteen month term which is both harmful and painful for the native who is in their second period of a Moon Firdaria.

Third Sub-Period
Donor – MOON : Recipient – JUPITER
(33.6 – 34.9 Years)

The third sub-period for the Moon brings relief and some breathing-space for the Moon from a beneficial source in the form of Jupiter.

The Moon can set an agenda for Jupiter which it is happy to follow, as it generates career advancement, strengthens relationships with superiors, improves reputation, and rejuvenates ambition in the diurnal nativity who has probably undergone a number of changes over the past three years.

Jupiter is an agent of the Sun, and vastly prefers day-time charts, so its sub-period can restore a level of normality for the native during the Moon's nine year reign, and the native may be relieved to feel they are once more in familiar territory.

Nor does Jupiter mind being under the direction of the Moon.

Although they belong to different sides of planetary sect, Jupiter asks the Moon for friendship, so that it can borrow Cancer (the Moon's sign) for its own exaltation.

In Thema Mundi, the Moon and Jupiter share the first sign of the Universe's Birth-Chart, and Jupiter is more than willing to be a recipient for the Moon during its major Firdaria period.

As the Moon's agenda also includes matters of the heart Jupiter, as the significator of children may provide marriage or the birth of a child if this is the native's desire at this time in their life.

This is also a better period for mother indicating good fortune for the native's parent and an improvement in mother's status, livelihood, or success in her accomplishments and the fulfilment of her own hopes and expectations.

Fourth Sub-Period
Donor – MOON : Recipient – MARS
(34.9 – 36.1 Years)

The middle period of the Moon's Firdaria is given over to Mars just prior to the thirty fifth birthday.

As a troublesome recipient, any task the Moon sets for Mars is bound to present drama, flare-ups, and experiences which generate tears and tantrums, both from the native and their loved ones.

Mars is neither gentle nor compassionate in its dealings with others, so there is a certain level of incompatibility between the two lords of this phase, especially given that both planets belong to the nocturnal sect, and will be uncomfortable working within the parameters of the Diurnal Firdaria.

If this is the case, then any nerves from the Moon can trigger a hysterical reaction from Mars, and a trifling matter can blow into a major disaster in terms of the native's life.

At best, Mars is likely to be over-enthusiastic in its desire to achieve results and risks ruffling feathers or creating enemies, which is the last thing the Moon desires from its sub-lord.

At its worst, Mars becomes truculent in its behaviour, with the native claiming emotional hostages rather than diplomatically fostering alliances.

For these reasons, Valens predicts dangers, physical weakness – often due to Mars driving the physical body too hard – accidents involving fire and bloodshed, family arguments, separations and unwanted confinement (as 'confinement' is also a term used to indicate the end of a pregnancy, this may be a difficult time to carry or deliver a child).

Fifth Sub-Period
Donor – MOON : Recipient – SUN
(36.1 – 37.4 Years)

The Sun takes over from Mars as the next recipient for the Moon's material desires and creates an unexpected result which was briefly discussed earlier in Moon's Firdaria. For most part the Sun is considering to be a benevolent force and its sub-period is usually anticipated to provide a time of benefit and advantage for the native.

Instead Valens says that the Sun taking on Moon's matter empties one's livelihood and produces the greatest expenditures, and should the Sun aspect any malefic planets, it shows ahead of time any hindrances to actions and empty hopes and divisions within the family.

Valens' delineation indicates difficulty for the native, and Robert Hand hypothesises that the Sun as the light source considers itself to be far superior to the Moon, which is normally the recipient of the Sun's reflected light. When the roles become reversed, the Sun is slighted when it must take the Moon's lowly tasks and try to apply them to its own lofty principles.

"In this example the Moon is the material component (matter) *and the Sun the formal component* (form). *Valens' delineation indicates difficulty. It would appear that the "stuff" of the Moon is not capable of living up to the demands of a solar form."* [136]

This is a case where the recipient, the Sun, believes the donor is beneath it in quality and standing, and as the Sun is insulted by the donation, it refuses to do much good during its sub-period.

Valens states:

"But for those who have reputation and stability of life, they begin to make journeys for purchases or the accomplishment and furtherance of matters, or for certain gifts and kindnesses." [137]

Only a last minute addition to the delineation can save this term, as it is obvious that the Sun in Moon's Firdar does not extend its goodwill to the Moon to either create or elevate the native's reputation.

However, it is required to maintain status, and to refrain from deliberately or spitefully destroying a pre-existing reputation.

Sixth Sub-Period
Donor – MOON : Recipient – VENUS
(37.4 – 38.7 Years)

The lord governing the Moon's sixth sub-period is Venus which is more accommodating than the Sun. Venus is inclined towards providing a pleasant fifteen month period, combining the effects of two social planets to produce accomplishments, alliances, sympathies and marriages for the native.

However, should either the Moon or Venus be *"uncongenially situated"* by sign, or in hard aspect to a malefic, then this will alter the quality of the women involved with the native. If this is the case then Venus' term becomes more unpleasant and is spoiled by envy, wastefulness, jealousies and breaches of faith with women, friends or family.

Similar to Mars' sub-period, the two planets concerned are naturally nocturnal but are working together in a Diurnal Firdaria. Venus may be better behaved than her fractious brother, but this does not guarantee her period will be totally smooth sailing either.

As Valens indicates there can be fallouts with friends and family members, and the native would do well to keep the peace during Venus' term.

A scenario of a different kind arises if Venus in the chart is connected to houses of health, that is, either good health via the first house, or the destruction of health via the sixth house.

Venus is a planet which is inclined to indulge in pleasures, but if they are excessive during her sub-period, the body may suffer harmful side-effects when the sensitive Moon is the major lord of the longer period.

If the diurnal chart belongs to a woman who has spent a significant number of years engaged in building a career, Venus' sub-period of the Moon's Firdaria can come as a reminder that her 'biological clock' may be ticking and the realisation of missing the opportunity to bear children may rear its head during Venus' shorter period.

Even if children are not part of the life-plan, and the chart belongs to either gender, Venus brings an awareness that friends and others around them are settling down to long-term relationships and this can make the native jittery if no such opportunity appears as an option for them.

A combination of Moon's material with Venus' form can tug at the heartstrings and cause the diurnal individual to wonder at the personal cost of independence, success and a full-on focus on career aspirations.

The desire to 'nest' during this sub-period is strong, especially if there are also powerful aspects at play in transits to either of these sentimental and emotionally driven nocturnal planets in the natal chart.

Seventh Sub-Period
Donor – MOON : Recipient – MERCURY
(38.7 – 40 Years)

The final period in the Moon's Firdaria belongs to Mercury, and this can be a time where past hurts are put aside, fences are mended and broken alliances are healed, but only if Mercury's diplomacy is prepared to work over-time.

The better Mercury's own alliances are with good planets such as Venus or Jupiter, the stronger it will work towards protecting the native's alliances and friendships. This may have a flow-on effect to the major lord, the Moon, who prefers emotional stability and the love and support of those whom it cherishes.

Unfortunately, the opposite effect stands true as well.

Should Mercury be entangled with Mars or Saturn, it becomes somewhat villainous in nature and is more inclined towards creating strife for the Moon. Mercury's mischief takes the form of lawsuits involving money, wrongly acquired assets (fraud) or inflammatory communication (libel), or in the field of accounting, taxation or merchantile matters.

Leader of the Pack . . . SATURN

"Throw me to the wolves, and I will return leading the pack."

Unknown

Fifth Diurnal Major Period lasts for 11 Years

Saturn is Lord from 40 – 51ˢᵗ Birthday

Saturn's Matter and Significations:

Physical barriers	Father	Separations	Responsibility
Time	Agriculture	The sea	Isolation
Management	Boundaries	Hardship	Obstacles
Health issues	Authority	Foundations	

Many of Saturn's significations carry a bleakness which is hard to deny and it is daunting to think that Saturn will have governance over the next eleven years of life.

It is difficult to find positivity or productivity from a planet with few redeeming features, and Saturn does little to encourage a host of potentials from a miserable donor whose list of tasks seem somewhat grim by definition.

It may be dependent for each of the remaining recipients to apply the qualities of their own nature to Saturn's major Firdaria and to bring changes or actions which are pleasurable, beneficial or productive for the native.

Saturn's Firdaria begins with the fifth decade of life.

Perhaps to coin a phrase 'Life begins at 40' is to recognise that the boundaries or restrictions one places on oneself are either ridiculously unfair, or no longer apply to life's circumstances. Saturn at forty grants us the freedom to say 'No' when we feel like it without having to justify our refusal with excuses or feel shame or embarrassment at our non-compliant behaviour.

Granted, it may take the entire eleven year period of Saturn's Firdaria to learn to say *'No'* gracefully and to really mean it, but certainly for Saturn, this fifth period is a time for reflection and consolidation.

Reflection on how the native's substance in life is measured and ranked by society, and consolidation of the combined energies from the two luminaries now that the native has experienced the Firdaria of both the Sun at birth – and the Moon – in the previous nine years.

Even though Saturn's qualifications as a peace-maker are somewhat basic, it is still familiar with the concept of fairness and balance through its exalted sign Libra, so perhaps it is the best equipped planet to synthesise intellect with emotion, and to perform the task of integrating the principles of Sun and Moon.

Saturn is the lord of Time, and during its eleven year period the native will decide whether Saturn's structures provide safety and a meaning to life, or they are suffocating and squeezing the vitality and all the pleasure from life.

Saturn's major period marks the years of the 'mid-life crisis' for the diurnal nativity, and it is no coincidence that transiting Saturn will oppose natal Saturn during Saturn's Firdaria at the approximate age of forty three years during the time when Mars will be the sub-period lord for Saturn's Firdaria.

Saturn's half-way point in its cycle puts added pressure on the native as reality steps in and life is evaluated, forcing a choice between whether they will fortify and fight to protect existing structures or they will tear them down in order to create new ones.

Make no mistake Saturn is a survivor, and it will take any hardship or rejection it encounters and learn lessons from the experience, working hard to turn a weakness into a strength.

Whoever crossed Saturn on the way down had better beware when it returns as the leader of the pack.

Saturn's one redeeming feature in a diurnal chart is that it is warmed by the Sun and becomes more temperate in its nature whenever a day-time chart places the Sun above the horizon.

The Sun's two qualities of light and heat have a moderating effect on the greater malefic, so that even at his harshest times, Saturn will still be more lenient on those individuals who are born during the day.

FIFTH Major Firdaria for the Diurnal Chart

♄ — 11 years

11 years divided by 7 = 1 year 6 months 26 days

Major SATURN 11 yrs Sub-Period	Combination of Major (1st) and Minor (2nd) Time Lords	Minor Time Period BEGINS—ENDS for 1 yr 7 months *(1.6) *months as %
1	♄ / ♄	40.0 – 41.6
2	♄ / ♃	41.6 – 43.1
3	♄ / ♂	43.1 – 44.7
4	♄ / ☉	44.7 – 46.3
5	♄ / ♀	46.3 – 47.9
6	♄ / ☿	47.9 – 49.4
7	♄ / ☽	49.4 – 51.0

Fig. 173 Saturn's Firdaria in the Diurnal Chart

First Sub-Period
Donor – SATURN : Recipient – SATURN
(40 – 41.6 Years)

Once again the longer period begins with the Firdaria lord taking the dual roles of major and minor lord for the first sub-period.

In this case Saturn is the lord for the first nineteen months, making this a time of vexation and inactivity, with an expectation of constant trouble with authority figures, and delays and hindrances for those projects which require a starting or completion date.

Valens warns that if Saturn aspects either Mars or Mercury in the natal chart, the troubles of Saturn will be based on the events which are signified by these two planets.

Mars suggests treachery, past adversaries and old wounds re-opened, whilst Mercury causes strife through the written word, subversion or chicanery (an old-fashioned term for funny business and trickery or fooling people) especially when they concern affairs or dubious dealings from former times.

During this period the native is advised to move forward gently and slowly, to be patient, and to deal honourably and honestly with transactions from the past, as Saturn's period is likely to involve issues concerning integrity, transparency and accountability.

Second Sub-Period
Donor – SATURN : Recipient – JUPITER
(41.6 – 43.1 Years)

Jupiter lightens Saturn's dark shadows and provides some light relief during the time it takes charge of the native's life.

The form provided by a benefic planet is more optimistic than Saturn itself is capable of providing, and surprisingly, the individual natures of these two planets are generally not in conflict, perhaps because they share a link through serving the same diurnal sect belonging to the Sun.

Saturn's material as donor may be scant in potential, but Jupiter is determined to make the best of it by highlighting events or actions which improve finances through the avenue of inheritance or legacies.

Jupiter also supplies elders to advise the native, or superiors who will recognise Saturn's industry and reward the individual for their hard work and past efforts.

Valens suggests that building projects can be successful, or acquisitions from businesses attached to water or the sea can be good investments, providing both Jupiter and Saturn are in good condition in the chart.

Jupiter also offers the ability to rebuild or demolish, and again, provides the opportunity to settle old matters and make amends so that the native's honour and reputation can be re-established during Jupiter's short term.

Third Sub-Period
Donor – SATURN : Recipient – MARS
(43.1 – 44.7 Years)

Valens is grim in warning that Saturn's secondment of Mars will produce the worst and most dangerous term, as he predicts weakness and treachery and distress, deaths and troubles from those closest to the native.

By nature, Mars is aggressive and highly competitive, and therefore makes a risky recipient for Saturn's woeful material.

This is not so much a problem of incompatibility as it is when the Sun or the Moon are involved with Saturn.

After all, Mars is exalted in Saturn's sign of Capricorn, but neither planet possesses the virtues of tolerance or gentleness, and neither applies diplomacy when it comes to dealing with other people.

The Greek philosopher Empedocles (c.490 – c.430 BCE) pre-dates Aristotle by almost a century. Empedocles is considered to be the father of the theory on the 'roots' or elements (as Aristotle re-named them) that we know as fire, air, water and earth in this order from lightest to heaviest element.

Empedocles believed that elements changed from one to the other through the forces of what he called Love and Strife.

Love was the natural desire for things to come together and to mix as one material with no beginning and no end, whilst Strife was a natural force which drove things apart and caused individuation and change.

For life to keep regenerating, there needed to be constant struggle between the two divine powers, as in previous times of inertia or non-growth, both powers existed alone and in separation from the other, but change, and life itself, could not begin to exist in this vacuum of non-competition.

Originally, Love was the more dominant of the two forces, existing within a perfect sphere, and Strife guarded the extreme edges of the sphere until Strife gradually broke through the perimeter and Life Began.

Love and Strife explained the elements' variations and their harmony in terms of the active qualities (hot and cold) and the passive qualities (wet and dry).

Cold was the separation of heat through Strife, and dry was the separation away from moisture through Strife's dividing force.

Alternatively, the force of Love attracted one active and one passive quality to create each of the four elements.

Fire (hot and dry), air (hot and wet), water (cold and wet) and earth (cold and dry) are the result of Love's uniting forces.

To relate this concept to the planets it is easy to see that benefic planets such as Jupiter, Venus, the Moon, and even the Sun to some extent, are programmed by Love to bring things together and to create situations for cohesion, cooperation and solidarity.

Malefic planets on the other hand, could be said to be programmed by Strife to create separation, disunity and change.

Saturn separates through its extreme cold quality, and Mars separates through its extreme hot quality.

Aphorism Number 90 of *The Centiloquy of Hermes Trismegistus* states,

"Saturn produces evil with slowness, but Mars produces it suddenly; and therefore Mars is reputed to be worse in harming." [138]

If this is true, then Mars' speed and capacity to create separation suddenly are exercised during its short-term period, and Mars is highly effective in producing a suitable form which complies with Saturn's long-term plan for separation and change.

Using Strife as its power base, Mars is the worse in harming through its usual avenues of anarchy, argument, heart-ache, illness or violence.

Valens predicts trouble from a variety of fronts.

He predicts friends who are ungracious, separations that are painful, open conflict with superiors, and poor health, or possibly the death of the father or elderly persons.

Mars' placement in the chart is likely to give some indication as to where the trouble will arise, and its condition will tell how severe or malicious the attacks from others will be, as well as how much long-term damage Mars will generate for the native.

Two things stand out in Mars' sub-period when it works under the control of Saturn.

Firstly, the fact that Mars is naturally better behaved in a night-time chart, and it is currently operating in a diurnal Firdaria, so it is likely to arouse fierce responses to its inflammatory behaviour.

And secondly, a reminder that the native will encounter Saturn's second opposition to itself during this time, and the stress created between a stationary Saturn and a transiting Saturn, is likely to produce pressure which will delight a mischievous or malevolent Mars.

Fourth Sub-Period
Donor – SATURN : Recipient – SUN
(44.7 – 46.3 Years)

The middle section of Saturn's major period belongs to the Sun and there are warnings for the health or safety of the father, who is jointly signified by these two planets.

Saturn may be an agent for the Sun under the rules of sect, but Saturn and the Sun are apprehensive in each other's company especially when yoked together for the purposes of Firdaria.

If the Sun was nervous of its association with an inferior material in the Moon's major period, then it must be appalled at having to provide form for Saturn's somewhat tarnished substance, where there is little potential for the Sun to shine brightly under Saturn's tutelage.

At best the Sun's term is a suspenseful year which can easily turn to fear, distrust or the questioning of others' motives.

Valens warns there can be a tendency towards being mean-spirited in relation to friends and relatives, and if Mars has made the previous phase difficult, then an arrogant Sun is an unsuitable candidate for patching up rifts with loved ones or business associates.

If the native is especially ruthless then one of the advantages of Saturn's major period is that a planet such as Saturn is single-minded to the point of obsessive.

If during Mars' sub-period years the native was 'thrown to the wolves', then the Sun's term marks the return of the outsider, who has not only survived, but has earned their rightful place as pack leader, and the cold-blooded nature of Saturn is likely to come to the fore when metering out justice to its former detractors.

The alchemical symbol of turning lead into gold is reminiscent of the Sun's attempt to serve its major lord, and to provide a valuable vessel by which Saturn's Firdaria can be put to good use during this nineteen month period.

Whether it is the actual material, or the spiritual symbolism that Saturn is seeking from the Sun, Schoener's interpretation of this sub-period is a little more optimistic than Valens' prediction for the same period.

Schoener says that the native will be increased in strength and worth and that they will have the dignity of constableship (authority) in judging men.

Sun's sub-period produces gold for Saturn as according to Schoener, the native will be happy and will rejoice concerning their house, fellowship and children.

The Sun rules the eyes so Schoener warns about suffering of the eyes and the eyesight but generally speaking, it is a more optimist view of the period than Valens is willing to provide for the native.

Fifth Sub-Period
Donor – SATURN : Recipient – VENUS
(46.3 – 47.9 Years)

The Sun vacates the chair after nineteen months as sub-lord of Saturn's Firdaria, and Venus takes its place without much promise or improvement in the native's lot, especially when Saturn entrusts its difficult and somewhat pessimistic makings to Venus, who foresees advancing pressure from a different direction to the Sun.

Rather than procuring breathing space and a respite for the native to enjoy some peace of mind, instead when Saturn donates to Venus, separations from wives or injustices from females seem to be the fallout of two planets with very different agendas.

Venus does not bear a grudge toward Saturn as she lends her sign, Libra, for his exaltation, and similar to Mars' relationship to Saturn, there is no natural hostility between them.

However, the principles of Saturn (separation) and Venus (unity) are at odds, and a combination of Saturn's material with Venus' form promises to set in motion misunderstandings, legal proceedings and poor judgement on Venus' part, at a time when she is his representative and is guided by his instruction.

Saturn is isolationistic in nature. Valens describes him as solitary, care-worn, downcast, secretive and miserable, and this is not great material for Venus to work with if she is going to make something of the period under her charge.

This task is made doubly hard by the fact that Venus is a nocturnal planet and she is forced to represent a diurnal lord in a Diurnal Firdaria.

This period is not an easy time for Venus.

She must deal with inconstancies in friendships and alliances, with friend turning to foe, and any chance of short-lived pleasures are potentially going to end in consequences which are heart-breaking and painful for the native.

Sixth Sub-Period
Donor – SATURN : Recipient – MERCURY
(47.9 – 49.4 Years)

The sixth sub-period of Saturn belongs to Mercury, who takes measures to add his own personality to Saturn's potential for position and advancement by dealing in matters concerning money and the management of property.

Mercury may be very savvy in business but directed by Saturn, it can bring resentments and enemies, especially when Mercury is ruthless or dishonest in its dealings with others.

Mercury rules over mysterious, mystical or secretive matters, and Valens warns of disputes over such significations should Mercury's machinations cause betrayals in confidences or reveal information that Saturn would prefer to keep hidden so that it can be used as leverage at a later date.

The native may *"become very learned and inquisitive during these days, and meet with pledges and gifts"*[139] but with Saturn at the helm, there are probably strings attached to any benefits Mercury procures for its major Firdaria lord.

Seventh Sub-Period
Donor – SATURN : Recipient – MOON
(49.4 – 51 Years)

The Moon is the final player in Saturn's Firdaria, during which time the native born during the daylight hours moves beyond the fifth decade in their lifespan and celebrates their fiftieth birthday, and looks forward to the commencement of their sixth decade.

Saturn directing the Moon's sub-period does not augment well for a happy final chapter in Saturn's rule, given that the two planets rule opposite sides of the zodiac in the astrological model of Thema Mundi and belong to opposing sides of the sect fence.

The native's health and general well-being are under considerable risk, and the Moon's condition in the chart will indicate the level of distress the Moon will encounter during the last nineteen months belonging to Saturn.

Emotional upheavals, bodily weaknesses, unexpected ailments and alienation from loved ones or family are foreseen for a term when the Moon is out-of-sect in a diurnal chart, and becomes a nervous recipient in the final stage of Saturn's Firdaria.

Saturn's potential to furnish a diversity of circumstances for the native to suffer separation and heart-ache means that the Moon is overworked when it is required to deal with the emotional fall-out and the practical repercussions of Saturn's efforts to initiate change in the individual's life.

The Moon also signifies the mother or a female relative so concerns over her health or her situation in life are part of the responsibilities faced by the native during the Moon's term.

The Light of Wisdom and the Guidance of Virtue . . . JUPITER

"Just as treasures are uncovered from the earth, so virtue appears from good deeds, and wisdom appears from a pure and peaceful mind.

To walk safely through the maze of human life, one needs the light of wisdom and the guidance of virtue."

The Buddha

Sixth Diurnal Major Period lasts for 12 Years

Jupiter is Lord From 51 – 63rd Birthday

Jupiter's Matter and Significations:

Growth	Children	Success	Knowledge
Prosperity	Ambition	Good Fortune	Love and Friendship
Authority	Freedom	Abundance	Politics

Jupiter follows Saturn in the Chaldean Order and after some bleak periods produced by the material of Saturn, it would be nice to think there is an improvement in life's conditions during Jupiter's rule over the next twelve years.

Jupiter's major period begins at the fifty second year, and for the most part, Jupiter is a beneficial donor to the other planets, although Mars and Saturn will always play the role of difficult recipients when they take over the minor periods at fifty two years of age for Mars, and sixty one for Saturn, with each sub-period lasting for a length of twenty months.

The diurnal chart is dominated by the Sun, a planet occupied with gaining acknowledgement, esteem and reputation for the individual, and Jupiter's twelve years is a perfect time to take advantage of the foundations carefully constructed by the preceding five Firdarias through the succession of first, the Sun itself, and followed in Chaldean Order by Venus, Mercury, the Moon and Saturn.

Jupiter's material offers the potential to increase prosperity, and its natural propensity to strive for advancement is canny in its ability to build friendships with great men, and to shrewdly take advantage of those friendships.

Jupiter's pursuit in attaining the mantle of authority, and the accompanying freedom afforded by wealth and privilege, are rich matter for the remaining planets to form their own opinion over how to best utilise Jupiter's material to create their own unique outcomes over the period of Jupiter's twelve years.

Whilst Jupiter promotes wealth and sharp business practices, it is worth noting that Jupiter's Firdaria occurs at a time in life when the individual can usually manage to find breathing space to reflect on the good fortune which has happened over the course of their lifetime.

Jupiter can afford to be generous with its experience, its knowledge, and its resources, and this twelve years may be the perfect opportunity to give back to the world through mentorship initiatives, community projects, or volunteer schemes.

If wealth has been Jupiter's gift in previous Firdarias then this period may be the time to acknowledge life's good fortune and return the favour through philanthropic contributions to others less fortunate than themselves.

The diurnal nativity needs to understand that a good relationship with the virtues of charity and generosity of spirit are just as important to its well-being as a wealthy lifestyle and the admiration of others. It would be a wise individual who uses Jupiter's Firdaria as the ideal time to nourish the light of the Sun's spirit and intellect within themselves and to find a way to exercise human nature's innate desire to do good deeds.

SIXTH Major Firdaria for the Diurnal Chart
♃ — 12 years
12 years divided by 7 = 1 year 8 months 17 days

Major JUPITER 12 yrs Sub-Period	Combination of Major (1st) and Minor (2nd) Time Lords	Minor Time Period BEGINS—ENDS for 1 yr 8 months *(1.7) *months as %
1	♃/♃	51.0 – 52.7
2	♃/♂	52.7 – 54.4
3	♃/☉	54.4 – 56.1
4	♃/♀	56.1 – 57.9
5	♃/☿	57.9 – 59.6
6	♃/☽	59.6 – 61.3
7	♃/♄	61.3 – 63.0

Fig. 174
Jupiter's Firdaria in the Diurnal Chart

First Sub-Period
Donor – JUPITER : Recipient – JUPITER
(51 -52.7 Years)

If Jupiter is in a decent condition in the diurnal chart, then Jupiter becoming both the major and minor lord during the first twenty months of its Firdaria should bring the consequences of a bountiful and joyous time for the native.

The individual's actions can be effective and beneficial, especially when supported and aided by friends, and the successful accomplishment of matters can occur if alliances with benefactors are maintained by Jupiter's efforts.

If Jupiter is connected to Mars by aspect or through the Terms, this first stage can be a little bumpy, but overall Jupiter's benefits are doubled during the period when Jupiter commences its Firdaria.

Second Sub-Period
Donor – JUPITER : Recipient – MARS
(52.7 – 54.4 Years)

If Mars does holds influence over Jupiter in the natal chart, then what began previously as a bumpy period, may accelerate to a term which feels somewhat treacherous, particularly in relation to people placed above the native in power or influence.

In a diurnal chart the planet Mars is a poor recipient for Jupiter's largesse, and rather than feeling the benefits of the potentially rich material presented by Jupiter, Mars can become arrogant or feel entitled to capture Jupiter's gifts and hold them hostage for its own use.

This type of behaviour is unlikely to find favour with others whose generosity in previous times has been helpful, and who now find themselves dealing with an individual who boasts of their own accomplishments and does not return the same generosity of spirit.

The combination of Jupiter as the driving force and Mars as its tool of application creates a stage for ambitious inclinations and single-minded purposefulness, especially if the native is engaged in public office or the military, but such a blunt tool can create enemies.

Valens warns that whilst Mars' term can be extremely effective in gaining professional advancement, a by-product of Mars' ruthlessness is that it produces fear, mistrust or suspicion within the native's mind.

Third Sub-Period
Donor – JUPITER : Recipient – SUN
(54.4 – 56.1 Years)

The potential presented by Jupiter will find a more gracious recipient in the Sun, especially if the native has contained Mars in the previous territory and directed it wisely towards projects or schemes which will benefit the individual's plans for the future.

Valens foresees a brilliant time in the Sun's sub-period, a time which is good for acquisition and an increase in popularity and advancement when Jupiter shares its material with the Sun, who absorbs the good fortune of Jupiter and creates a form by which the native can gain glory, reputation and an elevation in social position.

The Sun's term covers the middle years of the sixth decade from fifty four to fifty six years, and the two lords hopefully produce a good period when the native can maximise the fruits of their labours.

A caveat always applies to predictions such as these, as the level of success, the manner in which it is achieved, and the likelihood of it being maintained, is strongly dependent on the placement and condition of both planets in the chart, as the good fortune suggested by the nature of Jupiter and the Sun can be diminished or quickly evaporate if either planet is in a poor state.

Fourth Sub-Period
Donor – JUPITER : Recipient – VENUS
(56.1 – 57.9 Years)

Venus becomes the mid-term lord for Jupiter's Firdaria after the Sun's period has been completed.

Hopefully Venus will take a form which accentuates the lighter side of life and the native can find relative peace in the eye of the storm produced by Jupiter's heightened energy and enthusiasm which gleans the most from every situation.

Jupiter delivers twelve busy and eventful years. Even when they are richly rewarding they can still be exhausting for the spirit and the body as the individual struggles to cope with Jupiter's many demands.

During this period Venus provides Jupiter with an outlet for its energy, so that the individual has the chance to pursue their own idea of beauty, or spend their hard-earned money on gifts and privileges for those whom it loves to spoil, whether it be themselves or others.

Regardless of whether the native is male or female, Venus accentuates the charm, grace and vitality of women, and the native is given opportunity over this twenty month term to benefit from, or to improve relationships with, a variety of women who are important in their life.

Fifth Sub-Period
Donor – JUPITER : Recipient – MERCURY
(57.9 – 59.6 Years)

The opposition which exists between Jupiter and Mercury in the Thema Mundi model suggests mixed blessings for this chapter in Jupiter's Firdaria.

Mercury's nature is tainted by a capricious desire to shake things up and to alter life's direction for its own amusement, especially when it is not concerned with whether it brings ease or hard times.

For this reason, traditional astrologers were nervous of how Mercury's involvement would affect the outcome of certain situations when the delicate balance of fortune could fall one way or the other.

Mercury's behaviour becomes more random when it is influenced by the other planets and it is wise to be aware of Mercury's situation in the chart, as this will greatly affect the success of its sub-period.

Associations with benefic planets can make Mercury a good recipient for Jupiter's potential, making the best of Mercury's skills in calculations, speech and writing and producing profitable and commercial success during Mercury's term.

However, should Mercury be associated with difficult planets, it will take on a more malefic form during the twenty months of its rulership. In this instance Mercury will create its own special brand of mischief through scandal, slander, lawsuits or trouble with those who have the power to influence the native's fate.

Sixth Sub-Period
Donor – JUPITER : Recipient – MOON
(59.6 – 61.3 Years)

Jupiter's sixth sub-period belongs to the Moon, and perhaps the fact that the Moon generously allows Jupiter to borrow Cancer for its own exaltation, suggests a time when the friendship of two planets means they can combine their resources to produce a spell of profit, stability, good health and happiness.

The Moon's form is feminine, making room for alliances and advantages to come from a variety of females, including women involved with the family.

Jupiter specifically searches for advancement and reputation, higher office and social standing, and gains from these areas may increase under the Moon's influence. However, the Moon is a variable force that waxes and wanes and is dependent on Fortune's whims.

In some ways the Moon is similar to Mercury in that it is particularly susceptible to disruption from the malefic planets, either in the natal chart, or via transits during its twenty month term.

Any external influence can result in a reversal of benefits during the Moon's sub-period and profit can turn to loss during this twenty month term.

Moon also belongs to the opposite sect, and it will be uncomfortable in a diurnal chart unless it gains benefit from the two other conditions of sect dignity.

Overall, Valens speaks of the Moon bringing deliverance from the woes of affliction, illness or heart-ache, especially if the native is willing to partake in reciprocal acts of kindness, generosity and compassion.

Seventh Sub-Period
Donor – JUPITER : Recipient – SATURN
(61.3 – 63 Years)

Saturn is the final recipient for Jupiter's fortunes and whilst there are warnings concerning their incompatibility – Jupiter is in fall in Saturn's sign – there can be intervals during the final twenty months belonging to Jupiter where Saturn is capable of completing the required tasks set by its donor planet.

Saturn will use Jupiter's material to provide for the future, always fearful that Jupiter is the perpetual optimist and must be protected against its own good nature.

Saturn takes a more pessimistic view of life, and the donation of Jupiter's material to Saturn is reminiscent of Aesop's Fable of the cicada (later to become the grasshopper) and the ant.

In the fable, the cicada's singing mocks the ant during the summer months when the ant is busy storing away food for the wintertime, and the cicada is idly playing its song.

When winter arrives and there is no food, the cicada begs the ant to feed it lest it dies of hunger, but the ant refuses to listen to the cicada's pleas for mercy and instead rebukes the insect for its idleness, cruelly advising it to dance the winter away.

Some versions, including the Bible's Book of Proverbs, laud the Saturnian virtues of hard work and the merits of planning for the future, and finish with moral messages such as *"Idleness brings want"* or *"To work today is to eat tomorrow"*.

In Classical times it was argued that the ant's smug taunt in the face of the grasshopper's starvation makes it appear mean-spirited and vindictive. The French poet Jean de la Fontaine (1621-1695) philosophised that the ant represented society whose role it was to protect and provide for the grasshoppers, or the artisans, so that they could mutually benefit from one another's skills – poets, artists and musicians would be fed, and in return society would gain refinement for its citizens.

Fontaine was himself one of society's grasshoppers, and he wrote an alternate fable more palatable for Jupiter, where the ant relents and welcomes the grasshopper to share his larder, thereby praising the positive virtues of charity and magnanimity.

In astrological comparison Jupiter's optimism represents the grasshopper, whilst Saturn plays the role of the hoarding ant, so that when Jupiter supplies way too much material, Saturn chides it for wastefulness. Rather than taking Jupiter's matter and applying itself industriously, Saturn becomes miserly and its sub-period is marred by defeat and dissension.

Whilst Schoener says *"he will give of his own to the poor"*, Valens' interpretation of this period favours the earlier version of the fable, citing the disobedience of the family, unstable partnerships and friends becoming enemies.

Valens says that the native is unsuccessful at finishing things, or that they do so with postponements, angry conversations and petitions to the authorities of wrongdoings.

All of these manifestations have a dampening effect at the closure of Jupiter's twelve year Firdaria, and are an ominous premonition of the woes to be had in the following Firdaria belonging to an out-of-sect Mars.

Stout-Hearted Old Warriors . . . MARS

"This is one of the stout-hearted old warriors:
he is angry with civilisation because he supposes that its
aim is to make all good things – honours, treasures, beautiful
women – accessible even to cowards."

Friedrich Nietzsche (1844 – 1900)

Seventh Diurnal Major Period lasts for 7 Years

Mars is Lord From 63 – 70ᵗʰ Birthday

Mars' Matter and Significations:

Conflict	Energy	Force	Ambitions
Focus	Bad Fortune	Leadership	Courage
Motivation	Masculinity	Competition	Physicality

The seven years of Mars is the last major period in the Firdar cycle for the diurnal chart which is completed at seventy years of age.

Mars is a forceful planet, and is usually engaged in conflicts that require an endless supply of energy and focus, so it seems odd to find it appearing at a later period of life.

By rights we might assume that the native should be permitted to enjoy a more sedentary way of life, one relatively free from the agitation that Mars is keen to provide over its next seven year reign.

Mars' role as the final Firdaria lord is due to its position immediately above the Sun – the initial Firdaria lord for the daytime birth – so that when the Chaldean Order is implemented Mars will be the last planet to complete the diurnal series of the Firdaria system.

Mars may feel like a perilous finish to what has been a long journey, particularly as this planet prefers the night-time and can present itself as a difficult donor with a list of tasks which are often irksome and unsettling for its recipient planets.

In terms of planetary sect, Mars is often referred to as 'the out-of-sect malefic' for a diurnal chart, and a measure of its potential to cause trouble will be greatly dependent on its condition and placement in the natal chart.

Mars' one redeeming feature may be that its Firdaria contains the only sub-periods which are easily calculated.

Seven years for seven planets means that each one rules for exactly one year, so that as each birthday occurs, another planet steps forward to serve Mars as its sub-period lord.

If only for the purpose of neatness, the Mars Firdaria works well alongside other older style predictive tools such as the Solar Return, which creates a chart yearly from the exact degree of the Sun, and also for the technique known as Profection, which works its way around the chart through the signs, and allocates a new planetary ruler for each successive year of life.

The Mars Firdaria begins after the diurnal nativity has completed six of the seven major Firdaria periods. For a youth-oriented planet such as Mars to rule at the end of life it is a reminder of years gone past when the individual has faced great peril, achieved great successes and fought battles that seemed unwinnable.

In times when the birthday cake was not so crowded with candles the individual had the desire and energy to fight to protect their young ones, to maintain their position professionally or to keep the younger competitors at bay.

Mars is also a highly sexual planet, so in younger years its passion and enthusiasm was spent in attracting the opposite sex and having the sexual prowess to satisfy lovers and keep them by the native's side.

All of these Martian energies are fading, and although the onset of Mars does not mean the diurnal nativity is at death's door, there is still the fact that interests wane, the same battles seem pointless, and bodies get tired under the demands of this planet.

The warrior is no longer young and this time can be a painful reminder that time is passing.

If past projects still require completion or extended battles need to be won or dreams are crying to be realized, then the native needs to employ cunning as well as wisdom to finish the tasks.

Not every project can be completed nor every battle won, so the individual must make their choices carefully and valiantly during Mars' seven year period.

And Mars may even provide the courage to release dreams back into the universe and remember that often they are not meant to be achievable – that is why we call them dreams.

In the delineations provided by Valens, there is supposedly only one bright year amongst Mars' seven year period for the diurnal nativity. This year belongs to Jupiter who rules the final year of Mars' Firdaria.

Schoener agrees with Valens with the only exception being that Venus' sub-period will be slightly better, as it denotes a time when the native is pre-occupied with bedding women of dubious character.

The point is that the native has the choice whether they will spend the last Firdaria of Mars being frustrated and angry at life like Nietzsche's *"stout-hearted old warriors"*, or they capitalize on Mars' seven years to squeeze the last juicy morsel from life, and make the old warrior's last battle the one where he or she experiences their finest hour.

The Nodes will take up the next five years, followed once more by the Sun's Firdaria, so life is far from over even in the seventies, eighties and nineties, but this last Firdaria belonging to the 'out-of-sect malefic' has the potential to set the tone for the last decades of life so it would be nice to think that they will be spent well, and not wasted on pointless rage or bitter regrets.

Perhaps Mars as the final Firdaria lord in this diurnal round would do well to heed the advice of American journalist Hunter S. Thompson (1937 – 2005) who once said:

> *"Life should not be a journey to the grave with the intention of arriving safely in a pretty and well preserved body, but rather to skid in broadside in a cloud of smoke, thoroughly used up, totally worn out, and loudly proclaiming "Wow! What a ride!"*

> From *The Proud Highway:*
> *Saga of a Desperate Southern Gentleman, 1955 - 1967*

SEVENTH Major Firdaria for the Diurnal Chart ♂ — 7 years 7 years divided by 7 = 1 year		
Major **MARS** **7 yrs** Sub-Period	Combination of Major (1st) and Minor (2nd) Time Lords	Minor Time Period BEGINS—ENDS for 1 year
1	♂ / ♂	63.0 – 64.0
2	♂ / ☉	64.0 – 65.0
3	♂ / ♀	65.0 – 66.0
4	♂ / ☿	66.0 – 67.0
5	♂ / ☽	67.0 – 68.0
6	♂ / ♄	68.0 – 69.0
7	♂ / ♃	69.0 – 70.0

Fig. 175 Mars' Firdaria in the Diurnal Chart

First Sub-Period
Donor – MARS : Recipient – MARS
(63 – 64 Years)

Mars hands over to itself and the first year is a double dose of Mars in the role of both major and minor lord. This presents as a year which is bound to be unpleasant and full of trouble for the individual born during the day.

Valens expands on this theory, saying Mars instigates conflict and causes rivalry and friction with others, abuse of public matters, or dealings with those who squander public funds.

The worse the condition of Mars, the more underhand, shady or even criminal the dealings can become, so that the native needs to be aware how their conduct at this point in time can influence the remaining six years of Mars' jurisdiction.

Second Sub-Period
Donor – MARS : Recipient – SUN
(64 – 65 Years)

Mars hands over its second division to the Sun, and this year can be dangerous for the father if he is living or for one likened to the father in their role as a past or present mentor or protector of the native.

The Sun's form indicates dealings with elevated persons or authority figures, and matters need to be carefully handled if contention is to be avoided.

When Mars is the major donor its entire duration of rulership holds Strife's dormant seeds, and according to the nature of its matter, Mars has the potential to gather together small slights and frustrations to quickly fan the flames of discord, or create open antagonism which can deteriorate into acts of verbal abuse or physical violence.

The Sun has an affiliation with Mars through its exaltation in Aries so it understands to a certain degree the passion and enthusiasm which is inherent in this volatile planet.

For this reason, the Sun can charter the difficult waters presented by Mars, and so long as it applies tact, caution or diplomacy to any situation generated by Mars, then honours, beneficial negotiations or an elevation in status are not goals beyond the Sun's reach during this year.

Third Sub-Period
Donor – MARS : Recipient – VENUS
(65 – 66 Years)

The potential for Mars and Venus to be at war with one another is a very real possibility during this year.

Their respective signs lie in opposition in the Thema Mundi model, and misunderstandings or friction in dealings with women are featured during a year when Venus is the sub-period lord for Mars.

Mars' propensity for ill-disciplined or irksome behaviour is difficult for Venus to fully represent with enthusiasm, so any strategic advantage gained in Mars' personal vendetta against the world can take a toll on the native's relationships, regardless of whether they are business dealings or of a more personal nature.

Venus also represents the mother in a diurnal chart, so this can be a perilous year for mother's health or well-being if she is still living.

Fourth Sub-Period
Donor – MARS : Recipient – MERCURY
(66 – 67 Years)

At the age of sixty six Venus is thankful to finish its term of duty and Mercury steps forward at the halfway mark of the Mars Firdaria to become the fourth lord in the last round of the diurnal chart's planetary rulerships.

The secondment of Mercury's skills by Mars is not, strictly speaking, a cause for concern.

However, given both planets' individual significations and the propensity for their combination to land the native in strife, heralds a year full of disturbances and losses on account of writings, speech, calculations or money.

Valens' translator uses the term *chicanery* to describe the kind of morally ambiguous trap the native can fall into when a slick Mercury becomes the recipient of Mars' dubious intentions.

Chicanery comes from the French verb *'chicaner'* meaning 'to quibble' or 'to prevent justice' and is described as clever, dishonest talk or behaviour intended to deliberately deceive people.

At the very least, this type of behaviour accumulates enemies and leads to legal proceedings, and at worst, places the native in danger of imprisonment, verbal abuse or physical violence if their dishonesty is outed.

Any leanings towards deliberately encouraging misrepresentation or the broadcast of misleading information needs to be curbed, regardless of whether Mercury believes that it can justify trickery or fraud, in order to meet the needs of a Mars wishing to gain a winning edge over its competitors.

Fifth Sub-Period
Donor – MARS : Recipient – MOON
(67 – 68 Years)

The Moon becomes the next recipient for the wish-list prepared by Mars.

Valens predicts this year to be one which is perilous and full of danger, possessing unsettlements and constraints, lawsuits and precarious travel abroad or attacks and insults from a foreign land.

The Moon signifies the mother or female relatives so battles with female members of the family, or separations from loved ones, can be the theme for a trying year under the Moon's care.

Both major and minor time period lords belong to the nocturnal sect, and the Moon is unlikely to be particularly helpful in fulfilling Mars' requirements.

Mars does not appreciate sensitivity, compassion or gentleness if these emotions stand in the way of a substitute planet achieving its aims, and the Moon may genuinely want to relieve Mars' agitation, but may not be strong enough to resist Mars' demands.

Schoener says of this period that the native risks being arrested, and that he can lose wealth or substance during the Moon's year, or anything he values will become spoiled.

This is a definitely a year in which transits to the Moon, along with the Solar Return and the Profected Lord require close examination, especially if the Moon is strongly featured in any of these predictive techniques.

Although neither Valens nor Schoener mention poor health in the Moon's year it is noteworthy considering that the Moon rules the health of the body, and if Mars is poorly situated in the diurnal chart, a decline in health, surgery, or sudden dramas concerning health might be anticipated during the Moon's term.

Sixth Sub-Period
Donor – MARS : Recipient – SATURN
(68 – 69 Years)

Saturn is the recipient for Mars in the sixth sub-period and the synthesis of two malefics is unlikely to provide a time of peace, good fortune or serenity for the native.

Valens says that it indicates a year 'that is the worst', and is a time given to a multitude of disturbances.

Whether the year consists of encounters in lawsuits and insults, losses and rejections, these 'stars of Strife' surround the native with violent and highly disturbing affairs.

Health concerns, physical weaknesses or injuries, the insurrection of enemies, hurtful and distressful travel abroad, and all manner of reasons to breed fear and distrust in the native's mind abound in this time. Unless the benefic planets can shield the native from harm, Valens says that Saturn causes wretched treatment, and ominously predicts that the native will be forced 'to submit to charges hardly touching the surface'.

Neither Valens nor Schoener take into account the fact that Saturn is working in a diurnal chart, and therefore, sect dignity might mitigate some of its worst characteristics in the Diurnal Firdaria.

Both traditional authors predict terrible things for the native during this year and it is difficult to find sanctuary from what appears to be a year fraught with danger or misery.

A Profected Lord in good condition may be able to soften the blows during the combined malefics' year, but like the sailors at sea caught in one of Saturn's storms, it may be a case of 'batten down the hatches' until the year has safely passed.

Seventh Sub-Period
Donor – MARS : Recipient – JUPITER
(69 – 70 Years)

Finally, a sub-lord that portends a year described by Valens as both fine and effectual, a relief after several years ruled by other planets with little idea on how to harness the energy of Mars.

Jupiter is the last planet to be seconded by Mars for the purpose of achieving its end goals.

If the naturally diurnal Jupiter has the power to control and direct the random and wilful energy signified by Mars, it has the potential to bring with it accomplishment and assistance from superiors, and to allow the native to rise through the ranks with good leadership skills and a talent for being both innovative and courageous in decision-making.

The individual approaching seventy may complain that Jupiter has left its run a bit late, and that career aspirations are far from the native's mind at this age, but many professional people are working well into their late seventies and early eighties, at a time when a good diet, exercise and medical advancements mean that older individuals are making changes for a fuller life, rather than winding down and waiting for Death to appear at their doors.

In recent years, a growing number of senior citizens are successfully competing in marathons and triathlons, and this is causing experts to rethink much of what they previously believed about age-related changes in physical capacity.

This last period of Mars' Firdaria may not be the ideal time to take up long-distance running, but there are a multitude of ways in which Jupiter can get the best from Mars' material.

With Mars as the originating source, Jupiter can take its passion and provide direction and purpose for Mars, so that the native can achieve the fulfilment of their expectations and morph the harsh lessons learnt in the previous six years into experiences of a more positive nature.

CHAPTER TWELVE

The Lunar Journey

The Firdaria and the Nocturnal Chart

"Each star is the ruler of its own "element" in the universe with reference to the stars' sympathy or antipathy or mutual influence.

The moon becomes the ruler of foresight,
the sun the ruler of light,
Saturn the ruler of ignorance and necessity,
Jupiter the ruler of rank, crowns and zeal,
Mars becomes the ruler of action and effort,
Venus the ruler of love, desire, and beauty,
Mercury the ruler of law, friendship, and trust.
These stars have their own effects . . ."[140]

Vettius Valens, *Anthologies, Book II*

For the Nocturnal Firdaria life's journey begins with the Moon and continues in the Chaldean Order with Saturn, Jupiter, Mars, Sun, Venus and Mercury each taking their turn as major Time Lords.

The planets' areas of expertise for Nocturnal Firdaria are identical to Diurnal significations as they remain the same regardless of whether the chart is classified as a daytime or a night-time chart.

It is recommended that the reader revisit the seven major periods in the section on planetary sect (Chapter Two) to familiarise themselves with the full extent of the planets' meanings according to Vettius Valens' delineations from Book One of his *Anthologies*.

The change in daytime or night-time Firdaria will not affect the planet's meanings and general significations.

However, sect will change the way in which planets operate when they are either the long-term or short-term Firdaria lord simply because they are members of one sect or the other.

For instance, the Nocturnal Firdaria will begin with the Moon (nocturnal planet), then Saturn (diurnal planet), then Jupiter (diurnal planet), then Mars (nocturnal planet), then Sun (diurnal planet), then Venus (nocturnal planet) and finally Mercury (either nocturnal of diurnal).

Therefore, just based on the first rule of sect this order of planets will feature an in-sect luminary (Moon), an out-of-sect malefic (Saturn), and out-of-sect benefic (Jupiter), and in-sect malefic (Mars), an out-of-sect luminary (Sun), an in-sect benefic (Venus), and an in- or out- of sect planet, depending on its position to the Sun (Mercury).

The planets which are out of sect (Saturn, Jupiter, Sun) will hopefully be diurnally placed (travelling with the Sun) or in masculine signs (fire or air) in order to provide them with some sect dignity so that when their time comes as major or minor Firdaria lords, they can bring some benefit to this period of the Firdaria.

The planets which are in sect will hopefully be nocturnally placed (travelling in the opposite hemisphere to the Sun) or in their correct gender signs (Mars in masculine, Moon and Venus in the feminine signs of water or earth) so that they can increase their strengths and produce beneficial results during their term as major or minor Time Lords.

As if this isn't complicated enough, the rulers of the Firdaria will also swap from one planet to the next in the smaller time periods in the same Chaldean Order, and will start the process according to which of them rules the longer period of years.

Sub-period lords will alter in the minimum of twelve months during Mars' seven year Firdaria and up to the maximum of twenty two months in Mercury's thirteen year Firdaria.

Valens does not differentiate between day and night births in his delineations on handings-over even though he is aware of the impact of sect on the malefic planets, and this has been discussed earlier in the introductory chapter on Firdaria.

His delineations take into account the general nature of both planets involved in the Firdaria and often the combination of whether the two planets are hostile or friendly towards one another, but the better or worse case scenario of sect dignity vs. sect debility is left for the reader to work through on their own.

Possibly it was assumed that sect was so basic a technique known and applied to both general astrology practice and specifically, to the idea of one planet handing responsibility over to another as Time Lords, that Valens believed it was fundamental to the reader's knowledge and therefore not worthy of mentioning in the text.

Johannes Schoener certainly mentions the differences between a day birth or a night birth when he delineates different Firdaria periods.

Valens states *"The benefic stars which are appropriately and favourably situated bring about their proper effects according to their own nature and the nature of their sign, with the aspects and conjunctions of each star being blended. If however they are unfavourably situated, they are indicative of reversals."*[141]

He makes the point that the benefics work to their best advantage when they are *"appropriately and favourably situated"*. That is, in signs or degrees of essential dignity, and placed effectively in the chart, either in angles, or in houses that aspect the Ascendant.

"with aspects and conjunctions of each star being blended", preferably with good aspects to other benefic planets and with no hard aspects (conjunctions, oppositions, or squares) to the malefic planets.

The text then continues:

*"In the same way even the malefic stars, when they are operative in appropriate places **in their own sect**, are bestowers of good and indicative of the greatest positions and success; when they are inoperative, they bring about disasters and accusations."*[142]

Similar to the benefics *"appropriate places"* refers to the malefics being placed in signs of essential dignity and in good placement in the chart which will bring some dignity to the malefics in the same manner as it does the benefic planets.

However, a further rider which is not included in the benefics' condition but is specifically added for the malefic planets' benefit, *"in their own sect"* refers to the fact that for Saturn to become 'accidentally benefic' it needs to be in a diurnal chart or diurnally placed.

Mars will turn from a malefic to an accidental benefic if it gains sect dignity by being in a nocturnal chart or nocturnally placed on top of being in signs which dignifies its nature.

If this happens then either Saturn or Mars are going to become *"bestowers of good and indicative of the greatest positions and success".*

But *"when they are inoperative",* in other words out of sect or debilitated, the malefics bring about disaster and accusations.

Saturn in the diurnal chart benefits from the Sun's heat and light, as the Sun's qualities warm Saturn and shine light on the areas where it is most ignorant or illuminates the darker recesses when Saturn becomes cold or insensitive towards others' suffering.

The Sun blesses Saturn with a touch of humanity whereby Saturn has the opportunity to move towards enlightenment, or at the very least, tolerance, and bestows good humour (albeit dry and biting) to situations where its presence is appreciated, rather than feared.

If Saturn does produce benefits, it is more likely to produce them for diurnal nativities in periods of the Diurnal Firdaria. Saturn has the ability to create position and success for the native if all its other conditions are met in the chart, whether this occurs during its major period beginning at forty years of age (Fifth Period of the Diurnal Firdaria), or acting as an agent for any of the other planets' in their sub-periods.

Saturn's dislike of the nocturnal chart can make life doubly hard when its eleven year major period occurs between the ages of nine and twenty years (Second Period of the Nocturnal Firdaria).

Diurnal charts have the opportunity to claim Saturn for their own benefit as forty year old adults, to work out for themselves what *"the ruler of ignorance and necessity"* might mean in their lives, but this wisdom of age is not available to the individual born during the night.

It is left to the teenager to grapple with a Saturn which is more likely to be projected on to authority figures such as parents, teachers, adult mentors, religious leaders, social workers, psychologists, doctors or counsellors. Or in worst case scenario, if the child is really struggling with Saturn, to law enforcement officers and the judiciary system.

Mars prefers a nocturnal chart, where it is better behaved when it is removed from the Sun's heat and light, as the Sun's qualities overheat Mars and causes it to become aggressive, agitated or destructive.

Mars cools down under the Moon's light and becomes more temperate, more thoughtful and sensitive to the fact that even though it is *"the ruler of action and effort"*, those actions have consequences, and the avenue for Mars' efforts can be chosen with care, forethought or deliberation in a nocturnal chart.

A more controlled version of Mars provides nocturnal nativities with the drive to perform without the unnecessary aggravation that often accompanies Mars' actions.

In the Nocturnal Firdaria, whether Mars rules the Fourth Period beginning at thirty two years of age, or acts as sub-period lord, an in sect Mars bestows good fortune by creating allies instead of enemies and directs the focus towards goals rather than wasting the native's effort or energy.

Nocturnal Firdaria

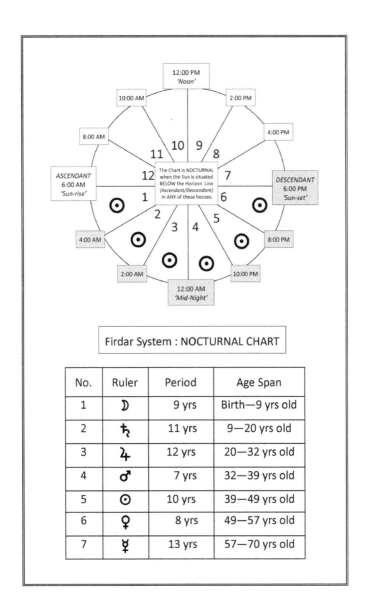

No.	Ruler	Period	Age Span
1	☽	9 yrs	Birth—9 yrs old
2	♄	11 yrs	9—20 yrs old
3	♃	12 yrs	20—32 yrs old
4	♂	7 yrs	32—39 yrs old
5	☉	10 yrs	39—49 yrs old
6	♀	8 yrs	49—57 yrs old
7	☿	13 yrs	57—70 yrs old

Fig. 176 Nocturnal Firdaria

But Life was There, A Transparent Pearl
. . . THE MOON

"Endless moons, an opaque universe, thunder, tornadoes, the quaking earth.

Rare moments of peace; forehead up against my knees, arms around my head, I thought, I listened, I longed not to exist.

But life was there, a transparent pearl, a star revolving slowly on its own axis."

Shan Sa, *Empress*

First Nocturnal Major Period lasts for 9 Years

The Moon is Lord from Birth to 9th Birthday

The Moon's Matter and Significations:

Life	Body	Mother	Physical environment
Appearance	Family	Children	Short journeys
Emotional state	Health	Women	Female relatives

The Moon is the first planet the individual will meet if they are born during the night-time hours as the Moon, not the Sun, is honoured as the primary luminary for nocturnal charts.

Under the guidance of a warm and loving mother-figure the nine year period after birth can be a constant unfolding of the physical world, especially when the carer meets the child's emotional and physical needs.

However, not all children are fortunate enough to have this early experience, and the Moon's period from birth to the ninth birthday could equally be a time when the child yearns for a safe environment and a loving supportive parent who has their best interests at heart when they are traversing the most vulnerable years of their life.

In Chris Brennan's paper on the Lots[143] he states that the nature of each luminary is fundamentally different, and that the Sun plays an active role in emitting or emanating its rays and its light, whereas the Moon plays a passive role in receiving and reflecting light.

Simply put, the Sun 'emits', and the Moon 'receives'.

No other planet can imprint on the Sun.

It is the sole source of light and energy in our solar system.

The solar child learns very early in life how to emit the Sun's rays. Sending forth sparks of light that will draw attention the child hopefully gains others' admiration and respect, so that depending on the state of the Sun in the chart, the child learns how to 'shine' from a very young age.

In a diurnal chart the child will follow the examples laid down by the Sun and will look for praise or acknowledgement from the strongest leader in their lives in much the same way as we bask in the Sun's light on a warm day in spring after a long cold winter season.

True, the native can experience some unpleasant side effects from the Sun's relationship with malefic planets, and Mars or Saturn can affect the quality of the Sun's emissions, but these effects are usually externalised and often projected onto another individual or a figure in authority.

This allows the native to direct its disapproval outwards and react accordingly, rather than collecting the malefics' negativity and directing it towards themselves.

Blaming another for one's shortcomings is a natural form of self-protection, and part of the process towards maturity involves the realisation that perhaps our own actions were also involved in the Sun's dilemma.

This natural defence is not so easily accessible to the child born during the night-time hours.

Their main luminary is designed for reception, both good and bad, and the lunar child has no such light or spark to direct them, only a weak reflected light from the Sun to lead them through the dark.

This child learns to rely on other senses besides sight.

Their ear picks up any slight nuances in voice inflection or alteration in sound.

Their minds vibrate with any change in the energy currents which surround them.

They manoeuvre through a world invisible to the adult, and even closed to the solar child whose senses are designed for more obvious signs.

The lunar child learns to cooperate with others and to gain strength from mutual trust rather than from individual brilliance.

This is the child who is conditioned to receive from others throughout life.

Gathering and collecting experiences, emotions and information, often intuiting between the gaps, so they can build a full and extensive model of survival which is uniquely their own.

Being on the receiving end means that any contact the Moon has with the malefic planets in the natal chart will filter through to the lunar child and become part of their intrinsic nature and the very fibre of their internal landscape through the body and the mind. Projection is a luxury that the lunar child rarely gets to experience as absorption, rather than expulsion, is their *modus operandi*.

The out of sect Saturn can have a dramatic effect on the child's first nine years of life as the Moon receives its negativity, and tries to both absorb it and find ways to survive its maleficence at the same time. Even Mars can be a battle even though it is the in sect malefic as the world judges a child and its parents harshly if speaking one's mind becomes rudeness, or wilful behaviour turns into uncontrollable tantrums.

The Jesuit statement of *"Give me the child until the age of seven and I will show you the man"* can easily be applied to the First Firdaria Periods of the Sun in a diurnal chart or the Moon in a nocturnal chart as both initial Firdarias contain the first seven years of life.

This boast on the moulding of an adult's character within the first square of Saturn (7 years) also applies to the Ages of Man which, similar to Firdar, uses the Chaldean Order for planetary periods and the Ages are discussed in detail in *A Tiny Universe* (Chapter Two).

The Diurnal Firdaria supports the solar child during the first ten years of life.

The diurnal child is the one who seeks to emulate the Sun's principles of light and warmth, gaining attention and praise at each small advance. Depending on the amount and quality it receives, the child either extends these qualities in adulthood or searches for artificial replacements to compensate for the lack of the Sun's qualities in their early years.

The Nocturnal Firdaria supports the lunar child during the first nine years of life.

This child is the one who follows the path of the Moon as its light increases and fades away, heavily relying on their five senses to cautiously explore any foreign territory it comes across in its wanderings.

The Moon ruling the first nine years gives its child constant experiences and opportunities to investigate and evaluate every nuance of the physical world – including their own body – using the lunar tools of instinct, emotion and intuition.

If the solar child is the glorious regent in a long line of monarchs, the lunar child is the explorer of an alien land who anticipates trouble at each new turn.

In many ways *The Little Prince* is a clever union of the two luminaries.

The main character is the solar prince who is granted entitlement through his royal lineage and who enjoys a state of total control over his environment by being his planet's sole occupant.

His imperial duty is the responsibility he feels towards the care of his asteroid, his volcanoes, his baobab trees, and his single red rose.

But he is also the lunar child who leaves the security of his planet to wander the universe, simply because he feels resentment towards the ungrateful rose whom he loves dearly and serves faithfully.

When the prince meets a snake (a symbol in the nocturnal world of death and resurrection) he points to his home-star and the snake remarks on how beautiful it is.

The snake then asks the prince what brings him to Earth, and the golden-haired boy answers

"I've been having some trouble with a flower", which means everything to him, but seems to the snake to be an opaque answer to a simple question.

Perhaps this fusion of light and dark is part of the reason behind the enormous popularity of *The Little Prince* which has been translated into over 300 languages and different dialects and is considered to be one of the greatest books of the 20th century.

This children's fable may have been intended for adults to reflect on their own yearning for the synthesis of two opposing forces that pull apart but ultimately seek unity. Perhaps we are as much invested in a peaceful resolution to *The Little Prince* as is its wandering alien child, its stranded pilot, its odd adult characters alienated on their own planets, and finally, its complex author, Antoine de Saint-Exupéry.

Sect acknowledges the chasm between the Sun and Moon, the day and the night, and confronts our ideas on how all features of the astrology chart will alter if we accept its separatist rules of dividing the planets into two distinct camps. For this reason, sect won't appeal to everyone's astrological tastes, but sect did not create the division.

Polarity, tension and opposition has always existed between the two luminaries, and techniques such as sect dignity and the Firdaria system allow for the two sides to measure their differences, rather than competing over which one is the more powerful force.

For the purpose of explaining the difference between the major and minor lords, Robert Hand has used the allegory of matter for the major, and form for the minor lord.

Of the seven planets the Moon is the closest example to truly raw material and the breadth and depth of the range of possibilities when the Moon's agents magically turn into form can be both amazing and humbling to the astrologer who observes its transformations.

From this treasure trove of material the planets dip into the Moon's reserves.

The lunar child searches with each subsequent sub-period for a representation of themselves which they can take forwards on their journey when the Moon's period is finished and the planets follow one another in the Chaldean Order.

A child born during the day will experience a Venus major period after the Sun at age ten, followed by Mercury at the age of eighteen.

For the child born during the night, their first nine year period needs to be rich in experimentation, intense and far ranging in emotional and physical experiences, as the planet which follows on from the Moon is Saturn, and the child is destined to meet a hard task-master before their tenth birthday.

FIRST Major Firdaria for the Nocturnal Chart		
☽ — 9 years		
9 years divided by 7 = 1 year 3 months 18 days		

Major MOON 9 yrs Sub-Period	Combination of Major (1st) and Minor (2nd) Time Lords	Minor Time Period BEGINS—ENDS for 1 yr 3 months *(1.3) *months as %
1	☽ / ☽	Birth – 1.3
2	☽ / ♄	1.3 – 2.6
3	☽ / ♃	2.6 – 3.9
4	☽ / ♂	3.9 – 5.1
5	☽ / ☉	5.1 – 6.4
6	☽ / ♀	6.4 – 7.7
7	☽ / ☿	7.7 – 9.0

Fig. 177 The Moon's Firdaria in the Nocturnal Chart

First Sub-Period
Donor – MOON : Recipient – MOON
(Birth – 1.3 Years)

The Moon's first sub-period when the Moon is both the major and minor lord is particularly sensitive to the circumstances of the child's natal Moon when the infant's early nourishment and their body is so small and delicate during the first fifteen months of life.

Valens' delineation on the Moon's sub-period is geared towards adult experiences, however, he does mention that a malefic in aspect to the Moon produces bodily weakness and sudden dangers.

In his delineations on the Moon's Firdaria Schoener allows for sect differences saying that if the Moon in a nocturnal chart is in an 'evil state', illness and injuries will happen to the infant, and sadly, *"his parents will shun him"*[144].

But if the Moon is in a good state, it signifies that the baby *"will be healthy in body and of good habits; his parents will love and honour him and will do good for him."*

The Moon's position as a recipient means that its susceptibility to another planet's influence in the chart is likely to be reflected in the child's own sensitivity to changes within its environment.

Schoener's words are a reminder of how easily a tiny life could slip away in earlier times of history when the medical profession was less informed and the birth process was dangerous for both mother and child, even more so when the family came from society's poorer sector.

Thankfully, modern medical practices mean that Schoener's words are not so dire for the infant of today's world, but it is worth noting that the Moon in poor state can indicate a weakness in the child's vitality and strength during the first year of life.

Second Sub-Period
Donor – MOON : Recipient – SATURN
(1.3 – 2.6 Years)

The Moon at the base of the Chaldean Order hands over to Saturn the highest-placed planet in the Order. This second period of the Moon's fifteen month sub-period can be gruelling for the nurturing parent who is experiencing broken sleep coupled with the reality of parenthood's endless responsibilities.

The Moon and Saturn are at odds in Thema Mundi because their respective signs are in opposition, and as both planets signify mother and father, any strain in their relationship can have repercussions for the nocturnal nativity, whose emotional radar is extremely sensitive to tension or discord between the parents even at this young age.

Valens looks at the adult and predicts that this interval will produce a year that is diverse and suspenseful for the native's mother, and, for the Moon who lends its material to Saturn, this is a time of withdrawal, illness or frustrations for the infant.

The diurnal nativity does not experience contact between the Moon and Saturn until the Moon's Firdaria when the individual born during the day is over thirty two years of age and the Moon donates its material to Saturn during its sub-period.

By this time the native has already navigated Saturn's Return and as an adult has achieved self-awareness to varying degrees, having had time to develop communication and reasoning skills, on top of achieving a modicum of power to control circumstances in life whilst Saturn has been orbiting their chart.

The nocturnal nativity does not have the same ability to react to Saturn's influence as they are barely past the first year of life.

The nocturnal nativity is placed at a distinct disadvantage given that they are governed by the Moon and are programmed to receive, rather than to emit like their contrary sect cousins who are ruled by the Sun. They must absorb the shock of the Moon and Saturn meeting for the first time through the Moon's Firdaria and as both planets signify the body – Moon as its general ruler and Saturn as the ruler of the skeletal system, the skin and the lungs – this period can show up any weaknesses in the infant's physical form.

Added to this is the fact that Saturn is generally perceived to be an out of sect in the nocturnal chart and its potential to be malefic is accentuated if there are no redeeming factors to counter against its loss of dignity in a night-time chart.

The infant does not yet possess adequate communication skills to express themselves, and the impact of Saturn's sub-period goes largely unnoticed unless there are dramatic health issues for the child.

However, this is the child's first contact with Saturn, and the effects are both physical and emotional. The awareness that mother and child are separate units can alarm the child, who suddenly becomes increasingly clingy and tearful if mother disappears from sight.

Saturn's term can mark the first period of separation anxiety, and as the demands of the child escalate and the mother becomes desperate to gain space or independence from a demanding child, the need for constant reassurance places both infant and adult in a stressful situation.

Saturn's sub-period is the time of 'two-year olds tantrums' and if the nocturnal child instinctively fears for their safety or feels rejected, then there can be an emotional backlash for future relationships in life.

If the Moon and Saturn are aspected in the natal chart, or if the Moon is in the latter degrees of most signs – Leo and Libra are the exceptions – then it is likely that the Moon is in the Terms of Saturn *(The Egyptian Terms, Fig. 167)*, and if this is the case, then Saturn responds to the Moon's material by taking a form which places the child's psyche on high alert for the first time.

Depending on the severity of the circumstances, a nocturnal Saturn can take the opportunity provided by the Moon's Firdaria to condition the child's Moon to anticipate the same cold feeling and emotional shut-down in the future, especially if triggered by Saturn's capacity to create situations of deprivation, fear or isolation in adulthood.

Third Sub-Period
Donor – MOON : Recipient – JUPITER
(2.6 – 3.9 Years)

The third sub-period for the Moon brings relief for both mother and child in the more positive form of Jupiter who brings opportunities to expand life's experiences and to provide a light at the end of a dark tunnel created by Saturn.

This is a better period for mother indicating an improvement in mother's status, livelihood, or her emotional stability and happiness.

Jupiter's term may bring increased socialising for the child, or the opportunity to explore an alternate environment other than the one in which the child is usually more comfortable or is better known.

If this exploration goes well, the child's confidence and skills can grow under Jupiter's watchful eye as Schoener predicts that the nocturnal child is increasing in every matter, that he is dearly loved, and that he brings joy to his parents.

Fourth Sub-Period
Donor – MOON : Recipient – MARS
(3.9 – 5.1 Years)

The fourth sub-period occurs at the mid-way point in the Moon's Firdaria and the Moon's material is placed in the hands of Mars, just prior to the native's fourth birthday.

The Moon is bound to be nervous when Mars steps forward to enthusiastically embrace its true form.

Firstly, Mars owns Scorpio, the sign least comfortable for the Moon as it is the Moon's sign of fall and Mars may meet a jittery Moon when it takes over from Jupiter. Secondly, the gentler nature of the Moon is not suited to the blunt tools that Mars can apply in order to create its own form and this difference in temperament is likely to add to the tension between the two planets.

Mars requires tougher stuff than the Moon is capable of providing, and this state is reflected in the delineations of both authors who suggest illness, injury and upheaval during Mars' short-term period.

The age of four brings bumps and scrapes as the toddler strains towards independence through the exploration of its physical environment and Mars may be kinder to the nocturnal child given the fact that it prefers the Moon's coolness and moisture to temper its own heat.

This phase of development may have already begun with Jupiter's sub-period a year earlier but the bravado that Mars feels honour-bound to display can challenge both the toddler and their carers during this term.

Tears and tantrums are the order of the day, and the carer as Moon's representative is bound to find manoeuvring through the mine-field which is the child's emotional state both vexing and exhausting, especially if a new sibling appears on the scene at this time.

The child's vocabulary is increasing by this stage so this may relieve some frustrations over not being understood. There is also the drama of the first year of education looming on the horizon at age five. The enforced discipline and order of school timetables can be challenging for the nocturnal nativity who fears new experiences provided by Mars during the fifteen months of its sub-period.

Fifth Sub-Period
Donor – MOON : Recipient – SUN
(5.1 – 6.4 Years)

The Sun's sub-period is one which Robert Hand uses for his example of the major lord as matter, and the minor lord as form.

Valens speaks unfavourably of the Sun's reaction to being asked to take over as recipient to Moon's matter.

Their natural roles are somewhat reversed, and in this sub-period the Moon acts contrary to its nature and emits (matter) whilst the Sun receives (matter) and is committed to produce results (form), which is not much to the Sun's liking.

For the diurnal birth, this particular combination of the Moon as donor and the Sun as recipient occurs during the Diurnal Firdaria's fourth major period when the native is between the ages of thirty six and thirty seven and a half years, and Valens warns that during this time one's livelihood is emptied, and that it produces a period of the greatest expenditures.

His delineation indicates difficulty for the native, and although the nocturnal nativity is still very young, it would be wise to keep his prediction in mind at a time when the child is moving away from the safety of a daily routine based at home, into an arena of foreign experiences and new authority figures represented by the Sun.

Schoener is more positive than Valens in his delineation of Sun's period, saying that the native will begin to go on journeys and that they will be changed from one status to another, and learning and intelligence will be increased – presumably travelling to school and gaining some independence and status by becoming a new student.

Schoener does warn that the child can be dogged by ill health during this period, but this is a standard expectation for the initial years of schooling, when children converge together and the lunar child's body is exposed to a variety of illnesses in a new environment.

It is worth noting that the Sun's period during the Moon's Firdaria once more involves two planets who represent mother and father (or grandfather), so there may be indications that one parent's actions or the events surrounding them has a profound influence on the parenting unit, and the extended family may need to deal with any unpleasant outcome during the Sun's tenure.

Sixth Sub-Period
Donor – MOON : Recipient – VENUS
(6.4 – 7.7 Years)

The Moon provides the material for Venus to take a more gracious and joyous form in the sixth sub-period, so one imagines that friendships, and an overall sense of well-being surrounds the child at this point in time.

If either the Moon or Venus are unfavourably situated, then friendships may be more strained, and instead of the native reaching out to socialise with other children, instead they can feel either emotionally or socially isolated from groups or activities.

This chapter can be a time when the native begins to understand there are differences between themselves and other children, and they may retreat to spend more time alone, or be painfully shy in making friends during these months.

One of the advantages of a parent being aware of a planet's influence during a particular Firdaria period, is that rather than pushing the reticent nocturnal child forward into a social situation which they feel ill-equipped to manage, it is far better to encourage Venus' involvement in another direction, whether it is through music, the arts, dance or imaginary friendships, especially if Venus in the child's chart is under duress from the malefic planets.

It would be far better for the lunar child to experience this period in a positive way and pass through it without added attention or stress from the parents.

This way, they feel neither pressured nor abnormally different from the children around them who are most likely going through a similar phase, but doing it differently according to their own individual chart or the chart's sect division. (The diurnal child is going through a Sun/Saturn sub-period at the same age and will be exploring their own state of social integration).

Seventh Sub-Period
Donor – MOON : Recipient – MERCURY
(7.7 – 9 Years)

The final period in the Moon's Firdaria is shaped by Mercury, who is generally quite prepared to take Moon's matter and to form opinions and judgements based on the native's knowledge of the family and the social environment in which they find themselves.

The variable fortunes of Mercury come into play here as life can change very rapidly during this fifteen month period when the Moon's volatile material is harnessed by an extremely fickle and unpredictable planet.

As a result, the native may find that there are sudden shifts in home environment or a change in schooling or social status as a consequence of one or both parents' situation.

The nature of the Moon donating to Mercury's form has the potential to create severe mood swings or behavioural changes in the child if the circumstances require them to explore a new landscape when relocation has taken place.

Their emotional pendulum is likely to swing between the two extreme positions, from excitement and anticipation at one extreme and back to the maximum position at the other end of the pendulum, where feelings of shock and fear of the unknown unsettles the child.

Both the Moon and Mercury are greatly influenced by natal aspects or by transits from the slower-moving planets. The nature of these planets has the ability to either alter the Moon's base material, or to change the form of Mercury.

Either way, this influence can create a situation which improves the native's lot in life and their sense of security, or suddenly snatches it away and causes life to become more complicated for the sensitive lunar child.

The High Art of Survival . . . SATURN

"I have a high art. I hurt with cruelty those who would damage me."

Archilocus, 650 BCE
Poet and Soldier

Second Nocturnal Major Period lasts for 11 Years

Saturn is Lord from 9 – 20th Birthday

Saturn's Matter and Significations:

Physical barriers	Father	Separations	Responsibility
Time	Agriculture	The sea	Isolation
Management	Boundaries	Hardship	Obstacles
Health issues	Authority	Foundations	

At first glance it would seem that Saturn's list of significations is better suited to adulthood when the native has a measure of control over how they will choose to accept Saturn's small print – its terms and conditions – on how life is going to be played out.

If an acceptance of Saturn's 'T's & C's' is not for the individual, life gets tough, and often the child moving into puberty feels resentment and rebellion as it rails against Saturn's restrictions. Puberty and raging hormones can cause the teenager to feel overwhelmed or exhausted by life's constant obstacles, so much so that depression and anxiety are part of their daily coping mechanisms.

The current trend of dividing the generations into *Baby Boomers, Generation X, Y, or Z*, and now the emergence of *Generation Alpha* is one of Saturn's ways of dividing people into groups via ageist stereotyping. At the same time it removes the individual's responsibility for their own actions and creates a mob mentality whereby one generation resents another, and all concerned believe that their woes are inherited from another generation's mismanagement.

For those who have been living on another planet, here are the definitions for the various age groups.

Boomers One (or Baby Boomers) were born after the Second World War (1946–1954); *Boomers Two (or Generation Jones)* are classified as being born between 1955 and 1965; *Generation X* is for those from 1966 to 1976; *Generation Y* became the group born from 1977 to 1994; *Generation Z* followed in the period between 1995 and 2012; and *Generation Alpha* is the last category to date with births occurring after 2012.

Gen X (1966-1976) is often described as the 'lost' generation, with the lowest voting participation of any generation and are a generation with a chip on the shoulder, blaming their parents for the elevation in their divorce rates and their own abandonment issues.

Gen Y (1977-1994) prides itself on being sophisticated, racially, ethnically and socially diverse in their politics, and are smug in the knowledge that they were born at the beginning of the technology revolution.

Gen Y attacks both ages of the *Boomers* for their materialistic ways, and the rise in today's real estate market, whilst the rebuke from the *Baby Boomers* is that *Gen Y* is spoilt, wasteful and self-indulgent.

Gen Z (1995-2012) is considered to be a more conservative and cautious group than their predecessors.

A US study found that *Gen Z* had the highest percentage of church attendance, has had less experimentation with alcohol or drugs at a young age, is more likely to wear their seat-belt in a car driven by another person, and has the lowest rate of teenage pregnancies when compared with the other generations at the same age.

They are concerned about the environment and clean energy and their ideal pin-up is Malala Yousafzai, the Pakastani education campaigner, who survived being shot by the Taliban, and who became the world's youngest ever Nobel Prize recipient.[145]

The new *Generation Alpha* (2012 - ?) has only just come into existence but they will have their own Saturn concerns as they grow up and alienate themselves from the previous generation, *Gen Z*, even though they are only a few years apart in age.

For every individual, regardless of what so-called Generation group they now belong to, the passage through the middle years between childhood and adulthood is a time when they trekked through this barren land alone and believed themselves to be uncared for, thinking that they are the only ones who suffered pain and rejection in their teenage years.

A large part of these painful in-between years is the memory of being incapable of relating to members of their own generation, so it really should not be surprising that the lunar child, a lonely child of pent-up emotion, visions and imagination, is required to travel through Saturn's landscape at a time when it is at its most inhospitable and frightening.

Saturn is the Lord of Time and is usually depicted as an emaciated and decrepit old man carrying the sickle of Death. This image carries a touch of irony (also Saturn's domain) that is not lost on the child who must battle through eleven years of Saturn, beginning at the tender age of nine years old.

The Ages of Man is another pattern of planetary periods which runs in reverse sequence to the Chaldean Order – beginning life with the Moon and completing its cycle with Saturn in old age – so there is plenty of time and a number of planets to pass before meeting the inevitable, when Saturn rules the final thirty years from sixty eight to ninety eight years of age.

Compare this scenario to the Nocturnal Firdaria when the child born during the night must jump from the comfort of the Moon's ample breast straight into the skeletal arms of Saturn and as his grip tightens, the lunar child receives his embrace and gets ready to learn his lessons in the next decade of Saturn's reign.

Saturn is the itinerant. The judge on his circuit, the vagabond on the road, the old man who is driven from his home, or the one who in their youth, chooses of his own freewill to 'jump before he is pushed,' and roams the world as a stranger, cut off from loved ones and the security of his own hearth.

In exchange for the comforts of home the traveller, often the pilgrim searching for truth, gains resilience and freedom for both mind and body.

As the traveller wanders with no clear destination, they witness all things foreign to their own ways and avoiding unfavourable comparisons or harsh judgements, they prefer instead to embrace the differences without fear or favour.

Today's travel industry really does not cater for this kind of traveller, instead charting peaks and lows in travel periods to accommodate the wishes and work timetables of its clients.

The same industry uses the term 'shoulder season' to describe the time interval that falls between the peak and low seasons, when fares tend to be relatively low.

The shoulder season is considered to be good value for several reasons.

The crowds are thinner, the locals are friendlier, flights and accommodation rates are lower than during peak season, and the days are usually more temperate than the peak season in the summer months or the snow season during the winter period.

Travelling during the shoulder season is desirable as it offers the visitor a combination of reasonable prices and fairly decent weather.

How much smoother would the transition be, if the lunar child could envisage Saturn's major period between the ages of nine and twenty, as nothing more than life's 'shoulder season'?

The days of the shoulder season are not without their drawbacks and can be somewhat bleak in nature.

The exhibits are often closed to the public, the weather is unpredictable, the choices in accommodation are restricted, and there is more time spent alone on deserted platforms where extra transport has not yet been put in force.

But there are also advantages in passing through this time unencumbered by excess baggage and others' inflated expectations of what travelling means for them, but what is mostly immaterial for the adolescent.

Freedom is a personal concept – it can describe childhood when the individual is free from responsibilities and worry about the future, or freedom can describe adulthood when the individual is free to make their own decisions and choices in life.

Either way, Saturn provides a breathing space, or a shoulder season, where the person can decide over the eleven year period what freedom means for them.

The nocturnal child is influenced by the Moon in the same way as the Moon influences the tides, and the ebb and flow of emotions can be easily disturbed under Saturn's Firdaria.

This period of adolescence can be difficult, confusing and often painful, and the fact that Saturn is uncomfortable within the confines of a nocturnal chart can mean that life's shoulder season can turn cold, alien and dangerous without any warning during the pre-pubescent years.

It is best to remember that common sense and a good grounding with plenty of support from loved ones is the best strategy to survive a planet geared to teach the child (or their parent) about the physical limitations of their world.

Time spent learning Saturn's lessons in sound qualities such as composure, self-sufficiency and pragmatism, may in the long run, be far more useful to the native, than the lessons the solar child is learning – parallel in time but not in essence.

Tutored by Venus from the ages of ten to eighteen, the solar child learns different lessons in diplomacy, social acceptance, craftsmanship and personal adornment which will aid the diurnal nativity in reaching their own goals in the future.

There can be no comparison between which is the 'better' path, as they are merely different expressions of the same planet under different conditions and experienced at a different time in life.

Thankfully, we are not capable of living two lives at the same time, or to contemplate why the moment of birth occurred during the night instead of during the day.

These are questions of fate, providence and destiny and are far beyond our mortal comprehension.

However, acknowledging the differences is something an astrologer *can do,* and taking these skills and this knowledge with them into the consulting room, has enormous potential to help the client recognise the signposts which are laid out for them through the lens of planetary sect and the two versions of the Firdaria system.

SECOND Major Firdaria for the Nocturnal Chart ♄ — 11 years 11 years divided by 7 = 1 year 6 months 26 days		
Major **SATURN** **11 yrs** Sub-Period	Combination of Major (1st) and Minor (2nd) Time Lords	Minor Time Period BEGINS—ENDS for 1 yr 7 months *(1.6) *months as %
1	♄ / ♄	9.0 – 10.6
2	♄ / ♃	10.6 – 12.1
3	♄ / ♂	12.1 – 13.7
4	♄ / ☉	13.7 – 15.3
5	♄ / ♀	15.3 – 16.9
6	♄ / ☿	16.9 – 18.4
7	♄ / ☽	18.4 – 20.0

Fig. 178 Saturn's Firdaria in the Nocturnal Chart

First Sub-Period
Donor – SATURN : Recipient – SATURN
(9 – 10.6 Years)

Beginning at nine years of age and lasting for nineteen months, the period where Saturn is both the matter and the form can be a hard for the native to find much relief, especially if the father figure (also represented by Saturn) is confronting his own demons during this time.

Whilst the native's parents may pride themselves in sheltering their child from the harsh realities of life, the nocturnal child's inner compass directs them towards uncovering emotional upheaval, no matter how well it is masked by brave smiles and gestures of normality.

This is a case where imagination can be worse than reality, and a parent's duty may lie in sitting down to explain the situation with truth and clarity as this may ease a child's worry about the future.

If Saturn should aspect either Mars or Mercury in the natal chart, the troubles are based on events signified by these two planets. Mars can bring flare-ups of overt verbal or physical violence, or Mercury can be more insidious in its nature – implied violence where the native 'reads between the lines', and fear takes hold within the child's mind.

Second Sub-Period
Donor – SATURN : Recipient – JUPITER
(10.6 – 12.1 Years)

From Saturn's dark matter is carved a brighter and more uplifting form belonging to Jupiter, whose natural tendency is to expand and lighten the nineteen month period for which it is responsible.

Saturn's severity is tempered by Jupiter's optimism, and this sub-period features a sense of expectancy and nervous anticipation for the native on the brink of their teenage years.

Schoener says that good things will happen for the native and that he will gain benefit from the favours bestowed on him by others.

If Jupiter is seconded by Saturn to ease its burden of responsibility, then Jupiter activates a certain bravado and self-confidence in the native, providing a welcome lull in schooling or learning as lessons are more revisionary than the next leap into secondary education.

The child tends to possess a somewhat cocky 'know-it-all' attitude around the first Jupiter Return, which will be modified or tempered by Saturn for its own use in the remaining years of its major Firdaria period.

Third Sub-Period
Donor – SATURN : Recipient – MARS
(12.1 – 13.7 Years)

Valens is bleak in his delineation of a period when two malefic planets oversee the events of life, predicting the worst and most dangerous term, as Mars becomes the instrument of Saturn's will and the potential is there for Mars to cause harm and distress.

This sub-period belonging to Mars stands at the threshold of the years of the 'puberty blues' and the emerging teenager of a nocturnal nature is experiencing every nuance of emotional highs and lows at this point in their lives.

This period is likely to be about the child's perception of the world around them rather than how it actually is, and Mars becomes a tool for self-protection, as the often belligerent behaviour of the pre-pubescent erupts internally and externally into a body they barely recognise as their own any more.

To the nocturnal child, Valens is not wrong in his prediction.

To the sensitive teenager on the knife-edge of drama, angst and the constant battle to maintain emotional normality, the term belonging to Mars *feels like a dangerous year.*

If they are the instigator of one drama after another then authority figures such as Saturn describes, are likely to come down hard on them, even at this young age.

If Juliet from Shakespeare's *Romeo and Juliet* had been born during the night, this would be the time in the story when she takes her own life because she believes that her lover is dead.

This period is bleak, reactionary and its problems are distorted.

Saturn's normal reasoning ability or its radar on reality is somewhat askew during Mars' sub-period, and patience and gentle handling are required by the Saturnian adults during this period of a child's life, especially when the combination of malefics are present in a nocturnal chart.

Valens predicts trouble from a variety of fronts.

Friends who are ungracious, separations or an unsettling period for family members, conflict with superiors, and poor health or the death of the father or elder persons.

Mars' placement in the chart will give some indication as to where the native perceives the source of the trouble to be, and perception will colour the severity or intent of the attacks. No amount of rationalisation by an adult will convince the child that the slights are minor and that the current disaster is not a permanent state of affairs and that 'this too shall pass'.

Fourth Sub-Period
Donor – SATURN : Recipient – SUN
(13.7 – 15.3 Years)

This sub-period describes two planets still in conflict through their signs of opposition, but Schoener's text of a Sun sub-period during Saturn's Firdaria is more encouraging than Valens' delineation on the same combination.

Schoener says the native will increase in strength and worth, and that they can gain success if they work toward a particular goal.

Valens calls Sun's term a 'suspenseful year' and warns of a threat to the health and safety of the father, who is jointly signified by these two planets, but this may be more a conflict over rules and boundaries set by the father, and rebelled against by the teenager.

Concurrent with the Sun's sub-period, is the time when transiting Saturn's opposition to its own natal position is at half-way point for the Saturn Return at twenty eight years of age.

The year between fourteen and fifteen is generally the period when transiting Saturn opposes natal Saturn, and power struggles between parent and child reflect Saturn's issues over control as the youth struggles to find independence and subsequently clashes with the older generation.

The Sun's sub-period can be an intoxicating time if the adolescent is winning praise or attention in the sporting or educational arena, and as much as a glimpse of their future potential is enticing, it also brings out protective behaviour in parents who know that a parallel development in maturity is necessary to accompany the teenager's budding potential.

The best hope for the mid-point period of Saturn's Firdaria is that a little magic may occur in this tough period. Like the alchemist who prays for the transmutation of matter, perhaps under modified sect conditions, with the perfect pressure applied, and just the right amount of love and care, then metaphorically speaking, Saturn's lead *can* be turned into the Sun's gold.

Fifth Sub-Period
Donor – SATURN : Recipient – VENUS
(15.3 – 16.9 Years)

When the fifth sub-period of Saturn's term arrives, Venus steps forward to take her place as Saturn's recipient. The alternating feelings of intense love and hate must give Venus the sensation that she has just sacrificed herself at the altar of Saturn, rather than stepped up for a different post in a new job.

Venus is the perfect form for Saturn to guide the native through experiences in attraction or repulsion, and the resultant heart-ache is a good opportunity for the Moon-orientated nocturnal child to exercise their emotions as they encounter Cupid's sharp arrows.

Crushes, whispered confidences, sly glances and break-up songs are par for the course during Venus' sub-period, and whilst adults are bemused by the levels at which teenage drama can quickly escalate, for the young adult it is a serious business.

If their heartfelt passion is ridiculed or reduced in importance by their peers or the adults in their life, the pain they experience is excruciatingly real, and the inability to express this inner pain leaves them feeling isolated, misunderstood and miserable.

Saturn is the material behind Venus' form in its desire to connect with others, or to form relationships. Saturn Venus is the period when a broken-hearted nocturnal Romeo discovers his dead lover and takes his own life.

Dark moments of despair cannot be underestimated, especially in these times where personal comments become fodder for social media exposure that can add further humiliation and suffering during Saturn's nineteen month period.

Valens' text can be modernised to include the deplorable act of absentee bullying in social media, especially when it is a coward's retreat for those who themselves are often isolated or rejected, and who in turn, target and persecute another human being, in the name of Saturn's dark donation to the socially-hungry Venus.

Sixth Sub-Period
Donor – SATURN : Recipient – MERCURY
(16.9 – 18.4 Years)

Mercury becomes the lord of the shorter term after Venus, and in modern times is finishing the upper years of schooling.

These are the years when serious studies take over from the concerns of the heart as thoughts turn towards the future, and the desire to become a functioning, productive member of society increases under Saturn's influence.

Saturn donates to Mercury who must fashion plans for the next few years after secondary school. Mercury is required to instigate conversations on what qualifications are needed for the future, how specialisation in courses can be achieved, and when copious discussions with parents, elders, teachers, and experts in their field are useful to help the school-leaver's future.

If study is not part of the future plan, thoughts of job interviews, applications and forms, living accommodation, driving licenses etc., all require serious thought and planning at this time in life. Mercury's form is driven by Saturn's need to get it right and the volatile nature of this sub-period lords is such that it levitates between mental exhaustion, anxiety about the future, and pure excitement as dozens of possibilities open up with the movement into adult territory.

Seventh Sub-Period
Donor – SATURN : Recipient – MOON
(18.4 – 20 Years)

This is the second time that these two planets have met in the shortest period of time – that is, if you call seventeen years a short period of time.

The first time Moon and Saturn met the individual was just over one year old when the Moon was the major planet who donated her matter to sub-lord Saturn, resulting in a difficult and exhausting time for mother (Moon), father (Saturn), and the native themselves, with the condition of the Moon in particular indicating how tough this year was for the entire family.

This time when the Moon meets Saturn, it is Saturn who is the master, and the Moon who is seconded into his charge, and it is she who is expected to comply with his wishes.

Again, it is likely to be the Moon's condition which dictates this period, but the difference lies in the fact that the Moon is a gentler form than Saturn is capable of providing, so whilst there are warnings of illness and difficult times for mother, the Moon is more sensitive to the needs of others and the native's emotional state at this time.

Part of the Moon's period involves leaving childhood behind, its friendships, alliances, confidantes, lovers, even enemies.

The loosening of bonds brings nostalgic times and frightening times, fear of the future, fear of failure, fear of not meeting family's expectations and fear of being suffocated under the weight of others' demands.

The Moon's sub-period is Saturn's last hoorah so far as its Firdar is concerned, and with the aid of the Moon, Saturn's Firdaria comes to full term with highly emotional experiences of cutting ties and voluntary or necessary separations.

At this time the native begins to dismantle the scaffolding which has supported them throughout childhood and begins the solitary task of building the first foundations of adulthood as they celebrate their twentieth birthday.

The shoulder season is finally over and the traveller returns to life, sometimes tired and jaded by their experiences in a foreign landscape, but this is not always the case.

Sometimes the traveller returns with a renewed faith in their own resources knowing that they have journeyed alone through inhospitable territory and have triumphed over sorrow, weariness and isolation.

It is hard to know if experiencing Saturn's Firdaria at such a young age is a blessing or a curse.

Perhaps the traveller's answer to that would be 'it's an interesting place to visit, but you wouldn't want to live there.'

The Level of our Success . . . JUPITER

*"The level of our success is limited only by our imagination,
and no act of kindness, however small, is ever wasted."*

Aesop (620-560 BCE)

Third Nocturnal Major Period lasts for 12 Years

Jupiter is Lord From 20 – 32nd Birthday

Jupiter's Matter and Significations:

Growth	Children	Success	Knowledge
Prosperity	Ambition	Good Fortune	Love and Friendship
Authority	Freedom	Abundance	Politics

The benefits produced by Jupiter may have a greater long-term effect for the diurnal birth who experiences the Jupiter/Jupiter period later in life at the age of fifty one, as they have often accrued wealth and achieved acknowledgement or success in their chosen field, after the previous years of Saturn's hard work.

For the nocturnal birth Saturn's period has been about growing up through the alienation and angst of the teenage years.

Building Saturnian foundations for Jupiter's triumph in the coming years through commitment to a career was not part of their experience, as there was little they had control over, and many of the decisions made during Saturn's previous eleven years were largely out of their hands.

Therefore, Jupiter's rich years will have a different expression for the nocturnal native, as the diurnal benefic is far more concerned with building for the future in the next twelve years, rather than in basking in the glory of the present or producing the fruits of Saturn's immediate past.

Jupiter can afford to be magnanimous in a diurnal chart.

Time is still precious but the years between fifty one and sixty three afford plenty of opportunity to reflect on one's own good fortune, and to act with generosity toward the younger generation, who are struggling to achieve the same levels of success and comfort as they have achieved.

For a nocturnal chart Jupiter's twelve years are expansive in a different way.

These are years of romantic yearnings and idealist visions of the future, as well as a time for gaining knowledge and expertise.

Jupiter is the material of optimism, countless possibilities and youthful potential where one is only limited by the imagination, and generosity of spirit is a badge best worn by those who have not yet been beaten down by life, or been made to watch others rise at the native's own expense.

This is not to say that all twelve years belonging to Jupiter will be brimming with joy and benefit as both malefics will take their turn along with the other planets.

But if Saturn's eleven years were hard on the soul, then with good fortune, kindness and the direction of well-meaning individuals, the native has the opportunity to find where they can best use their considerable skills and to find out where their service is most beneficial.

It is too simplistic to say that the Sun serves one-self, whilst the Moon serves others and that each luminary pursues happiness and satisfaction through these avenues.

We live in a solar system where the planets, including Earth, depend on the light source which is the Sun, whilst the Moon, a satellite of Earth, has no energy source save the projected light of the Sun.

One luminary emits, and the other one receives.

Jupiter belongs to the sect with the luminary that emits and will naturally take the light of the Sun and expand it into areas of success, authority, ambition, knowledge and politics.

If Jupiter has to serve the luminary which is naturally tuned to receive, it will do so by promoting the Moon through its other significations, such as love and friendship, children, good fortune and abundance.

The years of Jupiter offer the nocturnal chart life's first painful experiences and its long-term period is as much about one's early failures as it is about one's successes.

Often our greatest learning curve occurs after a dismal failure and the passing of Jupiter's longer period to the remaining planets is an opportunity for each one to teach the young adult about their own concept of pass and fail.

Valens' list of the planets' effects at the beginning of this chapter can be applied to the idea of falling or failing according to each planet's nature.

Jupiter is the ruler of rank, crowns and zeal and as the first participant in Jupiter's Firdaria at the age of twenty, the nocturnal youth's idealism on how swiftly they will rise through the ranks is likely to be punctured during this term. The belief that the world has been waiting for them is quickly followed by the realization that it is going to take more than zeal to get ahead in life.

Mars is the ruler of action and effort and Mars is the second sub-period lord. At twenty one some actions are going to be useful and others will be a waste of time. Likewise, some efforts are fruitful and Jupiter can work from these beginnings and others lead nowhere and frankly – are not worth the effort.

The Sun rules light but exposing our mistakes and foolish behaviour to the world can be humiliating.

Venus rules love, desire, and beauty and there are so many hits and misses in relationships during Jupiter's middle period.

Mercury is the ruler of law, friendship and trust and during Jupiter's Firdaria Mercury can provide opportunities to explore any or all three of these possibilities. Whether they are good experiences or more of Jupiter's 'learning curves' is largely up to the individual.

The Moon rules foresight but Jupiter's Firdaria may teach the young lunar adult that intuition can sometimes be wrong and trusting in the Moon's 'sixth sense' can lead them into poor decisions or heartache.

Saturn rules ignorance and necessity and it takes its turn as Jupiter's final sub-period lord at the age of thirty so perhaps this in an ideal time to contemplate on what reveals our ignorance and what we believe to be necessary in life.

THIRD Major Firdaria for the Nocturnal Chart
♃ — 12 years
12 years divided by 7 = 1 year 8 months 17 days

Major JUPITER 12 yrs — Sub-Period	Combination of Major (1st) and Minor (2nd) Time Lords	Minor Time Period BEGINS—ENDS for 1 yr 8 months *(1.7) *months as %
1	♃ / ♃	20.0 – 21.7
2	♃ / ♂	21.7 – 23.4
3	♃ / ☉	23.4 – 25.1
4	♃ / ♀	25.1 – 26.9
5	♃ / ☿	26.9 – 28.6
6	♃ / ☽	28.6 – 30.3
7	♃ / ♄	30.3 – 32.0

Fig. 179 Jupiter's Firdaria in the Nocturnal Chart

First Sub-Period
Donor – JUPITER : Recipient – JUPITER
(20 – 21.7 Years)

This first period where Jupiter is both the donor and the recipient bodes well for the native according to both sources.

Valens says that Jupiter distributing to itself produces a time which is good and effectual, whilst Schoener says that the native will be changed from a low state to a good one.

They will go forth from every trouble to every good fortune, his wealth will increase, and happiness is a distinct possibility for the native's state of mind.

The sign and placement of Jupiter as well as the houses it rules in the natal chart, will give an indication of how and where the native may find the freedom and confidence to enjoy this period which lasts almost two years.

Support and aid from friends and mentors may help to guide the native towards finding benefit and purpose.

Schoener says that this time is especially beneficial if Jupiter is in Sagittarius, or happens to be in its own terms, or the terms of Venus.

Valens mentions *"release from bonds"* and *"freedom"* in his own list on Jupiter's significations, and this may be the greatest gift of Jupiter's first sub-period when it is both material and form.

The release from Saturn's bonds, liberation from the pressure of rigid timetables enforced by childhood schooling, and relief from total dependency on parents are reasons enough for the celebration of freedom.

Even if only for a short period until reality sets in and thoughts of the future encroach on the exhilaration of being free, and instead turn toward the responsibilities of taking care of oneself.

Second Sub-Period
Donor – JUPITER : Recipient – MARS
(21.7 – 23.4 Years)

Jupiter hands over the reins to Mars and at twenty one years of age, a heady mix of these two planets can produce an interval that is poorly handled by the inexperienced young adult.

The force and power which naturally drives Mars may catch the youth unawares as they do not have years of experience behind them to manage Mars' full-on energy.

The diurnal chart experiences this same combination at the age of fifty two, and whilst the nocturnal youth has the advantage of physical prowess to withstand Mars' onslaught, the diurnal individual owns the discipline to direct Mars towards a focused, productive or positive form during its twenty month stint under Jupiter's supervision.

Jupiter driving Mars in the chart of a twenty one year old suggests a donor with incredible power attempting to direct a recipient whose principle significations include force, violence, banishment, anger and quarrels.

Physical safety is one of the concerns during Mars' sub-period, as the combination of the two planets in a nocturnal chart can result in risk-taking to the point of stupidity, or pushing the physical limits through speed, force or an imagined concept of bravery or courage.

This is not a time to 'play chicken' with one's life as Mars will take the excesses of Jupiter, and add its own dangerous qualities to create a potentially deadly mix if common sense or self-preservation is missing in the nocturnal youth's psyche at this age.

Mars denotes masculinity and lightening reflexes, and Jupiter's galvanising energy creates the astrological equivalent of a huge injection of testosterone just itching to prove itself, especially if it is operating without the control or direction of Saturn.

Mars creates a force of incredible energy which can place the native in the way of harm, usually of their own volition when they are pitted against friends, superiors or enemies.

The nocturnal child often mimics the Moon's irregularly lit path and, unlike the Sun-child, struggles with setting clear goals and staying the course, so when the dozen years governed by Jupiter appears at a young age the number and variety of choices is intoxicating for the native.

When Mars adds its own bravado to Jupiter's matter, and as Valens says *"It controls the hard and the abrupt"*, Mars oscillates between actions which challenge the world around them, and deep-rooted insecurities based on a crisis in identity or a misconceived belief in life's futility.

This fluctuation in the young male or female adult's attitude and behaviour often leads to an escalation in situations where the native feels they are beset by trouble, enemies, diminished finances, and worries over stable employment.

No matter that their own actions may have led to a number of these stressful situations. A sense of perspective and a realisation of one's own mistakes is definitely not a trademark of the Jupiter major period with Mars in control.

The *'act of kindness, however small'* which Aesop speaks of as an accompaniment to the limitlessness of the imagination, is a little scarce on the ground during Mars' term, so it is left to the Sun to repair any lingering damage in the sub-period which follows in the wake of Mars' destruction.

Third Sub-Period
Donor – JUPITER : Recipient – SUN
(23.4 – 25.1 Years)

During the third sub-period the Sun takes Jupiter's material and forms its own interpretation of success, personal achievement and productivity.

Jupiter has been aware of the rise in the native's potential over the past three and half years of its major period, but it needs the Sun's brilliance to illuminate the nocturnal personality and lead it into the light.

The Sun's phase brings the possibility of fostering self-confidence and activates dormant ambitions, providing a clarity of mind and a conscious awareness of the native's role in society, a fact which may have been hidden, or completely absent, during Mars' sub-period.

The Sun's role as the Universe's principle source of light and warmth shines perhaps for the first time on the night-time person, and sometimes increased attention or enthusiasm can be overwhelming for a highly emotional individual.

Schoener predicts a marked improvement in honours and wealth which is to be expected during the Sun's sub-period.

However, he also says that the native's understanding will increase, and whilst he may have been referring to an increase of a scholastic nature, the Sun also has the ability to bless the native with self-understanding and a desire to commit to the adult world.

This Sun period can be very powerful for the young nocturnal searching to find a suitable place within the solar world where they feel comfortable, or if they so desire, where they can take their place as a useful and productive member of society.

Fourth Sub-Period
Donor – JUPITER : Recipient – VENUS
(25.1 – 26.9 Years)

The middle period of Jupiter's Firdar belongs to Venus, and this is a time when the native's natural ability to work within a world where emotions, intuition and a good sense of the 'unspoken' comes to their aid as they form strong alliances.

This is the time when the night-born can use their considerable social skills to gain advancement, social advantage, and even fulfil Venus' desire for love and happiness.

Schoener says the native gains the attention of powerful friends and superiors, and that if they conduct their affairs well and wisely, they can gain good fortune during Venus' twenty month period.

The level of good fortune will greatly depend on Venus' condition in the natal chart, and poor condition because of sign, or aspects to malefic planets, can quickly dissolve good luck and turn benefit into scandal and disrepute.

Although the predictions are for the good, a word of advice on moderation and self-restraint comes with Venus' sub-period.

The nature of Jupiter's excessive material in combination with Venus in the form of flaws in the character, such as indolence or self-gratification, can bring about the native's downfall through hedonistic behaviour.

Venus in debility has the potential to describe morally or socially corrupt behaviour and any suspect dealings or associations with the criminal element or intemperate individuals, will likely lead the individual into trouble, or damage the native's reputation.

Jupiter's protection may not be enough if Venus is hell-bent on self destruction, or becomes infatuated with lovers and friends who do not have the person's best interests at heart, but will discard them at the first sign of trouble.

Fifth Sub-Period
Donor – JUPITER : Recipient – MERCURY
(26.9 – 28.6 Years)

There are mixed blessings for the liaison between Jupiter and the fifth sub-lord, Mercury, as their natural opposition can cause poor communication between the two planets.

Jupiter's material is somewhat overwhelming for Mercury, who constantly changes its form to accommodate the current moment in time.

Mercury's eagerness to communicate Jupiter's wishes may not always work out well as Schoener remarks that this is a time when the native will display good morals, and that he will be patient and benign, but that his good-natured temperament will be tested by a poor business environment which works to his own disadvantage.

Schoener states that *"he will stand firm in vain"* and that he will have to face the ordeal alone as *"his own friends will fly from him and will become his enemies"*.

This text suggests that Mercury's usual prudence has deserted the native and they may need to put aside a gentle or kind temperament in order to protect themselves during a difficult period when others are busy seeing to their own needs, or wilfully destroying the native's reputation for their own advancement.

An early Saturn Return during this phase may upset Mercury's plans or add a quality of mental stress, anxiety or worry to this period, especially if promises of assistance are abandoned or blockages and autocratic red-tape frustrates Mercury's crafty schemes which are egged on by Jupiter's unrealistic dreams of success.

Sixth Sub-Period
Donor – JUPITER : Recipient – MOON
(28.6 – 30.3 Years)

The following twenty month patch belongs to the Moon and there is a level of affinity between Jupiter as a beneficial donor, and the luminary that lends Cancer to Jupiter for its own exaltation.

This situation suggests that Jupiter has a good working relationship with the Moon, and should Saturn's return to its natal position occur at the beginning of the Moon's sub-period, the major sect luminary will settle the native's nerves during this time of upheaval and guide them through a re-evaluation of their priorities in life.

The Moon is eager to please Jupiter as it feels supported by the greater benefic, even though they belong to different sides of the fence in terms of planetary sect.

Jupiter means no harm to the Moon, so that when she relaxes she comes bearing gifts and benefits for the native.

The Moon's term should be a time when there is breathing space on all levels – physically, emotionally and psychically – if the native is proceeding through their Saturn Return at this time in life.

If changes must be made for Saturn to relinquish things that it no longer needs, then it is best that it occurs during a Firdaria which supports the health and well-being of the native.

There may be a need for isolation, withdrawal for reflection or a necessary separation during Saturn's year of return but a Jupiter Firdar with the Moon as its helper will hopefully provide a counter-balance for a difficult year when letting go can be painful.

Jupiter's ability to 'see the big picture' may flow through to the Moon, who shields the nocturnal's sensitive feelings by adopting Jupiter's philosophical view, and on a practical level, provides the native with respite and a reasonably quick recovery from Saturn's ills.

Seventh Sub-Period
Donor – JUPITER : Recipient – SATURN
(30.3 – 32 Years)

A few months after the thirtieth birthday Saturn, who has been previously occupied by its own Return, presents itself for duty as Jupiter's final sub-period lord.

Schoener predicts a poor finish to Jupiter's Firdaria, warning that the native will be shunned by their brothers, friends and comrades who will put all their efforts into causing harm and evil for the native.

The saving grace of this final period lies in this being a time when the individual's resolve and character is tested through delays and postponements as they enact changes wrought by Saturn's Return.

It may not feel like the perfect time to pause and reflect on the past ten years but Saturn, as the lord of Time, sets up its own schedule and is not bothered if we are not happy with its choices.

Jupiter is prepared to keep the material coming thick and fast for Saturn to fashion into a range of trying experiences designed to test the mettle of the individual.

Jupiter's donation to Saturn is not always easy to accept and it requires a strong heart and an iron will to withstand the onslaught of Saturn who is bent on inflicting some measure of loss, injury or despair during its twenty month period of Jupiter's Firdaria.

The Dance of Battle . . . MARS

"The dance of battle is always played to the same impatient rhythm.
What begins in a surge of violent motion is always reduced to the
perfectly still."

Sun Tzu (544 – 496 BCE)

Fourth Nocturnal Major Period lasts for 7 Years

Mars is Lord from 32 – 39th Birthday

Mars' Matter and Significations:

Conflict	Energy	Force	Ambitions
Focus	Bad Fortune	Leadership	Courage
Motivation	Masculinity	Competition	Physicality

Mars belongs to the same planetary sect as the Moon, so for the nocturnal individual Mars is better behaved and has more potential for positive actions.

It does not have the same 'bite' as it does for the diurnally born individual, and a tempered Mars may begin its seven year Firdaria *"in a surge of violent motion"*, but hopefully, under the gentle guidance of the Moon, there will also be times during this long-term period when Mars will be *"reduced to the perfectly still."*

Only then might its true potential be examined and as the donating principle, perhaps other planets will be able to move in as recipients, free from the damage caused by Mars' impatient dance of battle.

Mars is more comfortable when it is removed from the Sun's glare as its own qualities are extreme in heat and dryness, so it prefers to be removed from the solar heat source.

Mars takes on a cooler and more controlled temperament in the chart of a nocturnal birth.

It is not so hot-tempered or impetuous in nature, and is more inclined towards defensive rather than offensive behaviour, especially in terms of attack and conflict.

The person born during the night will have the opportunity to fully experience Mars' benefits and drawbacks during what is effectively, the middle period of the Nocturnal Firdaria experience.

Mars' long-term period is the pivotal point in the Nocturnal Firdaria, and is met by the much younger individual in a night-time chart, than the diurnal birth which experiences Mars' Firdaria between the ages of sixty three and seventy years of age.

The virility, the heightened level of competitiveness, the sexual and physical energy created by Mars in the night-time chart meets a younger warrior from the ages of thirty two to thirty nine years.

These are the years when a person focuses on their ambitions, and competition with peers and work colleagues is often the impetus which causes the individual to strive a little harder, aim a little higher, to make their mark in business and personal relationships.

Mars' Firdaria can highlight ruthless business tactics, accelerated career advantages, and movement between jobs and employers and these can be exhausting actions especially if they are occurring at the same time as establishing a young family or purchasing real estate. Risk-taking may be more appealing to the younger model in the forms of stock market speculation or investments as Mars thrives halfway along the Nocturnal Firdaria between the event of birth and the celebration of the seventieth birthday.

FOURTH Major Firdaria for the Nocturnal Chart ♂ — 7 years 7 years divided by 7 = 1 year		
Major **MARS** **7 yrs** Sub-Period	Combination of Major (1st) and Minor (2nd) Time Lords	Minor Time Period BEGINS—ENDS for 1 year
1	♂ / ♂	32.0 – 33.0
2	♂ / ☉	33.0 – 34.0
3	♂ / ♀	34.0 – 35.0
4	♂ / ☿	35.0 – 36.0
5	♂ / ☽	36.0 – 37.0
6	♂ / ♄	37.0 – 38.0
7	♂ / ♃	38.0 – 39.0

Fig. 180 Mars' Firdaria for the Nocturnal Chart

First Sub-Period
Donor – MARS : Recipient – MARS
(32 – 33 Years)

Although Valens is aware of the impact of sect on the two malefic planets, he does not allow for the change in their behaviour according to whether they are working within the parameters of their own favoured sect.

He does not compensate for a well-tempered version of Mars directing its energy towards successful outcomes in a nocturnal chart.

Instead he says that this term will be unpleasant and full of trouble and that Mars instigates conflict, and causes rivalry and friction with others, abuse of public matters, or dealings with those who squander public funds.

Schoener's Mars fares no better, saying that during the Mars sub-period the native will behave in the manner of an evil-doer, and because of this, they will be involved in long legal conflicts and that family will turn against them and their enemies will multiply in number.

The only chance of leniency from attack is if natal Mars is found in the terms of Jupiter or Venus.

Second Sub-Period
Donor – MARS : Recipient – SUN
(33 – 34 Years)

Schoener's text suggests a poor relationship between Mars and the Sun which may be more significant in the chart of a diurnal birth. He predicts that during Sun's period the native's friends and brothers will shun and flee from him, and that he will be arrested because of his comrades.

At first glance Mars donating to the Sun seems to bring little relief from trouble; if anything it causes difficulty for the father figure, or brings contention with elders or those in authority.

However, a nocturnal Mars has an interesting relationship with the solar luminary as the Sun is no longer a damaging force for Mars. Rather than an over-heated Mars being agitated or unrestrained and running the risk of alienating powerful people, the Sun may be able to use this version of Mars to produce a more beneficial outcome for the native during its term.

Whilst this may be the case, it is worth noting that the Sun has a certain level of intolerance with being the recipient of either malefic planet's material, and even struggles when it is sub-lord for the Moon.

It seems the Sun considers the material presented by these planets is inappropriate or is deemed to be inferior for the Sun to create a form to its liking, and this will mean trouble for the period under its jurisdiction.

Third Sub-Period
Donor – MARS : Recipient – VENUS
(34 – 35 Years)

The signs belonging to these planets are natural opposites in Thema Mundi, and for this reason Venus' phase should indicate tensions within relationships on both personal and professional levels.

However, Mars and Venus share a commonality in that they both prefer the Moon as their prime luminary, and would be considered to have accidental dignity in a nocturnal chart.

For this reason, the improved material donated to Venus by Mars has the potential to bring forward Venusian forms which favour beauty, games, songs and all manner of pleasurable pursuits.

Transactions with women are prominent during the time belonging to Venus, and provided that Mars is honourable, respectful and fair in its dealings, exchanges can be mutually beneficial for both parties.

Fourth Sub-Period
Donor – MARS : Recipient – MERCURY
(35 – 36 Years)

Mercury becomes the sub-lord for Mars in the native's mid thirties, and neither Valens nor Schoener speak well of an interval when Mercury is needed to provide form for a donor which is known for being wayward and fractious in temperament.

Even in the best of conditions, Mercury requires clear direction and good management if it is to be seconded for a particular task during this year, and Mars may not be able to supply stability or focus for Mercury, even if it is required by the nocturnal native.

Schoener states that hardship and injury will happen to the individual, mainly due to the evil whisperings of others against their good name.

The damage and impact of others' mischief will greatly depend on the condition of Mercury in the natal chart, as any extra contact with the malefics via sign, aspect or Term rulership can accelerate the danger.

Valens is more direct at placing blame directly at the native's door, warning that if their own actions are recklessly or dishonest, then they can expect to be accused of wrongdoings and be appropriately punished for mismanagement or criminal acts.

Together the two cause hostility, lawsuits, reversals in good fortune, malice and the betrayal of others for their own profit.

Fifth Sub-Period
Donor – MARS : Recipient – MOON
(36 – 37 Years)

The fifth sub-period belongs to the Moon, the prime luminary in a chart for night-time births, so by rights it should follow that the Moon is highly capable of providing good care for the native during its term.

Unfortunately this does not appear to be the case.

From the delineations of Valens and Schoener, it would appear that the base material of Mars has already been corrupted in some way, and when the Moon takes that material, trouble occurs in the areas of both the physical and emotional domains under Moon's jurisdiction.

Mars holds the potential for what happens during its major period, and each successive planet is crucial to how the ruling planet's quintessential nature will play out in the native's life.

For the Moon to be fully engaged in Mars' antics, it will become involved in battles, and separations or emotional disturbances within the family. Friendships and professional life also suffer under the Moon's direction, and as much as Mars may be the initial cause, it is up to the Moon to smooth things over and try to reinstate equilibrium, so that broken bonds can mend or be created in a different form.

Mars' extreme qualities may have been tamed by the Moon, but its predisposition towards encouraging recklessness with little concern for the consequences or long-term effects of its behaviour, means that there is still the possibility of injuries and accidents to the body during the Moon's year.

The Moon also indicates the mother, and this can be a trying year in her life when the native feels obligated to be patient or supportive of her needs, especially when their relationship is likely to be strained by Mars' lack of tact or its selfish behaviour.

Sixth Sub-Period
Donor – MARS : Recipient – SATURN
(37 – 38 Years)

When two malefic meet under the circumstances of Firdar, they are likely to bring out the worst in both behaviours.

Under the terms of sect, one prefers daytime, the other the night, and in this case Mars is the better donor to a poor recipient in Saturn, as Saturn's qualities are usually improved by the warmth and light of the Sun in a diurnal chart.

Saturn is both dark and cold under the Moon's light, so a full examination of where Saturn resides in the chart, and the condition that Saturn is afforded through its sign and Term rulership can define how unmanageable this period can become, given that Mars is trying its best to provide acceptable material for its sub-period lord.

Schoener predicts trouble for both the native, and the native's father, as Saturn is an indicator for the males and superiors in the individual's life.

A downturn in finances is the least of their problems as ill health, family disturbances and afflictions of all manner are supposedly present during Saturn's year.

When Saturn falls under Mars' rule, there is hostility from all sides and reversals in good fortune, and only if Saturn is sound and strong in the chart can some of these woes be avoided or turned to the individual's advantage.

In this case, the trouble may surround the native and his male relatives, but not directly affect their emotional or mental state of mind. They may even be called in as experts, seen by the less powerful as capable of shouldering the responsibilities of others during this trying year.

Seventh Sub-Period
Donor – MARS : Recipient – JUPITER
(38 – 39 Years)

Jupiter's bias obligates it to make the best of a bad situation, so that when it becomes the final lord under the direction of Mars, the delineations of both Valens and Schoener list this last of Mars' seven years as a time when the native will be exalted. If they do not currently have 'any financial worth', then their financial returns will grow, and profit will come from legal matters, or from any associations with Mars, i.e. from weaponry, fire, war or surgery.

Valens calls this year effectual for advancement and opportunities for leadership, especially in the military, whilst Schoener says that the native will not tire from any work or magisterial duty.

Jupiter appears to lend better properties to Mars by providing opportunities and directing Mars' energy towards goals which are advantageous for the ambitions, reputation and wealth of the native.

Given the variety and extent of strife provided by earlier sub-lords who struggled with the material placed before them, Jupiter's period is a pleasant way to finish the seven years of Mars on a high note.

Moving from Darkness into Light . . . THE SUN

"I am a child of the Moon
being raised by the Sun
in a world walked by stars
and a sky drawn by flowers."

- Zara Ventris

Fifth Nocturnal Major Period lasts for 10 Years

The Sun is Lord From 39 – 49th Birthday

The Sun's Matter and Significations:

Brilliance	Action	Self-awareness	Good fortune
Father	Respect	Power	Acknowledgement
Intelligence	Authority	Judgement	Public Reputation

Once the nocturnally-orientated Mars has finished its seven year period, the Sun becomes the major lord for the next ten years of life.

Up until now, the native born at night has only met the Sun as a sub-lord who is in charge for shorter periods in each planet's Firdar.

The Sun's sub-period for the Moon begins at five years of age when the child is usually moving away from the insulation of the family unit, and learning new routines and information though the avenue of early schooling.

The child's identity is extended beyond their family, so they are becoming aware for the first time of differences between themselves and other children.

Information such as surnames, the careers, nationality and social standing of their parents, even an awareness of where they live, is all part of the journey towards the process of individuation.

The Sun's next sub-period begins halfway through their fourteenth year when Sun stands in for Saturn.

Valens calls this a suspenseful year, and as it is the same time as the first Saturn opposition, conflict with parents and authority figures are again part of the journey towards autonomy.

The Jupiter Sun sub-period begins just after the twenty third birthday and continues through the period when the native experiences their second Jupiter return.

Valens and Schoener predict a brilliant chapter in the native's life when honours are bestowed, aid is available from superiors, and increases in leadership and rank are a distinct possibility.

The most recent short-term period for the Sun began at the age of thirty three, when the Sun became the recipient lord for Mars, and this was a time when the Sun was at its most uncomfortable as a representative for Mars' forceful and often unbridled nature.

Trouble with superiors and those in authority, and illness or strife for the father was predicted during the time when the Sun was required to act on Mars' behalf.

These sub-periods were only snippets of the Sun's power and now the nocturnal chart meets the full strength of the Sun for the first time.

During the next decade from the age of thirty nine to forty nine much of Valens' delineations on the Sun's planetary periods are easily translated into the adult years when a nocturnal chart will experience the longer-term Fifth Period belonging to the Sun.

The Sun is often associated with long journeys simply because it is considered to be in its joy in the ninth house and therefore gains accidental dignity in this house which signifies journeys and religion.

For the person born during the night, it can feel as though the Sun's Firdaria involves a long journey of a different variety, as moving into the light can feel perilous and exposing for the individual who prefers to stand back and allow others to shine.

When Firdar was first being practised in the late 1990's, this was the time when it was thought that the Nodal Axis interrupted the passage of the planets between the Mars Firdaria and the Sun Firdaria.

The sudden exposure that nocturnal births experienced around the fortieth birthday was thought to be an expression of the Nodes, but since the discovery of new translations on Firdaria it has been proven that the Nodes do not come into play until all the planets have completed their major Firdaria Periods.

The jolt which the lunar person receives around the age of forty originates from the Sun, not the Nodes.

The dividing line between youth and middle age is no longer seen to occur at forty as improved nutrition and an active lifestyle has raised not only the age of death, but also the age which was believed to be the half-way mark.

A change in career direction at forty may have seemed almost pointless in days gone by but today it seems an unspoken condemnation of limited skills, intelligence, or a personality problem, if several changes have not taken place before, during or after the Sun Firdaria period.

Serious study or advancement in qualifications is another area that would have seen unlikely candidates after a person's mid to late forties, but mature age students are common on university campuses all over the world, and are no longer an oddity or the subject of curious discussion by younger students fresh out of high school.

The feeling of having to stand up and show oneself to the world during the forties decade springs from the Sun's Firdar, not from the Nodes.

Learning to emit light, if only for a decade, rather than having a lifetime of receiving light, causes the nocturnal individual to feel as awkward and as gangly as it did during its puberty years, when Saturn, another diurnal planet, governed their lives.

This ten year period can be extremely challenging for the nocturnally-inclined, and what comes naturally for someone born during the hours of light, is similar to operating whilst someone shines a bright light into the eyes.

Rather than gaining the advantage of light, the feeling of losing one's night vision is frightening and the thought of being blinded by something which makes one feel more exposed, more blind, and more likely to stumble on the first obstacle it comes across, is not a good feeling.

Sudden light does not make the world safer or less frightening. It just adds to the feeling that there are more things out there to fear.

The sharp distinction between light and darkness is foreign to the night-time chart, and it takes time to adjust to the light.

The diurnal person met the opposite luminary during the Moon's Firdaria at an age when they were ten years younger (at age 31), and perhaps this small age discrepancy has given them an advantage over their sect adversaries.

After all, they have had a chance to balance the two luminaries for a full decade earlier than the nocturnal birth who gains the same opportunity to walk on the other side of sect when they turn forty.

But the nocturnal person might argue the opposite point of view.

Their advantage lies in having had ten extra years to explore the parts of themselves which they now value beyond all worldly gain, and they have been able to find it without the distraction of needing others' opinions to validate their existence.

There are fewer interruptions, less noise and a lull in activities in the evening and during the early hours of the morning.

These hours are precious as they belong to the person who sits quietly, and bravely, through the hours of darkness in order to contemplate the mysteries of life.

Being alone in the daytime is a rare privilege, one that creates feelings of guilt at time wasted during the light when there are so many other people moving about their daily tasks.

Being alone at night is sometimes a curse, and sometimes a necessity, and the label will change with the emotion which drives the experience behind the state of aloneness.

The five senses are faculties by which humans and animals perceive stimuli originating from outside of the body. Sight, hearing, smell, taste and touch begin to readjust as the Sun slides beneath the western horizon.

Sight is diminished and becomes less important during the night, making way for the remaining senses to come to the fore.

Food shared with friends or family and eaten leisurely in the evening tastes different from rushed lunches and food scarffed down during the day to stop cravings and replenish the body's energy.

The night smells different from the day and a walk outside in the clear night air captures scents and re-awakes memories from times past.

Touch becomes intimate, exciting and pleasurable, when it is not just for the sake of convenience or safety, and hearing becomes more acute when the volume of the day is turned down and the subtle noises of the night take over.

These are the hours of stunning lunar landscapes, of whispered secrets and laughter with loved ones, of smelling jasmine in the cool of the evening breeze or listening to the quiet of the night and gazing up at the stars in awe.

These are the hours of feeling small, not because someone has diminished our efforts, criticised our work, or written *TEKEL* on our spirit and judged us to be wanting, as Daniel read on the walls at Belshazzar's feast.[146]

We feel small when we gaze at the night sky because we want to be as small as the little prince and to look up at the stars and point to our own, or to be as insignificant as the airman and hear five hundred million little bells tinkling as the stars look down and laugh at us.

Maybe those ten extra years of night vision are worth it after all.

FIFTH Major Firdaria for the Nocturnal Chart
⊙ — 10 years
10 years divided by 7 = 1 year 5 months 4 days

Major SUN 10 yrs Sub-Period	Combination of Major (1st) and Minor (2nd) Time Lords	Minor Time Period BEGINS—ENDS for 1 year 5 months *(1.4) *months as %
1	⊙ / ⊙	39.0 – 40.4
2	⊙ / ♀	40.4 – 41.9
3	⊙ / ☿	41.9 – 43.3
4	⊙ / ☽	43.3 – 44.7
5	⊙ / ♄	44.7 – 46.1
6	⊙ / ♃	46.1 – 47.6
7	⊙ / ♂	47.6 – 49.0

Fig. 181 The Sun's Firdaria in the Nocturnal Chart

First Sub-Period
Donor – SUN : Recipient – SUN
(39 – 40.4 Years)

When the Sun is both the donor and the recipient, Valens predicts brilliance, but is careful to add conditions which will affect the repercussions of their advancements.

When the birth occurs at night, the benefits are reduced or somewhat tarnished, and there is accompanying trouble with the native's rise in reputation or rank.

The native is warned of the dreadful accusations of others, the production of enemies who oppose the native's increased power, and false judgements which can be made against them.

If a malefic planet should also be connected to the Sun through aspect or dignity (as dispositor or Term Ruler), Valens predicts a diminishment in livelihood, or a reduction of reputation, precarious travel abroad, and trouble or danger for the father.

Schoener is more positive in his declaration on the night-time chart and sets no conditions, instead foreseeing praise and honour above all of the native's relatives, and wealth or riches, and says that happiness and joys increase during the Sun's shorter term.

Second Sub-Period
Donor – SUN : Recipient – VENUS
(40.4 – 41.9 Years)

Venus follows the Sun in the Chaldean Order and this sub-period is likely to be a pleasant chapter in the Sun's Firdar, given that Venus prefers a nocturnal chart and the native enjoys a respite from the Sun's ambitions and aspirations.

Schoener says that for a nativity by night, the Venus sub-period signifies that the individual will escape from trouble, they will produce beautiful things, and will rejoice in their partner and children.

Finances will not be a problem and the native may be inclined to buy property, and will also be generous and give alms to the poor.

If the Sun directs Venus towards journeys, then they are likely to be profitable, and the native will be honoured perhaps for the sake of religion.

If the Sun's seventeen month period has previously been difficult, the native will be able to rid themselves of concerns and every accusation according to Schoener's text on Venus.

Third Sub-Period
Donor – SUN : Recipient – MERCURY
(41.9 – 43.3 Years)

The Sun donates to Mercury in the next stage of the Sun's Firdar and there are mixed blessings during Mercury's sub-period.

The planet signified by finance and business dealings is somewhat fickle in its fortunes, and although Valens has a more positive attitude to Mercury than Schoener, saying Mercury can provide a good, effectual, prospering and sociable phase in the native's life, he also reminds the reader that Mercury is easily influenced by the other planets.

Good planets connected to Mercury bring good fortune, but should a malefic have any involvement with the same planet, it will introduce lawsuits and confusion, fears on written matters, and anxious times due to increased paperwork, legal documents or correspondence. Rather than bringing prosperity and productivity, instead Mercury experiences inopportune expenditures and losses.

Schoener notes that if the nativity is nocturnal, the native will have much loss and will encounter lawsuits because of lies and false witnesses.

He does not elaborate on Mercury's engagement with other planets, but presumably benefic planets means the lies will be uncovered and the native's reputation will be repaired, and malefic planets means the trouble is extensive and longer lasting in its ability to do damage to the reputation and cause a down-turn in the native's fortunes.

It is also worth noting that Saturn will experience the second opposition of its Saturn cycle (the first opposition occurred around fifteen years of age) and this can bring reality back with a jolt.

Saturn will require honesty and integrity from the native when this event occurs, and Mercury as the Sun's sub-lord may be reluctant to supply Saturn with full disclosure on some of its more nefarious business dealings.

The nocturnal individual who thinks their actions are covered by nightfall can be rudely exposed during Sun's major period, and if there are any irregularities in business or criminal activities then these will be illuminated at some time during the Sun's ten year period.

What better opportunity could there be for the Sun to expose the lunar personality and place it squarely under scrutiny than when transiting Saturn is halfway through its second cycle at age forty-two, and to have Mercury's shady dealings unmasked?

Truly a rude awakening for the night-born if integrity has been compromised somewhere along Sun's Firdaria.

Fourth Sub-Period
Donor – SUN : Recipient – MOON
(43.3 – 44.7 Years)

The Moon takes over from Mercury a few months after the celebrations of the forty third birthday. The Moon creates an interesting time when the two luminaries meet in reverse situations to when the native was a child of five years old, and the Sun was required to create an appropriate form for the Moon's matter.

The ancients believed the light-bringer did not consider it appropriate to be seconded by the Moon, a mere beneficiary of its light, and there was a certain resentment and lack of grace by the Sun to supply its form to Moon's matter. However, when the roles are reversed, the Moon is more congenial and is willing to contribute its version of form to the Sun's matter.

Valens predicts that when the Moon applies its practical knowledge of the physical world to the solar principle, it heralds a phase in the native's life which brings fruitful results.

The Moon signifies prudence and a keen sense of perception of what is going on beneath the surface, so this combination of Sun plus Moon furnishes the native with an instinctive intelligence and a willingness to cooperate in others' schemes. Good timing and a gentle approach towards others produces alliances and friends can bring good fortune as well as benefits from those with foreign connections.

Schoener says that the native's income will increase as profits flow from a secret place, and that they will associate themselves with nobles and men in high places.

However, he also adds a warning for a nocturnal birth. He says that tension between the two luminaries provokes a time which is sometimes harmful to the native's health.

Also, the Moon's natural compassion means the native will needlessly expose themselves to danger or unpleasantness, as life becomes complicated if they unwittingly become involved in the problems of others.

Fifth Sub-Period
Donor – SUN : Recipient – SATURN
(44.7 – 46.1 Years)

The Sun and Saturn are natural enemies, so this interval which spans a year and a half in the middle of their forties is likely to be tense and worrying for the native.

An adversary such as Saturn is unlikely to be a good candidate for the Sun's matter, and this is not aided by the fact that Saturn is considered to be the 'out-of-sect' malefic in a nocturnal chart.

If there were problems of a Saturnian nature during the Mercury sub-period when Saturn's opposition to natal Saturn took place (around age 42), then these hurdles may reappear in Saturn's own sub-period.

The Moon's involvement in the intervening spell may have lulled the individual into a false sense of security, or caused them to believe that the issue has disappeared and simply died a quiet death when the Moon took over from Mercury.

However, when Saturn's sub-period follows the Moon's, the native can see them re-emerging to cause trouble, and this time they may not be able to ignore impending lawsuits or possible dismissals for questionable business dealings.

Whilst there are other mitigating circumstances which may improve Saturn's behaviour, this planet is intrinsically uncomfortable working in the light-deprived environment of the night, and it should be remembered that Saturn causes Strife through coldness, stealth, and the slow unravelling of things we mistakenly believe to be totally under our control.

For this reason Valens predicts a grievous and frustrating seventeen months of delays and inactivity, as hindrances come from the direction of superiors, institutions and bureaucracy's red tape.

Those in authoritative positions are particularly vexing for the native. Any action on their part to hurry the process or re-commence stalled projects, is met by resistance and threats of appropriate consequences in response to the native's inappropriate actions.

Both planets signify the father so this time can be perilous for the parent or male relatives.

Schoener predicts sadness and injuries during Saturn's sub-period, and again the level and severity of Saturn's influence will greatly depend on its condition in the natal chart.

This combination has the potential to feel like the reversal of alchemical design, i.e., the depressing situation of turning gold into lead, and a prize is of little benefit to the native when something precious is lost in the process through neglect, poor management or heavy-handling.

The native would be wise to remember that once something is changed for the worst into a form which has little merit or no longer has true value in their lives, it is very hard to reverse the damage and return it to its golden state.

Sixth Sub-Period
Donor – SUN : Recipient – JUPITER
(46.1 – 47.6 Years)

Thankfully, Saturn hands over to Jupiter after its own troublesome period as the sixth short-term phase of the Sun begins. The Sun can relax a little knowing that it is now in the hands of the greater benefic, even though Jupiter's benefits will be somewhat dampened by the fact that it will be out of sect in a nocturnal chart.

Jupiter is not by nature harmful, so in general its sub-period is a good time for an increase in the Sun's significations of self-worth, strength, nobility and fortune.

If the Saturn period has been particularly difficult and peppered by adversities, then Jupiter's term will instigate the beginnings of victory and dominion over enemies, and those who wish the native harm.

If the situation has gone beyond redemption then perhaps Jupiter is the perfect time to start afresh and look for opportunities from another direction. If nothing else, the native can use this time to catch their breath and recuperate a little before re-entering the fray when the next malefic, in the form of Mars, becomes the last sub-lord for the Sun.

Seventh Sub-Period
Donor – SUN : Recipient – MARS
(47.6 – 49 Years)

Schoener says that during Mars' term the native will be changed from one state to another, and they will move from one place of power and influence to another.

He does not indicate whether the changes will be good or bad, as this will depend on the condition of the planets in the natal chart and the state of their relationship.

Once more, journeys are mentioned in relation to the Sun's major period, but the journeys have an alien or unfriendly quality, and Mars' influence produces hardships and misfortune from travel, rather than pleasures, during the final seventeen months of the Sun's Firdar.

Mars belongs to the nocturnal sect, so the trials, quarrels and injustices that Schoener associates with its sub-period should by rights be either trivial, or short-lived for the nocturnal nativity.

In many ways, Mars is an appropriate representative for the Sun, as the planets' individual significations can either overlap or complement one another, especially if the native is required to be courageous or self-confident when reaching for great heights.

Even though the Sun rules the contrary sect to Mars, it is exalted in Mars' sign of Aries and this implies an alliance between these two planets which means that Mars is more than capable of taking Sun's brief and achieving a good outcome during its short-term period.

Sect dignity improves the quality of Mars in a nocturnal chart, so much so that its actions are more effective and more likely to be met with success.

Under the Moon's influence of a nocturnal chart, Mars is direct, rather than aggressive, and does not waste unnecessary energy on anger, rash behaviour or meaningless gestures.

The final stage of Sun's Firdaria can be the perfect time to reflect on the events of the previous ten years. It may seem strange for Mars to be the vehicle for reflection and perhaps introspection is a better way to describe the courage and honesty which is necessary to be able to look backwards in hindsight at one's life as the half-century approaches and the fiftieth birthday is not so far away.

Reflection requires a careful examination of the facts which were available from the environment of the past and to try to understand why things panned out in a certain way.

Introspection is a deeper and more personal form of reflection.

Introspection requires the observation and examination of one's mental and emotional state of mind.

Soul searching is what sums up the essence of this solar term and the nocturnally-inclined Mars is a perfect candidate to lead a synopsis on the state of one's soul at the termination of Sun's Firdaria.

Under Mars' sharp knife the self-analysis of one's foibles, personal traits and philosophical beliefs can expose if not gaping holes, then at least some wear and tear, on a psyche made battle-weary by life's inconsistencies.

The gentle hand of Venus as the Sixth Firdaria lord may be needed to comfort the soul and the next eight years dedicated to the nocturnal benefic may be as much about learning the lessons of self-love, as it is about commitments to improve or foster relationships with loved ones, family and friends.

The Fountain of Youth . . . VENUS

"There is a fountain of youth: it is your mind, your talents, the creativity you bring to your life and the lives of the people you love. When you learn to tap this source, you will truly have defeated age."

Sophia Loren (1934 -)

Sixth Nocturnal Major Period lasts for 8 Years

Venus is Lord From 49 – 57th Birthday

Venus' Matter and Significations:

Social graces	Women	Self-appreciation	Mother
Relationships	Acceptance	Femininity	Pleasures
Beauty	Movement	Adornment	Artistic skills

Venus is the third planet which is affiliated with the nocturnal sect.

The subtlety of the night's light is extremely flattering to a more mature Venus, and she enjoys the flirtations, games, music and entertainments with a level of confidence which was lacking in the younger years of her previous five sub-periods under the tutelage of other planets whose instructions may not always have been to Venus' liking.

Venus is too genteel to openly oppose Saturn, the Sun, or even Mars, her fellow nocturnal companion, but inwardly she may have balked at the material donated by these major lords during their long-term Firdarias.

The Moon's Firdaria at the beginning of life was a tad wasted on Venus' talents at two years of age when a wet smile is all that Venus can muster but the sub-period during Jupiter's Firdaria between the ages of twenty and thirty two will have been much more fruitful for Venus to exercise her pout and perfect her sexual preening in the native's mid-twenties.

Now Venus gets to provide the material and she relishes the opportunity to turn the tables on her fellow planets and finally play the role of donating planet.

Venus is in agreement with the feminine qualities of the Moon and collectively the Moon, Venus and Mars represent the appetites of humankind when they are relaxed or at peace with themselves.

The Venus Firdar occurs later in life for the night-time birth, commencing at forty nine years and finishing at the fifty seventh birthday.

A woman's breasts can no longer be described as 'perky' unless the plastic surgeon has been at work, and buttocks are no longer firm or inviting to prospective lovers of either gender. Likewise, the male body is also deteriorating as bowed legs and pot-bellies show the effects of gravity on a body that has survived for over half a century.

For most people these are not exactly years conducive to experimental sex requiring the manipulation of one's body into intricate knots or prolonged hours of physical exertion.

I may be wrong, but at this age a good book and a hot cup of tea begins to look far more appealing than hours of 'sexy-time' with one's intimate partner, especially a partner who has shared one's bed for the past few decades.

For the night-births to encounter Venus' long-term period in the Sixth (of seven) Nocturnal Firdarias may seems a little unfair and a further blow to the person who faced Saturn's full force in their teenage years. This is an odd time of life for a goddess who is eternally the maiden to finally show her face, especially when she was kinder to the diurnal chart who experienced its own Venus Firdar through the coquettishness and youthful dalliances of puberty at the same time as the nocturnals were battling Saturn's demons.

Having made the point on Venus' poor timing, it may be that Venus still has much to teach the mature individual about love and desire, and this may in fact be the perfect time for the individual to lose their self-conscious hang-ups about their body and instead learn a little about self-acceptance.

The order in which the Nocturnal Firdaria reveals itself means that much of the night-time nativity's life has been spent learning about the darkness of matter, and the nature of what it is like for the soul to embrace a physical form.

It seems a natural progression – after all the other planets have had their opportunity to interpret physicality from their point of view – for Venus to reveal to the individual how they can find the love from within to appreciate and accept their own body as well as cherishing the love of others and admiring the beauty which surrounds them.

To quote a blog written by Michelle Combs (obviously a woman in her Venus Firdaria) on the Huffington Post website entitled *What Not to Wear After Age 50: The Final Say:*[147]

"You are over 50 . . . Wear whatever you want.

If you've made it to 50 and still need to consult articles on how to dress appropriately then you are so missing out on one of the best things about being over 50.

One of the best things about getting older is realizing that we don't have to spend our energy worrying about what other people think and we get to be comfortable in our skin with our own freak flags."

The blog's author continues by advising women not to wear psychologically damaging attire such as 'the weight of the world'; 'shame and regret'; 'rose-coloured glasses'; 'a stiff upper lip'; or 'too many hats'.

Like most media blogs the tone is facetious and intended to amuse the reader.

But it does make a point.

SIXTH Major Firdaria for the Nocturnal Chart ♀ — 8 years 8 years divided by 7 = 1 year 1 month 22 days		
Major VENUS 8 yrs Sub-Period	Combination of Major (1st) and Minor (2nd) Time Lords	Minor Time Period BEGINS—ENDS for 1 year 2 months *(1.1) *months as %
1	♀ / ♀	49.0 – 50.1
2	♀ / ☿	50.1 – 51.3
3	♀ / ☽	51.3 – 52.4
4	♀ / ♄	52.4 – 53.6
5	♀ / ♃	53.6 – 54.7
6	♀ / ♂	54.7 – 55.9
7	♀ / ☉	55.9 – 57.0

Fig. 182 Venus' Firdaria and the Nocturnal Chart

First Sub-Period
Donor – VENUS : Recipient – VENUS
(49 – 50.1 Years)

Venus begins her major period with fourteen months under her own care, and both authors writing on the Venus Firdar decree good fortune, joy and happiness, as well as profit and possible marriage, or a renewal in romantic love and friendship.

Whilst Venus signifies good times and romance, Valens warns that any interference from Mars or Saturn will either blight or dim the chances of happiness, as each in their own way will bring conflict, separation or rejection to the native.

Mars is tempered by the nocturnal chart, so disagreements may be resolved and trust reinstated but Saturn is not a friend of the night-time chart and can bring obstacles and hindrances that thwart the native's chances of happiness.

Second Sub-Period
Donor – VENUS : Recipient – MERCURY
(50.1 – 51.3 Years)

There is quite a discrepancy between the delineations of Valens and Schoener when it comes to the following sub-period under the direction of Mercury.

Valens presents a positive vision of Mercury's representation of Venus, citing an effectual year for commerce and friendships, and encourages public debate and advances in education.

According to Valens, Mercury is well equipped to accept Venus' matter, and fashions a form which suggests joy and pleasure in all things of a Mercurial nature.

Schoener, on the other hand, is cautious of Mercury's term. He warns that it is a time of foolish investments, and money will be lost on whims and desires which have little financial merit.

As well as predicting foolish expenditures, Schoener warns the native that they will be overcome by enemies who will tread them under foot, and that they will encounter many troubles in this fourteen month period when anxieties of the mind will vex them, and illnesses of the body will occur due to bad food or poor digestion.

At first glance the difference between the two interpretations seems startling, but there are reasons as to why Valens predicts a good period and Schoener forecasts the opposite scenario.

Valens is inclined to base his interpretation on each planet's individual significations as demonstrated by his delineations of the planets in Book One of *Anthologies* (Chapter Two on Sect).

For instance, when he describes Venus as desire and love and Mercury as education, reasoning and intelligence, the significations of both planets seem compatible, and from this base the time periods they share, regardless of who holds the major period, is interpreted as a time free from worry or conflict.

Schoener's interpretations apply the basic planetary significations in a like manner, but he also takes into account the relationships of the planets according to their essential dignities of rulership and exaltation.

Venus and Mercury have no conflict in rulership as their signs are not connected in the Thema Mundi chart.

However, Venus is exalted in Pisces and Mercury is exalted in the opposite sign of Virgo.

This situation of opposing rulerships results in both planets being in the debility of fall in the sign of the other's exaltation, and this is enough to cause tension between the two planets who share this time zone.

The same scenario happens between the Sun and Saturn, both in rulership and in exaltation signs, and this is reflected in Valens' and Schoener's delineations of their joint Firdaria periods.

There is also some difficulty between Jupiter and Mars, when Jupiter is exalted in Cancer and Mars is exalted in the opposite sign of Capricorn.

This explains why, when Mars becomes the sub-period lord for Jupiter, the delineations predict aggravated strife, heightened fear and an increased level of sadness during Mars' shorter term.

Third Sub-Period
Donor – VENUS : Recipient – MOON
(51.3 – 52.4 Years)

The next fourteen months is shared between the two feminine nocturnal planets, Venus and the Moon.

Moon is the recipient for Venus' material so that it would seem obvious that women and relationships are featured during this chapter of Venus' Firdar.

The Moon borrows Venus' sign for its own exaltation, so there is little doubt that she wants to do well by a donor who operates on two levels.

Firstly, Venus is the permanent donor of Taurus for the Moon's exaltation, and secondly, to please a fellow sect member of feminine gender who has donated matter which the Moon can easily transform into an appropriate form for her nature and significations.

Schoener says that the native will go forth from their misery (incurred during Mercury's term), and that their situation and business dealings will begin to improve under the Moon's tutelage.

A possibility of marriage or romantic attachments is also envisaged if the native is single, as well as the ability to have dominion over their equals.

Valens is more cautious as he warns that the Moon's condition in the natal chart will greatly affect its ability to meet Venus' requirements during the Moon's fourteen months of secondment.

If the Moon is connected to the malefics, there is still an indication of beneficial outcomes.

However, others are jealous or envious of the native's good fortune, and will work towards unsettling relationships, alienating friends and allies, or finding a way to destroy the native's happiness by other nefarious methods.

Fourth Sub-Period
Donor – VENUS : Recipient – SATURN
(52.4 – 53.6 Years)

Saturn becomes the fourth recipient for Venus and the out of sect malefic is the mid-term lord for Venus Firdaria's eight years. Saturn is seconded by Venus to meet her needs, and is required to fulfil her wish-list now that she has arrived at the centre of her major period.

The little prince's relationship with his beautiful rose comes to mind when imagining how these two planets might work effectively together.

The fox in the story tells the prince *"You become responsible, for ever, for what you have tamed.*

You are responsible for your rose."[148]

Saturn becomes responsible for Venus' care during its sub-period, but Venus must first decide how this care can be defined in terms which Saturn might comprehend, and therefore be capable of successfully accomplishing on Venus' behalf.

At this midpoint in Venus' eight year period, it is worth reflecting on what Venus is trying to teach the native during the passage of her Firdaria.

The noun 'desideratum' comes to mind when Venus is in charge of the native's Nocturnal Firdaria between the ages of forty nine and fifty seven.

'Desideratum' is derived from the Latin word *'desiderate'* meaning *"to wish for or long for"* and means something needed or wanted, almost to the point of desperation.

Venus' desideratum is her real need to be loved and accepted, and above all to feel a deep connection with others.

Venus initiates these connections through a mutual pleasure in music, dance, movement, beauty, the arts or any number of entertainments, whilst she builds steadily towards a meaningful relationship with another human being.

Venus' desideratum is the matter from which Saturn must find an appropriate form which is true to its own identity, but this is a planet which is ill-equipped to deal with Venus' sweet nature and what it deems to be her trifling demands.

If this were a secondment, then both parties are unlikely to leave the fourteen month term feeling satisfied with the results.

Venus is bruised by the experience, and Saturn is dissatisfied with his employer and probably feels that his talents have been either wasted or under-appreciated during his temporary transfer under her supervision.

Saturn is extremely uncomfortable in a nocturnal chart and, if there are no redeeming factors through the secondary rules of sect which can soften his maleficence, then taking orders from Venus is going to produce a haughty, sullen, or uncooperative subordinate. One who deeply resents being under the control of someone (Venus), who neither deserves the honour of leadership, nor appreciates Saturn's terrifying rank as 'the star of Nemesis'.

Saturn is the second planet to borrow one of Venus' signs for its own exaltation, but while the Moon, Venus' previous sub-lord, is grateful for Venus' generosity and uses Taurus to hold on to those it loves (which Venus would approve of), when Saturn possesses Libra the loving principle moves away from warmth and kindness, and instead signifies the unflinching scales of Saturn's justice.

The Roman poet Manilius is the author of one of the earliest surviving treatise on astrology, so when Manilius writes on those born under the sign of Libra, he probably has Saturn in mind rather than Venus in rulership:

"He (the Libran) *will be acquainted with the tables of law, abstruse legal points, and words denoted by compendious signs;*

he will know what is permissible and the penalties incurred by doing what is forbidden;

in his own house he is a people's magistrate holding lifelong office . . . whatever stands in dispute and needs a ruling the pointer of the Balance will determine."[149]

Perhaps Saturn shares a similar attitude to the Sun when it is the sub-lord for the Moon.

Both the diurnal malefic planet and the diurnal luminary may affect an air of superiority when it comes to the major lord being a member of the opposite sect, that is, a nocturnal planet.

Rather than being cooperative, these two show disdain and disrespect for what they believe to be an inferior planet and this haughtiness is displayed through their sub-period delineations which imply difficulties for their respective major lords and calamities for the native.

On a practical level, Schoener foretells a time when there is much grief, hardship and trouble in life during Saturn's short term which may feel much longer in the mind of the beleaguered nocturnalite.

Female relatives and loved ones are plagued by illness and quarrels, strife and contentions to the point where he says *'his wife will place horns on him"* presumably meaning she will see her husband as the Devil incarnate.

Fifteenth century Schoener uses the old-fashioned technique of addressing himself directly to the male reader so that he writes only in the masculine – the native is always of male gender – which is annoying to the ears of the female astrologer. Genderless text is not a part of traditional writings but Schoener is particular irritating in this respect.

None of his delineations are more obvious in his gender bias than when he writes on the Saturn sub-period. 'He' (the native) is presented as the masculine Saturn figure whose behaviour burdens his female counterpart with disrepute, illness, shame and misery.

These conditions are exactly the opposite to what Venus anticipates for her desideratum so she must be greatly relieved when Saturn's destructive months are complete, and Saturn hands over to Jupiter to help Venus fulfil her requirements for the next fourteen months.

Perhaps Saturn would do well to remember that love and responsibility go hand in hand.

The little prince regrets his resentment at having to care for the rose once he has tamed her, and for abandoning her when the burden of her care became too much for him.

He laments *"In those days I understood nothing! I should have judged her by her deeds and not her words. I should have guessed the tenderness behind her poor little stratagems.*

Flowers are so contradictory!

And I was too young to know how to love her." [150]

Age is no excuse for Saturn in the nocturnal chart's Venus Firdaria.

As the Second Saturn Return approaches once Venus is finished, Saturn will meet itself for the second time during the early stages of Mercury's stint as the Nocturnal Firdaria's last Lord.

It would serve Saturn well to remember that abandoning responsibilities can also be about abandoning those we love, and the Return need not be themed on past separations, or regrets and lost opportunities to care for something or someone.

Fifth Sub-Period
Donor – VENUS : Recipient – JUPITER
(53.6 – 54.7 Years)

Jupiter is the lord for Venus' fifth sub-period, and there should be some stabilising effects during a time when Jupiter is called to act on Venus' behalf.

Jupiter may prefer the daylight hours, and would promise greater honours and confer near-royal status on the diurnal chart, but this does not mean that it cannot bring benefits of a lesser nature to the nocturnal chart.

The material of Venus is well-suited for Jupiter to mould a good year, and one which is suitable for acquisition and strong alliances with those who wish to promote the native in some manner.

Venus still signifies the finer things in life, and even if Jupiter is prevented by its natal condition in elevating the status to dizzying heights, there is still the joy and bonhomie that accompanies a period when the two benefic planets join hands to govern the native's life for a short period of time.

The only warning comes from Jupiter's tendency to indulge in lavish behaviour, and if Jupiter's form begins to swell from an excess of good living, then the native may feel the burn from a less than tolerant Mars who takes over in the following period.

Sixth Sub-Period
Donor – VENUS : Recipient – MARS
(54.7 – 55.9 Years)

In correct Chaldean Order the next planet in line to serve Venus is its natural adversary, Mars.

If Venus' desideratum involves the gentle art of love, war-mongering Mars is not inclined to provide a suitable form by which it can achieve Venus' longings, at least not without creating a little madness and mayhem along the way.

Both planets belong to the nocturnal sect so hopefully Venus will be a little more tolerant towards Mars' boisterous nature, and Mars will be a little more considerate and restrained in its behaviour.

Unhappily, this is definitely not the message delivered by Schoener's delineations.

His text does discern between diurnal and nocturnal births, but there is little difference in the level of misery Mars is capable of creating for the native during its term as Venus' representative.

For the nocturnal nativity, the native's miseries will be multiplied (in comparison with the diurnal chart at age sixteen). Remember Juliet who fakes her own death and then fails to warn Romeo of her clever scheme?

Plot spoiler – Juliet dies twice, once by poison and then by dagger and Romeo dies by poison having first murdered Juliet's fiancée who is mourning her first 'death'.

It's not hard to see which planet signifies our young male hero in Shakespeare's story of unrequited love, and who is signified by the hapless Juliet.

Venus (major lord) sets the scene but Mars (minor lord) is too obtuse to follow her hints and it all ends in tragedy.

The individual experiencing Mars' chapter during Venus' Firdaria will be associated with powerful men, but they will create drama and grief for their brothers and comrades.

Mars makes the native ambitious, warlike and ruthless, totalling lacking in Venus' diplomacy, tact, or charm which seems to have dried up under Mars' extreme heat.

Interestingly, the word tact comes from the Latin *tactus* meaning 'touch, or sense of touch' and is such an appropriate word to identify with Venus.

Mars possesses none of Venus' gentle touch as it is often heavy-handed, indiscreet and rude in its dealings with people so Schoener's bad tidings should come as no surprise.

If women are featured during Mars' term they do not fare well, and disagreements, separations and injustices are done both by them, and to them, as Mars' single-mindedness wreaks havoc on family relations, friendships and professional associations.

In the first days of their acquaintance, the little prince asks the airman of what use are the prickly thorns to his beautiful rose if a sheep is able to eat the thorns and destroy the flower.

The airman is frustrated in his attempts to fix his damaged plane and answers the question distractedly by saying *"Thorns are of no use whatsoever; they are simply a flower's way of being spiteful"*.

Mars' sub-period is the thorns to Venus' rose.

If a nocturnal personality has spent Venus' sub-periods and much time in between them searching for love or desideratum and has been bruised by the experience, then perhaps thorns are necessary to protect the tenderness of one's rose-coloured heart.

The airman's careless answer angers the little prince and he retorts with bitterness,

"I don't believe you! Flowers are weak, they are naive. They reassure themselves as best they can. They think they are being frightening, with their thorns."[51]

Perhaps Venus thinks it is being frightening when she uses Mars' spite to reassure herself that her naivety is protected by his sharp thorns.

Seventh Sub-Period
Donor – VENUS : Recipient – SUN
(55.9 – 57 Years)

The final sub-period for Venus belongs to the Sun who adds its form to Venus' material desires.

This may be a nocturnal chart, but the Sun has demonstrated in the previous major period from age thirty nine to forty nine, that he is capable of administering power and reputation, especially if he is given free rein.

In this instance, he must take direction from Venus and the Sun is capable of using its warmth and charm to forge new friendships and fortify old ones.

The Sun's term is not without some disruption as Schoener warns that there is a lowering in the native's vitality from an illness, but it should not be serious as the native will be healed.

In terms of bringing material happiness, the Sun provides an increase in substance, servants, women and associations, and there will be extra money for beautiful fabrics and adornments which should please Venus' vanity.

There are alliances with influential or learned women mentioned in his text *"he will be united with one (a woman) who knows how to write"* and the native will be happy, will receive many gifts, and will be the victor over their adversaries.

Don't Complicate Your Mind . . . MERCURY

"Life is one big road with lots of signs
So when you riding through the ruts; don't complicate your mind.
Flee from hate, mischief and jealousy.
Don't bury your thoughts. Put your vision to reality."

Bob Marley (1945-1981)
Opening Lyrics to *Wake Up and Live!*

Seventh Nocturnal Major Period lasts for 13 Years

Mercury is Lord From 57 – 70ᵗʰ Birthday

Mercury's Matter and Significations:

Intelligence	Memory	Rational thought	Opinions
Education	Reasoning	Business pursuits	Speech
Numbers	Sport	Supervision	Marketing

Mercury's Firdaria is thirteen long years.

This should be ample time for the mind to grow and learn through new experiences, to take on new ideas, to retrain the mind to discard negative thoughts, or to free itself from the poisonous seeds of hate, mischief, jealousy or malice.

The same thirteen years can just as easily be occupied by complications born from past memories and thought patterns that crystallize into shards of bitterness, frustration, envy and spiteful actions.

Mars rules the final major period in the Diurnal Firdaria due to its position directly above the Sun in the Chaldean Order. Mercury shares the same honour in the Nocturnal Firdaria as it sits one sphere above the Moon in Aristotle's seven planetary heavens, and it is Mercury who is responsibility for thirteen years of the nocturnal's life from fifty seven to seventy years of age.

After Mercury the Nodes will rule for five years and the Moon will begin the cycle again at age seventy five to recommence the Nocturnal Firdaria.

For the diurnal nativity, Mars represents the old warrior who navigates the last seven years before the sequence of planets which began with the Sun has been completed, and the five years belonging to the Moon's Nodes begins at the age of seventy.

Mercury's rule is almost twice the length of Mars' major period, and each planet will be the sub-period lord for almost two years.

This longevity provides each of the planets with an opportunity to reflect on life's journey through the lens of their own personalities and their own choice in form, but always with Mercury's agenda in mind as Mercury is the long-term lord who directs their passage through the last Firdaria.

It may be too simplistic to quote Marley's opening line to *Wake Up and Live!* (wisdom in its own right), but life is a big road and for astrology, and particularly, for the Firdaria, there are lots of signs which are placed along the journey to help steer the native's course.

Each planet will set its own sign according to its essence, its characteristics, its qualities, its significations, and the form it chooses to take as sub-period lords in the sequence of either the Diurnal or the Nocturnal Firdaria.

Perhaps Mars is the ideal planet to complete the diurnal series for the Sun as old warriors relive past glories and contemplate the Sun's list of failures and triumphs in the previous sixty years of life.

By no means is Mars ready to pack up and leave during the final Firdaria as there is still plenty of passion and desire to enjoy the rest of the road. If all is going well for the diurnally-inclined individual Mars has the drive and energy to put the last of their visions into reality.

On the other side of sect, Mercury is the perfect planet to finish the Nocturnal Firdaria as straightforward communication and logical thought processes are not natural qualities for the night-born psyche.

Emotions, gut feelings, perceptions, fractured visions, dream interpretations and intuition are the language which comes most easily to the Moon's people who filter information through the opaque lens of their inner emotional landscape.

Mercury can provide precious time to record one's thoughts and experiences, to pass on knowledge and expertise, and to gently ease from one stage in life to the next with pleasant reminiscences, a sense of humour or gentle self-mocking, thankful for all that has gone before and excited for what is still to come.

SEVENTH Major Firdaria for the Nocturnal Chart

☿ — 13 years

13 years divided by 7 = 1 year 10 months 9 days

Major MERCURY 13 yrs / Sub-Period	Combination of Major (1st) and Minor (2nd) Time Lords	Minor Time Period BEGINS—ENDS for 1 year 10 months *(1.9) *months as %
1	☿ / ☿	57.0 – 58.9
2	☿ / ☽	58.9 – 60.7
3	☿ / ♄	60.7 – 62.6
4	☿ / ♃	62.6 – 64.4
5	☿ / ♂	64.4 – 66.3
6	☿ / ☉	66.3 – 68.1
7	☿ / ♀	68.1 – 70.0

Fig. 183 Mercury's Firdaria in the Nocturnal Chart

First Sub-Period
Donor – MERCURY : Recipient – MERCURY
(57 – 58.9 Years)

The first period belongs to Mercury whose job it is to set the agenda for the entire thirteen years.

Valens says that a double Mercury period is effectual and beneficial, and that it makes the native shrewd concerning whatever he puts his hand to, that they have good verbal delivery and are more excellent than their opponents.

Presumably many of Mercury's interests mentioned in Valens' earlier quote (Chapter Two on Sect) have the potential to be finely honed, skills such as working with numbers and accounts, marketing skills, and a career in one of the professions mentioned by Valens.

Those individuals who derive their health and happiness from making speeches or delighting in calculations are well served in Mercury's sub-period, especially if Mercury should be in a favourable sign or in aspect to Jupiter or Venus.

However, if either of the malefics aspect Mercury, the mind becomes fearful and the advantages of Mercury can be lost, so much so that debt instead of gain can occur during the two years governed by a Mercury whose woes may be doubled by its lone influence over this period.

Valens warns that Mercury can be capricious, and the anticipated outcome may never eventuate in profit or success if Fortune steps in, in the form of one of the malefics.

Saturn's second Return is likely to appear during this Mercury sub-period, or at the beginning of the Moon's sub-period depending on Saturn's speed through the signs, and will return back to its original position in the chart.

If the First Saturn Return at age twenty eight concerns itself with the individual taking responsibility for themselves as adults, then the Second Return at fifty eight can carry the theme of relinquishing control and letting go of the reins, so that younger versions of oneself can begin to take over and make their own mistakes.

Depending on Saturn's condition in the chart, the ease of this transition may be smooth and occur without drama, or the changing of the guard can be painful and fraught with fears of a bleak future, rather than being seen as a natural progression in life. This is especially the case if the person is fighting the adjustment and feels betrayed by others' involvement in the process.

This may be especially true for the diurnal birth as the Sun never enjoys relinquishing power and Saturn's Second Return occurs during the time when Mars is in charge of the Diurnal Firdaria.

In a nocturnal chart Mercury may be able to ease the worries of a troubled mind by planting new ideas and promoting plans for the future so that the nocturnal birth readily releases its authority in order to move forward to the next adventure with feelings of anticipation and a positive state of mind.

Whether Saturn's Return takes place during Mercury's sub-period, when plans are made and projects require focused attention and wise decisions, or during the Moon's sub-period when the sect's major luminary creates a more emotional response to the event, it is worth remembering that Saturn is averse to a nocturnal chart, and may use this opportunity to produce depression, anxiety or a sense of isolation for the night-born native.

Second Sub-Period
Donor – MERCURY : Recipient – MOON
(58.9 – 60.7 Years)

The following sub-period for Mercury belongs to the Moon, and good fortune will very much depend on how the Moon is situated in the chart.

If the Moon is a well-placed recipient for Mercury's wishes, then there are profitable alliances and prosperity.

Troublesome matters may find themselves being rectified, and the native encounters sympathy and support for their causes as both parties, Mercury and the Moon, feel content with the relationship.

During this phase Mercury strives constantly for expression and for success, and if the Moon is able to be of service to Mercury the native feels self-satisfied and happy.

However, should the Moon be uncongenially situated, if it aspects Saturn or Mars, or is in the Terms of the malefics then it is a poor recipient for the demands of Mercury.

Schoener says there can be an abundance of eating and drinking during Moon's sub-period which can adversely affect the health.

He also warns that relationships can be frustrating, that the body can suffer injuries or illnesses during the Moon's term, and issues with tradespeople and those in the native's employ may occur in this two year period.

Third Sub-Period
Donor – MERCURY : Recipient – SATURN
(60.7 – 62.6 Years)

If the Moon's interval has been difficult because of its own poor condition in the chart, then the time belonging to Saturn may not provide much relief for the native.

The potential for happiness and success hinted by Mercury is unlikely to find a sympathetic recipient in Saturn, that is, unless Saturn is in an excellent condition (in spite of its loss of sect dignity in a nocturnal chart).

If Saturn is faring well in the chart, then there is promise of an improvement in reputation or status, although there are still warnings of delays, postponements and unexpected expenditure involved in the process.

Schoener is quite dismal in his predictions for this period, as he says that whilst the native's substance (money) may increase, it will not buy happiness and the behaviour will tend towards miserliness, rather than Saturn being purely cautious or prudent with money.

If the native does give aid to another, the recipient will take advantage of their kindness and should they travel, hardship and troubles will happen along the journey.

The reduction of finances, the loss of one's home or possible hardship are worrying prospects during Saturn's term, as employment can become an issue if retrenchment has been one example of Saturn's ability to create Strife in the native's life.

Arguments, disagreements and poor attention to the fine-print conditions in contracts, can cause trouble during this twenty two month period when Saturn provides form for Mercury's material.

Saturn's form is often one of accountability, and if Mercury has played the role of trickster, or has been genuinely naive in the previous two sub-periods, then the native can come under the scrutiny of those in authority when their activity incurs losses, insults, or the dismantling of a structure.

Valens states that Saturn's sub-period can manifest in a state of weakness or wasting and disease. This is built on sound astrological lore as a combination of the two planets – Mercury who signifies the workings of the mind and Saturn which produces a variety of physical ailments – can damage the health and lay the native low with illness or a re-occurring health problem born from anxiety, depression or stress.

Fourth Sub-Period
 Donor – MERCURY : Recipient – JUPITER
 (62.6 – 64.4 Years)

Mercury handing over to Jupiter promises some respite for the native as they reach their mid sixties.

Jupiter is a more encouraging recipient for Mercury's list of possibilities than Saturn and successful ventures may restore confidence and improve finances.

Reputation and health can steadily be restored, and if isolation has been a theme of the past few years, the pressures of busy schedules, work commitments and family obligations may be lessening and Jupiter may find more time to rebuild old friendships or create new alliances.

If the individual's ambitions involve administration or commerce, then this time can be productive in supporting these ambitions.

There is one drawback in these two years which is due mainly to the ambiguous relationship shared by these two planets given that their signs are oppose one another in Thema Mundi.

If Mercury is a diurnal planet in the chart then both planets belong to the opposite sect and may cause problems for the native.

Valens warns of foolish decisions, poor advice from duplicitous financial advisors, or gambling with risky business ventures during Jupiter's phase of the Firdaria and this can put finances in jeopardy.

Fifth Sub-Period
Donor – MERCURY : Recipient – MARS
(64.4 – 66.3 Years)

Mars is a poor recipient for Mercury, as this is a planet which is known for its volatility and lack of grace.

Mars is a planet famous for its quick temper, rash decision-making and desire for battle and if a highly critical Mercury supplies Mars with reasons to over-react, it does not make for a good combination during its two years. If the native is going to be constantly expecting trouble they will be suspicious of others' motives and actions, and this constant stress can leave them in fear and turmoil if they cannot control their thoughts.

Mars may be more controlled in a nocturnal chart, and be less likely to fly off the handle and take offence at others' opinions, but arguments, upsets, betrayals, losses and disputes amongst family is a time which Valens states simply as 'not good'.

Schoener predicts that this period will involve the native in quarrels with people who are *"base men who have less strength"*.

The strength may be physical but this is not that uncommon given the native's age during Mars' sub-period.

However, the term Schoener uses tends to suggest those whom the native looks down upon as inferior to themselves, either because of social or economical reasons.

Mars may need to take care not to adopt an arrogant or superior attitude if it wants to keep its allies on side.

Schoener also warns of failings in commercial undertakings, and money lent to friends who defraud the native, and leave them to suffer the consequences, so that there is trouble with the authorities or possible imprisonment.

Sixth Sub-Period
Donor – MERCURY : Recipient – SUN
(66.3 – 68.1 Years)

The Sun is the recipient for Mercury in the sixth sub-period from the years of sixty six to sixty eight.

The Sun's chapter may take the form of retirement from full-time work, but may still be interested in short-term projects, part-time employment or consultancy work.

Schoener says of the Sun's term *"Each day the native's merriment, joy, profits and his vigour will be increased; and his men and comrades will be multiplied."*

If the health is sound and the individual's attitude and mental state is good, the two years belonging to the Sun can be fruitful, and this may be a time to pursue interests and hobbies that are external to the working life.

The individual may use the Sun's need for acknowledgement to join groups with humanitarian interests or philanthropic projects as this helps to maintain the Sun's needs to feel useful and productive despite the advancing years.

Reputation is vitally important to the Sun and it is hoped that if the Sun, or Mercury are in poor condition, or in the Terms of the malefics, that gossip, innuendo or another's spite does not harm or tarnish the individual's reputation at this point in their lives.

The Sun's sub-period can indicate a two year period when Valens predicts the native will be shrewd in their business dealings, social, effectual, and their company and advice will be sought by superiors.

The Sun may belong to the opposite sect, but it does not intend harm for the nocturnal individual.

Valens finishes his prediction by saying *"And the natives excel at most matters by finishing them in a mysterious manner and with good verbal delivery."*

I will leave it to the reader's imagination to work out what this phrase may possibly mean.

Seventh Sub-Period
Donor – MERCURY : Recipient – VENUS
(68.1 – 70 Years)

The final placement in the longest major period in the Firdaria system belongs to Venus, and she is happy to provide an upbeat finish to a thirteen year period with plenty of ups and downs.

Venus takes Mercury's list of possibilities and turns them into occasions for celebration, and a time for giving and receiving gifts and adornments.

Schoener says of Venus' two year term that the native will be associated with women. He will remove himself from the company of men and he will love women and rejoice in them.

Valens says that this last Mercury period belonging to Venus will indicate a time good and effectual for giving and receiving, and for purchases and amorous intercourse, and a time beneficial for those things that are gained through speech or education or administration. There are signs for new alliances, friendships and intimacies, and it is a time to be 'beneficent towards their own.'

Jean Shinoda Bolen is well known to those astrologers and lovers of mythology through her popular books from the 1970's, *"The God in Everyman"* and *"The Goddess in Everywoman"*.

In these two books she uses her background in Jungian psychology to explore several archetypes drawn from Greek mythology and explains how the ancient gods and goddesses live on through events and how unconscious behaviour patterns are duplicated by the myths in the modern world.

Whilst passing through her fifties Jean altered her perspective on life, changed her writing style, and produced books of a highly personal nature about her own experiences as she grew older.

From these experiences came a book titled *Crones Don't Whine: Concentrated Wisdom for Juicy Women.*

In the book she outlines thirteen qualities which the crone, a woman who has passed into the post-menopausal years, might like to develop in order to achieve the greatest joy in her later years.

These qualities identify the crone as a juicy older woman with zest, passions, and soul.

Qualities such as the fact that crones don't grovel or whine, that they choose their own path with heart, that they savour the good in their lives, and that they are fierce about what matters to them, are just a few of the characteristics which define juicy, wise women (and exceptional men who also come under the label of crones).

Shinoda Bolen continues by saying,

"It is in cultivating these qualities that the third phase of life (maid, mother, crone) *becomes a culmination time for inner beauty and wisdom.*

It is the perspective that makes the prime years of this phase of life an especially rich time to enjoy who we are, what we have, and what we are doing.

It is a time when wisdom calls upon us to use our time, energy, and vitality well." [152]

These words are proof that a combination of Mercury with Venus can create wonderful, positive images of beauty.

Images which move beyond superficial attractiveness to reach deep into the soul and radiate from a mind which is vital, alive and appreciative of the world's riches, regardless of the advancing years and the experiences, both good and bad, which have preceded this last piece in the Nocturnal Firdaria.

Endnotes

1   Hand, Robert, 1995, *Night & Day: Planetary Sect in Astrology,* published by Archive for the Retrieval of Historical Astrological Texts (ARHAT), p. 2

2   Paulus Alexandrinus, *Introductory Matters,* Project Hindsight, Trans. Robert Schmidt, Ed. Robert Hand, The Golden Hind Press, Greek Tract, Volume 1, p. 15. Footnote on terms by Robert Schmidt.

3   The Emerald Tablet of Hermes, http://www.sacred-texts.com/alc/emerald.htm

4   Alleged Plato quote, https://www.brainyquote.com/quotes/quotes/p/plato384673.html, but the quote is rejected as genuine by Dr. Dave Yount, http://www.mesacc.edu/~davpy35701/text/plato-things-not-said.html

5   Claudius Ptolemy, *Tetrabiblos,* Ashmand version, published 1822, Book One, Ch. VII, Diurnal and Nocturnal, p. 15

6   Hand, Robert, *Night & Day: Planetary Sect in Astrology,* p. 6

7   Ibid, p. 21

8   Paulus Alexandrinus, *Introductory Matters,* p. 15-16

9   Abu'l-Rayhan Muhammad Ibn Ahmad (known as al-Biruni), *The Book of Instruction in the Elements of the Art of Astrology,* TransR. Ramsey Wright, Luzac & Co, London, 1934, Notation 348, p. 211

10 Ibid, Notation #385, p. 234

11 Robert Hand, *Night and Day,* p. 7

12 Ibid, p. 7

13 Vettius Valens, trans. Robert Schmidt, ed. Robert Hand, 1995, *Anthology, Book II (Conclusion),* Project Hindsight, Greek Tract, Volume VII, The Golden Hind Press, USA, p. 45

14 Ibid, Footnote by Robert Hand, p. 45

15   al-Biruni, Notation 497, p. 308

16   http://www.hellenisticastrology.com/2010/12/15/full-translation-of-
      vettius-valens-anthology-released/

17   Robert Hand, *Night and Day,* p. 7

18   http://www.astro.com/astro-databank/Goethe,_Johann_Wolfgang_von

19   al-Biruni, Notation #497, p. 308

20   Firmicus Maternus, Julius, Jean Rhys Bram (trans.), 2001, *Matheseos
      Libri VII* (Eight Books of the Mathesis, or Theory of Astrology), *Liber
      Tertius,* Spica Publications, Aust, (orig, 1975, Noyes Press), p. 106

21   Robert Hand, *Night and Day,* p. 27

22   Maternus, *Matheseos,* Book 4, p. 106

23   Ibid, p. 108

24   Robert Hand, *Night and Day,* p. 23

25   Ibid, p. 23

26   al-Biruni, Notation #385, p. 234

27   Claudius Ptolemy, *Tetrabiblos,* Book One, Ch. VII, p. 14

28   Robert Hand, *Night and Day,* p. 26

29   Robert Hand's Webinar. Transcribed from a lecture on Sect held on
      27th July 2015 entitled *Night & Day: The effect of daytime & night time
      on Birth charts,* accessed from www.arhatmedia.com

30   Claudius Ptolemy, *Tetrabiblos,* Book One, Ch. VII, Diurnal and
      Nocturnal, p. 15

31   Ibid, Book II, Ch IX, The Quality and Nature of the Effect, p. 60
      (Ashmand translation)

32   Ibid, Book III, Ch XVIII, The Quality of the Mind, p. 108

33   Article by John Jeremiah Sullivan, Venus and Serena Against the
      World, 22nd August 2012. Accessed July 2015: http://www.nytimes.
      com/2012/08/26/magazine/venus-and-serena-against-the-world.
      html?_r=0

34   Robert Hand, *Night and Day,* p. 7

35   *Venus and Serena,* a documentary film produced by Maiken Baird and
      Michelle Major, Vendetta Films, Magnolia Pictures, K5 International
      M&M Films, 2011

36   *Venus and Serena,* Maiken Baird and Michelle Major, 2011

37   Julius Firmicus Maternus, *Matheseos,* Book Four, p. 107

38   Robert Hand's webinar. *Night & Day: The effect of daytime & night time
      on Birth charts,* www.arhatmedia.com

39   Robert Hand, *Night and Day,* p. 23

40 Book Title *"One Thing Leads to Another—Everything is Connected: Art of the Underground"*, Charlotte Bonham-Carter (ed.), Louise Coysh (ed.), Tamsin Dillon (ed.), Artwork Title by Richard Long (2009), 2013, Black Dog Publishing, London, UK

41 Hand, Robert, 2005, *On Matter and Form in Astrology*, Article from the conference in York, UK, published on the website, http://www.ncgr-turkey.com/on_matter_and_form.htm, Accessed 26th Jan 2015

42 https://todayinsci.com/A/Aristotle/Aristotle-Nature-Quotations.htm. From *Physics, Book II*, Part 7, 198a 21-26. As quoted in Stephen Emerson, 'Aristotle on the Foundations of the State', *Political Studies* (1988), 36, 89-101. Reprinted in Lloyd P. Gerson (ed.), *Aristotle: Politics, Rhetoric and Aesthetics* (1999), 74.

43 https://todayinsci.com/A/Aristotle/Aristotle-Nature-Quotations.htm. From George Henry Lewes *Aristotle* (1864), 231. Quote by Aristotle *"Among natural bodies some have, and some have not, life; and by life we mean the faculties of self-nourishment, self-growth and self-decay. Thus every natural body partaking of life may be regarded as an essential existence; . . . but then it is an existence only in combination."*

44 Fabry, Merrill, article for Time/History, *Now You Know: Which Came First, the Chicken or the Egg?*, 21st Sept 2016, http://time.com/4475048/which-came-first-chicken-egg/ Accessed July 2017

45 Hand, Robert, *On Matter and Form in Astrology*, Article from the conference in York, UK, in 2005, p. 3

46 Aristotle's Four Causes Diagram from http://art3idea.psu.edu/boundaries/bolagrams/aristotle.html

47 Firmicus Maternus, Julius, *Matheseos*, Book Three, Chapter One, p. 61

48 Hand, Robert, *On Matter and Form*, http://www.ncgr-turkey.com/on_matter_and_form.htm

49 Paulus Alexandrinus *Introductory Matters*, Trans. Robert Schmidt, Ed. Robert Hand, Project Hindsight, Greek Tract, Volume I, The Golden Hind Press, 1993, p. 24

50 Ptolemy, Claudius, *Tetrabiblios, Book One*, Ashmand translation, p. 26

51 Firmicus Maternus, *Matheseos*, Book Two, Ch. 29, footnote by translator Jean Rhys Bram, p. 51

52 Al-Biruni, Notation 377, p.277

53   Paulus Alexandrinus, Gieseler Greenbaum, Dorian (trans.), Hand, Robert (ed.), 2001, *Late Classical Astrology: Paulus Alexandrinus and Olympiodorus with the Scholia from Late Commentators,* ARHAT, Reston VA, p. 19

54   Ibid, p. 19

55   Ibid, p. 19

56   Al-Biruni, *The Book of Instruction In the Elements of the Art of Astrology,* p. 228

57   Manilius, Marcus, G. P. Goold (trans. and ed.), 1977, *Astronomica,* Loeb Classical Library, Harvard University Press, London, England, Book Two, Paragraphs 788 – 808, p. 145 - 147

58   Antiochus, with Porphyry, Rhetorius, Serapio, Thrasyllus, Antigonus et al. Robert Schmidt (trans.), 2009, *TARES, The Astrological Record of the Early Sages: Definitions and Foundations, Volume Two, Project Hindsight, The Twelve-Topic System of Places,* The Golden Hind Press, Cumberland MD, p. 305

59   Manilius, Marcus, *Astronomica,* Book Two, Paragraphs 808 - 841 p. 149

60   Ibid, p. 149

61   Ibid, p. 149

62   Ibid, p. 149

63   De Saint-Exupéry, Antoine, T.V.F. Cuffe (trans.), 1995, *The Little Prince,* Penguin Books, London, UK, Introduction, p. xi

64   Article published 7th April 2017, http://www.ctvnews.ca/entertainment/the-little-prince-becomes-world-s-most-translated-book-excluding-religious-works-1.3358885, Accessed August, 2017

65   Ibid, Introduction, p. viii

66   Ibid, Introduction, p. viii

67   James, Barry, Book Review of Paul Webster's book *ANTOINE DE SAINT-EXUPERY: The Life and Death of the Little Prince.* Review written October 28, 1993, http://www.nytimes.com/1993/10/28/style/28iht-book_16.html. Accessed June 2016

68   Ibid

69   Schiff, Stacey, article on Antoine Saint-Exupéry entitled *Par Avion,* written June 25, 2000 http://www.nytimes.com/books/00/06/25/bookend/bookend.html, Accessed June 2016

70   Riding, Alan, article written June 6th, 2000, *Romance of a Prickly Rose and a Starry Prince,* http://www.nytimes.com/library/books/060700little-prince.html. Accessed June 2016

71   Julius Firmicus Maternus, *Matheseos*, Book Three, p, 101 (#71): and Book Two, p. 40 (#79)

72   Langley, David, http://www.aviation-history.com/airmen/exupery.htm Accessed August, 2017

73   Paul Webster, June 24, 2000, Accessed June 2016 http://www. theguardian.com/books/2000/jun/24/biography.books

74   Ibid

75   Ibn-Ezra, A, Meira Epstein (trans.), 1998, *The Beginning of Wisdom*, ARHAT Publications, USA, Chapter Eight, Note 87, p. 125

76   Riding, Alan, 2000, *Romance of a Prickly Rose and a Starry Prince*

77   http://www.theguardian.com/books/2000/jun/24/biography.books

78   Riding, Alan, 2000, *Romance of a Prickly Rose and a Starry Prince*

79   Julius Firmicus Maternus, *Matheseos*, Book Three, p, 101 (#71): and Book Two, p. 40 (#79)

80   Ibid, p. 41

81   Ibid, Book 3, p. 64

82   Schoener, Johannes, Robert Hand (trans. and ed.), 1994, *Opusculum Astrologicum,* Project Hindsight, Latin Track, Volume IV, The Golden Hind Press, Berkeley Springs, WV, p. 34

83   al-Biruni, Notation 447, p. 261

84   Ptolemy, Claudius, *Tetrabiblos,* Ashmand translation from Proclus (1822), Appendix No. III, p. 153

85   Ibid, p. 156

86   Birth Data for Marlon Brando: 3rdv April 1924 at 11:00 pm in Omaha, Nebraska (AA Rating): https://www.astro.com/astro-databank/ Brando,_Marlon

87   Bonatti, Guido, *Liber Astronomiae Books One, Two and Three with Index,* trans. Robert Zoller,1994, Spica Publications, Queensland, Australia, 1998, p. 92

88   Julius Firmicus Maternus: *Matheseos Libri VII* Book Two, p. 38

89   http://www.astro.com/astro-databank/Gauguin,_Paul Paul Gauguin's birth data: 7th June 1848, 10:00am, Paris, France

90   Clifford, Frank, 2003, *British Entertainers the astrological profiles*, Flare Publications, Cornwall, UK, p. 52. Richard Branson birth data .....

91   http://www.moneycrashers.com/richard-branson-quotes-business-success-life/, accessed October 2015

92   Ibid, Top 10 Richard Branson Quotes About Business, Success and Life, quote no. One

93 http://www.astro.com/astro-databank/King,_Rodney, Rodney King's birth data: 2nd April 1965, at 7:00am in Sacramento, California, US

94 http://www.npr.org/2012/04/23/150985823/rodney-king-comes-to-grips-with-the-riot-within, Accessed October 2015, article by Karen Grigsby Bates

95 Alexander Fleming's birth data: 6th August 1881, at 2:00am in Loudon, Scotland

96 http://www.bbc.co.uk/history/historic_figures/fleming_alexander. shtml Accessed October 2015

97 Hamaker-Zondag, Karen, *The Yod Book,* Samuel Weiser, Inc, Maine, US, 2000, p. 317

98 *Time* magazine's article on *100 Most Important People of the 20th Century,* published in 1999, http://content.time.com/time/magazine/article/0,9171,990612,00.html

99 http://www.biography.com/people/alexander-fleming-9296894#early-career-and-world-war-i

100 John Belushi's birth data: 25th January 1949, at 5:12am in Chicago, Illinois, USA

101 Coretta Scott King's birth data: 27th April 1927, at 4:00pm in Marion, Alabama, USA

102 http://www.thekingcenter.org/about-mrs-king, Accessed October 2015

103 Jean-Dominique Bauby's birth data: 23rd April 1952 at 5:25am in Paris, France

104 http://www.theguardian.com/lifeandstyle/2008/nov/30/diving-bell-butterfly-florence-bensadoun, Accessed October 2015

105 http://www.nytimes.com/books/97/06/15/reviews/970615.mallon. html Accessed October 2015

106 Paulus Alexandrinus, *Introductory Matters,* Trans. Robert Schmidt, Ed. Robert Hand, Project Hindsight, Greek Track, Volume One, The Golden Hind Press, Berkeley Springs, USA, 1993, p. 25

107 Walker, Barbara, *The Woman's Dictionary of Symbols and Sacred Objects,* first published 1988, published by Pandora in 1998, London, UK, p. 9

108 Ibid, p. 153

109 Birth Data for Rodney King: 2nd April 1965; 7:00 am; Sacramento, California, Rated AA, https://www.astro.com/astro-databank/King,_Rodney

110 Birth Data for Coretta Scott King: 27th April 1927; 4:00pm; Marion, Alabama, Rated AA, https://www.astro.com/astro-databank/King,_Coretta_Scott

111 Ovid *Fasti* I 130-40 states his double head means he as *"caelestis ianator aulae"*, gatekeeper of the heavenly mansion, can watch both the eastern and western gate of heaven, https://en.wikipedia.org/wiki/Janus#cite_note-41

112 Varro apud Augustine, *"De Civitate Dei" VII 2, https://en.wikipedia.org/wiki/Janus#cite_note-120*

113 Omar of Tiberius, trans. Robert Hand, Ed. Robert Schmidt *Three Books on Nativities* (Project Hindsight Latin Track Volume XIV, 1995), Introduction by Robert Hand, p. 93

114 Janus image is a print from French Benedictine monk Dom Bernard de Montfaucon (1655-1741), *"L'antiquité expliquée et représentée en figures (Band1,1)* depicting a variety of different images of Janus, https://en.wikipedia.org/wiki/File:Janus.xcf Accessed July 2016

115 Julius Firmicus Maternus, *Matheseos*, Book Two, Diagram V, p. 39 (#79)

116 Review by Barry James in New York Times on the book *"Antoine de Saint-Exupéry: The Life and Death of the Little Prince,* Accessed July 2017, http://www.nytimes.com/1993/10/28/style/28iht-book_16.html

117 Antoine de Saint-Exupéry, trans. T.V.F. Cuffe, 1995, original English translation in 1943, *The Little Prince,* Penguin Books, London, p. 6

118 Ibid, p. 93

119 Hand, Robert: *Firdar, Alfridaria, or Alfridaries,* Copyright 1998 – 2010, ARHAT Media, Inc, updated July 2012

120 Al-Qabisi (Alcabitius), Keiji Yamamoto, Michio Yano, and Charles Burnett (eds.), 2004, *The Introduction to Astrology, Editions of the Arabic and Latin Texts with an English Translation,* Warburg Institute Publications, London. Reference courtesy of Robert Hand's Article *Firdar, Alfridaria, or Alfridaries,* revised June 2012, Copyright 1998-2010 Arhat Media, Inc

121 Vettius Valens, *Anthology*, Introduction to Book IV, Robert Hand, p. ix-xi (#121): and Volume XI, Ch 17, pp. 45 – 60 (#131)

122 Vettius Valens, *Anthology,* Robert Schmidt (trans.), Robert Hand (ed.), 1993, Project Hindsight, Greek Tract, Volume XI, Introduction to Book IV by R. Hand, p. Ix-xi

123 Ibid, Ch 17. Concerning the Giving Over of the Stars and Lots and *Horoskopos,* pp. 45 - 60

124 Ibid, Introduction, Book VI, Editor, Robert Hand, p. ix

125 Robert Hand, Article entitled *Firdar, Alfridaria, of Alfridaries,* Copyright 1998-2010 Arhat Media, Inc, Revised June 2012, http:// www.arhatmedia.com/firdar2.htm

126 Valens, *Anthology,* Book I, Riley Translation, p. 2

127 Ibid, Book II, The Triangles, p. 25

128 Antoine du Saint-Exupéry, T.V.F. Cuffe (trans.), English version, 1995, *The Little Prince,* Penguin Modern Classics, London, p. 73

129 Ibid, p. 20

130 Ibid, p. 72

131 Vettius Valens, *Anthology,* Introduction to Book IV, Robert Hand, p. ix-xi (#121): and Volume XI, Ch 17, pp. 45 – 60 (#131)

132 Astrology Website, http://www.hellenisticastrology.com/articles/ Vettius Valens, *Anthologies,* Book VI, p. 57

133 Ibid, p. 57

134 Hand, Robert, 1995, *Night & Day: Planetary Sect in Astrology,* published by Archive for the Retrieval of Historical Astrological Texts (ARHAT), p.26

135 Chris Brennan, *The Theoretical Rationale Underlying the Seven Hermetic Lots,* revised June 2010, originally published in the *Tradition* journal, issue 2, spring 2009.

136 Valens, Introduction to Book VI by R. Hand. p. x

137 Ibid, p. 48

138 Holden, James Herschel, 2008, *Five Medieval Astrologers, Chapter Three, Hermes Trismegistus: The Centiloquy,* published by the American Federation of Astrologers, Inc, Tempe Arizona, p. 105

139 Valens, *Anthologies,* Schmidt and Hand, Volume XI, Ch. 17, p. 51

140 Valens, *Anthology,* Book I, Riley Translation, p. 2

141 Ibid, p. 2

142 Ibid, p. 2

143 Chris Brennan, *The Theoretical Rationale Underlying the Seven Hermetic Lots*. Revised paper available online on The Hellenistic Astrology website

144 Robert Hand, Article entitled *Firdar, Alfridaria, of Alfridaries,* Copyright 1998-2010 Arhat Media, Inc, Revised June 2012, http://www.arhatmedia.com/firdar2.htm

145 Article in The Telegraph by Harry Wallop, 31st July 2014, *Gen Z, Gen Y, baby boomers – a guide to the generations,* http://www.telegraph.co.uk/news/features/11002767/Gen-Z-Gen-Y-baby-boomers-a-guide-to-the-generations.html, Accessed September 2017

146 King James Bible, *""You have been weighed on the scales and found wanting." (Daniel Ch 5: verse 27).* Mentioned in Chapter Five on Aversion

147 Michelle Combs, Huffington Post, 2/11/2015, Updated 6th December, 2017; *What Not to Wear After Age 50: The Final Say;* https://m.huffpost.com/us/entry/6656902?ncid=engmodushpmp00000003

148 Antoine du Saint-Exupéry, *The Little Prince,* p. 72

149 Marcus Manilius, *Astronomica, Book Four, 203,* Edited and translated by G.P. Gould, Loeb Classical Library, Harvard University Press, London, UK, original copyright 1977, reprinted 1997, p. 239

150 *The Little Prince,* p. 31

151 Ibid, p. 25

152 Shinoda Bolen, Jean, 2003, *Crones Don't Whine: Concentrated Wisdom for Juice Women,* Conari Press, an imprint of Red Wheel/Weiser, Inc, York Beach, ME, p.

Lightning Source UK Ltd.
Milton Keynes UK
UKHW010634051021
391704UK00001B/7